AFR

RICHARD DOWDEN was Executive Director of the Royal African Society from 2002 to 2017. He first went to Africa as a teacher in 1971, and then as a journalist in 1983, working for *The Times*. In 1986, he became Africa Editor of the *Independent*, and then in 1995 took up the post of Africa Editor of the *Economist*. He has also made three television documentaries on Africa, for the BBC and Channel 4.

From the reviews of *Africa*:

'Hugely readable . . . Dowden writes with the rigour of an academic but the immediacy and personal observation of a first-class reporter unravelling the paradoxes of Africa's recent history' *New Statesman*

'His account of the origins of the Rwandan genocide is the best I have read. His explanation for how oil-rich Angola transformed from Portuguese colony to Cold War proxy and finally into an oil-rich kleptocracy is brilliant. His optimism about Africa – the infectious humour, the natural beauty and the extraordinary resilience of the people – shines through the book in spite of the many horrors he has witnessed' *The Times*

'[A] fine overview . . . The strength of Dowden's book lies in his depiction of small details alongside broad brushstrokes . . . Dowden's greatest asset is that he knows better than to think he has any final answers' *Telegraph*

'Richard Dowden distils a lifetime's travel in, and study of, the world's most surprising continent into this authoritative but readable survey of Africa today . . . In this eye-opening book, from Sudan and Somalia to South Africa and Kenya, Africa talks' *Independent*

'Mr Dowden maintains the reader's interest by skilfully interweaving his research on the economic effects of AIDS and international aid into stories of myriad encounters with Africans rich and poor' *Economist*

'Vivid, informed and darkly humorous prose' *Scotland on Sunday*

'Dowden's experiences as a journalist over three decades are blended with summary historical analysis and a sprinkling of more wide-ranging insights' *Guardian*

'[A] superb collection of essays . . . Dowden's journalism is provocative and refreshing, intelligently picking over the AIDS debacle, the inefficacy of UN activities, the catch-22 of relief aid and China's fast-growing influence' *Financial Times*

'Part memoir, part personal portrait, this is also an enthralling attempt to explain an Africa of incredible complexity and contradiction' *Scotsman*

'Combines the edginess of good reportage with a sympathetic and intelligent analysis of the continent's future. His thirty years of sub-Saharan travel give witness to many crises and challenges, but his persuasive outlook is optimistic' *Independent on Sunday*

AFRICA

Altered States, Ordinary Miracles

NEW EDITION

Richard Dowden

GRANTA

First published in Great Britain by Portobello Books, an imprint of Granta
Publications, in 2008
Paperback edition published in 2009
Revised edition published by Portobello Books in ebook in 2014 and in
paperback in 2015
This new revised edition published by Granta Books in 2019

Granta Publications
12 Addison Avenue
London
W11 4QR

9 8 7 6 5 4 3 2 1

ISBN 978 1 84627 703 0 (paperback)
ISBN 978 1 84627 314 8 (ebook)

www.granta.com

Text designed and typeset in Galliard by
Avon DataSet Ltd, Bidford on Avon, Warwickshire

Printed in Denmark by Nørhaven

To Penny who let me go and welcomed me home and
Isabella and Sophie who endured my long absences.

Contents

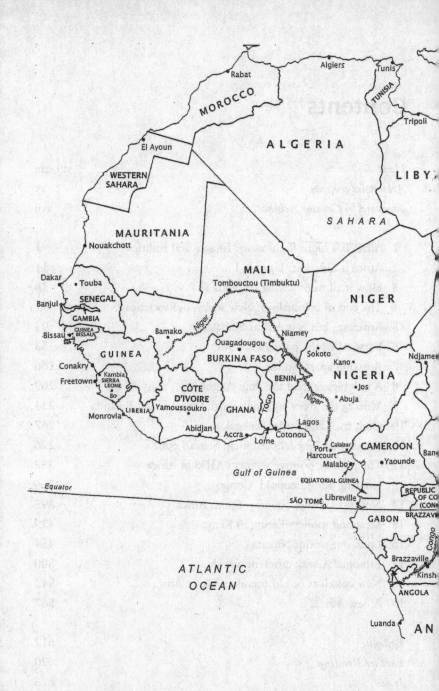

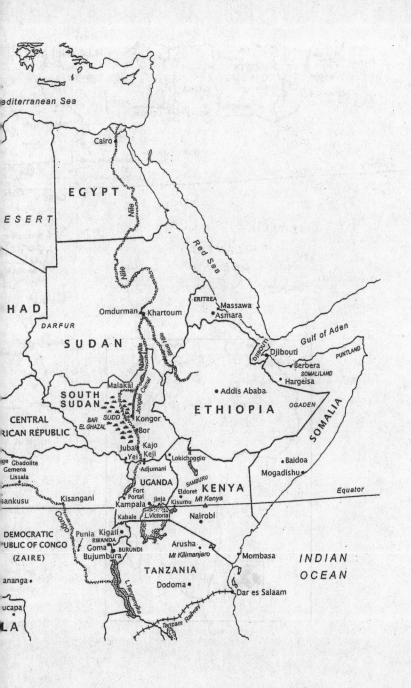

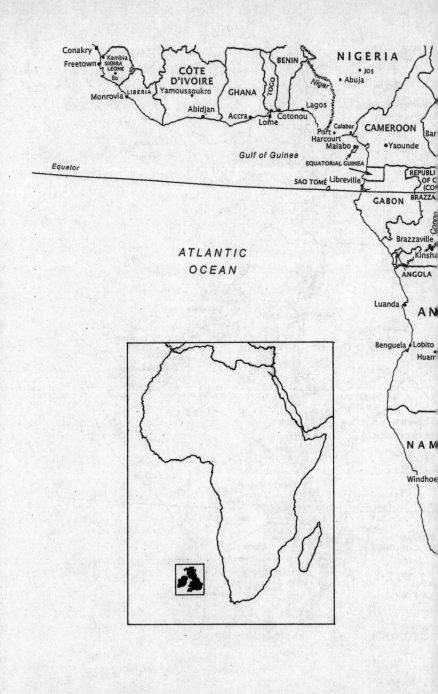

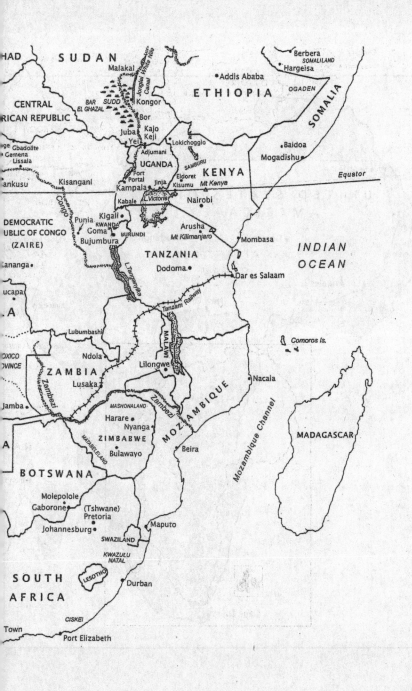

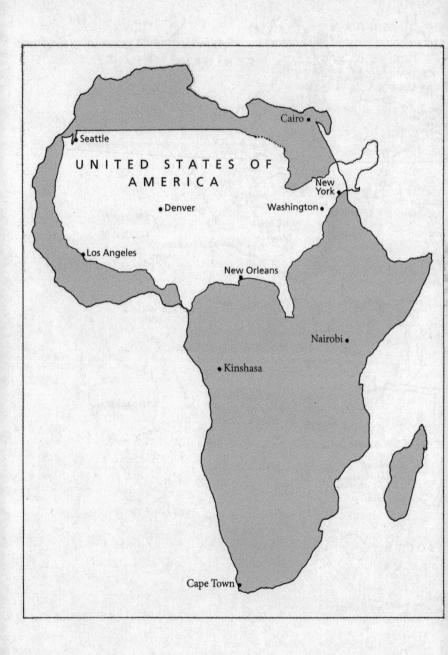

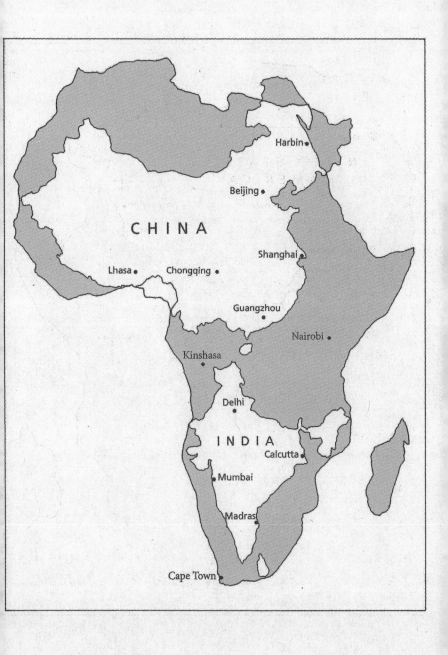

Acknowledgements

My life in Africa began with the Lule family in Uganda and they have always made me welcome in Kampala, particularly Michael Nsereko – *Webale Nyo*. I would also like to thank the many Africans, from drivers and market women to professors and presidents, who helped me to understand why Africa is the way it is. Without their patience and many kindnesses, this book would not have been possible.

I am deeply indebted to the late Anthony Sampson who believed I could write this book and told me to get on with it. A particular thank you to fellow journalists Koert Lindyer, my travelling companion for many years, as well as Karl Maier, Michael Holman, Michela Wrong, Peter Sharp and William Wallis, who were also there in bad places at bad times and still – in varying degrees – love and believe in Africa.

Stephen Ellis shared his striking insights into the continent and refined the manuscript.

This book covers many years of travelling in Africa as a journalist so I would like to thank those who helped me go there: Ivan Barnes at *The Times*, Andreas Whittam-Smith, Stephen Glover and especially the late Nick Ashford at the *Independent*, and Bill

Emmott at *The Economist*. Thanks too to all at the Royal African Society for their patience as I finished the manuscript.

The following also contributed, wittingly or unwittingly, to its creation:

Peter Adwok, Bernard Awazi, Nickson Bahati, Zainab Bangura, Dr Titilola Banjoko, John Battersby, Paul Borland, Maria Burnett, Cecil Cameron, John Carlin, Chukwu Emeka Chikezie, Sir Paul Collier, Abdi Dahir, Alex de Waal, Susana Edjang, Ilona Eveleens, Chris and Rhoda Gibbons, John Githongo, Anthony Goldman, Robin Gorna, Ann Grant, William Gumede, Heidi Holland, Renee Horne, Donald Kaberuka, Razia Khan, Joel Kibazo, Donu Kogbara, Matthew Kukah, Daniel Large, Margaret Lindyer, Ali Mazrui, Smangaliso Mhkatshwa, Miles Morland, Nkosana Moyo, Michael Nsereko, Ben Okri, Dapo Oyewole, Trevor Page, Tajudeen Abdul Raheem, Adam Roberts, Andrew Rugasira, Betty Senoga, Tim Sheehy, Patrick Smith, Henry Ssemanda, Alfred Taban, Camilla Toulmin, Pat Utomi, Bill Walker and Alan Whiteside.

Thanks also to my editors at Portobello, Philip Gwyn Jones and Laura Barber, to Christine Lo and Sarah Wasley in the editorial and production team there and to Jonny Geller and Gordon Wise at Curtis Brown.

Foreword

Africa is a vast continent, a continent of people, and not a place of exotica, or a destination for tourists. In *Africa: Altered States, Ordinary Miracles*, it is clear that Richard Dowden understands this, and one could not ask for a more qualified author to explore Africa's complexity. It helps a great deal that he has travelled extensively in Africa, his work having taken him to nearly every African nation, and that throughout his distinguished career he has committed himself to Africa's advancement as teacher, journalist and executive of the Royal Africa Society in London.

Africa, as most people are aware, has endured a tortured history, and continues to persevere under the burden of political instability and religious, social, racial and ethnic strife. Many chroniclers of the African condition often find Africa overwhelming. As R. K. Narayan once said about new stories: 'there are often too many stories out there to be told.' The writer is often faced with two choices: turn away from the reality of Africa's intimidating complexity, or conquer the mystery of Africa by recognizing the humanity of African people.

Richard Dowden makes the brave choice. In *Africa: Altered States, Ordinary Miracles*, he tackles Africa's problems without fear, sentimentality or condescension. The work benefits from Dowden's deep knowledge of African history, and his writing is often most powerful when he delves into Africa's struggle with corruption, poor leadership, poverty and disease. The treatment of the impact of colonialization on Africa is particularly novel, and the analysis of the continued foreign apprehension about Africa is inspiring. His dissection of familiar themes such as the collapse of nation states like Nigeria, the role of post-colonial political ineptitude and oppression, particularly under tyrannical regimes, is presented with a fresh perspective.

Before I am accused of prescribing a way in which a writer should write, let me say that I do think decency and civilization would insist that the writer take sides with the powerless. Clearly, there's no moral obligation to write in any particular way. But there is a moral obligation, I think, not to ally oneself with power against the powerless. I think an artist, in my definition of that word, would not be someone who takes sides with the emperor against his powerless subjects.

The triumph of the written word is often attained when the writer achieves union and trust with the reader who then becomes ready to be drawn deep into unfamiliar territory, walking in borrowed literary shoes so to speak, towards a deeper understanding of foreign peoples, cultures and situations. In this and so many other respects, Richard Dowden's *Africa: Altered States, Ordinary Miracles*, succeeds marvellously, and is a welcome addition to the growing library of serious critical analysis of Africa.

Chinua Achebe
Annandale-on-Hudson, New York
June 2008

Africa is a night flight away
Images and realities

I have watched the sun set, shrunken and mean, over a cold, drab London street and stood outside a mud hut next morning on a Kenyan hillside and seen it rise in glory over the East African plains. Africa is close.

Few go there. Africa has a reputation: poverty, disease, war. But when outsiders do go they are often surprised by Africa's welcome, entranced rather than frightened. Visitors are welcomed and cared for in Africa. If you go you will find most Africans friendly, gentle and infinitely polite. You will frequently be humbled by African generosity. Africans have in abundance what we call social skills. These are not skills that are formally taught or learned. There is no click-on have-a-nice-day smile in Africa. Africans meet, greet and talk, look you in the eye and empathize, hold hands and embrace, share and accept from others without twitchy self-consciousness. All these things are as natural as music in Africa.

Westerners arriving in Africa for the first time are always struck by its beauty and size – even the sky seems higher. And they often find themselves suddenly cracked open. They lose inhibitions, feel more alive, more themselves, and they begin to understand why, until then, they have only half lived. In Africa the essentials of existence –

light, earth, water, food, birth, family, love, sickness, death – are more immediate, more intense. Visitors suddenly realize what life is for. To risk a huge generalization: amid our wasteful wealth and time-pressed lives we have lost human values that still abound in Africa.

Back at home in London I sometimes ask visiting Africans what strikes them most about the way Londoners live. Sani Umar, a journalist from Sokoto in northern Nigeria, gives a typical answer: 'People walk so fast. And they do not talk to each other. Even first thing in the morning they do not greet each other. I came to the office in London and the people working there did not even greet me or each other.' And the most puzzling thing? 'I was lost and I walked up to a man and asked the way. He did not reply. He did not even look at me. He just walked away. Like that.' When Sani goes home to Nigeria and tells that tale they will not believe him. There they know that some Europeans are not kind to Africans, but to be so trivially inhuman to each other is shocking. Even in London or New York or Paris, Africans do not easily lose the habit of catching your eye as you pass. Raise an eyebrow in greeting and a flicker of a smile starts in their eyes. A small thing? No. It is the prize that Africa offers the rest of the world: humanity.

This is not what most outsiders associate with Africa. The image Africa conjures up in most people's minds is the Dark Continent, the heart of darkness, a place of horrific savagery: inhumanity. You can find that in Africa too. Hell has seized parts of the continent in recent times. In the mid 1990s thirty-one out of Africa's fifty-three countries were suffering civil war or serious civil disturbance. By 2016 the figure had risen to thirty-six countries. In these conflicts hundreds of thousands of people died, not necessarily from bullets, but from hunger, bad water and disease. In such wars the armies, be they government or rebels, live by looting. They target civilians and villages. The direct combat casualty rate is often low; the incidental death and destruction rate horrifically high. Only a tiny number of these wars have been between countries; most have been internal – battles for power and wealth within states, usually between different ethnic groups.

Their chief cause has been a lack of a common nationhood. Africa's nation states were formed by foreigners, lines drawn by Europeans on maps of places they had often never been to. They carved out territories, cut up kingdoms and societies of which they had little idea. All but two of Africa's concocted countries combine several ethnic groups. Some, like Nigeria and Congo, harness together hundreds of different societies with their own laws and languages. They lack what we take for granted: a common conception of nationhood.

Beneath the surface of Africa's weak nation states lie old cultures, old societies and communities and a deep sense of spiritual power. This is not a residual superstition, the vestige of religion. Nor is it a neurosis induced by insecurity or poverty. The spirit world, Muslim, Christian or traditional, lies at the heart of many African societies, a core belief in the power of spirits that can be harnessed by mediums. This belief partly explains Africans' lack of political or social agency. It can undermine personal responsibility and weaken communal solidarity. At worst it can inspire the most horrific brutalities – though not on the scale of mass murder inspired by fascism, Communism and nationalism in twentieth-century Europe.

But the traditional beliefs also provide immensely powerful defences against despair and hopelessness. Amid Africa's wars and man-made famines and plagues, I have found people getting on with life, rising gloriously above conditions that would break most of us. In Africa even in the worst of times you do not hear the tones of doom and despair that characterize some Western media reports on the state of Africa. Africa always has hope. I find more hopelessness in Highbury where I live in north London than in the whole of Africa.

'It's the fault of the media,' says the young PR man. 'The image they give of Africa is just wars and famine and disease. We can change that. What Africa needs are success stories. We are going to re-brand Africa.'

A smartly uniformed waiter – a Ghanaian from his accent – wheels the breakfast trolley to our table and offers us paw paw, mango, pineapple and other African fruits. And of course that African drink: coffee. Our tip for the waiter for bringing us that coffee pot will be more than a week's income for the family in Africa who grew the coffee. We are having breakfast in a smart London hotel with starched white tablecloths and heavy silver cutlery. So that's the way to change the world. If you don't like one image, find another one. Changing reality is as easy as flicking channels on TV.

Some outsiders campaign to change Africa's image and accuse the media of creating a false impression of Africa's reality. Some even suggest there is a conspiracy against the continent by foreign journalists. Say 'Africa' to people who have never been there and they will describe a sick and starving child and men with guns. News from Africa is almost exclusively about poverty, wars and death.

Would it be better if journalists did not cover the bad news out of Africa? As a reporter on *The Times* in 1984 I received a call from a contact at Oxfam who warned me that a huge famine was building in Ethiopia. I asked the editor, Charles Douglas-Home, if I could go. 'I don't think people want to read about starving Africans,' he drawled. 'We saw quite enough of that in Biafra.' Later that year *The Times* was forced to scramble another reporter to Ethiopia to catch up with what was one of the biggest stories of the decade. At that moment I vowed to try to get the reality of Africa's wars and famines covered in the press as well as they would be if they happened in any other part of the world.

Now, more than twenty years on, I sometimes find myself accused of giving Africa a bad image. My first reaction as a journalist is to say: 'Did I make this up?' The cynical slogan of many newsrooms is: 'If it bleeds it leads' (the news agenda). But the media must make room for context and connection as well as action. It must ensure that people watching from Europe or America are not left with the impression that this story is the story of all Africa. Journalists must engage with and understand what is happening but also make clear that what is happening in the Congo, for example, does not affect Kenya.

Most Africans are neither fighting nor starving. The majority have never known hunger or war and lead ordinary, healthy, peaceful lives. But that is not news. Editors want breaking news but many have little interest in explanations, let alone explanations and context from an African perspective. Journalists are sent to get 'the story' – or not, if the editor is like Douglas-Home. And even if they do go, some editors and journalists do not dig into the complexities of Africa. 'Keep it simple' is the message. All the rich history, culture and complexity of Africa is missed. Few in the media have felt the need to dig deeper into Africa. It is easier to describe it as chaos. Africa may often look like chaos and madness but there is always a comprehensible – if complex – explanation. A group of us, journalists who covered Africa full time, decided that we would ban the word chaos from our reporting and never give up the search for rational explanations for what was going on. Our watchword was, 'If you describe it as chaos you haven't worked hard enough.' That worked well enough until I told a Nigerian editor of our pact. 'It does not work here,' he said gloomily. 'Nigeria is chaos. But the chaos is created, organized by the government. Chaos allows it to stay in power.'

Africa has many realities. The media image dismissed by the young PR man is not untrue, but it is only one African reality, incomplete. Stories of war and disaster are only a slice of the reality of Africa. The new Africa is mobile phones in the village, well-organized elections, Chinese suits in the market and African multinational companies investing, but they get little coverage.

The media's problem is that, by covering only disasters and wars, it gives us that simple image of the continent. We have no others. When we see floods causing havoc in New Orleans we do not think that all of America is permanently under water, or when we see fighting in Burma we do not think all of Asia is at war. We know from other images we see and stories we read that there is a functioning and thriving America and a peaceful and successful Asia. But we have no other ideas of Africa, no sense of ordinary Africa. Persistent images of starving children and men with guns have accumulated into our narrative of the continent: Africans are gun-toting, mindless warriors or hopeless, helpless victims who can do nothing for themselves, doomed to endless poverty, violence and hunger. Only foreign aid and foreign aid workers can save them. The endlessly repeated images of guns, oppression, hunger and disease create the impression that this is all that ever happens in Africa. The stories of Zimbabwe and Congo and all their predecessors have become the story of Africa. We think all of Africa is like that – always.

By their nature victims need pity, not respect or understanding. 'They are just like us but without money,' we are told to believe. 'Give money and all will be well.' Aid and development agencies, from the smallest NGO to the World Bank and the United Nations behemoths, have little interest in understanding African difference, how Africa works. Aid agencies, Western celebrities, rock stars and politicians can help but cannot save Africa. Only Africans can develop Africa. Outsiders can only help if they understand it, work with it. Africa's history and culture, Africa's ways, are the key to its development, but they are as little acknowledged and understood now as they were in the nineteenth century when Europe colonized the continent. Some would argue that disregard for Africa and Africa's voice in its own development is as destructive today as territorial imperialism was 150 years ago. The policies the aid and development agencies have for Africa are not always bad – they often represent the highest aspirations and idealism of the rest of the world – but they take no account of the human reality on the ground. From the socialist and statist models of the 1960s, to the free market ideology of the 1980s, the Washington consensus of the 1990s, and the aid-driven Millennium Development Goals, there has always been a missing element: the Africans.

So journalists are not the only ones to blame. The aid industry too has an interest in maintaining the image of Africans as hopeless victims of endless wars and persistent famines. However well-intentioned their motives may once have been, aid agencies have helped create the single, distressing image of Africa. They and journalists feed off each other. The deal, mostly unspoken but well understood, is that aid workers tell journalists where disaster is breaking. The aid agencies provide plane tickets, a place to stay, vehicles, a driver, maybe a translator – and a story. In return the journalists give the aid agencies publicity, describing how they are saving Africans and using images of distress and helplessness to raise money. This deal excludes the efforts of the local people to save themselves. It is easier – and more lucrative – to portray them as victims dependent on Western charity.

In the early 1990s, several aid agencies appointed attractive young women to act as press officers in disaster zones to appear on

TV and raise income. A decade later, they went further and invited celebrities to visit these places, bringing the media along to follow rock singers and film stars wandering through refugee camps, hugging starving children and pleading for more aid. Celebrities are even less well equipped than journalists to provide a coherent understanding of what is happening in Africa, but it worked for the aid agencies. 'Saving African babies' is now big business, but it has also become the entry point from which the rest of the world sees the continent. Bob Geldof first experienced Africa in Ethiopia when he bullied the world into delivering food aid to the starving. Twenty years on, he resurrected that crusade and persuaded Tony Blair to join it. Though he had paid only a fleeting official visit to the continent, Blair proclaimed a 'passion for Africa'. He referred to it as a 'scar on the conscience of the world', deeply offending many Africans. His messianic mission to save Africa was reminiscent of the nineteenth-century missionary zeal. That set teeth on edge. It sounded like saving Africa from the Africans.

Life – as John Lennon sang – is what happens to you while you're busy making other plans. Travelling around Africa since the early 1970s I began to glimpse deeper truths about the continent, caught out of the corner of my eye as I went in search of the big stories. History books will tell you about momentous events and complex politics. Memoirs and travel books give you the feel of a place from personal experiences. In this book I have tried to combine the broad history with the local and personal, telling stories of incidents, actions, characters that hopefully give something of the feel of Africa, demonstrate its huge diversity of peoples and places, and go some way to illuminating why Africa is the way it is, both positive and negative.

I hope Africans will recognize their continent and themselves in these pages, but I write chiefly for outsiders, those who have not been to Africa but would like to know more about it. The best way to find out is to go, not as a tourist in a bubble of Western luxury and safety, but as a traveller to meet people and engage with them. It is easily done. But beware. Africa can be addictive. *Les fous d'Afrique*, the French call them, those who become mad about Africa.

This is a book about Africa south of the Sahara. I have not written about North Africa: Islamic, Arab-influenced and bordering the Mediterranean. The history and culture of the countries of the Maghreb have only tenuous connections with the rest of the continent. The Mediterranean linked North Africa with Europe, the Sahara desert blocked the route south to the rest of Africa. Few North Africans regard themselves as African. Nor does this book deal with Africa's islands and archipelagos, seven of which are independent countries, including Madagascar – two and a half times the size of the United Kingdom and a world apart with its own unique character. While influenced by Africa and counted as part of the African region, these islands too are different.

This is not to imply that Africa south of the Sahara is all the same. On the contrary, it is the most diverse zone of planet Earth. From the rainless deserts of Namibia to the diminishing snows of Kilimanjaro, from the Sahelian scrublands to the lush tropical forests of the Congo basin, Africa has an extraordinary range of climates, flora and fauna. And it is among African peoples that the greatest diversity occurs. Africa has more than 2000 languages and cultures and, despite the fact that we all share a single African woman as the mother of the human race, there is more human genetic diversity in Africa than in the rest of the human race combined.

Africa is often spoken of as if it were one small uniform country. Yet in comparison, Europe is homogenous, America monotonous.

Who would dare make generalizations about Asia based on Bangladesh? Or about Europe based on Greece? Perhaps Africa only exists as a piece of earth defined by the oceans, a mere shape on a map whose peoples and cultures have as much in common with other parts of the world as they do with each other. Even if you divide Africa in three: Africa north of the Sahara, South Africa and its orbit, and the zone in between, there are few common factors within these regions. What is Africa then? Not even the distinctive pale terracotta soil of Africa covers the whole continent. The lean brown African dog is common but not ubiquitous. Music? Maybe. I have yet to find an African community – or an African – which does not celebrate with music. But music is universal and African music varies widely. Africa's social systems, beliefs and culture are as diverse as its peoples and as disparate as its climates. West Africa feels quite different from East Africa, and even within West Africa you could never mistake Nigeria for Senegal. And neither of them seems on the same planet as Mali. Every time you say 'Africa is . . .' the words crumble and break. From every generalization you must exclude at least five countries. And just as you think you have nailed down a certainty, a defining characteristic, you find the opposite is true in other places. Africa is full of surprises.

2

Africa is different
Uganda I

It is hard to remember what images of Africa I grew up with. In the early 1950s my grandfather went off to Ghana, then called the Gold Coast. We were told he had gone to 'count the natives'. He had worked in the Births, Deaths and Marriages office at Somerset House in London for most of his life and came out of retirement in his late sixties to do something different. He returned a year later a rich brown colour and brought back beautiful silver spoons with an emblem of an elephant and a palm tree. He told tales of camping out in the bush and being stoned by an angry crowd. Later I learned that he had insisted on going third class in a steamer, sleeping in a hammock in a communal cabin, and had been carried ashore on an African's back at Accra. At school aged six I remember a nun from Congo. She had a lovely smiling face and smelt wonderful but she could be very severe. I loved her and feared her in equal measure. Throughout the late 1950s the solemn BBC news from our dark brown radio told of murder and some horror called Mau Mau in 'Keenya' – as it was pronounced then. Later, in the early 1960s, I heard tales of mayhem and massacre in the Congo. Along with Korea, Malaya and Cyprus, Africa seemed distant and dangerous.

Soon afterwards a wave of colonial exiles invaded Worcester, where my family lived. Tanned, smart and very particular about social etiquette, they had been district officers and policemen in Kenya, Uganda or Ghana. The men wore blazers with gold buttons, club ties and moustaches and drawled in accents of superiority. The women wore flowery cotton dresses and heavy perfumes and were haughty and complaining. They all whinged endlessly and pompously about the 'natives' or 'the African'. Over and over again I heard: 'They just aren't ready for independence,' usually followed by tales of bloody revolution, Communist take-over and servants stealing the sugar. But these pompous, frightened people also exuded a huge sense of sadness and loss. As their skins paled in the chilly Worcestershire climate, their souls burned with a yearning for Africa, their lost Eden.

Their arrival coincided with my own teenage breakout from these domineering old bores and I naturally identified with anyone also oppressed by them. They were the generation who had won the Second World War and they behaved as though they ran the world. In a muddled sort of way I identified my search for personal teenage freedom with the 'FreeeeeDOM' call of the African crowds I heard on the radio news. These colonial administrators had been defeated by Africa, and to my mind that made Africa powerful and alarming. After the Labour victory in the 1964 General Election, these old colonials were as terrified by the prospect of being ruled by socialists as they had been by the idea that Africans should rule in Africa. Many went back to Africa, but to Rhodesia, as Zimbabwe then was, or to South Africa, where the natives were still kept in their proper place and civilization prevailed.

Like almost everyone else who went to university in 1968, I became further radicalized by the Vietnam War but I felt too self-conscious to go on marches and wave banners. Nor could I bring myself to believe demonstrating would make a difference. I wanted to do something real about poverty and suffering. I believed that to change the world you had to go there, live with the poorest and change their lives. But after three years of learning about European history, what did I know that could possibly be of use to Africa?

The only thing that my education qualified me for was passing it on: teaching. Government-run urban schools were too much part of the 'system' for me and I imagined that out in the rural areas I would find the 'real' Africa. I was looking for freedom and authenticity. In London I met a group of White Fathers, Catholic priests who work in Africa. They were cheerful, kindly people, but with a radical streak. I felt inspired by their love of Africa and their life-long commitment to it. Through them I found a place as a teacher in a village school in Uganda.

I arrived in Africa on 18 May 1971. My new home was a tiny house on the edge of a hill called Kabuwoko in south-west Uganda. From my window I could see Lake Victoria shining in the distance across rolling green hills of banana plantations and forests. This part of Uganda is like English downland, only bigger and always green. It has two rainy seasons, but the huge lake creates the weather here and brings rain all year round. In the September rainy season massive meringue-puff clouds bubble up from the glistening water. Then the dark stormy mass suddenly rushes inland, flinging lightning around the sky and burying the hills and valleys in thunder and rain. But within an hour or two all is clear and still again and the warm sun returns. You never mind getting wet in Uganda.

Unlike English downland, the bottoms of the valleys are swamps, and so people live on the lower slopes. They don't live together communally in villages but dotted around on smallholdings. Homes are rectangular mud huts with thatch or – in richer households – corrugated iron roofs, each set in its own grove of bananas, with coffee plantations and a kitchen garden. The ground around each hut is bare, swept meticulously clean every day. Approach a home through the grove of bananas and coffee and you drown in the luscious perfume of coffee flowers, wood smoke and the dull scent of steaming bananas. You do not walk up and knock at the door. You stand a few yards away on the swept earth and call out a greeting. There is always someone to welcome you.

'Eradde?' the Baganda say. (It rhymes with day.) 'Is the lake calm?' 'Eradde – The lake is calm.'

Greeting in Luganda, a Ugandan language, is an age-old pattern of question and answer, of iteration and reiteration. Its rhythms establish relationship and order and peace, the replies repeating the questions in different tones:

'Bwera?' – Is there plenty of millet? 'Bwera' – There is millet.

'Mirembe?' Is it peaceful where you are coming from? 'Mirembe' – It is peaceful.

'Balamu?' – Are your people in good health? 'Balamu' – They are in good health.

'Kulika ekkubo' – Thank you for coming. 'Awo' – I have made it.

'Wasuze otyanno' – Good morning. 'Musula mutya?' – How are you?

'Bulungi. Ggwe osula otya?' – I'm OK, and you? – 'Bulungi.'

Even if you are at death's door the replies are the same. Bad news only emerges later, discreetly, in conversation. You do not greet people with anything except good news.

Uganda has the perfect climate, and since it is a microclimate created by the lake, it is not yet clear how global warming will affect it. The Baganda have never known anything else and, whatever else is going on beneath the surface, they live as if life is always good. Being with people, talking, making others laugh are what matter. Their language, Luganda, sounds sweet and subtle, its rhythms punctuated by cooing and hums. An early British visitor, keen to bring the Christian virtues of progress, civilization and hard work to the Baganda, protested that they had little need to work since nature provided food with minimum human effort. They spent their days, he complained, drinking beer, dancing and gossiping. This pious visitor was infuriated that when God had cast Adam and Eve out of the Garden of Eden, he had somehow allowed this charming but good-for-nothing people to remain. Meanwhile his Chosen People, obviously the hardworking, God-fearing, Protestant English, had been dispersed to a wretched faraway island to suffer the miseries of British weather. Mysterious – and irritating.

While the people live in valleys, the tops of the steep, grassy hills are left for herds of long-horned Ankole cattle – direct descendants of those great beasts you see in tomb paintings from earliest times in Egypt. An attendant flock of pure white egrets follows the cows, perching on their backs or darting around their hooves, stabbing at ticks and insects. When I arrived the hill also hosted a pair of crested cranes – the country's national symbol – and a hammerkop searched for frogs in the pond that formed near the house in the rainy season. Traditionally the hilltops, close to the sky, were left to the spirits. Near my house was a strange lump of rock the size of a tall bar stool protruding from the ground like a menhir. It was called the Nkokonjero, the White Cock. The students told me that a young girl was swallowed up by it when she was going to her wedding. She was still inside it and no-one should go near it as the rock might be hungry for more victims. I used to sit on it, but I never found out whether I, as a foreigner, was regarded as immune from the local spirits or whether they thought I was very stupid but very lucky.

At Kabuwoko, as elsewhere in Uganda, the Christian missionaries set their churches on hills, perhaps to colonize the citadels of the spirits as firmly as their political counterparts had taken over the land. They built a huge barn in pale red brick with gothic touches here and there and a bell tower at the eastern end. It made the hill habitable by providing water, channelled off its great corrugated iron roof into huge tanks. Without them it was a long steep climb down to a spring in the valley.

The missionaries also planted the hill with flowering trees and lawns, built a clinic and school blocks and levelled a football pitch. In colonial times the Churches and their surrounding parishes became powerful centres, political and social as well as religious. When the European missionaries handed over to African priests and nuns that role continued. All over Africa the parish today means schools, health clinics, workshops and an indigenous postal service. In most of Africa the Churches have delivered real development to people, matching or even exceeding what the governments, the World Bank and aid agencies have invested. Africa's networks of priests, nuns and Church workers are one of Africa's more effective organizations. When states like Congo, Ghana, Angola, Mozambique and Uganda itself collapsed, the self-sufficient parishes used their moral authority to provide protection. Like the monasteries in Europe during the Dark Ages, they kept civilization going. And unlike foreign aid workers or businessmen, they do not fly away when there is trouble.

But the missionaries not only imported a new religion, education, Western medicine and football. They also brought their own insane history to Africa and to Kabuwoko. The Catholics took one end of the hill, the Anglicans the other. In 1911, Catholics and Protestants fought a terrible battle on the ridge in the middle. Fifty years later at independence this religious conflict had been reduced to a fierce annual football match between the rival schools and a few weekend scuffles between pupils in the trading centre at the bottom of the hill. But there is still more than a whiff of Northern Ireland's religious divisions in Ugandan politics.

I shared the house for a while with another British teacher and a nephew of the parish priest, Henry Ssemanda. Most whites in Uganda, teachers in state schools, doctors and aid workers, kept their distance from Africans. They showed no inclination to challenge their position in society and live like the people. Many distrusted Africans deeply. I could not work out whether this superior position was accorded out of politeness or inherited or still demanded by most whites. I decided to try to break down the barrier. My diary from my first months in Africa shows an obsessive campaign to join African society, become part of Africa. 'Everyone seems to have accepted the prison the Africans have made for the *wazungu* (white people) here and everyone is continually playing to an African audience,' I wrote after one month. 'I certainly intend to test the walls of the prison to check for myself if they are solid but it is so hard to confront Africans without insulting them or losing face and therefore their respect.'

When I came to Uganda the African dream of a future of wealth and prosperity was reaching a dizzy climax. The students at the school were mostly the children of subsistence farmers, desperately – too desperately – keen to get education certificates. Coffee growing gave their families enough to provide the £15 a term school fees for one or two children. The size of the school roll varied according to the coffee harvest. Many could not come until the crop was paid for and the school fees settled. Boys were in the majority as they provided a better return on investment in education than girls. Ages varied from about twelve to twenty-two in four forms which occupied the five rooms of a single long block. Each had a blackboard, desks and chairs, but there were almost no books or other teaching equipment. Some of the students walked five miles to school every morning, five miles back in the evening, and not all could afford candles or an oil lamp to study by at night.

The students had a terrifying misconception of what the school was for. They came from families who grew what they ate and ate what they grew. Chickens scratched around outside the house and a cow might be tethered under the trees. Their only source of income

– unless they worked for each other or sold extra food crops – was coffee. Each *shamba* – piece of farmed land – had a few coffee bushes, and the harvest was sold to pay for the extras of life: sugar and salt, clothes and oil for the evening lamps. Most Ugandans never drink coffee, though some keep a tin of Nescafé for visitors. School fees, like weddings, were predictable expenses. The unpredictable and often devastating expenses that everyone faced sooner or later were medicine, weddings and funerals. The last were very costly. The dead are important and their spirits demand a good send-off. A big funeral can cost half a year's earnings. That is another reason why HIV/AIDS was so devastating in Africa. Families, already impoverished by the long sickness of parents in the prime of life, were ruined by the cost of funerals. The Churches in Uganda urged families not to spend too much on them.

But that was all in the future in 1971. The coffee price was good then and the new hard-top road from Kampala had opened up the area. There was poverty but there were also possibilities for anyone who worked hard. To me, life here seemed like rural heaven. But my students disagreed. They called the village 'primitive', 'uncivilized'. Was that their own concept or had someone told them that? And if someone had told them that, why did they believe it? To them, the good life – or high life, as they called it – was to wear a suit and tie, carry a briefcase and drive a car to an office in town. Escape. Africans dreamed of a modern Western utopia in those days. My shoeless students were going to be airline pilots, surgeons, astronauts and bishops. At the very least they would work in an office job in town. They were certainly not going to learn a craft like carpentry or building because that meant getting your clothes dirty. Nor could they go back home and dig the shamba. It was not a matter of escaping from the grinding boredom of peasant subsistence – compared to the lives of peasants in pre-industrial Europe, life here was far easier.

The students simply despised all work on the land. They wanted a city life.

The headmaster, Joseph Lule, could see that most of them would never get jobs in town and would have to stay on the land. He believed that farming and growing food for the school should be a school activity. He would try to lead by example, picking up a hoe himself and slamming it into the earth with great vigour. But even he found it very frustrating trying to get the students to do manual labour. The other teachers would quietly disassociate themselves from Mr Lule's attempts at getting farming onto the school timetable. This was not helped by the fact that digging was also a severe punishment. Not that it was tough working the earth with a hoe under a midday sun. It was humiliation. Digging was simply beneath their dignity as students. For them, that was precisely why they were at school: so they would never have to work with their hands.

Students with pale skins and soft hands were envied by others because these were signs that they did not have to dig in the sun. Like everyone else, black people do turn darker in the sun and paler out of it. One very black boy called Katongole, who had no shoes, was mocked because he was black and poor. They called him 'coalman'. With extraordinary charm Katongole rolled with it. He laughed with them and was the only student who cheerfully worked the garden. 'I am poor and black. I'm not proud of it but that's who I am,' he seemed to be saying.

Most students were embarrassed by their origins. I told them I grew up on a farm, but they immediately asked if there were tractors there. When I admitted there were, they gave that knowing look which said: 'Well, there you are then. That's different.' I sent home for posters or pictures that showed white people digging with shovels. They were met with incredulity. Many students were ashamed of their parents who had to work with their hands. We tried to set up a meeting with them, but the parents were even more in awe of the school than their children, and few came. One day the father of one of the pupils arrived during the day to pay school fees for his daughter. He was without shoes and bowed and scraped and endlessly hummed and thanked and blessed. I felt furious with the students for despising their parents who had slaved to give them schooling.

One day some students asked me how much I sent home to my parents every month. I was then earning £25 a month, slightly more than the African teachers in the school. Nothing, I told them. They were puzzled. 'You are the one with a job in your family. Why don't you help them?' they asked. Smugly I pointed out that it was rather the other way round. Both my parents worked. They were sceptical about this. Later I learned from Henry Ssemanda that many thought I was lying. Others wondered darkly why, if I was from such a rich family, should I have left home. Why was I cruel to my parents, refusing to help them with money? Had I done something terrible that I had to go so far from home and live in Africa? I decided that if my students were to believe that I was either a murderer or a missionary, it was better to be a missionary.

Like most outsiders arriving in Africa for the first time I was confused by the way people referred to their families. When a pupil wrote about his mothers and fathers, I corrected him. He promptly corrected me, pointing out that he lived in a house with three fathers and two mothers.

'Yes, but you have only one father and one mother,' I told him.

'No, I have three fathers and two mothers at our house,' he replied. 'One of my mothers is my mother's sister and one of the fathers is her brother.' In Africa any relative who looks after you as a child is a mother or a father. Even cousins several times removed are called brothers and sisters.

Family is central to life in Africa, but the African family is nothing like the neat nuclear family of Europe. Africans find the European family a paltry, cold affair. In Africa – the whole of Africa – the family extends to relations Europeans would no longer have any knowledge of. And you hold onto the family especially when they are old. Grey hairs are respected and obeyed in Africa. The elderly are not pushed aside as they are in Western countries. The downside of respect for age is that the old retain power over their families until they die. A young individual cannot kick over the traces of tradition and make a fresh start.

The self-made man does not exist in Africa. If the motto of Europe is individualism: 'I think therefore I am,' Africa's would be communalism: 'I relate, therefore I am.' In southern Africa this is the concept of Ubuntu, the idea that no one exists as a human being in isolation. You can't be human all by yourself. We are all connected. In Zulu there is a saying: 'One is a person through others,' or, as John Mbiti, the Kenyan theologian, put it: 'I am because we are and, since we are, therefore I am.' Africans know who is family and know where they come in it, both vertically and horizontally. A man without a family is no-one. He is nothing.

Families impose duties and obligations, so it is important to gather as many people to you as possible. Extending your family is the best way, but Africans are also great joiners of brotherhoods and sororities. Clubs, freemason lodges, religious organizations, Rotary Clubs, co-operatives, political parties are all hugely popular. You join as many societies as you can because membership of a group is always rewarding. That extends to the family too. Traditionally in Europe when a daughter married and left her family, she was given a dowry, a pay-off to settle her elsewhere. In Africa the money goes the other way. A suitor must pay bride price. He is not just ensuring, since she is valuable, that she will be respected and treated well, he is also binding their families together.

In Europe families shed people, in Africa families acquire people. Perhaps this is because European societies had too many people and not enough land, whereas in Africa there was always plenty of land but not enough people to control it. In crowded, bloody Europe people stood and fought for land. In Africa wars were fought for pillage: for slaves, for cattle, for control of trade. Very rarely did people fight for a piece of land. It was not necessary. There was always lots of space. If villagers did not like a chief they tended to move away and walk over the hill to start afresh. As personal identity could be expressed only by membership of the group, so ownership of land was always communal, not individual. Several different people, farmers and pastoralists, for example, can claim the same piece of land for different purposes. Wandering cattle keepers who might compete with settled farmers for land or water sources could strike a deal that allowed each to use the same piece of land according to the seasons.

The downside of the African family is that, at that time, distant relatives could claim from richer members. Any money that one member earned was expected to be distributed throughout the rest of the extended family. Distant cousins could call on someone with a salary for money – for medicine or school fees or a wedding or funeral. Their requests could not be refused. Franco, a teacher at Kabuwoko and barely out of secondary school himself, with a salary of less than £20 a month, was expected to pay the school fees of two cousins. As Africans have become more urban and better educated this practice has diminished but when there is a wedding or a funeral relatives who would be regarded as very distant in America and Europe will expect to be invited.

The school had football and netball teams and we encouraged students to stay on at the end of lessons and practise. Most of the students had a long way to walk home and only one set of school clothes. Only a few had shoes. In a society where 'putting on smart' was all-important, they were unwilling to risk getting their precious shoes dirty or damaged. We set up a volleyball court and played a hilarious kind of thirty-a-side volleyball each evening, but if anyone fell over or muddied themselves they would hurry off in distress. We also tried to make new goal posts for the football pitch and cut a small tree for them. But nature holds sway in Uganda. One post grew and turned into a tree. The other was eaten by termites. Termites eat only the inside of the wood, not the bark, so no-one noticed until a visiting striker hit the post with a devastating shot. The post disappeared in a puff of dust and the crossbar came down, nearly putting our goalkeeper in hospital.

That was typical of the sort of delicious insanity that enlivened life in Uganda. These stories might seem patronizing to some. Laughing at African foolishness? But the laughter was all theirs – gigantic, handslapping, fall down, helpless, luxurious laughter. It was a clash of civilizations all right, but one that resulted not in hostility but hilarity. The jam fermented and became alcoholic. We had a record player that went faster and faster the closer the needle got to the centre of a record. And we had a small dog and a white cockerel that were blatantly racist and chased Africans from the house to our intense embarrassment and to the amusement of everyone else except the person being chased. Laughter at someone else's expense is no crime in Africa.

We assumed the dog must have had an owner who did not want visitors or hated Africans, but the cock? Later it died in a horrific invasion. I had heard about marcher ants but had seen only the smaller version – little lines of skittering ants that sometimes crossed the paths on the hill. One night I was woken by the sounds of scuffling and a shout from Henry Ssemanda who slept in a room opposite our front door. He had heard our new-born puppies crying. He grabbed a torch and its beam picked out a seething river of black and red monsters the size of earwigs flooding into the shed where the puppies were. They were yelping pathetically, their eyes a wriggling mass of ant pincers. We rushed to the hut and grabbed the puppies, nipping and tugging the ants away and getting some nasty bites ourselves. Ants were beginning to climb up our legs. Stamping on the column did nothing to deter it. More and more came hurrying on. Henry knew what to do. He ran off and found some lengths of rubber and built a small fire with them and then flung them, burning, into the column by the hut door. Eventually the column like a giant snake turned back on itself and began to move away from the house. We saved the puppies but in the morning we found the cockerel half eaten.

Instead of the harsh life I expected to be sharing with poor Africans, I found myself treated as a god. The freedom I had imagined I would find was an illusion. Instead I found a society more restricted by tradition and Catholic prudishness than Victorian England, whose values Africans seemed to admire. I imagined that the immense welcome of dancing and clapping and speeches when I arrived was merely a traditional formality and that afterwards I would get down to real life. It never happened. Real life turned out to be the formal, mannered relationship that Africa imposes on strangers. I could reject it or damage it but I could never escape from it. 'You are a muzungu – a white man,' it said. 'And you must think like one, behave like one. You must be respected, bowed to, blessed, fawned on, presented with gifts, pampered and begged from. And kept firmly apart.'

As the impossibility of getting closer to Africa dawned on me, my disillusionment turned to fury. I raged at the whites for refusing to recognize it as an issue and I raged at Africans for keeping me out. My attempts at 'being myself', an important part of the cultural baggage I had brought with me, were disastrous. In my early enthusiasm to identify with local people I bought a *kanzu*, a long plain white robe introduced to the Baganda by Muslim traders in the nineteenth century. Kanzus are worn by Baganda elders with a tweed or linen jacket over it. Anyone wearing a kanzu is accorded unquestioned honour and behaves with corresponding dignity. I was encouraged to wear one to formal meetings. Also living on the hill were Rwandan exiles, Tutsi cattle keepers who had been driven out of Rwanda by the Hutu uprising in 1959 and now worked as day labourers, mainly looking after cattle for richer Baganda. The Tutsis wore brightly coloured wraps called *kikoys*. The Baganda–Tutsi relationship was a complex one. The Baganda looked down on the Tutsis because they were foreign and poor. The tall, proud Tutsis looked down on the Baganda because they were unreliable, lazy – and short.

I was unaware of this mutual lack of respect for each other. On my first big gathering of local bigwigs at the school I wanted to show how much I identified with my new world. I wore a kanzu with a kikoy over it. The effect was alarming. Some laughed, some were insulted, and all thought I was crazy. Mr Lule gently told me it would be better to dress normally.

On another occasion I went to visit a village some way off the road. They knew I was coming and decorated the path to it with banana leaves and sprigs of bougainvillaea, the usual welcome for a 'Big Man'. Elders lined up to greet me; the long handshake, leaning forward in a deferential bow, the left hand holding up the wrist of the shaken hand as if it might be enfeebled by the touch of such a great man. Women fell forward onto their knees before me. This deference was not reserved exclusively for white foreigners; the bishop, the local district commissioner and any powerful man, Ugandan or foreign, got the same deferential treatment. I was then placed on a dais on a special guest's chair with the priest, the headmaster of the local primary school, the chief and an old man with service medals from the Second World War pinned to his kanzu.

There was bottled beer and local beer in calabashes and *kiganda* dancing, a gorgeous display of women flicking their bottoms from side to side while they walked slowly back and forth, the rest of their bodies hardly moving. The best dancers could do it balancing a bottle of beer on their heads. The people sang and clapped in time as the drummers beat out the rhythm louder and louder and faster and faster and the bottoms flew back and forth more and more vigorously until the dance rose to an orgasmic climax. Then suddenly it stopped and everyone fell about laughing and slapping hands with each other. There followed a huge lunch of goat stew, beef stew, roast chicken, groundnut sauce, greens, potatoes and heaps of steaming *matooke*, the banana mash which is the staple food of the Baganda. Indeed, matooke is more than a staple. It means food. If you have not eaten matooke you have not eaten.

Then there were long speeches of praise for everyone, God, the government, me – Europeans in general. Finally it was time to go, and I was presented with a live chicken trussed by the legs. This village was poor. The lunch they had already provided must have severely strained their resources. A crowd of poor people hung around the dining table looking longingly at the leftovers. As I was leaving I picked the poorest person I could see and handed him the chicken. The reaction was startling. Smiles fell away from faces; people who had greeted me warmly averted their eyes and would not look me in the eye. The farewells were abrupt and perfunctory. They were insulted and, for once, showed it. They had laid on the best the village could offer and treated me like a king and I had given their present away to a worthless person. I had treated them and their gift as if they were not good enough.

It was one of many incidents that showed the gulf in understanding. The simplest of actions could be misinterpreted. I was trying to understand Africa but it did not occur to me to imagine how my own behaviour could be misunderstood. I assumed what I did was 'normal' and obvious. Once I went for a walk down the hill and through the shambas scattered along the hillside and swamps. It was partly for inquisitiveness and partly for exercise. At every hut I passed I was showered with astonished greetings, 'Eh! Muzu-ungu? Eh! Eh! Osibie Otyanno,' and requests to come and sit down. Mostly I refused. That evening a puzzled Henry Ssemanda came and asked why I was looking for workers. I discovered that my walk had been interpreted as a search for people to come and work on my shamba. No-one would believe that anyone went for a walk just for the sake of walking. Thanks to hours spent talking to Mr Lule and Henry Ssemanda I was beginning to get my mind around some of the attitudes and beliefs and learn how to behave.

Other cultural gulfs tormented me. One was the lack of personal privacy. Like most (Western) people, I like to be on my own sometimes. In Africa to be on your own means you are sick or upset. If I went and sat alone in the sun, people would ask me what was the matter and no-one thought anything of coming to my house and waking me once the sun was up. It was a social duty to make sure that I always had company. Another was the contrast between the social formality and apparent Catholic – almost Victorian – morality about sex and the extraordinarily sexually explicit traditional dancing. I was all for keeping traditions alive, but was there a connection between the sex-with-clothes-on dance and the number of girls who were forced to leave because they became pregnant?

I discussed these issues with Mr Lule and he discouraged me from trying to be part of African life. The best contribution, he said, was to be a teacher and be myself. Mr Lule contradicted the Baganda stereotype. The Baganda tend to be heavy, slightly overweight. He was tiny, bird-like. They move with languid grace, he bounced around with jerky, electric movements. They have a tendency to discourse in mellifluous bullshit. He was abrupt and blunt to the point of rudeness. Resignation would typify most Bagandas' attitude to life. Mr Lule was a man of boundless action based on perpetual optimism. Ask him how things are going and he would pause and think, then give one of two answers: 'Things are improving' or 'Things will improve soon.'

In 1985 I had become a journalist and returned to Uganda. Much of Kampala and other towns had been sacked by murderous, looting soldiers. I visited Mr Lule at his home on the outskirts of the capital. Some soldiers had come to his house late a few nights before and banged on the door. He, his wife and children were on their knees praying while the soldiers rampaged around outside commanding them to open the door or else they would shoot. The family stopped praying and fled to another room and waited in silence in the dark. Then, inexplicably, the soldiers left and attacked and killed their neighbours instead. When I asked Mr Lule how things were going, the pause was slightly longer than usual, but the answer was the same: 'Things are improving.' Then he added: 'Glory be to God.'

A teacher all his life, he admired learning and discipline. He was of that generation which benefited hugely from Western education, science and administration, but he was no apologist for colonialism. His attitude to the British before independence was, 'Thank you, but now treat us as equals and do not stay on to oppress us.' He had thirteen children and made sure every one, girl and boy, got as much education as possible. Each one has been successful in one way or another. His eldest daughter, Josephine Namboze, was Uganda's first woman doctor, one son the local head of a transnational corporation, another a civil engineer, another a senior medical doctor working for FIFA.

That family represents what Africa could have, should have become. In two generations the Lule family produced world-class professionals and had confidence and a sense of worth. It was the answer to Frantz Fanon's thesis that the most damaging effect of colonialism was psychological. Fanon argued that Africans and black people in general were so deeply scarred by the experience of white imperialism that they had lost their pride, their self-respect. Until they stood up, proud of being black and African, they would always be – or make themselves – victims, and fail. Here was a family who proved Fanon wrong.

Uganda's nightmare began in 1970 and fifteen years later, after a decade of Idi Amin's rule, Mr Lule's grandchildren were headed for a lifestyle more like that of his own parents. The professional classes had fled. Uganda's institutions withered. Subsistence survival seemed the best most Ugandans could hope for. Across Kampala and other towns little vegetable gardens started to spring up in municipal flowerbeds and other urban spaces. A generation was lost. Only at the beginning of the new century, nearly forty years later, could Mr Lule's grandchildren and great-grandchildren pick up the potential and possibilities that he had.

Although he was only eleven or so, Ssemanda had an instinctive understanding of Europeans and their peculiar ways. He taught me Luganda and interpreted for me. More important, he explained the thinking of local people. He told me how they would interpret what I did and said. Gradually I was acclimatized to Ugandan culture and ways of thinking. It was a painful process. My youthful arrogance lay not in thinking I knew better, but believing that principles such as equality were universal and self-evident. For example, I had believed that truth was more important than politeness, but now I began to learn how to live in a deeply unequal society where politeness ranked far higher than truth. Mr Lule, being an old man and deeply respected, could get away with being blunt and straightforward. I could not. I had to play by local rules.

The rules were complex and I realized I would never learn them fully, never become part of society except on its terms. But I learned how to get by without causing offence. That meant, first, avoid confrontation. Tease, joke, cajole, don't demand or command. Don't always seek a definite resolution of a problem; sometimes it is better to leave things unresolved. Don't expect the truth and don't blurt it out. Hint at it, work round to it, leave it understood but unspoken. Never, never get angry. Anger never works and loses you respect. Above all be patient. Everything takes more time in Africa than elsewhere. Good-hearted outsiders, idealists who truly want to help Africa, often find themselves mysteriously impeded by Africa because, in their enthusiasm to get things done, they come across as rude or domineering. These lessons have saved me a lot of trouble. They do not apply to Somalis, to white South Africans or in parts of Nigeria.

Gradually I began to learn to live in my gilded cage and put up with the fawning and gift-giving. It was not easy. 'What am I doing here? I am giving nothing to Africa. I am merely swirled around by it,' I wrote in my diary, and my letters home became less and less informative about what Uganda was really like. I just could not find points of reference that my family and friends would understand. Life in Africa was very, very different.

It was hard to see how Uganda or Africa itself could develop without a transformation of those attitudes and belief systems. Africa might be able to produce the best, talented and capable, but could they operate in Africa as they would in America? For example, in Africa every event has a spiritual cause or actor. Success in exams or football games, and disasters such as disease or death, all have agents, human or divine. There is no such thing as chance. Wealth and progress are obtained with the help of spirits or magic medicine. A Big Man has power, and that power cannot be challenged or ques-

tioned because behind his wealth or position lies spiritual power that
enables him to accrue wealth and an important job. That sense of spiritual power is common to almost all of Africa, a whole dimension that
outsiders ignore at their peril.

Another aspect that outsiders find difficult is the responsibility
that comes with being a wealthy outsider. I received a constant
stream of requests from people coming to my house asking for
money and sometimes for work. Little folded notes, torn from an
exercise book, would be delivered to me. They read something like:

> *Dear Master, I am graciously asking you for the help. My farmily is*
> *very poor and we are many and the moneys are few. God grant*
> *that you help us with the school fees for me. My only hope is in you.*
> *In return let me be your servant forever. May God bless you. Yours*
> *faithfully.*

> *Dear Mr Richard,*
> *How are you these days? Thank you for your work. Sir, I am*
> *writing this letter to help me that if you have any clothes which is*
> *old what you don't want sir help me and give it to me. Goodbye sir.*
> *Your friend*
> *D. Wasswa.*

One particularly sycophantic boy used to address me as My Lord.
'Good morning, My Lord. How are you, My Lord?' he would greet
me on the way to school. One day I told him this was not right, My
Lord was what you called bishops and lords in the old days. He
looked at me solemnly but said nothing. A few days later I met him
coming along the path from school. He beamed hugely and said:
'Good morning, Your Majesty.'

It was all very charming, particularly for Westerners who were
seeking love. Many were. Maybe I was one of them. Many young

Westerners went to Africa because they believed – or asserted – that they went for religious, ideological or moral reasons. But their conscious reasons often masked a deeper psychological one. Often they had fled Europe because they felt inadequate there or did not fit in. They did not love their own culture and despised their own history. In many cases they despised themselves, but externalized it in a rebel cause. Identifying with Africa justified these feelings, gave them an alternative base and a cause to fight for. For some it justified almost masochistic self-denial. Some were frustrated revolutionaries; some thought that by going to Uganda they could fight apartheid in South Africa. Others were suffering from broken love affairs. I recognize some of these feelings in myself at that time; a huge sense of (self-) pity, the love of a cause, the desire to lose oneself in another culture, to feel whole and good by being with the poorest, trying to share their lives.

Instead I found myself loved for the very reasons I despised. I was loved because I was white and came from the rich world. I had come to bring its benefits to Africa, had I not? 'So please Sir, Mista Richad, Masta, Teacha, My Lord, Your Majesty, help me for school fees, help me for medicine, give me clothez.'

'No, that is not why I am here,' my heart screamed. 'I have come to protect innocent Africa from Europe's greed and arrogance and make amends for slavery and imperialism. I want to preserve African values, stand in solidarity against Western materialism.'

But this was a point of view not easily understood by the children of African peasants. To them I was someone who had come to help kill off old Africa and replace it with European ways and Western goods. They despised the old Africa and wanted to be Western and 'put on smart'. I had an image of two people running towards each other with arms outstretched, each thinking they were about to fall into the other's arms, but instead looking beyond each other at a mirage and missing each other completely. 'All they seem to have kept from the past is beer and drums,' I wrote in my diary. 'Africa is fleeing from itself as fast as it can go. If this is the revolution of rising expectations, I don't want a part in it. But I am part of it. I am paid to feed it, to help it along its way.'

Africa wanted the trappings of Western wealth without understanding anything of the culture and values that created it or could sustain it. Instead of building on what they had and developing their assets and talents, they seemed to snatch at Western goods, turning themselves into beggars in a mad scramble to acquire symbols of Western wealth. 'Masster help me for shart,' they cried. 'Aid me with medisin,' 'Give me clothez. Give me moneys.' It makes you, as Paul Theroux has it, 'a wallet on legs'. It is also a paradise for aid agencies and donors. They ask; you give. But Mr Lule was tough and told me not to give anything for nothing. 'Whatever you do, do not let it be known you are giving out money. It will cause problems,' he said.

I grew more and more angry with Africans for abandoning their culture, fleeing from their traditions and becoming beggars. The main aim of all the students I taught seemed to be to get out of the village, away from their roots, and adopt Western ways, or at least acquire Western luxury goods and display them ostentatiously.

The brightest boy in the first year was Willie Kiyingi. And he knew it. His clothes were beautifully clean and well pressed every day, but they were always the same clothes. Close up you could see they were frayed and mended. He was very particular about them. Once he tripped while playing football and muddied his shorts. He stopped playing immediately. The other children respected his cleverness, especially when he caught me out in class, but they resented his arrogance and mocked his self-importance.

Kiyingi was rare in Africa. He was an only child and lived with his mother. I don't remember what had happened to his father. There were whispers that his mother was a prostitute, but others tut-tutted and said she was a hard-working farmer who barely survived on her own and put everything she had into her son's future. His school fees were partly paid for by the school, a sort of bursary because he was bright and had no other way of getting education.

One day about £10 went missing from the staff room. So did Willie. There was no sign of him all day. Then in the late afternoon there was a commotion down in the village. Willie was back. He had hired a taxi for himself all the way from the nearby town and stepped out of it in a shiny, ill-fitting suit, a garish tie and new shoes. He paraded down the row of little wooden shops while everyone ooohed and aaahed and laughed. Willie Kiyingi, they said, was now a Big Man. He went to the bar and bought everyone drinks and then the money ran out. Mr Lule expelled him the next day.

Willie would have done well at school and could have got one of those coveted office jobs. In the course of one afternoon, for a moment's madness, he had blown it, thrown his life away. I hated Willie for it. I pondered bitterly on what must have gone through his mind when he was buying those ridiculous clothes. What had he felt as he stepped out of the taxi and paraded down the street? He must have known he would be identified as the thief. I hated him because he seemed to reinforce those smug white cynics who said Africans never think ahead. 'They live for the moment. Give them money for a week and they'll spend it in a day.' Perhaps it is a feature of poverty. You work all your life to get out of poverty and suddenly you see a short cut. Never mind what lies beyond the short cut. You're there. You are wearing new clothes and that will make people admire you. Boom.

Now, nearly fifty years on, I think of Willie and wonder if he was not, after all, an aberration but quite typical of that first generation of African rulers and the grotesque extravagant pomp of many of them. I think of the Ghanaian minister who had a gold bed made for him, the insanity of the imperial coronation of Jean-Bedel Bokassa in the Central African Republic, the basilica bigger than St Peter's in Côte d'Ivoire, and Mobutu Sese Seko, drinking pink champagne every day and hiring Concorde to fly his family to New York to go shopping.

I tried once to discuss all this with a group of African teachers. I suggested to them that they had a pretty good way of life here in Uganda and it would be stupid to throw it all away in a mad scramble for Western materialism. They got very angry. How dare I suggest that Africa should not have what Western countries had. Weren't Africans as good as Europeans? If I had come here to stop Africa developing I had better get back to England where I belonged.

What I did learn was that the gulf in understanding between Africans and Europeans was immense. An old Dutch priest who had worked in one district of Uganda for thirty years said to me, 'I would give all of that again to have thirty minutes in the mind of an African.' At the time I was shocked, but he was not disillusioned or bitter and he certainly did not feel his life had been a waste. He was just puzzled.

Before I went to Uganda an old Africa hand in Britain had told me that stealing was common. I tried to argue that it was the traditional sense of communalism. He laughed. I called him a racist. After a few months in Uganda I began to see that my 'communalism' meant asking to borrow something, promising to return it but never quite managing to do so. Villagers and students took stealing very seriously. They kept everything under lock and key and were loath to lend anything.

Even petty theft could mean death. Necklacing, putting a tyre soused in petrol round someone's neck and setting fire to it, had not yet spread from South Africa, but thieves were chopped up with machetes or just beaten to death. What horrified me was that it was done casually, almost gleefully. Two English girls who taught in a nearby girls' boarding school told me that a man who had stolen bananas from the school plantation had been caught. The students had joined in beating the man to death, and laughed and joked about it. When my friends burst into tears, their students were embarrassed, not for what they had done but for their teachers' tears.

In 1907, Winston Churchill visited Uganda and described it as a Shangri La: 'beautiful, rich, temperate, a paradise on earth'. But he also sensed evil there. 'It must be too good to be true,' he wrote in *My African Journey*. 'It is too good to be true. Behind its glittering mask [Uganda] wears a sinister aspect . . . a sense of indefinable oppression . . . a cut will not heal, a scratch festers.' He called it 'a garden of sunshine and deadly nightshade'.

Occasionally I caught hints of that evil in the school. Boys would sometimes bully a girl. All they had to do was pick up a stick and shake it at her to reduce the girl to hysterics; kneeling, pleading, whining, begging them not to kill her. At first I thought it was an elaborate charade. One day a group of boys armed with knives and machetes went down to the home of a teacher who had upset them. He fled and would not return until negotiations had taken place. He had cause to flee. They would have killed him. Soon I would witness much more casual cruelty and killing as Uganda's institutions collapsed and soldiers began to realize they had absolute power. Later I was to see the same happen in Somalia, Nigeria, Mozambique, Angola, Ethiopia, Congo, Rwanda and Burundi, and then in Sierra Leone, Liberia and Côte d'Ivoire. The thinly rooted colonial states collapsed and violence ruled.

But Uganda was where I first knew the paradox of Africa's beauty and evil. Here I lost my virginity, physical, spiritual, moral, and found Africa's huge patience and humanity – and its cruelty and violence. Almost everything I know about why Africa is the way it is, I learned first in Uganda. In my second year I travelled through East Africa down to Zambia and found the same mad scramble for a Western lifestyle, the same rejection of African culture, yet a stubborn African way of doing things. At the rate their economies were developing at that time, African states would take decades to provide a Western lifestyle for more than a tiny minority. The majority were still subsistence farmers, but the young, aspiring to escape from rural drudgery through education, were caught in no man's land. They could reach that Western shore only in their dreams. They had abandoned their rural culture but only a tiny minority ever got near their dream. While populations soared, states collapsed or sank into economic decline. Ordinary Africans survived only by clinging to family and faith. Meanwhile, with criminal optimism, the World Bank and other Western aid donors continued to sell the idea of rapid development. Like the young PR man at breakfast, they blithely believed that if you change the message, you can change the reality.

The reality then was that Uganda was already in the early stages of a catastrophe. Idi Amin was already in power and Uganda was to suffer nearly fifteen years of tyranny and civil war. Idi Amin ruled for almost a decade. The burgeoning professional middle class fled and Ugandans, their dreams shattered, were about to become miserably poorer. Nearly all other African countries went the same way for a time. Development went backwards. Even worse, another horror was brewing that none of us knew about at the time. Only a few miles south of our little school in southern Uganda lay the first hot spot of the greatest catastrophe to hit humanity since the Black Death 600 years ago: Acquired Immune Deficiency Syndrome.

3

How it all went wrong
Uganda II

I last saw Idi Amin in Kampala by the roundabout on the Entebbe road in December 1972. He was driving his own Jeep and stopped to let us pass. His huge bulk made the Jeep look like a toy and he was dressed in casual military green with his favoured tartan forage cap, borrowed from a Scottish regiment, perched on his head. Catching sight of a white person, he smiled and waved gaily.

Amin became the stereotype of the African dictator, but in some ways he was not typical. The typical dictator would not have been driving himself. He would have been in a fast-moving, heavily armed convoy that would have driven – or shot – every other vehicle and pedestrian off the road. In Nigeria under military rule I witnessed the Vice-President's convoy in Lagos, a motorcade of some fifteen vehicles including an armoured car, an ambulance and two truckloads of soldiers. We were forced to stop as it roared past, sirens blaring and soldiers hanging out of the trucks pointing their guns at bystanders. I asked my taxi driver what would happen if the man just walked to work. The driver looked airily into the middle distance and said softly: 'We would kill him.'

Idi Amin at least had courage. He was a product of empire, a bizarre and unstable mix of British military discipline and African culture. The Uganda army had emerged from the King's African Rifles, which had seen action in Burma in the Second World War. KAR soldiers were mostly recruited in northern Uganda from the 'warrior tribes', as the British dubbed them. That included Amin, a street kid from West Nile who grew up in an army camp. The British turned him into a tough sergeant. There is a photo of him and another young sergeant standing to attention next to a crisp British officer in shorts and bush hat: the very models of the *bwana* and his 'boys'.

Amin became a sort of faithful pet to the British officers, patted and patronized. He played the role well even as President. He used to drop in for a beer at the Kampala Rugby Club, sit at the bar, play the accordion and sing Scottish ballads and rugby songs. The club was a very British outfit. After independence it admitted a few Ugandan members (if they had been to British public school). Idi was always welcome. As a young man he had been a match-winning wing for the Jinja rugby team. 'Just give Idi the ball and point him in the right direction and you could put your feet up,' the old East Africa hands used to say. Idi knew how to please such chaps. He was their sort of African. But others recalled that after the game they would pass beers to him through a hatch in the clubhouse wall. Africans were not allowed in the bar.

No-one seemed to ask what that might do to a man psychologically. After independence the British officers left and the new government Africanized the army's officer corps, promoting Amin to captain, major and colonel in rapid succession. He loved the glamorous British hierarchies. He created some spectacular new honours and orders for Uganda – and awarded them to himself. So simple Idi Amin became His Excellency Field Marshal Idi Amin Dada, President of Uganda, Conqueror of the British Empire, Victorious Cross, Member of the Excellent Order of the Source of the Nile, Distinguished Service Medal, State Combat Star, Long Service and

Good Conduct Medal. When he met Emperor Jean-Bedel Bokassa of the Central African Empire (now a mere Republic again) the sight was spectacular. Bokassa, a former French army sergeant, had fought in Vietnam and had also come to power in a coup. He too was addicted to giving himself – and wearing – bizarre awards and honours. The two men stood side by side in full dress uniform as if competing to see who could fit the most sashes, stars, medals and ribbons on their fronts. They were like moving display cabinets. Amin, with his vast frontage, won easily. Bokassa was barely five foot tall.

How had Amin come to power? Uganda had been one of the more peaceful British territories. Because it was a protectorate, not a colony, most land was still in African hands. Only a handful of settlers were allowed, so there was no bitter anti-colonial struggle for land as there was in neighbouring Kenya. But its politics were typical of post-independence Africa, an example of how, innocently, ignorantly but inevitably, the seeds of catastrophe were planted by imperial rule. The country's name comes from Buganda, the powerful and sophisticated lakeside kingdom founded around 1500 and ruled by a hereditary kingship, the Kabaka. At the end of the nineteenth century the British made Buganda the core of a bigger state, Uganda, extending the protectorate north, east and west to include other ethnic groups, some of whom had been at war with the Buganda kingdom before the British arrived.

Britain's policy of indirect rule co-opted the local kings and chiefs to carry out their orders but left the execution of the orders to traditional local systems. In Uganda the British designated the Baganda as the 'most advanced tribe' and so used them – and their sophisticated local government structures – to rule other parts of Uganda. That stored up problems for the future. Ethnic groups north of the Nile were utterly different by race and culture, about as similar to the Baganda as the English are to the Chinese. These groups resented the Baganda overlords. They were also in a majority, and as independence, democracy and political parties neared, the demography ordained that the Baganda would not win. The Protestant Baganda political elite was far more concerned to restore the Buganda kingdom and self-rule than promote Ugandan nationalism. The Catholic Baganda forged a new nation-wide movement, the Democratic Party, but it did not have the numbers to win nationally. Uganda, however, could not be stable with the Baganda in opposition.

At independence in 1962, Britain attempted to leave behind a Westminster-style democracy in the tropics with a President and a Prime Minister. Maybe they thought they had cleverly created harmonious balance. They might as well have left the Ugandans the instruments of the London Philharmonic Orchestra and told them to play Beethoven's Ninth Symphony. An election gave victory to a northerner, Milton Obote. He became Prime Minister. The counterbalancing presidency, a ceremonial post like the British monarchy, was given to the Baganda king, the Kabaka, Frederick Mutesa. The Democratic Party was left in the wilderness. The British walked away. Disaster was only a matter of time.

That election in Uganda opened up the seams and split the country along ethnic and religious lines. The system wobbled along for four years, then, in 1966, Obote lost patience with Baganda attempts to gain greater autonomy and drove out President Mutesa in a coup, making himself Executive President. He gathered all power to himself, made Uganda a one-party state and planned radical socialism.

But in using the army to overthrow the constitution, he had involved the soldiers in politics. Idi Amin was the army chief and had led the attack on the king's palace. The British High Commissioner described Amin as having just enough intelligence to know he couldn't run the country. Obote's own assessment was more prescient. He knew the army, and Amin in particular, were a threat.

Obote tried to get rid of him, but Amin was canny and dangerous when threatened. He cultivated the rank and file soldiers and recruited many from his own area. After a mutiny several soldiers were sacked but Amin quietly re-recruited them, making them beholden to him. As Obote went off to the Commonwealth Conference in Singapore in January 1971, he left orders that Amin be arrested.

It has always been assumed that the British had a hand in the coup that brought Idi Amin to power. Obote after all was a socialist and was threatening to nationalize British interests in Uganda. He also accused Britain of selling arms to apartheid South Africa. But was that sufficient motive to overthrow him? After all, in neighbouring Tanzania, President Julius Nyerere had nationalized British companies and was also a fierce critic of Britain's protection of apartheid, but Britain backed Nyerere, putting him back on his throne when an army mutiny overthrew him. The British Foreign Office papers suggest it was Israel that put Idi Amin in power but Britain, it is clear, did have a hand in it.

Since independence the Israelis had been training the Ugandan army, including Amin. They befriended him and took him to Israel on a paratrooper training course. Amin was also the link between the Ugandan army and the southern Sudanese separatist group called the Anya-Nya, which means 'snake venom', fighting for secession, an uprising in which Israel had an interest. Sudan had joined the Arab cause in the 1967 war and helped formulate the hard-line Arab policy towards Israel. Israel's revenge was to support the Anya-Nya fighters by supplying them with weapons. Uganda, Sudan's southern neighbour, was the conduit, and Idi Amin was the agent. Amin came from an ethnic group that bridged the Sudan border. Though a Muslim, he was naturally committed to the southern Sudanese cause and, contrary to Obote's pro-Khartoum policy, acted as Israel's arms supplier to the Anya-Nya. At the end of 1970, Obote flew to Khartoum to try to negotiate peace in southern Sudan between the Anya-Nya and President Numeiri. That worried the Israelis. They wanted the war to continue.

The organizers of the coup were Colonel Bar Lev, an Israeli officer who had worked in Uganda for five years and had become close friends with Amin, and Bruce Mackenzie, a former British bomber pilot and very close to the UK defence establishment, who had settled in Kenya and become a minister in its first independent government and 'foreign affairs adviser' to President Jomo Kenyatta. In the lead-up to the coup Bar Lev neutralized all the pro-Obote army units. That was easy since the Israelis had provided Uganda's military communications network. The Israeli colonel was seen on the eve of the coup with Amin. In the early hours of 25 January 1971, while Obote was in Singapore, the government was overthrown. Ugandans awoke to the slow, sonorous, uncertain speech of Idi Amin Dada announcing he was the new 'temporary' ruler. He then drove around Kampala in his Jeep with Colonel Bar Lev at his side. Uganda's nightmare had begun. Amin was driven out by the Tanzanian army nine years later, but stability in southern Uganda took a further six years. The north was ravaged by war for almost thirty years.

Not many people saw it at the time. Many Ugandans welcomed Amin as a liberator. In Kampala the Baganda bedecked their cars with flowers and drove around, horns blaring. Then they danced all night. Uganda's Asian community was among the first to congratulate him. Israel provided him with close protection, handled his communications and immediately supplied him with weapons.

Officially the British were bemused but relieved that one of their toughest critics had been removed. The Foreign Office papers reveal that Richard Slater, the British High Commissioner, had apparently not been informed beforehand. His telegrams suggest he was taken unawares on the morning of 25 January. But old colonial officials and British officers who had known Amin were delighted. 'Good Old Idi' had scored again. They thought they could keep him happy with some guns and aid – just as they had him in the palms of their hands when they passed him pints through the hatch at the Rugby Club. He would still come to heel when the white man snapped his fingers.

According to sources who knew Mackenzie well and who were there at the time, the plot to overthrow Amin was put together with the Israelis in Mackenzie's house in Nairobi. Mackenzie had direct access to the Prime Minister, Ted Heath, as well as to the Foreign Secretary, Alec Douglas Home, and senior military figures in the UK as well as in MI6, although he got on badly with the local MI6 officer, Frank Steele.

'We now have a thoroughly pro-Western set up in Uganda of which we should take prompt advantage. Amin needs our help,' reads a Foreign Office assessment from the early days of the regime. Being on 'our side' in the Cold War was priority number one for Western countries. Only Richard Slater warned that Amin might not prove the saviour that London wanted and drew attention to the massacres in the north. But he was glad to see the back of Obote.

Amin immediately reversed Obote's socialist policies, which would have led to the nationalization of some fifty British businesses in Uganda. The *Financial Times* declared Amin 'Man of the Week', the *Daily Telegraph* called him 'a welcome contrast to other African leaders and a staunch friend of Britain'. It encouraged the government to give him weapons. The government obliged. It even considered selling Amin Harrier jump-jets. Meanwhile in South Africa, the apartheid regime was delighted with the coup.

The Idi that the world saw was the cheerful, no-nonsense soldier who drove himself around town, fearing nothing. In the area where I lived Amin was popular because he had removed the Bagandas' arch enemy, Obote. He delighted them further by bringing home the body of Frederick Mutesa, who had died in exile in London two years earlier. Amin went round the country preaching traditional values and respect for the elders – and for British teachers. At a rally I attended he embarrassingly singled out us whites in the crowd and told the people to respect and thank those who had come to help develop Uganda.

In southern Uganda, Amin's first year in power did not feel like a reign of terror. On the contrary, many people said the country was freer than it had been under Obote. As a volunteer at that time you could live well on £5 a week. Hitchhiking around the country, you usually got where you wanted to go – eventually. And if you didn't, you would always find a meal and a bed. Ugandans were proud of their reputation for friendliness and hospitality and most Europeans wanted to be there because they loved it. A couple of hours' drive took you to game parks or treks in the hills. Everywhere music poured out of street bars and at the weekend wandering Congolese bands played in every town, their music as warm as the night air.

After a year I fell in love with a beautiful Ugandan girl and we spent most weekends at her family's home near Kampala. Betty worked at a bank but her ambition was to write the great African novel. My ambition was to start a new African tribe with her. Her family was typical of the new Ugandan professional class. Her father, Moses, was a primary school headmaster, her mother worked for the Save the Children Fund. They lived in a large bungalow surrounded by a garden which provided a lot of their food. Betty's brothers and sisters went to good schools and they had a car.

At Christmas we hitchhiked to the Kenyan coast, staying with whoever gave us lifts on the way. In Kampala we went everywhere together. Such relationships were accepted as part of the new Africa. The wealth gap between white and black in the cities was not great. In fact Betty earned more than I did and we were accepted together as equal members of the new rich elite.

Yet beneath the cheerful surface horrible things were happening. Soldiers from Obote's ethnic group, the Langi, and Acholi officers, the backbone of the army, were butchered. They were replaced by people from Amin's area. Two American journalists disappeared. Remnants of their bodies were found in an oven in Mbarara barracks. The Chief Justice, Benedicto Kiwanuka, disappeared. I had attended his silver wedding anniversary, a full Catholic High Mass followed by a sumptuous feast in his village a few miles away along a bush track. In the African heat he wore a top hat and tails and his wife a wedding dress. Kiwanuka had been Uganda's Prime Minister before independence and was one of the most respected elders in the country. But he had given a ruling against an army officer and a few days later soldiers dragged him from his court. He was never seen again. Nasty stuff, but was Amin responsible? No-one was sure. And anyway, who cared about human rights in the Cold War, let alone democracy? They were not on the West's agenda.

In February 1972 Amin began to change tack. His first state visits had been to Israel, then to Britain where the Queen welcomed him and gave him a ride in an open-top royal coach. (Even as he dined at Buckingham Palace, truckloads of murdered soldiers were being dumped in the Nile.) Then he went to Libya and met Colonel Gaddafi. Maybe it was Gaddafi's charm or his money. Perhaps he suddenly reacted to a lifetime of being patronized by Europeans or maybe he realized that they were not going to give him what he wanted. They might even try to get rid of him. When he returned he suddenly cast off the Israelis and the British and adopted the Arab cause, fervently denouncing 'Zionist imperialism' and 'British neo-colonialism'.

The buffoon was still there. First item on Ugandan television news every night was what President Idi Amin Dada had done that day. It also showed him winning swimming and athletics contests that he had organized. He ordered whites to kneel before him and carry him around in a litter. He proposed marrying Princess Anne as a way of patching up Anglo-Ugandan relations. But the buffoon was also a monster. Later he is said to have killed one of his wives and eaten parts of her. They found her remains in his fridge. Amin became the proto-type African military dictator and clown, the jumped-up sergeant who ruled like a profligate king in a wasteland of terror and destitution. His image became the emblem of Africa for decades.

On 6 August 1972 Amin announced that all Asians who did not have Uganda citizenship were to be expelled and their businesses given to Ugandans. Between August and October some 50,000 were forced out and went to Canada, America, Australia and Britain. On their way to the airport the army stripped them; rings, watches and jewellery, anything they fancied. Their expulsion was wildly popular. The Asians, most of them petty traders, were not liked. They did not mix with Africans and many Asian businessmen exploited them bru-tally. So when Amin expelled them, many thought that they would be given Asians' businesses, cars and homes and be rich.

The day the Asian exodus began, a force of Amin's opponents invaded from Tanzania and tried to fight their way towards Kampala. They expected a popular uprising but it did not happen. The army, loyal to Amin, beat them back and they got no support from the local Baganda who did not want Obote to return. The invasion almost reached Kabuwoko Hill and I was confined to the house for nearly a month. The only news of what was happening around us came from local gossip and the BBC World Service. On the ground all was confusion. It was impossible to know who was a rebel and who was a government soldier or who was winning. We kept the compulsory picture of Amin on the wall but I kept the old picture of President Obote hidden behind a cupboard. When soldiers came to the school we had to guess which one to put up.

Mr Lule stayed in Kampala but the parish priest assured us that if the worst came to the worst, he could hide us in his house. The invaders were defeated and driven back, but this short war made Uganda's army paranoid and aggressive. Roadblocks were set up everywhere, manned by jittery and explosive soldiers who used their new power to take money off people. Often they were drunk.

Masaka was put under the command of a terrifying Major Maliamungu. One day he decided to end the practice of overloading taxis – sixteen in a Peugeot designed for eight was not uncommon. When no-one paid any attention to his order, he went down to the taxi park, took the first driver with an overloaded vehicle and shot him dead. The other taxi drivers went on strike until he threatened to have them all shot.

As Amin became more and more anti-British and the British fumbled about trying to find a way of curbing him, mixed relationships became more and more dangerous. One day he denounced Ugandan girls who had white boyfriends as unpatriotic. A friend of Betty's who was seen with a white man was nearly beaten to death by soldiers. Betty's family, with huge sadness and embarrassment, told me I could no longer come to the house. Neither of us had telephones so we relied on letters and visits to communicate. We met in secret and fear, pretending to ignore each other in public.

A few Britons were arrested as spies and paraded in public. In school the students became disquieted. They listened to Uganda Radio and believed it. Some asked me if I was a spy. Others asked if the Ugandan army would beat the British army if it invaded. I decided to stay on, partly because I thought I was too out of the way to be of any interest to Amin and partly out of bloody-mindedness. I went into town as little as possible. Rumours told of daily new atrocities by Amin and his soldiers. The British government-sponsored teachers, doctors and aid workers were withdrawn. Only missionaries and a few older white people who had made their home in Uganda stayed on.

Hard though it is to imagine now, Uganda was becoming self-sufficient at that time. It aimed to be self-reliant, free of aid by 1974. Western governments would have continued to fund particular projects but the Uganda government should have been able to raise its main revenues from taxation. Africa has not always been an aid-dependent beggar. The Asian miracle of the 1980s could have been the African miracle. Instead the 1980s were Africa's catastrophe. Nor was Uganda the only country poised to stand on its own two feet in the 1970s. Others with more natural resources were doing even better. Thirty years on some of them are beginning to get back to the levels of wealth of the early 1970s. But many of them, like Uganda, have become aid-dependent. By 2008 more than half of Uganda's budget came from Western donors. So what went wrong?

The economists blame Africa's failure on the fall in price of the continent's key commodities. They started falling in the 1970s and went on down until around 1995. When Africa started earning more again, life began to get better. Worsening terms of trade certainly added to the mix, but the theory doesn't explain why Asian countries which produced the same commodities as Africa did not also collapse in civil war or become completely impoverished. Development experts blame Africa's failure on policy: the wrong policies, or the right policies badly implemented. But it was not policies that messed up Africa. It was politics. The deadly combination of internal competition for power and outside interference wrecked Africa. As an individual, Amin was extraordinary. What he did to his country was not.

In November I went to a dance in Masaka in a large hall. The invasion had interrupted the weekly Saturday night hop, but nothing could stop the wonderful Congolese bands coming across the western border in large cars stuffed with amplifiers, drums and guitars. Masaka was one of their first stops on their tours of East Africa. Dances were old fashioned in a way. Men and women sat separately from each other and men would ask women for dances, and sometimes giggling girls would ask a man for a dance. But no-one was left out, everyone danced, even if they danced alone. There would also be scores of beautiful girls, many of whom were *mbalassasas*, named after the gorgeously coloured Ugandan lizards. They were fun-makers, out for a good night with music, beer and, if they could get one, a man who would pay for their evening out.

That night some of Major Maliamungu's soldiers came to the dance in uniform. One of them wore a thick red canvas belt. The music went on, no-one paid them much attention, but there was a stiffening of the atmosphere. The major tried to take a girl. There was a fight. Someone grabbed the red belt and tore it off. The major and his men were thrown out, but a few minutes later there was a rumour they were returning. A shot was fired and the dance hall emptied in screams and panic. It was the last dance.

A month later Amin declared all whites in our area to be spies who had uniforms and guns hidden in their houses. It was time to go.

I arrived back in dark, cold, wet December London. It was as if I had been woken from a magnificent dream or dragged out of a wonderful theatre and thrown into a dungeon. I had 50p in my pocket and no winter clothes. Friends put me up and lent me a coat. Three days later I was working in a warehouse near Euston station. But the physical discomfort was nothing to the anguish of leaving Africa. I had left behind the girl I loved, with little prospect of meeting again. People had warned me about the culture shock of going to Africa. Nothing prepared me for the culture shock of coming the other way. No matter how much I talked no-one understood what I was saying. I sank into deep depression and vowed to get back to Africa.

4

The end of colonialism
New states, old societies

Three words come to mind when people try to explain the failure of Africa's first generation after independence: leadership, tribalism and resources. They are not bad starting points, but they do not fully explain why Africa, free at last, endowed with enormous potential wealth and peopled with bright, optimistic men and women, failed.

Leaders do not emerge from nowhere. Could it really be coincidence that all of Africa's forty-odd leaders who came to power at independence were bad rulers who took bad decisions? Not all of them were corrupt tyrants and many were decent men who believed that what they were doing was for the best. The new presidents inherited total power from the colonial rulers, but the states they ruled were made up of old African societies, once self-governing and still held together by their own networks of power and influence. Trying to use the tools of a Western-style state to control these rooted societies was like trying to herd cats with a dog-training manual.

In Africa – as anywhere else – ethnicity and culture are important. Imagine if, after two world wars that have slaughtered some 90 million people, America and the Soviet Union, exasperated by tribal warfare in Europe, create a single country called Europe. They impose it from above, creating provinces by drawing lines on maps with no regard for the identity of the people living there. Today a Slovene President is trying to broker a border dispute between the provinces of France and Germany. Under France is a vast pool of oil, but some of it is also under Germany – the Germans are all Muslim by the way. Meanwhile the ancient tribal hatreds still cause frequent massacres among Greeks and Turks, Basques and Spanish, and in parts of north London where rival football tribes called Arsenal and Tottenham are clashing in the streets. Tribalism is not an exclusively African disease.

Imagining a 'tribal' Europe gives you some idea of what African citizenship is like. The European Union has only 23 languages. Africa has at least 2000, and between 6000 and 10,000 political or social entities, each of which once had its own governance and legal system, its leadership and customs and culture. And, like an imagined Europe unified by force by outsiders, Africans played no part in the creation of their nation states. Their boundaries were drawn on maps in Europe by Europeans who had never even been to Africa, with no regard for existing political systems and boundaries. Half a century later Africans were given flags and national anthems, airlines and armies, and told they were now independent: Kenyans or Nigerians or Chadians.

In these newly independent countries the easiest way for a would-be ruler to gather supporters was to mobilize his own ethnic or religious group against others and impose his will by force in the name of establishing national unity. What might Africa have been like if the Europeans had not taken it over? What political systems might have evolved from Africa's traditional, subtle systems of power and monarchy if European contact with Africa had remained purely mercantile? Would it have been a United States of Africa or hundreds of mini-states, each based on an ethnic group?

But the tribalism factor, while certainly important, is not the whole story. Take Somalia and Botswana, two countries where almost everyone belongs to the same ethnic group with the same culture and language. Somalis are also bound by the same religion, Islam, but Somalia exploded in the worst war any country has suffered. It is still trying to restore itself. Botswana, the home of the Tswana people, is a success story, peaceful, democratic and wealthy. It is also the answer to the 'resource curse' theory – that Africa's very wealth makes politics a mad, winner-takes-all scramble for gold or diamonds or oil. Botswana had nothing at independence except a few cows and a lot of bush. Diamonds were discovered and mining was developed from 1967. Since then the country has earned billions from diamonds. In two decades its wealth increased by 500 per cent. Per head of population, Batswana had $122 each in 1970. This grew to $7480 by 2011. And Botswana's elected government has spent the money on giving its people improved education and health and better roads and water. Visiting Botswana makes you realize what all of Africa might have become.

Back at the beginning of human history, Africa north of the Sahara was part of the Persian and early European worlds, linked easily by trade across the Red Sea and the Mediterranean. It was as much part of the Roman Empire as Britain or Germany. That link was cut by the Arab expansion in the Middle East and into the Maghreb in the eighth century. Africa was cut off from other traders and influences for 700 years. Asians were the first to come with a visitation by the Chinese fleet to the East African coast in 1405 and in subsequent years. But they went away again and did not return. A mere fifty years later the Europeans first arrived in sub-Saharan Africa, working their way down the west coast. Unlike the Chinese they were aggressive, destroying existing trade routes and taking what they wanted by force. They came in greater and greater numbers and they settled. From the early days of trading, through the slave-trade centuries and the imperial take-over at the end of the nineteenth century right through to today, Europe dominated Africa. Now that domination may be coming to an end with the re-appearance of the Chinese. Recently they have come seeking raw materials and as traders and may transform Africa as profoundly in the twenty-first century as Europeans did in the previous two centuries.

When European rulers suddenly decided to take over Africa's hinterland at the end of the nineteenth century, they did not want any unseemly fights in front of the natives. That might give them the idea that the white man was vulnerable. Better to share out the continent amicably and convince Africans that whites were their new masters. So the whites sat down at a meeting in Berlin in 1884 and carved up Africa by drawing lines on maps. In some areas white explorers had not even set foot on the ground where they now drew borders. Most states were formed from the ports and forts that European traders had secured on the coasts of the continent over almost four centuries. In the seventeenth and eighteenth centuries they had come in search of gold and then slaves. Now they wanted the land. In West Africa the European land grab ballooned out of the coastal trading posts into the vast unexplored continent – hence the shape of West African nation states today. Ethnic groups, local identities and even natural borders such as rivers and mountains were ignored as the mapmakers guessed where watersheds lay between river sources. The imperial powers then sent in their frontier forces to crush resistance and establish their rule.

The Europeans conquered in the name of Christianity, Civilization and Commerce. Was it possible to bring Christianity – stronger today in Africa than almost anywhere in the world – without the eradication of the beliefs and culture of ancient societies? Could the Europeans have brought 'civilization' – the rule of

European law, the benefits of education and health – without the destruction of social and political structures? Could it have been possible for commerce – wealth-creating trade – to benefit Africans instead of reducing them to labourers for the imperial powers? In theory, yes, of course. In fact the Europeans, believing they were superior beings, imposed their systems of trade, belief and finally rule, with devastating violence.

Had Africa been more amenable to European settlement, the invaders might have wiped out the existing populations or reduced them to the margins – as they had done in the Americas and Australia. In Southern Africa and Algeria and for a while in Kenya that is what they tried to do. Where Europeans did not settle as colonists their rule was imperial. They made treaties with friendly kings and chiefs who sought short-term advantage from their new, well-armed white allies. But Africa's rulers were also marginalized and swallowed up in the new territories. A tiny elite of Europeans took control. They did not try to displace the population – often they simply left the people alone under the control of now subservient local rulers – but they took whatever natural resources they could find. Africa's economies were twisted to serve Europe's needs. With the missionaries and colonial governors came the destruction of Africa's political systems, religions, culture, dignity and self-worth.

The brutal but brief conquest of Africa, particularly south of the Sahara, left it somehow stranded between tradition and Western modernity. While some African peoples were almost wiped out by the arrival of imperial troops and colonists, others were barely aware of the arrival of the Europeans or their departure half a century later. In contrast Indians, who were ruled by Britain for more than a century, absorbed British institutions and systems and made them their own. At independence Indians inherited reasonably good infrastructure and a capable civil service. In Africa the European powers had been strong enough to destroy or subdue traditional African political systems but did not stay long enough to create new ones. Perhaps it would have been better for Africa if they had remained longer.

As in India, the British used the system of indirect rule. The kings and chiefs stayed on, allowed to run local affairs in traditional ways as long as they did not conflict with imperial policy or create problems. Land disputes, marriages and suchlike matters were dealt with by the traditional system. On bigger issues the British provided 'guidance' to the chiefs who became, in effect, paid civil servants. Where there were no chiefs the British invented them or deployed chiefs from other 'superior' ethnic groups to rule over them.

While the British never pretended that their subject nations would be British, the French and Portuguese based their empires on the Roman Empire, planning their colonies to be as French as Paris, as Portuguese as Lisbon. They created administrative systems in Africa similar to their own domestic structures. They tried to turn the chiefs into official administrators. In practice they still had to deal with the chiefs as traditional rulers. Under all imperial systems traditional kings and chiefs had little direct power, though they could exert considerable influence. If they co-operated with the imperial rulers they could became local dictators without the checks and balances of Africa's traditional political systems. On the other hand, if they disobeyed the orders of their imperial bosses, traditional rulers were removed and replaced. Most pursued their own interests, helping, hindering or obstructing the imperial power as it suited them.

In his memoir, *Remote Corners*, Harry Mitchell, a district officer in Kambia, Sierra Leone, illustrated the difference between British and French imperialism. He was given a district on the troublesome Guinean border to administer. There was, he says, no policy at all beyond preventing problems arising. Mitchell saw it as his role to bring some development to the region, encourage schools and health programmes. His fellow administrator in a neighbouring district took the opposite view. He saw it as his role to protect Africans from the modern world, preserve their way of life and prevent anything that might change it. Neither approach seemed to find approval or disapproval from their overlords in the Colonial Office. Across the border in Guinea, says Mitchell, the French 'appear to have taken a pride in ruling over a huge area of the continent and to have regarded themselves as the modern successors of the Romans'. French policy was a mission to 'civilize' Africa and make its people French.

Whatever dreams the imperialists had for their new possessions at the end of the nineteenth century, they were never able to fulfil them. Europe took over Africa when most of its own bloody disputes had gone quiet. The industrial revolution had made Europe rich. Supremely self-confident, the Europeans were ready to rule the world. But thirty years after the Berlin conference the First World War broke out, followed by economic depression and then a second global war. Much of Europe's economic resources were destroyed. The First World War in Africa cost 100,000 military lives, 45,000 of them African. The civilian toll was uncounted but it was certainly many times the military toll. Thousands of African men were forced to become bearers and workers in the war effort, leaving their families to starve and their villages to struggle. In the Second World War, African regiments were formed and fought in Burma and elsewhere. Their experience of seeing white men fight each other and die had a profound impact on the way in which Africa viewed itself when they returned. Although parts of Africa did well economically during the Second World War, Britain and France were devastated by it and, when it ended, they no longer had the resources to manage, let alone develop, their colonies as they had planned half a century before. America now ruled the Western world and America opposed European imperialism. Besides, the lessons of genocide in Europe and the contribution of Indians and Africans to the defeat of Nazi racial ideology were not lost on subject peoples. Self-rule became inevitable.

'Seek ye first the political kingdom,' said Kwame Nkrumah as the first stirrings of African self-rule began. His words inspired a generation of African nationalists to demand independence from the imperialists immediately and on Africa's terms. When demands for independence in India – the jewel in the imperial crown – became irresistible, Britain was forced to 'shoot or get out'. At first, faced with the shock of losing this pillar of empire, Britain thought that Africa could be their new India, but India's independence in 1947 itself inspired other nationalisms among all colonized peoples. In 1952 the British accepted Nkrumah as Prime Minister of the Gold Coast. That made it inevitable that it would become independent Ghana. When Egypt seized the Suez Canal in 1956 and America forced Britain and France to stop their attempt to overthrow President Abdul Nasser and win it back, the days of European imperialism were numbered. Uprisings in Palestine, Malaya, Aden, Cyprus and Kenya sent Britain the message that staying on would be costly. France fought and lost bloody wars in Algeria and Vietnam. The fear in London and Paris was that anti-imperial rebels would harness the support of the Soviet Union and China and they would be faced with nasty, long-drawn-out and ultimately unwinnable guerrilla wars in all their territories. Better to get out quickly. They opened the floodgates.

If only we had had more time, said many of the departing colonial administrators. With more time and resources they felt they could have created viable states in Africa instead of being forced to hand over power immediately, often to populist and unscrupulous leaders. They complained that weak, cynical governments in London and Paris had given up too quickly, glad to be rid of imperial burdens. 'They just aren't interested in those potty little places any more,' one colonial officer was told on a visit to the Commonwealth Office in London in the mid 1950s.

More than half a century of imperial rule was shuffled off in just four years. Between 1960 and 1964, twenty new entities were pitched onto the international stage as nation states. In sunset ceremonies in ten British colonies and protectorates, the Union Jack was lowered and hastily devised national flags raised to the clink of teacups and the strains of an equally hastily composed national anthem. As the British scrambled out of one African country after another the new states received an army, an airline, a mace for the parliament and stamps. The French, who still clung to the idea of France overseas, were more reluctant to leave. They tried to create a 'French Community' in which Africa's new states would be autonomous but still somehow part of France. It failed, and France too was forced to invent new nation states and find them flags and anthems.

Independence officially restored power in Africa to Africans, but the countries created and the systems that the Europeans imposed on Africa as they left were not rooted in African culture or experience and not strong enough to contain social and ethnic pressures that lay immediately beneath the surface. European influence – indirect and sometimes direct – remained strong in Africa, and the Europeans were joined by Russia and America, who wanted to ensure 'stability' by propping up dictators in the new states to serve their strategic interests and protect their economic stakes in Africa.

In French territories, apart from Guinea which went its own way, the transition was peaceful and the new rulers seemed to accept the explanation of their French masters that they had suddenly become mature enough to rule themselves. The French remained directly engaged with Africa after their colonies became independent. They officially handed over administrative control in formal flag-raising ceremonies, but not all their officials left their former territories.

France held together its shadow empire in Africa to gain votes at the UN, but mainly to project its own self-image of a world power. The shadow empire was run secretly through shady deals and clandestine networks. For fourteen years formally – and many more years informally – it was run by Jacques Foccart, a secret service agent known as Monsieur Afrique, who headed the *réseaux*, a network of informers and enforcers based on the systems of the French Resistance. From 1960 almost until he died in 1997, Foccart made sure that no government changed hands in francophone Africa without his say-so. In his memoirs he admitted to murdering one opposition leader. There were almost certainly many more. The French also controlled their former colonies' economies by creating their currency, the CFA (the *Communauté française d'Afrique*), pegging both versions of it, the West African and the Central African, to the French franc and now to the euro. The French government also made bilateral military agreements with its former colonies and until recently kept about 9000 troops in its African former colonies. Under the agreements the troops were stationed in French-controlled bases providing training and arms and sometimes intervening to keep their chosen ruler in power. In 2008 President Nicolas Sarkozy, embarrassed by France's outdated relationship with its former African colonies, offered to renegotiate the agreements.

Three decades after independence there were more French people in the francophone territories than there had been in colonial times. French companies still got all the major contracts. Most ministries in francophone Africa still contained a French official lurking in a back office to ensure that things did not go awry. That also meant Paris was kept fully informed of what was happening. For a long time it seemed that former French-ruled Africa was far more successful than former British Africa. In reality the problems were only delayed by continued French intervention.

In the late 1990s this began to change as francophone African leaders sought alternative partners and France seemed to lose interest in Africa. For most French people, Africa was becoming an immigration problem. For the young emerging middle class in Africa, France was a domineering neocolonialist. But France remained dependent on Africa for much of its oil and uranium – and for votes at the United Nations – so political, commercial, military and intelligence links were maintained with the ruling elites. In 2002, when civil war broke out in the jewel in the crown, Côte d'Ivoire, French troops intervened and France took the political and military lead right through to the final ousting and capture of the president who refused to give up power, Laurent Gbagbo.

In contrast, the end of the Belgian, Spanish and Portuguese empires in Africa felt more like expulsion. Two days of bloody rioting in Congo in January 1959 sent the Belgians scuttling out by the thousands. Independence, targeted notionally by Belgium for the twenty-first century, came within eighteen months. Spain could not stay on in Equatorial Guinea when everyone else was leaving, and departed in 1968, allowing its other possession, Western Sahara, to be seized by Morocco and Mauritania in 1974. Ironically Spain, the least of all the European colonial powers, is the only European country to still own a part of Africa: the two tiny enclaves, Melilla and Ceuta, in northern Morocco.

The Portuguese had been in Africa longest and had the most colonists there. They declared Angola, Mozambique and Guinea-Bissau to be part of the Portuguese state, not colonies, and refused to abide by United Nations decolonization resolutions. They did not leave until a modernizing military coup in Portugal forced them out in 1975. Like the Belgians, they fled in bitter defeat. For a long period both Belgium and Portugal failed to establish even the semblance of friendship with the governments that took over their former colonies.

The bitterest battles were fought where colonists had taken the land or where local resistance movements had battled on throughout the colonial period. Colonies with substantial settler populations like Algeria, Cameroon, Kenya, Zimbabwe and the Portuguese colonies experienced serious uprisings. But these were not necessarily liberation movements. Some were local, ethnically based and inspired by loss of land. Only in some cases did these local battles consciously develop into national uprisings against outside political domination.

Like Algeria, South Africa at the other end of the continent underwent an attempt at total colonization based on race. In both cases the land was seized and the indigenous population driven to the margins and reduced to servility. The settlers, French in Algeria and Dutch in South Africa, lost all family links with their original homeland. The Dutchmen made a virtue of it, proudly calling themselves after the land they had conquered, Afrikaners. They were defeated by the British but in 1909 the Union of South Africa was created. In a British concession to the Afrikaners, all non-white people lost their land tenure and voting rights. Africans fought back, founding their own political movement, the African National Congress, in 1912. They got nowhere, and after the Second World War the Afrikaner National Party came to power and formalized racial discrimination as *apartheid* – separateness. Britain and other Western countries disapproved, but continued its trade and strategic alliance with South Africa. Only when the Cold War ended did they feel confident enough to withdraw that support from the white minority.

In countries which had few European settlers and no removals from the land, there were almost no nationalist movements. Independence came to their inhabitants as a surprise, not as a liberation. Here political and economic pressure from the United States was more important than African agitation in forcing Britain and France to get out. Their inhabitants were told they were going to become independent before they had expressed any demand for it. A group of French territories including Côte d'Ivoire and Senegal wanted to remain part of the French empire. The first President of the Seychelles, James Mancham, fought hard to keep the islands British.

The imperial powers took down their flags and left. But it was one thing to say that the British should stop ruling the Gold Coast, quite another to create a country called Ghana. Hoisting a new flag did not create a new nation state. What did Africans feel about suddenly being Nigerian or Ghanaian or Senegalese? Or indeed about being African? What did it mean? Europeans had claimed racial superiority to justify slavery and then imperialism. African culture, knowledge and values were despised, African dignity and self-worth eroded. Africans were not allowed to develop their own political and social systems to engage with the modern industrial world. They were forced to abandon their own beliefs, identities and values and become imitation white men. In the end, the greatest impact of European imperialism in Africa may have been neither political nor economic. It may have been cultural and psychological: the destruction of African self-belief.

Through the flow of Africa's historical struggle for self-rule are two swirling currents. One is Marxist, based on the belief that imperialism is about economic exploitation. The Marxist strategy was to change the structures and seize political power so that the economy could be run in the interests of the masses. The other was Africanist, a reaction to racial oppression. The Africanist philosophy was less about seizing power in order to change economic structures and more about freeing Africans from alien rule. One of its greatest exponents was Steve Biko, the South African revolutionary, murdered by the police in 1977. For him the most important battle in the struggle against apartheid was for individual Africans to free themselves from the mental and spiritual bonds of oppression. The two currents,

Marxist and Africanist, powered the struggle for African liberation. They sometimes followed similar but separate strategies and even crossed over, Africanists sometimes being more hard-line Marxist than the Marxists. The Marxists often played the race card. Sometimes they formed rival camps that offered opportunities for the Europeans, Russians and Americans to play divide and rule.

For the new African rulers, the new nations states were a psychological and cultural problem as well as a political one. For a start, the citizens of the new nations had played no part in creating them. Somehow the new rulers had to invent nationalism. Like anyone else, Africans feel their identity grows out of family, language and culture – ethnicity. All but a few African countries are made up of several ethnic groups. Nigeria, for example has some 400 different languages and three huge ethnic groups – nations even – which compete fiercely for power.

These new states also contained the remnants of leadership from precolonial states: kings, emirs and chiefs whose power may have been eroded or discredited by colonial rule but who still exercised considerable influence at local level. Why did power not revert to these traditional systems at independence? In Lesotho and Swaziland, micro-Southern African kingdoms inside South Africa which more or less matched old African states, it did. These states had kept separate from South Africa under British rule. But in neither case has traditional rule worked. From independence Swaziland had a king who ruled sensibly, taking into account both tradition and the need to modernize. However, his British public-school educated successor, King Mswati III, rules like an old-fashioned African dictator. Perhaps that is how he imagines his ancestors ruled. He treats parliament as an advisory body, ignoring it when he does not like its advice, and uses state funds to buy his several wives trinkets such as new BMWs. In Lesotho, elections divided the country between a hereditary monarch who did not accept the position of ceremonial king, and an elected Prime Minister who was a traditional chief. In its early years, party politics based on splits in the royal family kept Lesotho as divided as any African country.

Elsewhere ethnic groups which might have had their own micro state or autonomous region were brought quickly under the new national governments. Groups that had signed special deals with the imperial rulers, like the Lozi in Zambia and the Bakiga in Uganda, rebelled. They had formerly agreed to 'protectorate' status, which had left them autonomous under imperial protection. Now, at independence, the British abandoned them and they were lumped in with their neighbours. These little kingdoms deeply resented it. They wanted their own separate state, but that suited neither the departing imperialists nor the new national leaders. Such potential ethnic-based nation states were quickly suppressed.

In other areas traditional rulers were caught flatfooted by the sudden collapse of imperial rule. As the demands for freedom grew louder, most of the chiefs were more and more identified with the ruling imperial system. The new African politicians like Nkrumah, Obote, Nyerere and Kenneth Kaunda in Zambia, whose authority came from academic qualifications not inherited position, attacked their corrupted office and painted their traditional role as feudal and backward. In rural areas the kings and chiefs might still hold sway, but in the swelling towns young nationalist leaders were creating political awareness and building a power base. They knew they had to break old loyalties to chiefs and kings and replace it with loyalty to themselves and their parties.

Only a handful of the new rulers came from the precolonial ruling class. On the whole they did prove better than those who had come from lowlier backgrounds. The prime example is Nelson Mandela, a Xhosa prince. The Ethiopian Emperor Haile Selassie was, until his later years, a dynamic and progressive leader with natural authority. Félix Houphouët-Boigny, first President of Côte d'Ivoire, and Julius Nyerere of Tanzania were also sons of chiefs. Seretse Khama, Botswana's first President, was another born to rule. He had inherited the throne of the Tswana Khama clan at the age of four and managed to secure a good education while a regent stood in for him. But when he wanted to marry a white English woman, Ruth Williams, he nearly lost his position. The regent, the Khama chiefs and the British overlords opposed the marriage. He defied them all, married Ruth, and stood as a candidate in the elections that led to full independence in 1966. He won and remains arguably Africa's most successful post-independence leader until Mandela.

So what of the others, the new giants breaking the fetters of colonial rule? What sort of men were they? Where had they come from? Leaders do not emerge from thin air. They are products of their societies.

The French system had allowed some Africans, like Houphouët-Boigny, to exercise real administrative power, but in the British territories there were few Africans with experience of government or administration. Indeed, the British had locked up most of the future leaders as troublemakers. There is no clear pattern to the backgrounds of Africa's first rulers beyond the fact they were all men. Africa had to wait until 2005 – when Ellen Johnson-Sirleaf was elected President of Liberia – to have its first woman president, though nine years earlier the unelected Ruth Perry was made Liberia's head of state.

Many of that first generation were the first in their families to receive Western education and came from the emerging class of mission-educated African professionals: clerks, teachers, doctors and priests. The parents of Jomo Kenyatta, Kenya's first President, were illiterate peasant farmers. He worked for the water board until he went to Britain on a mission to fight for Kikuyu land, and stayed in exile for fifteen years. After the Second World War he returned home on a wave of African nationalism. A period in prison as a suspected leader of the Kikuyu Mau Mau rebellion gave him the status of undisputed leader of Kenyan nationalism.

Kwame Nkrumah's father was a goldsmith and he was born in a village called Nkroful in the western Gold Coast. After a Catholic mission education he became a teacher and then went to study in America, returning to Ghana on a worldwide wave of demands for freedom in 1947. Prison – though for less than a month – also confirmed him as national leader. Houphouët-Boigny in Côte d'Ivoire went to medical school and worked for the health service until he formed a political movement to protest at the favourable treatment given to large white-owned cocoa plantations over small African producers in French West Africa. He was elected to parliament in Paris and served for fifteen years as a minister in six French governments. When some sort of self-government became a possibility, he campaigned for Côte d'Ivoire to remain in political association with France, but when full independence became inevitable, he became President. Houphouët-Boigny remained close to Paris for the rest of his life. The French ambassador in Abidjan was always jokingly referred to as Houphouët's representative to France.

In the eyes of the world he was a great statesman and French politician. Like others of that generation, he suffered from that schizophrenia that bedevilled Africans who had been brought up to admire all things European and despise African culture and thought. On the site of the village he was born in, Yamoussoukro, he began to build a new capital city. At its edge in virgin bush he decreed a repro-baroque cathedral modelled on St Peter's in Rome, but taller. A series of stained glass windows depict kitsch scenes from the life of Christ and Catholic saints. Amid the myriad stained glass angels and saints there is only one black face: that of President Houphouët-Boigny himself, kneeling in prayer before a traditional European-featured Virgin – hardly the image of an African leader forged in the furnace of anti-colonial struggle. When he died in 1993, Houphouët-Boigny was buried in a magnificent ceremony in his basilica. Soon afterwards weeds began to appear in the paving around the church and ants started to build little mounds of red earth nearby, mocking the mighty dome of stone and lead. Cracks and damp patches appeared in the vast masonry. It was symbolic of what was happening in the country. Côte d'Ivoire, France's model colony, was also beginning to fall apart.

Patrice Lumumba, Congo's radical first Prime Minister, was mission-educated and worked as a clerk before getting involved in politics. His nemesis, Joseph Désiré Mobutu, was the son of a cook. Mobutu became a policeman and then a journalist. He was of the Africanist mould, changed the name of Congo to Zaire and forced the Zaireois to drop their European names and adopt African ones. But under his rule, independence became no more than a change in the colour of the face of the ruler. He ruled as greedily as King Leopold, the Belgian founder of Congo.

In Guinea, Ahmed Sékou Touré, first President and the only francophone African leader to reject the idea of a French community in West Africa, was the son of a peasant and rose to power through trade union activities. As President he was bloody and repressive. Fulbert Youlou of Congo-Brazzaville was a Roman Catholic priest who was soon overthrown. Leopold Senghor, the philosopher king and poet of Senegal, was a university lecturer. He tried to reconcile the African and the French by seeing Africa as his mother and France as his father. Julius Nyerere of Tanzania was a university-educated schoolmaster. He kept the title Mwalimu – 'teacher' in Swahili – and tried to guide Tanzania towards a model of Christian socialism. He remains one of the most respected – and loved – of all African first presidents.

Under such men independence was accompanied by a symphony of optimism despite catastrophe in Congo and worrying rumblings beneath the surface in other countries. The image of Africa then was a continent freed, master of its own destiny. The incubus of colonial rule had been removed and all that was needed to allow Africa to take off and fly was a little aid to get industries going and improve agriculture. In the late 1960s, Africa was seen as the future. Asia was a hopeless continent with too many people and not enough food. Africa, in contrast, was inhabited by a dynamic population, stuffed with valuable minerals and blessed with good agricultural land. A common cartoon image of the continent at the time was of a black giant in chains waking up and breaking his bonds.

It was the writers, not the economists, who got it right. Chinua Achebe, the Nigerian novelist, accurately prophesied the true nature of African politics in the next era. In his novel *A Man of the People*, published in 1966, he described the coming of independence in Nigeria:

> *We ignore man's basic nature if we say, as some critics do, that because a man . . . had risen overnight from poverty and insignificance to his present opulence he could be persuaded without much trouble to give it up again and return to his original state. A man who has just come in from the rain and dried his body and put on dry clothes is more reluctant to go out again than another who has been indoors all the time. The trouble with our new nation was that none of us had been indoors long enough to be able to say 'to hell with it'. We had all been in the rain together until yesterday. Then a handful of us – the smart, and the lucky and hardly ever the best – had scrambled for the one shelter our former rulers left, and had taken it over and barricaded themselves in. And from within they sought to persuade the rest through numerous loudspeakers, that the*

*first phase of the struggle had been won and that the next phase – the
extension of our house – was even more important and called for new
and original tactics; it required all argument to cease and the whole
people to speak with one voice and that any more dissent and
argument outside the door of the shelter would subvert and bring
down the whole house.*

Most Africans have been in the rain ever since. Nkrumah's battle cry
for self-government, 'Seek ye first the political kingdom,' was indeed
taken up by ambitious African politicians. In most African countries
the elite grabbed the postcolonial state for themselves and boarded it
up against the people. They embraced all the repressive colonial
laws and changed very little except the size of their bank accounts.
From within, but in the name of the people still out in the rain, they
continued to foment civil wars and coups and repress their enemies.
It is their loudspeakers that stir up divisions among those still
outside. Even when an outsider succeeds in uniting people and
breaking into the house, he soon closes the door again and adopts
the style, manners and policies of the previous occupiers. Meanwhile
most of their people, still in the rain, die young, often sick and
hungry. So when people say, 'African solutions to African problems,'
or 'Let the Africans sort it out for themselves,' or 'You must help
Africans,' I reply: 'Which Africans? Those inside or outside the house?'

That may not make African rulers any different from rulers anywhere. What makes them different may be that elsewhere rulers are
constrained by constitutions, institutions and pressure groups that
prevent them becoming megalomaniac, kleptocratic dictators.
African politics are all local and personal. They have had little to do
with *how* Africa is to be ruled and everything to do with *who* is to
rule. Ideology, principle, political parties and policy have been merely
disposable weapons in a battle for power between individuals and

power blocs. And having obtained the political kingdom, the winners hold onto it at any price – sometimes even at the cost of destroying the country itself.

Some argue that Africa's dictators were simply imitating their predecessors in deploying all the pomp, grandeur and mystique of European imperial rule. Britain's power was largely an illusion projected by display and ceremony and the occasional brutal military strike. French rule had more physical and cultural presence. But after the 1920s, apart from the odd plume and topi on official occasions, European commissioners and district officers tended to wear shorts and open shirts. Some travelled their domain by bicycle. Their successors as local governors in many parts of Africa today wear dark suits and travel in armoured vehicles or black Mercedes Benz escorted by heavily armed military convoys. Anyone on a bicycle is driven into the ditch.

Others suggest that the growth of dictatorship in Africa was a return to a traditional African style of rule – the tyrannical village chief. Certainly many new African rulers cited African tradition to justify their dictatorship. But were the tyrannies of men like Amin, Mobutu, Bokassa, Abacha and Mugabe a genuine return to traditional African forms of government? Some African empires in precolonial times had elements of totalitarian dictatorship. In the Zulu empire in Southern Africa, the Ashanti kingdom in West Africa and the Buganda kingdom, the kings were virtual gods. But these empires were the exception to African governance rather than the rule. Most precolonial African political systems contained strong democratic elements. African kings and states were constrained by checks and balances such as committees of elders or spirit mediums. They made sure the king ruled well and in accordance with custom and religion. Even in hereditary kingships, counsellors chose a successor from among a dead king's sons. The spirits of the ancestors did not always speak through the ruler. If a king ruled badly he could be deposed.

The essence of democracy is not at all alien to Africa. Although few African societies were pure democracies, some, like the Igbo of Nigeria and the Acholi in Uganda, were almost egalitarian, at least among men. They did not have kings or chiefs and decisions were taken after debate at meetings of the male elders. Discussion tended towards consensus rather than adversarial debate. If your population is small it is important not to split the group. Governance in such societies tended towards compromise rather than leaving victors as conquerors and vanquished as adversaries.

Nowhere is the African view put better than in Barbara King-solver's novel *The Poisonwood Bible*. Set in pre-independence Congo, it highlights the profoundly different ways of African and Western thinking, especially when it comes to an election. 'To the Congolese it seems odd that if one man gets fifty votes and the second forty-nine, the first one wins altogether and the second one plumb loses. That means almost half the people will be unhappy and . . . in a village that's left halfway unhappy you haven't heard the end of it. There is sure to be trouble somewhere down the line.'

First-past-the-post, winner-takes-all parliamentary democracy suddenly imported from London or Paris does not suit African culture or the multi-ethnic states of Africa. For a start, the concept of a loyal opposition was not fostered by colonial rule. On the contrary, there was no doubt where power lay in those times and no opposition, loyal or otherwise, was tolerated. So Africans had little preparation for electoral choices or the alien concept of leader of the opposition. They were suddenly expected to work a system in which parties competed vigorously for power in an election, the winner became President and the loser was allowed to continue to attack the winner but not try to take power. Opposition candidates in Africa are frequently told, 'I will vote for you when you are President.' The implication is that the President is the President. People would no more vote against him than British people would demand a vote every five years on whether the Queen should remain monarch.

It was fertile ground for misunderstanding. In 1988, Neil Kinnock, the leader of Britain's Labour Party, then in opposition, toured Southern Africa. Over Mutare his plane was forced down by bad weather and he landed unannounced at a small airstrip in the bush. Zimbabwean soldiers detained the plane and questioned the visitor. When he proudly announced that he was the leader of the opposition in Britain they arrested him. They were thrilled. The soldiers thought they had caught a really important terrorist.

Multi-party democracy produced other unexpected results in Africa. In the wild and undeveloped north-east of Uganda, Karamoja, there was only one Karamojong with Western education in 1961. He had adopted a strange mix of European and Indian names: Maximillian L. Choudry. The 'L.' was a mystery. No officials from any of the three parties contesting the pre-independence election penetrated so far north, and Maximillian L. Choudry applied for and was endorsed by all three parties including, bizarrely, the party of the Baganda monarchists, Kabaka Yekka. He changed his name slightly for each candidacy; Maximillian L. Choudry, L.C. Choudry and Max Choudry. Professor James Barber, who became a distinguished Africa scholar, was then the young district officer in Karamoja. Bemused, Barber summoned Mr Choudry and asked which party he intended to represent. 'Whichever wins,' came the logical reply. Maximillian L. Choudry was duly elected, and became a junior minister in the government.

Other examples abound of the way first-past-the-post, multi-party democracy does not suit African culture. Of the 1957 election in Sierra Leone, Harry Mitchell wrote in his memoir:

The traditional African method of election or of dealing with any contentious matter is to gather together to 'hang heads' and, after heated discussion, reach a unanimous decision. This practice was adapted to modern times by having meetings before polling day of all the voters of a village who would agree, were it not an already foregone conclusion, on the candidate for whom they would vote; later they would walk to the polling station in a body to register their ostensibly secret votes.

A colonial officer in Zimbabwe, then Rhodesia, reported the same phenomenon of communal African politics at an election there in the mid 1960s: 'Voters would hold a meeting to agree on the candidate for whom they would vote before going to the polling booth.'

In Uganda, President Yoweri Museveni tried to introduce a 'no party' system. He did not ban parties but neither did he allow them to campaign nor to field candidates in elections. Candidates had to stand as individuals. The people were encouraged to join his 'movement' and play an active political role in the area. Freedom of speech was pretty much guaranteed. Museveni pointed out that Western parliamentary democracy developed in Europe where society is divided horizontally on class lines. People could change their voting pattern as they grew richer or poorer and their class interest changed. In Africa, however, ethnicity is more important than class. Parties tend to be ethnic based, dividing societies vertically. At independence, when new, national identities were still foetal, winner-takes-all elections threatened to confirm the largest ethnic group as rulers for ever. Other groups were forced out of power and into possibly permanent opposition. Museveni's idea made sense in theory. But after nearly twenty years in power he was forced to allow other parties to operate. However, with all the state resources at his disposal as well as the army, police and security organization and his wife as his virtual deputy he could still win elections. He tried to make his son his successor and freedom of speech and political space were reduced in many ways. When a young singer, Robert Kyagulani, known as Boni Wine, a singer from a ghetto who became a member of parliament, challenged Museveni he had him beaten up and hospitalized.

Leadership has proved a problem in all post-colonial states in Africa, not just in politics. In society – as opposed to politics – I have often witnessed an endless capacity to talk, to keep discussing until everyone is on board. It seems to be a continent-wide phenomenon where decisions have to be taken by a group rather than an individual. But once a decision is made everyone is expected to fall into line. Even after today's presidential elections the winners like to bind losing candidates into the system by giving them powerless positions in government. Only if this is rejected do they try to obliterate the losers.

In businesses structured on Western lines you still often find Western managers or Africans who have trained abroad – even among African-owned businesses. Leadership and management skills were, until recently, very rare on the continent. Age could be a reason: younger men cannot tell older men what to do. The average age of African presidents in 2011 was 64, four years older than the world average. Ethnicity is also a problem in some countries. The Chinese have found the same difficulty. Despite talk of Chinese treating Africans as equals, in their burgeoning businesses in Africa there are, as yet, almost no Africans in management positions in Chinese operations.

Multi-party democracy was abandoned in most African countries soon after independence, but it was not replaced by any other system of accountability to the people. In some cases political parties other than the ruling party were simply banned; elsewhere the parties merged voluntarily under the umbrella of the ruling party. Dissidence was suppressed. The justification was always national unity. Nyerere in Tanzania put the best spin on it when he argued that Africa's traditional way was democracy under the trees, seeking consensual communal democracy. Adversarial party politics were inappropriate. The job in hand was national development, and unity was essential to achieve that. Nyerere argued that Tanzania could not afford the luxury of party political power games at the expense of getting on with development. He instituted a one-party state with elections for individual candidates rather than parties. Other African rulers did the same for the more obvious reason that they wanted total power, making themselves 'President for life' at the same time.

After independence many African economies were taken under state control. Before free market ideology carried all before it in the 1980s, governments everywhere played a much greater role in trying to manage national economies. It was not only socialist governments that set up marketing boards and ran state companies. Most European countries believed in the mixed economy, with a lot of state-owned or state-subsidized industries and services. Africa at the time was no different. Backed by the World Bank, African rulers nationalized key industries, established new ones and created marketing boards to establish state control over the means of production and distribution. Self-sufficiency in everything was the watchword. The ideological argument was that political independence was not complete without economic independence. But the nationalization of companies, foreign and locally owned, also destroyed an alternative political power base that might have supported an opposition. The parastatal companies became vital sources of patronage, providing jobs for favoured groups.

Africa's one-party states increasingly became one-man states – the Big Man. All tyrants suffer from the same apocalyptic monomania, but Africa has provided some of the most spectacular examples. In his book *Dispatches from a Fragile Continent*, the American journalist Blaine Harden described the classic African President:

> *His face is on the money. His photograph hangs in every office in the realm. His ministers wear gold pins with tiny photographs of Him on the lapels of their tailored pinstriped suits. He names streets, football stadiums, hospitals, and universities after himself. He carries a silver-inlaid ivory mace or an ornately carved walking stick or a flywhisk or a chiefly stool. He insists on being called 'doctor' or 'conqueror' or 'teacher' or 'the big elephant' or 'the number-one peasant' or 'the wise old man' or 'the national miracle' or 'the most popular leader in the world'. His every pronouncement is reported on the front page. He sleeps with the wives and daughters of powerful men in his government. He shuffles ministers around without warning, paralysing policy decisions as he undercuts pretenders to the throne. He scapegoats minorities to shore up popular support. He bans all political parties except the one he controls. He rigs elections. He emasculates the courts. He cows the press. He stifles academia. He goes to church.*

With few exceptions this portrait remained accurate until the end of the twentieth century. The vast gap between rulers and ruled in Africa strikes outsiders forcibly. The Big Man likes to demonstrate how far he is from the squalor that most fellow citizens live in. He uses conspicuous displays of wealth to show that he has escaped from ordinary life: that he is powerful and rich, a benefactor blessed by God, lord of the people whose love and obedience he takes for granted. Such Big Men dress as do only the fattest cats – or would-be fat cats – of the Western world. I often think back to Willie Kiyingi, the boy at the school in Uganda who blew away his future for one day of dressing up. Those with the most expensive Savile Row suits and

Rolex watches are often those who argue most fiercely for Africa's traditional way of doing things. Big Men rarely show pride in anything African. Visit a Big Man's house and you will find it stuffed with gaudy imitations of dull, old-fashioned European art. You sit on baroque plush furniture, drink from crystal glass or French porcelain and try not to spill anything on the white leather sofas made in Milan. The only African presence in such houses are the servants. In front of their employers they behave more like slaves.

Nelson Mandela argued that poverty is the cause of Africa's Big Man syndrome. In a speech at the London School of Economics in 2000, he reminded his audience of the backgrounds of most African rulers: 'Children go to school without any learning aids. Taught in a language which is not theirs, by teachers often not so very qualified . . . Poor children eating porridge in the morning, porridge at lunch, porridge as their dinner, unable to concentrate. Large families with little room to move about. A child who shares a room with about three or four others. No table, no chairs. Doing their homework on the floor.' Mandela begged understanding and asked that Africa's rulers should not be judged by Western standards because they had grown up in poverty. 'When you assess the achievements and failures of Africa you must keep this background in mind.' Do not, he said, 'judge us on the same basis by which you judge opinion makers in the old and advanced industrial countries'.

Mandela tried to persuade his audience that people who had grown up without shoes could not live a simple lifestyle when in power. But he could have argued it the other way. He might have said that memories of childhood poverty should have left Africa's Big Men with an understanding of the problem and a sense of solidarity with the poor. Perhaps even a feeling of 'there but for the grace of God . . .' Instead he chose to ask for understanding and patience for oppression and greed. For once his words have not been heeded. Luckily.

With all the powers of statehood at their disposal, doling out jobs, declaring states of emergency, deploying the police, the Big Men demanded and often got blind obedience. They identified personally and totally with the power of office. The President became the presidency with no distinction between the self and the office. *L'état c'est moi*, the dictum of France's King Louis XIV, was also a good if well-worn joke in Moi's Kenya. He lived far removed from everyday Africa, sweeping from palace to limo to plane to palace surrounded by grovelling attendants and bodyguards without ever touching African soil. If he travelled by car to a remote village, a new road was built for him so that he would not be troubled by potholes. Listening to the old-style presidents like Robert Mugabe or Paul Biya of Cameroon, I have often wondered if they know anything of what happens in their countries or in Africa at large. They do not see Africa any more, and who would dare tell them what it is like?

Mobutu Sese Seko, who ruled Zaire, now renamed Congo, was the ultimate Big Man. He gave himself a string of titles that outdid even Idi Amin. His name means 'The Cock that Covers all the Chickens', and his full title read, 'Father of the Nation, Guide, Helmsman, Chief, Messiah, the All-Powerful Warrior who Goes from Conquest to Conquest, Leaving Fire in his Wake'. Mobutu promoted *authenticité*, a return to African values – though there was nothing made in Africa in his palaces, and he began each day with pink champagne. He treated the country as its founder, King Leopold of Belgium, had done: a private estate that he owned outright, its people his slaves. He stayed in power by leasing out state contracts, offices and positions to other political players. In return they had to pay him homage and a percentage. All officials, from ministers to soldiers, were allowed to steal whatever they wanted through bribes or theft from the ordinary people. In terms of statehood, the country was no more than a Congo-shaped blank on the map. Everything else had been stolen, sucked upwards and outwards. Mobutu was kept in power by the West, given loans by the World Bank and rescued from rebellion more than once by French and Belgian troops.

Dictatorship was not exclusive to Africa in the Cold War. Throughout the 1970s and 1980s much of Asia was ruled by powerful military men backed by the West. They were also very corrupt. Yet several Asian countries began to industrialize and develop during that period. Why did Africa not do the same? The difference between Asia and Africa may be that the Asian dictators invested their stolen wealth in the country. They bought factories and plantations and started businesses. They believed in their countries and had a plan to develop them.

By the late 1980s, outside Botswana, Senegal and Gambia, Africans lived in one-party states, mostly ruled by Presidents for life. African states were simply crumbling away like old colonial mansions that had fallen into desuetude. The elites who had seized the instruments and symbols of power from the departing imperial powers had stopped the process of democratization dead. The house of Africa looked exactly as Achebe had predicted.

African elites did not see the development of the countries to be in their interest. Presidents always made sure their own people were allowed to 'eat' – receiving a bountiful expenditure of state resources in their home area such as a tarmac road and airport (Museveni), an airport and a university (Moi), a collection of grotesque palaces (Mobutu), or a whole new capital city (Houphouët-Boigny). Development elsewhere could create other centres of power, alternative sources of wealth that might challenge the rulers. Instead they kept a tight grip on what wealth there was and shipped it out of the continent to Swiss, French and British banks. According to the World Bank in 2016 there were more than 7000 African multimillionaires and 145,000 Africans with holdings of approximately $800 billion. But some 60 per cent of privately owned African wealth was kept outside the continent in 2016 – double what Africa was receiving in aid at the time. Others put the figure as high as $150 billion. Presidents and ministers looted state funds and stuffed the money into offshore bank accounts. They bought luxury flats in London, Paris, New York or South Africa, and sent their children to school and university in Britain, France or America. They had become the modern looters of Africa. Or as Romuald Hazoumé, the Benin artist, says, 'They are the slave sellers of our times.'

In the 1970s, the Big Man often became A Big Military Man. Africa suffered at least forty military coups in its first two decades of independence. Western diplomats, who sometimes had a hand in the coups, would often extol the popularity of military regimes. The line was, 'Of course we don't like military governments, but it is stable, less corrupt and more popular than what was there before.' In a few cases, that might have been true. Coups against bad civilian governments always brought cheering crowds onto the streets. All of Nigeria's military coups were popular when they happened, though their popularity didn't last long. One that did was in Burkina Faso. Captain Thomas Sankara seized power in 1983 and was genuinely popular. He had shown none of the usual traits of African Presidents, driving around the capital in a Renault 5 and listing his guitar when he declared his meagre possessions. He was murdered in 1987, almost certainly at the prompting of the French and Houphouët-Boigny, who was godfather to the wife of Sankara's deputy – and successor – Blaise Compaore, who became one of Africa's richest men.

In most cases, military dictators looted their countries, impoverished their peoples and charmed Western visitors. At the time their people grumbled and occasionally rioted, but rarely were military governments challenged. For outsiders, the passivity of Africans in the face of appalling oppression was depressing. It was embarrassing that South African blacks, who were physically better off and freer than most of their fellow Africans, were organizing mass resistance while in the rest of Africa, where criticism of the government could mean death and people were in desperate poverty, there was merely resignation. In Nigeria more than 100 million people were ruled for twenty-nine years by an army officially 70,000 strong, of which probably only two-thirds were effective. That meant only one soldier for more than 2000 Nigerians. And yet in all that time there was not one popular democratic movement of significance.

That applies to most of Africa. Only three times did Africans rise up against military governments in a popular movement. The first was in Sudan in 1985, when the people of Khartoum rebelled against President Jaafar Numeiri and drove him out. The second was in Togo in 1991. People came onto the streets and pushed the soldiers back to their barracks, but the military dictator, Gnassingbe Eyadema, backed by France, outwitted the civilian politicians and stayed in charge. The third was in Côte d'Ivoire in 2001, when General Robert Guei put his troops on the street to try to stay in power but was thwarted by masses of young supporters of Laurent Gbagbo.

At the heart of African politics is an attitude to power. Power whether used for good or evil, is widely revered for its own sake. The Big Man is given great respect because he has power. Many African societies traditionally had little sense of equality, and even today you can be shocked to see people prostrate themselves before their superiors. That does not just mean the little people who line the roads to cheer the Big Man. Ministers who usually behave like gods themselves become lowly servants in the presence of their President, bowing and hunching their shoulders in deference.

Power is not just about physical strength or wealth or status. It has a spiritual dimension. A well-educated teacher in Mobutu's Zaire admitted to me that although he hated Mobutu, he feared him, 'because Mobutu has been to the pyramids in Egypt. He obtained some divine power so he always knows what I am thinking. I know this sounds crazy to you but I believe it. I can't help it.' In Liberia the same fear of magical powers kept Charles Taylor in power. People hated him, but they feared to act against him because somehow he would find out through his mystical powers and come and kill them. Jonas Savimbi in Angola was believed by many to have powerful magic that enabled him to know what everyone was thinking. A President's secret opponents will often admit that, despite the evil that he has done, they admire him as well as fear him. I have often waited for an African President, chatting to African colleagues who openly expressed their disgust and hatred for him. Yet when the Big Man emerged, the same journalists ran forward, grasping his hand, fawning on him and throwing back their heads to howl with laughter at his jokes. Hypocrisy? To Western eyes, yes, but they were simply showing due diligence by respecting power.

Another important tradition that the Big Men rulers manipulated was the family. They liked to be called Father, Tata or Dada – like Idi Amin. The first generation of African leaders called themselves 'Father of the Nation'. Some African rulers brilliantly exploited this reverence for patriarchal power in the home. The traditional father is a god-like figure, procreator and provider. His children treat him with immense respect and speak only when spoken to. His wives are his appendages, obedient in all things, acting as intermediaries between a father and his children – the people. By portraying himself as a father, the President instils in the minds of people that they must fear him, love him, obey him and believe they are completely dependent on him.

Both sides in the Cold War embraced and fêted these dictators. On the agenda of the West, fundamental principles for which it sup-posedly stood – such as democracy and freedom of speech – took second place to which side you were on: Moscow or Washington. The West's top priority was to make sure the governments of these new nation states did not fall into the hands of the Soviet Union. So while they complained about corruption, theft and oppression, the task of Western diplomats was to keep those governments loyal. The Soviet Union protected its own protégés equally carefully. One of Africa's tragedies was that most of it became independent as the Cold War was getting colder. East and West vied for every inch of territory and sea on the planet.

Some argue that Western countries deliberately imposed these dictators on Africa because it suited capitalism to keep the continent poor and weak. Capitalism needs markets and Western governments would have undoubtedly preferred successful states to emerge in Africa. On my journeys in Africa, I was often depressed by the attitude of Western diplomats, resigned to the fate of their former colonies and powerless in the face of oppression and corruption. Western companies were gradually forced out of Nigeria when a succession of coups brought in governments that wrecked the economy. They were sad to go. West Africa had been a profitable market. The idea that these representatives of Western interests were secretly pulling the strings to keep Africa poor and oppressed is preposterous.

So was the idea that these rulers were mere puppets. That would be to deny that these dictators had any power of their own. As one American diplomat ruefully said when Jonas Savimbi, the American-backed Angola rebel leader, had committed another atrocity: 'The trouble with puppets is they don't always jerk when you pull the strings.' Few puppets served the interest of their backers beyond denying their country to the other side. Mobutu's Zaire was hardly an advertisement for the benefits of capitalism. Indeed, Western capitalist companies lost out badly in the destruction of the Zairean economy. Nor was Angola a good advertisement for Communism.

The ruling MPLA basked in luxury and allowed the poor to starve. It was hard to see what Angola gave the Soviet Union apart from bad debts and sun in winter for its generals. Its oil, assiduously protected from American-backed rebels by the Cubans and Russians, went to American companies. Its diamonds were sold secretly to De Beers which controlled the global market in gem diamonds. Sometimes Cold War logic was hard to follow.

Most African countries found diplomatic space to manoeuvre between Russia and America. They ducked the question, 'Whose side are you on?' by calling themselves 'non-aligned'. They chose a middle way, playing off the superpowers against each other or floating cleverly between the two. Many used Marxist anti-colonial language to justify their rule, portraying themselves as leaders of the oppressed masses struggling against capitalist imperialism. But language was the only thing they borrowed from the Soviet Union. They invested their money in Swiss, French or British banks. And they knew where their best interests lay when the chips were down. Jomo Kenyatta in Kenya, once the scourge of British imperialism, employed Bruce Mackenzie, the white South African-born MI6 agent, as Minister of Agriculture and then as his foreign affairs advisor: when Kenyatta became incapacitated in old age, Mackenzie virtually ran the country. Even Nyerere, who spoke in the most virulent anti-colonial language, had to ask the British to put him back on his throne when he was overthrown in an army mutiny in 1964 (the British obliged). In francophone Africa, Presidents treated France as their protector. Maintained in power by French soldiers, Houphouët-Boigny spoke of 'nominal independence' from France.

Many African rulers survived by ducking and weaving, but those who failed became victims of military coups sometimes plotted with the help of East or West. Western countries and companies propped up their favoured regimes in Africa or disposed of those they did not like. The French in particular liked to select their own African rulers and posted French soldiers to protect them. The Israelis cut their own deals. They needed international allies, but felt far less domestic pressure than Britain, France or America to behave decently. The Israelis provided support for several of Africa's worst dictators as well as for apartheid South Africa. Apart from putting Idi Amin in power, they gave close protection to Nigeria's Sani Abacha, Mobutu and Laurent Kabila in Congo and José Eduardo dos Santos in Angola.

Some countries, like Somalia, were strategically vital and the superpowers actively vied for their allegiance. Across the Red Sea from Saudi Arabia, Somalia was valuable and vulnerable at the same time: valuable because both sides courted it, vulnerable because the other side might try a coup or back a rebellion. But the superpowers were not always in the driving seat. Mohammed Siad Barre, Somalia's ruthless President from 1969 to 1991, achieved the astonishing feat of changing sides in the Cold War – and surviving. But it left his country an arsenal of guns and bullets. When civil war began in the late 1980s there were more guns than people in his country. In most African countries diplomats – East and West – settled for 'stability', a neat label that covered the horrors of Mobutu's Zaire, Bokassa's Central African Empire, and even Idi Amin's Uganda. As parliaments were abolished, civil services ignored, judiciaries overruled and universities closed, the Western powers, supposedly fighting for worldwide freedom and democracy, shrugged and blamed Africa.

The paternal relationship between African rulers and the former colonial powers is one of the most poisonous legacies of colonialism. It is often correctly portrayed as evidence of an enduringly patronizing attitude on the part of the former colonialists. But as Nkosana Moyo, a former minister in Zimbabwe, has pointed out, Africa rulers also like to maintain that paternalistic relationship. For years they played the role of neglected offspring, children of an imperial father, and begged for aid and support from the former colonial powers. The 'Emperor' of the Central African Empire, Jean-Bedel Bokassa, used to weep when he met General de Gaulle of France and call him Tata – Daddy. A white visitor will sometimes be accosted in the street in Africa and asked for money with the words: 'You are my mother and father.' That attitude, says Moyo, is self-serving: 'Africa has structured its relationship with the outside world as a family relationship. Support for your family is unconditional and in families you do not expect to be paid back.'

Only in recent years have African leaders, largely led by South Africa, begun to become masters of their ship. They now push back against Western demands and display their dislike of what they see as Western interference in Africa by showing solidarity with Zimbabwe's dictator, Robert Mugabe. This became possible because at the end of the twentieth century a powerful new player had arrived on the continent: China. African rulers suddenly had an alternative partner. China does not lecture them about democracy and human rights. On the contrary, it deals directly and only with the governments and pays no attention to what those governments do to their people. Non-interference is the Chinese watchword but it is increasingly obvious that Chinese interests are not always best served by allowing African governments to do whatever they like. Behind the scenes, China is more proactive – for example, in Sudan, when North and South went to war in 2012, Beijing applied heavy diplomatic pressure to stop them.

At the end of the Cold War, Africa was virtually abandoned as Western governments and companies turned away to concentrate on new opportunities in Eastern Europe and East Asia. The collapse of the Soviet Union was seen as a triumph of both democratic and free market values. Western political victory also presented an opportunity for Western business to expand into former Communist states.

In the rush, Africa was left a backwater. By the mid 1980s no African country, with the possible exception of Botswana, had delivered anything of value to the majority of its citizens. Almost all Africa's economies were going backwards. Whatever the political system, the vast majority of ordinary people were as poor as ever if not poorer. This was partly due to the terms of trade: Africa's commodities had fallen in value while the price of manufactured goods from overseas had risen. But Asian countries faced with the same predicament had diversified their economies and begun to prosper. They had even started producing some of Africa's traditional crops and, while African production stagnated, Asia began to gain market share.

The West abandoned Africa at the end of the Cold War in the early 1990s, leaving a last message: end political interference in the economy and follow the free market and the rule of law, dissolve one-party states and hold elections. Dictators and coups would no longer be tolerated. An unfettered market would sort out everything else. Control of Africa's economies was left in the hands of the World Bank and the IMF.

For the next decade, World Bank and IMF economists flitted in and out of Africa dismantling state-owned enterprises, privatizing assets and letting currencies find their own level. They applied formulas they imagined were universal, rarely giving a thought to the social or political implications of what they were doing. For a start, most African states were already privatized. They were the property of the President. There was no rule of law, no framework within which to privatize properly. State structures were also controlled by the elites. African states had no basic rule of law or system of government beyond the whim of the President. So privatization did not create a 'free market'. It was not even a free-for-all. It was a free-for-some: the President and his cronies. Rich and powerful, they now grabbed state assets they had already robbed and run down.

With bank loans and partnerships with foreign firms they grew even richer. As their currencies were allowed to wither under IMF instruction, the ruling elites kept their wealth safely in dollars outside the country. Meanwhile salaried professionals, on whom state and society depended, could no longer afford to retain their day jobs. As IMF Structural Adjustment Programmes removed what little state support they had, the salaried were made destitute. The poor naturally became poorer.

Impoverishment at a moment of weakening state control thawed social and political energies that had long been frozen. With no new leadership or organizations to channel it, pent-up energy frequently exploded in violence. By the mid 1990s more than half of the countries of sub-Saharan Africa were suffering wars, major civil disturbance or complete breakdown.

Gradually however, multi-party democracy began to spread, and although it did not bring down all the old dictators, elections opened up democratic space. Free markets meant a free press, and all over Africa local radio stations sprang up broadcasting more and more of the truth about Africa's rulers. Mobile phones and the Internet meant news could spread rapidly and immediately. South Africa's election in 1994 gave the process a huge boost. In fact that election was more like a ritual to seal a deal, a symbolic referendum to transfer power from white to black. But it was so spectacularly successful that reluctant African leaders who had held up or manipulated democratization were forced to take the plunge too. It seemed then that the age of the African dictator was almost over.

In varying degrees of free and fair, almost all African countries now hold some sort of poll to choose leaders. Even presidents who had taken their position for granted had to find new ways of justifying their rule to an increasingly sceptical population. Those who had given themselves grand titles or divine justifications had to give more modest reasons. Democratic principles were enshrined in the African Union Charter of 2000, although there was no mention of elections. It also promoted human rights. After 2000 there were hardly any military coups and when troops seized power in Mauritania in 2005 the African Union suspended its membership and insisted that elections were held as soon as possible. The country returned to constitutional rule in 2007. The demand for free and fair elections came from above and below but presidents, old and new, learned how to manage them. In some states still ruled by the old dictators, the elections were mere play-acting.

Elsewhere elections provided rich opportunities for the urban youth to take money to protect – or break up – rallies. There were not many profound policy debates. In most countries campaign speeches were promises and lies, clichés and bribes. Suddenly crucial marginal areas were promised a new road or a water supply. In a few cases the promises were kept. Meanwhile distant rural constituencies were sometimes barely aware of elections or the battles that raged in and around the towns. The media, mostly radio, found their revenues boosted by party advertising and their audiences were keen to phone in and join the national debates. Politics south of the Sahara had never been so lively since the struggles for independence thirty years before. In north Africa however the dictators had managed to stay on.

But on 17 December 2010 in a small town in Tunisia, a young, educated man forced to earn a living as a fruit and vegetable seller had his barrow of goods confiscated by the police. Bouazizi Mohamed complained to the municipal authorities but was rebuffed and humiliated. He poured petrol over himself and lit it and died shortly afterwards. Twenty-eight days later President Zine Ben Ali stepped down and fled the country. The spark started a revolution that roared across North Africa and spread into the Arab world, with mass anti-government demonstrations in capital after capital.

President Hosni Mubarak was overthrown in Egypt. Libya was plunged into civil war that resulted in the overthrow and death of Colonel Muammar Gaddafi in October 2010.

The Arab Spring burned fiercely in the Arab world but appeared, at first, to have little impact on Africa south of the Sahara. In fact it shook African rulers and their states deeply. Young Africans were following the events in North Africa on social media networks such as Facebook and Twitter, sharing their own frustration and passing on messages of protest. With the death of Colonel Gaddafi, the strongest force against Islamic fundamentalism in North Africa and the Sahel was removed. That gave a great boost to Al-Qaeda in the Mahgreb and to militant Islamist groups in Nigeria and other African states of the southern Sahara and further afield. But why did young Africans in black Africa not take to the streets as their counterparts north of the Sahara had done? Some claimed that Africa had had its 'spring' after the Cold War ended and the super-powers withdrew their support for African dictators. But while the youth in some countries took advantage to establish political parties and call for elections, the drivers were primarily external, not internal as in the Arab Spring.

I suggest two reasons for the lack of an All-Africa Spring. One was that the leaders of the uprisings in the Arab world were mainly the children of the middle classes. Like Bouazizi Mohamed, they saw their future as hopeless. They would be worse off than their parents, all their education wasted. In sub-Saharan Africa the equivalent middle class was much smaller and newer. This younger generation believed they would be better off than their parents. They still had hope. Second, they knew that, unlike the soldiers of Egypt and Tunisia, their national armies would shoot them down in the streets without a second thought. They stayed at home, but by blogging, texting and tweeting, they reflected on these events, shared their vision and created ideas and solidarity.

Only in Uganda in 2011 were there serious street demonstrations, comprising a Walk to Work campaign, a mass movement in the capital Kampala to protest against rising prices. President Yoweri Museveni crushed it by force but when one of his aides asked him what he saw as the threat, he is reported to have replied: 'Mubarak.'

After the Arab Spring in 2012 many north African states held free elections, and by 2013 it looked as if Somalia would hold one. The last ones had been held in 1968. Even dictatorships like Angola held elections in 2008 and 2012. By 2013, only Libya, Swaziland, Somalia and Eritrea had not given their citizens any say in who ruled them.

In some states the elections were mere play-acting. Old dictators like Omar Bongo in Gabon, Sasso Nguesso in Congo-Brazzaville, Paul Biya in Cameroon and Robert Mugabe in Zimbabwe performed ritual elections but would never allow themselves to be voted out of office. In these countries the ruling party was both government and state. When Mugabe lost the first round of the 2008 election in Zimbabwe, the results were not announced for five weeks. When the opposition went to court to force the government to produce them, the ruling party cheekily demanded a recount to delay them further. In these countries the presidents have turned into kings, absolute monarchs presiding over any officially organized endorsements. But in others, like Congo in 2007, elections could have gone either way and it really mattered who won.

By the end of the decade, elections resulting in a peaceful transfer of power had occurred in ten sub-Saharan African countries. But elections, far from affirming national statehood, revealed that African societies could be divided by their politicians along ethnic or regional lines. Some elections opened up those seams at terrible cost. In Kenya, Mwai Kibaki, seen as a harbinger of reform when elected as part of a broad coalition in 2002, had, once in power, become the very model of a Big Man dictator, surrounding himself with cronies from his own ethnic group and allowing corruption and theft to flourish on a grotesque scale. After the 2008 election he claimed to have won again amid credible reports of rigging and other electoral violations. The country exploded. The violence – like Kenya's politics – immediately became ethnic. More than 1,000 people were killed and 300,000 were displaced. It almost destroyed Africa's most sophisticated country outside South Africa.

But when the violence died down a 'never again' consensus pushed the ruling elite to hold a national debate about the constitution. A meeting was held at the Bomas conference centre led by Kibaki, the politicians and prominent members of Kenya's civil society. A new constitution was drafted, devolving some power to a local level based on ethnic territories. This raised a continent-wide question. In countries defined by lines drawn on maps by outsiders and with populations of multiple ethnicities, is a first-past-the-post, winner-takes-all, multi-party election the best way of choosing a ruler? Maybe there is a version of democracy that is better suited to Africa. With more than 40 per cent of Africa's population under fifteen years old, the pressure for change can only become more intense.

5

Amazing, but is it Africa?
Somalia

Somalis. People times ten. From grief to laughter, from love to hate Somalis seem turbo-charged. Hyper-driven with life force.

It is easy to see Somalis as a product of their landscape: craggy, hard, arid, a vast griddle, scoured and scorched daily by the sun for thousands of years. Look into the hawk face of Abdillahi Yusuf, who was elected President in exile in 2004 and was carried to Mogadishu by the Ethiopian invasion at the end of 2006: it is easy to see how such a land might breed such a man. Two black eyes, hard as stone, glitter in a face that makes a vulture look gentle. An army colonel who nearly captured Addis Ababa in 1978, then a rebel against Siad Barre, Somalia's dictator from 1969 to 1991, Yusuf spent years in jail, but emerged to become the dictator of the self-declared statelet of Puntland in north-east Somalia. When I visited him there they were celebrating their first year of 'self-rule', but it seemed more like a birthday party for Abdillahi. In 2006 he underwent a liver transplant in London. He joked with a friend afterwards: 'They gave me the liver of an IRA terrorist. Now I am a real killer.'

Most of Somalia is a desert of rock, stone and sand, flat as the sea from horizon to horizon with a sudden explosion of mountains flung skywards, like a bunch of fists punching defiantly at the sky. For most of the year that sun allows nothing to grow except cactus and vicious thorn scrub. Yet when rain comes, the plains and hillsides and valleys gently green and flower, and camels, sheep and goats gorge themselves on grass. That too reflects another side of the Somalis, their tender, witty poetry about love and the beauty of their camels and women.

Before the digging of wells and bore holes for irrigation, Somalis were nomads, searching for grazing for their herds in perennial wanderings. Other nomads who live on Africa's desert fringes may share their toughness and individualism, but few have that extra dimension, the Somalis' idiosyncrasy. Africa is a tough place and life's cruelties often evoke laughter, but Somalis meet misfortune head on and stab back at disaster with barbed, black jokes.

At the beginning of the nineteenth century Britain fought a war against Mohammed Abdille Hassan, Somalia's resistance fighter against colonialism, known to the British as the 'Mad Mullah'. The story goes that a wounded Somali staggered into the British-held town of Hargeisa from a battle nearby. He had a bullet wound in his leg and a spear stuck in his stomach. The doctors examined him and pronounced they would operate on his leg first because it was going gangrenous. 'No, no,' said the man, 'fix my stomach first. It hurts when I laugh.'

That spirit lives on in Somalia. One abiding, horrifying, but typical image stays in my mind: a young Somali dressed in T-shirt, flip-flops and *macawiis*, the traditional skirt-like wrap, running at an American armoured Humvee firing an AK47 from the hip. Bravery, ten points. Stupidity, also ten points. He was cut to shreds.

Most African peoples do not like fighting and avoid it whenever possible. Somalis have created a culture of war. Their poetry reveres bravery and revenge. One of their songs composed during the 1978 war with Ethiopia runs: 'If I do not wash the face of the land with the blood of the enemy, I am not a Somali.' Gerard Hanley, who tried to survive there during the Second World War, called his book about the Somalis *Warriors*. It opens with a harrowing account of Hanley finding a murderer standing over the bloody corpse of his victim and demanding that Hanley carry out immediate justice and shoot him on the spot:

> *I never saw a Somali who showed any fear of death, which impressive though it sounds, carries with it the chill of pitilessness and ferocity as well. If you have no fear of death you have none for anybody else's death either, but that fearlessness has always been essential to the Somalis who have had to try and survive hunger, disease and thirst while prepared to fight and die against their enemies, their fellow Somalis for pleasure in the blood feud, or the Ethiopians who would like to rule them, or the white men who got in the way for a while . . . The Somali really did want to die, totally satisfied with himself after waiting for his enemy for over a year. Instead of being about a camel, this death was about a woman, something of far less value than a camel.*

When you first hear Somalis talk you think they are having an argument. They usually are. Their language sounds 'as if they have swallowed sand', as Nuruddin Farah, the Somali novelist, says. It is as harsh as their arid homeland. But it is not just words. When most people argue they listen to the other person's point of view and, without conceding their main point, try to establish a common understanding. I once tried to argue with a Somali friend who runs a human rights organization. As the 'discussion' developed she simply reiterated her argument more stridently. She changed down a gear and tried to drive straight over my argument, crushing it under a pounding of words that grew louder and louder. Later, after I had spent longer in Somalia, I realized she was not being rude, she was being Somali. Challenge, fight, win. Only when you have used up all your ammunition do you begin to look for accommodation.

For every generalization about Africa, Somalia is always the exception. And Somalis know it. Somalia is one of two countries on the continent that has only one race, one ethnic group, one language, one religion, and one culture. It is possible to talk about a Somali race. They do. I wonder if their distinctive and often extraordinarily beautiful physiognomy has been preserved by their xenophobia. Their creation myth goes something like: God created the white people and was quite pleased, then he created black people and was also quite pleased. Then God created Somalis and he laughed.

The Somalis are Cushitic speakers like the Afars and Saho people of Ethiopia – all very different from their Bantu-speaking neighbours. In a continent in which so many names of countries were invented by the imperial powers, Somalia is at least named after the Somalis. Reuniting Somalis remains a national aspiration. The Somali flag is a white, five-pointed star on blue background. Each point of the star represents a part of Somalia carved out of the territory by the imperial powers. Italian-ruled Somalia, British-ruled Somaliland, Djibouti, the eastern lowlands of Ethiopia known as the Ogaden, and much of northern Kenya. Few Somalis do not believe that one day all these areas will be reunited, by force if necessary.

In many parts of Africa people lack a sense of identity, ethnic or national. They are culturally uprooted, unsure of who they are and what they want to become. The old ways forgotten, many Africans have not yet worked out new ones. As Romuald Hazoumé, the Beninois artist, says of the slave trade and today's Africans: 'They did not know where they were going but they knew where they came from. Today we do not know where we are going and we have forgotten where we came from.'

Somalis know who they are; they are born with self-respect. The nomadic life engenders self-sufficiency. When the British took over their northern coast in order to provide food and other resources for Aden, the port across the Red Sea and a vital imperial staging post on the route to India, they found the Somalis made excellent travellers and recruited thousands of them into the British merchant fleet. That is why today there are substantial and long-standing Somali communities in British ports like Liverpool, Cardiff and east London. Somalis also became drivers on the fleets of trucks that ply the routes into Africa from the continent's eastern ports. I met them when I hitch-hiked from Uganda down to Southern Africa. They all carried clubs and daggers. Nobody messed with them.

Some would call that self-sufficiency and self-respect arrogance, but that is a compliment in Somali. It was that very arrogance which destroyed the Somali nation state.

Somalis do not think of themselves as Africans. In precolonial times southern Somalis raided into what is now northern Kenya and enslaved the local Africans, bringing them back to work on the land in the Juba valley. Released from bondage under European rule, the 'Africans' remained a separate lower caste, never incorporated into the Somali clan networks. Soon after Somalia imploded in 1991 I went to Somaliland, the former British-ruled northern part, to witness its declaration of independence from the rest of the country. Throughout Africa and the Middle East I have never seen more devastation. The capital of the north, Hargeisa, resembled Berlin or Hiroshima at the end of the Second World War. There were not more than one or two houses still standing. As the rebel movement attacked, the government had used artillery as well as MiG fighter bombers flown by former Rhodesian pilots to destroy rebel-held parts of the city. The airport is close to the city, so the hired pilots flew dozens of sorties every day. Then one night the entire remaining population of the city and surrounding area – some 300,000 people – walked out of the city and in a biblical migration over three days made their way into Ethiopia.

When Siad Barre fled the country and rebels seized the capital, Mogadishu, the army abandoned Hargeisa and some of the population returned. About three-quarters of it was rubble and where walls still stood there were no roofs. Government troops had pillaged the entire city before they left, ripping off roofs and pipes and, with unbelievable vindictiveness, had planted anti-personnel mines in houses and gardens for the day the people returned.

Trying to find something optimistic to write about, I visited the newly appointed Somaliland minister of tourism and wildlife. He produced a map of the country showing designated game parks that would, he assured me, soon be filled with tourists. That in itself would have caused a bitter laugh in the rest of East Africa, where the Somalis have a reputation as the continent's worst animal poachers. Trying to keep a straight face, I asked him about United Nations help for the project. He sighed and said: 'The trouble with the United Nations is that if we ask them for help they will send us some African who has already destroyed his own country and then will come and mess up ours too.'

I was sitting in a teashop in the small town of Boromo when two bearded old men approached me. They wore beautifully made sandals and macawiis and turbans and carried the long forked sticks of nomad herders. They asked if I was English and when I said yes, they bought me tea and demanded a conversation.

'You see,' one said, 'we want to say sorry – make apology for you.'

'To me?'

'Yes – you are Briteesh. In nineteen sixty we make terrible

meestake. We demand unity with Somalis in the south. The Briteesh warn-ed us but we not listening. You see – in the north we had Briteesh rule. We had justice and lo'aw and fair play. In the south they had the Italys, spaghetti and Mafia. That make southerners terrible people. They are cheaters and, you know, some of them are not even Somalis at all. They African!'

Apart from war, camels and themselves, Somalis love poetry. Unsurprisingly their poetry is largely about love, war, camels and themselves. Camels come top. One poem by Cumar Xuseen 'Ostreeliya' says:

> A Somali may gather great wealth
> Diamonds he may have and houses too . . .
> But he has no legacy to leave behind him
> Unless he rears the beast whose necks bear wooden bells . . .
> A man who has reared no camels will always be a pauper!

There is a passionate love poem by Maxamed Ibraahim 'Hadraawi' about a fellow poet who died of love for a girl called Hodon. In the poem the dead poet sends a message to his friend saying that he does not think about Hodon any more because in Paradise he is surrounded by houris 'who encompass me in the inner borders of their robes'. But, even better, 'A herd of sturdy camels is thronging towards me now.'

Camels or women? No contest for a Somali man.

You can imagine the young Somali herder warriors on long nights under the stars by the campfires of their camel camps. At the end of each day they prayed to Allah, drank camels' milk and chewed *khat* outside their tents. It is a mild amphetamine and acts like strong coffee; it frees and speeds up the mind slightly. Then they began to sing their poems about camels, the women they missed and the enemies they hated. Absence made them idolize the women and demonize the enemies. Nomads never have to accommodate neighbours. People who live in settled communities and never move have to come to terms with the people next door, make fences and boundaries. The neighbours will be there tomorrow and the next day, always. You may quarrel, but in time you define separate areas: physical, legal, mental and social. But if you are a nomad you meet your 'neighbours' only once a year in the grazing grounds. There are no agreed boundaries in the great expanse of desert. Last year maybe another family abducted your favourite sister and stole three of your best camels. Now you have a whole year to sit under the stars and make up poems about how much you miss your beautiful sister and your wonderful camels and how much you hate your neighbour and exactly what you are going to do to the thieving bastard when you run into him this year. That is what most Somali poetry is about. It is the meaning of life in Somalia.

Somalis are Sunni Muslims, but always followed the Sufi tradition with individual 'saints' from the past passing down their sanctity through lineages to communities today. Their religious spirit is tolerant of different strains and is mixed with elements of Somali's pre-Islamic Cushitic beliefs. Although Somalis retained their traditions more strongly than any other group in Africa, in recent years their culture and religious practice have been undermined by Arab Wahabi preachers and Saudi money. Until recently Somali women played a major role in society, dressed in bright colours and did not cover their heads nor arms. Today Somali women are expected to dress in the full Saudi black *niqab* and obey their men.

Somali society is divided along clan and family groupings that go back to an individual founder. After independence all African leaders preached against tribalism in the cause of national unity. Siad Barre went further and banned clans, even forbidding mention of them. In the rest of Africa the denigration of tribalism made people shy of say-ing which ethnic group they belonged to. In many countries, it is politically incorrect to ask someone what ethnic group someone is from, though it remains an important reality. A Somali who worked as a civil servant in the first administration after independence told me that he did not know the clans of his colleagues. At that time they were all just Somalis. Today only a few idealists refuse to say what clan they are and insist it doesn't matter. Most will tell you as proudly as they will tell you their name.

And then they endlessly discuss clan politics in all its mind-numbing complexity and hierarchies of loyalty. Clan A is aligned to clan C and has always fought clan B. But if clan E attacks clan C then clan A will join clan E and clan B will join clan C. Then you have the sub-clans and the sub-sub-clans, and then the powerful families who also have complicated histories of love and hate stretching back into the mists of time. Somalis cannot even agree which clan derives from which or how one clan relates to another. Once the conflict started at the end of the 1980s the leaders played on these fractious loyal-ties. They set up numerous political parties and movements, the Somali National Movement, the Somali National Salvation Front, the United Somali Congress, but they were never anything more than political packaging for the clans. Mere fig leaves covering clan armies.

In the old days these clan wars were fought with spears, arrows and muskets. A skirmish would leave a few dead and wounded and then the elders would meet and talk – Somalis are as good at talking as fighting. For the first half of the twentieth century the imperial rulers, Italy, France and Britain, mediated or put down clan quarrels by force. Siad Barre may have banned the clans in public but in prac-tice he played them off against each other. As soon as one clan becomes dominant, the others resent it and form a counterweight.

The relationship between clans in the past has been described as a great wheel that brings one clan to power and then brings it down again. For a while Siad Barre froze the wheel with his clan, the Marehan, at the top. He also undermined the status of elders of the other clans, corrupting them by bribes. But when he fled in January 1991, the pent-up anger burst out and the wheel began to spin. It spun out of control and the country was torn apart. It has not yet been put back together again.

I got a flavour of that 'electric violence', as Hanley called it, in Mogadishu in January 1992. I hitched a lift in a small plane bringing in medical supplies from Nairobi for the four NGOs still working in the city.

The airport is frequently shelled when planes try to land, so the pilot coasts in with the engines running as quietly as possible. We leap out and local aid workers feverishly unload medical supplies. Then the pilot slams the engines to full throttle and blasts off down the runway. As the wheels leave the ground he flips the plane over on its wing tip and zooms out over the ocean at a right angle. I get a lift from the Red Cross and we drive through the blasted streets. People walk fast carrying bags and bowls on their heads. Some are pushing wheelbarrows piled with possessions or carrying a wounded or aged relative. Mogadishu's richer citizens have deserted the city and the few aid agencies who have stayed have the pick of the houses – and the cooks. The Red Cross has a huge secluded mansion with a neat little garden of scented flowers behind high walls and sheet metal double doors. In normal times it would have been a perfect place for doing nothing.

Here everyone is frantic. A chain of Somali staff unloads medical supplies from a truck to the house, which is already packed with people and stores. The balcony has been turned into sleeping quarters with beds and mosquito nets. A radio crackles with messages. Among the pot plants on the veranda I grab a few moments with Verena Krebs, a Swiss Red Cross nurse, who has seen it all: Cambodia, Yemen, Angola, Afghanistan, Kuwait and now Somalia for the second time. Verena runs through the figures; an estimated 10,000 deaths since November. Seventy casualties yesterday, ten so far today, and it is only 10 a.m. Someone bangs on the gate. Two men are let in, one of them clutching a wad of cotton to his head. Nurse Krebs goes down and allows him inside and finds a storeroom with enough space for a mattress.

The boy lies down calmly. He is about seventeen, good-looking, tall and straight. His clothes are clean. He doesn't look like a fighter. Verena lifts the cotton wool wad from his head. Just above his left eyebrow is a neat hole which seeps a little blood. Above the left temple is a dark bulge where a bullet is lodged beneath the skin. Verena and I stare. 'Christ! How can he be alive?'

The boy shows no more sign of pain than if he were suffering from a headache. He lies perfectly still while she dabs the wound with disinfectant but she can do nothing now. 'Come to the hospital tomorrow,' she says and she bandages his head and gives him some painkillers. We help him to his feet. He is steady as a rock and climbs up the stairs and walks off, occasionally touching the bandage as if it irritates him. 'The threshold of pain here is high – very, very high,' says Verena gazing after him. Just how high I discover the next day.

Mogadishu is now divided; the south is held by the fighters of General Mohammed Aideed. The war for the city has been bubbling on since Siad Barre fled the capital a year ago after his army was defeated by Aideed in the south-west. Aideed's army of young, rural fighters approached the capital, terrifying the inhabitants. Aideed is Habr Gedir, a sub-clan of the Hawiye. The city is also mostly Hawiye but their sub-clan is Abgal. They are petrified of Aideed, a brutal military man backed by bands of wild bush fighters. The city did not allow him to claim the prize – the presidency of Somalia. The Abgale elders quickly formed a committee of businessmen called the Manifesto Group and established an interim government to block him. Both sides said they wanted to share power but men like Aideed do not do sharing. He marched into the city and before long the centre was a war zone.

All the traditional Somali warrior mentality now comes to the fore, but modernized. Much of central Mogadishu is rubble or shell-holed, blackened buildings. Small groups of fighters are dug into the rubble, firing rockets and machine guns. Behind them tanks and artillery pound what they believe to be enemy strongholds. Thanks to Somalia's strategic position in the Middle East, with good harbours and dockyards on the Indian Ocean and the Red Sea, there are masses of arms in the city. Both the Soviet Union and the United States had been generous with weapons for Siad Barre who changed sides in 1978. The weapons supplied by both superpowers had been supplemented by Somalia's age-old enemy, Ethiopia, who provided more to rebels. By the end of the 1980s, when Somalis went to war with each other, Somalis were living on one of the world's biggest arms dumps.

Tanks, rocket launchers, artillery and anti-aircraft guns abound. In Mogadishu's Bakara market, between the meat and cosmetics sections, there is an emporium of weaponry: thousands of guns on open stalls – AKs from Russia and China, G3s from South Africa or Germany, FNs from Belgium, M16s from America, rocket launchers, landmines and mortars from everywhere. And stacks of crates full of bullets for all of them. It is said you can even buy a tank there. Every male Somali seems to have a gun.

The favourite weapon is the 'technical', a four-wheeled drive vehicle, usually a Toyota Land Cruiser, sawn off at steering wheel level and with a bazooka or heavy machine gun mounted on the back. The technical tactic is to park in a side street off a main thoroughfare, then zoom backwards into the main street, tyres screaming, loose off a burst, slam into second gear and zoom back into the side street to reload. The bullets of such weapons go a long way. A family in a little cement block house on the outskirts of town will suddenly be blown to pieces. Stray bullets, known as Yusufs because of the swishing noise they make, frequently cut down a child far from the street fighting.

Tonight a huge new battle for Mogadishu begins. I have gone to the Save the Children house run by David Shearer, a tall, laconic New Zealander. The only other person in the house is Jama, who has lost his wife, two daughters and two sons in three separate hits on his home. He speaks little as he cooks us a full meal, carefully laying the table with napkins and cutlery at each place. None of us is hungry. Conversation is sporadic. We are trying to listen to what the shelling is telling us.

The barrage goes on through the night, each side firing two or three shells a minute across the city. I lie on my bed trying to listen to Vaughan Williams' *London Symphony* on a Walkman, but the house-shaking crash of outgoing and incoming shells makes it impossible. David is not even trying to sleep. We put on a video of an All Blacks–Australia rugby international which takes our minds off the battle for a while, but the generator closes down at midnight and our universe becomes darkness, gunfire, shell bursts and fear-filled silences. The base of the stairwell is probably the strongest part of the house. We agree to camp there if it gets worse.

I am startled out of sleep by the generator coming on just before light and I realize the battle must have stopped in the early hours. At 7.45 the first shell comes whistling in from the north and lands a couple of blocks away. Then another. The local artillery is not slow to respond. It all feels less dangerous in the light somehow. Breakfast is green bananas, coffee, cornflakes with powdered milk and dough-nuts. I go upstairs to see where the shelling is coming from. It is a beautiful day with bright sun and a gentle breeze from the sea. Apart from dark smoke from a few fires, the city looks surprisingly normal at rooftop level.

At mid morning I drive over to the Digfer hospital which is close to the front line. On the dashboard of the SCF Land Cruiser a printed note reads:

Security Guidelines
- Do not wear a seat belt. You may need to get out of the car suddenly and this will restrain you. And if you are stopped and you reach down to undo the seat belt it may be interpreted as a move for a gun.
- If stopped – don't move suddenly. Put an arm out so as to make it clear that there is an expatriate in the vehicle.
- All vehicles carry sterile bandages for shell and bullet wounds.

In the back of the vehicle two gunmen perch with AK47s at the ready, their spare ammunition clip bound to their guns with sticky tape marked 'Save the Children Fund'. The driver tells me enviously that Médecins Sans Frontières have hired a 'proper technical' with a big gun on the back. He regards the SCF as wimps. We roar off. Travelling slowly might indicate that you are up to no good.

At the hospital gate a crush of desperate people is shouting and screaming. A man tries to push through carrying a young girl in his arms. A woman with a terrible leg wound is carried by relatives. An unconscious old woman is bumping along in a wheelbarrow. The guards try to block them, but pain and despair are stronger and the crowd suddenly pushes through the gate and into the courtyard. At that moment a 'technical' screams up, horn blaring. It almost crashes into the crowd. The young men on the back fire their weapons in the air and the crowd scatters in panic. The 'technical' shoots forward through the gate. Three men leap out shrieking and dash into the hospital carrying a comrade gushing blood from his mouth.

I follow them. The trail of blood splashes leads along a corridor lined with wounded. Most have relatives around them holding their hands, brushing the flies away from their faces. On a mat a beautiful girl lies, eyes shut, face concentrated. She is one of the lucky ones. Her sister holds a saline drip bag over her and strokes her face. My shoes squelch and stick in the blood.

The emergency room is bright, hot, tense. Highlighted under powerful lamps, doctors in green surgical aprons are gathered round the operating table, like priests performing a sacrifice. They wave the flies away as if blessing the young man bleeding on the table, releasing his soul. They are removing a bullet from his leg. You can see the shattered shin bone white against the red gore. The surgeon is digging into it vigorously. On the other table a man lies face down, his back almost torn off. On the side two more lie groaning in pools of blood. One, covered in flies, looks as if the top of his head is missing. Two other bodies lie unmoving under blankets, waiting for the earth, not the operating table. Another twitches horribly. On the bench beside the crude operating table are blood-soaked bandages and clothes and a pile of shaved matted hair glistening red.

The heat and smell are unbearable. One of the surgeons is an American, Bill Moore, a former army doctor who wears a T-shirt that says 'African Paradise'. He wants the window open. He argues that if a shell bursts nearby the window will shatter. The Somali doctor says if they open the window they will let in infection and more flies. They open it for a moment but the noise of battle and the screaming crowd at the gate is terrifying. As if to make the American's point, a shell slams into the hospital wall not far away and the building rocks. The doctors pause but do not stop.

A Somali nurse tells me without looking up from her work:

> We have no anaesthetic gases, no painkillers. We use local anaesthetics for amputations. Sometimes we use spinal anaesthetics for anything below the waist, but a lot of abdominal surgery is carried out without anaesthetics. We have picked up 680 bodies from the streets in the last two weeks – we used volunteers. Everyone has lost someone. Whole families are wiped out.

Mogadishu's water supply is destroyed, so water has to be brought to the hospital in barrels. Ordinary people walk miles through the dangerous streets in search of muddy pools to scoop a few mouthfuls of water to drink. The children's ward is full of dysentery cases and there are fears of cholera. Everyone asks how long food supplies will hold out. Famine has already struck Somalia's food-producing areas. Already there is hunger in Mogadishu. It will be only a month or two before the city starves.

By midday there are forty casualties. 'It's going to be a long day,' says the nurse. The Somali doctors here have not been paid for a year. 'We have had this for fifty-six days now,' says Dr Abdi. 'Sometimes I do not sleep for twenty-four hours. But I have to stay. I could not leave my people.' Foreign doctors working for NGOs agree that it is the Somali doctors who keep the whole operation going. The hospital deals with up to 200 casualities a day: faces slashed by flying glass, stomachs and lungs ripped open by bullets, arms torn off by shrapnel, legs smashed by falling masonry, and small neat bullets in brains. But there is no time to record what the doctors do. The only record of this war will be the hospital store log: the count of bandages, swabs and suture thread.

Dr Abdi, a Somali doctor, talks as he works: 'People are fatalistic here. When they die they accept it; it is the time. There is nothing you can do about it. Some of the fighters are just boys from the bush. They enjoy it . . . they have no food, no home. They live to kill.' Bill Moore tells me, 'I never saw anything like this in Vietnam.'

As I leave, a shell bursts by the gate and the road becomes a mass of dead and dying. Everyone alive is screaming, tearing their hair as they stand over victims, unable to do anything. The market nearby empties and a tank and a multi-barrelled rocket launcher come hurtling up the road. We leap into the vehicles and dash back to the house.

After another noisy night I go to visit General Aideed's house, which is only two streets away. An imposing, thuggish-looking man who seems unaware of anyone else around him, he has no charm. But he does have the twisted Somali sense of humour. When I complain about the shelling he tells me this is the safest place in the city because they are aiming at his house. He wanders into the room in his sock feet, pushing past a crowd of people who have come to beg favours. He carries a silver-topped cane and dresses in a black denim jacket and a straw hat. One of his officials takes the fan from the room. Aideed shouts at him. Amazingly, the man shouts back and they row. Aideed wins and takes back the fan.

He launches into a high-pitched husky monotone, explaining why he must be President because of this resolution passed at that congress and that resolution agreed in this party meeting. His juggernaut of resolutions, technicalities and protocols grinds on relentlessly. I try to engage him in a more personal conversation. He smiles insincerely, a brief flash of acknowledgement, and presses on again with more self-justification. He shows no interest in compromise or peace, but reassures himself by repeating the litany of his cause. Stopping to see if he is persuading me is not a priority. The appalling war in the streets is as nothing beside this man's ambition to rule.

The rant goes on for two hours. He sees himself as a freedom fighter, a military liberator. He talks of freedom and a multi-party system and human rights. 'I am working hardly in order to develop my country very goodly with intellectuals and those who fight for the country,' he concludes. 'Have you made any mistakes?' I ask. 'No. I haven't made any. The Manifesto group started fighting us. Our aim is not to seize power but to liberate the country.'

I am dismissed. The rant is suddenly switched off and he turns away with a perfunctory handshake. Shelling is sporadic when I leave his house, but as I walk back I try to judge which burnt-out car or broken wall I will dive for if a shell comes close.

At the house the heads of the four aid agencies remaining in Mogadishu are meeting. They are divided over whether to pull out or stay. All admit they can no longer do what they came to do, but should they stay on in solidarity with the people? A month ago a Belgian aid worker, Wim van Boxelaere, was killed. A dock worker got angry over some food being delivered and shot him. Wim's guard threw himself in front of his body to protect him, but the bullets passed through him, came out spinning and tore into Wim. The guard survived, but Wim died four days later on a plane taking him back to Belgium. Somalis were outraged and ashamed that a foreigner who had come to help had been killed in their war. That inspires some of the aid workers to stay on. Fear underlies the discussion. But there is also a macho competition not to be the first to cut and run.

Another factor unites them. Everyone despises the UN. Somalia cruelly exposed the myth of the world organization that would protect the suffering masses. When the government collapsed in 1991 the powers that control the UN – America, France, Britain – were embroiled in the battle for Kuwait. Kuwait has oil. Somalia does not. The UN, humanitarian workers included, pulled out. Now UN workers receive $100 a day extra for being off base. Many are staying in holiday hotels on the Kenya coast. While the NGOs have to budget carefully, flight by flight, to bring in their supplies, the UN occasionally flies in a plane with just one person on it to see what is going on. They bring no supplies. 'They don't even tell us they are coming,' complains one NGO boss. 'They could at least bring in some supplies for us.'

Then an argument breaks out over food aid. Four people have died this week of starvation. Some NGOs want to use the hospitals as distribution points, but the medical NGOs say no. 'Give us the money and we'll find the food.' They argue that hungry people will be attracted to the hospital and fill it, stopping casualties getting in.

The Red Cross rule that it relies only on its flag for the safety of its staff has collapsed here. It has been forced to accept protection from locally hired gunmen. Too many foreigners have been kidnapped and their equipment and vehicles stolen at gunpoint on the street. Headquarters in Geneva pretend this is only to guard the vehicles, not the staff. The staff here have the usual contempt for headquarters, but they are frustrated. They spend most of their time locked in their house surrounded by high walls. Bringing in medical equipment for the hospitals is just about their only useful role, but they admit it probably does not need foreigners to do this.

More disturbingly, someone asks the question: does a regular supply of bandages, drips and anaesthetics to the area make the Red Cross anything more than General Aideed's medical corps? They cannot get supplies across the line to north Mogadishu, though there is the possibility of a new airport opening up on the north side of the city. I had already seen at the hospital how the fighters always took precedence over civilians. Could the Red Cross presence be prolonging the war?

'It's time to go,' says one staffer. 'There's no point in putting ourselves at risk when we can't do anything anyway.'

'We have to stay – we can't just leave because it gets hot,' comes the reply. 'It's the very time we should be here.'

The argument boils down to what each agency does. None of their headquarters insists that they stay, but there is pressure to hang on – not least because of the unspoken need to raise funds. As long as strong media images of suffering are coming out of Somalia, any aid agency with a spokesman on the ground is going to get media publicity and be able to raise cash. The Red Cross decides to continue breaking its rule, but to move to the edge of town to get away from the artillery battle. The three others choose to stay put and watch developments.

This discussion about front-line intervention has since been repeated again and again in Africa: Rwanda, Burundi, Congo DRC, Congo-Brazzaville, Sierra Leone, Liberia, Côte d'Ivoire, Sudan, Mozambique, Angola have all thrown up wars in which humanitarian aid workers intervene only to find themselves caught up in the same terrible dilemma. There is no such thing as neutrality. Intervention is interference. Whatever aid workers' motives, their intervention has military and political effects. The aid agencies' dilemma was stark in Somalia and two years later even starker in eastern Congo, where the aid workers went to help the great exodus from Rwanda. There, most of the aid agencies chose to ignore the problem and ended up feeding and protecting the perpetrators of Rwanda's genocide. They even provided surplus food aid which was grabbed by the killer militias who sold it and bought new weapons with the profits.

In Somalia, after endless negotiations, UN troops did arrive that year, a small group of Pakistanis who got no further than the airport. The war spread to the south and the areas that usually grow the nation's food were hit by famine. In Mogadishu children started to die of hunger. In December 1992 President George Bush decided to send in the marines to stop the fighting and clear a path through the warlords' territory to deliver food to the starving. Bush called it 'God's work' that could not fail. How could it? – God's work backed by American firepower.

If they had really wanted just to feed the hungry, the Americans should have come six months before when the famine was at its height. The worst-hit area was south-west Somalia, easily reachable by road from Kenya. The Americans did not need to go near Mogadishu to feed starving people. It is very unclear what exactly the mission was, but I suspected that Bush wanted another imperial display of American military might and decided on a frontal assault on the capital.

The Americans facilitate scores of journalists to come to Mogadishu and on the evening of 8 December 1992, General Frank Libuti and Robert Oakley, the American special envoy to Somalia, brief the journalists in a villa in Mogadishu. It belonged once to Chevron, the American oil company, but at this time is being looked after by Osman Atto, a Mogadishu businessman who is bankrolling General Aideed. General Libuti deliberately lets slip that if we sleep that night we might miss something.

That night the airport building roof is an extraordinary sight: cameramen, camera bags, tripods, wires, lamps, photographers, more wires, laptops and bags and bags of food and booze. This is going to be a long wait. Some journalists have not seen each other since the Gulf War and there are lots of whoops and high-fives and hugs. They stroll across the runway to the beach, reminiscing and story telling. From the shore the media circus on the airport roof shimmers under powerful arc lamps like a film set with too many technicians and no actors.

At about 1.45 a.m. a cameraman trying out a night sight suddenly spots something out to sea. Everyone rushes down to the beach to find four frogmen in wet suits swimming ashore. The US Navy Seals are coming. What nobody seems to have told the landing party is that the beach and the airport are swarming with journalists. The Seals wade through the surf and onto the beach – straight into the flashing cameras and microphones of the journalists. Like celebrities emerging from a nightclub, the Seals try to shield their faces and slink away. One, face painted green, flees towards some sand dunes at the top of the beach and starts to pack his wet suit into a rucksack and put on chocolate chip camouflage. Caught with his trousers down, he is hounded by the media horde, lamps held high and a barrage of shouted questions. He tries to ignore us, but eventually turns and pleads, 'Please leave me alone.' He is like a child playing hide and seek, begging the adults not to give him away.

'Go away or we'll shoot,' shouts another one trapped in some bushes. 'Shoot away,' someone shouts. 'We're rolling.' Three little Zodiac speedboats come whizzing ashore and disgorge more Navy Seals, while the journalists have been reinforced by other crews running down from the airport building. By now the Pakistani force is getting interested, and a Jeepload comes hurtling across the runway to find out what the fuss is about. Eventually a major emerges from a patch of shrub and calls the journalists. 'We were not expecting this,' he says frankly. 'Please leave us alone to get on with our work.'

I have been told that the main body of the invasion force will sail straight into the harbour, so I drive to the port with my Somali crew: translator, driver and two gunmen. My life depends on Abdi Dahir, Nur and Abdi, the guards, and Mohammed, the driver. Cheerful and cynical, they are ever ready to expound on the complexities of Somali society or to kill for me. This morning they are hyper, fascinated by the Americans and their guns and equipment. But will the Somalis welcome them or shoot at them? Amid shrieks of laughter, they explain that 'seal' means 'vagina' in Somali. Our pick-up has flashing Christmas lights around the windscreen and plays Brahms's *Lullaby* when it reverses. The windscreen and dashboard have three bullet holes in them and I notice the driver's seat also has a hole through it. 'My brother was driving at the time,' says Abdi Dahir quietly. 'He died.' Nur, one of the gunmen, carries an impossibly heavy G3 rifle in one hand. He lost his other arm when his father, a soldier in the Somali army, took him aged ten to the front in the 1978 war against Ethiopia to show him what it meant to be a warrior. He was hit by a sniper.

I wander down the jetty on my own to watch two black-headed terns hovering and diving in the tranquil early-morning light. Suddenly two sparks fly past my head. Then the crack, crack of a rifle. I am being shot at. I fall over, feeling rather stupid. A couple of marines sprint up to me screaming hysterically. 'Stay down, you fucker. Don't fucking move,' one shrieks. 'Roll over. Put your hands out flat.'

I see boots next to my face and lift my head. Immediately a rifle barrel is jabbed into my ear and my head slammed down onto the tarmac. I feel another gun sticking in my back. 'Identify yourself!' screams the soldier.

'I . . . I . . . I'm a British journalist,' I say, not very confidently.

'He says he's a British journalist,' the marine parrots back over his shoulder, turning swiftly back as if the meaning only sunk in when he shouts it. 'You're a what?'

'I work for the *Independent* newspaper of London. What's your problem?'

He is silent for a moment. Another marine pulls my bag away and is searching it. I look up.

'Get your fucking face in the dirt,' he screams again, but then seems to run out of conversation and waits for someone to tell him what to do. That is difficult as a helicopter thunders in over the containers and hovers just above us. Its downdraught whips up clouds of dust and drowns out the commander's orders.

More soldiers run up. They too are hysterical. I try to calm them. 'Go easy. There's no trouble up there, they're all friendly.' But my captor shrieks back: 'Get your hands above your head and walk ahead up the jetty.' Another of his comrades flings himself flat and fires a burst up the jetty to where other journalists are sitting.

'Don't be stupid – there's only journalists up there,' I shout, but as the words leave my mouth I realize that my crew are there too. They have guns and they are Somalis. I have paid them and we have a deal. They will die for me – and kill for me. If I call them they might come out, guns blazing. I walk up the jetty, my hands held high, with two soldiers moving nervously behind me while others sprint and drop, sprint and drop from container to container each side. I approach the nervous little gaggle of journalists and their Somali helpers. Then I see my two gunmen recognize me and reach for their guns. Now I scream, 'Put the guns down. Don't shoot. Don't shoot.' They look confused, as if to say, 'Why did you hire us then?' But they obey.

Everyone waits stock still as the marines approach. The Somalis look bemused. The marines order them to lie on the ground to search them while we whites are searched standing up. A wave of sullen anger passes across their faces. 'Treat us like human beings,' shouts one. 'We are human beings.' The Americans do not listen. From that moment I know they will be defeated by Somalia.

That was the only time I was ever assaulted in Africa.

Almost a year later, an American special forces team went into the centre of Mogadishu to try to capture General Aideed. They had tried to get him several times before, but each time believed false information and got it wrong. On two occasions they attacked UN buildings after false tip-offs. One of their informants clearly had a great sense of humour. So did General Aideed. When the American commander of Operation Restore Hope, Admiral Jonathan Howe, offered $25,000 bounty for Aideed, the General offered a similar amount for the Admiral's head. That night was no different. They did not find Aideed, and two special forces units were trapped in the middle of Mogadishu with two Black Hawk helicopters shot down. There was no rescue plan and eighteen Americans died horribly. Hundreds more had to be rescued by Malaysian UN troops – the only force in Mogadishu with hard-skinned vehicles.

More than 1000 Somalis were killed that night, most of them women and children hit by bullets and rockets from helicopter gun-ships which circled the trapped men, spraying the flimsy Somali houses with guns that fired thousands of rounds a minute.

Next day, the body of one of the Americans was dragged through the streets and Reuters filmed it. The footage hit the world's TV screens and America froze. A couple of days later I got there and went with my crew to the site of the crashed helicopter and watched scrawny Somali kids swinging and bouncing on the broken blades. We found a woman and her children who had been taken hostage by the trapped Americans. In the film of the incident, *Black Hawk Down*, the Rangers are shown protecting the woman. She told a different story. The soldiers had seized her and her children and held them in front of them with guns to their heads as human shields to try to escape.

After a while Abdi Dahir, my translator, suggested we move away quickly. I asked why. 'The crowd, they think you are American,' came the reply. As I got in the vehicle I said: 'What if I was American?'

'They would kill you,' he says with a smile.

A month later the Americans cut and ran. President Clinton

brought the US troops home and stopped funding the UN force in Somalia so it too was forced to withdraw, leaving Somalia to years of bloodshed and death. That punished the ordinary Somalis, the people the Americans had supposedly come to help, leaving them at the mercy of the gunmen. But the real victims of the Somali debacle were the Rwandan Tutsis. After Somalia Americans gave up on the UN. They blamed everyone else and punished Somalis for their own debacle. But when in 1994 the genocide started in Rwanda, the memory of Somalia made America allergic to intervention in Africa. The United States, backed by Britain and Belgium, forced the UN Security Council to cut the peacekeeping force as the genocide plan was rolled out across Rwanda. Nearly a million people were murdered.

In 1999 I went back to Somalia to see what had happened. Considering that there was no state and the civil war sputtered on, life was not as bad as I had expected. In some ways it was a lot better. Those few aid agencies that stayed on were no longer run by expatriate overlords but staffed by Somalis. Not many foreign aid workers wanted to be there. Somalis had also managed to get the economy going – without a single cent from the World Bank or the IMF. The new economy was largely built around a worldwide telephone banking system – a truly free market system and, at the time, by far the world's cheapest and most efficient. Several Somalis who had worked in telecoms in America bought dishes and telephone equipment and set up phone booths in small towns. From here, for a dollar a minute, people could call cousins and aunts and uncles all over the world. They also set up cheap telephone and email shops in cities in Europe, America and Australia so that Abdi in Vancouver can hand the phone company $103 and $100 will be given to his aunt Mariam in Galkayo the same day. Somalis all over the world began to pour remittance money into Somalia to rebuild the country's ruined cities. Nothing is written down, everything is on trust. Somalia – within the clans – is a very high trust society. Cheat and you die. It works well.

In contrast to the high-tec New Somalia, I want to see how the traditional pastoralists who live under the sun and stars with their herds of camels and sheep have survived the war. A veterinary organization in Hargeisa which tries to help the nomadic herdsmen gives me a guide and a Land Rover and we drive south from Hargeisa into a world of sand, rock, thorn trees and plastic bags. Given away free in markets, millions of blue and pink thin plastic bags blow across Somalia like confetti from a giant's wedding. Almost every thorn tree has at least one in its branches tugged by the wind. Thousands more are flattened against rocks or caught in sandy gullies. The vets complain that goats and camels sometimes eat them and die.

Here you can feel the bones of the planet. In this vast landscape you are touching its naked body, unprotected by soft layers of soil and vegetation. Plateaux have been pushed up, tilted, cracked, eroded. You can almost feel the aeons of heaves and cracks in the earth's crust. All is rock and thorn but in gullies and pans, thin sandy soil has accumulated to allow hardy grasses and tough-skinned plants to cling to life. Grass seems to grow under the thorny scrub only where sheep and goats cannot reach it. My guide says that there was once more grass and more soil but over-grazing has eroded them. Everywhere trees have been cut down or their branches hacked through to provide a few mouthfuls of thorny leaves for the animals.

The sandy track takes us a few miles south of Hargeisa to a small trading post of makeshift wooden shacks and a stone mosque. I step out of the car into unbreathable heat. Gusts of wind do not cool but waft even hotter air into your lungs. They bring dust too, drying mouth and eyes. People walk to the village to drink tea or buy a minuscule bag of salt or a single cigarette. Then they wander off into the sand and scrub. A lorry laden with firewood stops and its driver and helper come into the tea shack. That is the biggest moment of the day. The population of the village changes by the hour. It is difficult to see who lives here permanently, if it can be called living.

In the tiny shack-shops women sell little balls of paper containing sugar or salt, soap, candles, batteries, biscuits and spaghetti and the usual odds and ends that represent commerce in poorest Africa. A deranged man with wild matted hair and crazed eyes wanders about in filthy rags, abusing everyone. The shop women shout back at him and give him sweets and a cup of tea. At midday the wife of the man who seems to be the boss of the place gives us lunch: spaghetti in a communal plastic washing-up bowl. She insists we wash our hands in a bucket of pale brown water.

At around four in the afternoon, as the heat begins to drain out of the sun, an old man, dressed traditionally with a red hennaed beard strides into the village. Wearing a macawiis wrap and thick leather sandals, his step is heavy but strong – like the camels he herds. He carries a herding stick across his shoulders in the traditional way, forearms drooped over the ends. His name is Aden and he has come to the trading post, as he does every day, to listen to the news on the BBC Somali service. He wears thick glasses in heavy frames, foggy with age. After a brief exchange through our interpreter, he agrees that if we bring a few bunches of khat, we will be very welcome at his camp tonight.

'How far is it?'

'Very close.'

'How close?'

'A few *gedis*.'

'What's a gedi?'

A gedi is the way Somalis measure distance. It is the distance a browsing sheep moves in a day. If you're a nomad it is the only distance that matters. It would, he says, take us about an hour. We gather our bags, buy khat and extra water and set off on foot. Two and a half hours later we are still walking. The old man carries the khat while we look like refugees weighed down with bundles of sleeping bags, blankets and a water container. The sun sets suddenly and stupendously behind us throwing up our shadows in front of us ten times our size.

The sun is gone and the earth is dark, but above us the sky is still pale blue. Eventually we reach the camp, two small dome tents of brown reed matting, protected by a hedge of fearsome inch-long thorns. One of these traditional Somali dwellings has a blue plastic sheet over it – a remnant of the miles of plastic sheeting brought in by the UN for displaced people. We are greeted by the scent of wood smoke, the ubiquitous, eternal smell of humanity in Africa. Two other men and two women have spotted strangers approaching and have come out to greet us; their cries of welcome carry in a distant, dreamy way in the vast landscape.

The men make a fire for us in a semicircle of cut thorn branches some way off from the tents and, after a while, the women bring us a washing-up bowl of spaghetti. We scoop out trailing handfuls and drop them into our mouths, slurping up the tails. It's how I always wanted to eat spaghetti as a child. By the time we have finished eating it is dark, and a wind hisses and screams in the thorn hedge around us and buffets the fire. Suddenly it becomes very cold and we are glad of the sleeping bags and blankets that we had joked about a few hours ago in the baking heat. Aden sits barelegged with only his cotton shawl draped around his shoulders. We pile more wood on the fire and move closer to it, drink tea, chew khat and talk.

The khat is working, keeping me awake. Even allowing for an old man's nostalgia for the good old days, Aden is clear that Somalia fifty years ago was a much greener, richer place than today, 'as different as heaven and the ground', he says. He talks of lions and leopards and ostriches, rain that was plentiful and regular, 'virgin grass higher than a man'. Dry seasons, he says, were worse in those days and the herds had to be taken to drink from the river at Hargeisa. Now there are several bore holes and wells in the area. There were fewer camels and sheep in the old days, but they were bigger and stronger than today and produced 'twenty times' the amount of milk. 'We used to pour it away on the ground,' he recalls, as a gambler might boast of a squandered fortune. The gedi, he explains, was longer in those days because the animals were stronger.

Somali herders move around in a yearly pattern. In the dry season, towards the end of the year, they go down to the coast as they have done for centuries to sell some of their animals to traders who take them across the Red Sea to the markets of Saudi Arabia. I have watched them at the port of Berbera, herds of camels and sheep driven to holding areas where herders have to buy fodder for them and pay for water at the market troughs. These herdsmen are at a big disadvantage while they wait to sell their animals. But the mobile phone has rescued them. They can call up traders in Jeddah directly to find out the market price of animals there. They now know when to come down out of the mountains and sell. A week later I watch a herdsman on the outskirts of Berbera driving his herd towards the port with herding stick in one hand and in the other a mobile phone – perfect technology for the nomad.

But economics is turning against their way of life. Sheep and goats for the markets for Jeddah and Riyadh are cheaper and cheaper, brought from as far afield as Australia. Who wants to lead a tough, dull life in the desert when all the attractions of town life beckon? What does Aden want from life now? He has sat cross-legged for nearly two hours in the firelight, wrapped in a thin shawl, his legs bare. Above us the stars glitter, millions of brilliant pricks in the darkness. I am snuggled down in a sleeping bag but my head is freezing.

'We just want rain and better animals. That's all I pray for,' he says, stroking his hennaed beard. Echoing the poem by Ostreeliya, he adds: 'We do not work for money and a house in the city. Our animals are the backbone of our lives in peace and war. Every race has some blessing from Allah and ours is our camels. Our wealth is our camels. We are not interested in gold or money.'

Education? 'Just some Koranic school so our children can learn to pray,' he says. I ask Aden if his way of life will survive. 'God has given us this life,' he replies. 'It is hard, but we want to continue.' One of the younger men adds that many people are leaving the towns because there is no work there now and they are heading back to a nomadic life in the plains.

'But what about the women?' I ask. He waves the question away with a gesture as if I was asking about how his dog felt about its life. 'They may prefer to be in the city,' he says. We offer to ask them ourselves, but the suggestion is dismissed with a laugh. The conversation switches back to the concerns of men.

'In the old days sometimes there were fights with other clans,' he says. 'The British would call us together and get us to talk, but if they failed to make peace, they would say, "OK, go and fight." And we did. Praise be to Allah. We took sheep and camels from other groups and women too, but only unmarried ones. When I was young I married two girls. I took them both by force to avoid paying a lot of camels to their families. Yes, I took my wife by force in an attack on another clan. I carried her like this.' Aden smiles hugely and holds out his arms in front as if he were carrying a baby. 'But then later we sent some animals to her family to make peace.'

He describes an attack on the Ogadenis, another Somali clan that sometimes comes to these grazing grounds. 'We were 1000 and at dawn we attacked. Many died, but we took between 800 and 900 camels.' Even now such battles go on, he says, but it is not like the old times. He dismisses the civil war that has destroyed Somalia in the last fifteen years as a small affair.

The khat keeps us going far into the night. It makes me feel extraordinarily interested in everything, and say extraordinarily interesting things. I made extensive notes but next day I could hardly remember the conversation. At last I ask the old man the question that I thought might reveal the secret of the nomadic life: 'What does he need from the rest of the world?' He thinks for a moment and, putting his head on one side, replies, 'Poison, so we can kill all the wild animals.'

After the old man and his son had retired to their tent, we lie back under the blankets, our feet cooked by the fire, our faces chilled by the wind, our brains fizzing with khat and our hearts among the brilliant shimmering stars.

In the morning the women are up first, bringing us tea. Then they milk the sheep and goats that have been kept in a thorn-fenced kraal overnight. Somali sheep all have white bodies and black heads and, tied together in a line waiting to be milked, they are an extraordinarily beautiful sight. Bent double the women move between them tugging tiny jets of milk from their teats into little gourd bowls.

We are invited into their tent and perhaps to impress us they then hold a special prayer meeting. It may also be because one of the younger men there is a wandering imam who is staying with the herders. I climb into the larger tent and squeeze down against the side. A rough grass mat thrown over bent branches, the tent looks flimsy. I am nervous of leaning against the side. The imam chants from a very battered copy of the Koran and I have a chance to look round the inside of a Somali home. The matting is secured over the round frame of branches tied together. These come from a particular tree, now becoming scarce and very precious. Hanging on the frame are a couple of blankets and sleeping mats, an oil lamp, a kettle, a flask and an old gourd. On the floor are sleeping mats and blankets, an enamel bowl and tin pans and a long wooden box full of salt. Tucked into a dark cranny at the back of the tent is an AK47.

For more than twenty years Somalia lay in pieces. The rest of the world either ignored it or intervened sporadically and violently with little understanding of its internal dynamics. Determined to create a Western-style sovereign state with an elected president, political parties, elections and a parliament, they funded peace talks and conferences. If talking could solve anything, Somalia would have been resolved years ago. Millions were spent on airline tickets, hotel bills and telephone calls to bring Somalis together in at least sixteen major international peace efforts to reach agreement. But like a Rubik's cube gone wrong, Somalia's politics seemed impossible to unlock. Every peace conference sooner or later became entangled with Somalia's clan rivalries or was undermined by other countries in the region. The neighbours watched peace conferences carefully, making sure that the peace they aspired to did not damage their interests.

Many Somalis despaired of ever achieving statehood again. Some said that perhaps Somalia's social structure would never permit a normal nation state in Somalia. Somalis, they said, should be happy with a loose federation of clan-based autonomous areas. The neighbours, particularly Ethiopia and Eritrea, used it as a battle-ground, each backing opposing camps. A divided, weak Somalia suits Ethiopia, its old rival. A conference at Arta in Djibouti in 2000, financed by the European Union, brought together representatives of all the clans. The President, Ismael Omar Guelleh, had the sense to lock them away in a sparse inhospitable barracks with no alcohol and – even better – no phones. He had seen the phone bills from previous attempts. The meeting reached agreement and a government was formed, but a year later the Ethiopians pulled it to pieces and persuaded the world to accept Abdillahi Yusuf as president.

The warlords continued to rule their areas, taxing, robbing, raping, killing. Although some businessmen who ran the remittance banking and mobile phone companies did well, most Somalis lived day to day, hand to mouth. Thousands fled the country, risking the Red Sea or the Indian Ocean in open fishing boats to find a future. Many were drowned or turned away by hostile patrols from other countries. Unknown numbers stayed at home and starved or died of simple diseases.

In 1991 Somaliland in the north-west declared independence from the rest of the country and set up a government. There, talking eventually resolved the war, and with virtually no help from outside an administration was formed, institutions were set up and elections held. Recognized by no-one and dependent on remittances from its own people in exile, it has remained peaceful and reasonably safe. Hargeisa, the razed city, has been rebuilt and is booming. The annual poetry festival has been restored and flourishes.

The north-east also established a measure of peace. Giving itself the biblical name of Puntland, it too had its own president, ministries and officials but it never succeeded in establishing the coherence, efficiency and solidarity that Somaliland has. And its 'independence' was only temporary, lasting as long as there was no effective government in Mogadishu.

Abdillahi Yusuf, the Puntland warlord, was not accepted as president in Mogadishu so he spent most of his time outside the country or in Baidoa, the town near the border with Ethiopia. The new government was kept out of the capital by the Islamic Courts Union. Politics had broken Somalia and years of suffering had driven many people to seek religion as a source of hope and solidarity. It provided order where there was no leadership. Always Islamic but never particularly religious, the Somalis began to find in religion a unifying factor which trumped the disunity of clans. Businessmen, tired of paying 'tax' to the warlords, also saw that the Islamic Courts could bring some order and peace. Business suddenly boomed across the country. As one Somali friend said: 'We could walk down the street using a mobile phone without fear of it being stolen, we could go to the market without fear of attack or rape. People respected each other.'

Meanwhile the Americans wanted the three men they said were responsible for the bombings of their embassies in Nairobi and Dar es Salaam in 1998. A Comorean, a Sudanese and a Kenyan, they were thought to be hiding somewhere in Somalia. Early in 2006 the CIA tried to hire some of Somalia's worst warlords to go and get them. Money and guns were flown in by plane to Isaley airstrip, north of Mogadishu. The news spread fast and the reaction was instant. Clan loyalties forgotten, Somalis flocked to the Islamic Courts to fight the warlords who had held Somalia to ransom for so long. Within days the warlords were chased out of Mogadishu. From there the movement spread across southern Somalia. Several other towns agreed to join the Courts movement without a fight.

The Courts turned into a popular uprising, the first viable movement to cut across clan rivalry and unite Somalis since 1991. But the Courts were not universally popular. Some said they had little power outside the Hawiye area and their power simply represented a peace agreement between the warring sub-clans of the Hawiye. Influenced by Saudi Wahabists whose Islam is at odds with Somalia's more tolerant Sufi tradition, the more extreme Islamists tried to enforce Sharia law, the veil and the drab colours of the fundamentalists.

Personal freedom became an issue. Some Courts were quoted as saying they would kill those who did not pray five times a day, and they tried to stop people watching television or chewing khat.

Somalis, renowned for their strong-willed individualism, argued back. No-one tells them what they can or cannot watch on TV. If there is one lesson from Somalia since independence in 1960 it is that Somalis will be governed only by consent.

But the Americans and British claimed that the leadership of the Courts was in the hands of extremists, protecting men wanted for 'terrorism'. They had assumed that because Somalia had no state it would be easy for 'terrorists' from all over the world to come and settle, even recruit there. After all these years, the Americans still had no understanding of the country and its people. Perhaps they did not care. Their one-eyed obsession with 'terrorism' ignored the local politics. They wanted the men who planned the embassy bombings and they wanted to avenge the deaths of the American soldiers in 1993.

The Ethiopian government was also concerned that Somalia might be reuniting – and reuniting under an Islamic movement. They said they had evidence that the Islamic Courts movement was supporting Somali rebels in the Ogaden and another Ethiopian rebel movement. Worse, they found their deadly enemy, Eritrea, was funding and supplying the Courts and other enemies of Ethiopia in Somalia. A Christian mountain empire surrounded by Muslims who also make up nearly half its population, Ethiopia has always feared its Muslim neighbours, especially Somalia in the east. Ethiopia blamed rebellion at home on Islamic fundamentalism. When the hotheads from the Courts rushed to Baidoa to attack the Ethiopian-backed government, the Ethiopians had their pretext. Ethiopian and American interests coincided, and on Christmas Eve 2006 the tanks rolled into Somalia.

The Islamic Courts fighters, armed with AK47s and rockets, were no match for tanks, helicopters and fighter bombers. They soon collapsed. Fleeing south-east, they were cornered, trapped between the sea, patrolled by the US Fifth Fleet, and the southern border, patrolled by the Kenyan army and American special forces. The Ethiopians swept across the country. Just as it looked as if the last remnant of Courts fighters would be captured, American AC 130s reportedly based in Ethiopia poured fire down from the sky, killing large numbers of people. Why did they kill rather than capture? And why the Americans, when the Ethiopians seemed to be doing the job perfectly well? They said it was the 'war on terror' – but none of the wanted men was captured or found in the rubble. Instead, more than a hundred Somalis had been killed in crossfire. Once again America seemed to be creating the very thing it claimed to be destroying.

Predictably the Ethiopian-imposed government was soon holed up in fortresses in Mogadishu, joined by Ugandan 'peacekeepers' who were also treated as invaders. In early 2008 the streets of Mogadishu were as dangerous as they had been in 1992. The civilian population fled to the surrounding area where they began to starve – a man-made disaster that killed hundreds of thousands of people.

By the end of 2011 the government still only controlled a small part of the capital, thanks to an African Union peace-keeping force. The battle for Mogadishu still flared occasionally, as it had for the past 22 years. But by July of that same year the country was gripped by the worst drought in 30 years. When the warnings sounded in November 2010, the rest of the world reacted to Somalia as it usually did, ignoring it until pictures appeared on TV of starving families trying to cross the border into Kenya.

Meanwhile, a new phenomenon had emerged: al-Shabaab. The word means youth and indeed many of its members had never known anything except gunfire and fear. Al-Shabaab's simplistic answer was a vicious version of Islamic order in which every non-Islamic influence was *haram* – forbidden. Many of its fighters were

Arabs and they linked up with Al-Qaeda. They started detonating car bombs in crowds of civilians as a way of undermining the credibility of the so-called government. Ethiopia and America had created the very thing they thought they were destroying in 2010.

At the same time, young men in fast speed boats began to operate along Somalia's unpatrolled coasts, seizing international shipping and holding the boats and crews to ransom. By 2012 the cost of piracy had risen to more than $3 billion, as nearly 50 substantial vessels had been seized, including two supertankers. Somali piracy became an international issue, although, as happens so often in Somalia, Western ignorance played a role. Huge fishing vessels from Japan, Indonesia and other countries were hoovering up enormous quantities of fish from Somalia's territorial waters. The British government's aid agency, the Department for International Development, wanted to give the Somalis control over their maritime jurisdiction and funded a maritime security company to train Somali coastguards. The training included the use of fast speed boats and weaponry. The coast guards promptly privatized themselves and extended their mandate to include any ships in reach of the Somali coasts.

The cost, particularly to Britain, which hosts the maritime insurance companies, was estimated at $7 billion in 2011. But when US, French and British forces began to patrol the sea routes around Somalia, piracy dropped dramatically. On the back of that, Britain took the lead in trying to bring an end to Somalia's 23 years of anarchy and war and establish a government. It wanted to replace Somalia's current crop of ineffective clan-based politicians with a more effective government which could stop piracy and defeat al-Shabaab. Incursions of Somali fighters and refugees into northern Kenya prompted Kenya's government to send its army into Somalia to create a buffer zone on the other side of the border.

With the Ugandans and the Burundians, this international, mainly African, force guided by the United States and the United Kingdom now went on the offensive. It seized the wealthy port of Merca from al-Shabaab and cleared the movement out of Mogadishu. By the end of the year, al-Shabaab had been forced underground and for the first time in 20 years, the formal meeting of the Somali parliament was held on Somali soil. Britain took the lead on the political front, putting a lot of effort into peacemaking and hosting the politicians in London. As a result, instead of being ruled over by the usual warlord president, Somali clan chiefs were encouraged to elect a civil society activist, Hassan Sheikh Mohamud.

In 2013 there were hopes that Somalia's civil war might be coming to an end. The questions that remain concern how long the country will have to rely on the Ugandans, Burundians and Kenyans as an occupying force in the south, and whether al-Shabaab was really broken or had just pulled back to regroup. There were several bombings in markets and other crowded places in Somalia and a deadly suicide attack on a shopping mall in Kenya in September 2013 killed more than 65 people.

But gradually islands of relative safety began to be established particularly around the centre of Mogadishu and the parliament building despite occasional deadly explosions by truck bombs. In February 2017 parliament elected a new president but he only ruled over a heavily fortified bastion in Mogadishu while two truck bombs exploded outside the zone killing 350 people. Shabaab can still cause murder and mayhem.

6

Forward to the past
Zimbabwe

In 1976 Notting Hill was not chic. Its grand terraces were uncared for, broken up into flats and single rooms and rented to the poor and black. Some were boarded up. In cold January rain I made my way through dark streets of cracked and peeling houses, streaked green from leaking drainpipes. I found the address and climbed down slippery steps to a basement flat. An African woman ushered me in without a smile. It was as if I were there to please someone else, not to be welcomed. She led me into a sitting room where four African men sat in armchairs huddled against the cold.

They acknowledged my presence rather than greeted me. The smallest was cradled in the largest armchair, wrapped in a dark over-coat many sizes too big for him. The woman introduced me. Robert Gabriel Mugabe peered out of large spectacles, intense, no pleas-antries, anxious to get on with the interview. For an African he was gauche and ill mannered; he did not have time. He was indeed in a hurry. Recently released from Rhodesia's top-security prison, he had immediately launched his campaign to lead ZANU, the Zimbabwe African National Union. Chinese-backed and the bigger of the two guerrilla movements fighting to overthrow the white government of Ian Smith, it had been riven with political faction-alism and was at odds with its backers among African governments.

The African cause had just received a huge bonus which would lead it to victory. Portuguese rule in Mozambique had collapsed and Frelimo, the nationalist movement, had taken over. ZANU was now able to open a new front in the east. Thousands of young men – 1000 a day, according to UN reports – were walking across Rhodesia's hilly eastern border, to get to training camps in Mozambique and return as guerrilla fighters. The white regime was all but surrounded by black African states.

Robert Mugabe had grown up poor, one of six children. His father, a carpenter, deserted the family when he was ten years old, an incident which may have affected him deeply. As a child Mugabe was reclusive, self-reliant, spending much of his time alone. He went to a Catholic mission school where his intelligence blossomed and the white priests provided alternative 'fathers'.

Turning down the idea of becoming a priest, Mugabe trained as a teacher. From there he went to Fort Hare, the university for blacks in South Africa, then on to study in Zambia and Ghana where he met his first wife, Sally Heyfron. He studied politics fanatically and became a convinced Marxist, but he did not engage in political action until he was thirty-six years old in 1960. While the older nationalist leaders wanted to pursue their cause by persuading the rest of the world to bring justice to Rhodesia, Mugabe opted for resistance and armed struggle. He survived three years as an activist before being arrested and sentenced. He spent nearly eleven years in jail. There he settled down to study law and economics, getting three degrees by correspondence course with London University, to add to the three he already had.

When he was released at the end of 1974, Mugabe had to fight for control of ZANU, a guerrilla liberation movement committed to coming to power through the barrel of a gun. But Mugabe had never had military training or used a weapon. He did not even pose as a guerrilla fighter. To this day he dresses like a banker in dark city suits and ties or plain safari suits. He relies instead on his razor-sharp mind, honed by his time in prison, and his clear, hard-edged voice which expounds his militant, no-compromise cause.

Mugabe's inflexible, military approach was not popular among African Presidents in the region, who still thought a deal could be worked out. After all, they had achieved independence with little bloodshed. But they had all faced an imperial power that had lost the will to rule. Mugabe was battling colonists who had settled and invested their lives in Rhodesia. These were two very different adversaries. Mugabe turned on the Zambian President, Kenneth Kaunda, denouncing him and accusing his army of killing and arresting his fighters. Only Julius Nyerere could influence him.

Ever since the white regime in Rhodesia had declared unilateral independence in 1965, the British, South Africans and Smith had tried to agree on a way forward that accommodated the country's black majority but fell short of allowing a leftist like Mugabe to come to power. Smith was stubborn and the Rhodesian army was – in the short term – brutally successful in counterattacking the black guerrillas. In 1971 the British proposed a settlement based on Smith's UDI constitution that would not have created a democracy until well into the twenty-first century. All the Zimbabwean leaders rejected it, though Britain persisted in trying to reach a settlement based on its proposals. Meanwhile the British maintained the fiction of sanctions, knowing that Portuguese-ruled Mozambique and South Africa were breaking them with impunity. The charade of the Royal Navy blockade of Beira was maintained until 1974, when Mozambique became independent.

Mugabe was tired of waiting for Smith, the British or anyone else.

In that dingy basement flat in Notting Hill, he told me he wanted liberation now, by military force, and that he would settle for nothing less than majority rule. He said he was no longer interested in interim measures in Rhodesia, and announced that there were thousands of newly recruited and trained fighters ready to go to war.

Trying to follow the battle for Zimbabwe from London was not easy. While rebels in Eritrea, Ethiopia, Uganda and Angola were happy to take Western reporters with them, the Southern African movements, Umkhonto we Sizwe, the guerrilla wing of the South African National Congress, Namibia's South West Africa People's Organization, SWAPO, and Zimbabwe's nationalist movements, ZANU and its rival ZAPU, the Zimbabwe African People's Union, never allowed Western reporters near their operations. So the accounts of the wars against white rule in Southern Africa were entirely one-sided. The international press based itself in Johannesburg and Salisbury, the capital of Rhodesia, now renamed Harare. Their language and perspective were mostly that of the white regimes. They described the rebels as Communist terrorists and denounced their attacks as atrocities. The armies of white-ruled Africa were said to be defending innocent civilians and freedom. Almost no reporter for the British press based in Salisbury questioned the language or the accuracy of the regimes' military reports. Most of them carried the reports verbatim, as if they were undisputed fact.

The journalists could argue that there was no alternative, since the African nationalist movements did not take them to the front line. Besides, the movements issued regular if wildly exaggerated bulletins describing the glorious victories of the struggling masses against the racist imperialist capitalist regimes. According to their figures, the armies of Rhodesia, Portugal and South Africa would have been wiped out several times over. So Western reporters ignored them. Did their one-sided picture have any effect on the outcome of the war? Probably not, but continuous skewed reporting creates layers of perception. Africans saw the Western media as biased against them and their cause. The rest of the world, including the British government and most commentators in Britain, came to believe in the late 1970s that the 'terrorists' could not win an election.

Mugabe's guerrillas began to pour back across the Mozambique border into Rhodesia. Smith tried to counter the invasion by setting up a destabilizing force inside Mozambique. The Rhodesian army created Renamo, the Mozambique National Resistance, a militia of Mozambican dissidents whose tactics were terror. It soon started ravaging the centre of the country, wiping out whole villages with appalling brutality. The Frelimo government did not have the capacity to protect the people, let alone deliver its promises of education and health. Mozambique was becoming too weak to allow ZANU to have bases there. Internally, Smith could keep the guerrillas at bay, but he could not win the war. In 1979, to buy time, he appointed Bishop Abel Muzorewa, the black African leader of the accommodating United African National Congress party, as Prime Minister. Smith remained in complete charge, of course. No-one was fooled, and the war continued.

But it was a hopeless cause. South of Rhodesia things had changed too. From 1974 South Africa had pushed for a negotiated settlement there. The Soweto uprising of 1976 had rejuvenated an internal African resistance movement in South Africa, dormant since the failure of the military and political campaign by the African National Congress (ANC) in the mid 1960s. Defeated by Cuban firepower in Angola in 1975, the shocked South Africans felt they were now facing what they called a 'total onslaught' from the 'Communist menace'. That was the language they used with America and Britain. Among themselves they used the Afrikaans *Swart Gevaar* – Black Danger. In 1978 P.W. Botha, the Defence Minister – known as the *Groot*

Krokodil, the Great Crocodile – became Prime Minister, and he increasingly saw things in a purely military light, the total onslaught requiring a 'total strategy' to keep South Africa white-ruled and Christian. Until then, Ian Smith's independent Rhodesia had been a buffer state against black Africa as well as a racial and ideological ally. Now the Afrikaners realized South Africa could not sustain an embattled Rhodesia any longer and began to put pressure on Smith to negotiate.

Western countries were also shifting to the right. In 1979 Margaret Thatcher came to power in Britain. Two years later Ronald Reagan was sworn in as President of the United States. Both had the defeat of Communism high on their agendas.

Although she had pledged to recognize Ian Smith and Bishop Abel Muzorewa's government and despite her intense opposition to what she regarded as Communism, Mrs Thatcher was forced to accept the reality of a rising tide of black African nationalism in Southern Africa. This reality now forced all players to negotiate and some bizarre relationships began to grow. The feeling that whites in Southern Africa were 'kith and kin' dominated the Conservative Party. They also supported Ian Smith because he had been a fighter pilot for Britain in the Second World War. Although she was very comfortable in Conservative circles, Mrs Thatcher broke the tribal mould of the Conservatives, making it an ideological party. She objected to apartheid and to a race-based constitution in Rhodesia, not because she supported black nationalism, but on free market grounds. She saw systems that discriminated against people's freedom on grounds of race as a hindrance to her free market, capitalist principles. The problem was that those who most vigorously supported the cause of one man, one vote in Southern Africa were Communists – the deadliest opponents of her beloved free market. The last thing on Mrs Thatcher's mind was to bring to power the likes of Robert Mugabe in Zimbabwe and Nelson Mandela in South Africa. Yet by one of the bizarre ironies of history, her policy helped do just that.

Despite intense opposition to what she regarded as Communism, Mrs Thatcher was forced to accept the inevitable realities of a rising tide of black African nationalism in Southern Africa, especially in Rhodesia. As those realities forced all the players to negotiate, some bizarre relationships began to grow. One was between Mrs Thatcher and President Samora Machel, the bearded, bright-eyed revolutionary ruler of Mozambique. He deployed his considerable macho charm on the British Prime Minister. She was impressed with the realism of a supposed Communist – and perhaps a little flattered. As a result Machel was persuaded to put heavy pressure on Mugabe both before and during the peace talks to do a deal with the Rhodesian regime. Meanwhile Zambia delivered the more pragmatic and flexible Joshua Nkomo and his ZAPU to the negotiating table. South Africa, which carried almost all Rhodesia's trading routes to the world, was pressed by the Americans to deliver Ian Smith to the talks.

From September to Christmas 1979 Ian Smith and the African Nationalist leaders attended talks in London at Lancaster House – the venue where many nationalist leaders of former British colonies negotiated a transfer of power. The British knew it was their only chance to end the war, hold an election and escape from the invidious responsibility for Rhodesian independence. Mugabe twisted and turned and threatened to walk out. In the end he was forced to sign when Machel told him ZANU would not be allowed to use Mozambique as a rear base unless he did.

Under the deal Rhodesia came under British rule again and sanctions were lifted. Christopher (later Lord) Soames was appointed governor general and sent out with full regalia to oversee an election in which the people of Rhodesia Zimbabwe – even the name was a compromise – voted for a Senate and a 100-seat Assembly of which twenty seats would be held by whites – 4 per cent of the population – for at least seven years. The nationalist forces – Mugabe's ZANLA, the Zimbabwe African National Liberation Army, and Nkomo's ZIPRA, the Zimbabwe People's Revolutionary Army – would be confined to camps monitored by Commonwealth troops led by a senior British general. But the Rhodesian army would provide the overall security.

The issue of land was unresolved. According to Lord Carrington: 'What was agreed to in the end by all parties was that willing sellers should be paid a fair price for their land and that the British and Americans would be prepared to finance this.' Property rights were made sacrosanct. Britain offered funds to help transfer some land, but it was not clear how much. Later, African participants said that £2 billion had been offered. The British have always been coy about the amount. Although they saw that some transfer of land was probably politically necessary, they were reluctant to encourage it. They feared it might send the wrong message to whites in South Africa and lead to a mass exodus of white farmers in both countries.

Maybe Mugabe, like the British, believed that he would not win a free and fair election in 1980. He did not play by the rules, keeping thousands of fighters out of the assembly camps so they could intimidate voters in the villages. Everyone else cheated too. But this was the one chance Britain had of escaping from its southern central African mess and it was not going to allow a bit of intimidation to spoil it. The cheating probably made little difference. What the electorate knew was that only Mugabe could end this war and he would end it only when he had won. Maybe many of those who voted for ZANU-PF were voting for peace rather than for Robert Mugabe.

On 27 February 1980 the polls opened, and five days later ZANU-PF was declared the winner with fifty-seven of the eighty elected assembly seats. The speech that Mugabe gave at Zimbabwe's independence in April was magnanimous. Calling for reconciliation and rejecting revenge, he said:

> *The wrongs of the past must now stand forgiven and forgotten. If we ever look to the past, let us do so for the lesson the past has taught us, namely that oppression and racism are inequalities that must never find scope in our political and social system. It could never be a correct justification that because the whites oppressed us yesterday when they had power, the blacks must oppress them today because they have power.*

He formed a coalition government including some members of the Smith regime and, following the pattern in the rest of Africa at independence, he pledged friendship to Britain, the former colonial power. Whatever he felt in his heart, he was forced to heed the advice of Julius Nyerere, Tanzania's President, and Samora Machel. He also amazed Lord Soames by seeking his advice on how to manage the transition and even asked him to stay on to help create stability. The smug British had – apparently – got away with it again. The man they rejected as a Communist and militant had secured an overwhelming electoral victory and had now become another Nkrumah or Kenyatta. Like them, Mugabe had begun as a militant, served his time in prison, forced the British to realize there was no alternative, come to power and then settled into a friendly relationship with the former rulers and pursued moderate economic policies. The British shrugged insouciantly at their God-given ability to win out against impossible odds, and Mugabe settled into State House. He even invited Ian Smith over to tea and asked his advice too. General Walls was kept on as army commander and Ken Flower, Smith's spy chief, became Mugabe's spy chief. Zimbabwe seemed like another colony which Britain had lost control of but that had somehow turned out all right in the end.

In 1981 the gods seemed to bless the Mugabe victory with sumptuous rains and a bumper harvest. Father Dieter Schultz describes that new dawn, recalling that at the independence day celebrations Julius Nyerere had greeted Mugabe with the words: 'You have inherited a jewel. Keep it that way.' In his memoir *Whatever Happened to the Jewel*, Schultz recalls:

> *At the donor conference which followed two years later, representatives from almost all Western countries literally fell over each other with offers of aid to rebuild the country ravaged by nearly ten years of civil war, which left an estimated 80,000 people dead. Dozens of non-governmental organizations were founded to respond to every imaginable need of individuals and communities, including the demobilized ex-combatants. To say that newly independent Zimbabwe was the darling of the international community is no overstatement.*

Zimbabwe seemed set for rapid development.

But what did Mugabe feel? He had frequently snapped at the British during the Lancaster House negotiations and said afterwards, 'I never trusted the British. Never at all. I do not think they meant well towards us . . . I do not think they wanted a liberation movement, and especially the one I led, to be the victor.' He may well have been right about that, but while he mistrusted the British government, he seems to have admired – adored perhaps – the Queen, British culture and the British upper classes. Mugabe stayed in touch with Soames long after he left and his presence at Soames's funeral in 1987 was seen as more than just an official mark of respect.

In 1987 Downing Street officials were surprised to receive a phone call from Harare requesting a meeting between President Mugabe and Mrs Thatcher. The President's wife suffered from kidney disease and was coming to London for dialysis. The President would like a private meeting with the Prime Minister. Since Britain was generally perceived as chief supporter and protector of apartheid South Africa, Mrs Thatcher was intrigued. The following Sunday night she welcomed Mugabe to Downing Street and spent more than an hour in the sitting room, she sipping whisky and he perched in an armchair drinking water. They talked about everything: global affairs, the state of Africa, politics and economics. And not for the last time. For the next couple of years, before Sally died, he occasionally dropped in on the Prime Minister for a chat.

Technically Mugabe kept to the Lancaster House Agreement, remaining Prime Minister until the seven-year embargo was up. But he made no secret of where he wanted to take the country politically. He maintained all the repressive laws that Smith had enacted to bolster his dictatorship, and even when he dropped the State of Emergency in 1990 he kept legislation like the Law and Order Maintenance Act which prevented people meeting and discussing politics without government permission. Mugabe wanted a one-party state and, steadily accumulating powers to the presidency, step by step he tried to create one.

He justified it on security grounds. Zimbabwe was in a rough neighbourhood and South Africa was on the warpath. Mugabe survived two assassination attempts, and undercover South African squads helped by sympathetic white Zimbabweans blew up ZANU-PF headquarters in 1981. The following year they destroyed most of Zimbabwe's air force planes, the only possible defence against South African raids. In Mozambique, Renamo and the South Africans went for Zimbabwe's jugular, blowing up road and rail bridges and the oil pipeline that linked Zimbabwe to the world through the port of Beira on the Indian Ocean. Zimbabwe's only alternative trade routes lay through South Africa.

Mugabe began to blame the whites, accusing them of 'acting in collusion with South Africa to harm our racial relations, destroy our unity, to sabotage our economy and to overthrow the popularly elected government'. He suspected them of being a fifth column, covertly helping South Africa. Some whites were detained and tortured. Ian Smith was arrested, then released. On the other hand, Zimbabwe was the first country in Africa where leaders who lost power were not killed or hounded out of the country or locked up and charged with minor offences, their wealth confiscated. Ian Smith went on living in his house in Harare. Even in 2001, when white farmers were being hounded from farms, Smith did not see any need to lock his gate or front door. He was never harmed.

But in the new Zimbabwe there was no truth and reconciliation commission as there would be later in South Africa. The past was allowed to lie and fester. Smith made no gesture of regret, let alone apology for UDI and the subsequent war that lasted seven years and directly killed more than 20,000 people. On the contrary, he took his place in parliament and attacked the government. In 1986 he gave an interview in London in which he said that black rule was ruining Zimbabwe. The following year he spoke out in favour of apartheid in South Africa. For this he was reprimanded by the assembly speaker and suspended, but the Supreme Court overruled the speaker and his position was restored.

What Smith did may not have been important to Mugabe. What the whites, as a group did, mattered a lot. In the elections of 1985 and again in 1990 the whites voted overwhelmingly for Smith, the man who had led the country to disaster in the first place. Mugabe felt he had offered peace to the whites and they had rejected it. They did not accept the spirit of reconciliation that he had apparently offered. While some were undoubtedly more respectful, even friendlier, to black Zimbabweans than they had been previously, most whites continued as before: aloof or outright racist. Above all the whites kept to themselves. They did not integrate.

Mugabe's main target in those early years, however, was not the whites. It was the Ndebele. Like all but two African countries Zimbabwe is ethnically divided. The Shona live in the centre, east and north and make up 80 per cent of the population. The Ndebele live in the south and south-west and make up 20 per cent. They speak different languages and have different cultures. They also have a history of enmity. In the nineteenth century the Ndebele cattle keepers clashed with the farming Shona and dominated them. In the struggle for independence, ZANU was largely Shona and ZAPU Ndebele. The leaders Mugabe and Joshua Nkomo managed to stick together at Lancaster House, but the rivalry was bitter and personal.

Despite the efforts of other African leaders to keep them unified, outsiders exacerbated the problem, the Russians backing ZAPU and the Chinese supporting ZANU. The two groups had united under the Patriotic Front in 1976, but Mugabe insisted on running a separate campaign in the 1980 election. Soon after the election their mutual mistrust and hatred burst out into the open with clashes between former guerrilla fighters on both sides while Mugabe and Nkomo exchanged barbed insults. Mugabe began to refer to Nkomo as 'a snake in the house' and spoke of the need to 'crush' or 'eradicate' ZAPU. In a speech in parliament in 1982, he threatened to take 'two eyes for an eye and two teeth for a tooth'.

The war on the Ndebele – their territory is known as Matabeleland – lasted four years. Mugabe claimed that elements in ZIPRA had become South African mercenaries, and were trying to destabilize his government. He may also have feared that the Russians, who backed ZAPU, might try to replace him with Nkomo. Whatever the truth of the origins of the war, Mugabe ordered the fearsome North Korean-trained Fifth Brigade into Matabeleland where it looted, burned, raped and murdered. The death toll may have reached some 25,000 people in a devastating campaign known as the *Gukurahundi* – the wind that blows the chaff away after the harvest. It is hard not to conclude that the result of the operation – the crushing of the Ndebele – was Mugabe's real intention. ZAPU and ZANU were officially 'merged' in the name of national unity. In effect ZAPU disappeared.

The Shona-based ZANU-PF became the sole political power in the land, and only those Ndebele who submitted to its rule were allowed a public role. Nkomo knelt before Mugabe, a broken man. He was given the title of Vice-President and played no further meaningful role in Zimbabwe's politics. His younger lieutenants were imprisoned and tortured. When they were thoroughly cowed, some were given ministries. The British, relieved to have disposed of the bothersome Zimbabwe Rhodesia question after so many years, said nothing. Zimbabwe was sorted out as far as they were concerned, and Mugabe had become their ally. They needed to work with him in the coming struggle for South Africa and they were not going to let a massacre or two spoil that.

Zimbabwe is not just another African country to the British. To this day it receives far more newspaper and broadcast space in Britain than, say, its neighbour, Zambia, or the huge and much more important Congo. Although Zimbabwe was not important in economic terms, it became part of the British political battleground along with fox hunting and public schools. The right was pro-white, the left and most liberals supported black majority rule. Today both sides still have a grief- and anger-ridden fascination with Zimbabwe. Those who supported Rhodesia and white rule feel vindicated by the treatment of the white farmers when their land was taken. And for its old liberal and left supporters, Zimbabwe has become the ultimate symbol of the failure of leadership and governance in Africa – a bitterly disillusioning experience.

How did it happen? In the late 1980s, Southern Africa was in turmoil. South Africa still ruled Namibia, the last colony, occupied since the end of the First World War and in defiance of United Nations resolutions since 1946. The apartheid government was lashing out at its neighbours, trying to punish and destabilize them to stop the 'total onslaught'. In Angola the South Africans and Americans backed the rebel movement, UNITA, while in Mozambique the South Africans took over the murderous Renamo from the Rhodesians and reinforced it. Zimbabwe was at the heart of this regional turmoil. It had the largest economy apart from South Africa and it was led by Robert Mugabe, the most militant and articulate adversary of the South Africans. But Zimbabwe was landlocked, dependent on routes through its neighbours or through South Africa.

South Africa's increasingly paranoid government seemed to be heading for catastrophe, choosing war when its Western friends urged diplomacy. In the mid 1980s, the Americans – of all people – had to spell out to the Botha government that there was no longer a Communist threat to Africa, let alone a 'total onslaught'. Mrs Thatcher's rejection of sanctions against South Africa – even as a threat – was rewarded by South African attempts to murder or kidnap African National Congress activists on British soil. In petty revenge for the trickle of arms and pinprick attacks by ANC guerrillas in South Africa, Pretoria repeatedly raided and sabotaged Angola, Zimbabwe, Botswana, Mozambique and Zambia. It mined the harbours of Mozambique, launched bombing raids on Gaborone, Lusaka and Harare and finally sent its army into Angola, calling up its 140,000-strong citizens' force to take on the Cubans there.

All the while the real war was happening in South Africa itself, through strikes and township uprisings aimed at making the country ungovernable. Television footage of South Africa's reaction of repression and reprisals made it difficult for even those most sympathetic to whites in Southern Africa to support the regime.

Mrs Thatcher's policy therefore risked making Britain apartheid's last supporter. She was gradually persuaded that she needed to add another dimension to her Africa policy beyond protecting South Africa from sanctions. Britain could not hold back the military-led South African government as it attacked its neighbours. Nor would the British use their military power to defend them, even though some of them were former British colonies and members of the Commonwealth. But neither could Britain leave them to the mercy of the South Africans. So, without lessening her opposition to sanctions, Mrs Thatcher began to support the front line states, especially Zimbabwe.

In the first years after Zimbabwean independence, Britain had opposed the formation of the regional grouping which later became the Southern African Development Community because it was aimed at reducing the region's dependency on South Africa's energy and transport systems. After 1986 Britain began to help Mozambique, Zimbabwe, Botswana and Zambia with aid to develop but also to defend their transport links against South African attacks. The following year Britain started to arm and train the Mozambican army as well as the Zimbabwean. If they could hunt down the Renamo guerrillas, or at least protect the railway lines from Zimbabwe to Maputo and Beira on the Indian Ocean coast, Zimbabwe would escape the South African stranglehold on its exports and imports. British development aid even provided an armoured train for the Maputo corridor and new weapons for the Mozambican army.

Like a naughty child who suddenly begins to do the right thing but refuses to admit it, Britain would not attribute its new policy to

South Africa's attempt to destabilize the region. British ministers ascribed the wars in Southern Africa to internal rebels: UNITA in Angola and Renamo in Mozambique. They refused to accept that some attacks were carried out by South African special forces or even that South Africa was helping these 'rebels'. Even when sea-going South African special forces launched attacks on oil installations in Angola and destroyed navigational aids in and around Maputo harbour in the late 1980s, the Foreign Office did not draw attention to South Africa's destructive role in the region. As late as 1989 Lynda Chalker, Britain's aid minister, pretended that Renamo was just another African rebel movement and refused to acknowledge South Africa's backing – even though the Americans had publicly accepted that it was little more than an extension of the South African army.

Mrs Thatcher was persuaded to visit Africa to sell the new British policy, and in 1989 she flew to Zimbabwe to visit the British army training camp at Nyanga in the eastern highlands with Mugabe and President Chissano of Mozambique. Newly trained Mozambican troops put on a display. Under a tree at the end of a shooting range covered in shrubs, the three sat awkwardly in armchairs wearing ear muffs, which made them look as if they did not want to hear what each of them was saying. Mugabe and Chissano slumped in their chairs. Mrs Thatcher sat bolt upright on the edge of her seat. At a given signal the bushes sprang to life, flung off their greenery and opened fire on targets about 100 yards away. Unfortunately the trainees were using tracer ammunition that made it look as if the bullets were actually coming the other way and, thinking this was some fiendish assassination attempt, several members of the entourage flung themselves down. Mrs Thatcher didn't flinch.

None of this convinced Mugabe. British duplicity seemed to irk him more and more. When he found that Britain did not respect him – perhaps love him as he psychologically needed – he felt betrayed and sought revenge. White farmers were the obvious target. Despite degrees in economics and an apparent passion for social justice, he did not care what happened to their land once the farmers had been driven out. Much of it became unproductive and almost none of it was given to the landless poor. But he spat in Britain's face and got away with it.

African leaders who came to power at independence in the early 1960s were inexperienced and sometimes rash, taking ideological decisions without thinking through the economic and political problems they might create. Mugabe came to power almost twenty years later and had plenty of time to learn the lessons of other African countries that had crashed, collapsed or just gently declined into backwaters. He also had the benefit of advice from leaders coming to the end of their tenures. During the first ten years of Mugabe's rule all the warning lights flashed, indicating that he was making many of the same mistakes.

In the early days he had pushed for a leadership code of conduct for ZANU-PF leaders preventing them having second jobs, renting out property or owning large tracts of land or businesses. Soon court cases and good journalism were exposing huge breaches of the code by Mugabe's own family and senior members of ZANU. He did nothing. Gradually the party leaders became like the pigs in *Animal Farm*, an elite above the law, in total political control and living the lifestyle of the world's richest. They awarded themselves huge salaries and grotesque allowances, using their political positions to gain contracts and take over businesses. They became as far removed from the lives of their fellow black Zimbabweans as any white Rhodesian had ever been.

I had known Chen Chimutengwende as an impoverished activist in London in the 1970s. A big man with a big smile, he dressed in a spectacularly large brown jersey and delivered fiery speeches against

Smith and Britain. Twenty years on, at the height of the farm invasions, he suddenly called me. Now Minister of Information, he summoned me to his suite at the Meridien on Piccadilly, one of the most expensive hotels in London. He welcomed me warmly and pulled a bottle of champagne from the fridge. Ebullient as ever, he informed me that all was going according to plan and Zimbabwe was at last on the right path. It was all the fault of the British from Cecil Rhodes onwards, and the government was merely taking corrective measures.

I asked him why Zimbabweans were now poorer than they had been at the height of the war in the 1980s, and 10 per cent poorer than they were at independence after years of sanctions. The answer was long and rambling but it was all the fault of the British. As I left he opened another bottle of champagne.

One of the usual reactions of outsiders to Mugabe is, 'He's gone mad, hasn't he?' The common impression is that Mugabe used to be a good guy and Zimbabwe did well in the early years. Then he went crazy and ruined it. Some have suggested that he was always evil, murdering rivals, manipulating supporters. But Heidi Holland, the Zimbabwe-born writer, has pointed out Mugabe's love–hate relationship with Britain was created by his own upbringing. The 'friendless clever little Robert' growing up in a fatherless family was adopted by an alternative 'father', an Anglo-Irish Catholic priest, and doted on by a white nun. He could never reconcile the two sides to his personality. He could not, says Holland, 'pull off the pretence of being both an Englishman and an African since the one despises the other'. All his life he has aspired to Britishness. He loves cricket, reflects fondly on his meetings with the Queen, formed a close relationship with Lord Soames and sought meetings with Mrs Thatcher. All these reflect his wish to be accepted. But he feels he is not and his anger at rejection drives his pursuit of power. Holland writes: 'His addiction to power and the bombastic, cruel way he exercises it reflects weakness rather than strength . . . and is probably due to his failure to develop a strong inner core in his deprived youth. The lonely child with long-buried grievances is still crouching inside Mugabe's old body, ever ready to take offence and inflict revenge.'

Mugabe has not gone mad. Nor was he always bad. He is a complicated schizophrenic man, driven both by respect for the Western mentality for logic and order and a passionate sense of injustice and rejection by whites. He has both a vision of wrongs to be righted, even revenged, and by the lust for power. When he became President he could have ripped up the Lancaster House agreement and seized the land there and then, or seven years later when the time clauses ran out. Or, if he wanted to do it peacefully, he could have drawn up a plan to transfer the land gradually, wooed the farmers into giving up part of their farms, trained black farmers, and sought international support for a coherent agricultural policy that would have brought subsistence farmers out of poverty and made them successful smallholders. He did none of these things. Instead he let the land issue, driver of the economy but a political time bomb, remain unaddressed.

That is, until 11 August 1997. Heroes' Day is a national holiday, when all Zimbabweans remember those who died fighting for independence. It was not the whites or Britain that finally provoked the showdown, but his own militant followers. Mugabe was in full flow at Heroes' Acre, the national cemetery, when a rowdy crowd shouted him down. Led by Chenjerai Hunzvi, the 'war veterans' were demanding pensions for injuries received on active service in the struggle. Hunzvi, a doctor and rabble-rouser, had taken over the leadership of the veterans – though his wife claimed he had never held a gun in his life. The party leaders, it had just emerged, had looted the war pensions fund, leaving the poor, who had fought the war, ragged beggars. Mugabe's usual reaction to demonstrators was to turn the riot police on them, but this time he dithered. These people were supposed to follow behind him. Instead they were in front of him, singing *his* anthems, chanting *his* slogans. He panicked and ordered the Finance Minister to pay the demonstrators pensions. That bust the budget, the final straw for the IMF and the Western donors. But for Hunzvi and his gang of thugs it was only the beginning. They had learned they could make Mugabe blink. Mugabe had defeated the white regime, he could defy the British and the South Africans, he had massacred the Ndebele and terrified Nkomo. But he could not cope with an attack from the left within his own movement. It threatened his party, it threatened his power. It threatened his soul.

Mugabe thought he had bought off Hunzvi, but he was also beginning to realize that an opposition movement was building in Zimbabwe. Over twenty years Mugabe had drawn more and more power into the presidency. He proposed a new 'people's constitution' that would have formalized this new power. The presidency would be limited to two terms of five years, but the legislation was not retrospective so Mugabe could run again if he wanted to. Opposition mounted from those who wanted to keep checks and balances. In 1999 the opposition formed a new party, the Movement for Democratic Change, with a former trade union leader, Morgan Tsvangirai, at its head.

In February 2000 a referendum was held on a new constitution. In Mugabe's mind the referendum was a formality. After all, ZANU held 99 per cent of the seats in parliament and he assumed a similar proportion of Zimbabweans would support him. Who could possibly oppose his will except a small unrepresentative gang? The answer was a population far better informed than he expected or planned. The referendum was defeated – a loss that hit Mugabe like an electric shock. Not only did he lose a bid to consolidate his power, he also found serious opposition to his rule. Worse: the opposition was being funded and partly organized by whites, his old enemies. They were now trying to make a political comeback through the ballot box by funding and organizing the No campaign in the referendum.

Mugabe had to defeat them at any price. That price included the destruction of the Zimbabwean economy if necessary. Anything rather than lose power. And he had at hand the weapon to do it: the 'war veterans' who had dared try to use his own ideology to attack him. He would simply set the 'war veterans' on the farmers and break the source of their political power: money.

The whites' wealth came from the land and from industries based on agricultural marketing and processing. The land bomb had been ticking away since independence. Although, in terms of statistics, land ownership in Zimbabwe is probably as unequal as it is in Britain, land had been at the heart of Zimbabwe's liberation war. Far more than human rights, democracy or self-rule, people had fought for their stolen land. It was about more than a piece of land on which to grow food or even that was valuable as real estate. As in many parts of Africa there was a spiritual aspect. The land belonged to the ancestors and their descendants, creating a bond between the people and the land. To the colonists it was simply real estate that could be monetarized under the independence settlement. But under the independence settlement, if the government wanted land it had to pay full compensation in a currency of the seller's choice. Only unused land could be taken without compensation, and in the productive parts of Zimbabwe that was in short supply. For twenty years Mugabe did little about the huge discrepancy in land ownership and allowed the principles of the 1931 Land Apportionment Act to stand. That had decreed 48 million acres reserved for 48,000 whites and 25 million acres – later reduced – for one million black farmers.

At independence, 6000 white commercial farmers held 39 per cent of the land. In 1990, only 8 per cent of this commercial land was owned by black farmers, most of them the politically well connected. Mugabe said he had done nothing about the land issue before because he did not to want to upset the delicate negotiations going on over the future of South Africa – the same argument the British had used to stay quiet on the land issue. But he did not even use up the money the British had set aside to buy land at a market rate. In 1991 the government created a law allowing it to seize land without compensation, but the process was slow and still had to be referred to the courts. Not much land had changed hands by the end of the decade.

So in 2000 Mugabe added extra clauses to the newly drafted constitution permitting the government to seize land without compensation. The British, he declared, were responsible for paying compensation and, if they failed to do so, there would be none. The land would simply be seized.

Although he appeared to accept the loss of the constitutional referendum gracefully, Mugabe immediately co-opted the 'war veterans'. Diverting them from their original target – his government – he encouraged them to attack white farmers and their 'puppets', the opposition MDC. He announced a 'third Chimurenga', the third time the Shona people had gone to war to defend their land. The previous occasions had been the uprising against the arrival of the white men in 1896 and the liberation war of the 1970s. The war vets – by this time largely unemployed poor directed by the secret police – marched onto farmland, killed animals, destroyed crops and burned buildings. Farmers and their families were beaten up, some were killed. One told me that he would not have minded so much if his own workers had taken over the farm. At least they knew how to run it. But those who were directed to take the land barely knew how to be subsistence farmers, let alone work the sophisticated irrigation systems and manage all the complex business of running a farm. Irrigation pipes were ripped up and sold as scrap metal, dams needing constant maintenance were allowed to collapse. So was the Zimbabwean economy.

How did the rest of the world react? Britain's chicken had finally come home to roost. It was payback time for two decades of diplomatic and development neglect of Zimbabwe and Africa. In the early 1990s I had accompanied Douglas Hurd, the British Foreign Secretary, on a visit to Zimbabwe and he asked me what I thought of Mugabe. I said I thought at heart he was a one-party-state socialist. 'His heart?' scoffed Hurd. 'You don't have to worry about a politician's heart.' The implication was that whatever Mugabe felt, his actions would be forced by circumstances – in this case, British demands.

When Labour came to power, relations rapidly deteriorated. In conversation with Tony Blair at the 1998 Commonwealth conference, Mugabe asked for more money to buy back the land. Blair not only refused, but repudiated any responsibility for Zimbabwe. Clare Short made things worse by telling Mugabe that she was Irish, also a nation colonized by the British. Peter Hain, the Africa Minister, thought he could shout Mugabe down with insults. Mugabe rebuffed their rejection with vigour. He always had the last word. After one visit to London the President was 'arrested' by Peter Tatchell, the Gay Rights Campaigner, straight after a meeting with Hain. Mugabe was convinced that Hain and the British government had set him up.

When Blair spoke of 'regime change' in Zimbabwe, Mugabe treated it as a declaration of war. He was terrified that the British would depose him. After that it was easy for him to blame Britain for everything else that went wrong in Zimbabwe and see a British hand in any opposition to him. Britain's cynical policy towards apartheid,

Rhodesia and Southern Africa in the past gave Mugabe plenty of ammunition, and his furious diatribes went down well in other parts of Africa, releasing anti-colonial feelings that had rarely been expressed in the independence era. Many other African leaders were also looking for scapegoats for the continent's ills. When Blair sent the British army into Iraq without a UN resolution, in support of George Bush's war on Saddam Hussein, it confirmed that Britain was still at heart an imperial power. President Ben Mkapa of Tanzania was a member of Tony Blair's Commission for Africa in 2005 but, like many other African presidents and politicians, he supported Mugabe. He called the land grab 'the price of transformation'. Sam Nujoma of Namibia cheered Mugabe on and promised a similar solution to Namibia's land issue, President Chissano of Mozambique began to complain but then withdrew. Only Festus Mogae of Botswana was critical, particularly because thousands of Zimbabweans fled across the border into Botswana.

The most important neighbour was, as before, South Africa. The two countries had never had an easy relationship. In 1923 Rhodesia rejected union with South Africa in a referendum, yet it was never quite able to escape dependency on its giant neighbour. South Africa was Rhodesia's main trading partner and controlled its trade routes. But in the 1970s the South African Prime Minister, John Vorster, under pressure from the United States and Britain, had finally made it clear to Ian Smith that he would not spend South African blood or gold to save a white-ruled Rhodesia. That spelled the end of Smith's bid for white supremacy.

But where Prime Minister Vorster had helped force Smith to surrender, President Thabo Mbeki stood firm. Putting his relationship with Britain on the line to protect Mugabe and keep Zimbabwe in the Commonwealth, Mbeki advocated an internal solution to Zimbabwe. He also urged 'quiet diplomacy', the policy he had denounced so vigorously when deployed by the Americans in dealing with the apartheid government. Mbeki allowed Zimbabwe to continue using South African electricity it could not pay for and spoke out against any international pressure on Zimbabwe.

Why did Mbeki protect Mugabe? Logic suggested he should deal with this scandal in his own backyard. Many saw it as the first test of South Africa's willingness to address Africa's self-inflicted wounds. The collapse of Zimbabwe is estimated to have cost South Africa some $2.6 billion a year for ten years. Even more was lost in credibility as South Africa's and Africa's failure to deal with the Zimbabwe crisis undermined faith in Mbeki's African Renaissance project. Mugabe's spectacular throwback to the old African dictators of the 1960s and 1970s, like Amin and Bokassa, occurred just as Mbeki was trying to sell a new vision of good leadership in Africa. When initiatives such as NEPAD (New Partnership for Africa's Development) and the African Union were put forward as African solutions to African problems, sceptics suggested that they would be credible only if they dealt with Zimbabwe. And the Zimbabwe crisis – particularly the expulsion of white farmers – received almost more publicity than the rest of Africa put together. This meant that the message of hope for Africa that many like Mbeki were trying to impress on the world was drowned out by howls of anger and derision over Zimbabwe.

Dealing with Mugabe was not easy. He had never quite adjusted to the peaceful transformation of South Africa. When the world gloried in the release of Nelson Mandela and instantly elevated him to the leadership of Southern Africa, if not the entire continent, Mugabe was put in the shade. He was no longer the militant anti-imperialist spokesman for Southern Africa. Mandela's stronger, big-hearted voice called out with a deeper message. He may have used some of the same militant Marxist language, but Mandela appeared far more human than the austere, angry Mugabe. On Mandela's first visit to Zimbabwe, the two men spoke from the same platform. Mugabe chose to stress that the struggle against white rule would now be redoubled. Mandela called for a peaceful settlement and was careful not to alienate potential allies. They did not get on in private either. In 1998 when Mandela was trying to mediate the crisis in Congo, he groaned to his assistant: 'Please don't tell me I have to speak to Comrade Robert again.'

One reason for Mbeki's stance was African solidarity. Post-apartheid South Africa, despite its strong trading links with the rest of the world, was determined to be seen as African and on the side of the African poor. It did not aspire to be part of the Western world, and the ANC government was terrified of being seen in the rest of Africa as the cat's-paw of the West or the bullying boss of the continent. Besides, Mugabe was a hero of the liberation struggle. When others, such as Kenneth Kaunda of Zambia, had wobbled, Mugabe had remained clear and steely. Even after victory, whenever he spoke crowds cheered and gave him a standing ovation. He appealed to the simple pre-1994 world of literal black-and-white politics.

Secondly, South Africa had a not dissimilar land problem. If Mbeki punished Mugabe for giving the land back to black people, he might light a fire in his own backyard – especially if he was seen to be doing it on behalf of the Western powers. Mugabe's anti-colonial rhetoric struck a deep chord among ordinary Southern Africans, all of whom had suffered white rule in living memory, and for the South Africans far more recently. Whatever they felt, the leaders did not want to swim against that tide. As one senior South African official told me: 'Mugabe is just too bloody popular in Southern Africa.'

While Mandela had risen above racial politics, Mbeki was trapped by them. Just as the whites in Britain and South Africa had sympathized with Rhodesian whites, regarding them as 'kith and kin', bound by ties of blood, so Mbeki spoke of 'our African brethren' in Zimbabwe. Even as Mugabe's thugs were chasing white Rhodesians off the land, Mbeki chose to see the land seizures in terms of historical injustice rather than deal with the current legal and political – let alone economic – issues.

And lastly there was a personal factor: Mbeki was but a young boy compared to Mugabe, and in Africa, age counts. In meetings Mbeki was reported to be nervous of Mugabe, even obsequious, fearing Mugabe's notoriously vicious tongue. He knew he did not have the personal strength to tell Mugabe what to do.

Yet Mbeki's claim that he and Mugabe were comrades in the liberation struggle is not borne out by the historical relationship between their respective movements. The ANC in South Africa and Mugabe's ZANU in Zimbabwe had very different origins and philosophies. Relations were not always as warm as Mbeki has made out. The opposing philosophies of their liberation movements, Africanist and Marxist, had made them enemies in the past. The ANC was based on Marxism, identifying the poor of Africa as Marx's working class oppressed by a capitalist ruling class. Once that leap of faith had been made it was simply a matter of adapting a revolutionary socialist solution to the imperial occupation of Africa. Followers of this philosophy were aligned to the Soviet Union, parties such as the ANC in South Africa, and Nkomo's ZAPU in Zimbabwe. So were the MPLA in Angola and Frelimo in Mozambique. Mugabe's ZANU was pan-Africanist, a philosophy which borrowed a lot from Marxism but did not follow Moscow's line. Its belief was that race, not class, was the ultimate dividing line. Their solution was a black take-over, not necessarily a class revolution. In this category were the Nkrumah pan-Africanists in Ghana, UNITA in Angola, the Pan Africanist Congress and Steve Biko's Black Consciousness Movement in South Africa. The ANC and ZANU did not fight alongside each other in the liberation of Southern Africa. In fact they frequently fought each other, the ANC shunned ZANU in exile and in power ZANU wiped out ZAPU, the partner of the ANC in Zimbabwe.

Mbeki's treatment of Mugabe was an echo of Mrs Thatcher's treatment of South Africa when she protected it from the demands for sanctions. He seemed more incensed by Britain's attitude to Zimbabwe – and Africa – than he was by Mugabe's behaviour. A stubborn man, Mbeki was prepared to risk the relationship with Britain and the US rather than be seen as the West's policeman in Southern Africa. He insisted on seeing the problem as an internal political spat between equals, Mugabe and Tsvangirai, that could be mended only by talks and reconciliation – just as apartheid had been ended in South Africa. The difference was that international pressure forced South Africa's white rulers to deal with the ANC. Mbeki applied no such pressure to Mugabe who had no intention of making a deal with Tsvangirai. He agreed to negotiate with him but never did so. The idea of South Africa brokering a deal between government and opposition in Zimbabwe as if it was a minor misunderstanding was ludicrous.

Had Mbeki's tactic worked none of this would have mattered. But it failed. Mugabe made a fool of Mbeki. Zimbabwe became more and more repressive and the economy spiralled downwards out of control. In 2005 Mugabe secured a resounding victory in a violent, rigged election, reversing many of the gains of the MDC in the previous election. His power secured for another five years and the opposition clearly beaten, Mugabe still felt it necessary to clear away even potential threats. At a terrible human cost, he launched Operation Murambatsvina ('Drive Out the Rubbish'), an astounding attack on informal settlements and squatter camps around the cities. On the edge of towns, owning nothing and resentful, these people could be mobilized politically by the opposition. Back in the villages they could be more easily controlled and could not organize effective political activity. They called it Zimbabwe's tsunami. Some 700,000 people were driven from their self-made homes around Zimbabwe's towns at the coldest time of the year. Their livelihoods, side-of-the-road stalls selling single cigarettes, balls of salt or soap and pieces of bread, were destroyed. They were forbidden to trade.

Despite a vigorous criticism of this policy by Anna Tibaijuka of the United Nations Environment Programme after a tour of the destroyed settlements, Mugabe managed to secure enough support to avoid censure at the UN. At the African Union too he escaped any criticism. African solidarity triumphed. Even people like Chief Emeka Anyaoku, former Secretary General of the Commonwealth, does not think Zimbabwe should have been expelled and thinks that Mugabe had to 'solve' the land issue in some way.

By 2006 Zimbabwe was broken. On average, Zimbabweans born at independence could be expected to live for fifty-seven years. In 2006 that had plummeted to thirty-seven for men and thirty-four for women, the lowest in the world.

In March 2008 those who remained in Zimbabwe went to the polls in local, parliamentary and presidential elections. The split in ZANU-PF had finally opened up and Simba Makoni, a former finance minister, ran against Mugabe. Few senior members dared support him openly but for many it looked like the beginning of the end of Mugabe's rule. The MDC, however, had also split and many of its best tacticians had fallen out with Morgan Tsvangirai because of his disregard for the party's constitution. But for once the opposition MDC was allowed to campaign in rural areas and the voting results were, for the first time, pinned up on notice boards at the polling station where the votes were cast.

The MDC won the parliamentary election and claimed

Tsvangirai was the victor in the presidential poll too, but the result was not announced. Was Mugabe preparing to step down? Of course not. After five weeks he allowed the world to know that Tsvangirai had led by 47.9 per cent to 43.2 per cent. Already he was preparing for the run-off, handing the country over to the Joint Operations Command – a body made up of security chiefs that had originally been set up by Ian Smith in 1972 to fight ZANU guerrillas. The army, police, party militants and paid thugs systematically combed Zimbabwe's rural regions, beating MDC activists and burning their homes. Often they used clubs wrapped in barbed wire. The very transparency of the March election allowed them to target every village that had not supported the president. After more than eighty people had died and tens of thousands had been beaten and displaced, Tsvangirai pulled out of the election. With Robert Mugabe the only candidate, it went ahead on 27 June 2008.

The day after Mugabe was sworn in African rulers met in Egypt for an African Union summit. It was their first clear test of the commitments the African Union had made to democracy and good governance for the continent. Led by Thabo Mbeki, they failed it comprehensively, urging dialogue and a government of national unity on Zimbabwe as if dealing with a minor dispute between adversaries of equal standing. They ignored the findings of their own election observer missions which said the election did not meet their standards.

Perhaps they did so not in spite of American and European pressure but because of it. Even if it was the right thing, they did not want to be seen to be doing the bidding of the West, especially against one of their own. Fifty years after most of Africa had become independent the colonialist mentality seemed more evident among the colonized than the colonizers.

Alone, vilified, attacked by Western governments but victorious –

Mugabe was at his happiest. Heading towards ninety, he refused to make any succession plans and a vicious battle started among his ministers. Many predicted that the day after Mugabe will be worse than anything we have seen so far. In August the Zimbabwe dollar was 'redenominated' by removing ten zeroes but in November inflation soared further to a global record 79.6 billion per cent. That made money meaningless. The country abandoned its currency, using US dollars or South African rand instead. By 2010 the country's GDP had shrunk to a fraction of what it once was. Between three and ten million Zimbabweans fled the country.

Britain and Western countries had to wait another five years to get their man, Morgan Tsvangirai, into office. In March 2013 a referendum on a new constitution was held. It limited presidents to two terms. But by then Tsvangirai had grown tired and distracted by a chaotic love life. He tolerated corruption and complacency among MDC MPs. Meanwhile ZANU-PF had reorganized and set about bullying and bribing voters. Many officials were ZANU-PF members and used their access to remove opposition voters from the electoral role. Diamonds were discovered at Marange in 2006 and immediately ZANU-PF and its political and military bosses were able to fill their pockets as well as the ZANU-PF coffers. In July that year Mugabe swept to power by a margin of 8 per cent, too wide to challenge.

Zimbabwe had obsessed Britain for more than a decade but Mugabe's victory represented the biggest defeat for British Africa policy since 1956 when the imprisoned Kwame Nkrumah was released from jail and asked to form a government following his overwhelming victory in the election for the Gold Coast's advisory council.

Mugabe thought Zimbabwe was his because he took it by force – exactly the same mentality as the brutal white colonists who seized it more than a century before. His aim, he said, was total independence but Zimbabwe had become more and more dependent on others' charity.

Increasingly his aggressive young wife, Grace, began to take big decisions in his name. She was filmed on a gargantuan shopping spree in South Africa at a time most Zimbabweans were facing starvation. At last part of the ruling political class and the army generals decided to make their move. On the night of 14 November 2017 tanks rolled onto the streets of Harare and Zimbabweans woke to the news that the president had been retired. Claiming that those close to the President were giving him bad advice, they said that it was time for the president to rest.

It was the gentlest, cleanest and most effective coup ever mounted in Africa. The presidential palace guard was disarmed and, in a state room sitting on a sofa, Mugabe was gently asked if he minded resigning. The army issued a statement saying that it was not a coup and that the President was 'safe' and all would return to normal after the army had dealt with the 'criminals' that had surrounded the president and had caused the socio-economic problems. That meant his wife and her militant followers. The new president was the man who had been Mugabe's right-hand man since the bush war started in 1964 and complicit in all his decisions and policies and activities: Emmerson Mnangagwa.

7

Breaking apart Sudan

The plane dips suddenly and Tony Trout, the Texan pilot, points to the left. I look down over a featureless grey-brown carpet of dried swamp stretching to the rim of the sky. Sliced across this monotony a trench shoots from horizon to horizon. The Jonglei Canal, begun in 1980, was conceived as a conduit to speed up the flow of the White Nile, providing more water to its lower reaches, especially Egypt. The canal was designed to take a quarter of its waters directly northwards from Bor to Malakal, cutting out the great 400-mile bend in the river. But that bend is home to the Dinka people and their cattle which feed on the tough clumps of grass in the Sudd, an immense swamp that floods from the Nile every year. The Dinka thought their grazing lands would be turned into desert, and the canal became a key reason for the southern rebellion to resume in May 1983.

Exactly ten years on I am visiting southern Sudan to see how close the rebels are to victory. Like most African conflicts, Sudan's war leaves relatively few direct military casualties from sporadic fighting, but creates mass civilian death through displacement, hunger and disease. The earth turns beneath us as we drop and I see the airstrip at Panyagor, a neat few inches of etched earth like a pin-scratch on a ballroom floor.

It is the only way into this zone of suffering. Thousands of ragged, hungry people have come here in the hope of food and safety. They are camped around a nondescript row of shacks and huts. When they hear the plane they look up and begin to move around. Some come towards the airstrip. Maybe the plane brings food. If those responsible for the crimes against humanity in Sudan in this war were put on trial, Panyagor would be a prime piece of evidence.

Every African country has its own colonial legacy, residues of alien rule. In many it is shocking to find how much remains, how things are still done in the old colonial way. Sudan is no exception. Today Sudan, until 2011 Africa's biggest country by area, is ruled as an empire exactly as it was 100 years ago when the British ruled and the Ottomans before that. The government in Khartoum, whoever it is, governs by neglect, repression and realpolitik. The word Sudan means 'the land of black people', but it has always been ruled by an Arabic-speaking, Muslim elite. In 2000 an anonymous publication appeared, known as *The Black Book*. It listed the origins of everyone in the Sudan power structure from ministers to drivers. They were overwhelmingly from three tribes from one area just north of Khartoum representing no more than 6 per cent of the population.

Some 134 languages are spoken in Sudan but among its ruling elite you will find only one – Arabic. Ask most members of the government if they are African and you will get an ambiguous reply. Ask them if they are Arab and they will say of course. They are in Africa but not of Africa. Looking north, not south, they see themselves – and Sudan – as Arab and Islamic. If they look south it is in the spirit of Islamizing or 'civilizing' the blacks who live there. Southerners are as physically and culturally different from northerners as Chinese and Norwegians. Black African, with a huge diversity of ethnicities and languages, the southerners have always felt neglected and exploited by the north.

Only imperial rule could have created such a non-nation as Sudan. Most of the south was first conquered under the Ottomans, then taken over by the self-proclaimed Mahdi, the charismatic military-religious leader, in the 1880s before his state was finally conquered by the British. The British motive for taking over Sudan had little to do with Sudan and everything to do with India, the 'jewel in the crown' of empire. When the Suez Canal opened in 1896 it allowed ships to sail from Britain to India through the Mediterranean and the Red Sea instead of sailing right round Africa. Britain bought the canal and put Egypt deep in its debt, controlling more and more of its politics until the take-over was complete. But that also meant taking over Sudan. A cunning French engineer had demonstrated that the Nile waters could be diverted, even stopped. So the British became convinced they must control the Nile from source to mouth in case another European power took part of it and threatened Egypt's water supply and thereby the route to India.

At that time Egyptian slave traders were moving further and further up the Nile, buying or seizing black Africans. Stopping slavery provided the British with another motive for moving into Sudan, but making Egypt, the main slaver, into the anti-slavery policeman was not easy. Britain had the power but ruled in the name of Egypt.

An outpost was established at Khartoum under the command of General Charles Gordon, but in 1881 the Mahdi, Mohammed Ahmed Ibn Sayyid Abdullah, led a militant Wahabi Islamic movement determined to destroy Egyptian Ottoman rule. The Mahdi was portrayed in Britain as a mad fanatic. Four years later the Mahdi surrounded the Anglo-Egyptian force in Khartoum and, after a siege of a few months, overran the city and killed Gordon. An expeditionary force coming to the rescue arrived too late. A classic heroic loser, Gordon stirred the hearts of the imperial British and they launched an army to destroy the power of the Mahdi. In one fell swoop they took revenge and Sudan.

The Mahdi had already died by the time the British force reached Khartoum in 1899, but the British made sure his army was destroyed and his successor killed. The battle of Omdurman was fought at a moment when technology in the form of machine guns and breech-loading artillery gave the Europeans brief but total military superiority over African armies. Both sides had rifles, but the British had new, long-range, quick-firing ones as well as Maxim guns and howitzers. The British cheerfully mowed down the Ansar, the followers of the Mahdi, who charged straight at them. The figures say it all. In one day the British counted 48 dead and 382 wounded. On the Mahdi's side 10,800 died and 16,000 were wounded. Afterwards the British general, Herbert Kitchener, had the body of the Mahdi dug up from its tomb in Omdurman and thrown to the dogs. British rule, even if it still flew an Egyptian flag alongside the Union Jack, was firmly established.

Sudan also provided the only serious threat of conflict in Africa between the invading imperial powers. Days after the battle of Omdurman the British got news of a French expedition that had marched north from the Congo and halted at a tiny village called Fashoda several hundred miles south of Khartoum on the Nile. The British could not allow their old enemy to have a stake in the Nile valley and General Kitchener immediately dispatched a force down river to confront the French. When they arrived, both sides simply stared at each other. Were they really going to fight to the death in this bleak swamp, miles from anywhere? They decided to check with their masters just to make sure they were supposed to slaughter each other. The obliging British allowed the French to send sealed letters up the Nile and on to Paris to speed up instructions. The two little armies then settled down together awaiting orders, sending presents to each other every day with the officers sharing their meagre reserves of champagne and brandy, but knowing at any moment they might be instructed to kill each other.

After seven weeks, orders finally arrived. The French government backed down and recalled its army to Senegal. The Nile, from Lake Victoria to the Mediterranean, was to be British. The French have never forgotten the Fashoda incident. The British never remember it. To this day every time the British gain an advantage over France in Africa, its ghost reappears. If the French hadn't blinked at Fashoda, southern Sudan might be a separate francophone country.

Sudan became an Anglo-Egyptian condominium, ruled in name by Egypt and Britain but in practice by the British. They ruled the north and south as separate entities. Northern Sudanese will tell you that this division is the cause of the divided nation which led to the 2011 north–south split. Southerners disagree. They tell you that northerners and southerners know each other perfectly well but northerners despise southerners and force them to become Muslim. Their memories go back to the times of the Arab slavers. The British made no attempt to forge a single nation state. For example, Christian missionaries were encouraged to go to the south while northern Muslim preachers were banned from going there. So at independence much of the south was nominally Christian while the north remained solidly Muslim. The two parts of Sudan were united only in 1947, a mere nine years before independence. The nation state was imposed. It did not grow out of a common identity. Northerners and southerners never established a common understanding of what Sudan is or what being Sudanese means.

The British had the guns to seize Sudan but not the manpower to rule it. So they used Egyptian civil servants and kept in place and retrained Sudanese officials who had served the Mahdi and Ottoman rulers. Outside the capital the British used the same tactic as they had in India, indirect rule. They co-opted local chiefs, sheiks and emirs and left them to rule as they wished as long as they did not cause trouble or expense and accepted the British as the ultimate power. Local rulers therefore continued to govern in their traditional ways as long as they did not create problems for Britain.

A new national school and military academy were set up to retrain the Sudanese civil servants, and at independence in 1956, almost all those Sudanese who took over the reins of power had been through these schools. Their qualification for doing the job of running an independent Sudan was that they knew how to do it. This was rare in Africa where those who took over at independence often had no experience of running anything, let alone a country. In Sudan the civil servants continued to rule as they had been taught to do by the British – by connections and deals with powerful people in the regions. And by force. The bosses in the regions relied on money and guns from the capital. But, as under British rule, neither group was accountable to the people of Sudan. As Mansour Khalid says in his book *The Government They Deserve*, their politics are derived from 'systems and methodologies of government more suited to colonial powers than to independent political "national" parties'.

This ruling group inherited a country in which 83 per cent of investment – public and private – was concentrated in the north, mainly around Khartoum and in Blue Nile province. Since the new rulers came mostly from these regions, they had no incentive to change anything.

Southern Sudan's first war began in 1955 and was fought for secession by a separatist group called the Anya-Nya. It ended in 1972 in a deal which gave the south more resources and more autonomy. But in 1982 the Khartoum government reneged on the agreement and a group of army officers, led by Colonel John Garang, picked up the southern cause. He formed the Sudan People's Liberation Army

(SPLA) and launched a new war in the following year. Although the SPLA was largely a southern movement and most of the war took place in the south, Garang's vision was a new, united, secular and democratic Sudan, 'based on equality, freedom, economic and social justice and respect for human rights for all Sudanese'. It did not mention secession, even though this was the real aim of most of the SPLA.

One reason that the SPLA did not initially demand a separate state was that its fighters were based in and backed by Ethiopia. The government there was fighting an Eritrean secessionist movement. It did not want to be seen to support any secessionist movements elsewhere in Africa. It is also true that Garang really did believe in a united Sudan, probably the only person in his movement who did. But he failed to bring in other marginalized groups such as the Fur in the west and the Beja in the east. It remained a Dinka-led southern movement.

The other strong supporter of the SPLA was Israel, which wanted to keep Sudan at war to weaken the Arab cause. It had supplied and trained the Anya-Nya rebellion in the 1960s. The American government was happy for Israel to feed its surplus weapons to the SPLA. It too was no friend of the Muslim rulers of Sudan.

The SPLA soon managed to operate throughout much of southern Sudan – hardly surprising, since it is the size of Western Europe and has no roads. To win and control territory would have taken a force twenty times the size of either the SPLA or the Sudan army. For the next sixteen years the pattern of the war remained unchanged. In the rainy season the SPLA would spread out from its bases, surround small towns and garrisons and sometimes capture them. In the dry season the Sudan army would counterattack, retake lost towns and restock its garrisons. Militarily the war went nowhere. The SPLA never managed to take the southern capital, Juba, or defeat the

Sudan army decisively. But as the war shifted back and forth, millions died, forced from their homes and fields and vulnerable to hunger and disease. Southern Sudan went back to the Iron Age.

In 1991 the SPLA split. Several senior members denounced Garang as a dictator and tried to overthrow him. The leader of the anti-Garang faction was a young Nuer chief called Riak Machar, married to an English woman. He said he stood for democracy and human rights. But his rebellion also had an ethnic flavour, since most of the commanders of the SPLA were Dinka and most of the rebels were Nuer or Shilluk or from minority groups. After several months the rebellion failed, and Machar and other leaders went over to the government side. They accepted jobs in Khartoum, and the government gave their fighters guns to continue their tribal war against Garang. This war within a civil war created havoc in southern Sudan. Guerrilla commanders became warlords, living off their own people by rape and pillage. In ferocity and barbarity this tribal war exceeded anything that the government and the SPLA had done to each other.

Panyagor's airstrip is the battleground of this conflict. Whoever can control the airstrip can fly weapons into the front line. A few months ago the Nuer seized Panyagor and the Dinka counterattacked, driving out the Nuer and killing a respected leader, Joseph Oduho. Now his death must be avenged, so the place has filled with Dinka troops as well as the hungry and homeless. The United Nations and the aid agencies want the Panyagor airstrip to deliver food aid. That makes it even more valuable to both sides. UN food and medical supplies are as important to their fighters as guns and bullets. But as soon as it is known that the UN may be dropping food here, ever more starving, displaced people drag themselves to Panyagor and sit in the merciless, timeless heat waiting for rescue.

The UN security officer, who hasn't actually been here recently, has decided it might be attacked again. UN food flights have been stopped and the hungry left to starve. A few have picked up their rag-tied bundles and trekked off to look for food elsewhere. Most have stayed put, lying around in groups day and night, waiting to die. A few aid agencies defy the UN ban on flights and find pilots like Tony Trout willing to take the risk. None will leave their planes on the ground overnight, so they drop a load of food and medicines and leave it for the SPLA to distribute.

I have come to stay in Panyagor to see what happens after the foreigners leave. Trout says he will be back sometime, hopefully in a few days. Phillip Aguer, the local head of the SPLA's social organization, welcomes me off the plane. So do thousands of ragged, exhausted people. I am like John the Baptist – a herald of hope. A white presence means that they may be fed.

At first I am given a grass hut on the edge of the settlement but then, as I am settling in, Phillip changes his mind and says I must come and stay with him. The reason is security but not, as I first assumed, fear of an attack by the Nuer. We stop at a hut that serves as a hospital where a little girl lies with a crude bandage on her head. Last night while she slept near that hut a hyena attacked and ripped off half her face. There are no painkillers here. She lies in her mother's arms, whimpering.

A collection of dilapidated brick and corrugated iron buildings that were once a school has been taken over by SPLA fighters, and I share a room there with Phillip. It feels like a furnace even though the sun is going down. I lay out my sheet sleeping bag over the grit and goat shit on the floor, but Phillip insists I take his grass mat – what he calls his mattress. Dinner is a bowl of maize porridge and I then spend an hour with my portable water filter, purifying a few mouthfuls of grey green water from the nearby well. Candles are rationed so I lie in the dark and listen to the screeching, sawing insects and mosquito whines. A rat scuttles over my legs.

In the grey pre-dawn I am woken by the dull thumping of bare feet on earth and a rhythmic chanting. In the vast silence of the Sudd the sounds are thin and distant. Jogging barefooted in step and chanting SPLA songs in unison, about forty fighters are doing early-morning drill round the school perimeter fence. As they stand, naked to the waist, tall, blue-black, long-boned and easy limbed, each with an AK47 strapped across his back, the magnificence of the Dinka fighters makes the huddled crowds on the edge of the settlement even more pathetic. The sun rises quickly and the dust kicked up by the fighters turns into a cloud of glorious gold. Dawn grows into glaring heat and the jogging and chanting cease. Their officers get up later and we have breakfast together, bread and porridge, sitting outside in the shade on comfortable new upholstered armchairs and a sofa that are inexplicably intact. How did they get to this derelict outpost? Another African mystery – like Magritte's bowler hat in the clouds.

I wander over to the feeding centre. The crowd has grown over-night, flopped in circles, silent, exhausted, expectant. When they get up they move like stiff old people. The women tend their zombie naked children, pot-bellied and stick-legged. Hope grows in their eyes when they see me. They nudge each other and point at me and smile. Word has spread that the UN is back, food is here, salvation is at hand. More and more will come. I thought I was an outsider, a detached reporter come to tell the world about the catastrophe here, but my very presence is helping to create it.

The cheery euphemisms given to southern Sudan's relief operations – Operation Lifeline, Operation Rainbow – cover a messy dilemma. Aid workers see their job as getting food into hungry mouths. They ignore all other considerations, even if it means feeding the devil as well. Some say it is not their business to judge – they just provide food. Others argue that you *must* feed the armies, government and rebels, or they will live off the people. Again and again in Africa aid has enabled wars to continue. By turning a blind eye to food and medicine being stolen by the men with guns, or straightforwardly furnishing them with such supplies, the aid agencies have again become part of the problem.

In south Sudan 20 million people have been cut off from the rest of the planet for almost twenty years. Copious guns and bullets arrive, but only a trickle of food and medicines. What little comes in is at the whim of both the government in Khartoum and the SPLA. Both sides must agree each flight – when and where it goes and what it carries. Each side wants to get as many flights as possible to their own areas so they can steal the food and medical supplies for their own troops and block flights to the other side. Neither side blocks everything going to the other side because then they will get nothing themselves. They play poker. The chips are the lives of Sudanese. Sometimes they deliberately create gatherings of hungry people to lure in the UN and then steal the food and medicine for their own fighters. The UN bleakly claims that it gets at least some food to hungry civilians. The price it pays, however, is that it also feeds the warring armies.

The UN's only weapons are diplomacy and a refusal to supply food where the government or the rebels want it. Here it is worse because the harvest failed two years ago and the local food supply has not recovered. And it is complicated because of the split within the rebel movement which makes Panyagor the frontline of two overlapping wars. The anti-Garang faction accepts weapons and ammunition from the government and is beginning to look like a purely anti-Dinka tribal movement rather than an attempt to bring democracy to the SPLA.

Women and children pay the heaviest price. At midday I wander over to the feeding centre which contains about forty listless children and their mothers and a billion frenetic flies. The starving children are tagged with white plastic wrist bands and sit on the bare concrete floor as if weighed down by their massive cannonball stomachs. Flies here do not flit nervously around your head like they do in Europe. This species flies straight onto your lips and eyeballs. As fast as you can brush them off, they zoom back again and crawl into your nose and mouth. Exhausted mothers vaguely waft the flies away from the faces of their babies but they come straight back. If only the relief flights were as persistent as the flies.

Today the mothers have come to the feeding centre in case a flight arrives. Suddenly I hear a distant growl – aircraft engines. At first people react with fear, almost panic, gathering up their meagre bundles ready for flight. The plane is an Antonov, a cargo plane that the Sudan government also uses to bomb them. They know the sound too well. Some start to hurry away from the camp, others just sit and wait, too exhausted and hungry to move. But the plane is coming in to land. I walk down to the airstrip. The UN says these flights, flown by aid agencies that refuse to seek government permission, jeopardize the whole operation. Not least because the planes they charter are often the same ones that the SPLA hires to fly in weapons. That gives the government an excuse to cancel all flights. It also creates bad blood between the aid agencies. At one starvation camp two rival aid agencies came to blows when they arrived simultaneously at the same feeding station.

The great silence of the Sudd is torn by a thunderous roar and the plane touches down in a cloud of dust and hope. It taxis to a halt and silence returns. The door opens and the pilot steps down in white shirt and dark trousers. The crew is Ukrainian, and as I welcome them I catch a whiff of vodka. Right behind them scuttle out four nuns dressed in white and grey habits. Irish, working for Goal, an Irish aid agency, they go wherever there is need, with complete disregard for the government, rebels, threats or their own safety.

The nuns acknowledge me with smiles, but no more formality or surprise than if we passed in a Dublin street, and they get on with supervising the unloading of sacks of food. The Ukrainian airmen have no enthusiasm for this business, and they stand around smoking as sacks of grain and flour tumble out of the plane's belly. Under the cheerful, sharp-eyed supervision of the nuns, bare-footed, bare-backed men heave them onto their shoulders and trot off to the store. The nuns then hurry off to the feeding centre and gather babies to their bosoms and start spooning milky gruel into their mouths. I observe, make notes. I close my notebook and go out, come in again, watch the children slowly coming to life. The nun nurses look at them quizzically, judging. Can this one survive? Is that one hopeless? I ask the sister what she thinks. She answers with a smile and hands me the baby she is feeding and a cup and spoon and tells me to get on with it. I feel a huge sense of relief, and although my eyes fill with hot tears, that bitter, ridiculous irony makes me smile. The little girl looks about three years old but she might be seven or eight. She sucks slowly on the spoon. I remember that my own daughters as babies used to wriggle and squirm and wave their arms and laugh with their eyes when they were fed. This child has a milky blue film over her eyes. I look into those dark eyes but she does not see anything beyond herself and the huge task she faces: staying alive. I hold up her arm. It is as thin as my thumb.

The next day two young fighters take me for a walk along a track to Kongor, the old administrative centre a few miles away. You can see the centre for miles, marked by great dark mango trees. The brick buildings are now wrecked and roofless. The fighters warn me against going into them because of snakes, but I can't resist seeing what is inside. In the second one three corpses in uniform lie sprawled on the floor. There are more at the back. My Dinka companions tell me they are Nuer fighters who died in the battle for this place two months ago. When I get back at midday I am exhausted by the heat and humidity and have to sleep. My companions laugh. 'That was short walk and we went slow,' they say. 'Sometimes we walk ten times that distance in a morning – fast.'

During the day the fighters keep themselves apart from the people. They wander around Panyagor but never come to the feeding centre, spending most of their time in the armchairs chatting. Mostly they just sit and stare, picking their teeth. Well fed, they do not seem to regard the local people as part of their war or their lives. They smile at the efforts of the Irish nuns who risk their lives to come in and feed their children. Every day two or three graves have to be dug for those who have succumbed to hunger, but this is done by volunteers. The fighters are nowhere to be seen. They live as a caste apart from their own people.

Two nights later I am woken by distant shots then shouts and the sound of a heavy lorry nearby. It is the first working vehicle I have heard since I arrived. Early next morning voices are raised, excited. There is an air of expectation. A Nuer group attacked in the night and the truck has brought in the wounded. They lie on the floor of one of the classrooms, bandaged and still. At midday I hear the sound of an aircraft and see Trout's white twin-engined plane sweeping low over the camp to make sure it is still in friendly hands. Then he turns and comes in to land, bumping onto the gravel strip. A nun climbs out, but this plane is bringing only a few boxes of medicine and dried milk powder. Trout and the nuns nod me a casual greeting. I feel I have not seen them for months. It is time for me to leave. We deposit the boxes in the feeding centre, but as we are getting ready to go, the commander appears and tells Tony to take some of the wounded to the Red Cross hospital at Lokichoggio, the UN base in northern Kenya. Tony is busy putting up mosquito netting around the feeding centre to keep the flies out. He goes on hammering in a nail and quietly refuses.

'I'm not allowed to carry anything or anyone military. Anyway there aren't enough seats in the plane.'

'If you do not take them you will take no-one, you will not fly at all,' replies the commander.

After a long argument Tony agrees to take three of the heavily bandaged young men. Silent, grey with pain, they are carried to the plane like sacks. Tony's face is tense as they are laid in the back. He knows we are overloaded but says nothing. He starts the engines and rams the throttle forward onto full power. He is pouring sweat and when we reach the end of the dirt strip we are only a couple of feet off the ground. The plane heaves itself away from the earth. I look back at the wounded fighter propped up against the back of my seat. He is about sixteen years old, I guess by the innocence of his face, but already long and lanky. A huge bloodstained bandage has been fixed round his chest with a safety pin. He gazes at me with soft, reflective eyes and smiles reassuringly. As we approach Lokichoggio he reaches out a long hand and takes mine as if trying to shake hands. But he does not let go and he grips it as we drop down through the bumpy clouds to the UN base. He is still gripping my hand when we land. When I turn round, he is dead.

No-one could have called Whisky Delta a soft-hearted or naive aid worker. He worked for the World Food Programme and his huge belly was indeed a waddling advertisement for food. If you met him for lunch or dinner he would say, 'Let's eat first and then talk.' And he meant it. He ate with intense, silent concentration, piling food into his mouth forkful after forkful and washing it down with beer.

Whisky Delta would hit the office in Kampala early, leaping out of his car and skipping up the steps, bulldozing down the corridor, his stomach leading the way. For such a fat man, Whisky Delta moved fast. Named after his radio call sign, he loved the radio almost as much as he loved food. During the day he worked steadily through meetings, warming up for the evening show. At around 4.30 the performance began. He reminded me of a rugby coach at school exasperated with coaching or refereeing. He wanted to play. Suddenly he would strip off his tracksuit and join in, grabbing the ball and running with it, scoring tries, saving tries, throwing in, taking penalties. The kids he was supposed to be teaching would be demoralized – and often flattened.

Holding the radio receiver to his mouth like some exotic fruit he was about to swallow, Whisky Delta would pace around his office calling round his workers scattered all over East Africa. Tonnages of grain, numbers of trucks, camps to be served, numbers of refugees, names of truck drivers poured out of his head into the receiver. Between calls he barked orders to his secretary. I never saw him consult paper or write anything down.

'Whisky Delta to India Mike. Are you receiving me? – Over . . . Roger. Has the truck been mended yet? Why not? – Over . . . I need it now – Over . . . Just do it. Roger.'

'Hello, Quebec Bravo. Where the fuck are you? – Over . . . Quebec Bravo, you should be in fucking Bujumbura by now – Over . . . Roger, but what are doing there? – Over . . .'

'How many tons? No no no no . . . I said sixty. Six zero. What do you mean, it was all you could get? I said six zero. Well it's your job to get them . . . I don't care about that. I'm not interested in excuses. Over and out.'

Bullying, sarcastic, patronizing, he was more like a gouty general from the days of the British Empire than the image of a compassionate, caring, modern UN aid worker. Even when he could find no fault with his staff he would give them a blast down the radio or telephone just to remind them he was watching them. I never heard him give a compliment. His staff hated him.

If he cared at all about the people he was supposed to help, he never showed it. The aid agencies feared him but depended on him for UN support. He had them at his mercy and sneered at their do-gooding dedication. Getting the job done was all he cared about. Delivery. If a few people got hurt on the way that was an added bonus. He had worked in war zones and with bloody dictators all over the world. Some said he was effective because he was as big a bastard as they were.

Whisky Delta was kind to journalists. He loved being on TV, having his name in the papers. He boasted of the times he had been on CNN. When I arrived in the region in early 1994 because of an upsurge in fighting in southern Sudan, he immediately offered me transport and communications. Over 100,000 people had been driven out of three makeshift refugee camps in South Sudan known as the Triple A camps. The entire population of all three had fled, trekking southwards through the bush towards Uganda like some biblical exodus. Until they reached the border they had no food and possibly no water.

On the way north we stop at the Adjumani camp near the Uganda border, crammed with tens of thousands of Sudanese refugees. Whisky Delta believed that the SPLA had exaggerated the numbers in the camp so it would receive more food aid. He discovered that the rebel movement was also taxing the refugees, taking a proportion of their weekly maize handout. Collecting the surplus, they sold it to a local businessman who sent it to Kampala for sale. Whisky Delta found himself buying the same grain over and over again. His reaction was swift and harsh. He cut back Adjumani's WFP food aid. Despite this we see no terrible hunger in the camp.

The Uganda border post at Kajo Keji is a mud hut at a point between two nowheres in the African bush. Next to a pile of rubble that had once been the customs post, a man in flip-flops has set up a school desk under a tree and wants to check our passports. He apologizes for not having a stamp but he inspects our luggage and insists on all the other formalities of statehood in SPLA-controlled South Sudan. He makes us fill in forms and pay for passes, laboriously writing out receipts. Then he discovers I am a journalist and decides to refuse me entry to Sudan. He won't even discuss it, so I pick a novel out of my bag and sit and read for a while. Eventually he realizes I am not going to give him money and he gets tired, so with no more explanation than he had given for detaining me, he lets me go. His last gesture of authority is to remind us to put our watches back one hour as we enter 'liberated South Sudan' and to drive on the right-hand side.

The road is deserted, but half-way to the camps we turn a corner and find the way blocked by a gang of about thirty men, dressed in grass, leaves and feathers and carrying spears and bows and arrows. As soon as they see us they disappear into the thick bush. When we reach the point where they were on the road there is no sign of them. Who are they? The driver shrugs: 'Hunters.'

We reach the first camp to find only flies. In the still air there is no sound except faint buzzing. Thousands of little thatch and blue plastic huts stand empty across the hot valley like a photograph. The camp has been ransacked, recent food supplies looted. Cooking pots have been tipped off fires, food still in them. Pathetic bags of clothes lie ripped open, tins emptied. Whisky Delta had speculated that the SPLA has attacked its own people in order to drive them back into Uganda so they can steal the recently arrived food. He could be right. On the edge of the camp we find two corpses half-eaten by animals. The bodies of two tall men in uniform lie splayed out on the ground as if still running, fixed in the pose they died in. They are too decomposed to reveal any facial scars that might give us a clue to their ethnicity.

We get a call from Whisky Delta ordering us back across the border into Uganda to an airstrip. A plane is landing, and when the door opens Whisky Delta himself emerges. He says he has come to see the situation for himself, even though his deputy is here. He is dressed as the caricature of a war correspondent: desert boots, pale slacks, khaki bush jacket with pockets everywhere, a slouch hat and a huge camera slung over his shoulder. 'Come on,' he shouts. 'Let's go check out Parajok.'

The SPLA is demanding that the UN provide food for this village where there is supposed to be a large refugee population. Whisky Delta says this is an SPLA scam to get food delivered directly to its fighters. He commandeers a Land Cruiser and off we go, but we frequently stop because Whisky Delta wants pictures of himself taken with his own camera: in front of a burnt-out village, beside a shot-up military truck, peering out from a deserted strong point.

Parajok has been knocked about recently, but luckily for us it is still in SPLA hands. Whisky Delta asks for the local commander, but he is asleep in a hut. Whisky Delta strides in and wakes him. Without the usual pleasantries and introductions, he launches into an interrogation.

'How many people are here?'

'Many.'

'OK, cut the crap. Let's get a figure, a thousand, ten thousand?'

'Many thousands.'

'I don't think you have a clue do you. Are they hungry?'

'Very.'

'Are they starving?'

'Many have died.'

'Show me the graves.'

'They are far.'

He poses for more photos and then, without a goodbye, Whisky Delta shoots off to his plane. 'That's the problem dealing with these lying bastards,' he says. After his plane has departed, Abdullah, one of the UN workers, tells me he has a message. He is shaking with anger. 'I know as well as anyone that these people tell lies, but for months I have been trying to work with them. If we want to feed these people we have to work with the SPLA. We must co-operate. Now they say to me: "Tell Whisky Delta that the SPLA never want to see him again. He is not welcome in South Sudan." Just tell him that.'

I try to tell him the SPLA should deliver their own message.

'No, it will come better from one of his friends,' says Abdullah with a look of contempt.

Two days later, back in Kampala, I sit down to a gargantuan meal at the best restaurant in town with Whisky Delta. As we finish eating I summon up my courage and begin: 'I have some bad news I've been asked to give you.'

'From the SPLA?' asks Whisky Delta, without looking up from a slice of creamy gateau.

'Yes.'

He laughs. He's already guessed. 'Well, you tell your friends in the SPLA: if they ban me from South Sudan, South Sudan gets no food. Get it?'

In 1991, after three decades of war, the Ethiopian government of Mengistu Haile Mariam was overthrown by Tigrayan and Eritrean rebels. The rebels had been supported by the Sudan government, and once these rebels turned rulers they immediately ended Ethiopian support for the SPLA and closed down its radio station. But Sudan and Ethiopia are natural regional rivals; the equation is strategic, not ideological. After a couple of years, strategic interest overcame political friendship and the Ethiopian government resumed its support for the SPLA in Sudan.

The new Ethiopian rulers were close to the United States, which was becoming increasingly concerned with the apparent rise of militant Islam in Sudan in the 1990s. Under the guidance of Hassan Turabi, a powerful militant Islamist, Sudan lurched towards the Islamist camp and gave refuge and military training areas to Osama bin Laden. Support for Saddam Hussein in Iraq after his invasion of Kuwait confirmed American fears, and in 1996 Sudanese agents tried to kill Egypt's President, Hosni Mubarak, during a visit to Addis Ababa. America identified Sudan as a 'terrorist' state and UN sanctions were imposed. In 1998 US planes bombed a pharmaceutical factory in Khartoum asserting, wrongly, that it manufactured chemical weapons. Sudan became a pariah state.

That year I went back to the south and met up with an old friend, Peter Adwok, then 'Deputy Secretary for Industry and Mining in the Government of South Sudan'. Peter's face is battered and crumpled like a gnarled old African mask. But it is not beaten into defeat or despondency. It says, 'There is no more suffering you can inflict on me. I have seen it all. Do your worst.' And when he laughs, Peter's face cracks wide open with the youngest smile imaginable. Tall does not quite reach Peter. His seven feet are made more ridiculous by being balanced awkwardly on one leg. Artificial legs do not come in his size and the one he has fits badly, so he swings around stiffly with a very long walking stick. One moment he curses with frustration, the next he is laughing at his own precarious movements.

When the war broke out in 1983 Peter was setting up the geology department at Juba University. He desperately wanted to fight, but he had a wife and four children under eight. So he waited three years. Then he left Juba to join the SPLA in Ethiopia. He had just been offered a Fulbright scholarship in America but, he says, 'I just had to go.' He told his wife to join him with the children as best they could but, he admits now, he doubted that he would see them again.

He nearly didn't see them again. Joining the SPLA is not like

joining a political party. When it started, Garang tried to force his followers to obey him blindly. Recruits, especially educated ones like
Peter who might challenge Garang intellectually, were forced to sit
for hours in the sun singing songs praising him. Worse, 'training' was
simply a process of dehumanization and humiliation. As an intellectual, Peter was given specially degrading treatment, forced to shit in
public and share sleeping quarters with illiterate boys who were
encouraged to humiliate him. Actual military training was brief, and
Peter was immediately sent on a raid into Sudan. They should have
crossed the border at night, but Garang delayed the order to move
and the unit found itself caught at dawn in open ground. The
Sudanese army was waiting for them and more than 100 were cut
down. Badly wounded in the leg, Peter managed to swim back across
the river into Ethiopia. By the time they got him to a hospital, his leg
had gone gangrenous and had to be amputated.

Peter's military career was brief, but he threw himself into the
politics of the movement with the same disregard for his political
safety as he had shown on the battlefield for his personal safety. He
spoke his mind to Garang, who had become a dictator expecting
unquestioning loyalty. When the movement split in 1991, he joined
the anti-Garang faction. But when the rebellion failed, Riak Machar,
its leader, and other senior figures joined – or were bought by – the
Khartoum government. Peter was left out in the cold. He tried to
bring the movement together again and went to talk to Lam Akol, a
fellow Shilluk, who had joined Riak and the rebels but had not gone
over to the government. Peter journeyed to Lam's home village, but
Lam promptly had him thrown into a cage in a pit and left there for
weeks. When he was let out, Peter went straight to Garang, who also
imprisoned him in a pit. Eventually he was released and accepted
back into the movement.

I meet Peter in Nairobi, and he stands up on his single long leg and greets me with a huge smile and a wobbly hug. I am clutching his midriff, trying to stop us both toppling over. 'Come to Sudan with me. I am leaving very soon,' he says. He explains that the SPLA has issued a gold-mining licence to an Israeli and he wants to find out what the man is doing. I accept his invitation with alacrity, but then I realize he has no means of getting to Sudan. He may be a 'minister' but he has no money. The Israeli might have some, so he thinks he can collect some tax to pay himself some salary. He phones around Nairobi to see if anyone is flying or driving there and has a spare seat. We could be waiting for weeks.

Two days later there are reports that a hospital has been bombed at Yei, a small town about forty miles north of the Uganda border. Ten are reported dead, fifty wounded. The Nairobi office of Norwegian People's Aid wants to fly medical supplies there and bring back the wounded. They are happy to squeeze in a journalist and give Peter a lift too. The plane leaves at dawn.

The only aircraft available is, bizarrely, one that used to belong to the Queen of England. Now it has been pensioned off and has the look of an aristocratic old lady who has decided to take a walk on the wild side. As boxes of medical supplies are lobbed up the steps and stacked inside, I try to imagine the royal corgies hopping up those steps. This plane, I am told by the ground staff, is also regularly chartered for running guns to the SPLA in Sudan and rebels in Congo.

This flight is illegal. The Norwegians, like the Irish nuns, refuse to belong to the UN consortium. When we land at the earth strip at Yei, everyone helps unload – fast. The Sudanese air force can pick up unauthorized flights on radar and sometimes attacks them. We stack the medicines while the pilot directs two men to knock down a new anthill that has sprouted out of the runway. A lorry backs up to the plane and a dozen stretcher cases are loaded on board.

The scene at the hospital is horrific. One bomb landed in the entrance to an underground shelter. An earth room roofed with tree trunks, the shelter was jammed with people who had been queuing in front of the hospital. Now it's a huge crater. Two tree trunks have been blown right off the bunker. Others are leaning at crazy angles. The orange earth in the bunker is still dark and wet with blood. A child's flip-flop lies on the bottom step.

Eleven people were killed instantly and twice as many have horrific injuries. Dr Ajak Bullen Alier shows me the remains of one small boy. He has no feet and his body is lacerated with deep shrapnel gashes but he is somehow alive. Another miracle lies in a coma beside him: a young man with the side of his head smashed off. Dr Ajak lifts the dressing to show me the exposed brain. Incredibly, when I come back a week later, he is still alive. The bombs have taken huge chunks of brickwork off the front of the hospital, blown off all the inside doors and brought down the ceilings. Dr Ajak, young, soft-spoken, laid-back, has already managed to get the essentials functioning again.

He explains how refurbishment of the hospital had finished only a few days ago. There is neither despair nor anger in his voice. He simply tries to work out how long it will take to repair. Then he stoops and picks up what looks like a twisted candy bar of steel about six inches long. I had already seen one embedded in a tree trunk by the entrance and wondered what it could be. Dr Ajak shows me another stuck in the brickwork. These are extra shrapnel that the Sudanese air force binds onto its bombs.

There is no question that the hospital was the target. Five bombs have fallen across it. The SPLA camp is at the other end of Yei on the far side of the river, military lorries and artillery clearly visible. Dr Ajak explains that they aim to frighten people out of the town and force them into the bush. They have succeeded. Yei has emptied.

Set on the edge of a valley in a rolling, wooded landscape with a near perfect climate, Yei must have been a beautiful town. 'Town' may be the wrong word. It is a pleasing collection of administrative offices built of soft red brick, plus church, bank and hospital providing a core around which little houses and mud huts gathered. Only the church and the hospital are still used. Other buildings sprout trees and grass. The streets are tree-lined tracks. Is this what London or York looked like in the fifth century after the Roman legions departed and the Britons were left squatting amid the ruins?

Peter wants to go in search of the gold-mining Israeli and collect some revenue. The deal is a two-year concession in return for $10 million worth of investment. Peter, the geologist, reckons he can mine six tons of gold in two years and must give half to the SPLA. Knowing the pace at which things are done in southern Sudan this seems unlikely, but Peter is optimistic.

We sleep in a mud hut, baking under its corrugated iron roof, and next day we set off southwards towards the gold mine. We pass through vaulting cathedrals of pale teak trees, first planted after the First World War by the British with imperial confidence. I wonder what must have been in the minds of the men who laid them out. What did they think this place would be like when the trees came to be harvested? In another attempt by the SPLA to bring outsiders to exploit the areas it controls, a South African company has set up a sawmill. As we pass, the workers are covering its shiny corrugated iron roof with branches and reeds. The ruse didn't work. A couple of weeks later it was hit by bombs and abandoned.

The gold mine consists of a couple of shipping containers, three broken-down tractors and a couple of thatched huts next to a stream. A pot steams on an open fire and some people sleep in the shade of a tree. No-one knows where 'the Jew' is. Peter is furious. But they give us their lunch of maize porridge, beans and a small deer they had trapped that morning and boiled in the pot. This does not look like gold-rush city. Apparently 'the Jew' had plans to divert the river and excavate the bed but a year into the project, there is no sign of it. Peter hobbles around and picks through the container to find a few old bedsteads and tools. 'This is just some old rubbish he has brought here, there is no proper mining equipment. He has deceived us.'

Next day we set off for Juba, the capital of the south and still in government hands, though besieged by the SPLA. This road cannot have been touched since the war started seventeen years ago. It is not comfortable with Peter's seven feet and an artificial leg squeezed into the front of a little twin-cab pick-up. Boy soldiers with AK47s perch on the back, thrown this way and that by the jolting, twisting ride. We rarely get out of first gear.

On the way we pass camps of fighters, most of them strolling on the road or lying under the trees. Why don't they repair the road? The answer is it isn't worth it. We are one of only three vehicles we see all day. There are only a handful of vehicles in the whole of southern Sudan. Ordinary people and fighters move around on foot, the aid workers and military bosses go by air. But there are only twenty usable airstrips in the whole of the south. No wonder this war has taken so long. It is like a boxing match on a football pitch.

Juba has been under siege on and off since the war started. Sometimes the SPLA moves a little closer and lobs some shells into the city, sometimes the government dispatches a force to chase the attackers away. Both sides send out patrols to make sure the other is still there. The merits and risks of seizing the southern capital have been debated endlessly by Garang and his commanders since the start of the war. Its capture would be of huge symbolic importance. Some even argue that the regime in Khartoum would give up the south if the southern capital fell to the rebels. But the city is heavily defended and supplied by river and air. It would be impossible to capture without hurting the population of southern refugees huddled in the city. And even if it were captured, it would be impossible to defend against air attack and recapture. So the strategy is to threaten Juba and force the government to keep lots of troops there, but to attack other targets in the south.

On most roads in Africa you always see people walking or cycling. But here, although the land looks green and fertile, we see almost no-one. Peter explains that people now live in the bush because SPLA fighters take food from the locals and pressgang their children into the army. The few people we do see are ragged and shoeless. Cut off from their main market, Juba, people can only buy manufactured goods that have been brought hundreds of miles from Kampala or Nairobi. And they have little to barter in return. Development is a very distant memory here.

We pass a vast herd of long-horned cattle coming slowly through the forest. More than a hundred file past with lumpy gait, driven by two slim Dinka boys with whips. Peter explains that they have walked from the vast swampy grasslands of Bar el Ghazal hundreds of miles to the north, heading to market in Kampala, another 300 miles. The trip will take them half a year and will bring back a little wealth. 'When they have sold the cows,' Peter explains, 'the boys will hire a truck and bring back sugar, beads, soap. And AIDS.'

The front line, thirty-two miles from Juba, at least looks like a front line. About thirty soldiers are sitting in a network of shallow trenches. Artillery guns and a tank are parked under a tree, though the tank has a neat hole punched through its barrel. We cannot actually see Juba from here, but we can hear a plane taking off from the airport. Most soldiers are asleep in the shade, so we keep our voices low so as not to disturb them. The sector commander, Abraham Wana Yoane, shows us round. Wiry, alert and half the size of most of his Dinka troops, Commander Abraham explains that the trenches used to be closer to Juba, but there was no spring for water, so they have to pull back in the dry season. The rains were poor this year and the crops have all but failed. There is not enough food, so he told some of his fighters to go home.

The only action, Commander Abraham explains, is a weekly raid by a government MiG fighter bomber, but it does little damage. The most damaging weapons are mines liberally scattered by both sides. The victims, however, are mostly civilians who try to slip in and out of the city at night. We walk a little way towards the town to some trenches where there had been a battle a few months before. Three burnt-out tanks, one with its turret flipped off, lie nearby. Strewn everywhere are spent cartridges, ripped-up copies of the Koran, broken ammunition boxes and rags of uniforms, some with bones still in them.

Suddenly there is a burst of machine-gun fire nearby. Commander Abraham looks alarmed. His troops leap from their slumbers. Someone shouts a question. From the bush comes a distant reply. Commander Abraham and his men relax. The afternoon government and rebel patrols have bumped into each other. The shots were simply a warning ritual. They managed to avoid each other and now everyone can go back to sleep.

On the way back, Peter suddenly orders the driver to turn off into elephant grass almost ten feet high. We nose slowly through the wall of grass stems that fold across the windscreen and enclose us. Peter insists there is a track, but it is invisible. Then suddenly we are through and crossing a little brick bridge over a small river. On the other side an avenue of pale giant eucalyptus trees leads up to some buildings.

At the end of the avenue, on top of a low rise, is a beautiful ruin, a double-fronted mansion like Sleeping Beauty's castle. But this is no fairytale. The walls of the abandoned house are black with soot from fires lit in the rooms and the walls are covered with crude graffiti and drawings of guns, bombs, sex and death. In the corners are piles of dried human shit. At the back a courtyard sprouts gladioli and roses that have somehow survived. We gingerly climb the rotten staircase and from the main room upstairs we step onto a balcony and find ourselves looking west across a stupendous landscape of hills and forests. Once they were rich tea and coffee plantations, Peter explains, owned by a Syrian merchant who built the house. He left during the first war in the 1960s and the forest reclaimed the land. Now it is taking back the house too.

Ten years later I was telling this story to a Syrian businessman who said he knew Sudan. 'You have just described the house I grew up in,' he said. Anis Haggar told me that the farm was called Iwatoka and was originally started by an Englishman called Maynard. In the local Keliko language, Iwatoka means the place where there are no elephants. Two fast-flowing rivers either side of the hill discourage them. Anis's grandfather, Mikhail Haggar, came to Sudan as a trader from Aleppo, towards the end of the nineteenth century. He lived in Omdurman but travelled south to sell his goods. Anis's father, George Haggar, settled near Yei around 1932, bought the farm and developed tea and coffee and then tobacco. Anis said the kitchen garden had twenty-seven different fruit trees.

The family was accused of helping the rebels in the first war in southern Sudan. Then the farm was expropriated in 1970 but returned three years later. When the second war started the SPLA 'invited' the family to leave. Now with peace, the family is hoping to return but local community leaders are asking for huge sums of money to allow the family back.

In one of the few villages that seems to have people in it we stop for a drink and meet Henry Stephen Danga, the local administrator appointed by the SPLA. He is wearing a T-shirt which reads, 'Avoid hangovers – stay drunk.' Our arrival prompts him to live up to his T-shirt slogan and he orders two bottles of local spirit. Slurred but impeccably courteous when we arrive, he rapidly becomes incoherent. He says he received some training in local government administration and development in Khartoum but there is, he claims, little here for him to do. 'We have achieved very little,' he says, with a degree of honesty rare among SPLA officials. 'There are no people here. Maybe they will come back now and we will have to re . . . rehalibitate.' He smiles amiably. I ask him if he gets paid. 'No, I don't get a salary,' he says ruefully. 'I am supposed to carry out policy but there's no people, no money and no policy.'

I look to Peter for a judgement. He shrugs and dismisses the man with a wave of his hand. 'No ideas, no dynamism, just drinking,' he says. Then he adds, 'But there's no-one else.'

War or disaster sometimes injects dynamism into a society. Since the genocide, Rwanda has become one of the most focused and dynamic countries on the continent. Uganda and Ghana too, freed from oppression and conflict, have forged ahead. War in South Sudan appears to have destroyed more than people and places. The will to make life better tomorrow seems to have been a casualty, too.

Back in Yei we meet a more inspiring person, Thomas Cirillo, once a major in the Sudanese army, now an SPLA commander. His brother Peter was a leading figure in the government, but fell out with them and is under house arrest in Khartoum. Their parents are in Juba. He tells me, 'As a child in 1965 I saw Juba burning. It is in my consciousness and we know that the Arab is our enemy. It is in everyone's consciousness here, so the will is there to free ourselves.'

That night I am invited to the SPLA barracks in Yei. Some 150 officers have assembled from all over the region to attend training courses. I am ushered into an open space brightly lit by spotlights. As my eyes adjust to the glare I realize hundreds of pairs of eyes are looking at me. I am the guest of honour, seated at the centre of a semicircle of senior officers. Beyond them, hundreds of men are sitting on school benches. Peter sits down with the officers and immediately starts an argument about Garang's leadership. He tells them he has brought me here 'because I wanted him to know the truth'. He accuses Garang of stupidity and incompetence. I realize at that moment that Peter is untouchable. He has experienced such suffering and still cares so much that he can speak the truth without a trace of fear. He is free. It is the others who are frightened.

After a while, about fifteen women emerge from the shadows carrying plastic buckets and huge bowls of food, meat and rice and sauce. The men queue up with plastic plates. As they eat, someone turns on a blaring, crackly tape recorder playing Congolese music. The cooks retire and huddle together on a bench. One of the commanders insists that I begin the dancing. 'Go and ask them to dance,' he says. I get up and two girls hurriedly rise and walk quickly towards me. The one that reaches me first is barely more than a girl, maybe fifteen or sixteen. We start to dance and she pulls me close to her. 'Kiss me, kiss me,' she says in my ear, pushing her face into my neck. She is sobbing and shaking.

'What's the matter?' I ask.

'Please take me with you, take me with you,' she begs.

'Did you come here because you were forced to or because you wanted to?' I ask.

'We were forced. I live in the town. I want to be at home with my mother but they made us come here. I know what will happen tonight – when the soldiers drink beer.'

So this is the new Sudan. I am guest of honour at a massive, officially sponsored gang rape. I disentangle myself from the girl and go to tell Peter. He looks grave and angry and says we should leave soon. Is there no way we can help them, I ask? He does not reply, but he is ashamed. This is one battle he is not going to fight.

*

At Khartoum the two Niles meet: the faster-flowing Blue Nile, creamy brown with mud from the Ethiopian Highlands, and the White Nile, pale, vast, sedate, like a long lake. But for the annual flush of the Blue Nile, the Nile would never make it to Egypt.

The centre of Khartoum was now a modern city and there are few remnants of the old British-built capital. Its faded red brick buildings with high ceilings, long corridors and cloisters were more like monasteries than government departments. Khartoum is three cities. On the west bank is Omdurman, where most people live. On the north bank is Khartoum North, the industrial city. Suburbs sprawl out into the desert, and beyond them on the bleak outer fringes vast squatter camps of plastic sheeting and cardboard are homes for more than two million people, mainly southerners, driven here by war. They have walked hundreds of miles to squat in the waterless rocky desert on the margins of the capital. Their survival is a miracle.

I set off to the foreign ministry in one of Khartoum's battered yellow taxis. It is 1988 and the city is home to models not seen in Europe and America for decades, all lovingly kept on the road long after they would have been scrap in the first world. The bodywork of this one is more dents and rust than paint, its ignition system is two bare wires and it lacks springs or shock absorbers. The dashboard is bedecked with Christmas tinsel, illuminated Koranic sayings and dusty tassels.

Khartoum's taxis blast out clouds of blue smoke and persistently beep their horns. It sounds aggressive, but then you realize that it is more a constant dialogue between drivers: 'Beep – I'm going left, Beep Beep. OK, I can see, but I'm going first, Beep. Fine, go on, Beep Beep Beep. Thank you. Have a nice day, Beep. You too. Beep.' They push in, pass, force others to brake, but there is no anger, no hurry, no frustration, although, judging from the dented chrome bumpers and the hammered-out door panels, there are a lot of mis-understandings.

You can divide African cities into those where it is safe enough to drive with windows open and those where you close them and lock the doors. Lagos, Nairobi and Johannesburg are Windows Closed cities: thieves will try to grab your watch or your wallet through an open window. There are tales of thieves brandishing syringes they say are full of HIV-infected blood and threatening to stab you unless you hand over your wallet. Khartoum is an Open Window city. You can walk the streets and drive with car windows open in safety – if you can bear the thick, baked air.

Khartoum is a city of dust. Sunrises and sunsets are stupendous, but the fine sand haze settles on your skin and turns your clothes a reddish yellow. It gathers on the sides of the roads, where gangs of women sweepers occasionally waft it back into the air with their brooms. After the dawn hour the only respite from the sun is provid-ed by the banyan trees that give a shade so dark that you can barely see beneath the great tangled mass of branches and hanging roots. Beneath them sit women at little school desks or an upturned crate, selling single cigarettes and sweets or tiny packets of salt and soap. At street crossings, great amphorae of cool drinking water stand in the shade. Small boys will serve you a plastic cupful for a few coins. How they are filled is a mystery.

I have come to see the most senior southerner in the govern-ment, Bishop Gabriel Rorich, Anglican bishop and Foreign Minister. He is employed to show people like me that the government does not discriminate against southerners. The Anglican Church dis-owned him for taking this job. At the outer gate, my polite cough wakes the receptionist asleep across his desk, and although I have an appointment, I have to fill in a form and wait. After half an hour I am led into the courtyard where three northern men dressed in bright white *jellabiyas* sit in the shade talking. Out in the sun two southern women with hand brooms are bent double, sweeping the walkways. At the next building I have to fill in another form. Then to a waiting room where an Arab woman, traditionally dressed, silently brings me sweet black tea and water. Another, a secretary dressed in Western clothes but with her head covered, bustles in to check on me. These women and the path-sweepers are the only people who seem to be doing anything that could be remotely described as work at the ministry.

After another lengthy wait I am led to the bishop's office. My attendant takes out the key, unlocks the door and ushers me in. Then he withdraws and locks the door behind me. The bishop appears to be locked in his office by his keeper. What does that make him? A caged exhibit? A semi-tame specimen, maintained and controlled? Gentle, solemn-faced, the bishop sits behind an almost empty desk, dressed in black with purple clerical shirt and white clerical collar. He welcomes me politely, and although I was ready to attack this stooge of the northern Muslims, I find it difficult not to like him.

He sees himself as a bridge-builder, a go-between trying to explain the problems of the south to the northerners. Surprisingly, he does not disagree that southerners are second-class citizens in Sudan, and it is hard to argue when he says the southern rebellion has failed and this only means more suffering for the south. That is why he is trying to make peace. When he turns away for a moment I peep in his in-tray. It contains old UN reports, one of which is about Sudan. He returns, but has grown weary of his routine speech. He says he has another meeting. Unlikely, I think.

A visit to another southern minister confirms my suspicions. Lam Akol is a southerner who was once John Garang's foreign spokesman and a key player in the SPLA. I had met him in those days. A clever, difficult man, he defected to Khartoum and is now Minister of

Transport with a grand office. Like the foreign ministry, it is staffed entirely by northerners except for the path-sweepers and tea-makers. Lam Akol may be Transport Minister but roads and air come under other ministries. That leaves him in charge of a defunct railway. I wait an hour in the outer office, but then I am told he is too busy to see me. Perhaps that is his one moment of power today in his neutered life.

I go back to the Acropole and sleep. An old-fashioned hotel, run by a Greek family who have lived in Sudan since 1922, it is more like an austere sanatorium. The rooms have plain beds, ancient wardrobes and stone floors. Bathrooms are shared. Air-conditioning is very recent. Its clientele is always interesting. This time there is a Japanese businessman, a Greek Orthodox bishop, a British television producer and an Italian doctor who underwent a deathbed conversion to Islam and, having survived, has come to live in a Muslim environment. He has been having problems making anyone in Khartoum believe a European could be Muslim.

At dusk, I wander down to the Omdurman Bridge over the White Nile and look at the sun setting over the two rivers. It is one of the most beautiful places in Africa. The muezzin call from a hundred mosques and the limpid light makes the rivers glow with a velvet sheen. A herd of sheep and goats wanders along the Nile bank as if out of some pastoral Arcadia. In the nearby zoo park families are out for the evening stroll. Young and old climb on the swings and gently rock. Every movement seems restrained, almost mannered. Courting couples very discreetly sit next to each other on the benches, but do not touch. As the light fades, families gather up their picnic things and greet me with friendly salaams. It feels like a city of eternal tranquillity; a world away from war and famine in the south.

For more than a century this vast disparate country was ruled by a small Khartoum-based elite, a club where everyone knows everyone else; often they are related through blood or marriage. As one clique took power, another would go to senior army officers who are also members of the club, and persuade them to step in. No democratically elected government lasted for more than a few years.

Although everyone in this complex society is Muslim, their Islam comes from different sources with very different practices. The Islam of Khartoum is the Islam of the Saudi peninsula which was brought down the Nile from Egypt or came across the Sahara desert with Arab traders. Most Sudanese Muslims, however, including the Fur, follow Islamic traditions that have been filtered through African cultures over centuries, having spread along North Africa and then continued south through the western end of the Sahara and back eastwards to Sudan along the Sahara trading routes. On the way they accrued an African flavour in their rituals and values.

Things changed when President Omar al-Bashir came to power in a coup in 1989. He appeared to be just another inarticulate tough, straightforward soldier without political skills. He called himself Chairman of the Revolutionary Command Council for National Salvation. The coup was not a violent overthrow or a defenestration but a subtle deposition.

Nor did Bashir seem interested in running the country. So the politicians were still given space to administer the country. The most powerful politician at the time was a subtle but militant Islamist radical, Hassan Turabi, officially speaker of the parliament. Sudan has swung between a democratic, multi-party state and a radical Islamist one.

Ten years on Turabi's lieutenants, mostly European-educated lawyers and doctors, realized that Turabi was a liability and that real power lay with the men with guns. He had treated his acolytes like children but they felt they had come of age. They also saw that Sudan had gone too far down the militant Islamist route. It needed to come in from the cold. Suddenly Turabi was deposed by his lieutenants leaving Bashir in sole control. He got to the top at the same time as the petro-dollars began to flow to the Sudan government from an oil reserve estimated at more than 6.8 billion barrels. The Chinese developed the oil concessions and suddenly the government had money. It could buy weapons – or peace.

The new Sudan government stopped attacking the United States, condemned the 9/11 attacks and offered information about Osama bin Laden. But in its dealings with Sudan, Washington was not only responding to Islamist attacks. The US government was also under pressure from two very disparate groups: conservative evangelical Christians and radical African Americans. Both were concerned about reports of slavery in Sudan, the Christians because those enslaved were Christian, the African Americans because they were black. The tales were spiced with rumours of crucifixions. And extra spice was added by two facts: the perpetrators were apparently 'Arabs', and the country had oil.

For once, the US government was under immense domestic pressure to do something about Africa. America put a huge effort into a peace process in Sudan and, after years of what seemed like fruitless negotiations, the war in the south paused and then halted. The Sudan government and the SPLA finally signed a treaty in Kenya on 9 January 2005 called the Comprehensive Peace Agreement (CPA). On paper, Khartoum accepted the possible separation of the south with a referendum in 2011.

In the meantime, the government and the SPLA were to share power in the run-up to the elections in 2009. The south was to receive 50 per cent of the revenue from oil in the south with immediate effect. The Americans and the rest of the world were serious so the referendum took place. A total of 98 per cent of southerners voted for independence and South Sudan, the world's 153rd state, was born on 1 June 2011.

The CPA dealt with the south but neglect, marginalization and violence are not exclusively southern issues. Sudan has always been run as an empire by the Khartoum elite. Its very lack of comprehensiveness drew attention to other subject peoples like the Beja in the east and the Fur in the west. These subject nations had been growing increasingly desperate, having been ignored and repressed for decades. In Darfur, clashes between the local Fur people and Arab-speaking groups had been on the rise for years.

Finally, in 2002, open rebellion had broken out. Darfur's 6 million people, divided into thirty or so ethnic groups, have a long, complex relationship with each other, but the Fur Sultanate that ruled the region from 1800 onwards had always treated Arabs and non-Arabs with equality, and people adopted multiple identities. Settled farmers, such as the Fur, have always had an alternately cooperative and competitive relationship with the Arabic-speaking pastoralists from the Sahara desert who live a more nomadic existence. In the dry season the nomadic groups would bring their camels and goats into the farming areas and their animals would graze on the harvested fields and fertilize them. Farmers and nomads would exchange grain for meat. But sometimes the pastoralists' animals would eat crops or drink scarce water at the wells, and small battles would break out.

Terrible droughts in the 1980s made life in Darfur more difficult for all. Access to land and water became restricted. Nomads found traditional routes blocked by fences, their animals turned away from watering holes. The government delivered no development or services and it also failed to mediate local disputes justly. Weapons poured into the area in the late 1980s as Colonel Gaddafi tried to take over Chad and create an Arab supremacy in the region. Fights in the past that might have left one or two dead became massacres.

Dating back to the trans-Sahara slave trade, 'Arabs' had always assumed racial superiority over the 'Africans' but in the local context of Darfur, Africans and Arabs were just another distinction in a fiendishly complex matrix of relationships between different groups which were always shifting and evolving. Many of them were cooperative as well as competitive but periodic droughts sharpened competition into conflict. Now, as each side attacked and counterattacked, a new Arab supremacist movement emerged: the Janjaweed, paid and supplied by Khartoum. It proceeded to pillage, rape and murder its way across Darfur.

There was also a copycat factor. How had the southerners achieved 50 per cent of the oil revenues and a seat at the top table of government? By fighting back. The very success of the southern peace talks contributed to the start of war elsewhere. One of the Darfur rebel groups had close links with the SPLA. The government saw that if Darfur was also given a seat at the top table, all the other peoples of Sudan would demand a slice of power and part of the new oil wealth. Its grip on Sudan would be weakened. Realizing that the rebellion in Darfur had to be suppressed at any price, the government followed the imperial tactic of turning an insurgency into a civil war. 'Only one of us will be left standing,' was the comment of a senior Khartoum official.

The rebellion began in earnest in October 2002 when the government sent in the army and also armed and deployed Darfur's neighbours, in this case the Janjaweed, already a formidable and well-equipped force. Mounted on camels and horses, they reached and attacked villages that the army could not reach. In the next few months some 4 million people were driven from their homes and began to starve. The lucky ones made it to refugee camps in Chad and along the border. However, some 200,000 died over the next twenty-four months.

The arrival of African Union troops in 2004 reduced the rate of destruction but the killings and the burning of villages continued. Beshir, claiming national sovereignty, did not want a United Nations peacekeeping force because he knew that the UN, unlike the AU, would bring journalists, and their reports would reveal that his government was supporting the Arab militias. He feared the UN might also try to arrest him for war crimes, on behalf of the International Criminal Court.

The tactics used by Bashir's government were no different from those used by other governments in Africa faced with rebellion. In wars in Congo, Sierra Leone, Liberia, Uganda, Zimbabwe, Mozambique and Angola, millions of civilians were driven from their homes by state armies and rebels. In those cases, the world sighed, resigned itself to bringing food and shelter, and muttered about violent Africa. But in Sudan it would be different. Already mobilized by the war in the south, black America and Christian America as well as liberal America were outraged by the plight of Darfur.

They saw it as 'Arabs' attacking 'Africans', and soon seemed to care more about Sudan, in which it had no direct stake, than it did about Iraq, which it had just invaded, with more than 4000 American soldiers killed in the subsequent occupation. 'Out of Iraq – Into Darfur' ran one slogan. Congress accused the Sudan government of committing genocide but, bogged down in Iraq and Afghanistan, America would not intervene.

The Sudan government had lost its militant Islamists but now it turned America's attacks to its own advantage. Portraying them as American attacks on Islam, the formerly isolated Sudan government was able to garner support among fellow Islamic and Arab countries and even some African governments. Besides, Khartoum had a new ally in China, which has invested hugely in Sudan and buys the bulk of Sudan's oil. Although the Chinese, under pressure from Western countries over Darfur, encouraged the Sudanese to accept a UN–AU hybrid force for Darfur, their principles of non-interference provided Sudan with an ally, investor and protector.

Sudan's ruling elite in Khartoum know that outsiders do not hold Sudan in their hands as the Ottomans or the British once did. The Sudanese know the rest of the world better than the world knows them. They have cleverly judged how far they can defy the United States and the United Nations and get away with it. When Bashir was indicted by the International Criminal Court for crimes against humanity and crimes of genocide and in particular war crimes in Darfur, he barely changed course or tactics and managed to rally support from other African heads of state.

On 9 July 2011, South Sudan, freed from war, celebrated its independence with joy and unbounded optimism. Blessed with oil and minerals and a perfect climate for agriculture, it could become one of Africa's most dynamic countries. But almost half a century of war had left a population without education or development. I paid a visit to Juba, the capital, soon after independence with one question in my mind: What have Southern Sudanese learned from watching the first 50 years of independence in the rest of Africa? I found Juba filled with enterprising young Ugandans and Kenyans willing to work long hours, while former SPLA soldiers of the same age were sitting around. One told me he would just live on his pension. 'I am a soldier. I do not work with my hands.'

The ruling elite, meanwhile, built a new four-lane highway that cut round the centre of Juba for their massive 4x4s to speed on. That is all it is there for. It has no pavements. I would guess about 5 per cent of the town's population had cars. The rest had to walk. When they reach the new road they either walk on it – dangerous – or in the ditch – dirty. My question about what the Southern Sudanese had learned from the rest of Africa was answered.

Almost immediately after independence there were border clashes with dissident rebels that were still backed by Khartoum. This grew into full scale war with both armies attacking civilians who were forced to flee. Ethiopia tried to mediate and a peace agreement was reached on the border, oil and trade.

The next disaster was created by President Salva Kiir who sacked his entire cabinet and decided to make himself dictator. That set off a Dinka–Nuer war at the end of 2013 that was even more vicious than the war for independence. Thousands were killed and Ugandan troops joined in to support President Kiir. More than a million South Sudanese fled into neighbouring countries.

It took three more years for peace to be established but by that time the country was wrecked. In 2017 famine was declared in parts of the country. The Nuer leader, a well-educated man, Riek Machar, returned to South Sudan and became Vice President but spent his time trying to undermine Kiir. The two Sudans live in a dangerous and duplicitous neighbourhood. The entire region may remain unstable. All the region's countries meddle in each other's politics. The Arab Spring reshaped the Arab world, most dramatically Egypt, Tunisia and Libya. The first two have managed to hold together but Libya remains broken in two. Traditionally, Egyptians have regarded the Nile as theirs and have treated Sudan like a recalcitrant younger brother who does not do as he is told. To the east, the old enemy, Christian Ethiopia, has a peace agreement with Eritrea to stop supporting each other's rebels and enemies. Eritrea has been assisting Darfurian rebels and helping dissident Ethiopian groups in Somalia. Ethiopia hosts armed Eritrean dissidents. To the west are the Central African Republic and Chad, both of which are now free of Gadafi's meddling but still linked, politically and ethnically, to groups and rebel movements in Sudan. Chad's president, Idriss Deby, is Zagawa, as are the rebels in Sudan. In the south-west is Congo, a lawless zone where no government's writ runs. And to the north-west is Libya, currently embroiled in its own political strife that could lead to civil war. In the past it sent money and guns through Sudan to fighters in Chad.

If the Arab Spring encouraged governments in North Africa to become more Islamist, Arab Africa and sub-Saharan Africa are likely to grow further apart. North Africa is likely to support Khartoum, while South Sudan is looking to sub-Saharan Africa for allies and trading partners. Its trade routes go through Kenya and Uganda and an oil pipeline to the Kenyan coast. Black Africa is sympathetic towards the SPLA government in Juba. Uganda supported the SPLA in the war. In retaliation, Khartoum supported Ugandan rebels like the Lord's Resistance Army in northern Uganda, one of the most brutal and politically aimless movements to have sprung up in Africa in the last fifty years.

Since 2012 there have been continual clashes as both sides tried to undermine each other and this could escalate to full-scale war. They seem to believe that war is necessary and continue to arm each other's rebels. Perhaps, after nearly 50 years of war, they know no other way. Without a radical change of attitude from both Khartoum and the SPLA, the region – increasingly infiltrated by a militant fundamentalist Islam – will become more unstable and violent in coming years.

8

A tick bigger than the dog
Angola

The polite applause for the speeches gives way to the sound of drumming. A snake of dancers, barefoot, wearing feather head-dresses and red underwear beneath their grass skirts, twists its way among the tables swaying and singing. I turn to the minister to ask where they are from. 'Angola,' he says proudly. 'Yes, but where from in Angola?' He pauses and turns to his neighbour to ask. Then he turns back with a shrug and says, 'They are not from anywhere in particular. They are our idea of Africa.'

We are sitting in an open-air restaurant in Angola's capital, Luanda. It is 1983 and the restaurant has been taken over by the People's Movement for the Liberation of Angola – Workers' Party, the MPLA-PT, which is a copybook reproduction of an East European Communist Party. The food is Portuguese and the restaurant decorated with arches of plastic European flowers. My host, like most of the ruling Angolan elite, has a Portuguese name, Alberto Ribeiro, and an African *nom-de-guerre*, Kabula. Dressed in a dark suit, he wears gold cufflinks, a gold tiepin and a gold watch. I ask him about our forthcoming trip to the east where the civil war rages. His government, backed by the Soviet bloc and Cuba, is fighting guerrillas of the UNITA rebel movement led by Jonas Savimbi. UNITA stands for the National Union for the Total Independence of Angola and it is backed by apartheid South Africa and the United States. The east, he tells me, is Chokwe country, an ancient African kingdom that produced great wood carvings. 'Those are our roots, the real Africa,' he adds.

Mr Ribeiro is a small brown man; but he looks African to me, so I am puzzled by his apparent coyness about Africa. I ask him where he is from. 'Luanda.' I do not want to ask him which ethnic group he is from. In many African countries in those days it was rude to ask about origins and ethnic groups – rather like referring to Africans as natives. So I ask him what language he learned from his mother. 'Portuguese,' is the reply. Mr Ribeiro speaks no African languages. Furthermore, I begin to see that he is immensely proud of having an old Portuguese name and a family history that goes back several generations in Angola. Although he likes the idea of Africa, I sense he is glad that he isn't a 'real African'.

When the drummers and dancers complete their last swirl and troop out, the tables and chairs are pushed back and the diners begin their own dance. The music is Portuguese and Brazilian, not the Congolese rhythms I associate with Africa. And unlike African dances where partners do not touch, these couples clutch each other European-style. They step back and forth, part, clap and advance. They are dancing an old Portuguese peasant dance.

I have been in Angola less than twenty-four hours, on the first of many visits I am to make in the years that follow. It is only later that I began to realize the significance of that first experience and what it told me about the impact of Angolan history on its current politics.

The European engagement with Africa took many forms. Broadly there were four types: firstly, the settler trader who perched on the coast and acted as agent or go-between for overseas businesses;

secondly, the settler farmer who actually took land and became self-sufficient; thirdly the imperial European administrator, who ruled over Africans but neither traded nor took land. Lastly there were – and are – the missionaries, teachers and aid workers who come to Africa to implant their faith or impart their knowledge. When independence came, the European administrators left, although some individuals took jobs with the new African governments. In parts of Africa – Kenya and Zambia, for example – the white settlers and missionaries stayed on and adapted to the new Africa. In Rhodesia, South Africa and Namibia the settlers refused to give up power and Africans had to struggle longer for their right to rule themselves. The Afrikaners in South Africa are the most striking example. For a long time these Dutch settlers supplied food and water to European ships sailing round the Cape of Good Hope. Eventually they took to farming and penetrated deeper inland, conquering and enslaving the local population as well as importing slaves from the Dutch possessions to the east in Asia. But unlike the Portuguese, the Afrikaners did not acknowledge their mixed-race offspring. Indeed, they enslaved them too and turned them into a caste – the Coloureds, keeping them separate by apartheid laws. In Namibia, they call them, and they call themselves, *basters* – bastards.

Settler communities and their mixed-race offspring exist all around the coasts of Africa and along its rivers. In the past most of these communities identified more with their 'home' country than with their black neighbours in Africa. In Freetown, Sierra Leone, descendants of returned slaves from America speak Krio English and identify with Britain and British culture. Banjul – originally Bathurst – in Gambia is a similar settlement. So is Calabar in Nigeria. On the other side of Africa, Arab and Persian families on the Zanzibar islands traded in slaves from the mainland and spices from the islands, intermarrying but keeping culturally and socially separate from Africans who were brought to the islands as slaves. The power of these trading families was broken only by brutal force and the merger of Zanzibar and Tanganyika in 1964. Another extraordinary settlement, though not created for trade, is Liberia. The Americo-Liberians, freed slaves from America, play a similar role in Liberia. Until recently they lived apart from the original inhabitants and often used them as slaves. The Liberian constitution until 1986 read:

> *We the people of the Republic of Liberia were originally inhabitants of the United States of North America . . . From time to time, our number has been increased by migration from America, and by accessions from native tribes . . . we have extended our borders by acquisition of land by honourable purchase from the natives of the country.*

The document accords no political rights to those 'native tribes'.

All round the coasts of Africa these new mixed-race communities became the go-betweens, seeing themselves as separate from the Africans and trading between Africa and Europe. As the relationship grew more and more unbalanced they became like leeches, sucking out slaves, then ivory, gold, rubber, wood and palm oil. In return they brought in manufactured goods from Europe. Outside South Africa and Egypt few African countries developed, or were allowed to develop, manufacturing industries to process or add value to their raw materials. In most cases that was done by the imperial power. Africa was kept as the source of raw materials for processing in Europe. The intermediaries based in Africa's ports dealt with the kings and chiefs in the hinterland and acted as agents for the European companies. In British or French colonies they benefited hugely from imperialism. But in the Portuguese colonies the settler group had a different history and a different relationship with Africa.

In the late fifteenth century Portuguese traders sailed their ships gingerly down the Atlantic coast of Africa in search of gold, silver and jewels. They were not Portuguese imperialists acting on behalf of the Portuguese state. Quite the opposite. Most were rebels or fortune-seekers with no loyalty to anyone except themselves. If anything they were seeking freedom from the Portuguese crown and its tax collectors, who were not powerful enough to control them. The Portuguese coastal traders' relationship to Africans differed from that of their counterparts from France or Britain. Luanda and other Angolan coastal cities were founded by settler colonists who intermarried with local women and created a new ethnic group known as the *mestiços* – the mixed ones.

Some traded back and forth between Africa and Europe, but others began to settle and farm or trade between communities along the African coast. They became embroiled in local politics, fought for kings and chiefs in local wars as mercenaries, married into local families and had mixed-race children. Their weapons and fighting skills were particularly useful and they provided weapons for local kings in return for slaves to work their farms and sell on the other side of the Atlantic. Britain's 1806 ban on slavery only applied to the north Atlantic so throughout the nineteenth century the Portuguese slave trade continued unhindered. Britain was unwilling to prevent its oldest ally taking slaves across the Atlantic to Brazil. This continued until 1903.

One group settled on the uninhabited island of São Tomé, off the coast of what is now Gabon, and planted sugar. Their workers were slaves from the mainland. They traded sugar in exchange for European guns, cloth, metal bars and beads. Slaves and sugar were exceedingly profitable businesses and Portugal tried to bring these adventurers under its control so it could tax them. It was a game of cat and mouse. In 1526 the King of Portugal imposed a governor on São Tomé and started to collect local taxes. The Euro-African traders moved south to Luanda, now the capital of Angola. At the same time new Portuguese merchants arrived in the area from Lisbon bearing charters, the *asiente*, that gave exclusive royal permission to trade in slaves. At the end of the sixteenth century Portugal took over Luanda in the name of the king, and the Euro-Africans were forced to move again, this time further down the coast to Benguela where they set up a slave market, making direct contact with Brazil. Again they escaped from Portugal's control. But they remained in constant danger of being squeezed out of the trade.

The Portuguese imperial venture had been more thoroughgoing than the British or French. Of all the European imperial powers the Portuguese were in Africa longest and penetrated it most deeply. Because they were trader-settlers, rejected by their own country of birth, they created a class of people in Africa, white, mixed-race and black, who had been de-Africanized, spoke no African language and who were, culturally, European. What baffled me was that in every other African struggle such a class would have identified with the colonists, the enemy. In Angola they became the liberationists, or at least claimed to be, formed into a Marxist liberation movement, their credentials approved by the Communists of Moscow and Havana.

How did this happen? Who were these people and why had they ended up on the African side in the war against European imperialism? The story of Angola tells us much about the relationship between Africa and Europe. The fundamental difference between the Portuguese adventurers who settled and married in Africa and the majority of British, Dutch and French traders was that the Portuguese depended for their physical survival on local kings and chiefs while the other Europeans maintained close links with their trading companies in Europe and demanded protection by their national navies. They did not become part of Africa in the way many of the Portuguese families did. The British in particular rarely married Africans and gave no acknowledgement to their mixed-race offspring.

Slave-trade profits for Europe were huge. Voyages could make as much as 200 per cent gains for their investors, though the average for the Royal African Company was around 30 per cent. While the traders grew rich, the effect on Africa was catastrophic. Before the Europeans arrived, slavery was already the norm in most of Africa. Most societies seem to have kept a group in slavery without the rights of property and family that regular members enjoyed. West and Central Africa were vulnerable to the trans-Saharan trade in slaves. Slaves were also traded along the coast and between kingdoms. But the colonization of America, North and South, created an astronomical new demand for slaves. The trade became an industry. With supplies of guns from European traders, local chiefs became despotic rulers. Local rivalries turned into full-scale wars. The supply of arms produced a chain reaction, upsetting local balances of power and resulted in new wars and the taking of yet more slaves. The European slave trade created a malign spiral in Africa. Whole communities fled their lands and in turn became another roving army that ranged across West and Central Africa seeking out more slaves and causing mayhem. Almost all other economic activity was stifled. The huge European sailing boats that bobbed at anchor in Africa's western ports dominated the hinterland for hundreds of miles inland. European slave captains in the late eighteenth century often claimed that Africans would be better off as slaves in America because life in Africa was so appalling. Conditions in some areas were so bad that they may well have believed this to be true. Few acknowledged their own role in bringing about this hellish cycle of war and chaos.

In Benguela and Luanda the slave ships disgorged metal bars, bolts of cloth, booze and beads, and took on board slaves and food and water for the voyage. Both slaves and the food and water were provided by the local Euro-African warlords who controlled the hinterland. One historian of the period, Colin McEvedy, writes in *The Penguin Atlas of African History*:

> *Older kings of the population centres, who based their rule on agricultural tribute and regional trade in locally-produced goods, fell to the military challengers who surrounded themselves with slave retinues and sold captives to Atlantic-orientated trading partners . . . Survivors, driven into cramped, defensible sites strained the capacity of battle-torn lands to support them. Such artificial shortages of land exacerbated the hardships of drought and enlarged the number of hungry refugees vulnerable to capture and sale. Captors might rationalize their enslavement as a last-ditch escape from death by starvation. The remaining population of slaving zones created extra people in order to survive and then came to survive by exporting its surplus members.*

The Portuguese-speaking Euro-African traders also managed the bureaucracy so they could control the times when ships docked and departed. That gave them monopolistic power. Delay could ruin a visiting merchant vessel. Even when the British ban on slavery took effect after 1850, they cut deals with British merchants who continued to ship people across the Atlantic illegally. When the British antislavery patrols began to close down the transatlantic slave trade, they turned to the new commodities demanded by Europe: wax, rubber and ivory. Africans were still needed to transport these bulky goods from the interior of Africa to the coast on foot. Slaves were also needed on the new plantations of cotton and coffee.

In Portuguese territories Euro-African intermediaries had ruled like kings, but after the Second World War they were dealt a terrible blow. Their old enemy, the Portuguese government, needing to solve a land shortage in Portugal, encouraged the migration of hundreds of thousands of poor rural Portuguese to Africa. They arrived on the back of a coffee boom and immediately began to take the jobs that had previously been done by the Euro-Africans. Gradually the old mixed-race families of the coast, with names like Dos Passos, Dos Santos and De Matos, were squeezed out by the new racist policies of Portuguese imperialism. Portugal claimed that Angola was as Portuguese as the Algarve and wanted it ruled directly from Lisbon. Less well-educated white Portuguese were given jobs that had previously belonged to better-educated Euro-Africans.

As they became increasingly marginalized in Angola, these families who had lived on the Angolan coast for centuries turned to the only people who would help them: the Portuguese Communist Party. By historical accident the Portuguese Communist Party was the most Stalinist party in Western Europe, closely allied to the Soviet Union. Being also anti-imperialist, it supported these new recruits from Angola and helped construct a Communist Party for them. It taught them socialist ideology and slogans. Thus was born the People's Movement for the Liberation of Angola, the MPLA. The bourgeois capitalist families of Angola who had grown rich from slavery became Communists, protected and supported by the Soviet Union.

The old slave-trading families had no problem pretending they represented the working class and the peasants of Africa. They were happy enough to chant slogans about solidarity and liberation if that was the price they had to pay for retrieving their birthright as the rulers and exploiters of Angola. Had they not always wanted freedom from metropolitan Portugal? The mystery of how these mixed-race Euro-Africans, who spoke no African language and dressed like wealthy businessmen, had come to rule Angola as Communists began to become clear. The MPLA might rule in the name of The People, but they were not of the people and certainly not of the African people.

In the 1960s Angola produced independence movements along the same lines as the rest of Southern Africa, divided between the black nationalist parties fighting simply to drive out the colonialists and Marxist parties which wanted an economic transformation as well as an anti-imperial struggle. The Marxist MPLA belonged to the second group. Hardly surprisingly the two other parties, UNITA and the FNLA, the National Front for the Liberation of Angola, were Africanist. The FNLA derived its strength from the BaCongo in the north who, in turn, drew inspiration from the militantly Africanist neighbouring state of Zaire, as Congo was called then. It was defeated in the late 1970s and re-emerged as a political force only in 1991 when political parties were allowed to function again. UNITA, led by Jonas Savimbi, split from the FNLA and drew support from his own highland Ovimbundu people. Its slogans were Socialism, Democracy and Negritude. Defenders of Mr Savimbi used to say that Negritude was the philosophy of Senegal's first President, the poet Leopold Senghor. He intended that African values should be stressed, but he was not anti-white or exclusive.

While France and Britain handed their African colonies over to African rulers in 1960s, Marcelo Caetano, the Portuguese dictator who succeeded António de Oliveira Salazar in 1968, decided to stay and fight. He claimed that Portuguese possessions were not colonies but part of Portugal. To maintain the Portuguese empire, Caetano had to send thousands of conscripted young men to war in Africa. By the early 1970s, nearly half the Portuguese budget was being spent on military efforts in Africa. The Portuguese generals knew the wars of independence were unwinnable and on 25 April 1974 they mounted a coup and overthrew Caetano. Portugal's African colonies were suddenly pushed into ill-prepared and precarious independence. In Mozambique, Cape Verde and Guinea-Bissau, Moscow-backed parties took over uncontested. But although Angola's three movements signed up to a power-sharing peace agreement, they almost immediately went to war with each other. The Americans backed the FNLA and later UNITA, the Soviets and Cubans the MPLA and the South Africans UNITA. The Cubans sent planeloads of troops, and in response the South Africans invaded Angola from the south with the encouragement of the Americans, but they were beaten back by superior Cuban firepower. With Cuban help the MPLA were installed in the capital and along the coast. The FNLA fell apart and UNITA withdrew to the south-east.

The Americans did not give up. This was the Cold War and every inch of the globe had to be contested with the Soviet Union. They wanted to deny Angola to the Russians not just because of its oil. Angola has good harbours on the Atlantic seaboard opposite America and the prospect of a Russian naval base there worried Washington. The presence of Cuban and Russian troops in Angola was also seen as a threat to South Africa. There was no doubting where America and Europe stood if they had to choose between apartheid and Communism in Southern Africa.

But the main motive and tactic of the Americans was simply to bleed the Soviet Union by making its Angola venture too expensive. In practice that meant bleeding Angolan peasants, the main sufferers in a war that lasted more than forty years.

Like many of the small civil wars of the Cold War period that appeared to be ideological, fought by proxies of the Marxist Soviet Union and the capitalist United States, the Angolan war was actually the continuation of a local historical conflict. To woo powerful allies, both sides cheerfully sang the hymns of the Soviet Union or the US. The superpowers were fooled into believing they had real disciples.

Naturally the MPLA also had the support of British Communists, who provided my minders on my first visit. Employed by the Angolan government to fill my ears with Soviet-speak, they smugly boasted the 'correct' interpretation of events amid the chaos of Africa. Puritanical and humourless, they prattled on about 'solving the problems of the people' and 'triumphing over capitalist imperialism'. They excused the special 'leaders shops', where you could actually buy something, as providing incentives to retain skilled people who were not necessarily committed to building socialism.

But the contradiction in lifestyle and outlook between the puritanical British Communists and their flashy Angolan employers provided endless entertainment. The Angolan ambassador in London lived in a luxury suite in one of London's most expensive hotels. He would occasionally host a lunch for British journalists in one of London's smartest restaurants. The British journalists and Angola's British propagandists would turn up in jeans and leather jackets. The ambassador would come dressed in a Savile Row suit, sporting a Rolex watch, dripping in gold chains and reeking of expensive aftershave. He was always more comfortable dealing with corporate oil executives than with his fundamentalist Marxist allies in London.

One of the government's claims was that racism did not exist in Angola. It just did not matter what colour you were, they said. There are more mixed-race people in Angola than in most African countries and, with lots of Russians and Cubans around, Luanda boasted a spectrum of colour between white and black. After a while you noticed that this applied only to the upper end of society. If you went to poorer parts of town, everyone was black.

The elite ruling class that had been at the heart of the slave trade for centuries found no difficulty setting up a Communist command economy. For them it was simply a continuation of the monopolies they had enjoyed in the good old days. They managed the economy in a way that made them exceedingly rich. For example, as government officials and ministers they were able to obtain dollars for travel or contracts overseas. They received the dollars at the official rate, 30 kwanza to the dollar. They would then go to the street and sell the dollars at the black market rate of 1200 kwanza to the dollar. With the profit they could buy more dollars at the official rate, go back to the street and sell them at the unofficial rate. Fortunes were made on this currency round-tripping. And since Angola's basic commodities, oil and diamonds, were traded in dollars for its most important imports, guns, it suited Angola's rulers and traders nicely. But Angolans who received fixed salaries in kwanzas were systematically impoverished. They had to pay grotesque prices to survive. In 1988 I found an apple in a Luanda market that cost the equivalent of $52 at the official rate.

At first American support for UNITA was secret, but in 1985 it became formal and overt with the official allocation of $27 million a year in aid. In practice the CIA had probably been supplying and helping the rebel movement since the mid-1970s. This war, American diplomats always made clear, was not winnable, however. There would have to be compromises and a government of national unity.

Savimbi posed as an ally of the West. Called 'the black Mrs Thatcher', he got to meet Ronald Reagan and George Bush in the White House. The right in Europe and America fêted him at dinners and receptions. A British journalist, Fred Bridgland, titled his eulogistic biography, *Savimbi: A Key to Africa*. There is no doubting Savimbi's brilliance. His ability to argue, cajole, charm brought him considerable support. He could switch from fluent Portuguese, to French, to English in mid sentence – not to mention African languages. He was usually described as charismatic, a powerful speaker with a great sense of theatre who gathered around him impressive commanders and spokesmen skilled in public relations.

His international representatives were highly intelligent, articulate people who knew that Westerners expected people to turn up to meetings on time and give quotable replies to questions in plain English – even if they were not particularly truthful answers.

To the MPLA and its supporters, Savimbi's message was more sinister. UNITA represented the deep resentment of the hinterland Africans against the coastal people. Savimbi seemed to be saying, 'We are the real Africans up in the hills and those half-castes down on the coast have been selling us into slavery and ripping us off for centuries. It is time to drive them into the sea and send them back where they came from.' He called for Angola to be rid of 'foreigners'. During the Cold War, foreigners meant Russians and Cubans, but it was always tacitly implied that it also meant the *mestiços*. Petrified by the threat of pogrom if UNITA ever reached Luanda, the MPLA called the members of UNITA primitive savages and whispered about witchcraft and cannibalism conducted by the natives in the interior. Some of it was true.

The contrast with the MPLA's ambassadors and officials, who made up in dress what they lacked in articulacy, could not have been greater. No wonder UNITA won the propaganda war. But the closer you got to UNITA the more worrying it became. The American belief that it represented a democratic movement, or the South African idea that 'blacks like these' should run Africa, was a grisly fantasy. However sophisticated, almost independent-minded, UNITA's representatives appeared to be, they would change into petrified slaves whenever Savimbi appeared. Waiting for him to attend a press conference, they would chat and joke easily with journalists, but as soon as he appeared they turned into grovelling courtiers bowing before their 'President'.

Savimbi's main weapon was always fear. UNITA's other members were mere servants to carry out his wishes. In September 1988 Tito

Chingunji, his able and charming representative in London, said in an interview with me that UNITA was a democratic movement that could change its leader if it wanted to. For this Savimbi recalled him to Jamba and executed him as well as eighteen members of his family.

I first met Savimbi in 1984 at Jamba in the area of south-eastern Angola the Portuguese used to call 'The End of the World'. He had summoned the press from Europe and America to witness the release of Czech engineers whom he had seized from a paper factory near Lobito the previous year. The Czechoslovak government sent a deputy foreign minister to witness their release and bring them home. There may well have been a ransom, too. Hostage taking was a technique that secured Savimbi publicity and made him seem merciful. But his mercy applied only to foreigners, non-African foreigners, that is. There were no MPLA prisoners as far as I could see. His Angolan prisoners were made to become porters, then either forced to join UNITA or shot. Some months earlier the British had been obliged to send a senior diplomat to secure the release of British miners also taken hostage by UNITA that year. Like many, Sir John Leahy was taken in by Savimbi's charm, danced to his drummers and praised UNITA.

The journey to Jamba reveals much about Western alliances in the Cold War. We fly to Kinshasa where we are met on the tarmac by UNITA representatives and Mobutu's secret police, then taken through the VIP lounge without going through immigration. We are driven directly to a house in a Kinshasa suburb and kept there under guard. The following morning before dawn we are taken to the airport again. This time we board an ageing and unmarked propeller-driven Viscount. The pilots are Portuguese. We fly first to Kananga, south-east of Kinshasa, to refuel, and then head south-east across the yellowing plains of an African winter. At sunset the plane turns and drops down into a flat, sandy landscape of dry scrub. There are no tarmac roads and it is hard to spot the landing strip. It is short and bumpy and when the engines reverse they throw up a great cloud of dust that covers the crowd of women dancers who have come to welcome us. As soon as the aircraft stops a gang of men rush out of the bushes dragging branches to pull onto the plane to hide it.

The drummers and dancers are still performing as we clamber into two large army trucks and set off down a rough bush track. If you stand or grip the sides you are in danger of being whacked across the head by low thorn branches or having your hands scraped off. If you lie down you are flung about the floor of the truck. It barely gets out of second gear all night. The night is brilliantly clear and freezing cold, so I wrap myself in a blanket and lie back to look up at the stars. But after a while I notice that we seem to be going in a circle. Orion's belt – in Southern Africa he is lying down – is on our right then turns and is behind us and ends up on our left. I wish I had brought a compass. Later I discover that the airstrip, closely protected by the South African Air Force, is just a few miles from the Namibian border. It is quite near to Savimbi's headquarters at Jamba, but to conceal its whereabouts and add to the drama, visitors are taken on a long night drive.

The dawn arrival is spectacular. The east turns purple, green, pink, red, and the vast ball of sun squeezes over the horizon. The track emerges into a camp beneath the trees and we pull up by a roaring blaze of logs stacked in a pyramid (so much for precautions against fears of being spotted from the air). We clamber off the trucks, stiff and cold, and UNITA soldiers in smart, dark green uniforms show us to our quarters. Each of us has a small grass hut with a wooden bed with sheets and blankets, a mosquito net and an enamel basin on a stand with a jug of water beside it. Nearby is a smaller grass hut with a camp toilet over a hole in the ground. When I get back to the fire a man in evening dress with white gloves is serving coffee from a silver pot. UNITA seems to be running luxury bush safaris, not a bush war.

After breakfast we are taken to the parade ground where, standing under a blazing sun, are rows and rows of UNITA troops, posed stock-still, legs apart, eyes ahead, as rigid as the guard at Buckingham Palace. Two hours later in the full morning heat they were still there. Around the parade ground huge posters in Portuguese and English proclaim UNITA's successes and the leadership of President Jonas Savimbi. The arrival of the fierce-looking bearded 'President' begins with cheering on the edge of the parade ground, and he appears wearing battle dress with his black beret stuck on the side of his head and a pearl-handled revolver at his hip. Big grin on his face and surrounded by his lieutenants, he swaggers through the crowd and skips up onto the podium. He is more like the owner than the leader. As he reaches the sunlight at the centre of the podium, the soldiers let out a mighty shout.

The impressive choreography of the daytime parade does not prepare me for the night spectacle. In the late afternoon Savimbi makes a great show of releasing the Czechs, shaking hands with each one and proclaiming friendship with the Foreign Minister, even though his Soviet masters are firmly committed to UNITA's enemy, the government. Finally the prisoners are put on a plane hired by the Red Cross and flown to South Africa. After dark we are taken to what seems like a stadium, but as we enter it we are blinded by bright arc lamps shining directly at us. It is impossible to make out anything and we are led to seats. At first the stadium seems empty, then as my eyes grow accustomed to the dark, I make out row upon row of eyes and then faces, all around the stadium. They keep absolute silence. Music starts up and searchlights flash and play across the crowd, finally settling on a team of gymnasts who run and skip into the arena to perform, leaping, vaulting and creating tableaux. They are followed by teams of dancers, choirs of women and children and displays of karate and unarmed combat.

As the show ends I am told that Savimbi will see me tonight. I wait in my grass hut until nearly 2.30 a.m. before I am summoned, and I am taken to a bunker, dug underground in the sand. It is plain and rough, looking every inch the headquarters of the guerrilla chief, but security is tight. For all his proclaimed popularity this man fears assassination. I am ushered into a room and he greets me warmly and sits in an easy chair surrounded by five or six of his lieutenants. Although I had spoken to some of them during the day and found them forthcoming, in his presence they are reticent, speaking only when invited. He is well briefed and knows I am no supporter of UNITA, but instead of haranguing me, he uses great charm and not a little humour as he tries to persuade me I am wrong. He does admit, one of the first times in public, that he is taking arms and assistance from South Africa. He justifies it in terms that 'my enemy's enemy is my friend'. He cites Churchill's pact with Stalin to fight Nazi Germany.

The enemy's enemy argument produces a ludicrous contradiction in Angola. At this time the Americans are not openly supporting UNITA, but when they do so in 1985, their policy in Angola results in this: American oil companies and workers and South African miners are protected by Soviet and Cuban troops from attacks by an American and South African backed rebel movement which calls itself socialist. Angola was one of the most bizarre sideshows of the Cold War and also one of the most murderous. America's interest in Angola could be judged by the contrast between its commercial and its political presence there. Chevron, the mighty American oil company, built itself a glistening new high-security block on one of Luanda's hilltop sites. The American embassy was a cramped collection of caravan trailers on a vacant plot on the edge of the diplomatic quarter. The US Congress objected to America building a proper embassy in a 'Communist' country. Most African rulers stayed in power by allying themselves with one side or the other, but some successfully played them off against each other or tried to stay friends with both. Others, like Siad Barre in Somalia and Jerry Rawlings in Ghana, even changed sides and survived.

In Angola, as soon as the Cold War ended the Americans began to organize a peace agreement as if the Angolan civil war had simply been an extension of the Cold War. The MPLA dropped the façade of Marxist-Leninism, allowed other parties to form and called an election. It was held in December 1992 and America backed UNITA to win. Even at this stage they got it wrong. The MPLA was declared the winner, Savimbi rejected the result and a huge bomb went off outside his headquarters in Luanda. UNITA supporters were rounded up and executed. The war restarted.

Did the Americans encourage Savimbi to return to the bush and continue fighting? Having confidently said that he would easily win a free and fair election, the Americans must bear some responsibility for what their man did next but, realizing he could not win, they switched sides and began to help the MPLA defeat UNITA.

And the coastal trading class, now freed from the rhetoric of Marxism, had a new African commodity to sell to the world: oil. After sugar, slaves, rubber, wax, ivory, diamonds, cotton and coffee, African oil, the most lucrative of all, was becoming a strategic issue. Combined imports of Angolan, Nigerian and Algerian oil are close to those of Canada, the United States' main provider. In the longer term the Gulf of Guinea could become vital to the US economy unless replaced by oil obtained in the United States by fracking.

In the mid 1990s, anxious to secure Angolan oil, the US abandoned its previously stated mantra that the war in Angola was not winnable by either side. Having changed sides, the Americans helped the government launch an offensive in 1999 to drive UNITA from its heartland in central Angola. The rebel movement had used the ceasefire period to rearm, and when the war restarted it turned itself from a hit-and-run guerrilla movement into a conventional army. Now it fought with tanks and artillery, held towns and airports and built up redoubts and strongholds. But, abandoned by the Americans, it lost support outside Angola. In 1996 its main ally in Africa, President Mobutu Sese Seko of Congo Zaire, was overthrown. Two years later the Angolan army moved into southern Congo, blocking supplies crossing the border. The Angolans bombed a power station in northern Zambia to warn the Zambian government off its support for UNITA. In Congo-Brazzaville, President Pascal Lissouba, Savimbi's last African friend, was overthrown with the help of Angolan troops. The government retook towns and captured strongholds. With no friendly neighbours or borders to cross to escape from the assault, UNITA was pushed further and further east and south, into the barren lands of Central Africa.

But Savimbi still proved elusive. Eventually the Americans and Israelis, with South African and British mercenaries, helped the Angolan army track down their former ally. Aircraft equipped with infrared sights, and originally provided to American oil companies in Angola to patrol their perimeter fences at night, were now allowed to be used all over Angola to find Savimbi. The information was immediately passed to the Angolan army and air force. The codes for UNITA's secure radio communication system, originally supplied by the CIA, were divulged to the Angolan army, so every movement UNITA made was known instantly by the government.

It paid off. On 22 February 2002 the Angolan government announced that Jonas Savimbi was dead. He had been caught on the banks of the Luvuei River in Moxico province and is said to have died in a fierce gun battle. But it is unlikely that even if he had allowed himself to be captured, Savimbi would have been allowed to live. Twenty-one of his guards died with him. Brigadier Wala, the commander of the unit that found his body, said he died with a gun in his hand, like a soldier, hit by fifteen bullets. A photograph of the body shows him lying on a rubber mattress, bootless and beltless, his underpants visible beneath his dark green combat dress. A soldier lifts a cloth from the body, another is walking casually by. Proof that Jonas Malheiro Savimbi was dead, nothing more. He was buried under a tree near where he fell. There was no gloating, no triumph, but it marked the end of the war in Angola after fifty-one years.

Savimbi was sixty-seven when he died. Why had he carried on? He could have taken his considerable wealth and gone to live in retirement in America or Morocco. He spurned the offer of the vice-presidency. Instead he betrayed every promise he made except that to himself: to be President of Angola. It was the only thing that ever meant anything to him. When the war restarted in 1993 his movement did not concern itself with hearts and minds any more, but brutally forced people to fight and carry for it. Savimbi abandoned his Maoist training, which had taught him to treat the peasants as the sea for his guerrilla fighters to swim in. Now his troops forced people to flee to the towns which he then surrounded and tried to starve into submission. UNITA shot down planes with UN or Red Cross markings carrying food aid. On the ground his soldiers planted land-mines near villages on paths to streams and fields as Savimbi pursued the last hopeless threads of his dream. The war had lasted over 40 years and cost more than 400,000 lives. For years later landmines continued to kill and maim.

And the victors? The MPLA now showed itself in all its greed and corruption. The word 'corruption' suggests a functioning system has gone rotten. In parts of Africa, corruption, like an advanced form of cancer, has taken over the whole body. It is the system. As John Robertson, a Zimbabwean economist, says, 'We imagine corruption to be like a tick on a dog. There are some places in Africa where the tick is bigger than the dog.'

Angola's few principled Marxists were sidelined or retired. Those who remained called themselves 'pragmatic'. Today many are extremely wealthy – the oligarchs of Angola. Human Rights Watch said that between 1997 and 2002 unaccounted funds amounted to $4.22 billion. At the same time, the UN funded some $6 billion worth of public and private initiatives in Angola but the government has never accounted for this money. Not much had changed by 2006 when Angola's income leapt to over $30 billion – derived from 585 million barrels of oil per day. In that year, Africa – the whole continent – received $32.62 billion in aid. And according to the IMF, Angola is expected to grow by 15–20 per cent a year for the next decade and maybe beyond. But the money stays with the top 5 per cent of the population. Spread out among all Angolans each one would receive about $2000 a year, putting it 63rd in the list of countries ranked by income per head and above Romania. In 2008 Angola was 162nd out of 177 countries in the Human Development Index. Ninety-five per cent of Angola's 16 million people were living on less than a dollar a day.

Examples abound of the elite's greedy grab for assets. Take for example housing in Luanda. Blocks of flats built in the 1950s and 1960s for the influx of Portuguese immigrants have housed the poor since 1974. After 2000, party bosses seized them and sold them to themselves for a few hundred dollars. The poor were evicted, the flats done up and rented out for thousands of dollars a month: $2000 a month for a two-roomed apartment in central Luanda is common. In 2011 and 2012 Luanda was the most expensive city in the world.

Meanwhile its health statistics are horrendous. A quarter of Angolans die before the age of five – in 2006 it had the second worst rate in the world for child mortality. Its education system exists only for the rich. Sixty per cent of Angolans are illiterate, but in 1995 the government spent more than a third of the education budget on scholarships and grants to send Angolan children overseas for university education. Guess whose children won the scholarships.

After the disaster of 1992 the MPLA did not hold another election for 16 years. When it did, it was a done deal, full of fraud and intimidation. The MPLA won 80 per cent of the vote and UNITA a mere 10 per cent. Angola's oil wealth protects it from Western pressure for democratisation. Another election was held in August 2012. UNITA increased its vote by 16 per cent and it was marked by a higher abstention rate, but never for a moment could anyone dream that the ruling party might be dislodged by people voting. Its wealth also enables it to buy off other political aspirants, so no popular leadership has yet emerged. And the MPLA has a new friend: China, the old supporter of its rival, UNITA. China's non-interference policy means it treats with good and bad governments in the same way. It does not ask any questions about how the country is ruled. As long as a government recognizes China and not Taiwan, Beijing has no interest in how it treats its citizens or whether the ruling elite steals from the public purse.

The IMF and Western donors had tried for years to get the Angolan government to be more accountable and transparent in its government spending. Just as it seemed Angola was about to give way and conclude a deal with the IMF, the Chinese Eximbank stepped in with a $2 billion loan at 1.5 per cent over seventeen years in return for guaranteed supplies of oil. President José Eduardo dos Santos and his cronies were allowed to continue business as usual. Donors who were trying to get the government to be more transparent in its accounting and to do something about poverty in Angola were sidestepped. The poor continued to be poor.

With such friends and finance, the Angolan ruling elite strengthened its grip on power. Maybe it feels confident it can buy people off and that the oil money will gradually lift the whole country out of poverty, eventually bringing benefits to ordinary people whether the government directs it towards them or not. But the evidence from other African oil states is that, unless the government consciously directs funds towards infrastructure and services that help the people, the rich get richer and the poor get poorer. An IMF report states that oil-rich African countries have no better record of lifting their populations out of poverty or reaching the Millennium Development Goals than countries without oil. Oil creates an enclave economy: the money comes directly into the treasury straight from oil companies and no mechanism exists to spread it around. Once again Angola's wealth is being ripped out by people perching on the edge of Africa who have more in common with outsiders than with ordinary Angolans. Angolans gain nothing from their country's oil riches, and if they want to change their lives they will have to fight. There is widespread anger and disaffection, but no sign yet of a national movement to challenge the government. But as a new generation comes through, feelings of anger at the oppression and lack of jobs will grow. This anger at the un-African elite is the one element of Savimbi's movement that may survive. Perhaps Angola needs a socialist party.

After the war ended I visited Luanda, and was passing through the lobby of the Meridien Hotel, the Mecca of visiting businessmen. Sitting waiting on a sofa, digging around in a smart black briefcase, was a bull-built white man who could only have been an Afrikaner. He had a face like a boxer's protected by puffy, hard, sunburned skin. He seemed to take pride in his battered, seen-it-all looks. I asked him if he had been in Angola before and he shot me a glance that said, 'Yes, but I am not going to talk about it.' I persisted and he admitted that he had been a South African special forces officer and had spent a lot of time in Angola's brutal bush war. 'Things must have changed a bit since those times,' I ventured.

'Ach,' he said with a shrug. 'The shit changes but the flies stay the same.'

9

Missing the story and the sequel
Burundi and Rwanda

Just when you think the Devil has conquered the earth, Africa throws up a Job, a saviour, one just man who redeems all.

It is 1994 and I am heading into the densely forested mountains of southern Burundi. There has been a massacre somewhere in these huge, hump-backed hills, we have been told, but in the capital, Bujumbura, no-one is sure of the name of the place or exactly where it is. At furious speed, we swing blindly round sharp bends on a new road that winds up into the mountains away from the lake. The driver, a big, ill-tempered man, ignores our pleas to calm down and flings the four-wheeled drive around like a rally driver, veering between sheer rock face on one side and sheer drop on the other.

No-one else is travelling this route `– bad people are on the rampage. In the past week vehicles have been attacked and their occupants slaughtered on this road. Suddenly we round a bend and there is a gang of children in front of us, naked to the waist. They seem to be carrying mini bows and arrows and spears. They are. As we flash past they stand back and stare. I realize they are not children but Batwa, pygmy people on a hunt. Further on, the road is still under construction and we pass a gang of about fifty Chinese workers in blue uniforms with dumper trucks, heavy rollers and excavators. They wave rather formally, seemingly oblivious to the fact they are in a war zone.

Rwanda 1994 is what the world now knows about. Genocide. But in Burundi too, politics conspired to create a narrative of racial slaughter and repeat it again and again and again. The country was ruled by Tutsis since independence in 1962. There were massacres here in 1965, 1969, 1972, 1988, 1991 and now this latest one triggered by the murder of the first ever Hutu President in 1993, a year after he was elected. After his election President Melchior Ndadaye had moved quickly to replace Tutsi dominance at all levels of government. He restored land taken from Hutus, brought back Hutu exiles and, most dangerous of all, tried to establish ethnic balance in the army. That was too much for a group of Tutsi officers, and they killed Ndadaye and other Hutu leaders and overthrew the government. The Hutus rose in fury and started killing Tutsis all over the country. The Tutsis, backed by the army in many cases, responded in kind. For a week, neighbour turned on neighbour and gangs armed with machetes, spears and sharpened bamboos stabbed and hacked and slashed. Women and children were not spared. Not even babies. No-one knows how many have died, maybe 200,000. Maybe more. A couple of months later it is still rumbling on.

We stop at an old mission church perched atop a massive hill like a toy crown. From here we can see for miles across rolling forests, grassland and terraced fields that drop more than 3000 feet into steep valleys dotted with huts and banana plantations. The priest is away, but nervous Church workers give us directions. A single Tutsi soldier in a red tracksuit is guarding a group of Hutus who have taken refuge in the old red brick mission buildings. He barely acknowledges us when we greet him, and when we ask why these Hutus are sheltering there, he asks truculently why we want to know. When we ask if people have been killed in the area, he giggles. The Hutu refugees do not want to talk at all. They look scared. Maybe they do not speak French.

We move on, and eventually we reach Musenyi, a steep green hill scabbed with the burnt-out remains of villages. The fields are intact but the huts are deserted and windowless – like blind people with black holes where once there were shining eyes. A smell of burned grass and wood hangs in the air and something else – foul.

We find a group of people picking through the remains of a homestead: broken pots and a charred mattress – people are so poor here they do not leave much behind when they flee or die. What we have been told seems to be true. A Tutsi gang came to this area and sought out all the Hutu homes. They caught Hutus and killed them, men, women and children. Then they stole their goods and crops and burned their homes. This is extermination, final. There is not much more you can say about it. The victims cannot speak, the perpetrators will not tell you the truth, a witness who survived would not dare.

As we are leaving our driver tells us that there are some survivors living in a house further down the hill. We turn back and head down to a perfectly kept pink brick house with a corrugated iron roof, a thick hedge round it and a neat well-swept avenue of pines leading up to the porch.

Jean-Baptiste Nteturuye is a retired policeman. Tall, dignified, aristocratic-looking, he wears an old, faded white jacket immaculately cared for, a French beret, and gleaming black shoes that have been stitched and restitched. Mr Nteturuye used to be a sub-chief in colonial times. Now he is an angry man. His back rooms are filled with Hutu families – thirty-eight people packed on the floor, terrified but alive. That in itself is not strange in these troubled times. Refugees and the homeless crowd into the houses of their relatives until they feel safe enough to return home. What is strange is that all the guests in Mr Nteturuye's house are Hutus but Mr Nteturuye is a Tutsi.

They are stereotypical in every way. Mr Nteturuye is tall, straight, long-faced and fine-featured, a typical Tutsi. His house, with corrugated tin roof and neat lawn, proclaims his professional status and hard work. His guests are small, huddled peasants and their homes are – or were – mud and thatch huts. He gave them refuge and when the Tutsi killers came, he barred the door and told them that if they wanted to kill 'his guests' they would have to kill him first. It worked. The killers backed off, daunted by the audacity of the old man. But now they wait and watch. He has no weapon, no defence. Only his personal authority stands between his guests and death. If they leave his house they will be killed. For the moment they are safe.

He shows me a list of the names of his guests and their children in his old-fashioned copperplate handwriting. Squatting in the back parlour of his house are men, women and children. They have filthy clothes and no shoes and they avert their eyes, reluctant to talk. One of the women says they were attacked by a group of Tutsis from the next hill. They killed four people in her family and burned the house. She and the children fled into the forest and hid until Mr Nteturuye gave them shelter. Why did he take in all these people? 'Because they are my friends,' he says. Isn't it dangerous? 'Yes, I am afraid. I have been sent a letter threatening me because I am protecting them.'

No-one, neither Mr Nteturuye, nor the Hutus, nor the soldier, could explain how the two groups had lived so close for so long with so much apparent hatred just under the surface. People do not like to talk about it. They shy away from the subject or speak fearfully, trying to avoid the emotions it evokes. Sometimes they just shrug in acceptance of the inevitability of it all: Hutus and Tutsis cannot live together. Against that dark inevitability, Mr Nteturuye seems like a tiny but brilliant spark of hope.

This is January 1994, the eve of things to come in Rwanda.

The relationship between Hutus and Tutsis is unique, complex and very difficult for outsiders to comprehend. There are no words in English to describe it. Caste, class, race or tribe do not match the reality. Its origins are hotly disputed. The colonial version was that Batwa pygmy hunter-gatherers were here first. Then came the short, dark, round-headed Hutu farmers, who settled the land. Tutsis were tall, long-faced cattle keepers who wandered down from north-east Africa in the sixteenth and seventeenth centuries and, according to this version, being a superior race, dominated the inferior Hutus and ruled over them. They formed two powerful kingdoms with similar but different political and social structures: Rwanda and Urundi – as Burundi was called then. When that even more superior race, the Germans, made the kingdom part of German East Africa in 1890, they set in law what they perceived as the racial hierarchy. They did not believe that primitive Africans could possibly have a complex society, and so they strengthened the racial hierarchy based on their interpretation of the height and features of the population. What had been fairly fluid and flexible categories, often overlapping, became rigid, absolute and separate. The Belgians, who took over the administration of Burundi and Rwanda from Germany after the First World War, classified every citizen as Hutu or Tutsi and selected the 'superior' Tutsis to be educated as teachers, priests and doctors.

The colonial view provoked a counter-interpretation. This maintained that before the Germans took over the two kingdoms, Rwanda and Burundi, Hutus and Tutsis lived together in harmony. Indeed, some even maintain that Hutu and Tutsi are not separate but one and the same people, but that the Tutsis became tall and slim through eating more meat and drinking milk. According to this version, it was the Belgian imperialists who separated them, categorized them and created antagonism between them so they could rule them more easily. What we do know is that formerly the two groups were socially integrated with some intermarriage between them. Families and individuals could even move from Hutu to Tutsi or vice versa, but the distinction was not blurred. The division did not make these kingdoms weak. On the contrary, there was considerable 'national' solidarity. In the nineteenth century both Rwanda and Burundi were strongly defended territories. Slave traders learned to respect them.

Whatever its origins, the Hutu–Tutsi division still exists in the psychology and culture of Rwanda and Burundi and also in other parts of the Great Lakes region of the Rift Valley. In Uganda the two groups are the Bahima – the Tutsi equivalent; and the Bahiru – the Hutus. In eastern Congo there are the Banyamulenge, a group of Tutsis who live up in the hills above Lake Tanganyika. They do not have a Hutu equivalent. In each area the relationship is slightly different.

Despite the best efforts of the present Rwandan government to pretend you cannot tell Hutu and Tutsi apart, the categories and the stereotypes are alive and well. There are some short dark Swedes and some tall blond Turks, but not many. It is impossible, even in towns, not to be either Hutu or Tutsi unless you are Batwa. Physical characteristics, however, are not always the determinant. During the Rwanda genocide when outsiders came to kill, they often mistook Hutus for Tutsis. Burundi and Rwanda are organized and administered not village by village but hill by hill, and neighbours on every hill know who is Hutu and who is Tutsi. Besides, in Rwanda until the genocide, national identity cards carried the tag, Hutu, Tutsi or Batwa.

It is easy to think of precolonial Africa as fixed and static, but of course it was as dynamic and changing as any other human society. There was intermarriage and social mobility, so Hutus could gain Tutsi status by owning cattle and Tutsis became Hutu if they lost their cattle. Most significantly of all, they speak the same language, have the same names, follow the same cultural customs and worship the same gods. In short, they were part of the same society, the same ethnicity. They cannot be described as separate tribes. Concepts of caste and class are present and – it has to be said – so are genes, race.

The complex relationship was based in the past on both inter-dependency and power. Cattle-keeping Tutsis traded milk and meat for Hutu farmers' grain and vegetables. The Tutsis formed a sort of aristocracy, but it was not clear-cut. In Rwanda a king, the Mwami, held the balance of power between them. In Burundi a princely caste, the Ganwa, were the powerful arbiters. On the whole the Tutsi, about one-sixth of the Hutus in numbers in Rwanda and Burundi, were the bosses. On some issues, however, Hutu chiefs were more powerful than Tutsis. In Rwanda there were traditionally three chiefs on a single hill, each dealing with different matters, one for marriage and family matters, one for land disputes and one for cattle. These chiefs could be Hutu or Tutsi.

Although mediated by many checks and balances, the relation-ship was not harmonious before the Europeans came. Occasionally violence broke out and people were killed. Although Burundi was technically a kingdom before colonial rule, the Mwami of Burundi was weak and the political arena was dominated by the Ganwa, who existed above the Hutu–Tutsi divide. One reason why the German take-over of Burundi was relatively easy was that the Ganwa were divided over who should be king. There was also considerable anti-Ganwa unrest, a sort of class war. Conflict at this time was not pri-marily between Hutu and Tutsi, though the division was at the heart of politics. The title of one Hutu leader was 'killer of Tutsis'.

In 1919 Belgium took over Rwanda and Burundi from Germany under a League of Nations mandate. They stratified Burundian soci-ety and strengthened the power of chiefs. The Belgians disliked and mistrusted the Mwami but they did not dare to get rid of him.

By 1929 all local chiefs were Tutsi, put there because of their Western education and connections with the Belgians. Their power did not come from any intrinsic or traditional authority. When there was an anti-colonial uprising, Tutsis were attacked because the people saw them as part of Belgian imperialism.

Independence came sooner than the Belgians had anticipated after the Second World War. The Catholic Church, the most powerful institution in the country after the government, backed the Hutu and democracy although most of the educated elite were Tutsi. In its last days the Belgian administration also switched support from Tutsis to Hutus. Tutsi leaders knew that if they waited for democratic elections, they would be destroyed by demographics. So they sought international support for a more militant anti-colonialism and demanded immediate independence. If they could exploit their current dominance and seize power quickly in a revolution as the Belgians departed, they stood a chance.

Politics and society in pre-independence Burundi became polarized around the Hutu–Tutsi divide. The Tutsis did not have the numbers to win an election. Violent events in Rwanda next door heightened the tension, and thousands of fleeing Tutsi arrived in Burundi, a portent of what might happen to the Burundian Tutsis. Political parties, somewhat mixed to begin with, became mere vehicles for Hutu and Tutsi power.

In the first years of independence the Mwami himself was the only unifying factor as he tried to create ethnic balance in the government. But after months of bloody battles and massacres, the Tutsi-dominated army and *gendarmerie* seized power in 1964 and executed the entire Hutu political elite. A few months later, Captain Michel Micombero drove out the Mwami, too, and took over as President.

Tutsi rule lasted until August 1993 when, amid a spate of post-

Cold War elections across Africa, Ndadaye was elected President, the first Hutu ever to become the ruler of Burundi. In October he was murdered by Tutsi extremists. His death was followed by the massacre of between 100,000 and 200,000 people in the space of one week as Hutus and Tutsis turned on each other. In addition nearly a million people, one-fifth of the population, were driven from their homes. According to an international inquiry into human rights violations in Burundi, Hutus and Tutsis were killed in about equal numbers. Reviewing the report, Réné Lemarchand wrote in *Burundi Ethnic Conflict and Genocide*:

> *A blind rage suddenly seized Frodebu militants and peasants alike in almost every province, and they killed every Tutsi in sight . . . the picture that emerges is one of unadulterated savagery. In one commune after another, scores of men, women and children were hacked to pieces with machetes, speared or clubbed to death, or doused with kerosene and burned alive.*

It was that sort of sporadic massacre and counter-massacre that I witnessed in January the following year. From independence until the late 1980s, Africa and the rest of the world had looked the other way. After the 1993 killings however, the United Nations became involved and tried to broker a peace agreement. The following year Julius Nyerere, the former President of Tanzania, took over the peace talks and in turn passed the process on to Nelson Mandela. Since then, regional and international players have remained closely engaged. In 2001 a transitional government was installed, but the most militant of the Hutu groups stayed out, either in the bush or in eastern Congo. Peace talks punctuated by sporadic fighting and massacres seemed to end in 2005 with two elections that both showed overwhelming support for power sharing. Another Hutu, Pierre

Nkurunziza, became President, but the reform of the army, the crucial internal factor since independence, was still unresolved.

Although driven by their own dynamics, Rwanda and Burundi are deeply affected by events in the region. In eastern Congo armed Burundian gangs can live well and have little incentive to return to a peaceful Burundi. Disarming militant Hutu groups hiding there and persuading them to return to Burundi in peace has proved difficult.

Like Burundi, precolonial Rwanda was riven by a power struggle. In Rwanda it was between the centre of power, the Mwami, and the periphery – especially in the north-west, where local Hutu kings still ruled independently. Less than 100 in number in 1914, the Germans could not rule absolutely. They had to play divide and rule, allying themselves with the king. As in so many kingdoms and states in precolonial Africa, the king, Mwami Yuhi Musinga, saw these white visitors as a useful short-term buttress to his power. The Germans – or at least white invaders – turned out not to be short-term visitors.

Although they strengthened the power of the king and created a simple hierarchy through which they could rule, the Germans began to manipulate, distort and rework what they would later claim was African tradition. Meanwhile they removed checks and balances and other complications and local variations. The Belgians continued the process, replacing complex and fluid Rwandan institutions with a centralized, tiered power structure, a hybrid of useful bits of Rwandan tradition blended with their own European model. They promoted the 'racially superior' Tutsis and in 1929 they abolished the system of multiple chiefs and replaced them with one, invariably a Tutsi, so that by the end of Belgian rule forty-three out of forty-five chiefs were Tutsis.

The Belgians introduced European feudal practice as well. Land, instead of being held by the people and supervised by the chief, became part of the king's gift, so that it could be 'granted' to certain chiefs, giving them much more power than they had traditionally held, though it was exercised only with the blessing of the Belgian overlords.

Only after the Second World War did Hutus begin to get education and advancement. Too late the Belgians realized that independence meant democratic elections and democratic elections would put power in the hands of the Hutus. By then the Tutsi–Hutu divide was *the* division in Rwandan society. In 1959 violence broke out and thousands of Tutsis fled the country, many to Uganda. In communal elections in 1960 Hutu parties won 84 per cent of the seats and in national legislature elections the following year they won 78 per cent. This led to the same bizarre contradiction as in Burundi. The Tutsi bourgeoisie and overlords, seeing their power diminishing rapidly, demanded immediate independence rather than a process towards democracy. So they aligned themselves with the Soviet Union and radical international anti-imperialism. The Hutus however, demanded elections rather than independence in order to demonstrate their numerical superiority. They were delighted at the results of the Belgian-organized poll. But independence led to more violence and the flight of hundreds of thousands of Tutsis. Rwanda became a Hutu-dominated state with the surviving Tutsis a shamed and oppressed minority.

The children of the Rwandan Tutsis who had fled north to Uganda from the genocide of 1959 grew up stateless, mainly in refugee camps. Radicalized by the experience, many were recruited by Yoweri Museveni, himself a Ugandan 'Tutsi', when he began his rebellion in Uganda in the early 1980s. In fact his National Resistance Army was led mainly by Rwandan Tutsis. Fred Rwigema ended up as chief of staff and Paul Kagame – who later became President of Rwanda – was head of military intelligence. They won the war for Museveni and became powerful ministers and officials in the new Ugandan government. But in their hearts they wanted to go back to Rwanda and rule their own country. When Museveni refused to give them land and full citizenship in Uganda, they decided to go home and kick the door down. Morally their case was unquestionable. Politically it was dubious. Militarily it was insane.

For thirty years the people of Rwanda had been fed the propaganda of the 'revolution' that kept Habyarimana and the Hutus in power. They were told that the former Tutsi overlords, lackeys of the colonialists, had been overthrown in that revolution and that the masses had triumphed. Tutsis were discriminated against in schools, in the job market and in the army. Now a Tutsi army was on the march, invading their homeland!

The Rwandan Patriotic Front was made up of Tutsis who had grown up in exile and did not even speak French. They tried to use the same military tactics they had used in Uganda: win over the local people by treating them well and explain why they were fighting; only then attack military and administrative targets. But a million Hutus in north-east Rwanda did not get the message and did not wait to hear it. They fled. By 1992 Kigali was swollen with huge numbers of internally displaced refugees in camps around its edges. As in so many African wars, sporadic fighting flared and died while the leaders and their officials met and talked about a deal. In Rwanda a ceasefire was signed in July 1992 and the final details of the establishment of a broad-based government, including representatives of both sides, were agreed by early 1993. Six hundred RPF troops were lodged in Kigali – a symbolic gesture of trust. Everyone knew the dangers – they had seen what had happened in Burundi that year. But when President Juvenal Habyarimana boarded his plane at Dar es Salaam on 6 April 1994 most people believed that peace was probable.

As the aircraft was coming in to land at Kigali airport, it was hit by missiles fired from the ground. Exactly who fired them and why has never been made public. His death triggered the most rapid genocide in recorded history. The killing began that night and ended six weeks later. By then some 800,000 people had been murdered, mostly with spears, knives and machetes.

By 1994 I had covered some twenty wars as a journalist, most of them in Africa. Rwanda's horrors made a mockery of the media clichés of death and destruction.

I am sitting in a bar on the Ugandan border. I have an hour to send my story. The journalist's thrill at telling an important story to the world shrivels in the face of what I have just seen and heard. I wait for the rush of adrenalin that comes with hitting the keys when you start a big story. Nothing happens. I feel numb. I light a cigarette and start again. Then have another cigarette, and then a beer. Time is ticking away. Nothing is happening. Images but no focus. No words. The mechanism in my brain that changes images into words is jammed. I begin to panic. The deadline is near. I start a message to the news editor to explain why the story is late and I begin it, 'I do not want to tell you what I saw today . . .' I stare at the words and realize this is the story. Why should my aged parents be presented with this vision of hell at their breakfast table? How could I tell my wife what I have seen and smelt? And what if my children should glimpse my name in the paper and read what I wrote as they got ready for school? Why should anyone need to be told these things?

Like an explosion so close that it numbs the brain, Rwanda left no immediate impression. Other journalists I have spoken to admitted the same sensation. Almost no reporters who covered the genocide as it was happening wrote anything memorable. For once, the journalists who came after and heard the stories second hand created the bigger, more vivid picture.

The massacres in Burundi the previous year suggested that the world would not be moved by mass murder in Rwanda. Not a single staff journalist from the British press had gone to Burundi as genocide happened. It barely made the headlines and was hardly reported in national newspapers or on national radio in Britain. Any news editor or desk officer who made a check through the records would have found that massacres of Hutus and Tutsis in Rwanda and Burundi were common in the second half of the twentieth century. The word 'genocide' was frequently used but no-one had ever proposed sending a UN peacekeeping army to stop the massacres. So why should they now? It was a train smash in a faraway country which no-one knew or cared about.

The US was still traumatized by its experience in Somalia, where eighteen of its special forces had died on a single night the previous October. As far as Washington was concerned Rwanda was Africa and Africa was Somalia. President Clinton was not going to allow the UN – let alone the US – to get sucked into local conflicts that might end in another disaster. But without America's airlift and financial muscle any UN peacekeeping operation would be stillborn. For London, Rwanda, a former Belgian colony, was of little interest to the Foreign Office, which had been forced to cut its staffing levels in Africa through the 1980s and early 1990s. Rwanda had no diplomatic, historical or commercial links with Britain and no media editor had put the story on the front page. Rwanda was ignored. As the crisis developed, the Foreign Secretary, Douglas Hurd, was being briefed by officials whose only source of information was CNN.

So two weeks into the slaughter the Clinton government, supported by Britain, pushed the UN Security Council to reduce the peacekeeping force in Rwanda to just 270 men, despite the pleas of its commander, General Romeo Dallaire, who insisted that a UN military presence could make a difference. Dallaire managed to hold onto 400 troops. The Americans and British tried to block the use of the word 'genocide' in the Security Council to describe what was happening in Rwanda, because it would, by international law, have forced them to act. Later Bill Clinton and Madeleine Albright, then his representative at the UN, expressed regret for this but their British counterparts, Prime Minister John Major, Douglas Hurd and Baroness Lynda Chalker, then Minister for Africa, said nothing. The pivotal player at the UN dealing with the dispatches from the UN force commander in Kigali at the time was Kofi Annan, then Under-Secretary General for Peacekeeping. He did not treat General Dallaire's reports and pleas with urgency. Annan went on to become Secretary General and his deputy and successor at Peacekeeping, Syed Iqbal Riza, became his *chef de cabinet*. Despite the retrospective breast-beating, no-one resigned over Rwanda and nobody's career was damaged.

With hindsight it is obvious that the world's political leaders and opinion formers failed Rwanda in 1994. Before the Rwanda genocide it was different. I regarded myself as someone who had pushed the plight of Africa in the mainstream media and covered wars that others had not bothered with. But years of dealing with tough-minded news editors who did not want to know about another small, incomprehensible and irrelevant war in Africa made me sceptical about getting Rwanda onto the front page. For most people Rwanda was just that – another incomprehensible and irrelevant small war in Africa. The antagonists spoke French. They had silly names: Hutu and Tutsi? News editors giggled and spoke about Tutus and Whoopsies in news conferences. Even when they took it seriously they came up against an extremely complicated history, and they doubted that readers needed to know about it.

But Rwanda became a turning point. The enormity of it began to sink in when the killing was almost over. Afterwards the UN and the northern hemisphere powers began to pay more attention to Africa and its wars. Burundi suddenly became a big issue;

intervention in eastern Congo was contemplated. In 2000 Britain intervened in Sierra Leone; France sent troops to Côte d'Ivoire in 2004. The cry, 'Remember Rwanda,' led to intervention in Somalia in 1992 – disastrously – and in eastern Congo and Darfur in 2003. The Americans pushed Darfur up the international agenda the following year. So the Western world did, it seems, learn something from April 1994, and in the 'never again' aftermath the concept of the Responsibility to Protect was born. The failure in Rwanda became a marker for subsequent conflicts when huge numbers of civilians were under threat.

On 7 April all major newspapers reported the plane crash that killed the President and followed it with reports of the murder of ten Belgian soldiers and then the evacuation of foreigners. There was little attempt to analyse Rwanda's particular politics beyond the fact there had been a civil war that had been frozen by the Arusha accords. *The Times* treated it as a 'wildlife in danger' story and ran several articles about the fate of the Rwandan gorillas. For most newspapers the foreign story of the moment was Bosnia, and its coverage was already stretching media budgets and staffing levels.

Besides, another global African story was developing: the end of apartheid and the first democratic election in South Africa. The mainstream Western press was not able to cover more than one Africa story at a time. In Washington, according to Madeleine Albright, not one question was asked about Rwanda at State Department briefings throughout that period. Many Western commentators were predicting a bloodbath in South Africa. They said that the African National Congress would break its promises and begin a campaign of murder and destabilization. Others pointed to the continuing violence in KwaZulu Natal, and predicted tribal massacres between Zulu and Xhosa. Chief Mangosuthu Buthelezi, the leader of the Zulu Inkatha movement, had not agreed to take part in the election, and more and more people were dying in the sporadic warfare between Inkatha and the ANC. Only days before the election, Buthelezi signed an agreement. South Africa went to the polls on 27 April, and voting was vast and peaceful. Journalists who headed to KwaZulu Natal expecting war were disappointed. They included most of the stringers for the world's press based in Nairobi who would have covered Rwanda. In the search for blood in South Africa we all missed one of the worst mass murders of all time.

Those who did go to Rwanda straight after 6 April accepted the diplomats' analysis that the killing of civilians was a renewed civil war that had become ethnic. This interpretation made some sense: Hutus were afraid that Tutsi rule would be restored if the RPF overran the country. They were attacking their Tutsi neighbours because they saw them as RPF supporters, a fifth column. After the killing of President Ndadaye by Tutsi soldiers in Burundi, it was easy to persuade Hutus in Rwanda that this was a Tutsi conspiracy to re-establish Tutsi supremacy in both countries. No-one knew for sure who had shot down the plane and killed President Habyarimana, but the government radio told Hutus that it was the RPF. The RPF abandoned the ceasefire and advanced. The civil war was resumed. In Kigali the presidential guard attacked the 600-strong contingent of RPF fighters that had come to the capital to protect opposition politicians who came into government as part of the Arusha accords.

At first the killings of civilians were reported in the context of renewed fighting between the RPF and government troops, not in the context of mass murder. In Kigali General Dallaire, who briefed the journalists every day, spoke not about genocide but about re-establishing the ceasefire. The journalists used language that reinforced the image of another African outbreak of 'tribal violence'. The local Reuters correspondent, Thadée Nsengiyaremye, reported 'gangs of youths settling tribal scores hacking and clubbing people to death'. He quoted Western diplomats as saying, 'continuing tribal slaughter between the Hutu majority and Tutsi minority in the Central African states was feared . . .'

Those early reports of 'tribal bloodletting' also implied that Tutsis were trying to take over Rwanda and were killing Hutus indiscriminately. The assumption was that the anarchy created by renewed fighting had allowed these 'ancient tribal hatreds' to burst forth and that they could be suppressed only by the re-establishment of a ceasefire. In New York Iqbal Riza at UN Peacekeeping was giving the Security Council similar descriptions of 'chaotic, ethnic, random killings'.

It was not until 12 April that Catherine Bond in *The Times* stated that 'Tutsis were the target plus Hutus who had made the mistake of supporting the [Arusha accords]'. Two days later she wrote:

The majority of the killings are carried out by militias, trained by President Juvenal Habyarimana. The militiamen belonged to two political parties which are opposed to power sharing with rebels from Rwanda's minority Tutsi tribe . . . Increasingly in the past two days the militiamen have appeared on the streets armed with guns and stick grenades given to them by the remnants of a government led by extremists from the majority Hutu tribe.

The only references to genocide in reports from Rwanda referred to past massacres. Only after a week did anyone report that this was not mayhem, but a well-organized genocide. Gradually throughout that bloody April, the language of newspapers changed from describing it as civil war to defining it as genocide. The name of the organized death squads, the Interahamwe, was first mentioned in the press only on 30 April by Reuters.

One reason that I did not fully comprehend the scale of the

organized killings was that I did not think Africa capable of doing it.
I had seen fighting in Uganda, in Sudan, Somalia, Sierra Leone and
South Africa, in Mozambique and Angola. I had seen horrible massacres and atrocities, but nowhere anything so organized, sustained
or final. I thought Nazi-style genocide like this was impossible in
Africa. Africans do not go in for such thoroughness, such dedicated,
supervised evil. The capacity of African governments to organize
their people at the best of times, or to command such obedience is
not great. Most African people do not believe or obey everything
they are told on state-run radio. Africa's wars had been about establishing a victor, then absorbing the vanquished into its ranks.
Massacres were part of that, but once the rage cooled, the lesson
taught, the enemy crushed, there was no point in continuing to kill.
Extermination was never the point.

The Rwandan genocide is now seen as a conspiracy that was
planned, organized and ordered. But it was more than that. The
majority of Rwandan Hutus probably killed because they were ordered
to. Some probably killed out of fear of being killed themselves if they
refused to take part. But the orders to kill Tutsis fell on fertile ground.
The Hutu refugees with whom I spoke in the camps in Goma later in
1994 mostly denied that any massacres had taken place, but the few
that did admit that Tutsis had been killed said that it had to happen.
'They were going to do the same to us,' one told me.

The orders from government resonated with fears and feelings
that went back a long way. In many villages there were no Interahamwe, but people went out and killed their Tutsi neighbours
anyway. The call on Radio Milles Collines to kill was more a permission than an order for huge numbers of Hutus. They went about it
with a will, even with glee. The awful truth about the genocide is
that it was democratic.

What would the world's reaction have been if the media had

reported that the killings were government-organized murder as well as 'tribal madness' – if they had portrayed the massacres not as an off-shoot of fighting between government and rebels, but as something well organized at a national level? It is hard to judge whether leaders such as John Major, François Mitterrand and Bill Clinton would have taken a different stand had they known what was going on or if world opinion had engaged sooner. Had the world's powerful governments understood at the time, would they have accepted sooner that genocide was taking place and ensured that the UN did not withdraw? As it was, when the truth began to emerge, the UN Security Council authorized Operation Turquoise, a French expedition to western Rwanda. That was aimed initially at propping up the government but, when it could not stop the rout, it did help slow the genocide. However, the French did also allow – some say encourage – most of the organizers and perpetrators to escape to Congo.

Earlier that year I had had a chance to blow a warning whistle. On the same trip as when I visited Burundi in early 1994, I stopped over in Kigali briefly on my way to Congo. All the diplomats, politicians and aid workers I spoke with there talked about the fragile but functioning Arusha peace accords, the complex power-sharing agreement between the Tutsi-led RPF, the Hutu-dominated Habyarimana government and several small political parties. After two years of fighting an agreement had at last been reached. The delicate and dangerous task of implementation was then reaching its final stages. Only one person in Kigali warned me that there could be genocide: Philippe Gaillard of the Red Cross. He told me that President Habyarimana was not really interested in peace, but was probably just waiting until the UN mandate ran out in March so he could go back to war. He still had the full support of the French, who regarded the invasion from Uganda as a British plot to take over their francophone territory. Gaillard also told me that the government was arming militias and that plans were being laid to promote mass killings of Tutsis throughout the country: the *Nettoyage Final* – the final clean-out of Tutsis.

I thought long and hard about writing a story under the headline, 'Genocide Looms in Rwanda'. It might have made the front page, but I had only one source. Everyone else I had spoken to sounded confident about the Arusha peace process. I did not sense anything sinister on the streets of Kigali that might have made me sceptical. And, as the world-weary diplomats pointed out, the worst that would happen if the agreement did not work would be another round of fighting. To write a sensational story about impending genocide would have been dishonest. It might even have helped to promote genocide. I went to Congo without writing anything.

Three months later, on 6 April, I was in London packing my bag for South Africa to cover the impending election. The *Independent*'s foreign editor, Harvey Morris, phoned to tell me that a plane crash in Kigali had killed President Habyarimana and the President of Burundi. It appeared that the aircraft had been shot down. After some discussion we agreed that I should continue to South Africa, but watch developments in Rwanda and Burundi. The next day ten Belgian paratroopers were murdered in Kigali by Hutu extremists and the killing of Tutsis began openly in the streets of Kigali. But these events still did not make big news. There were no television pictures. I quickly wrote a background article about Rwanda and caught the plane to Johannesburg. For three weeks the newspaper carried agency reports on Rwanda. As the South African polls closed at the end of April, I flew to Kampala to try to find out what was happening in Rwanda.

Getting there is not easy. There are no flights to Kigali or anywhere else in the country. The route through Congo in the west is impossible, since President Mobutu Sese Seko is allowing journalists into the country only by special invitation. To try to get in from the south through Burundi might be dangerous, since that country, too, has been destabilized by the death of its President. The other possible routes are through Tanzania to south-eastern Rwanda – a journey of three days – or across the Ugandan border, which is officially closed. However, the World Food Programme is running a cross-border operation to eastern Rwanda. The RPF, who control the border on the Rwandan side, are encouraging journalists to come across.

The WFP lends me a vehicle and a driver and we drive south into Rwanda. Once inside, the RPF keeps me waiting near the border for a couple of days. Eventually they give me a guide and bodyguard and on 2 May we drive down through Rwanda to the Kagera River on the Tanzanian border. The route, through hills covered in huts and villages, is almost completely deserted. Africa's roads, especially in a crowded country like Rwanda, are usually teeming with pick-up trucks, walkers and cyclists. In two days of driving we see no more than a dozen people.

On the first evening it is raining and overcast, and we stop at Kayonza for the night. The town is deserted, and many buildings have been broken into and looted. Others are chipped and spattered with bullet holes. RPF fighters move cautiously through the town in small groups. As I walk into the main street I catch the scent of rotting bodies. I follow my nose, and behind a garage come upon several contorted corpses flung across the ground like discarded clothes. Suddenly there is shooting close by, and I hide behind a tree. Some soldiers come down the road, shouting and waving. One of them is the long thin figure of Paul Kagame, the RPF leader whom I had known from Uganda. He greets me calmly and reassures me that there is no problem. I feel if he is prepared to walk openly in the street so can I, and we go back to the school where we are staying overnight.

The next day we drive on south through a deserted countryside. But the driver is cautious, stopping and talking to RPF patrols at every opportunity to learn whether the road is safe. Eventually we reach the border, where the swollen Kagera surges eastwards over waterfalls and down into Tanzania. Out in the current I suddenly see what looks like a porpoise; shiny, wet and yellow-grey, floating through the flood. Then another, and another. Corpses, hundreds of them, are swirling and bobbing downstream. Sometimes the belly button has popped outwards with the gases of decomposition and points at heaven like a tiny accusing finger. At the rate I see them – one every three or four minutes – it means that hundreds of people are being killed every day. At the bridge the river tumbles through a narrow gorge, and you can see more bodies spinning slowly in the eddies below, bumping against each other. In one pool there are so many they are packed like dead fish in a tub. It is hard to get close enough to see the cause of death, but some seem to have their hands tied together behind their backs. Others are without feet. Later I discover that the killers hacked off the feet of their victims before killing them, to cut the tall Tutsis down to size. Some said they had so many to kill, they cut off their feet to stop them running away while they waited their turn to be butchered. Dumping them in one of the many tributaries in Rwanda that flow into the Kagera was the fastest way of getting rid of them. It was also said to be a way of sending the Tutsis back to Ethiopia where they supposedly came from.

From here we drive across to the refugee camps on the Tanzanian side, leaving our RPF guide and guard in Rwanda. Thousands of exhausted, sullen Hutus have fled here from eastern Rwanda. Their leaders tell us that RPF Tutsis are murdering Hutus and they have come across the border to escape. Later I see some journalists accept this story at face value and publish reports saying that the RPF are the mass killers. My instincts are confirmed when two people separately draw me aside and whisper that what I am being told is untrue. They are clearly frightened, but desperate to tell their story. They say that it is these refugees who have done the killing and they have fled to escape RPF revenge.

Back in Rwanda I am taken on a tour of massacre sites where piles of hundreds of bodies lie in ghastly postures in halls and churches. The sheer number of corpses begins to convince me that something enormous, diabolical has happened. This is no small, meaningless war in Africa. We turn west to Kigali and join the RPF front line in the hills overlooking the city from the north-east. The RPF are methodically building up their weaponry and ammunition around the city, preparing to attack. But not today. From a distance, the city looks normal and peaceful. Later I learn that, even as we stood there, looking down across the peaceful green hills to red-tiled churches and shining corrugated iron on homes, schools and clinics, the city is one huge slaughter house. Tutsis are being rounded up and killed. Many are holed up in schools and churches where the killers will, sooner or later, come for them, call them out or throw grenades in. Then the men will be shot or cut down, the women will be raped and stabbed to death and the children bludgeoned with spiked clubs. It is not at all like a frenzied madness. Every later account reports how methodical, organized, determined it is. A task, a communal task, is being performed by all: chopping, beating, cutting, slicing. These are not people that are being butchered, they are bushes being slashed and cleared or new terraces being cut into the hillsides. They call it *kazi* – work.

These days in Rwanda I am being accompanied by Major Ndore and Valence, a shy eighteen-year-old fighter who speaks no English and little French. In fact he hardly speaks at all. He goes nowhere without his gun. He hugs it in the car, takes it with him when we stop to pee or to eat and sleeps with it under his blanket. He appears to have no other possessions except his clothes. One day, as we are getting back into the car from a break, the door slams shut on his fingers. He grunts in pain and there's a sudden rush to open the door again. His fingers are badly crushed and split, possibly broken. Major Ndore examines them and says we will get him some medical attention as soon as we can. Spartan-like, Valence holds the hand under his arm. I watch Valence's face. It never moves. 'Do you feel pain?' I ask. 'Yes,' he says but not a flicker crosses his eyes. 'It's the way we train them,' says Major Ndore.

The next day we come to a town near Valence's village and he suddenly recognizes two girls walking in the street. He shouts out and we stop, and he runs to the girls. They greet each other warmly and I watch them talk for a minute or two. Then he turns and comes back to the car and gets in. He says nothing, but his face is strained. I ask Ndore what news, and he talks to Valence in Kinyarwanda. I see him flinch for a moment. There is silence. Ndore says: 'His whole family were wiped out, mother, father, brothers, sisters, not one left. All dead.'

I turn to Valence and say I am sorry to hear his terrible news. I try to reach for his hand, but he pulls back and mumbles a reply. For the next hour he stares out of the window, but there is no sign of a tear. Not a glimmer of emotion. When we are alone next, Major Ndore says, 'He is a fighter. When he meets his enemy he will remember his family.'

It is impossible to send my story to London without leaving Rwanda. There are no telephones that work and mobile phones are still a few years in the future in this part of the world. It means returning to Uganda, a day's journey on very rough roads. Once out it might be impossible to get back in again, since the WFP vehicle has to go back to Kampala and no other vehicles are available. I decide to send a report, even if it means not staying in Rwanda. I cross back into Uganda and make for Kabale where there are telephones. But when I try to write, I cannot find the words.

Fearing represals from the RPF, Rwandans abandoned their homes and headed west into eastern Congo. Whole families, communities, towns – hundreds of thousands of men, women and children with only what they could carry – arrived in Goma to be fed by the UN in refugee camps. A whole nation fled out of its borders. By then the media and the NGOs had latched onto the Rwanda story. The mass migration made wonderful television, and the story became one of pity for the huddled masses in these camps who had been forced to flee their homes to avoid the war.

Drawn by these images, the aid agencies piled into Goma in huge numbers. Their competition for media coverage turned to greed and lies. They plastered the town with their logos. I had a fantasy of newly arrived refugees like Oxford Street shoppers pondering on whether to go for Care's rehydration mixture or the Red Cross's cholera package. Should they queue for Oxfam's water or World Vision's food? The logos were of course not for the refugees – they were to catch a cameraman: a flash of your logo on *News at Ten* could bring in hundreds of thousands of pounds.

At the joint press conferences every day, the aid bosses competed with each other over the death toll in the camps, knowing that the highest figure would make the news bulletins and bring in the money. And cash poured in to 'save Rwanda' appeals. But these people in the camps were not the passive victims of genocide. They were the perpetrators. The aid agencies ignored the survivors of genocide across the border inside Rwanda. Instead, they swamped the camps with so much food that the defeated genocidal army encamped nearby was able to gather it up, sell it and buy guns and ammunition. The aid industry contributed to the continuation of genocide.

Kagame and the RPF remained ambivalent about outside inter-vention to stop the genocide. Its bottom line seemed to be that it would allow an international force to stop genocide as long as this did not also prevent it from taking over the whole country. Many Tutsi survivors of the genocide claimed afterwards that the RPF was far more interested in seizing power than saving their lives. When he became President, Paul Kagame cleverly exploited Western guilt to obtain political and economic support for Rwanda on his own terms. In conversations with Western politicians, diplomats and journalists, he always claimed the high moral ground and never stopped playing on Western failure to intervene. As a result he also managed to obtain large amounts of aid and, more importantly, a free political and military rein in the region. The genocide has become a fact – The Fact – of Rwandan history and that history is being recon-structed around that fact. Critics or questioners are instantly smeared with allegations that they are sympathetic to genocide or even sup-port it. Kagame also plays on the patronizing Western habit of seeing African leaders as either goodies or baddies. But the fact that Hitler committed genocide did not make Stalin a saint.

In 1996, with Western, particularly American, support the Rwandan army crossed the border into eastern Congo and forced hundreds of thousands of Hutu refugees back into Rwanda, splitting them away from the defeated former Rwandan army that was sta-tioned next to the vast refugee camps around Goma. That army, a mixture of Rwandan soldiers of the former regime and Interahamwe killers and their women and children, fled deeper into Congo. The new RPF government in Kigali carried out hot pursuit raids to chase them. The new government's policy was simple. If you returned to Rwanda you would be screened and vetted and, if there was nothing against you, allowed to return home or be resettled in one of the new village settlements. If there were suspicions about you, you were locked up. Some 100,000 were imprisoned. Many were held for more than ten years without charge or trial. But if you turned west, deeper into Congo, you were a *génocidaire* to be hunted down and killed. Despite protests from the UNHCR and numerous NGOs, the Rwandan army massacred whole groups of unarmed Hutus who had fled the wrong way. I encountered one group of about 400 mostly women and children near Punia in central Congo in late 1996. They settled down for the night in a disused factory, half-starved, exhausted and ragged. 'We must leave again at dawn,' said their leader. 'We have to keep moving or we will be killed.'

Almost no-one thought that Kagame's troops would stay in Congo for long or go deeper into the country. This intervention was about chasing the *génocidaires* and protecting Rwanda's border. But the Rwandans and their Ugandan allies went deeper and deeper, claiming President Mobutu Sese Seko was supporting the Rwandan killers. Dressed in dark olive uniforms and green wellington boots, carrying AK47s and a few spare banana clips, they pushed on westwards and disappeared into the great forests of Congo. Six months later they reappeared close to Kinshasa. The ailing Mobutu fled. One of the reasons that he had let Congo's roads disintegrate was to keep the country divided and to prevent the army taking over. The Rwandans did not need roads. Lightly armed and travelling across the continent on foot, they had taken over a country eighty-nine times the size of their own.

They deployed the same tactics they had used when they fought for Museveni in Uganda a decade before: avoid big battles, respect the local people, find out as much as you can about your enemy, surround him but always allow a gap for him to run away. The RPF had learned that a demoralized fighter is more use than a dead one. He spreads fear. It was an incredible feat of organization and determination, matched only by their arrogance in installing Laurent Kabila as

President. The Tutsi stereotype had been confirmed a thousand times over.

Kabila had been a supporter of Patrice Lumumba in the 1960s, and although he had never given up, he had spent the intervening years in exile as a bar owner in Tanzania. Desperate to find a Congolese to front their invasion, the Rwandans and Ugandans picked him to head a puppet government. Two years later, when Kabila began to wriggle out of Rwandan tutelage and build his own political military power base, the Rwandans tried to do the same thing again. They accused him – like his predecessor – of supporting the Interahamwe, and invaded Congo. This time they airlifted troops across the continent to an air base within easy marching distance of Kinshasa. But Kabila was cunning, and persuaded Congo's other neighbours to come in on his side. The Rwandans were thwarted. Well-trained Zimbabwean troops and battle-hardened Angolans, backed by jet fighters and gunships, suddenly joined Kabila's side. The Rwandans had never faced air attack before and took heavy casualties. Fighting the unpaid, ill-trained troops of the dying Mobutu regime had been easy, but they could not take on a professional army. Eventually they were rescued by UNITA, the Angolan rebel army, based on the Congo–Angolan border. For years UNITA had been supplied by the Mobutu regime, but it now gave its support to the Rwandan army that had overthrown Mobutu. UNITA troops held the road south to an airstrip inside Angola and from there the defeated Rwandans were able to fly back to Kigali.

With this second invasion Rwanda and Uganda overplayed their hand, and lost the diplomatic battle in Africa. Everyone had cheered when they overthrew Mobutu in 1997. No-one complained about that first invasion. But because they teamed up with UNITA and received support from elements in the American government, particularly on the military side, they were now branded Western puppets.

Although he had never fought a single minute during the invasion, Kabila was good at singing the old anti-imperialist songs. He portrayed himself as a champion of Africa standing up to the puppets of Western imperialism. That was a travesty, but it made the utterly useless Kabila a continent-wide hero. Rwanda and Uganda ended up as the bad guys.

But they did not give up. At one period in 1998, Angola, Zimbabwe, Namibia, Burundi, Rwanda, Uganda, Sudan and Chad all had combat troops in Congo. There may have been others. Drawn into the vast, ungoverned vacuum at the heart of Africa, they all wanted a piece of Congo. There was now no way the Rwandans could reach Kinshasa again and install another puppet government. Then they fell out with their Ugandan allies and fought two pitched battles in Kisangani, causing huge loss of life and livelihood and destroying much of the town. Rwanda won the battle but the local allies they and Uganda had spawned turned into rebel movements taking on the weak Congolese state. In 2012 a UN report revealed that Rwanda and Uganda had supplied and supported rebels who were killing, raping and looting at will. Meanwhile, senior Rwandan and Ugandan officers created fiefdoms where local people were forced to dig coltan, gold and diamonds, which they then took across the border and sold. The Ugandan officers became rich, and so did many Rwandans, but the Rwandan state took the bulk of the booty, justifying it on the grounds that the war in Congo had to be paid for.

The war on Congolese soil went on and on. It is said to have killed more than four times the 800,000 people murdered in Rwanda in 1994. This was not a second genocide, but responsibility for those deaths lies partly with Kagame and Museveni.

At home, the RPF tried to create a new Rwandan ethos in which the names 'Hutu' and 'Tutsi' were no longer spoken. The government's new version of history claims that the Hutu–Tutsi division was created by colonial rule and that from now on everyone is just a Rwandan. To question who is Hutu and who Tutsi in Rwanda these days is to be 'divisionist', or even a promoter of genocide. The blasts of self-righteousness coming from Kigali neatly obscure the fact that Rwanda is now ruled by a small elite of formerly exiled Tutsis who hold all the powerful – though not necessarily senior – positions in government. Hutus co-opted into government must remain subservient. At the slightest hint that they might develop a power base of their own, they are sacked, denounced, imprisoned or forced into exile. Not a few have been murdered.

This presented the Western donors with a real dilemma. Rwanda and Uganda had become their new darlings. Suddenly they found that both countries were supporting very nasty rebel movements in Congo, giving them weapons and equipment and even sending orders and seconding senior officers to them. The UN report forced the donors to suspend aid. This was a blow to Britain in particular, which needed to spend money in places like Rwanda to meet its aid targets. The British especially liked Rwanda because Kagame shares the Western view on many issues. Kagame is also a close ally of Israel and supports American foreign policy. Rwanda also takes the Millennium Development Goals seriously, setting its own realistic targets. Rwanda's government delivers on its commitments and doesn't steal aid. Its army does peacekeeping in Africa and Rwandan officials are focused, hardworking and determined. They fill top posts in pan-African institutions, often the most effective civil servants. But Congo has vast potential in minerals and as a market. In the long run it will be more important than Rwanda to the West.

At a local level the new government has built schools and clinics and tried to raise educational and health standards – not least because it believes that a better-educated population would be less likely to carry out another genocide. But the schools and clinics that it builds are part of its villagization policy that has forced people to leave their homes and live in closely laid-out settlements. This makes them handy for the schools and clinics. It also makes them easy to control. Everyone is monitored as carefully as in the old Soviet Union. The press is not free. Human rights and political space are very limited.

To bring to trial more of the 100,000 imprisoned people accused of genocide, the government adapted a traditional justice system called *Gacaca*, justice on the grass. The accused are tried in their villages by committees. But this applies only to the genocide. Atrocities and revenge killings committed by the present government as it came to power are excluded. Many Rwandans who were not involved in the genocide in any way argue that this is not sufficient to bring about true national reconciliation. They argue that the government too must confess to mistakes and submit itself to justice.

But the Rwanda government will admit to no crimes and apologize to no-one. Rwanda was one of the first countries to step forward and offer to be monitored by the African Peer Review Mechanism, the monitoring mechanism of the African Union's New Partnership for Africa's Development. The first stage of the process is a self-critical national – not just government – assessment of the economic, social and political state of the country. The Rwandan government promptly stuffed the committee with its own supporters. Government officials wrote a glowing appraisal of the state of Rwandan democracy. It found nothing to criticize and ignored Rwanda's role in Congo and well-documented human rights abuses at home. It skated over the lack of separation of powers in the constitution. No better example exists of Rwanda's self-confidence and arrogance, knowing they can hide behind the genocide to attack any critics who might suggest they are not quite a democracy.

Today Rwanda is ruled as tightly as ever. The Tutsis, only 13 per cent of the population, are in power. Guaranteeing their survival is their top priority. Rwanda's rulers track down any Rwandan any-where who poses a threat to them, even targeting dissidents in London. But it is not former *génocidaires* plotting to overthrow the government who are being targeted. It is former allies and close asso-ciates of Kagame who have fallen out with him. In order to ensure its own survival, the Tutsi regime is trying to create a 'new Rwanda' with a dynamic gold-standard development programme, a new his-tory and a harmonious political culture in which there is no Hutu and no Tutsi. But can a government based on the former ruling caste change a whole country, a whole society, by a mix of repression and re-education in a single generation?

In 2017 Kagame changed the constitution to win a third term as President with 98.8 per cent of the vote but whether that figure is 'the will of the people' will emerge through time. He even felt strong enough to free some opponents. America and Britain support him but until Rwandan society feels free to discuss the country's history openly, it is hard to read Rwanda's future.

10

God, trust and trade
Senegal

In 1895 the Senegalese Islamic mystic and poet Cheikh Amadu Bamba Mbacke got out of the boat that was taking him to exile in Gabon and, kneeling on a mat that appeared miraculously in the water, prayed to Allah. Then he walked across the water back to Senegal and founded a global African trading company based on Islamic principles. Those who work for it are known as Mourides. In any city in the world today, if an African street trader offers you jewellery, belts or bags, he is almost certainly a Mouride, a follower of Amadu Bamba. Mourides are scattered all over the globe from Paris to Los Angeles, from Hong Kong to Dubai. They possess in great abundance a commodity that much of Africa lacks: trust.

Born into a strict Muslim family in the Baol region of Senegal in 1853, Amadu Bamba was drawn to the *tassawuf* style of Sufi mysticism. Its precepts are purely religious and it shuns the world and its politics. But his early life witnessed the progressive French encroachment into the old Wolof kingdom that ended in the annexation of his country when he was thirty-seven years old. He became a symbol of Islamic traditions, and although he never directly challenged the French interlopers with their mission to 'civilize' the Africans, his very existence became a threat to their colonial domination. They exiled him to Gabon in 1895 and then to Mauritania, but the discontent this caused forced the French to allow him back. He returned to Senegal in 1907 in triumph. In Senegal they tell you he walked home across the water.

The movement he founded is based on three rules: follow God, work and provoke no-one. He believed that prayer, study and work would protect people from the corrupting and dehumanizing influence of France and French culture. Among his followers he promoted the values of humility, endurance and sharing. He required them to attach themselves to a Sheikh and obey his every command. Later his followers founded *dahiras*, prayer circles where they could meet, socialize and read the Koran and Amadu Bamba's poems. They were also required to pay a subscription to help fellow members in trouble and to contribute to the expenses of the whole movement and its leader. In that way it is not unlike the Freemasons. They even have a special handshake. When the master founded the movement, most of its followers worked as labourers on his farms to support the movement, but when their sons began to migrate to the towns, the movement started to take off. Bamba had some 70,000 followers when he died in 1927. Now there are an estimated three million.

For rural people arriving in town for the first time, the dahira provides a base and a network. The subscription enables new members to find accommodation and work. If one of their number dies, it gives money to bring the body home for burial. The Mouride brotherhood offers a secure bridge from rural to urban, from ancient to modern. The wealth it gathers from all its members provides a welfare system. Richer members also provide capital for fellow Mourides to start up trading enterprises.

It is 2000 and I am sitting by a well in a walled, well-swept courtyard in the dappled shade of an old tree. The women of the house in wrap-around skirts, flip-flops and T-shirts are chatting as they wash pots and plates, sweep and pick the bad bits out of trays of rice. I am waiting to talk to Ahmadou Lo, a senior Mouride and a Marabout, Islamic holy man. This is Touba, a city of more than a million people 100 miles east of Senegal's capital Dakar, where Amadu Bamba chose to base his movement.

At first you would not notice anything different from any other dusty Sahelian town. But Touba is very different. It is a state within a state. This is election time and every wall in the rest of Senegal is plastered with party posters. '*Changement* – Change,' scream the ruling Socialist Party hoardings. '*Sopi* – Change,' shouts the opposition. But there will be no change in Touba. Nor are there any posters here. Politics is not banned, but posters are forbidden and rallies and meetings discouraged. As you come into town, there is no checkpoint, no security men checking your papers, because there are no policemen. And no taxmen, local officials or courts either. Banks are not necessary. If a trader here wants to buy, he can call up a fellow Mouride anywhere in the world and ask for goods to be sent. The money is paid here in Touba to the trader's family. Trust is the key to the Mourides.

I wander through the streets of glaring, baked sand and dust and speak to some of the shopkeepers selling hi-fis, computers, TVs, bags of rice and flour or bolts of brightly coloured cloth from their cool, dark, cavernous stores. One shopkeeper in a long robe and Muslim kufi, selling music CDs and tapes, tells me that he came here and joined the Mourides because no-one pays tax in Touba. 'Touba is not part of the state,' he says.

> *If there is a problem that requires money the Marabout calls a committee and they ask everyone to contribute. And immediately everyone gives, it's called Adiya. They give because they follow the Marabout but also because if they give, people know the road will be*

> *fixed and the water will run again. This is not like Dakar . . . It's*
> *all one family here. If you believe in the father, you believe in his sons.*
> *Then there is the money you pay for the poor here – two and a half per*
> *cent of your profit, so no-one suffers. The Marabouts give good*
> *direction and make us work to help others. They organize and they*
> *have connections. But the big hope is for the next world – Paradise.*

I ask if there are thieves here and corruption.

> *There is no corruption, none. Everything is transparent. But yes,*
> *there are thieves here sometimes. We don't cut hands off, we believe*
> *in tolerance, but if someone steals we form a committee to judge the*
> *person. If they are guilty we beat them. If it is serious we might*
> *consider taking them to a law court in another town but it's better*
> *just to beat them.*

Amadu Bamba is buried at the huge marble-clad mosque of Touba. His magnificent tomb with a ceiling of gold is a place of annual pilgrimage. More than 2 million people congregate in the city for the great Magal every year, the two-day ceremony that commemorates his return from exile. The days are spent in prayer and the evenings in feasting and listening to the Sheikh's poems and the *griots* – the praise-singers. People are accommodated by the town and use the visit to buy tax-free goods more cheaply than anywhere else in Senegal. During the Magal delegations from the government and political parties are received by the Khalifa – a recognition of the political status of the Mouride leader. From independence until the late 1980s these meetings symbolized the collaboration of state and religion. The support of the other-worldly Mourides for the ruling party was taken for granted. Just as Amadu Bamba had reached a compromise on mosque and state with the French, so his successors accepted and supported the independence governments – even though Senegal's first President was a Catholic Christian. But after the riots of 1988 the new Khalifa decided to keep his distance from the government. The lack of explicit Mouride support may be the chief factor that cost Abdou Diouf the presidency in 2000.

Ahmadou Lo comes eventually and greets me warmly. Dressed in a checked robe, he is in his mid fifties and has a few reverend white hairs in his sparse beard. He ushers me out of the courtyard and into a plain but well-polished house, a one-storey square building with a corrugated iron roof. This is not the house of a Big Man, and he is greeted with deference and respect by the women of the house but not awe or abasement. In the main room, painted white, a huge copy of the Koran takes pride of place on a lectern. There are two beds, one covered with a torn starched white sheet, a large steel trunk under the other. A telephone and an old-fashioned radio from the 1960s sit on a wooden table, and around the walls are framed photographs of Marabouts with a large portrait of Amadu Bamba in the middle. A gaudy carpet patterned with Arabic writing covers torn green linoleum on the floor.

We sit on plain old chairs and he tells me that his father worked for Amadu Bamba, so he came to Touba sixteen years ago to learn the Koran and become a Marabout. 'If your father is a Marabout then you must become one too,' he says. He does not claim the Mourides have the only correct interpretation of the Koran, in fact he admits their interpretation is slightly different from others, 'but there is no difference in substance. Bamba wanted people to work harder for God. So you submit yourself to one Marabout absolutely and then you have nothing else to worry about. You will never do anything wrong. There are two types of Mourides, those who are trying but not yet convinced and those who are ready to die for it, the militants.'

Ahmadou Lo has some 2000 to 3000 followers. He does not know all of them personally but knows the heads of each family. 'They join to get to Paradise, but the movement also helps them if they have problems on earth such as lack of money or a job. Then you can go to the President or you can turn to the Koran. If you do the right thing you will be all right.'

As I leave he shows me the Mourides' peculiar handshake – pressing the back of my clasped hand to his face. The next time I use it is a year later by the Ponte degli Scalzi in Venice, and it brings astonishment from the two young African men selling Barbour handbags, trinkets and jewellery at a stall. They are even more astonished when I tell them I have been to Touba. They have been in Venice two years and will go back only when they are summoned. We all shake hands again and one says with a smile, 'Now you are also Mouride.'

When a Mouride visits a city for the first time, he will go straight to the dahira, which will provide him with somewhere to stay, credit to trade and social support. In New York the dahira was founded by Bamba's great-grandson in 1985. Senegalese Mourides traders had begun importing African art and jewellery in the early 1980s and selling it on the streets. From New York they sent electrical goods and clothes – tax-free – to Touba and sold them all over Senegal and West Africa. The Mouride network then started bringing hats, watches, sunglasses, umbrellas and leather work from all over the world into New York. A simple trust-based money transfer system meant that all transactions between America and Africa could be done by telephone with the minimum of official scrutiny or paperwork.

The lack of trust that exists in most of Africa is reflected in the atomized African diaspora in Europe and America. Very few organizations exist beyond the family and those that do, for example school associations for Ghanaians and Sierra Leoneans, professional associations among Nigerians and Churches among West Africans generally, are social or religious in character. When money becomes involved they often break up bitterly.

The only other African group that operate a high-trust commercial operation like the Mourides are the Somalis, providing the same low-cost money transfer systems linked to their telephone companies and based on trust. They too run global trading networks, moving goods from the Middle East and Asia to Somalia and East Africa. Both have a strong Islamic element, but where the Mouride systems are purely faith-based, the Somali systems are family- and clan-based, so they are unable to expand in the way the Mourides do by drawing in new recruits. The Somalis have another element. When I praised their high-trust banking system to one Somali friend he said, 'Yes, but you mess with those guys – they kill you.'

In 2002 the New York Mouride community was estimated at about 7000 and Harlem has its 'Little Senegal' area, complete with mosque, library and school. As in Touba, Bamba's feast day is celebrated with a Grand Magal each year and New York now has several dahiras and an umbrella organization which provides support for Mouride families in trouble and deals with the city council, the police and local politicians. If you die, the Mouride organizations will fly your body home to Touba for burial. It is where all Mourides want to be buried. The Mourides also handle remittances to send back to Touba, donating some $8 million towards the completion of a modern hospital there. At the turn of the century the worldwide Mouride community was sending back an estimated $15–$20 million a year – about one-fifth of what Senegal received in direct foreign investment.

About one-third of Senegal's population – and all the leading artists, musicians and businessmen – are Mourides. They put into a religious institution all the trust and taxes, obedience and commitment given by citizens to the nation state in most countries.

And the religious organization fulfils many of the functions and services of a welfare state as well as channelling its followers' commercial energies. They also willingly give the Mouride movement a hefty 'tax' on all their dealings. Unlike the Somalis, the trading and social care network has not grown out of a collapsed state. Senegal is one of the oldest European colonies in Africa. It sent deputies to the French parliament in Paris in 1848 and its borders were established in 1890. Apart from its southern province, Casamance, it has been stable since independence, with Abdullai Wade only the third head of state. There has never been a hint of a military coup. Nor have there been bad rulers: Léopold Senghor stood down as President in 1981 and, after nearly two decades in power, his hand-picked successor, Abdou Diouf, lost the 2000 election to Wade and accepted the result. Under Wade, life for ordinary people has got tougher. Services and infrastructure have deteriorated, as has trust in the government, and there are few jobs for skilled young Senegalese. But you cannot talk about Senegal and somewhere like Nigeria in the same breath. They may be on the same continent but in Senegal there is justice, a police force and a tax system. At one moment Wade seemed to threaten this by ruling more and more autocratically, treating the opposition with contempt and trying to bribe an IMF official. In February 2012, aged 86, having failed to enable his son to succeed him, he announced he would run for president again, although he had promised in 2007 that he would not seek another term. Tens of thousands took to the streets to protest, and in the April 2012 election he was defeated by his former Prime Minister, Macky Sall.

Under Diouf and Wade, Senegal did not feel the wind of economic growth that started to blow around 2000. It already had a poor economic record, with economic growth between 1975 and 1995 at only 2.2 per cent, slower than its population growth of

2.8 per cent. It slowed even further between 1986 and 1996, which meant the Senegalese were getting poorer per capita at a rate of 1 per cent a year. But in the next decade, 1996 to 2006, growth picked up to 5 per cent and from 2014 the economy picked up, posting a 6 per cent growth rate in 2017. But despite its comparatively good governance and lack of conflict, not even Senegal seems to inspire civic national commitment. Rather than trust their state, many Senegalese seem to invest their future in a religious body instead.

According to the economic historian Angus Maddison, Europeans were only three times richer than Africans at the beginning of the nineteenth century. In 2000 they were twenty times richer and the gap was getting wider. Ireland's 4 million people, once the world's poorest, produced more wealth than 200 million West Africans, including the mighty Nigerians with their abundance of oil and gas. The entire continent south of the Sahara, apart from South Africa, produced less than tiny Belgium.

The figures tell the story that the living standards of most Africans fell during the last three decades of the twentieth century. But in around 2000 African economies started to grow, some, particularly the oil producers, at extraordinary rates. However, that did not necessarily affect ordinary Africans. In 2008, on the UN Human Development Index, the world league tables that measure human well-being, African countries fill twenty-eight of the thirty bottom places for health, education and per capita wealth. Some African countries are beginning to improve, but most Africans are still worse off than they were thirty years ago. In 2010 some 388 million Africans out of almost a billion were living in absolute poverty, 73 million more than 10 years before despite the economic growth. Only 15 per cent lived in 'an environment considered minimally adequate for sustainable growth and development', says Paul Collier of the Centre for the Study of African Economies at Oxford. According to the World Bank, it will take at least a decade of strict policies and sweat to achieve and maintain growth rates of more than 7 per cent. This is the target if Africa is to get back to the levels of prosperity that African countries enjoyed when the imperial powers left at the beginning of the 1960s. In terms of growth rates, some countries are achieving this, but retaining that wealth within the country and using it to improve the lives of its citizens does not seem to be happening in many African countries.

This is what the number-crunchers at the World Bank and the UN tell us. It is the stuff of NGO appeals and the justification for pouring aid into Africa. And there are places which are poor – or rather impoverished. You need only visit a slum on the outskirts of Kinshasa or Nairobi to see people in rags picking through piles of rubbish. Away from cities, where a rapidly increasing population has taken every inch of land, or where there is drought or harvest failure, you see people stretched by hunger, their children sick and listless. Above all, where war has forced families to flee their homes you see unconscionable suffering and casual death. But this is restricted to specific places and times. It is not all of Africa. Most African families get by, meet their needs, eat well enough, have a radio, save for a TV, have time for family and friends, leisure and talk, go to church in a suit on Sundays or to the mosque on Fridays. Given half a chance they earn enough to improve their homes, maybe buy a second-hand car. There is little depression, no loneliness. Sunshine makes life more open and shared. It's not such a bad life.

Most people like this whom you see on the streets of African cities are counted as absolutely poor by the UN Development Programme: living on less than a dollar a day. That sounds very poor to anyone living in the Western world, but wealth comes in many forms and maybe there is wealth in Africa that is not measurable in economists' dollar calculations. And that does not just mean valuable human capital that cannot be measured in monetary terms. When mobile phones went on sale in Africa, people suddenly found the money. Millions of Africans suddenly turned out to be richer than the economists and developmentalists said they were. A lot richer. How much more wealth is hidden in Africa uncounted by the official figures? In 2010 Ghana decided to change the baseline year for its official statistics from 1993 to 2006. So much new economic activity had not been picked up in the original baseline, such as mobile phone use, that Ghana was suddenly catapulted from a poor to a middle-income country. Other countries are following suit. I have always suspected that all the economic figures in Africa are wrong but now we know for certain: the continent is a lot richer than we thought.

Nevertheless, the fact is that Africa's margin of safety when it comes to poor harvests, disease, war, climate change or other disasters is narrow. Africa has done less well than Asia, and I always have the feeling in Africa that it could be – should be – a lot better.

So what went wrong? At independence in the 1960s Africa was portrayed as an awakening giant, casting off the chains of colonialism and exploitation and bursting with energy. At that time Asia, including China and India, was seen as a basket case where overpopulation, bad government, lack of entrepreneurial spirit and fatalistic religions seemed to produce economic stagnation, endless famines and hopelessness. In 1965 the average income in Africa was twice that of Asia. Countries like Ghana, blessed with raw materials and a well-educated elite, were seen as particularly dynamic.

By the end of the century Asia had leapt ahead while Africa had gone backwards. Many Asian states started from a lower economic baseline than Africa in the early 1960s, but then made rapid progress in the 1980s with hi-tech industrialization policies implemented with rigid political, social and educational discipline. Economic policies, technology, social organization and, above all, attitudes had changed. Within a couple of decades Asian countries were able to sustain increasing populations and offer them a future. More of their children survived, more families had clean running water and electricity, more were going to school, were learning to read and write and were able to find jobs when they left school. Korea, the Philippines, Malaysia and a new and mighty China began to become the world's manufacturers, making better and cheaper cars, textiles, ships, plastics, radios, toys and computers. Life got better for more people in Asia in the 1980s than at any other time in the history of human development – although in 2010 there were still more poor people in India than in the whole of Africa. Latin American countries, led by Brazil, also progressed to become middle-ranking economic powers.

In the same period, with the possible exceptions of South Africa and Botswana – and Mauritius if you count the island as African – the continent was going backwards. Africa was once just one part of the third world: those non-industrialized countries that had mostly been under imperial rule in the nineteenth century and emerged as independent states after the Second World War. The third world was defined as the left-behind countries, behind the first world, the capitalist European countries and America, and behind the second world, the Communist countries of Eastern Europe and China. The third world was the rest: most of Asia, Africa and Latin America, poor and 'backward'. There was widespread agreement that what the third world needed was aid and advice so that it could 'catch up' the first world. A decade into the twenty-first century Asia still contains huge numbers of very poor people, but when people think of the third world now they think of Africa. Once an economic classification, 'third world' became a geographic area and then a problem.

Now it is commonly used as a term of contempt, shorthand for failure. And it means Africa.

The causes of Africa's failure are hotly debated. Is it caused by the rest of the world: unfair trading systems, international capitalism and its agents, the World Bank and the International Monetary Fund? Is Africa the victim of a neo-colonialist conspiracy to keep it poor, a continuation of imperialism and exploitation that dates back to the slave trade? Or did Africa's leaders cause Africa to fail? Aid agencies, the elites themselves and Africans outside the continent tend to blame external factors, mainly the IMF and the international trade rules. Africa's poor and middle classes – at least those who are not part of the ruling elites – tend to blame internal factors, mainly their leaders. So do most people who do business in Africa.

The external factors begin with bad geography and bad history. Africa is endowed with natural resources, minerals, forests and, parts of it, water in abundance. It is a rich continent with a lot of poor people. But economic development in Africa was designed to benefit outsiders, not Africans. Look at the railway systems. All go from a coastal port inland to a mine. They were not built to link peoples or towns or regions, they were designed to extract Africa's mineral wealth as quickly and cheaply as possible and ship it overseas.

Political geography made matters worse. Africa's borders do not fit natural boundaries or lines of demarcation between peoples. The European powers carved up the continent at the end of the nineteenth century, drawing those lines on their maps of places they had never been to. In many cases the maps were blank. They had no idea what lay on or under the ground in vast lands they were claiming as theirs. The lines, which in time hardened to demarcate nation states, cut through peoples and natural boundaries and blocked traditional trading routes. The lines gave birth to Nigerians, Ivoireans, Ugandans and Tanzanians who had little in common with many of their new fellow citizens. Although they paid lip service to the unification of Africa, few leaders were prepared to merge their countries into larger units. African rulers were no more or less willing to cede power to regional bodies than politicians anywhere.

Bad history undermined African societies. Before colonization there were traders, artists and farmers and a ruling class. After colonization there were only farmers and a small random group that had secured their status through Western education or by being soldiers – a status unrelated to traditional power structures or the rest of society. A huge gap existed between the professionals and the people. A class of skilled artisans, urban and rural, seemed to be absent. African societies were becoming deeply fractured. That could have worked in its favour, freeing up societies and releasing creative entrepreneurs. The opposite happened.

The colonial legacy made African economies primary producers of raw materials. Manufacturing was done in Europe. Raw materials gave Africa a guaranteed income, but that income fell steadily from the 1970s to 2000 as the prices for those primary products – except for oil – fell in relation to manufactured goods. Between 1980 and 2000 the price of cotton fell by 47 per cent, coffee by 64 per cent, cocoa by 71 per cent and sugar by 77 per cent. Africa's share of world trade fell from 6 per cent in 1980 to 2.4 per cent in 2016. And although Asian producers dominated the market, Africa's commodities are being exported in increasing volume.

The only way Africa could make up these losses is by building its own manufacturing capacity, training up its people and adding value. Asian countries did just that and explored how to make and sell goods more cheaply than the rest of the world. Their economic miracle depended on a combination of skilled, disciplined but cheap labour, a port near the factories for export and a stable government that investors trusted. Very few African countries had all of these factors and many had none. Apart from Mauritius none of them had the vision to take up the opportunity. South Africa also had a substantial manufacturing sector, but its race policies curbed its trade potential.

Many people blamed European and American trade barriers for Africa's failure to build factories to process raw materials and develop exports. Indeed, the playing field was not level. Heavy import tariffs discouraged the export of African manufactured goods into Europe and America. In addition Europe and America undermined African agricultural producers by giving their own farmers fat subsidies that lowered the world price of many African farm products. In 2016 America handed out nearly $300 million to its cotton farmers. In the same year the UK's total agricultural subsidies were £35 billion – more than three-quarters of the total GDP of sub-Saharan Africa. The US cotton subsidies directly affected Africa by lowering the price by up to 14 per cent, affecting a million African cotton growers. Furthermore, the Americans and Europeans dumped their subsidized produce on Africa, undercutting local producers and destroying local markets. On the Senegal coast the local dish consists of fish, rice and tomatoes. The rice for this traditional dish now comes from Asia, the tomatoes from Holland – both exported at subsidized prices – while the fish is missing altogether because massive European fishing boats suck up all the fish in Senegal's coastal waters, leaving nothing for the locals.

All this is true. But these conditions affected Asian countries just as much as African ones. The Asians however, developed strategies to find a way round them and get their manufactured products into Europe and America. The truth is that while Asian countries were eyeing up and measuring global markets, African governments were looking inwards, working on self-sufficiency and import substitution and taxing exports. They lacked the ambition to see what African manufacturers could offer American, Japanese or European customers. For them rich countries were aid donors, not markets.

Asian countries did not limit their development to manufactured goods. They also started producing traditional African commodities in greater quantity and better quality than Africa. From the late nineteenth century up to the 1960s Nigeria was king of palm oil. In 1957 Malaysia sent a team to Nigeria to examine its palm oil production. They learned what they needed to know, went away and expanded their own palm oil production. By 1998 Malaysia accounted for nearly two-thirds of world production. It exported 85 per cent of its palm oil, some of it to Nigeria where production had collapsed. The same collapse in African production occurred in Congo and later in Côte d'Ivoire. Meanwhile other countries began to catch up African producers of cocoa and coffee. Between 1990 and 2000 Uganda increased coffee production from just over 100,000 tonnes a year to just over 200,000. That had fallen back to 150,000 tonnes in 2007. In the same period Vietnam increased production from just under 100,000 tonnes to over 1.275 million tonnes.

And meanwhile Africa's greatest asset, its land, was ignored. My experience in Uganda in the mid 1970s seemed to be confirmed across the continent throughout the 1980s. No-one with any education wanted to stay in a rural area and make things grow. Working the land and selling the produce was for peasants, the life that everyone tried to escape from by going to school. A few rich Africans, especially in Kenya, bought land, but they rarely invested in it, preferring to build a mansion than create a working farm. Only a few imaginative souls – Mr Lule was one – started medium-sized agricultural enterprises. Those who did made money.

While external conditions did not help, Africa's loss of market share in its strongest exports and its failure to develop a manufacturing industry were caused primarily by internal factors. When it came to economics Africa's rulers were mostly either socialist idealists or greedy dictators. Men like Kaunda and Nyerere had been deeply influenced by Christian socialist missionaries, who had strong feelings about how the fruits of the earth should be shared but little idea about how economic systems worked. When African countries became independent, most of their leaders believed the next stage in nation building should be government ownership of the economy. The new rulers argued that political independence would not be complete without economic independence. They saw themselves as liberating Africa from colonial rule and wanted to gain control of their production as well as their governance. In country after country mines, land and businesses were nationalized. It was seen as Africa reclaiming its inheritance. Nationalization policies received substantial support from the World Bank and donors.

In 1967 President Nyerere ordered that the National Development Corporation take a majority share in all large businesses. In Zambia – it seems gaspingly bizarre now – President Kenneth Kaunda wrote a letter to foreign companies politely asking them to 'give the state at least 51 per cent interest in their enterprises'. It was not just the socialist-orientated countries like Tanzania or Zambia that created huge state companies such as national mining houses and marketing boards, called 'parastatals'. Senegal, Kenya, Côte d'Ivoire and Malawi, held up as Western allies and examples of mixed-economy successes, also mortgaged their countries' wealth to fund state-run companies. By the mid 1990s, it is estimated that capitalist Nigeria had more than 600 state companies. Kenya had 360. In Zimbabwe before the economy collapsed about 35 per cent of it was under the control of state-run companies.

The stated aim of nationalizations was to bring the whole economy in line with a national development plan and prevent capital being exported. The effect was to give leaders total control of the money. Nationalization gave them a vast barrel of patronage, allowing them to reward political allies and pay off enemies. The parastatals also provided a slush fund for the President's pet projects and removed any other wealth base in the country that might have been tempted to fund an opposition. Andrew Sardanis was a businessman appointed by Kaunda to run the Zambian parastatal companies. In his memoirs, *Africa: Another Side of the Coin: Northern Rhodesia's Final Years and Zambia's Nationhood*, Sardanis claims that although Kaunda insisted in public that the companies should be run for profit without political interference, the President and other ministers continually sent him notes telling him to give X a job or give a loan to Y.

While parastatal jobs and contracts went to cronies, the state companies were run for explicitly political ends, such as keeping politically important sectors of society happy. In Zambia making food cheap in the cities was a top priority. If the cities went on strike or rioted they could create political problems. Rural areas could not. So farmers were paid a tiny proportion of the world price for their goods by the state agricultural marketing boards, while the cities ate subsidized food. The parastatals bled Africa to death.

More paranoid African rulers, like Hastings Banda in Malawi or Siaka Stevens in Sierra Leone, felt threatened by wealth in any hands except their own. Successful businessmen worried Presidents as much as political opponents. In Zimbabwe, Strive Masiywa, a young telecom entrepreneur, was chased out of the country by death threats from Robert Mugabe's cronies. The contract he sought was given to the President's nephew. In Ghana, Jerry Rawlings, the blunt-talking military dictator who ruled from 1982 to 2000, forbade Sam Jonah, head of Ashanti Goldfields, Africa's most successful indigenous mining company, to have a private jet until he himself had an even bigger one. Successful entrepreneurs like these would be regarded by most governments as national heroes and role models for the rising generation. In Africa they were mistrusted and either forced to lie low or hounded out of the country.

Africa produced no Lee Kuan Yew – a leader with a vision of wealth creation. On the contrary, the worst rulers fulfilled the Kenyan proverb: 'It does not matter how thin the cow gets if you are the only one on the teat.' Men like Daniel arap Moi, Idi Amin, Sani Abacha, Hastings Banda and of course Mobutu Sese Seko dedicated their lives to looting the state and staying in power. They were quite prepared to let their countries' economies die as long as they were rich enough to buy off or eliminate potential rivals. At the heart of the failure was bad politics. As far back as 1986 Rawlings stated bluntly that Africa should not blame outsiders. 'We broke the pot,' he said.

Few in Western countries expressed much dissent at the time. Cold War loyalties were their prime concern. These days Western donors proclaim themselves global champions of 'traditional values' – democracy, the rule of law, human rights and the free market – but these are new inventions. In the 1960s and 1970s the Western countries and their institutions such as the World Bank wanted to know whose side you were on: the Soviet bloc or the West. They would rather risk having a ruler like Idi Amin or Mobutu than have a change of government which might lead to a country aligning itself with the Soviet Union. So they supported bloody dictatorships in the name of 'stability'. The departing imperial power usually owned the main businesses in Africa and in many cases struck a deal with the incoming President to protect its commercial interests. What happened to the rest was of little interest. Most Western countries themselves at that time had mixed economies and many industries were state-run. Their governments had no difficulty going along with nationalization, state-run companies and managed economies in Africa.

It is hard to believe anyone thought they would work. Stanley Please, who worked for the World Bank in the 1950s and 1960s, said that everyone there knew full well that it was funding the whims of African dictators. The donors, he said later, were giving them just enough rope to hang themselves, but that was the way it was at the time. The World Bank helped the Stalinist Ethiopian ruler, Mengistu Haile Mariam, forcibly to resettle millions of northern Ethiopians in the south to prevent them falling under the influence of rebel movements. So did Oxfam. And there were plenty of Western economists sympathetic to the concept of national economic planning to support the new nationalizations. For the donors to refuse funds on the grounds that these policies were economic suicide would have been to deny that these rulers were independent. That would have been neo-colonialism. In the Cold War that would have played into the hands of the Soviet Union. So Western countries found themselves funding wasteful or even destructive projects they knew would fail, and embracing bloody dictators.

In most African countries trade was run by particular groups among whom trust levels were high. In Senegal and parts of West Africa it is the Mourides. Though they lack the Mourides' religious and communal ideology, the Malinke, an amorphous ethnic group also known as Mandingos, also set up trading networks across West Africa. The largest businesses in the continent were corporate transnationals. European business used to be far more extensive, but throughout the late 1970s and 1980s smaller European businesses gradually withdrew or collapsed, unable to sustain themselves through political and civil disruption. They also found their markets shrinking with Africa's dwindling economies. Until the late 1990s medium-sized businesses in West Africa were run by Lebanese, brought in by the French and British as a mercantile class during colonial times. In East Africa, Indians ran all the import–export businesses. In Southern Africa, whites ran quite small shops and factories. In Sudan and parts of Congo, it was Greeks. Until recently Africans in most of Africa operated only downstream trade. Some became wealthy through political connections that gave them lucrative state contracts but, always a potential threat to those in power, they remained vulnerable to political whims. Today, with more legal protection, successful and wealthy African businessmen are expanding out of their local areas and building business empires. And the Chinese, Indians and other Asians are moving in.

Many African friends who tried to get a business enterprise going all reported the same problems: workers did not turn up on time, they had no urgency and they delivered sloppy work. Often they found themselves blocked by rivals. The elites who made money out importing and exporting had an interest in preventing the development of local manufacturing or processing. They sometimes got their political partners to use red tape to obstruct rival businesses that might threaten their monopolies. And poorly paid or greedy customs officials at ports and airports were often obstructive, threatening delay or entangling exports in a jungle of regulations so as to elicit bribes from frustrated businessmen.

There were sometimes social and cultural elements that blocked the development of trade and business. I often heard Africans say that Africans can't do business. There is not enough trust between them. Leave that to the Lebanese, Asians and others. And in some parts of Africa an item had to be made in America or Britain or France for it to be thought any good. No-one wanted to buy something made in Africa. In Nigeria in the 1980s that even applied to food. Apparently only foreign-grown rice was edible. No-one wanted to buy Nigerian rice. In the 1980s and 1990s, I searched in vain for a successful family business in which brothers, or a father and sons, or a man and wife shared responsibilities. Recently I have found some, but in the past African businesses tended to be one-man bands in which other members of the family were mere messengers. When the father, founder, owner and boss died the family pulled the business to pieces. Contrast that with the Asian businesses constantly sharing the workload and responsibilities and lending family capital to younger sons to start new ventures.

With the end of the Cold War, Western donors were freed from the need to prop up African dictators and switched their aid to Eastern Europe. Meanwhile the old African 'Fathers of the Nation' were dying off and a new generation was emerging in Africa that demanded the same political freedoms as the West enjoyed and which were now spreading to former Communist countries. The West's new agenda for Africa was democracy, human rights and the establishment of the free market. But Western capital saw the free market as the most important. As Herman Cohen, the American Assistant Secretary of State for Africa in the early 1990s, told me: 'If you get the third one right, you get a discount on the other two.' I think he was only half-joking.

In the minds of Western leaders, multi-party democracy and a free market were both the cause and the prize of their victory over Communism. Since most African countries were one-party states that controlled their economies, the assumption was that they too would profit from free market solutions. The aid donors saw how the corrupt, top-heavy, state-controlled bureaucracies of Africa blocked both democracy and economic progress. The International Monetary Fund and the World Bank, both controlled by representatives of Western governments, provided them with the policies and machinery that they believed would engineer a free and flourishing Africa. Accountable to no-one, they moved in.

The new design was euphemistically named the Structural Adjustment Programme – aptly nicknamed SAP – as if it were no more than tinkering to fine-tune a misfiring economy. The prescription was handed out to one country after another. In fact it meant a thoroughgoing economic transformation: sell off state enterprises, float currencies (many of them sank like stones), cut public expenditure (including health and education), sack thousands of state employees. Those who remained were kept on their original salaries which sometimes became worthless. Economies that had been in the hands of kleptocrats were now in the hands of World Bank bureaucrats.

The reforms imposed on Africa in the late 1980s and 1990s went far further and far faster than any reforms that any Western countries would have dared impose on their own people. They even went further than the reforms implemented in post-Communist Eastern Europe. African governments complained that it was very hard for democratically elected governments to implement such harsh measures but they did not argue back. One World Bank official who had come to Africa after working in Latin America and Asia said that while other countries argued to and fro over the details of Structural Adjustment Programmes urged on them by the Bank, African governments did not come up with an alternative plan – or any plan at all. They resisted for a while then signed up to SAPs without a murmur. He thought that this either meant they did not have the expertise or confidence to argue economic strategy with the World Bank or that they had signed up with no intention of actually implementing the programme.

No-one had thought through the immediate impact of such dramatic programmes on African states. The economic theory, known as the Washington Consensus, was that once economies were free from meddling government bureaucracies and the sacred laws of the free market – Western style – had been put in place, all would be well. Investment would flow in, economic activity would increase and African economies would bloom. They assumed taxes would be collected and state-centred corruption would be reduced. The government would then be able to spend the taxes on public goods. But their theory also assumed that the states had a legal framework that would enable the market to function freely and transparently. Meanwhile no-one thought about the effect on people. Classic economic behaviour happens in states only where there is the crisp rule of law, a national government to enforce it and transport and utility infrastructure in place to enable economic take-off. By the early 1990s, many African countries no longer functioned as normal nation states and their economies were too far gone to be revived by a dose of 'structural adjustment'.

The theory also ignored all the networks and systems of influence that lie under the surface in Africa. Most of the officials of the IMF and World Bank never bothered to find out about how these economies actually worked before they set about fixing them. Many never thought of getting out of their air-conditioned offices except to get into their air-conditioned cars to return to their air-conditioned houses. They simply had no idea of the realities of Africa. Or maybe they thought it was not their business. I met one young woman who had worked at the IMF. Her first job there was to write the economic reform programme for Mozambique, which she did straight out of a textbook. She never left Maputo, the capital.

Secondly, these new principles were not imposed uniformly. Western countries continued to pursue their own interests and protect their allies in Africa. Their economic interests still came first and countries like Kenya, where Western nations had strategic interests, were given a far easier ride than poor, weak countries of little interest to the West. After the bombing of the Twin Towers in New York in 2001, the West's agenda changed again. Two new factors entered into the equation: the 'war on terror' and oil. African countries no longer had to respect human rights or hold elections at all if they produced oil and co-operated with America in its war on Al-Qaeda. Libya, for example, formerly regarded as a rogue state, became a Western ally but its dictator, Colonel Qaddafi, stayed on, as repressive as ever.

The collapse of the currencies reduced the salaries of senior civil servants to around $50 a month. The very people who were supposed to implement the reforms were themselves impoverished. Naturally many of them left, to either America, France or Britain, or got jobs in the new private sector that paid in hard currency or the equivalent. This meant that many African states lost the only people who could run them. The machinery of government, never very effective, ground to a halt. Lack of capacity in Africa resulted in scores of foreign consultants being brought in at huge expense, many of them with no experience or knowledge of Africa and how it works. Africa was further marginalized from its own development.

In addition to the collapse at the top of the civil service, thousands of minor state employees, often supporting large extended families, were now laid off. Those who remained were rapidly impoverished by collapsing currencies. Scores were reduced to clocking into their offices then moonlighting as taxi drivers in the official car or helping their wives sell food on the streets. Naturally they needed cash, and many sold their services. Petty corruption increased hugely. In Kenya they call it *chai* – tea, in West Africa it is *dash* and in Congo *un petit sucre* – a little sugar. Under these circumstances I think of these requests as a sort of personalized VAT, irritating but widely practised and, as long as services are delivered, neither immoral nor illegal. Normal throughout most of Africa today, these practices were inevitable as Africa's currencies plummeted and civil servants on salaries were paid less per day than the price of a loaf of bread.

Still pushing the idea that states were the problem, aid donors attempted to get aid directly to the people by bypassing government bureaucracies and giving aid to non-state agencies such as international and local NGOs. African governments became less and less able to provide the basic functions of government such as security and justice. Health and education systems collapsed. Poverty soared while the newly wealthy NGOs operating in African states found themselves becoming mini governments, responsible for everything from providing food aid to employing their own private armies. In some places it looked as if the free market agenda imposed suddenly and uncompromisingly on Africa would result in the dismemberment of the continent, dividing it between warlords and NGOs.

Privatization was strongly resisted at first by governments. Then, aided by bank loans, the elites who had been running the country and its parastatal companies and assets, began to buy them up – assets they had wrecked and looted while they were in government. And they made sure that the price stayed low. The rules of privatization often included local ownership, and when Western companies began to reappear in Africa, they needed someone local to hold their hand as they tiptoed into Africa's bureaucratic jungles. Who better than a local powerful politician? So the fat cats of the old state-controlled regimes now became the even fatter cats of the privatized companies. Everything changed and everything stayed the same. The old rich became the new rich. The poor stayed poor. Or, as that acidulous South African in Angola said, 'The shit changes but the flies stay the same.'

The old elites put their new fortunes to good use: politics. The second part of the new Western agenda for Africa was multi-party democracy. Keeping political power was essential and under the new Western-dictated rules it was quite easy. Many of the ruling elites were now dollar multi-millionaires and the electorate was poor. Far from the free market separating the state from the economy, the new world order kept them together as solidly as they had been under state-controlled systems. The bosses and their cronies still ran – and now owned – the country.

Western governments, the World Bank and the IMF were desperate to prove that their remedies were working. They anxiously sought 'success stories' among those who had taken the medicine and were beginning to resurrect their economies. At the start of the 1990s Uganda and Ghana were held up as models of well-governed countries following good economic policies. Yoweri Museveni, the Ugandan President, was fêted in Western capitals as one of a new breed of African leaders. He was joined by Paul Kagame, the man who took over Rwanda's government after the genocide in 1994, and by Meles Zenawi of Ethiopia and Issaias Afwerke of Eritrea. These military philosopher-princes had come to power through the barrel of a gun, but they turned out to be pragmatic men who eschewed ideology and promoted what Western countries saw as sensible economic policies. At first power did not seem to go to their heads. All but Rwanda had suffered economic catastrophes in the mid 1980s and had bounced back, so the figures under the rule of military reformists began to look good.

These prize pupils, promoted by Western governments, did not turn out as hoped. In 1998 Meles and Issaias went to war, ostensibly over a piece of desert that was barely big enough to bury those who died fighting for it. The war cost tens of thousands of lives and ruined the economies of both countries and the reputations of both men. The following year the armies of Museveni and Kagame clashed at Kisangani in Congo in a squabble over whose army was going to grab the country's fabulous resources.

The World Bank and the International Monetary Fund then held up Botswana and Mauritius as models for the continent. Mauritius, though a member of the African Union, is an Indian Ocean island which looks more to India than Africa. Its government was determined to end its dependency on sugar and put all its efforts into diversifying into textiles. Despite a long and difficult struggle

Mauritius remains a success story. Botswana too. Its tiny population of one and a half million grows richer mainly because of diamonds which produce nearly 90 per cent of the country's foreign exchange earnings. Some say that Botswana's success and lack of strife is due to its single ethnic group, the Tswana. They say it does not suffer from tribalism like other African countries. There is some truth in this, but it is not entirely correct. A quarter of Botswana's population are from different ethnic groups and do not speak Setswana, the language of the Tswana people. The mono-ethnic argument does not hold either. The other country in Africa that is supposedly mono-ethnic is Somalia; hardly a model of peace and prosperity. The people of Botswana got richer because the government did not steal the diamond money but spent it on things that benefited the country.

Throughout this second post-independence period, which lasted from the mid 1980s to the late 1990s, only five countries in sub-Saharan Africa had economic growth rates high enough to produce a better life for the next generation. Three of them, Congo-Brazzaville, Angola and Rwanda, were emerging from terrible civil wars and were growing from a very low base. The economies of Congo and Angola were growing particularly fast as oil producers – which was the main reason for their terrible wars. Oil investment revenue created nice-looking economic statistics that cheered up the World Bank and the IMF, but oil is notorious for destroying other economic sectors. In Nigeria and Angola oil smothered other economic activities and made corruption a way of life.

The rest of Africa south of the Sahara suffered drastic economic decline. Debt mounted, incomes fell, the capacity to produce growth diminished. People began to ask whether the state could survive in Africa. The lesson from that decade was that there were no model pupils. Africa's new leaders were – a bit like ordinary human beings – neither entirely good nor entirely bad. None of them completely followed the West's new rules: the free market, democracy and respect for human rights. Some followed the free market but had no democracy. Others were democratic but had appalling human rights records. In the end Africa's rulers did what rulers anywhere do: they did whatever they could to stay in power. But Africa has fewer checks and balances and fewer options for former leaders other than exile or death. When the chips are down in Africa and rulers have to choose between following Western policies or risk the loss of power, the local imperative always wins out.

In many cases the centre did not hold. Weakened by economic reforms and political demands, several African countries exploded in rebellion and war. In the 1990s thirty-one African countries, three-quarters of the nations of mainland Africa, suffered wars or violent social upheaval. There were fears that some of these collapsed states would simply disappear. In Sierra Leone, Liberia, Sudan, Angola and Congo, rulers and rebels had become like competing warlords, seizing as much of the economy as they could to further their war aims. No side could boast legitimacy; many governments controlled little more than the capital and could not deliver security or development to their people even if they had wanted to. Rebels lived by rape and pillage, happy to leave the care of the people and other state functions to the United Nations agencies and NGOs. As long as their fighters had food, shelter and women, they had little interest in the rest of the population. Whatever the motive for starting the war, the pursuit of resources – diamonds and other minerals and timber – sometimes became an end itself. This looked like war without end, a hellish vision of economic, political and moral collapse. Outsiders like Robert Kaplan saw Africa as 'The Coming Anarchy' or more simply – as the *Economist* said – 'The Hopeless Continent'.

Times were bad but whatever evils Africa suffered then, lack of hope wasn't one of them.

11

Dancers and the leopard men
Sierra Leone

Apart from Rwanda in 1994 I have never encountered hopelessness in Africa. Amidst the direst catastrophes – war and death, famine or just slow decline – Africans don't do hopelessness. I am walking an earth track leading up from a great river towards a group of huts nestling under a vast airy tree. Glorified by the setting sun, the earth glows a rich purple red, the trees are green fire. Woodsmoke and song drift softly on the still evening air, scent and sound mingling in unbearable sweetness. In a strong quavering voice, a matron chants the line of story-song and her companions throw back a refrain; strident, repetitive, unanswerable. Yet she answers it. And they reply to her again. 'What did hare tell the elephant's mother?' – 'Cook soup for me!' They clap and sing in time to the booming beat of poles thudding into a deep wooden pestle. It is the heartbeat of Africa. The song ends with a whoop! and a peal of laughter. A shrill bird call applauds from somewhere in the forest and then silence and the low voices of the women talking.

This idyll of Africa is Sierra Leone in 1993, just as the civil war is reaching its horrific nadir. There are tales of armed robbers on the road, killers in the night, villages burned and children with guns and knives who kill their parents, rape their aunts and cut off hands and feet. There are even rumours that they rip out human hearts and eat them, hot and pumping.

The singer stands, adjusts her wrap and sways to the rhythm of the song. The girl pounding the maize pauses and leans on her pole. Another jumps up from the bench to take her place and the singing resumes. Spread comfortably over white plastic chairs, the men hold a spasmodic conversation that trails off into long silences. The main hut is a smooth square of clean brown mud with a roof of rust-brown corrugated iron. The others are thatched. Nearby is a plot of maize and a few coffee bushes. Some utensils lie on the ground: a hoe, cooking pots, a rusty old lorry wheel. Here is an African family: father, wife, his mother, her mother's sister, two sons and four daughters, two cousins – called daughters too – and a couple of other relatives from far away also staying at the house.

They are poor in money. The family sells a little coffee and sur-plus maize but they must buy salt, sugar, cooking oil, clothes and kerosene for lamps. The big expenditures are school fees, weddings and funerals. Any one of these can cost more than a year's income and put a family in debt for ever. Then there are shocks like medical bills. Over the years the work of their hands has bought fewer and fewer goods from the industrial world.

Some, usually the younger ones, long to escape to the city, to Britain or America. Adversity is what they know and how to live with it, survive it. If you arrive unannounced they will feed you without question, not entirely in the hope that you will do something for them one day. Africa is rich in manners. Politeness. Every meeting begins with a long greeting. And when you go they will give you a gift. This is a family that could be anywhere in tropical Africa. What has Africa to offer the rest of the world? Patience, hope, civility – and music. If you judged the peoples of the world by their music, Africans would rank the most hopeful and contented. If music were wealth Africa would be rich. Africa gifted modern music to the world through America. All the rhythms of rock and jazz, reggae and soul have their roots in Africa. Africa's music is defiantly self-confident, irrepressibly strong. Life is good, the bubbling rhythms throb. Love life, cry its floating songs. African music expresses African culture more strongly than anything else. Walk down any dusty, litter-strewn street in a poor part of a broken African town and the thick warm air tingles with tunes like jewels threaded on a subtle silver wire of rhythm. Music mingles with the smoke of roasting meat at roadside charcoal stoves and the dust and fumes of cars and buses.

How can such irrepressible optimism come from Africa, supposedly the violent, suffering, despairing continent? If Africa produced the relentless rage of rap or the brutal speed of grime music no-one would be surprised. But there is not a whiff of stress or despair. There is no word for depression in most African languages. Africa's upbeat music is not some chin-up, always-look-on-the-bright-side pep song, nor an underground resistance movement, a defence against hopelessness. African music is hope. Its dances are life. Africa is ruled more by its music than its misery. Is there some secret source of joy in Africa that the rest of us have forgotten or never knew? Maybe. In *Talk Stories*, Jamaica Kincaid, the African Caribbean writer, puts it like this:

> *Now, there are a few cultural traits that black people may want to deny (why, I will never quite know), but there are some that they just can't escape. For instance, they can't deny that they know how to make dancing music more than any one else, that they give better parties than anyone else, that they are better at dancing spontaneously than anyone else.*

African music catches a spirit, a profound talent for living, enjoying life when it is good and surviving the bad times. The paradox is perfectly balanced: terrible times produce huge strength. Grief enhances joy. Death invigorates living.

Here you see death, disease and pain every day. It is out in the open, not hidden away as it is in Europe and America. At funerals the coffin is open. At the market animals are slaughtered with axes and the blood runs into the gutter. The beggar with stick legs performs his handstand in the street then swings his shrivelled limbs towards you – and laughs. The leper takes you by the hand. You will hear appalling tales: a lost identity card that cost a job and weeks of hunger for the family, a theft of five years of savings, an illness that cost a family its land, a sudden storm that destroyed a home and its crops, a painful death from an unknown sickness. Africa lives with death and suffering and grief every day, but to be alive is to talk and laugh, eat and drink – and dance. If you didn't dance you would curl up and die.

The rainforest around Mokaba is the jungle of your nightmares where you are lost and being chased. A village not much more than a clearing in dense West African rainforest, it lies by a tributary of the mighty Sewa River. A group of gleeful boys bathe naked, diving and chasing each other in and out of the water with shrieks and laughter. A group of women wash clothes, beating them on the rocks. Further up the river a fisherman stands knee-deep, with string tied to the end of a rough-hewn branch.

Two days earlier I had stood on the old stone bridge over the River Clun at Leintwardine in Herefordshire watching my children trying to catch minnows in a net and a fly fisherman in waders waiting for a trout. Two thousand years ago the Romans built a marching camp at Leintwardine and there has been a stone bridge there ever since.

Why is there no bridge at Mokaba? It needs one. The people have to cross the river to reach their fields. There is plenty of stone nearby, but the bridge here is made of lianas and branches, a perilous walkway strung across the river that swings and wobbles when you step on it. Every year it gets washed away in the rainy season and every year the villagers rebuild it. I watch a blind man led by a child trying to feel his way across. He gives up and turns back. Women carrying goods on their heads – the only method of transport here – cannot cross it either. They pause and unload their things into smaller bundles. Why not build a stone bridge that would survive the annual floods? Why doesn't Mokaba look like Leintwardine?

Poverty is not an answer. Nature has endowed the area around Mokaba stupendously. The earth of central Sierra Leone is so rich and the climate so good that, as in Uganda, a seed or stick half-planted in the ground grows astoundingly fast. The land crops twice a year. The rivers are full of fish. The forests provide wild fruits and bush meat. Beneath the earth God has seamed the rocks with gold and strewn the river beds with diamonds. This is a land where you do not have to work hard to live comfortably. With hard work you might get rich. But this place is poor. And there is no bridge. In Europe people adapted the environment, broke it and remade it. In Africa people accepted the environment and adapted to it. Is that the answer? If so, what does it say about 'development' in Africa?

Right now I sense a lack of trust here too, a poison seeping into society, a fatal ending. On the way the bus stopped at a roadblock manned by soldiers, some no more than ten or eleven years old. Beneath a roadside tree, surrounded by discarded beer bottles, their commander lay asleep. His kid soldiers shouted orders, waved their AK47s at the passengers and forced the women to bring their bundles down from the top of the bus and untie them. The passengers were marshalled into a queue to have their papers checked by a young corporal sitting at a school desk under a tree, while the soldiers picked through the bundles, taking things at whim. When a woman complained a soldier raised a stick to strike her. A young man's identity card was torn up in front of him.

When my turn came to hand my passport across the school desk, the sergeant ordered the soldiers to search me. Two of them started to feel my pockets, but from the queue behind me an old man in a tweed jacket and cap stepped forward and intervened on my behalf.

'Who are you?' they sneered.

'You too young to ask me dat,' he replied. 'Dis man visitor and my friend. Show respect.'

Surprisingly it worked. A shred of respect for older people still remained. The sergeant waved me through.

The soldiers were supposed to be searching for guns and supporters of the Revolutionary United Front (RUF), an incoherent rebel movement that was causing mayhem in the east. But Sierra Leone's new young military rulers had simply pressganged street kids in Freetown, given them uniforms and guns and sent them up country. There they were turning into what came to be called 'Sobels'; soldiers by day, rebels by night. They had suddenly gone from being the lowest kids in the land to men with power. They cared little whose side – if any – they fought on. Most just used their guns to steal, rape and kill.

For the rest of the journey I sat next to my rescuer. Dan Bindi is a retired headmaster living in Bo. He fears deeply for the future. He sees the conflict as an apocalyptic struggle between good and evil, but the more he talks the more he seems to present the conflict as one between civilization and barbarism in which Western civilization is driving out African barbarism. He refers to 'we' – him and me – as being in the civilized Western camp. The rebels – and these boy soldiers he sees as evil – uncivilized, African. Mr Bindi and others of his age and class from Freetown regard themselves as superior to Africans in the 'interior', as they still call the rest of the country outside the Freetown peninsula. It is a view that has grown out of the history of Britain and Sierra Leone – a history every Sierra Leonean knows and hardly a single Briton.

The first British encounter with the country was in 1562 when John Hawkins, pirate, slaver and British sea hero, sailed into the huge estuarine lake that is now Freetown Bay and seized some locals as slaves. He sailed across the Atlantic and sold them in the Caribbean, marking one of the first instances of the trade in African slaves that was to create vast wealth for Britain. Hawkins did not return, but later British traders established good relations with the kings who ruled the harbour zone and the peninsula.

Sierra Leone re-entered British history more than two centuries later when Britain had one of its periodic fits of immigration panic. At the outbreak of the American war of independence, thousands of black slaves fled from their masters and joined the British loyalist side, encouraged by promises of freedom. In 1772 Lord Mansfield, England's Chief Justice, had freed a runaway slave called Somerset who had escaped from his owner during a visit to Britain from the West Indies. Until then there had been contrary legal rulings about the legality of slavery in Britain. Officially there was none, but the question arose when a slave owner in America brought a slave temporarily to Britain. Some rulings had permitted Britons living abroad to visit with their slaves. The Somerset case finally established that slavery was illegal on British soil. Fear that this ruling might be imposed on America too was a crucial but much overlooked motive for the white American bid for independence. It certainly ensured that the vast majority of black people in America supported the British cause in the war of independence, believing that they stood a better chance of emancipation under British rule than under the colonists. They formed a whole regiment to fight for the British crown as well as providing assistance to other British troops.

Britain lost the war and retreated, but while white colonists who fought on the British side were able to pay their way back to England, the former slaves could not. Many were caught and executed or re-enslaved, but some fled north to Canada and settled in Nova Scotia. Gradually and despite the callous indifference of the British government, thousands made their way to Britain, almost doubling the numbers of black people already living there. With no skills or support, many became beggars on the streets of London, Bristol, Plymouth and other ports. It was eventually proposed that they be settled in a colony at Sierra Leone, a solution that the former slaves, the anti-slavery movement and the government accepted. But each had different ideas about how it was to be done. The anti-slavery activists who funded the project imagined that the blacks, who had mostly been born in America, could simply be returned to Africa and live there as they had before. Crooked government contractors failed to deliver the promised supplies and the blacks were divided among themselves, fearful of being returned to slavery or just abandoned.

In April 1787, after long delays in which many died of hunger, cold and disease, three ships with more than 600 on board sailed from Plymouth. But not all of them were black people wanting to return 'home' to Africa. Just before the ships sailed the London authorities rounded up prostitutes and criminals, plied them with drink and 'married' them to the departing Africans.

Arriving in West Africa as the rainy season began, the settlers suffered from hunger and disease. The seeds they planted would not grow, their animals grew thin and died. So did they. Within a year there were only 130 survivors. The new colonists were ruled by a British-appointed governor, but the local king, King Tom, exploited their weakness and seized some, selling them as slaves to a passing French slaver. Others joined local slaving agents themselves. Two years later the whole settlement was burned to the ground.

In 1792 1000 black former soldiers and their families who had fled to Nova Scotia after American independence were sent to the settlement. Many of them also died, but the group now had a chance of survival and for a while it progressed. But as things got better the settlers became impatient with being ruled from London and rebelled – successfully.

Unfortunately for them however, there had recently been a slave revolt in Jamaica. A group of rebels known as Maroons had fled to the hills and threatened British rule. The governor talked the men into surrender with the promise that they could return to Africa. In 1800 the Royal Navy took them back across the Atlantic and sailed into Freetown harbour just as the rebellion there was in full swing. The British promptly armed the newly arrived settlers and turned them on the rebellious settlement. Thus ended Sierra Leone's first attempt at independence. To this day there is bad feeling between Sierra Leoneans of Nova Scotian and Maroon descent: the Montagues and Capulets of Freetown.

The troubled colony continued to suffer, attacked and looted by the French and rarely at peace with neighbouring African settlements and slaving stations. Meanwhile in Britain the anti-slavery movement had grown in strength and in 1807 a law was passed outlawing the slave trade. As the world's leading naval power, Britain took its own law seriously and the following year Freetown became the base for the Royal Navy's West African anti-slavery patrol. The fort on Bunce Island in the middle of the harbour, built by the Portuguese as a slave fort, was rebuilt and for the next century Freetown became Britain's main naval base in the east Atlantic. In the overgrown graveyard on Bunce Island you can still see the graves of young British naval officers who died of fever on the anti-slavery patrol. The British legacy in Sierra Leone is mixed.

The anti-slavery patrol freed slaves from French, Portuguese and

Dutch ships on the West African coast and deposited them at Freetown, giving it a cosmopolitan feel. The town turned into a prosperous port supporting a lively colony. Like Falklanders and Gibraltarians, the inhabitants felt close economic and emotional ties to the colonizing power, closer than they felt towards their neighbours. In the nineteenth century many Freetonians were well-off traders, living in three-storey houses and sending their children overseas to British public schools. The people of Freetown still feel a strong bond to Britain and – like Mr Bindi – identify strongly with British values and culture.

Until the late nineteenth century the British had merely made forays into the rest of the country, maintaining its hegemony in the region but making no attempt to extend its rule beyond the Freetown peninsula. In 1896 the rest of Sierra Leone was established within its existing borders as a British protectorate but ruled from the Freetown colony. The cosmopolitan people of Freetown saw themselves as pioneers in the interior. In the protectorate people resented the Freetown colony with its superior ways and ruthless exploitation. Freetown, with its magnificent harbour, golden beaches and lavish hotels, still feels like a European settlement perched on the edge of Africa. Like many of the continent's ports it also seems sometimes like the end of a great pipe, sucking the wealth out of Africa. The rebellion of the 1980s and 1990s owed much to a nation-wide resentment of Freetown's corruption and domination.

Independent Sierra Leone's path to ruin is a well-trodden one. Party politics in its first few years set Freetown Creoles against the chiefs in the interior. After coups and counter-coups Siaka Stevens, thief and thug, emerged as the victor. In 1978 he made it a one-party state. Two years later he bankrupted the country by spending almost a year's government revenue on a lavish summit for his fellow African heads of state, providing them with new hotels, a conference centre and hundreds of new vehicles. The economy never recovered.

Stevens tortured and killed his opponents but died in his bed, having handed over power to a charming but indolent old general called Joseph Momoh. Feeding on aid and corruption, Momoh took the country further downhill throughout the 1990s. The ultimate prize lay in the centre and east of the country, along its rivers: diamonds. Sierra Leone has some of the best diamonds in the world, but very little revenue came to the state treasury. Tiny, hard to find but of immense price, diamonds are easily stolen and easy to hide, smuggle and sell anywhere in the world. Very corrupting. Diamonds were once the mainstay of Sierra Leone's economy, providing the bulk of government revenues. Gradually theft, illegal diggings, smuggling and corruption reduced the government's take to nothing. In August 1993 the Minister of Finance, James Jonah, told me that the total tax for the Sierra Leone Treasury that month was $8,000. Some diamonds were taken by the Revolutionary United Front, the rebel militia, which swapped them for guns provided by the Liberian warlord Charles Taylor, later to become President of Liberia. Others fed into networks organized by Lebanese traders who smuggled them out to Antwerp, usually with a 'dash' of money to the President and a few officials in the chain. The Lebanese had been encouraged to settle in Sierra Leone during British rule to encourage trade and build the economy. Now they were sucking the country dry, leaving it a corpse, the people destitute. Britain propped up the government with aid.

The little shiny stones have transformed Mokaba from a peaceful riverside village into a squatter camp of frantic and fractious immigrant diggers. Every morning scores of young men leave their shabby huts of scavenged wood and corrugated iron and make their way down to the riverbank. It looks like a building site of earthworks and diggings. Stripped to the waist and working in pairs, the miners dig down to where the gravel is heaviest. Sometimes they build a wide pit, sometimes a shaft with chambers and tunnels running off it. Children are sent down the tunnels to scrape together bucketfuls of the heaviest gravel they can reach. The mushy gravel often collapses. Diggers complain they frequently come across the bodies and bones of children from old workings.

I watch two young men come down to the river carrying ropes, a long hollow bamboo pole and a bucket. One strips, ties the rope around his waist and wades into the torrent. His mate holds the other end of the rope. He plunges out into the water and lets the current carry him down to the end of a rapid. Then he dives downwards holding the breathing pole above him like a periscope. Nearly a minute later he re-emerges further down the river and his mate hauls him back towards the bank. His precious load is held aloft. Among the gravel and sludge in the bucket may be a diamond washed down the river over the millennia and lodged in the gravel beds and the shallow rock pools beneath the rapids.

In Angola, where diamonds were mined by large foreign companies, they simply dammed the river, diverted its course into a new channel and excavated the river bed. I watched them at Lucapa on the Luachimo River. Using mechanical buckets and JCBs, they worked down through the gravel and rock and dug out the ravine at the base of the river's course. On the edge of the ravine were armed guards, their guns pointing at the workers. They watched for anyone who might slip his hand to his mouth to hide a diamond. The heaviest mineral, diamonds sink through the sand and gravel and at bedrock, they gather in pools scooped out by aeons of flooding. In such places miners have been known to find millions of dollars' worth in a few minutes.

Here in Sierra Leone all is done by hand. Along the riverbank bare-backed men work in pairs. In the mornings they work the gravel pits along the river terraces. The afternoons are for washing the gravel in the river. One stands thigh deep in the river holding a fine sieve like a tray that he dips into the water and spins and shakes. The other shovels gravel into the sieve from a pile on the bank. From time to time the siever stops and peers at something, picking intently at a pebble, then he chucks it into the river and continues. I watch them for ages but I never see a diamond. 'You won't,' says the local doctor later. 'If a man finds a diamond here, he'll slip it into his mouth before you'd notice. If people know you have found a diamond, you are in mortal danger. That is the problem with this place. There is no trust – not even between these brothers who dig together. We have many killings. A lot of people disappear.'

After a couple of days in the village I have still not seen a diamond and I ask a digger to show me one. He furtively takes me round the back of a hut and looks around to make sure no-one is watching. Then he opens his mouth for a fraction of a second. On his pink tongue I get a glimpse of what looks like a piece of broken Coca-Cola bottle.

Watching them I wonder if this is what California was like in the 1840s when thousands of young men trekked to the area in the hope of finding gold. Many did and the result was prosperity, transport, law and the creation of a magnificent new city, San Francisco.

Here they call it the resource curse, and judging by the way the miners live, it brings nothing but poverty. The young men from miles around and beyond leave their homes and farms to come and dig. Without them their families become poorer. Even if they find a valuable stone they will be cheated by a dealer or even killed for it. What money they receive they spend on flashy goods to prove they are rich.

I continually hear tales of miners who have found a big stone.

Every story has the same ending. Whether from the diamond rivers of Congo, Angola or the Central African Republic, the same stories have the same ending. The man found a stone. He got paid $1000, $100,000, $1 million, $2 million. He bought a Mercedes Benz, a smart suit, a gold watch, and built a big house in the city. He had many wives, many children. He was very popular. He had many friends. But he drank. He lost his money. He lost his car, his house. Then his wives and his children turned against him. They stole from him. Then they left him. Now he is back digging again. You can meet him if you like.

Several African countries are cursed with diamonds: Angola, Congo, Central African Republic, Sierra Leone. Only in South Africa, Namibia and Botswana, where mining is tightly controlled and the revenues used well, have they created wealth. Elsewhere they have fed wars and created poverty. In Angola's civil war the government had oil, the rebels diamonds. In the end there was no contest. In 2001, the year before the UNITA leader Jonas Savimbi was killed, oil gave the government $3.18 billion. Jonas Savimbi's diamonds brought in a fraction of that. He lost.

A diamond the size of your little fingernail can be worth hundreds of thousands of dollars. But there is no shortage of them. The price of diamonds, however, has been kept artificially high by control of the supply. Until recently the market was controlled by one company: De Beers. The British-based South African mining company owned the Big Hole at Kimberley in South Africa, the first mine in the world where diamonds were mined on an industrial scale. As more and more diamonds came on stream from Africa and elsewhere, De Beers bought the mines or forced their owners to regulate supply and sell only to the De Beers marketing organization, the Central Selling Organization.

The cartel controlling supply from mine to manufacturer ensured that a rise in production would never cause a fall in the price. The 'diamond is for ever' slogan fed the myth that the value of diamonds can never be questioned by the market. Not even America's Anti Trust laws could break the De Beers monopoly, though for years no senior member of De Beers dared to go to the US for fear of arrest. Did they break the US laws? As Eleanor Fox, a New York lawyer, told me in an interview in 1993:

> *It's a very interesting question whether consumers of diamonds want the price to go down. People buy diamonds because they want a scarce, valuable gem . . . [If the cartel is broken and the price goes down] people who have bought diamonds will be greatly aggrieved and the people who are buying a scarce, beautiful gem tomorrow may find the diamond is no longer such a gem. There seems to be no consumer clamour to break up the diamond cartel.*

Or, as one New York dealer put it, 'When a guy buys the girl a diamond, what he really wants is to get into her pants. And he reckons the more he pays, the better his chances.' The value of diamonds perhaps lies in sex rather than supply.

Apart from some fluctuations in the 1930s, the price of diamonds never went down between the 1890s and the end of the twentieth century. When demand was slack or production rose, De Beers stockpiled diamonds in London – $4 billion worth in the late 1990s. If market demand did not soak up production, a line in the De Beers contract forced producers to stockpile the surplus unsold until De Beers chose to buy it when demand picked up. Even at the height of the Cold War De Beers bought diamonds from the Soviet Union. Both sides wanted to avoid bad publicity – the Russians by dealing with capitalists based in South Africa, and De Beers by doing business with Communists. So the two sides met discreetly in Hambro's Bank next door to the De Beers complex in Holborn, London.

At the other end of the process De Beers fed the stones onto the market at a rate that ensured they made maximum profit. Carefully vetted dealers were invited to become 'sight holders' and buy directly from De Beers at their London headquarters twice a year. But this was no normal market. The sight holders had to disclose all their financial details to De Beers and supply them with everything they knew about the market. Before the twice-yearly sights at De Beers headquarters at Charterhouse Street in London, the sight holder made a wish list of quantities of stones according to size and quality. De Beers might – or might not – supply them according to what its research thought the market would bear. On the day of the sight each sight holder was closeted in a small bare room with a table, chair and lamp. Their box of specially selected diamonds was brought to them to examine. They would find that in addition to what the buyers asked for – which may or may not have been supplied – the buyers were also given a whole lot of other stones they had not asked for and on which they could make little profit. De Beers terms were take it or leave it – the whole box or nothing. So the company could punish or reward their sight holders, playing them off against each other, impoverishing one, enriching another according to how subservient they were. Buying outside the De Beers sights was frowned on. And knowing the financial health of every individual, the company would know exactly what each sight holder could buy. They could refuse to buy once or twice, but if sight holders continually refused to buy, they would be struck off the list.

If they were jewellers running a cutting factory with an expensive wage bill, diamond dealers needed a regular supply of diamonds, so they had to accept De Beers' terms. The alternative was buying on the open market – supplied by diggers like those at Mokaba and their

Lebanese controllers – but that could not guarantee a regular supply. And the open market was not necessarily cheaper. De Beers also took care of that. Their buying offices in Antwerp purchased just enough to soak up the open market supply if it threatened to bring down the price.

How did De Beers manage to do this? The company was – and in part still is – owned by the Oppenheimer family who at the time also owned Anglo American, the South African gold mining giant. When the world was feeling insecure and needed to save, it bought gold. When the world was feeling rich and spendthrift, it bought diamonds. Sunshine or rain, the Oppenheimers won. From that they moved into almost every other business in South Africa from newspapers to nuclear fuels. When the Johannesburg stock exchange had its big bang in 1995, more than half the companies quoted, some 600, were owned or controlled by the Oppenheimer family.

The wars in Angola and Sierra Leone came to be seen more and more as wars over resources with no further political aim. The scandal of 'blood diamonds' threatened to do to the diamond industry what pictures of cuddly furry animals being slaughtered had done to the market in fur coats. At the same time Russia and Canada were producing diamonds in such quantities that De Beers could no longer afford to buy them up and stockpile them. The company was forced to rethink its whole diamond operation. In 1998 it separated from Anglo and in 2000 De Beers closed its buying operation in Antwerp and got rid of the stockpile, introducing a policy of 'supplier of choice'. Although it still sells diamonds to other dealers, the company started to market them directly to the public, setting up a shop in London's Piccadilly that sells specially marked diamonds with certificates to prove they are from legitimate mines that are not in war zones.

*

In Sierra Leone General Momoh was overthrown in 1992 by junior officers who promised to clean things up. Did anyone believe they would? 'We have to,' said one woman I spoke to in Freetown, 'because they are so young. By taking over they have overturned the Sierra Leonean social order. Older people have been robbed of their position and status. People no longer respect them. So if these young men fail we will have no-one to turn to.'

One of the first orders the young soldiers gave was to restore the tradition of Saturday cleaning. From colonial times it had been a tradition that all Sierra Leoneans went out to clean the streets on Saturday mornings. On the orders of the young junior officers the rotting rubbish on waste ground or blocking open sewers was suddenly swept away. Bright flowers were planted in public places. And Freetown's bare walls – usually used for pissing against – were smartly painted by Alusine Bangura, a junior prison officer with a gift for painting faces from memory. Before long Freetown's walls were adorned with pictures of the Pope, John Kennedy, the Queen of England and Mike Tyson along with famous Sierra Leoneans.

This gave the people hope that the country too would be cleaned up and put back on its feet. But things got worse. Captain Valentine Strasser and the gang of junior officers seized power simply because they resented fighting the RUF in the east of the country while the greedy and corrupt grew fat in Freetown. As soon as they took power they became as greedy and corrupt as those they had overthrown. And – with the possible exception of Strasser himself – far more violent. I interviewed John Benjamin, the finance minister and only civilian in a senior position in government. While I was talking to him Captain Karefa Kargbo, the Secretary of Foreign Affairs, strode into the room without knocking. Benjamin leapt to his feet and rushed deferentially to him like a servant. Which indeed was what he was – and one who would be shot, rather than fired, if he failed to deliver.

The RUF had begun as an idealistic Marxist movement, led by students from Fourah Bay College. But once they took to the bush the students lost control to Foday Sankoh, a former army photographer, who turned the RUF into a movement of pure terror. Politically the RUF proclaimed a vague message of liberation and played on the hopelessness of Freetown's street children and village kids up country who had just enough education to understand that they would never see any benefit from the riches around them. But it quickly resorted to forced recruitment, initiating young new members in horrific ways that prevented them ever returning home. Sometimes they were forced to rape their relatives or kill their own parents. The children became 'other', no longer themselves. Many say the RUF became their mother and father controlling their lives, enfolding them totally in its world. Their alienation from the rest of society was complete, reinforced with rituals such as drinking human blood and eating human flesh. They were told such rituals would make them spiritually powerful and protect them from bullets. The young fighters were also fed drugs. 'Brown brown' was one such concoction, made of cocaine and gunpowder.

The movement's tactics were murder and rape. Its speciality was cutting off hands. With no hands you cannot vote in an election, the victims were told. Sometimes they cut off feet as well.

Sierra Leone has a history of such militias. Secret societies are common, brotherhoods such as the *Poro* which indulge in rituals and vows of secrecy. One tradition from Sierra Leone and Liberia going back to the nineteenth century is the 'leopard men', in which men could 'become' leopards and kill with impunity. The leopard men were controlled by the secret societies, and if they sanctioned someone's death, the chosen killer would dress in a leopard skin and mark the corpse with real leopard claws or claw-shaped knives. But he would also 'become' a leopard to carry out the act. Possessed by the leopard spirit, he was not himself and could not be held responsible for the death. The British rulers had great difficulty finding witnesses in cases of leopard men killings. In retrospect it is hard not to see a link between those societies and the practices of the RUF. It too acted like a secret society, enforcing absolute obedience through fear.

In January 1996 Strasser was ousted in a coup and the British arranged for him to go to Birmingham University to study. They also persuaded the new leader, Julius Maada Bio – much against his will – to hold to the original promise of elections. The soldiers tried to stop them, harassing candidates and attacking queues of voters on polling day, but the election went ahead. Ahmed Tejan Kabbah, a lawyer and former civil servant, was elected. Later that year he signed a peace agreement with the RUF.

It didn't work and Kabbah too was overthrown the following year by another young military man, Johnny Paul Koroma. But military coups were becoming unacceptable to the rest of the world in the late 1990s. In Sierra Leone, where the military were seen as part of the problem, a coup was particularly unwelcome. The regional West African organization, ECOWAS, the Economic Community of West African States, led by the Nigerians, sent 'peacekeeping' forces to Sierra Leone. They fought their way into Freetown and restored Kabbah to power. But the war in the rest of the country got worse and Koroma, driven out of Freetown, now linked up with the RUF and formed his own militia, the West Side Boys. They roared into Freetown at the end of 1998 killing, raping and looting. The city centre became the battleground and the city was saved only by fierce defending by Nigerian troops. Some 3000 people were killed.

The war ended in a messy compromise. But it ended. The Reverend Jesse Jackson, the American special envoy, strongarmed President Kabbah to sign a peace deal with Sankoh which brought

Sankoh into government as chairman of the country's diamond commission. Since Sankoh had stolen huge quantities of the country's diamonds on behalf of his ally, Charles Taylor, it was hard to see whether this was a bad joke or a naive attempt to make Sankoh a responsible member of the government. Released from house arrest in Nigeria, he came to Freetown and moved into a house protected by his own guards. The RUF, still out in the bush, scented victory and seized some 500 pathetically under-equipped and untrained UN troops.

That provoked a peace demonstration in Freetown which marched on Sankoh's house. His bodyguards opened fire and some demonstrators were killed. Sankoh fled but was captured days later and imprisoned. Meanwhile eleven British soldiers were also captured by Koromo's West Side Boys near Freetown. British special forces flew in to rescue them and wiped out the West Side Boys at the same time. This demonstration of firepower so impressed the rest of the RUF that they released their hostages. The movement disintegrated and its members melted away.

Sankoh died in prison, but the question remained: should those responsible be held to account and punished? The United States government said yes. But having failed to support the International Criminal Court and seen what an expensive disaster the special court for Rwanda had been, the Americans set up a hybrid court, a joint UN and Sierra Leonean government institution. This court indicted eleven men from the RUF, the Armed Forces Revolutionary Council of Johnny Paul Koroma and the Civil Defence Forces which had fought the RUF but often used similar tactics. When Hinga Norman, the leader of the Civil Defence Forces, died in prison during his trial many felt that he should have been treated as a national hero rather than a war criminal. In 2007 eight were convicted, but the most important defendant, the former Liberian President Charles Taylor, had to be tried in The Hague – though under the jurisdiction of the Sierra Leone Court.

Given some of the atrocities that have occurred in Africa's wars, I am always struck by the spirit of forgiveness when they end. Sierra Leone has its own ways of dealing with the past. Many RUF fighters did return to their homes and villages and others walked free on the streets of the capital – untouched. I heard only one story of retribution in a village against those who had fought with the RUF. 'We washed them in the river,' I was told. Another wonderful African ritual of reconciliation, I thought. An almost biblical cleansing. But no. The villagers had tied the children to stakes in the river at low tide and let the rising tide drown them. The river had killed them. No-one had to take responsibility.

Elsewhere in Sierra Leone to this day mothers see in the market the men who murdered their sons or raped their daughters. Children see senior RUF commanders who slaughtered their parents. Sometimes they see the very people who cut off their hands or feet. Yet there are astoundingly few reports of retribution. Africa seems to have a talent for reconciliation when wars finally end. In Nigeria after Biafra there was a policy of 'no victor, no vanquished'. In Kenya after Mau Mau, in Zimbabwe at independence and in South Africa when Mandela came to power, new governments urged people to forgive the white former rulers and leave them in peace. They did. Once wars stop in Africa there is little or no revenge.

The most remarkable story is that of Bience Gawanas, a Namibian lawyer and a member of Swapo who was sent to Britain in the 1980s to do education work about the struggle for Namibian independence. It was a thankless task going around British schools trying to tell them about Namibia, but she remained cheerful and well liked by everyone she met. In 1988 she went to Angola where Swapo and most Namibian exiles were based, to visit her ten-year-old child. When she arrived she was arrested by the Swapo secret police and tortured horribly. (The liberal establishment in Britain, to its eternal shame, knew her and knew of her arrest but said nothing about it because they thought it might damage the anti-apartheid struggle.)

Bience was released eventually but was deeply traumatized. She returned to a liberated Namibia and one day was driving along the main street. A beggar stopped her at the traffic lights and she recognized him as the man who had tortured her in Angola. She wound down the window and their eyes met – 'There was definite recognition,' she said, though they said nothing. She gave him 20 Rand (about £5). 'It was a beautiful moment,' she said. She became Namibia's ombudsman and an Under-Secretary-General at the United Nations. Stories like that of Bience Gawanas are not uncommon in Africa.

In Sierra Leone peace and a semblance of government were restored. But the deeper problems that had caused the rebellion have not been treated. Sierra Leone's conflict was not about tribalism or a battle for land. It was a battle for wealth and power, power over the country's resources and who should benefit from them.

In Mokaba in 1993 all these horrors are ahead. Thanks to the chief's son, I am staying in a small thatched wooden house with shutters but no glass in the windows, no electricity and a million mosquitoes. The mosquito net is full of holes. The massive bed is covered with thick woollen blankets that make the heat and stale air unbearable. I lie on a sheet naked trying to bring my temperature down by willpower. Night is total darkness, a cacophony of insect scrapings and chirpings and the frequent whine of mosquitoes. Sleep is impossible.

In the morning I open the shutters and examine the room. On one wall hang the faded, ant-eaten remains of a 1965 calendar of the Sierra Leone Central Co-operative Society. Around the calendar are photographs of the white office-holders: President 'Pa' Hill and his successor, Kelvin Nicholson Esq. BSc, 'The Pushfull'. They look like a couple of typical imperial bureaucrats: short slicked-down hair, bold moustaches on stern faces. But the use of their African nicknames on an official document suggests they might have identified with Sierra Leoneans more than their official position required. The calendar's inscription says that the Sierra Leonean Society of Co-operatives was an offshoot of the British Co-operative Movement and that the Central Province branch had 138 local societies, over 6000 members and a fund of over £30,000 – a lot of money in those days. Across the bottom of the calendar was printed: 'We used to be at the mercy of cruel money-lenders . . . Co-operatives have proved to us that poor peasant farmers like ourselves, individually weak and without influence, can overcome our poverty by making common cause with honesty, loyalty and determination.'

In Freetown on my way back home I check out the fate of the co-operative movement in Sierra Leone. It drowned in debt soon after independence amid allegations of theft and fraud. Today people talk about introducing the 'new' concept of microcredit to Africa.

As I am leaving Mokaba I get a taste of just how far Sierra Leone has fallen since those days of 'common cause with honesty, loyalty and determination'. I tell the chief's son that I want to thank his father personally and give him something for his hospitality. As we go to his father's hut, I ask the young man how much I should give for the use of the wooden house and for his own time in guiding me around the village. I say I will give the money directly to his father.

'No,' says the young man, 'don't give it to my father, he will never pass it on to me.'

'But,' I suggest, 'if I give him an amount and tell you how much

I have given then you can ask him for it. That way he will have to give it to you.'

'No,' says the son again. 'My father will say I am lying or there is no money from you. Give the money directly to me.'

When a chief is not trusted by his own son, the basic bonds of society have all but withered away. In their place something evil is building like the storm clouds that gather every evening over the distant hills, erupting like distant nuclear explosions. I move on to Bo, a small town that serves as district capital of central Sierra Leone, and make for a small hotel, the Black and White Bar. The bar got its name in times when Africans and Europeans used to drink in separate places. It was the first bar in Bo for everyone – black and white. Now it is a white bar only again because a beer costs as much as a week's salary for a local teacher or doctor. The money, the Leone, is 425 times less valuable than it was ten years ago. In the evening the only customers are a Danish dentist, an Irish Catholic priest and a young mining engineer from Cornwall who is trying to rehabilitate an old gold mine nearby.

Next evening I run into Mr Bindi again, the old man who rescued me at the roadblock. He is still wearing his tweed jacket and matching cap, flannel trousers and shiny brown shoes. For a moment his solemn eyes light up and I invite him for a drink. We sit on the first-floor veranda looking out across the city, watching the evening settle across the town. In the west white clouds tinged with pink pile up from the dark forest into a light blue sky. Somewhere beyond them lightning flickers in dark clouds. A loudspeaker blares from the mosque, drowning out Whitney Houston on the jukebox. A strong smell of drains wafts up from the street and mixes with a musty smell from the kitchen behind the bar.

We take a walk down the dusty street. The street sellers are making their way home with huge trays of goods balanced on their heads.

A mangy dog scuttles out of the way of a boy kicking a tin can along the road. Kids clamber over the rusty frames of old cars abandoned by the roadside. The town feels neglected, impoverished except for shops that have 'Diamond Dealer' newly painted over the doorway and a big flashy diamond on the wall. Mr Bindi explains that the Lebanese dealers rent out equipment to diggers but demand everything they find in return, paying the finders 'chicken change' for the diamonds. Gangs of thugs enforce the contract. From verandas above the diamond shops, pale-skinned women with covered heads peer warily onto the street. They seem anxious and ill at ease, hiding their faces when I look up at them.

As we make our way to the hospital, Mr Bindi tells how proud of it the town used to be. Its sturdy practical buildings are laid out in a series of courtyards. Now it is a filthy ruin with green fungus growing on the walls below broken gutters. It smells of must and wood rot. The paint is cracked and riddled with worm holes. The floors are covered with bat shit and grit from the disintegrating ceilings, stained brown and sagging from leaks in the roof. Water pipes have been stolen so water is brought daily in an ancient tanker from a well a mile away. Sometimes the tanker has no fuel. Electricity is occasional but it is not reliable enough to run fridges. No vaccines can be kept there. If doctors or nurses need light they bring their own light bulb and remove it when they go. Even the wiring gets stolen. Beds are merely iron frames. Mattresses and sheets are a memory. Patients bring grass mats to cover the rusting frames and springs.

Amazingly each ward is more than full with families camping out on the floor with a sick relative. It is they, not the nurses or doctors, who provide food, comfort and most of the care. They cook on little fires in the neglected hospital garden and wash in plastic bowls on the grass. One operating theatre is working, and here the large and cheerful former army major, Dr Dennis Williams, carries out cataract operations for river blindness. He injects the affected eye ball with anaesthetic from an old syringe, then he slices into the eyeball, scrapes away the cloudy film over the iris and stitches it up again. All the while he sings Methodist hymns in a deep baritone. River blindness is partly caused by the scramble for diamonds, spread by a little black fly that lives near water. As more and more people have abandoned farming to dig for diamonds by the rivers, the disease has spread rapidly.

With a heavy heart Mr Bindi shows me the remains of the regional administration building, a charred ruin with trees sprouting through it. Built in the 1960s with Russian aid, it had a huge Communist hammer and sickle monument by the entrance. Shortly afterwards, protesting students burned down the building and carried off the hammer. Now the giant sickle, slightly askew in front of this ruin, hangs like a huge question mark the wrong way round. Why does it have to be like this? it seems to say.

On the way back we pass a newly built mud hut wreathed in smoke and we peer inside. A charcoal fire silhouettes a hunched old man wearing shorts sitting cross-legged, working a pair of bellows made from sticks and sheep stomachs. He is smelting iron building rods. What is he making? we ask. 'Knives, spears, machetes,' comes the reply. We watch mesmerized as the squatting old man pumps the bellows and turns the glowing bar with tongs, pulling it back out of the fire onto a flat rock to beat it. 'And you know where those rods come from?' asks Mr Bindi sadly. 'The hospital.'

Sierra Leone seems to be turning away from modernity and retreating into the Iron Age. I had felt the same sensation in Uganda, in Congo, Angola, Mozambique, Nigeria, Sudan, Ghana and even in some countries like Senegal and Kenya that had not suffered a complete political breakdown. It is as if everything manufactured – bricks, cars, engines, paper, plastic bottles, oil cans – had been carried into Africa on a tide that is now retreating. The strange imports lie like rusting and rotting flotsam beached on an alien shore. Africa is strewn with buildings and machinery that were supposed to bring development but somehow got adapted or transformed into something else or now lie broken and useless in the sun. And it is not just things. Sometimes the very nation states themselves, with their borders, flags, airlines, presidential palaces and government offices, seem to be disintegrating and dissolving. I hear a wise old African saying with a polite smile: 'Thank you for these things but they do not last long and they really are not suitable for Africa. It is better we rely on what we know: mud and wood, fire and a little smelted iron.'

As if to confirm Mr Bindi's apocalyptic view of Africa, a furious drumming and blowing of horns start up. Around the corner comes a group of swirling devil dancers. In the midst of them a frenetic figure swathed in grass and a fierce mask leaps and stamps. He dances towards us, advancing and retreating, coming closer and closer. A look of unconscionable fear and horror spreads across Mr Bindi's face. The grass figure steps right up to him and then stands stock still. Slowly he lifts his arm and runs his forefinger down Mr Bindi from the top of his peaked cap to his shining brown shoes, as if cutting him in half. Then the figure leaps violently into the air, spins round and rejoins the other dancers. Mr Bindi is pale and shaking.

'What did that mean?' I asked.

'Nothing. Nothing,' he says faintly, but quickly says goodbye and hurries off home.

Mr Bindi and his generation have spent their lives trying to stamp out these practices in Sierra Leone. He wants to be proud of Bo, its mayor and his gold chain, its clock tower and offices of administration, its churches and schools and the hospital, shops, football team and markets. It even has a Rotary Club and a Cheshire Home. Now these savages from the forest have dared to come to town, parade through Bo and brazenly affront him. It is clear he is not frightened of what they could do to him physically. He already proved his courage when he rebuked the child soldier at the roadblock. But he is afraid of their supernatural power, their spirits.

If that betrays more than a residual belief in the power of the traditional religion, Mr Bindi is not alone. Belief in God and the world of spirits is universal and powerful in Africa. In all the years travelling in the continent I have met only two Africans who said they did not believe in God. These days most Africans are enthusiastic followers of the Koran or the Bible, but before they discovered these texts, most believed in an all-powerful creator who made and controls the world. Interpreting that figure as the Christian God or Islamic Allah was not a difficult leap of faith. Most however did not lose all trace of traditional religion. In addition to Jesus Christ and the Prophet Mohammed, many also still believe in powerful local spirits who control destinies and inhabit special rocks, trees, rivers, springs and animals. At the heart of Africa with all its physicality, immediate in its pain and joy, close to life and death, lies a deep sense of the numinous and supernatural.

Some might say this is simply a product of the universal African predicament: the uncertainty of life. But it is not only rural people at the mercy of the weather and nature who believe these things. The fastest growing religious movements in the world are evangelical Christian Churches and preachers in cities and African communities in the rest of the world. They offer health and wealth, protection and security in this world as well as salvation in the next.

Traditional African religions were denigrated by the European Christian missionaries and imperial rulers who frequently saw them as devil worship and tried to stamp them out. In West and Central Africa and in South Africa these religions or their offspring sects are strong and open, but in East Africa they are hidden, not spoken of in public.

Africa never went through the philosophical and social revolution of Europe in the eighteenth century which sought scientific explanations for the world and put science and spirit in separate boxes. The modern Western view of the world distinguishes between the physical world and the spiritual world, some would say 'real' and 'unreal'. This view is actually quite new in Europe – only about 250 years old. Before that, most Europeans would have thought – and acted – much like Africans when it came to religion. Europe has lost that sense of the numinous, the spiritual. Africa has not. Life remains one in Africa and life includes the divine and the mystical as well as the objective physical world. In Africa body and soul are one and the soul lives on.

While Christianity teaches that only humans have souls, African religions hold that all objects, animate or inanimate, can be moved by spirits. Africa senses spirits in animals, trees and rocks as well as people. So the river and the spirit of the river are one and the same. The spirit allows the substance to change, the person to become something else. A friend in Port Harcourt in Nigeria told me that one day in 2001 a noisy crowd gathered under a tree and he went to investigate. There he found a man being roughed up by the crowd. When he asked what the man had done, they claimed he had been a bird sitting in the tree and when a young boy threw a stone at it, it fell down. The bird hit the ground and turned into man. The crowd wanted to kill this witch, this skin changer. A policeman appeared and my friend assumed the man would be saved. In a way he was; the policeman stopped the crowd killing the man and arrested him instead. When my friend asked what he was being charged with, the policeman said, 'Changing his skin.'

Steve Biko, the South African writer and activist, wrote that religion in Africa was not a specialized function observed only on one day a week in a special building, but 'it featured in our wars, our beer drinking, our dances and customs in general'. That is something the Western world has lost. So is belief in the power of ancestors. The importance of the ancestors, who can be traced back to the first man and woman in most belief systems, seems to be universal to sub-Saharan Africa. If the ancestors are angry they must be placated. Traditionally that means keeping them in mind all the time, living by their rules and, in some parts of West Africa, pouring the first drops of palm wine for them. Libations and animal sacrifice are common elsewhere too. Christopher Ejizu, a Nigerian religious scholar, says in an article on Igbo rituals that ancestors are the connecting mechanism between the ordered objective world and the spirit world, the world of the past and the future. The present, objective world also bears a relationship to the spirit.

Modern Westerners regard spirits and myths in our culture as somehow psychological, real only in the mind. As the Nigerian novelist Ben Okri says, Homer, Jesus Christ and Shakespeare would have been far more at home in the African world of spirits, gods and mystical powers than in our modern Western world. Africans have no problem with the stories of Homer when he writes of gods turning into birds, the sea rising up on the command of a goddess or a man's destiny being fixed by an enraged spirit. Shakespeare would have found it easier to talk with modern Africans than modern Europeans and Americans who have no sense of anything beyond the physical realities of Western urban culture. Africans understand Shakespeare's woodland inhabited by sprites and fairies or by ghosts of dead fathers and other mystical apparitions. Living in harmony with the other world is important.

The spirits of Africa are usually morally neutral. Africans tend not to be Manichean and divide the world into good and evil. There is no hell in African religions, but a rather detached God is the source and controller of everything in this world. The spirits are powerful but can be assuaged or placated by offerings. In a world ordered by destiny and spirits, it is important to know who is employing which spirits and how to counteract their influence. Everyone wants to know the future and obtain charms and fetishes to bring success and happiness, to honour the ancestors, gain the love of someone, pass exams or win at football. They also want to ward off evil or bring it upon their enemies. Spirit mediums, marabouts, the holy men of West Africa who mix Islam with African traditional religion, and what are called witch doctors have become big business. (The words 'witch' and 'witch doctor' are common in Africa, but they mean something different from the images they convey in Britain. The witch doctor is the finder of witches who are generally regarded as evil. The witch doctor can provide protection against witches and their magic.)

In Africa every apparent accident or illness is attributed to bad spirits who have been employed by another person, dead or alive, who is trying to inflict the evil. When people fall sick with AIDS, the first port of call is not the clinic; more often it is the spirit medium to find out which enemy has sent the deadly disease. I am frequently struck by the immediacy and directness of the power of spirits in Africa. The spirit world is closely linked to the practical world. People contact the spirits to know what the future holds. If some evil such as a death has befallen the family, spirit mediums or witch doctors are consulted. These mediums will discover the witch who has used his or her powers to cause misfortune or death and who has employed them. The eye specialist at the hospital in Bo working on a river blindness campaign told me that he thought he had achieved a breakthrough when he persuaded some villagers suffering from river blindness that it was not caused by an enemy employing a witch but by the little black fly that comes from the river. Then someone asked, 'Ah, but who sends the little black fly to bite me?'

A poem by the Nigerian writer Chinua Achebe describes how a car knocked down an old man and apparently killed him as it passed through a village. The enraged villagers pulled the driver from the car and beat him to death. Then the old man regained consciousness. The villagers promptly beat the old man to death too, because he had 'made' them kill the driver of the car. Such stories are not uncommon.

In *The African Child*, the Guinean writer Camara Laye described the phenomenon in his childhood:

> *In the past, in the great overgrown villages of Kouroussa in Upper Guinea, there is no doubt that the air, water, earth, and savannahs were really and truly inhabited by genii who had to be propitiated with prayers and sacrifices. There really were people who could bewitch you, and there were formulas for averting the ill effect of their charms. There were innumerable amulets that could be worn for protection. There were tellers of hidden things, there were healers, some of whom really did effect cures . . . All these things were current yesterday in Africa and they have greatly astonished the Europeans, although they then possessed their own mysteries, which, though they were different, should nevertheless have taught them to accept the existence of ours.*

Laye talks of yesterday, but such beliefs are prevalent today and are now being absorbed by the evangelical Churches who find plenty of stories from the Old and New Testaments to match these beliefs. So laying on hands, casting out devils, speaking in tongues and hearing the voice of God talking directly to people are used to subdue or placate the traditional spirits that still possess people and cause pain and suffering. Nowadays this is done in the name of Christ, and some pastors demand substantial fees for their ministry.

In many cases such 'pastors' are crooks exploiting the vulnerability of societies under great strain. Seeking answers from the spiritual world sometimes results in terrible consequences. In Angola and Congo there has been a spate of 'child witches': difficult children or children who have been brought into a new family from a previous relationship. They are often accused of witchcraft or of being possessed by devils that bring evil on the family. Unscrupulous 'pastors' charge fees to drive the devils out, often by stigmatizing the child or inflicting horrifically painful treatment. In South Africa witch doctors are believed to be able to smell out witches, and there has been a number of witch burnings as a result.

Given the prevalence of traditional religion, it is strange that few prominent Africans identify with it in public. How different from Japan where Shintoism – in many ways similar to aspects of African religions – is widely practised. In Japan respect for the ancestors is expressed by millions of Japanese visitors to ancient temples to salute the ancestors. Many Japanese proudly display in their homes the souvenirs of the holy shrines they have visited. Tourism? Partly. Busloads of Japanese descend on the famous shrines and take photographs of each other. But they also come to stand before the temple gate and bow and clap their hands together, and make an offering of a few coins as tradition demands. In Africa religion may be central to beliefs but its leaders and rituals still remain in the background. Only in South Africa are there shops in the high streets selling *Muti*, traditional medicine, and only in South Africa does a traditional *Sangoma* – priest – take his place at state functions along with Christian archbishops, Islamic mullahs and the Chief Rabbi.

Africa's spiritual feel for the world gives it great strength – the feeling that the ancestors will always be with you, their spirit reborn with each new child in the family. It helps people to live in harmony with the world around them, welcome visitors and strangers. It makes the individual part of a universal spirit. That numinous feel for the world has given us the extraordinary writings of authors like Wole Soyinka and Ben Okri. But a belief that the power of spirits is greater than physical reality can be used for all sorts of ends. While it creates a majestic acceptance of fate, it can also mean that people do not have to take personal responsibility for their actions. 'A bad spirit made me do it' is a common defence.

African leaders – especially in West Africa – have their spirit mediums and marabouts close at hand and consult them regularly. The man or woman who can harness the spirits is powerful indeed. Wherever you go in Africa you hear the word 'power' again and again. But in Africa the essence, the origin of all power, physical, political, even economic, is seen as spiritual. 'He is powerful. You must be careful,' people say of a rich man or a leading politician. He may be a chief, a businessman or a politician but his strength does not derive from his office or his status, but from within him. It means he is full of power and that means he is supported by spirits that have given him this position. And a Big Man likes to demonstrate that he is strong and fat with many wives and children and an army of dependants. His wealth, his power, must be on display for all to see.

One reason that African traditional religion and beliefs are hidden is that in many parts they are still associated with evil. Today hardly a week goes by without some report from Africa about witchcraft or the killing of witches. Africa's local press is full of them, the details reported as factually as a politician's speech or the football scores. Witchcraft and suspicions of witchcraft are not limited to backward rural areas. Any materially successful individual risks being denounced as a witch, another reason why some parts of Africa are hostile to the successful entrepreneur. Fear of being pulled down by the community keeps everyone in line, quiescent and conformist. In a village in Zambia I came across the story of a man who had been driven out of the village because he had become too successful and created jealousy. He was a teacher, married with children, whose wife died. He married a younger woman and then became an entrepreneur, breeding chickens and extending his farm to grow food for the nearest town. He bought a new truck. But then the rumours started. They said he had killed his wife by witchcraft. His new wife was a witch, that was why he was successful. The man was forced to flee, abandoning his businesses.

Cannibalism is another favourite theme of African newspapers and street gossip. Interviewing opposition politicians takes up a huge amount of a journalist's time. Often, having listed the President's economic follies, political failings and repulsive personal life, his opponent will lean towards me and say – *sotto voce*: 'and another thing. You know he is a cannibal. He eats people.'

So Idi Amin, Jean Bedel Bokassa, Charles Taylor, Daniel arap Moi and scores of others have been denounced as cannibals. Who can ever know the truth? Cannibalism was practised in Africa, but largely for spiritual reasons. It was not about eating people as if they were animals. This may not affect the morality of it, but cannibalism's spiritual aspect shows that, far from being an act of contempt for the victim, it showed respect. It was not a question of chicken, beef or human for dinner. To eat the vital organs of someone is to absorb their spirit into you. The nutrition is spiritual, not physical. So, traditionally, a warrior might eat the liver of his dead enemy to absorb his spirit, become part of him. There is also a belief that a spirit will not haunt itself, so if you eat part of the body of a dead enemy, his spirit will not come back to haunt you. It is not so far from the Aristotelian Catholic belief in transubstantiation in the Eucharist: eating the real body and blood of Christ but in the form of bread and wine. The idea is the same: eating ordinary food makes it part of you, eating God – or another person – makes you part of the devoured.

As I left Sierra Leone I took the ferry across the harbour to the road which leads to the airport. The ferry was packed with petty traders taking back city goods packed in boxes and bags, and noisy families on their return from a trip to the capital. I looked back on Freetown nestling like a very English town under the great peaked range of mountains that gave the country its name. And I looked across to Bunce Island with its history as a slave fort and then as the base for the anti-slavery patrol. From Hawkins's visit onward Britain had done terrible things and a few good deeds here. For good or ill, my country had moulded Sierra Leone over the preceding 400 years. More than any other people in Africa, Sierra Leoneans still look to Britain for friendship and support. The tragedy to me is that only a handful of people in Britain have even heard of it, let alone could point to it on a map.

As I looked down into the water, a woman shouted to me from the cabin door, 'Don't look into the water. The river devil will see you and pull you in.'

12

The positive positive women
AIDS in Africa

The heart-stopping view from God's Window in the KwaZulu hills of South Africa sweeps north and south, east and west, overlooking massive mountain ridges and deep twisting valleys to the endless plains beyond. 'Lovely beyond any singing of it,' is how the South African writer Alan Paton described this landscape.

A few steps downhill from this divine vista bring you to a glimpse of something more like hell. There stand three round mud and thatch huts which were once home to a family of seven. Now only two young boys live here: Manuel, aged fourteen, and his brother Malatji, aged eleven. Everyone else has died or disappeared. Manuel sits on a low mud wall, kicking his bare heels in the dust and tugging at his dirty torn shirt. He looks at the ground as he speaks, his face contorted with pain, his voice barely audible. We talk about his favourite classes in school and what he would like to be when he grows up. Then we broach the terrible subject.

When Manuel was four his father went off to Johannesburg to look for work. 'No, he never sent us anything,' he says, 'not even money for school fees or clothes. But I would like to see him again.' When he begins to talk about his mother his face crumples and he dissolves in sobs. He tries to wipe the tears away with a grubby hand but he doesn't want to talk any more. His aunt tells me that his mother fell sick in March. She had constant diarrhoea and lay in the hut until she died in May. Soon after his grandmother also fell ill and went to a hospital some forty miles away. She has not been seen since. In the hut where Manuel's mother died is a low wooden bed, blankets, a pile of worn out clothes, a sack of corn meal and an oil lamp. Nothing else. His aunt lives close by and comes to wash, cook and collect firewood for the boys, but she also has children of her own to look after.

Africa remains the epicentre of Acquired Immune Deficiency Syndrome (AIDS) and millions of Africans have failed to get treatment. UNAIDS categorizes the different impacts of the epidemic and classifies the Southern African states as suffering hyper-epidemics of over 20 per cent prevalence. The plague peaked by 2017 but 25.7 million Africans were still living with AIDS. An estimated 1.3 million died. Ask anyone between the ages of fifteen and fifty in Southern Africa how many relatives and friends of their age group have died in the last few years and many will say as many as twenty or thirty. But ask them what they died of and they will say TB or malaria or endless diarrhoea. Few hospitals in Africa separated out the AIDS patients from the rest. No-one wants AIDS to be written as the cause of death. Nobody knows exactly how many people die of AIDS because AIDS destroys the body's immune system so the sufferers actually die of tuberculosis, malaria and innumerable other diseases and infections. 'AIDS is clever,' as Sibanda, a Zimbabwean traditional healer and AIDS activist, says. 'It doesn't kill people, it hires others to do that for it.'

By 2007, more than 20 million Africans had died of the disease and the prevalence rate was around 6 per cent. Ten years later, according to UNAIDS, 940,000 people worldwide died from AIDS and 36.9 million people were living with AIDS, more than two-thirds of them in sub-Saharan Africa. But the spread is not uniform. Southern Africa is the worst hit with one-third of the global total of victims. A sixth are in South Africa, the worst-hit country in the world, where the government response was feeble. President Thabo Mbeki did not accept scientific evidence on AIDS and did not allow anti-retroviral medicine to be provided, so millions who could have been kept alive died. Mbeki was forced from office in 2008 and replaced by Jacob Zuma who allowed the treatment to be made available.

By 2017, almost 5 per cent of Africans were living with HIV. In 2010, 25.9 per cent of Swazis were infected, 24.8 per cent of Tswana, 23 per cent of Sothos and 17.8 per cent of South Africans. An unknown number of Africans, maybe 20 million, have already died from diseases that the normal human immune system copes with easily. UNAIDS reckoned that in 2007, 2.1 million Africans died of 'AIDS-related diseases'.

Among the five countries in sub-Saharan Africa with the largest HIV epidemics, four – Ethiopia, South Africa, Zambia and Zimbabwe – as well as eighteen others – had reduced new HIV infections by more than 25 per cent between 2001 and 2009 and Nigeria's HIV epidemic had stabilized. New infections in West Africa have not gone on rising.

Women are more than twice as likely to be affected as men but by 2012 the number of new infections was in decline. AIDS is no longer a fatal disease. Anti-retroviral drugs have made it a chronic condition, debilitating but no longer deadly – although it will contribute to eventual death. In the mid-2000s some 2.2 million people were dying each year from AIDS-related causes. This fell to about 1.8 million in 2010. UNAIDS reckons that a total of 2.5 million deaths have been averted in low- and middle-income countries since 1995 due to anti-retroviral therapy. In most other parts of the world these drugs are provided or are affordable. More than a million

Africans were on ARVs by 2007 and the number is growing rapidly but for most Africans ARVs are still something they hear about only on the radio. AIDS is still spreading devastation: homes abandoned, hospitals packed with emaciated young people waiting to die and children struggling to perform the tasks of adulthood.

In Southern and East Africa AIDS is wiping out the last fifty years of gains in health. Average life expectancy in 1955 was about forty. In 1990 it was about fifty-five. In the mid-2000s it was below 40 again. In Zimbabwe, where the epidemic was compounded by economic collapse, life expectancy in the mid-2000s for women was thirty-four and for men it was thirty-seven. In the rest of Southern Africa infection rates levelled off but many people still die younger because of AIDS. In 2005 nearly 40 per cent of Batswana were infected and in the rest of the region 21 million were infected. In its wake the pandemic is leaving millions of orphans like Manuel and Malatji. Already there are more than 12 million in Africa.

In 2003 I visited areas of Southern Africa badly hit by AIDS to get an idea of the future. For many young people there wasn't one. As you read this they are already dead.

Several steep miles from a tarmac road, Mandla, aged twenty-one, and his fourteen-year-old sister, Badelisile, lie dying in their hut watched over by their grandmother. Mandla sits up painfully, wraps a check shirt round his pathetically thin arms, grasps my hand and gives me a huge welcoming smile. After completing fourth grade he left school and worked as a security guard. He has been ill for about a year and was diagnosed with TB, but after two months the doctors said he was not responding to treatment and there was nothing more they could do for him. He was sent home to die. Badelisile cannot even raise her head from her mattress on the floor. She has been persistently sick since she was two years old and was probably born with AIDS. Their mother died four years ago and their father deserted home leaving only their mother's mother to care for them. The old woman – though she may not have been more than fifty – sits by the door wrapped in a blanket, too frail to dig their little plot of land. Unless helped, this family will die of starvation.

Not far away a collection of crumbling huts on a bleak, arid hillside is home to Eliza Zungu and her three grandchildren, all under fourteen. Wrapped in a filthy rug, Eliza too is wizened and weak and sits upright, her legs stretched out straight on the bare earth floor of a crude stone hut. She supports her grandchildren with her pension of 540 Rand (then £36) a month. Their father died a few years ago, and their mother fell sick from AIDS and suddenly went off to visit a traditional healer several miles away. She has not come back. Her children were forced to become adults: cooking, sweeping, washing, playing the roles with intense solemnity as if they were on a stage. But this is the land of *Lord of the Flies*. Children are not adults.

The two older children, Vania and Khangisa, are in school but they will probably have to leave to look after themselves and Lungile, the youngest girl. Lungile has vicious pink blotches on her face and arm where she was splashed by hot porridge as she tried to lift the pot from an open fire. The children are not strong enough to dig and grow their own food so they depend on their neighbours, an elderly couple looking after five orphaned grandchildren of their own. Every day the children have to walk for almost two hours to fetch water from the nearest source about a mile away. It is a steep climb down, then back up a rocky slope, all three with a four-gallon plastic container on their heads. Soon the children will have to walk even further for water because drought is beginning to dry the spring.

While I am talking with them my guide has been with the neighbours and comes back with a tale that makes *Lord of the Flies* seem like a bedtime story. Two months ago a gang of youths attacked the house and stole Eliza's precious pension book, money and other documents. Then they raped the old woman and beat her up. The crime was reported but no policeman or official has visited.

I want to ask, who were they? What actually happened? What did the children do? How do they feel about that? But the journalistic questions that would normally flow in such an encounter die in my throat. I leave them some money and walk away. For the second time in my life in Africa I want to keep walking, lose my notebook, tell the editor there is no story. The other occasion was the Rwandan genocide.

The unconscionable tragedies of people like Eliza Zungu and Mandla have catastrophic implications for the future. Mass murder and wars have an end. After the killing a new start is possible. But AIDS destroys the future.

We know for sure that a lot of people – some 25 million in Africa – will die much sooner than they would otherwise have done from diseases connected to AIDS. Anti-retroviral drugs may delay this extermination but they can't prevent it. Countries' usually pyramid-shaped populations have been hollowed out at the middle and bottom as the young and middle-aged die off and fewer children are born. The mature, productive middle generation is getting sparse and Africa's demographic shape will change dramatically.

This means that households like those of Eliza and Mandla are now common throughout Africa. In some places they are the norm. In rural areas where people eat only what they can grow, many will starve to death because the very old and the very young do not have the strength to dig and grow food. The 2004–5 food crisis in Southern Africa was partly due to the enfeeblement of the rural subsistence population. In cities Africa's weak economies may suffer as absenteeism and death create a shortage of skilled labour, and overall there could be a steady decrease in the accumulation of wealth as breadwinners die and money is spent on medicine and funerals.

When a family breadwinner dies, the family is doubly impoverished. The family loses its income and it must pay for a funeral. Tradition demands rituals of respect for ancestors and their spirits. That makes funerals expensive affairs and means destitution for the survivors. People will spend half a year's earnings on a lavish coffin, funeral rites and a feast for all their relatives and neighbours. Many are now urging that relatives cut down on funeral costs for the sake of those left behind.

In some African societies a dead man's widow traditionally becomes part of her husband's family and marries one of his brothers. These days that tradition is often used as a cover to grab the widow's inheritance: home, land, cattle and possessions. The widow and her children are often left destitute, especially if she has no education. When a mother dies of AIDS, daughters take over her tasks and drop out of school. Without education, the girls grow up poor, powerless, more vulnerable to predatory men and AIDS, more likely to get pregnant and give birth to HIV-positive children. Then they may die young, leaving more orphans. Even if they survive they may not be able to educate or protect their children. The spiral of death and deprivation spins on down: parents die young, orphans grow up in poverty with no education or skills and vulnerable to HIV. They too will have children who grow up even worse off and die early.

In the past, uncared-for orphans were rare in Africa. Traditionally children were an unquestioned blessing. Everyone had many fathers and mothers and families were always happy to bring another child into the home. When the AIDS catastrophe started many Africans proudly said that the traditional African family would take care of the children left behind. It was a nice idea, but was it realistic to expect even the broadest-reaching family to embrace the numbers of children orphaned by AIDS? The communal family system has come under intense pressure. In urban areas it is impossible to extend living space and costs like food and school fees to extra children. Richer relatives send money to poor cousins, but now there are tales that a few years ago would have been shocking. Impoverished families are turning away the children of their relatives. The extended family – Africa's great heritage, its strongest mechanism for human survival – is under severe stress.

Grandmothers have brought up the first generation of AIDS orphans. Those who would expect to be cared for in old age have become the main carers again. Magnificently they are bearing the brunt of the AIDS crisis, caring for those who should have cared for them. But what will happen in the future? As this generation of parents dies young, many families will have no grandmothers. This problem will grow incrementally as one unparented generation breeds another. Caring for AIDS orphans is going to be one of the most costly and difficult tasks in the twenty-first century. However, the good news is that incidence in South Africa was falling among the 18-year-olds from 1.8 per cent in 2005 to 0.8 per cent in 2009, and had fallen among women from 5.5 per cent in 2005 to 2.2 per cent by 2008.

In a thousand small ways the task of managing the victims has already begun. In the hills of Swaziland, seventeen-year-old Sonnyboy Dlamini looks after his two younger sisters. Their mother left home in 1993 but died shortly afterwards, almost certainly of AIDS. Five years later their father died. Two older sisters left home for South Africa but he has not heard of them since. He works in his neighbours' fields or cleans for them in return for food, but he earns no money so he cannot go to school. Sonnyboy is trying to teach himself from old textbooks. His sole ambition is to get back to school. The village chief and others have recently called a meeting to identify the orphans in the area and see what can be done for them. At more than 25 per cent, Swaziland in 2009 had the highest adult prevalence in the world.

At Molepolole in Botswana, an afternoon care centre has been set up for orphans and vulnerable children, most of them victims of AIDS. But helping is not always easy. When it started, a bus with the red ribbon of the AIDS programme painted on the side used to drive to the town's schools every day and pick up the children. Before long they found none wanted to board it. Those who went on the bus were ostracized in school, branded as sinners because they had AIDS or were AIDS orphans. The red ribbon and the name of the charity were quietly removed, and instead of going to the school, the bus stops at prearranged pick-up points around town to bring the children to the centre every evening. There they can get a proper meal and relax and do their homework.

Since 2003 the rest of the world has become more aware of HIV in Africa and most African governments have adopted national plans and strategies for dealing with it – though they are not uniformly implemented. Some countries do better than others. Unicef has set up national programmes for orphans with feeding centres, formal home care for child-headed families and communal fields in villages set aside for growing food for AIDS orphans.

The numbers of people on ARVs is also rising rapidly as the World Health Organization and donors pour money into free distribution. About a quarter of people who need ARVs now have them. In Botswana the death rate has stabilized and fallen slightly since the state ARV programme kicked in. For the rest it is a problem less of supply and cost than of the inability of African government health systems to distribute the drugs. And many HIV-positive people are afraid to come forward, get tested and claim the drugs.

But what of those who are not helped? If they survive at all what will they be like – a generation of human beings who have never known a mother's loving cuddle or a father's guiding hand? These children will learn life skills in institutions rather than imbibe them from parents. Organizations working with orphans report that some children are withdrawn or depressed, many have been forced to leave school because they cannot pay fees, some are ostracized by their peers because of the stigma of AIDS, others cannot feed and clothe themselves. Orphaned boys, adopted by uncles or guardians, are kept out of school and made to work for nothing on farms. Young orphaned girls are often sexually abused. Words that a few years ago were rarely heard in Africa like abandoned children, child abuse, depression and even child suicide are now heard daily.

In his pamphlet *AIDS, Economics and Terrorism in Africa*, Trevor Neilson argued that without caring adults children 'can be manipulated into doing almost anything' and cited horrors from several African countries including Liberia, Uganda and Congo. He claimed that 'terrorist organizations establishing a foothold in Africa will find it rich for recruitment'. This scary portrayal of Africa paints a picture of a generation of orphans growing up semi-feral, deprived of socialization or education, lacking the fundamental human attachments of family, owning nothing but the rags they stand in and unable to keep themselves alive except by theft and violence. In a continent whose economic growth rates barely keep up with population increase, Neilson predicts this scenario could turn into a development disaster on a vast scale. A generation of unparented orphans could easily become a pool of ruthless warriors for power-greedy politicians in Africa's fragile states. Child soldiers already play a big part in many of Africa's wars, but with no family hinterland at all, AIDS orphans could become a terrifying and uncontrollable force. According to this scenario, whole regions of Africa, already poor and made poorer by AIDS, could be destabilized.

However, there is no sign of this happening yet, despite more than 13 million orphans. The problems most associated with AIDS orphans are not dehumanization and aggression but withdrawal and depression. This scenario also misunderstands the motivation behind Africa's recent wars. Despite AIDS these wars are currently diminishing, not growing, in number and scale. All Africa's conflicts remain intractably local and political in their causes and aims.

Could AIDS itself become the cause of one of these wars? Imagine if an earthquake had killed a million South Africans and the government's response had been as half-hearted as that of Mbeki's government in South Africa to AIDS. If the ensuing disaster was widely perceived as preventable, surely there would be revolution in days. Yet the South African government and all African governments who do little about AIDS sleep easily in their beds. There were several mass demonstrations in South Africa demanding ARVs and treatment but this did not transform into a national movement against Mbeki's leadership. He knows that sickness and death from AIDS will have no more mobilizing effect on their populations than poverty has done in the past. The sick, like the poor, might demonstrate but they are not going to overthrow governments or the social order. Outside South Africa there have not so far been many public demonstrations demanding anti-retroviral treatment. AIDS sufferers are a disparate group who are not naturally brought together or able to communicate with each other. As Alex de Waal argues convincingly in his book *AIDS and Power*, there will be no radical political fall-out from AIDS.

Logic rather than empirical experience dictates that the best strategy to combat AIDS is to prevent it spreading by getting the message through to everyone, especially children before they reach puberty. The message is encapsulated in the 'ABC' slogan: Abstain from sex, Be faithful and use Condoms. Everyone is encouraged to talk openly about sex and to convince children to delay having sex until they are older, then stick to one partner and use condoms. African children are bombarded with explicit messages about sex from their earliest years. The message is relentlessly pounded out from TV and radio, posters, newspapers, T-shirts, even soft drink cans and crisp packets.

This approach is based on the idea that the first thing to do when you have a problem is express it, share it. Is this an African way of doing things? Not in my experience. Time and again in Africa I found an unwillingness to deal with problems by blunt acknowledgement. Maybe that is a strength that outsiders do not comprehend. Maybe it is a weakness that explains many of Africa's failings.

Take Priscilla, a bright-faced eleven-year-old pupil at a private school in the centre of Botswana's capital, Gabarone. She and her friends are dressed in crisp white shirts, burgundy red uniforms and shiny shoes. I meet them on an AIDS Awareness Day which brings the whole city centre to a standstill with troops of dancers, singers and performers. Thousands of school children have been brought in to listen to the message and be given leaflets by smiling young workers manning the booths set up by the shopping mall.

'What is AIDS?' I ask her.

'It is a fatal disease.'

'How do you get it?'

'From sexual intercourse or blood products.'

'How do you prevent it?'

'You abstain or you condomize.'

When she says sexual intercourse she does not even blink. There is not a hint of a giggle from her friends when she uses this economical new African word, 'condomize'. But Priscilla and her primary school friends answer as if quoting from a manual learned by heart, like a times table. They have learned the slogans and songs. That allows officials and AIDS workers to tick their boxes in an AIDS awareness programme. But is it real? Does it change behaviour?

Campaigns against the spread of AIDS that worked in Brazil and Thailand failed in much of Africa. Here, despite huge AIDS awareness campaigns, the rate of infection went on rising until people were dying in shocking numbers.

The glimpses that Africans get of the Western world from radio, hearsay and the occasional television pictures leave an impression of unreality. Their lives are so far removed from glossy clothes, flashy cars and soaring, shining buildings that these glimpses portray the rich world as a fantasy, a heaven you can escape to in your head. You may desire it desperately but have no idea of how to reach it or live in it. In school, as I found as a teacher, students learned some of the skills, disciplines and information, the building blocks needed to take part in such a society. But these learned texts and rules hardly affected the students' attitudes, their approach to life. Their two worlds – school and home – did not link up.

I was beginning to find the same phenomenon when it came to AIDS education. Many people I spoke to in Africa said they had decided to practise safe sex only after someone close to them had died of AIDS. They had not taken AIDS education programmes seriously. In Botswana AIDS is called the radio disease – people hear about it on the radio but they do not necessarily connect it to their daily lives. Most Africans live close to more imminent dangers, like malaria, car crashes and wars. Indeed, some claim these kill more people than AIDS. Millions die every year from uninvestigated and unrecorded causes. AIDS is just one more agent of death. But AIDS is also difficult to connect to death because it kills so slowly.

Plagues that have struck humanity in the past killed people quickly. The clear connection between disease and death forced people to change. The Black Death killed within days. So did the 1919 flu epidemic which killed huge numbers in Africa as well as Europe and Asia. Although people did not know that fleas carried bubonic plague, they moved away from afflicted areas. AIDS takes years to develop, so it is hard to persuade people that it exists and even harder to persuade them that it spreads through life-giving sex. In Cameroon they call it *le poison lent*, slow poison. Indeed it is technically a *lentivirus*. Its effects on society, social and economic, are even more long term. Read the AIDS statistics and they look like a tsunami, a vast wave inexorably sweeping towards us and drowning millions upon millions of people.

Along with the erosion of the extended African family, traditional African methods of teaching young people about sex are also dying out. In traditional rural areas, young people grow up and perform the age group rituals such as circumcision for boys and prenuptial discussions with elder sisters and aunts for girls. Without them Africans – like people anywhere – do not find it easy to talk about sex and AIDS. Even as the pandemic hits their societies many find it impossible to face up to it and teach their children preventive measures. When I visited remote northern Swaziland in 2003 the infection rate may have been as high as 40 per cent and hundreds were already dying. In 2007 the epidemic in Swaziland was still growing.

In South Africa Paul Bhembe, the headmaster of Ekuphakameni secondary school, tells me that AIDS is not a problem. 'We don't know why these people are dying but it is not because of AIDS, not in this area. It is not a problem here.' There is, he says, no programme for AIDS education in the school – the timetable is already full. AIDS education is, he says, 'something from outside, something imposed on us'. When I press him further Bhembe admits he and his teachers are too embarrassed to talk to his students about AIDS and sex. 'It is part of the way we have been brought up. Talking about things that are not talked about and breaking out of the inhibitions is difficult. It is an issue of culture. Not even parents talk to their kids about it.'

This refusal to face up to AIDS is not confined to Africa. AIDS first came to world attention on the west coast of America and was associated with homosexuals and drug users, already social outcasts. Known as the 'Gay Plague', AIDS was taboo. President Ronald Reagan mentioned it only once in public to announce his intention of putting HIV-positive people on the 'undesirable' exclusion list. Religious puritans rejoiced in what they saw as God's punishment on the immoral – a theme picked up by African Christian leaders who tend to interpret the Bible more literally than their Western counterparts. With a few notable exceptions, African leaders did not talk about it either. When the reality became too widespread to ignore, some chose to believe it was a conspiracy by the United States and other Western countries to wipe out black people. It reflects a common belief in Africa that disease can be perceived as the symptom of a spiritual or moral problem, not a purely medical one. So there must be a conspiracy behind it. Even the Kenyan Nobel Prizewinner, Dr Wangari Maathai, believed this. AIDS, she said, was deliberately created by 'evil-minded scientists' to kill black people so that outsiders could recolonize Africa.

Africa's spiritual view of the world plays an important part in the failure of prevention campaigns. In the scientific and maybe post-religious Western world, illness is seen as random bad luck which must be countered with science and medicine. No further questions are asked. But in Africa traditional thinking and culture remain strong. In addition to the What and the How, there is always the Why in Africa and then the Who. Sometimes disease, misfortune and death are accepted passively and gracefully as the unquestionable will of God. But more often people want to know more. Why am I cursed and who has cursed me? To find the answer they seek a divine or human agent. Many AIDS workers agree with Philile Mlambo, a volunteer counsellor in KwaZulu, who says, 'The first reaction when people fall sick is to ask who has bewitched them. They go to the witch doctor to find out which enemy has sent the sickness. Or they go to traditional healers. So they do not find that it is AIDS until it is too late.'

Western medicine is just one alternative among many competing responses to illness in Africa, often second choice to the witch doctors, spirit diviners and traditional healers. Witch doctors and spirit diviners – the distinction, if there is one, is blurred – will detect which enemy has sent evil spirits to bring sickness and deploy charms, rituals and other manifestations of the spirit world to counter the evil spells. Healers will know which herbs and medicines to use. Some may be honest and use effective cures but others are unscrupulous. All have made fortunes out of cures for AIDS. President Yahya Jammeh of Gambia claims to have discovered – and patented – a cure for AIDS.

Strange ideas grow in an impoverished, marginalized world that has been suddenly devastated by disease. In some countries those who have AIDS are seen as possessed by bad spirits and either ostracized or subjected to terrifying and painful rituals of exorcism. One common belief is that a man infected with HIV will be cured if he sleeps with a virgin. According to a survey by LoveLife, a US-funded AIDS awareness campaign body, one in four South Africans believes this. This monstrous fantasy may be connected to a spate of child rapes – even baby rapes. Schoolgirls are often targeted. Another belief is that condoms do not protect, they spread AIDS – a bizarre idea but apparently believed by a senior Catholic archbishop in Rome. Cardinal Lopez Trujillo, President of the Pontifical Council for the Family, told the BBC in 2004 that condoms don't help because the HIV virus is small enough to 'easily pass through' condoms.

In Africa traditional concepts and social controls have been weakened or forgotten, but they have not necessarily been replaced by a new moral code to fit the world's new realities. For example, female virginity is still very much valued almost everywhere, but male virginity almost never. On the contrary, men are expected to be sexually active from puberty and are regarded as odd if they are not. When I taught in Uganda the boys regarded the hunt for girls as one huge hilarious game with no rules or responsibilities. If girls got pregnant, they were expelled. The boys giggled. Mr Lule, the headmaster in my school in Uganda, was exceptional because he expelled boys who had impregnated girls as well as the girls.

Having lots of children has always been regarded as a measure of success and prosperity in Africa. I have never met an African, man or woman, married or not, who did not think that children were intrinsically good things. Claiming 'African tradition', Big Men in Africa like to have several wives – more than twenty is not uncommon among Very Big Men – and scores of children, acknowledged or not. The more the better. While mainstream Christian Churches battle to establish monogamy and the nuclear family, some of the new indigenous Christian sects claim that Christianity allows several wives (though not several husbands). Polygamy – though not polyandry – is socially acceptable too. Many men will have a wife and family in both their town and their village and wealthy men will set up girlfriends with flats or houses. It is common for a man who has had a child outside marriage to bring that child into the home and for his wife to bring it up as one of her own. The reverse situation – a wife bringing a child by another man into the home – would be unthinkable.

Mention of abstinence as a strategy against AIDS in male company is greeted with guffaws of laughter. Impossible. Women too find it impossible – because of the men. Condoms, which have helped stop AIDS spreading in most countries, are also problematic in Africa. Many African men are deeply reluctant to use condoms, believing they somehow reduce masculinity. President Museveni in

Uganda, whose record on AIDS awareness was excellent in the early stages of the pandemic, later began to deride the use of condoms as un-African. Whether this was a result of his wife's evangelical American Christianity or because he adopted a macho African mentality is unclear. But the President's support for abstinence and faithfulness as the only prevention methods encouraged leaders of the Catholic Church in Uganda to follow the same line. Cardinal Emmanuel Wamala of Uganda believes that a woman should have unprotected sex with her husband even if she knows he is HIV positive rather than use a condom. Until 2004 the Catholic Church in Uganda, probably the most powerful non-government organization in the country, had avoided the debate about condoms as an AIDS prevention strategy. But in 2004–5 it joined the anti-condom campaign and during that period the rate of decline in the number of new infections in Uganda slowed and halted.

Despite massive campaigns to supply condoms everywhere, in rural areas many people have never seen or even heard of condoms and some will be too poor to buy them anyway. The free distribution systems often do not reach that far. In urban areas too, where condoms are often freely available, people are also too poor or too ill-organized to use them. And poor people everywhere are reluctant to throw away anything that can be recycled. As a Ugandan doctor told me, 'If a man's shirt is torn you can be sure his condom is torn too.'

A study of prevention programmes in South Africa in the early 1990s showed that even the very best education programmes do not necessarily produce a change of attitude or behaviour. Conducted at a mine near Johannesburg, the study found that men facing daily danger and tough physical conditions down the mine, indulged in highly risky sexual behaviour. It suggested that compared to the dangers they faced at work every day, the danger from sex – preferably the intimacy of 'skin to skin' sex without condoms – did not register with them. Having several partners was an expression of men's power and machismo, a maleness denied to them in almost every other aspect of their powerless lives. The study suggested that something much deeper than just information and education was needed. More fundamental circumstances and attitudes had to change before the men changed their behaviour.

Although South African mine workers are obviously not typical of all of Africa, many of the same attitudes prevail among the poor masses. They have so little control over their existence, so little sense of agency or ability to change their lives, that acceptance is the most common response to external forces. The AIDS awareness campaigns can reinforce that sense of powerlessness. One common narrative runs like this: 'We are told that you get AIDS from having sex. I have had sex so I must have AIDS. If I have AIDS then I will die soon. So why should I care what I do now?'

In societies where people die all the time from disease and road accidents, such an attitude is not surprising. Death, as Hamlet says, 'will come when it will come. The readiness is all.' You just accept it.

And you accept it because you are not exclusively the captain of your ship. Africans do not see humanity in terms of Western individualism: self-sufficient men and women floating free from past and future. In Africa the chain of humanity stretches back to the first ancestors and beyond into future generations. As Tony Barnett and Alan Whiteside describe it in their book *AIDS in the Twenty-First Century*, individuality for a woman 'may be less important than her lineage which provided a vital aspect of her identity . . . lineages which are in principle infinitely existing entities – and perceived as such by those who are part of them. Looked at in this way individual infection and risk take on a different complexion.' The authors point out that whatever women may want for themselves, 'the pressures of lineage, family, gender roles and a short life expectancy may be for sex now (preferably reproductive, fertile sex) rather than for deferred sex and the use of a condom'.

It is these vital cultural perceptions that outsiders miss when they rush to save Africa from the HIV/AIDS pandemic. They bring with them quick, slick jingles and images thought up in San Francisco, New York, London or Paris and try to impose them on slow, communal, rural and shanty-town Africa. Often they do not even know they are imposing anything. They have no idea that they are in a different cultural world. When the results don't work they become frustrated and angry and start muttering about stupid Africans. In KwaZulu I visited a LoveLife programme for young people, funded by the Kaiser Foundation in America. What do young people like? they had asked themselves. Their American experience had told them: computers and basketball. So they built beautiful new youth centres like the one I visited, with basketball courts and a roomful of computers, and they trained local youth workers in the AIDS awareness patter.

A handful of young men are hanging around the centre when I arrive. It feels as if they have nothing better to do. The youth workers are keen to give me their well-learned answers but a glance at the carpets underneath the computer desks and state of the door jambs shows that the computer room is hardly used. The boys kick a football around the basketball court – basketball is not a particularly popular game in South Africa. Meanwhile the posters – all in English even in townships that were predominantly Zulu or Xhosa speaking – shout slogans that might make people in Los Angeles pause and think and maybe smile. In South Africa they cause bewilderment and sometimes offence. One reads: 'South Africa needs more oral sex – talk about it.' Here is the old aid problem in a new form – a neat, well-cut slice of America parachuted into Africa.

Although LoveLife claimed high rates of knowledge of its message and programmes, the rate of infections was steadily rising. Once again the message from Africa was clear and simple: you cannot achieve anything in Africa unless you work with Africans. To do that you need to understand Africa and how it thinks and works.

In Uganda and Senegal governments were positive and proactive in promoting an AIDS awareness message. In Senegal the infection rate stayed low. Uganda suffered the first wave of the epidemic in the early 1980s. In those days there were no education programmes, no condoms, just a disease called 'slim'. By the mid 1980s, when the civil war was in full swing, thousands were dying, including large numbers of Museveni's fighters. That may explain his vigorous and open education programme. Although we still do not know exactly what element of the message people picked up, governments' attitudes to AIDS seem to be crucial. Government encouragement of others to conduct public education is another vital element. In Uganda radio and newspapers carried daily AIDS stories and promoted AIDS education. The infection rate fell in the 1990s from between 25 to 30 per cent in urban areas and about 18 per cent in rural areas to 6 or 7 per cent in 2009, though there is some evidence that HIV infection is on the rise again. Experts argue over the data, past and present. Perhaps, some say, the numbers were exaggerated in the first place. In Senegal the government and Muslim leaders – the country is 95 per cent Muslim – launched a mass education campaign. Male circumcision also played a part there. Circumcised men are far less likely to become infected than uncircumcised men.

Kenya and Zimbabwe are also showing signs of a decline in the numbers of new infections but, again, it is unclear why. In Zimbabwe it may be connected to the country's general decline, lack of food and the early death of sufferers. The Botswana government had both the political will and the resources to inform its population about AIDS and spread the 'best practice' messages far and wide. It has done well in providing ARVs and preventing mother-to-child transmission. The country still struggles, however, with prevention. By 2010, 24.8 per cent of the population, some 300,000 people, were infected, giving Botswana the second-highest incidence among adults in the world, after Swaziland. But now it seems that the incidence of the epidemic has declined by 25 per cent or more with increased condom use. The Botswana government also managed to supply 80 per cent of those infected with ARVs – which also help prevent AIDS spreading.

The debate about the effectiveness of public education campaigns carries on, but where political leaders stay silent about AIDS and sex, people do not change their behaviour quickly. It is not clear whether mass government-backed public education programmes do change behaviour, but when political leaders speak openly and honestly about AIDS they encourage others to do the same. They enable personal communication, especially among friends and family, and that changes people's minds. If people who trust each other talk to each other about AIDS then public information helps get a clear message into the public arena. Public education programmes on their own do not enable people to understand the disease better or change their lives. The success of Uganda in bringing down infection rates in the 1990s was due in part to President Yoweri Museveni's willingness to speak out about AIDS and encourage others to campaign. Another key player was Philly Bongole Lutaaya, a singer who announced he was HIV positive and encouraged others to do the same. In the months before he died he toured the country with a song called *Alone* which called on people to stand up and join the fight against AIDS. As he was dying he used his music to warn others.

Until recently, South Africa's political leadership on AIDS has been disastrous. In 1992 Alan Whiteside, South Africa's leading AIDS expert, warned of an impending catastrophe but said that it could be avoided if education programmes were started immediately. They weren't. At that time South Africa was embroiled in the final collapse of apartheid and AIDS was not high on any politician's agenda. A decade on, the country adopted one of the best anti-AIDS strategies in the world – on paper. But it was not implemented. Only after Jacob Zuma became president in 2007 were there nationwide programmes of AIDS education and anti-retroviral drugs.

President Thabo Mbeki took a philosophical view of AIDS as if it were an interesting theoretical proposition. He read about it widely on the Internet and enjoyed debating the context and politics of AIDS on his party's website. 'How does a virus cause a syndrome?' he liked to ask semantically, and he derided those who warned of impending catastrophe as scaremongers who did not want South Africa to succeed. He put well-known dissidents who deny the link between HIV and AIDS on his presidential AIDS advisory panel and pointed out that traditional diseases were bigger killers than AIDS in South Africa. In 1997 Mbeki praised an 'African drug' called Virodene which turned out to be a fake made of industrial solvent, and the following year the government announced that a real drug to combat AIDS would not be available to pregnant women who were HIV positive because of the cost and side-effects. The outcry led to the foundation of the Treatment Action Campaign. In his book *After the Party*, Andrew Feinstein, a former South African ANC member of parliament, quotes Mbeki saying at a party meeting in 2000, 'If we say HIV + AIDS then we must say = drugs. Pharmaceutical companies want to sell drugs which they can't do unless HIV causes AIDS, so they don't want this thesis to be attacked.' The President then suggested that the CIA was involved and that the US was giving loans to African governments in order to buy its drugs. 'We must be aware of the AIDS agenda and the IMF agenda,' he concluded.

Mbeki suggested that AIDS was more linked to poverty than sex. Studies from Kenya and Côte d'Ivoire show this to be untrue. AIDS hits rich and poor equally, but evidence suggests that richer people are more vulnerable because they tend to have more sexual partners and the epidemic has spread more quickly among them. When William Malegapuru Makgoba, a distinguished South African scientist and the first black head of the country's Medical Research Council, responded by reiterating orthodox science on AIDS, Mbeki's allies accused him of 'betraying his race'.

Until the Supreme Court overturned the ban, Mbeki's government refused to allow the drug Nevirapine to be administered to pregnant mothers and newborn children. Nevirapine can help prevent transmission of HIV from mother to child. One South African official was even quoted as saying that it was cheaper to let the children die than to care for them as orphans. The government did not appeal the ruling but President Mbeki said he had not changed his views – though exactly what he really believes is still unclear. Without his support the provision of Nevirapine was chaotic. By 2003 it is estimated that more than 35,000 babies were dying of AIDS every year because of mother-to-child transmission. In a defensive and nervous interview, Jacob Zuma, the Deputy President, told me, 'What has happened is that people have mixed the President's personal views with the policy of the government . . . he is a thinker, a political scientist. It would be wrong for me to say "Mbeki, stop thinking" . . . [but] government policy is based on the premise that HIV causes AIDS.'

No country can win a war if its leaders continually express doubts about the cause. Mbeki's questioning of the link between HIV and AIDS and his opposition to HIV awareness campaigns and outsiders' solutions, not to mention his promotion and support for ministers who were AIDS sceptics, encouraged those who denied the existence of AIDS and undermined the fight against the disease. His minister of health, Manto Tshabalala-Msimang, urged people to eat beetroot and garlic to ward off AIDS, making South Africa the laughing stock of the world. He fell out with Nelson Mandela and Archbishop Desmond Tutu over the issue and agreed to keep quiet only when businessmen told him South Africa was losing the confidence of business because of its AIDS policy.

It would never have been easy in South Africa, where government institutions and structures were inherited from the apartheid system. After years of oppression black South Africans were slow to trust government institutions, despite having had a democratically elected government since 1994. But at least the South African government has a system that can deliver services and information right down to village level. Had the government taken the pandemic seriously, that system could have been used far more effectively to combat AIDS. In some other African states government structures barely function at all and their impact on people's lives is minimal.

As the then chairman of the National AIDS Council, Zuma gave me perfectly reasonable answers to my questions, but when he was charged with rape in 2006, he claimed in court that he had slept with the woman but with her consent. He knew she was HIV positive but, said Zuma, he had showered afterwards to protect himself. Ironically, however, under Zuma's leadership the country pursued a more vigorous campaign against HIV/AIDS than it had under Mandela and Mbeki. By 2011 South Africa was able to provide sufficient drugs for 90 per cent of HIV-positive mothers, thereby making elimination of that route for infection possible.

As funders of the big AIDS awareness campaigns, outsiders have immense influence – both positive and negative. By April 2008 the Global Fund to Fight AIDS, Malaria and TB had approved more than $10.1 billion for 136 countries. The US committed $15 billion over five years to the President's Emergency Plan for AIDS Relief, PEPFAR, which committed $39 billion in 2011 to bilateral HIV/AIDS and TB programmes as well as to the Global Fund to Fight HIV/AIDS, Tuberculosis and Malaria. Although the plan states that it 'emphasizes correct and consistent condom use, where appropriate' , the Bush government, heavily influenced by its fundamentalist Pentecostal Christian supporters, wanted to block funds to campaigns that permit abortion or promote condoms. This has begun directly and indirectly to undermine the ABC message: Abstain, Be faithful, use Condoms. The 'C' is becoming C for Celibacy. African rulers – many of whom already saw condoms as an insult to Real African Men or did not accept that AIDS was a threat to their populations – have been happy to go along with this.

How will AIDS affect Africa in the medium and long term? Theorists have put forward wildly varying AIDS scenarios ranging from improved economic growth to complete social collapse. Some economists came close to suggesting that the pandemic would be good for Africa. They argue that since Africa has a labour surplus, population decline will mean fewer mouths to feed and so a higher per capita GDP. Others predicted the total collapse of economies within twenty years as skills shortages and the indirect costs of AIDS undermine economic development. Others such as Trevor Neilson argued that African states would collapse in anarchy.

In South Africa a think tank called the Bureau for Economic Research predicted that decreasing productivity through death and illness and the increasing cost of health care and insurance will take half a percentage point a year off South Africa's growth rate in the next fifteen years. In 2006 the South African Business Coalition Against HIV/AIDS reported that 40 per cent of manufacturing companies and 60 per cent of mining companies reported tangible losses due to AIDS. But at the same time another South African organization, the Joint Economic AIDS and Poverty Programme, claimed that AIDS does not have a significant impact on the economy. Their survey, conducted in 2005 as the South African economy boomed, showed that out of a list of ten concerns of small and medium enterprises, AIDS came ninth. Nearly two-thirds of those questioned said they had never discussed AIDS issues with their staff and only a quarter provided any services connected to HIV/AIDS. The rest of Africa, already severely short of skills, will be further depleted by AIDS. In areas where there are no ARVs, many AIDS sufferers will die in their thirties and forties, the most productive part of most people's lives. Where these are people with vital experience and skills, they will be difficult to replace. Life expectancy has gone down by ten years or more in some places. That will certainly slow development progress in the medium term. There is little sign that African governments are aware that they will have to train twice the number of teachers, doctors and nurses to replace those who may die of AIDS (not to mention those who seek work outside Africa).

The HIV/AIDS pandemic may have peaked in Africa but the battle is far from over and complacency could allow infections to start rising again. There is talk of new strains becoming resistant to ARVs. There were always signs of hope and encouraging stories but the contours of the landscape of AIDS, the accumulative data of recent reports, and the tales of AIDS workers close to the ground now suggest that the pandemic has peaked. My own feeling is that Africa's survival instinct and the myriad hidden ways in which it keeps going through the toughest times will again enable it to come through the AIDS pandemic. There will be terrible suffering and many people will die before their time, children will grow up without parents, everyone will be poorer because of it, but somehow African societies will endure unaided, as they have always survived drought and famine, floods and war.

Out in the bush, deep in the rural areas, scattered through Africa's shanty towns and shack cities, Africans cling on as the tsunami hits. In a thousand small but effective ways, women are banding together to help their stricken neighbours. As if with their bare hands – they often have little more – they are holding back the devastation of the AIDS pandemic. Travelling through Southern Africa to gather the stories of AIDS orphans, I kept finding little glimmers of hope where undefeated human beings – almost always women – found strength even in the worst catastrophe. Alan Whiteside argues that AIDS is a long-wave event, spreading over several decades, and there is no longer some monolithic global AIDS strategy to stop it now. 'It's about doing lots of little things better at grass roots level, the emphasis on *doing* . . . there will be many ordinary people who will become heroes and heroines.'

I call them the 'positive positive women' because many of them have been transformed by the experience of discovering they themselves are HIV positive. Led by the grandmothers, these heroines – backed up sometimes by the odd hero – are beginning to emerge. Many have brought up their own children, watched them fall ill, nursed them and seen them die. Now they are bringing up their grandchildren, some of whom will also die before they reach school age. Some bring up their neighbours' children too. Hundreds of thousands of children across the continent now depend for survival on women, many of whom have already brought up one family and should be retired and cared for. Instead, as poor as they have ever been or even poorer, they walk miles to collect firewood and water, cooking and cleaning for another generation. In South Africa and Botswana, Africa's only sub-Saharan countries rich enough to pay old age pensions, ten or more people may be relying on one old person's allowance.

Wherever I went I found ordinary people made extraordinary by the AIDS crisis. Faced with the shock of discovering they were HIV positive and knowing they were going to die, they decided that before they died they would change the world. The trauma of discovering they had AIDS gave them a focus for living. That experience inspired them to help others faced with the same unspeakable crisis. They had the authority to speak out on AIDS prevention. Their message was confrontational – a blunt defiance of the traditional relationship between men and women. If women want to avoid AIDS they must be in sole control of their bodies. Day to day the women visited people with AIDS getting what food and medical help they could, checking their children were in school and preaching the message of safe sex. These small, local campaigns are fundamentally revolutionizing the relationships between men and women in Africa. The positive positive women will change African societies as deeply as the AIDS pandemic itself.

Siphiwe Hlophe in Swaziland had just turned forty in 1999 when she won a scholarship to study agricultural economics in Britain. She had four children, the eldest twenty-two years old and the youngest eleven. One of the conditions of the scholarship was an AIDS test which she took not thinking there was a problem. She turned out to be HIV positive. Her husband left her, she lost her scholarship and she thought she was going to die. Then she decided to do something for people living with AIDS. She formed a group called SWAPOL, Swaziland for Positive Living, made up of mostly HIV-positive women, and quickly built it into a 150-strong body. Walking, talking, singing and dancing with the swagger of conquerors, they visit terminally ill people in their homes, ensuring they get medical care and a healthy diet. Siphiwe laughs. 'We are so busy. Now I'm going to live to my retirement.' I met her on a visit to London in 2011, still going strong and still fighting government inaction.

Joanna in Soweto did not want her full name revealed. A couple of years before she had been a homeless, HIV-positive single mother who did not have enough money to buy milk for her baby. Her father left home when she was four and her mother when she was twelve. She dropped out of school and when she went for treatment for genital herpes she was persuaded to have an HIV test. She recalled the terrible moment when she received her death sentence. 'I saw my name in the book before the nurse told me. I saw I was positive,' she said.

Joanna went to a herbalist, a traditional healer, believing that she could be cured. Then she discovered she was pregnant. Her boyfriend did not know she was HIV positive and would not go for a test. There were complications when the baby was born. Unable to breastfeed for fear of passing on the virus, she was also afraid to bottle-feed for fear of revealing she was HIV positive. She moved in with her boyfriend's family but they fell out and he started to beat her up. But there was nowhere else to go. Thinking her father would help, she went in search of him, but when she moved to his house he sided with her boyfriend and would not help. Now she was homeless and broke and very sick. She was close to death.

The baby showed signs of malnourishment but she still would not breastfeed her. She got to a hospital where the nurses referred her to a clinic that specializes in AIDS and she began to regain her health. The clinic sent her for training in counselling other HIV-positive women and she now has a full-time job at the centre helping others affected by AIDS.

At last she summoned up the courage to have her daughter tested. 'The day I took her, she was nearly two years old, she was vomiting and I was certain she was positive,' said Joanna. 'Then they told me she was negative. I felt like telling everyone, putting up a billboard to tell the world: my daughter is negative. I have lived with

HIV for six years and maybe I am going to die soon. Before I prayed that I would live to see my daughter walk. I prayed that I would live to see her talk. Now I pray that I will see her go to school.'

Helen Mhone was the director of Botswana's biggest AIDS NGO. As I enter her office, slightly late, she looks at her watch and tells me I have thirteen minutes for the interview. That is about the rudest thing you can do in Africa and I protest. She laughs, then replies fiercely, 'With AIDS time is vital.' She is a big, strong woman, already in her forties with three grown-up children. Divorced, she was working as a manager in a hotel chain, when someone close to her died of AIDS. 'I went for a test and tested positive . . . I had always thought AIDS wasn't for me so I went through all the stages: anger, shock, grief, blame, denial. Then I went to a conference for people living with AIDS. I decided to become educated about AIDS and I declared my status in 1995. A lot of people then came to consult me and the government wanted to use me to educate people about AIDS.'

In 1999 Helen founded the Coping Centre for People Living With AIDS (Cocepwa) to educate people about AIDS and help the families of victims. It began in a hut by the main hospital in Gaborone and soon had centres throughout the country. 'People are still hiding from AIDS,' she says. 'We know we have thousands of people who are HIV positive but less than ten in Botswana are open about it.'

Helen's deputy in Cocepwa and the national organizer was Onnie Moyo, twenty-eight years old, bright and fast-talking. She dropped out of school and took a job. A few years ago she fell sick. 'I had non-stop diarrhoea, all day and all night,' she says. 'The director of the company I worked for was very kind and suggested I should know my HIV status. I had not thought of it until then. I was too afraid.' Onnie went to visit a friend who was dying of AIDS.

She had been very heavy but now she was very thin. She had messed herself, she was dirty, so I cleaned her up, washed her and changed the sheets. I said to myself, that could be me tomorrow. That convinced me to get a test.

When I went to get the results the doctor was holding them up and I could see through the paper. I could see that I was positive. My CD4 count [the level of cells that control the body's immune system] was 200 – it should be above 500 – and the viral load was 64,000. I could not retain food. I was very thin but something told me I was going to fight.

I started looking at the books and talking to people. I came to realize I am HIV positive – I have to live with that. I have to live with the virus as a friend. I talk to it. I feed it when it is hungry. If you fight it you will lose.

While Onnie was still sick, an old boyfriend, Edison, started calling her and wanted to go out with her again. She had to tell him she was HIV positive. 'I said it as a way of repelling him. We had known each other since 1988 and now he wanted to be with me. I had to get him to back off.'

But Edison had already anticipated that. Instead of being repelled, he asked Onnie to marry him. Why? 'Because I love her,' he replies without hesitation. Edison was tested but is negative. Both want children, but as Onnie explains, 'My duty is to make sure he does not get infected by me. If you want a baby there is a lot to weigh up. You could get sick and die and leave an orphan or you could infect the baby. How do you decide? It's hard but we want to try.' They married in August 2002.

In 2008 they are still happily together and they succeeded in having two HIV negative children. Sadly, however, their daughter died in a fire.

Cocepwa's funding dried up because donors were not happy with its accounts – a common tale among African NGOs. Helen is trying to revive it but meanwhile her own family has been devastated by HIV/AIDS. She has recently lost her daughter, her granddaughter and her sister whose four children she now looks after. Her other daughter was diagnosed HIV positive in 2009.

13

Copying King Leopold
Congo

When the light is almost gone, the note of the boat's engine deepens and we swing sideways into the immense pull of the current. The sky slowly drains of light and darkness seeps out of the forest, drawing the riverbanks closer together. The river glows in the dusk as if charged with some inner power. It hisses and sucks at our tiny wooden shell. As we draw closer to the bank, the sugary scent of the river mingles with the sour smell of vegetation. We struggle towards a break in the cliff of jungle where a flickering fire silhouettes tiny human figures beneath the monstrous legs of the forest. It feels like entering a vast silent cave of night, an entrance to the underworld.

It is the end of a second day crammed in a dugout canoe. From a distance the Ubangi River, a kilometre wide here, looks slow and sluggish but it surges along, a terrifying flood. Weighed down by nine people, weapons and ammunition crates, the rough-hollowed tree trunk lies low in the water, only a couple of inches to spare. At first it feels as likely to remain upright as a floating barrel. My stomach spins every time it wobbles and the water in the bottom slops up the sides. If we overturn should I hold onto the canoe or swim for the bank? But which? Sometimes both banks are almost a mile away. I try to guess how far I could swim.

Steering with a rough-hewn paddle, the helmsman tries to keep in midstream where the current is fastest. Here we glide sedately past clumps of floating water hyacinths. But closer to the bank the current seems to flow faster. We flash past sandbanks and reeds, dodging the massive trees that have toppled into the stream. Now it tugs their trunks and branches, trying to rip out their roots that still cling desperately to firm ground.

As if some primordial green god had ordered it to take over the world, the forest erupts out of each bank. A silent, still profusion of greenness thrusts out of the earth: trunks, branches, foliage, tendrils. The giant trees stretch their branches out over the river as if trying to reach the other side. Swags of lianas pull them back and drag them to earth. Where a tree has leant too far and fallen in, others immediately take its space, pushing upwards and outwards as if frantically trying to escape some deadly suffocation in the dark cauldron of the forest below.

We see no animals. Occasionally an eagle hangs over the forest searching for a kill, or a hornbill flaps like a wooden toy across the treetops to seek a new perch. Sometimes we catch sight of a pin-legged heron poised like a statue in the shadows by the bank. It feels as if we are the first humans here. Only the jagged clatter of our little outboard motor tells us we are in the modern world. There is nothing else here from the third millennium. Two centuries of industrial man have made no mark. When outsiders first came here they found no wheel, no written language. Forest and river rule here as timeless as the sky, as they did a hundred years ago, a million years ago. Just as they did at the Creation.

Hunched in this carved-out log sliding downstream, I am in search of an ugly, forgotten war, pursuing rumours of a massacre. Earlier we had passed a huge ferry wedged on the eastern bank, four decks high, with a flat-topped barge attached to its bow. It is black and brown with fire and rust. The government had stuffed it with weapons and ammunition and 1000 troops and sent it up the river. A perfectly aimed shell had punched a hole directly under the bridge. Then shells and bullets had poured in and it burned down to the water line. There cannot have been many survivors.

We city people yearn for the wilderness and hate to see it destroyed, but the ghastly strength of aboriginal river and forest is terrifying. We make a detour around a line of wooden floats stretching across the river but we see no-one and no trace of a village on either shore. I long for signs of humankind. I think of the Thames at Marlow, try to imagine its homely hotels at the water's edge and windsurfers and bikini-clad water-skiers riding the river. Marlow was once swamp and forest. Could there be houses, hotels and cruisers here one day?

A soldier keeps lookout, perched on an ammunition box in the prow with a long-barrelled Chinese machine gun. Whenever he spots a shoal or dead branches beneath the surface he shouts and shoots out an arm and the helmsman turns the boat away from the snag. A sudden rainstorm drenches us and threatens to fill the boat and we put into a quiet bay and shelter under the trees.

Three other soldiers, dressed in camouflage, are at the back of the dugout. The helmsman wears a wig of long black nylon hair. Another tends the old outboard motor that roars coarsely and frequently hiccoughs. In front of them sits the minister, a flaccid, anxious man in military uniform who lies back on a crude low chair like a nervous potentate. Behind him are three other journalists, Congolese, Dutch, Ugandan. Primo, the Congolese, cheers our spirits with jokes and old French pop songs that he sings in a high-pitched falsetto, adding an African rhythm by drumming the sides of the canoe. The Dutchman watches stoically into the distance, occasionally making notes or taking snuff. The Ugandan is silent and grim-faced. He cannot swim.

I crouch as low as I can and watch the water in the bottom of the canoe shift and swirl each time we sway. After a while I notice the dark water mark inside the boat does not grow. The pilot and the soldiers move around quite freely, shifting position, even standing up to pee over the side. I want to shout at them to stay still, sit down, but slowly I realize that for these men of the river it is like riding a bicycle. As soon as the boat tips one way, they instinctively lean to balance it. My fears are unfounded. I trail my hand in the warm, velvety water. It smells musky. I lick some from my fingers and it tastes sweet, seductive. There is no point in struggling against Africa. Ineffably gentle, it is too powerful and deadly. I begin to relax, trust the Africans around me. But it is more like surrender than a sense of safety.

The night before we had stopped at a tiny village and the ragged inhabitants gathered at the bank to stare at us. Yet it was not an aggressive or even inquisitive stare, more like the blank glassy-eyed look of wary cattle. What do they want from us? they seemed to ask. They called out greetings and when we stepped ashore, shook hands with each of us in turn – as everyone always does in Africa. But we had passed the blackened remains of several riverside villages that day. Visitors here were obviously not as welcome as they once were.

An old woman fried bananas and hunks of goat meat on a barbecue made out of an oil drum covered by a grid. We bought them all and ate greedily. I wondered whom she had been cooking for. Who were we depriving? Who could have money here to spend on such luxury?

As I sat and ate I wondered what I would do if I had to stay here. Supposing we were marooned like Robinson Crusoe? If the ancient motor roped to the back of the dugout broke down and no other boat came, we could be here for months, or years. Had I got any useful information or skill these people did not have? Had all my education, my life in high-tec Western society given me anything that I could reproduce here? What single piece of knowledge could I impart to people here that could make their lives better? What technology could I reproduce that could change their world? Could I build a car from the trees or make an electric cell from the river? Could I even build a water wheel?

Stranded here, cut off from the rest of the world, I would not know what to do to survive. I would be dependent on these villagers, on their knowledge, their skill, their kindness. I would still have a different mentality, knowing that things could be changed, made better. But I would be a visitor, an outsider looking in, understanding very little of what I saw. And if I did not understand the people here, how could I persuade them that change was possible? Or even desirable? And if I could not, how long would I continue to believe in my culture of progress? How long before my stories of computers, mobile phones, cars, televisions, even water pipes, wheels and candles became the fantasy tales of a foreign madman? I would be one of them, fishing the river, hacking the forest, digging the earth and placating the spirits of forest and sky and river. Could I learn to survive in Africa?

Survival is Africa's greatest talent. All over the continent Africans get by with skill and perseverance in conditions that would kill off other human beings in a few days. Africa may be where mankind began but it's a tough and unpredictable place for humans to thrive. Its indigenous crops did not support *Homo sapiens* well, and man could not domesticate its indigenous animals. Today all Africa's farm animals – with the possible exception of cattle – are descendants of animals from outside the continent. So are the staple foods: maize, bananas, cassava all come from elsewhere. The climate is erratic, often unbearably hot or humid. One year drought kills your cows and withers your crops. Next year a flood washes away your soil.

Plagues of grasshoppers and bugs suddenly emerge from the earth and strip your fields. Parasites eat your cattle from within. Harmless European plants have African cousins with terrible thorns or poisonous sap. Your children suffer from worms and bacteria or die of malaria. Nature can be vicious in Africa, and that is not just the lions, leopards and poisonous snakes.

Living in such a fickle world makes African societies conservative, controlled by the elders, tradition and thousands of proverbs. Proverbs – wisdom distilled into sayings – reinforce the old ways. At one time they had to. Survival margins were narrow; doing something different was risky. People were forced to accept whatever nature threw at them and appease the spirits that controlled it. Do not try to change things. Accept and adapt. These have been the watchwords of the human inhabitants of the world's most fecund ecosystems. Maybe in the past Africa's toughest environments dictated that this was the safest way to live. Obedience to the risk-averse elders was a Darwinian survival mechanism. But the qualities needed to survive are opposite to the qualities needed to develop. To change the world around you, you must take risks, be open to new ideas and allow young people to experiment and break away from the old ways of doing things. But even today young Africans are frustrated by the power of grey-haired old men. 'He is too young to be President,' Africans say of aspiring fifty-year-old politicians. African rulers are, on average, the oldest in the world. We Westerners admire the way Africa respects and cares for old people. But it comes at a cost.

Towards the end of the day the lookout calls and in the distance we see a man who seems to be standing on the river. We inch towards him, a fisherman standing naked in his dugout, hurling his silk-light net over the water. He watches it float onto the surface, lets it sink, then draws it in, checking it for a catch before hurling it out again. We have reached other human beings. If some catastrophe destroyed my home in Britain I know where I would want to be: here in Africa. New ideas and new ways may not always be welcome but people always are. The stranger is greeted and fed. Here I would survive.

The engine is turned off and as we glide towards the bank, a crowd gathers to stare at us. The prow of the canoe crunches into the sandy beach and we come to a halt. The men shout greetings to our soldiers and watch us cautiously. Children with shining night eyes prance and wave to us then dive back giggling into their mothers' skirts. There is a sense of excitement. But we are not the only recent visitors to this village. This is where a terrible massacre is said to have happened a few days earlier. Stiff and tired, we get up gingerly. I clutch my way down the boat and onto the beach. Another arrival in Africa.

We walk wet-footed up a steep pitch-dark path away from the river into the forest. The path is slippery, rutted by rain channels. With only a half moon for light, we feel our way in single file trying not to trip on tree roots and rocks in the path. The sour smell of the forest mixes with the smell of burned wood. We pass smashed and roofless huts and a burnt-out truck. After about twenty minutes we come upon a clearing with a small fire silhouetting several figures seated on rough benches. As we approach they call out greetings, give up their seats to us and offer us beer and bananas. Exhausted, we ask to be excused the celebrations and be allowed to sleep.

A short way into the forest we come into a clearing lit by moonlight. In the middle stands an old two-storey European house. Glass and plaster crunch underfoot as we approach and push through huge sticky cobwebs splayed across the doorway. The windows are long gone and the ceilings down. This is the house that Achebe described in *A Man of the People*: the one seized from the colonialists by the elite, 'the smart and the lucky and hardly ever the best'. Now they have fled and the house is a ruin.

Inside we find an ancient sofa, an armchair and a massive wooden bed with broken springs but no mattress. Nervous of snakes, we move around the room and stamp the floor; then, too tired to care, slump amid the wreckage to seek sleep. Africa's frantic night orchestra of insect scrapings and sawings and the moan and bark of beasts in the forest make it nearly impossible. But after a day hunched up in a canoe, the feeling of just lying out flat is wonderful. The mosquitoes attack and there is nothing to be done except pray that the anti-malarial pills work.

It is September 2000 and this journey began a week before at the old airport at Entebbe in Uganda. I wrote a letter to the head of Uganda's military intelligence service requesting that we be allowed to visit their army on operations in Congo. A day later it came back to me with a signature and an order to be at the old airport at eight the next morning. When I hand it to a soldier on the gate he scrawls something on it, stamps it and the gate swings back and we are in the old airport.

Twenty-four years after the famous Israeli raid on Entebbe, the old control tower and the airport buildings are still in ruins. Great holes have been blasted in the walls by rocket fire and the facings are spattered with hundreds of bullet holes like a crazed join-the-dots picture. Small trees sprout from the roof of the control tower and grow through the smashed windows. The tarmac is a rubbish dump of broken fuselages and rusting wings tipped at crazy angles. Derelict helicopters and fighter planes lurk in the long grass like prehistoric monsters. But the main runway is usable and three huge white Russian-built Antonovs crouch ready for take-off. In a war fought on foot in a far-off jungle these planes are the only supply route.

A neat middle-aged man with thinning black hair, a small moustache and dark glasses gets out of a pick-up truck, talking into his mobile. He speaks low and fast in English but I cannot hear what he is saying. This is Fitidis, a Greek Cypriot from Paphos, who hires the Antonovs and the Ukrainian crews that fly them.

While we wait for permission to fly we sit and chat in the shade. Born in Congo, Fitides has lived there most of his life but left three years ago when Mobutu was overthrown and Laurent Kabila took over. He supplies the Ugandan army with food and ammunition and flies anywhere in Congo under its control. His main route is to Kisangani, the city at the centre of the Congo on the bend in the big river. If he has space he takes soap, sugar and salt to the market there. Salt does well these days. You can buy a bag for $8 in Nairobi and sell it for $40 in Kisangani. 'But insecurity is bad,' he says. 'In Kisangani everyone says he is the boss or the mayor. It seems to change every couple of weeks so you never know who to bribe.' For the return journey he brings back dead and wounded Ugandan soldiers and whatever he can buy: coffee, minerals or hardwoods.

'Diamonds?' I ask.

He quickly denies it. 'No – you have to really know what you are doing and I don't know diamonds at all.'

I am not sure whether to believe Fitidis and I cannot see his eyes behind the dark glasses. Few businessmen would refuse diamonds: so abundant around Kisangani, so easily hidden and some worth more than the plane.

He brings these planes from Kiev to Sharjah in the Gulf where they pick up goods then fly to Nairobi and on to Entebbe. Since Ukraine is one of the biggest makers of arms for Africa's wars I doubt if they fly empty from Kiev either. This time his client is the Ugandan army, but it could have been any one of nine national armies and as many rebel groups involved in this war in Congo.

After the Rwandan genocide in 1994 more than a million Hutus fled Rwanda into Congo to escape retribution from the invading Tutsi army. With them came the defeated government army which camped with more than a million refugees near Goma on the border. The new Rwandan government said the Hutu soldiers were planning to return and continue the genocide. It accused Mobutu, the President of Congo, of supporting them. Suddenly in October 1996 Rwandan troops with their Ugandan allies invaded eastern Congo and drove most of the refugees back into Rwanda. But some, together with the Hutu soldiers, fled west, further into Congo. The new Rwandan army pursued them, ostensibly to hunt down the *génocidaires*. That was only one part of their motive. The other was to overthrow Mobutu. They walked halfway across the continent, fighting all the way to Kinshasa. Mobutu was forced to flee and the Rwandans installed Laurent Kabila as President.

Kabila was a failed rebel who had been running a bar in Tanzania, but he was the nearest thing to an alternative Congolese leader that the Ugandans and Rwandans could find. Lazy, greedy but able to make speeches about the legacy of Patrice Lumumba, Congo's murdered Prime Minister, Kabila shook off the control of his backers and – according to them – started supporting the defeated Hutu army as Mobutu had done.

In 1998 the Presidents of Uganda and Rwanda, Yoweri Museveni and Paul Kagame, invaded again but this time they did not find it so easy. Kabila's anti-colonial rhetoric and Museveni and Kagame's closeness to London and Washington brought other African leaders in on his side. Suddenly the Rwandans and Ugandans were facing Angolan and Zimbabwean planes and guns. Eleven African countries became embroiled in Congo's conflict.

Today we are bound for Gbadolite – pronounced Badoleetay – the birth village of Mobutu, where he lived in later life and built himself several palaces and a luxurious airport that could take Concorde. Now it is the headquarters of Jean-Pierre Bemba, who leads one of the rebel movements against Kabila. Mobutu's old cronies have made their way here from their chic apartments in Brussels and Paris in the hope of being on hand in case there is a new government and new opportunities for getting even richer. Bemba is also a friend of the government of the Central African Republic whose capital, Bangui, is just across the river. Fitides tells me that his planes refuel in Bangui.

An hour later the hefty cargo plane is grinding across Africa, its hold stuffed with drums of fuel, crates of ammunition, spare weapons parts and medical supplies. Perched on the piles a dozen soldiers are splayed out sleeping or talking quietly. The officer among them clutches a heavy suitcase. Later I learn it is full of dollars. Three young women, one of them with a child at her breast, crouch among the drums with several trussed chickens, whole sticks of bananas and cloth bundles.

The deafening monotony of the engines never changes. Below the forest stretches to the horizon in all directions like a vast head of dark broccoli, broken only by snaking slate-coloured rivers. Look down two hours later and nothing has changed. It is as if the plane hasn't moved. Occasionally you spot the mark of man in the endless primordial forest: a cleared patch of pink earth like an unhealed scar on African skin. From above, flying over the forest, there are no signs of roads or even paths. It is like looking at Africa from afar. Outsiders love to label Africa or preach about what Africans should or should not do. But the view from above does not see the African ways beneath the surface. Unless you go there and walk the paths you cannot know how Africa works, how Africans live and think. Down there beneath the canopy, the forest is veined with paths, a filigree mesh of human systems and networks.

Congo is not just another African country in a mess. It is the vast, rich, troubled heart of the continent with all its problems and strengths as well as some special ones of its own. Africa cannot succeed if Congo fails. It is a rich country. Its earth contains deposits of minerals that have only been guessed at. Its fertile soils could feed Africa, its huge rivers charge it with energy. But Congo is one of the poorest countries on earth. Its cities are not linked by roads or railways. There is no police force, no civil service, no government. Its people live closer to the Iron Age than the twenty-first century.

In 1999 Congo was an immense carcass being hacked to pieces. For the invading armies and the scavengers who came in their wake, in a country more than ten times the size of Great Britain there was plenty to go round. The war turned into a scramble for Congo's sumptuous resources and every invader found a local warlord willing to gouge out diamonds, gold or coltan in return for guns and ammunition. This war in Congo does not involve huge armies and terrible battles. A few guns can send hundreds of thousands fleeing from their homes. And when they flee they perish. The biggest killer is not the bullet. The Horsemen of the Apocalypse in Congo are hunger and simple diseases like diarrhoea.

You can see why novelists created Congo as a place of physical and spiritual horror. It is the setting for *Heart of Darkness*, *A Bend in the River*, *A Burnt-Out Case* and other terrifying novels of degeneration and nihilism. And as if trying to live up to this stereotype, Congo contributes its own horrors. It throws up sudden outbreaks of Ebola and Marburg, flesh-eating viruses that make you bleed to death in hours. It is almost certainly the swamp where HIV/AIDS spawned.

The International Rescue Committee estimates that more than 5 million have died as a result of this war. That, Stalin would have said, is a statistic, not a tragedy. And it is a guessed statistic. It could be even more or it could be a fraction of that. No-one knows how many there were in the first place and how many would have died had there been no war. Life expectancy was only fifty in the mid 1990s, and that was a guess too.

Anyone with a gun, a mobile phone and an airstrip can become a wealthy warlord. Ripped out of Africa, the loot then floats gently through the international free market system and comes to rest in the window of a jewellery shop, on the fingers of innocent lovers. Africa is close to us.

And vast. Lay the map of Congo across the map of America, with its eastern end on New York. The western border is beyond Kansas City. North–South is the distance from the Canadian border to New Orleans. Now it is no more than a Congo-shaped blank on the map. It is not a nation state and never has been. Slaves, rubber, ivory, timber, copper, gold and diamonds: the mouth of the Congo River sucked the guts out of the continent. Before King Leopold of the Belgians seized it, Congo was pillaged by the armies of the coastal slaving kingdoms that fed the American demand for slaves. Leopold carved out a private empire for himself. His predatory companies looted its rubber, ivory, timber and minerals. His agents cut off hands and heads and burned villages to force the inhabitants to deliver its riches to him. His grab for the huge heart of Africa sparked the imperial take-over of the continent by France, Britain, Germany, Portugal, Spain and Italy.

The public outcry against the rape of Congo forced Leopold to give it to the Belgian state, which turned it over to administrators and missionaries. With a mission to save the Congolese from slavery and sin, the Belgians took it upon themselves to crush African culture and reconstruct Africans as black Europeans. In the African museum outside Brussels built in 1921 a monumental statue portrays a bearded white priest holding a naked African child, clasping another under his cloak. Another shows a mean-looking Arab trampling a child under foot and dragging a naked African woman by the arm. A third shows an African on his knees gratefully clasping the knees of mighty Belgium, portrayed as a Roman soldier.

The Belgians exploited Congo ruthlessly, but they also built roads and a railway and hospitals and schools. That led to social and demographic change but the Belgians blocked any political development, so when Congo was suddenly pitched into independence in 1960, the African elite was tiny, inexperienced and angry. There was chaos. Congo nearly broke up but out of the chaos emerged Mobutu Sese Seko, one of the more grotesque figures to rule in independent Africa. America and Europe backed him because they saw him as anti-Communist, but he turned into Leopold's true successor, treating the country as his own personal possession and looting it. He renamed it Zaire, treated the treasury as his bank account and allowed the powerful and greedy to feed off the state.

Mobutu was the supreme master of what has come to be known as the shell state. Zaire was a one-party state but one in which all citizens were members of the ruling party by birth. It meant everything and nothing. During his thirty-two-year rule, Zaire had ministers and a cabinet, ministries and governors, officials and diplomats. These appeared to make up the structure of a government. In fact, they were a façade. The real rulers were members of Mobutu's personal networks, through which they picked out whatever they wanted from the treasure house.

I realized how it worked when I visited the Ministry of Mines in the capital, Kinshasa. A 1960s block in the middle of town, the building is empty except for one floor. Its officials use their position for the perks: status, an office with a telephone, perhaps a car. During office hours, however, they engage in other business. The front desk is guarded by soldiers – 'A little sweet for us, please,' they ask each visitor. You walk up several flights – the lifts have not worked for years. On the top floor the minister presides with his secretary. The waiting room is packed with people lounging in armchairs and sofas. Many are from rural areas, mostly relatives from the village come to beg for money for school fees or a funeral. The men wear ill-fitting, worn-out suits, some of the women are barefoot. Two or three are asleep. When the secretary ushers one group into the minister's office, they fall on their knees and clutch his hand. Keeping their distance from the beggars, two European businessmen sit upright clutching bulging briefcases, tight-lipped and staring straight ahead. They do not acknowledge each other. They are seeking mining permits, the personal gift of the minister. He is a one-man state, taxing the rich and gift-giving to his family and friends. He has done well but he is not at the top of the food chain. If Mobutu needs cash, the minister will have to disgorge some of his takings.

Mobutu used tax farming – a system giving someone the right to collect taxes, hand a share to the state and keep the rest – to reward loyalty and buy off rivals and trouble-makers. If anyone became too greedy or powerful enough to challenge him, he would have them seized and thrown into prison for a while. When they had learned their lesson he would release them and give them another lucrative post to feed off. Mobutu's Zaire was a wheel of fortune on which individuals could rise and fall several times in a lifetime. The system was cultivated chaos. On two occasions when the army became disgruntled and he had no money to pay them, he told the soldiers to help themselves. The *payage*, they called it: pay yourselves. The soldiers promptly rampaged through the commercial areas of Zaire's cities and looted everything they could carry away. With the President's blessing banks were robbed, cars hijacked and shops broken into. Fridges, televisions, computers, anything and everything they wanted was carried off. Junior officials, soldiers and policemen robbed ordinary citizens in the street. Mobutu promptly used the chaos as an excuse to postpone elections and make his rule indispensable.

Why didn't the Congolese rise up and overthrow him? One reason was that his rich, powerful network could silence or buy off any discontent. He also had the protection of America, France and Belgium. Cold War logic led them to send troops on several occasions when Zaire was attacked by rebels based in Angola, then a Soviet ally. Another reason he survived was that most Congolese took a pragmatic view. They may have felt great anger but no institutions existed that could act as a focal point for opposition. So their rage exploded from time to time but could not be sustained. Discontent was often directed against a rival ethnic group rather than at the government and Mobutu was happy to leave his people fighting among themselves.

Another reason was that Mobutu had cultivated an aura of power in an African sense. He tapped into that sense of personal, spiritual power. A Congolese teacher with a degree from Brussels told me that he could not bear to say or even think bad things about Mobutu because Mobutu would know. 'He has been to the pyramids of Egypt,' he told me. 'He got some power from them, the power of that eye in the pyramid. He can see what I am thinking.'

The year before he finally fled he went to France for treatment for the cancer that was to kill him. When he returned a few months later the rebels had almost reached Kinshasa. Everyone knew he was sick and that his rule was over. But he drove from the airport into Kinshasa in an open-topped car waving to the huge crowds that gathered along the route. No-one threw a stone or even shouted at him.

When Mobutu's rule ended in 1997, Zaire as a nation state was dead. Theft and corruption ruled. Once the system is corruption and corruption is the system, it is impossible to operate without it. The local boss of one big British corporate company went to great lengths over an expensive dinner to explain to me that Mobutu needed one – just one – clean foreign company that he could do business with and that was his. He said to me that Mobutu had never asked for a back-hander. Later I learned that every Monday this man flew to Gbadolite with a briefcase of dollars and handed them personally to the President. One day things may change, but at present no company, local or foreign, can do business in Congo and avoid corruption.

The local Congolese take a pragmatic approach to surviving from day to day. Jean Bosco Sangolo is a junior judge who lives in a mod-est house in Kinshasa. He explains that the judges fall into three categories on this issue. 'There are those,' he says, 'who give their judgements without taking any bribe. These are very rare. Then there are those who call the litigants and ask for a bribe. The judge-ment goes to the highest bidder. Lastly there are those who give an honest judgement but then afterwards they go to the winner and ask for some money.' M. Sangolo puts himself in the last category. What would you do on a salary worth $10 a month?

The only national organization that survived Mobutu and the looting was the Catholic Church. Its voice is still powerful and it cre-ates an uncorrupted space for discussion and debate. The Church is also the largest 'aid agency' and provider of health and education in the country. In Kisangani, the headquarters of the Catholic archdio-cese, known as the *Procure*, is a huge brick fortress with massive iron doors. But far from being a bastion to keep out the world, it is hos-pital, school, clinic, food store, shop, bank, hotel, post office, airline, workshop, garage and church.

Archbishop Laurent Monsengwo of Kisangani was seen by many as a potential saviour and did much quiet diplomacy to hold the coun-try together at the worst of times. When Mobutu was forced to accept multi-party democracy in 1990, he encouraged as many parties to form as possible. Nearly 400 registered. Mobutu asked Monsengwo to preside over a national debate. Foolishly Monsengwo accepted. The National Conference went on for months, years, as delegate after delegate rose to make a long elegant speech about the glorious future of the country. Meanwhile Mobutu sat in Gbadolite making his ministers play musical chairs with the departments and going on picnics with his family.

Gbadolite is a collection of bizarre presidential palaces and grotesquely grand mansions that seem to have been dropped into the remote African bush. They have. We are staying with Olivier Kamitatu, the urbane secretary general of the Movement for the Liberation of Congo (MLC), Bemba's group, which was created and sustained by Uganda. He lives in a pleasant two-storey mansion on one of Gbadolite's boulevards. The town has been comprehensively looted by the villagers and a succession of armies and militias, but not completely destroyed. There is even electricity from a power station, built especially on the river a few miles away to service Mobutu's palaces.

Mr Kamitatu, Congolese and Belgian, is the son of a prominent politician who once worked with Patrice Lumumba and then with Mobutu. He speaks good English but prefers to speak French. He tells me that the MLC has nothing to do with former Mobutists or officers in Mobutu's army. He also says that there are no Ugandan troops fighting in the war, only helping with supplies. After a long chat with him I wander upstairs to find a man in military uniform slumped in front of the television watching Eurosport. He introduces himself as the minister of defence of the Movement. And what was he before that? 'I was a colonel in Mobutu's army,' he says proudly.

The room above Olivier's office serves as a breakfast and dining room and has a working TV with a satellite dish. In this village where very little happens, there is always a chance that someone you are looking for is here. Even if they aren't there you will always find a collection of businessmen who work the tricky fringes of arms dealing or mining, a journalist or two and lots of attractive women. Breakfast is a particularly good meal. All the ingredients, coffee, eggs, sweet cakes and sausage, are flown in from Belgium. Olivier apologizes because they aren't fresh. Above his place at the table a bullet has kicked a hole in the plaster. Perhaps the pastries were a bit stale one morning.

Grandiose, grotesque, gross – you run out of superlatives trying to describe the monstrous mansions that Mobutu built for himself and his family in his mother's home village. As if spraying his territory, he built a palace in every major town in Congo, but at Gbadolite there are three. The rest of the town is simply there to serve them. So it has an international-sized airport so that Mobutu's family could hire Concorde to go shopping in Paris or New York and a Coca-Cola factory in case they needed a drink. Mobutu's ministers also built mansions – respectfully smaller – in and around Gbadolite to be near the 'all-powerful warrior who goes from conquest to conquest, leaving fire in his wake'.

And in the middle of town on a low hill is a palace for Kosia, the twin sister of Mobutu's wife, Bobi. In public the twins accompanied him, dressed identically. In private, I am told by a former guard, it was a different matter. Bobi was very possessive and when Mobutu wanted to spend time with Kosia, he would tell his wife that he was going to Kinshasa. The presidential convoy would swoosh off to the airport but Mobutu would sneak back to Kosia's palace. A Mobutu lookalike, complete with leopard hat and cane, would mount the steps of the plane and wave to Bobi – you can see the runway from the presidential bedroom – then the plane would leave for Kinshasa. A few days later the process would be done in reverse. The guards at Kosia's palace were under separate command from those at the President's house and were forbidden to talk to each other on pain of death. Here anything is believable.

Kawele Palace was the private home. The entrance is a triumphal arch and at the back there is a vast swimming pool on two levels and a banqueting hall of royal proportions. From the terrace you can see across to what was once Mobutu's private zoo and a European-style farm with cows flown in from Switzerland and sheep from Argentina. All are now dead and eaten and the farm is returning to bush.

Then there is State House, an attempt to build Versailles in the jungle. It was still under construction when the dying Mobutu fled in 1997 (they say some of his guards blocked the runway, stopping his plane taking off until they were paid more money). The classical frontage is pink and white marble. Inside a grand ballroom is lined with mirrors and lit by enormous chandeliers, the ceiling delicately moulded rococo plasterwork. A massive staircase leads to more state reception rooms. Outside a garden of ponds and fountains was once lit by coloured lights that flickered and changed in time to music.

Most mind-boggling of all, there is the Chinese city – an attempt to reconstruct the imperial palaces of Beijing in the bush. With curving roofs of heavy green tiles, it is built over a lake. The ceilings, pillars and beams are decorated with hand-painted birds and dragons and Chinese landscapes. The centrepiece is a gilded pagoda.

When Mobutu's first wife, Marie Antoinette, died he had a modern church built for her with a great sarcophagus in the crypt beneath the altar. Even the church has been smashed and looted. A bullet hole has made a neat circular pattern in one of the glass panels in the altar rail. Reverentially I climb down to the crypt. Some leakage has created a lake around the great marble tomb. I wade across to it and stand on tiptoe to peer in but the tomb is empty. Resurrection? Looted? Or did Mobutu have time to take his first wife's body with him when he finally flew to Morocco?

Every single block of marble and stone, each tile and brick and pane of glass and every grain of cement for all these buildings was flown from Europe. They say only the sand for the concrete was local. And Mobutu, the man who claimed he had restored dignity to Africa, allowed nothing of Africa near him. Everything is in imitation of Europe. And often bad imitation: wood painted to look like marble, gaudy plastic instead of glass. It is as if he had spent a billion dollars in a DIY store. And the bigwigs of the World Bank and the IMF continued to come here and fawn on him and shovel money into his mouth.

Today all is in ruins. Every movable object was looted when Mobutu fled: gold taps ripped from the bathrooms, tiles gouged from the floors, walls stripped of mirrors, switches and sockets. Now they are redecorated with obscene graffiti and drawings. The marble floors are covered in broken glass and the excrement of goats and bats. Grass sprouts from every crack in the stonework and creepers reach through the broken windows. Birds and spiders make their homes in the leaking roofs. At the back of State House a family has set up home; the mother cooks on an open fire that has sent a streak of soot up the white marble. Clothes are spread out on the stonework to dry and barefoot children play in the colonnade. Africa laughs and takes its mocking revenge.

After a couple of days Olivier announces at breakfast that the MLC has captured Dongo, a small town on the River Ubangi, and that we can take a boat from Lissala to witness their victory. We are worried about time. We had set aside three days for Gbadolite and have already used two. He assures us we can get there and back in a day. It is only about three hours down river and a little longer back, he says.

We go to the airport, only five minutes from the centre of this non-town. The Antonov is being refuelled. This time I manage to exchange a few words with the thick-set puffy-faced Ukrainian pilot who is standing under the wing smoking a cigarette.

'Is this plane safe?' I ask him.

He puffs on his cigarette.

'Very old.'

'Old? How old?'

He tried to express dates in English. In the end we agree it must be mid 1960s.

'But no maintenance,' he adds with a shrug. 'Need new veels. Need new engine. Need new vings.'

I see what he means when we arrive at Basankusu. We bump onto the dirt airstrip and immediately the brakes are jammed on and we are flung sideways as the plane skids and judders to a halt. When we get out there is smoke coming from the wheels. 'We need 2000 metres to land,' the pilot says, 'but this airstrip only 1400. Is problem.'

He calls for water which they feed into a little hole in the wheel hub. There is a hissing noise and clouds of steam rise. More water is sent for. While I am watching this, an altercation breaks out between a moustachioed major and a large woman in uniform. The major is shrieking at her and she is giving as good as she gets. Suddenly the major lunges at her, trying to slap her face, but she quickly puts up her hand and parries the blow. In fury the major pulls out his revolver and tries to load it but spills the bullets onto the ground. The crowd doubles up with laughter and the girl doesn't flinch. Beaten, he smiles too, and makes a comment that makes everyone laugh more. Then he turns on two men who are lugging buckets of water towards the plane and shrieks at them to run. But they kept walking. So he draws his revolver again and points it at them, but again the bullets fall out. The crowd love it and dance and clap, doubled up with laughter.

At Gemena we stop again and find another Russian plane on the strip surrounded by men in battledress. The two Ukrainian crews are delighted to see each other and give each other huge bear hugs.

Around the other plane lie half a dozen bandaged soldiers on stretchers. One of them thrashes around screaming. The walking wounded stand around with bandaged arms or heads. Some look bad. Out of the sun, under the wing, are two body bags. These are Ugandan troops from the elite Scorpion unit who had been fighting Zimbabweans south of Basankusu.

Our plane is ready to go. The wounded are being taken aboard the other aircraft but as the doors are closing about five men carrying others on their backs run across the tarmac as if in some piggyback race. One cries out in pain at the jolting. But they are turned back. No hospital in Kampala for them. More likely a slow gangrenous death on an earth floor in Gemena.

The next stop is Libenge and we are met at the airstrip by Ugandan officers who take us back to the mission station in their Korean Jeep. The boss at the mission is Sister Marie Ollina. She left Sardinia thirty-three years ago to come to Africa, and has been at Libenge for ten years. Smiling, waving and chattering rapidly in French, she hurries around finding chairs and Coca-Cola for us on the mission veranda and insists that we eat. She says the mission was bombed by a government plane last week but it missed the house. While she waits for the rice to cook she does the ironing and talks about life in Libenge. The rice is plain and comes with two sardines each. It is to be our last meal for four days.

We reached Dongo after three days in the dugout canoe and I am woken from a fitful sleep by the sounds of early morning. The birds do not sing but make cautious little whistles and plinks as if testing out the world to see if it is safe to leave the trees. Their sounds mingle with the gentle thump of a pestle and the soft swish of someone sweeping. Voices sound close but quiet. It is a moment of delicious calmness.

I wander back towards the river and hear male voices singing, soft, uncertain. In a clearing nearby are about twenty dejected men standing awkwardly to attention in two rows – prisoners, dressed in old green uniforms. Most are barefoot, others have frayed trainers or wellington boots. A rebel officer is trying to get them to sing the anthems of the Movement for the Liberation of Congo. The words proclaim the prowess and principles of Mr Bemba. The men do not sound enthusiastic. But they will be forced to fight for their captors. The major later explains to me that their commanding officer committed suicide, shooting himself two days after he surrendered the village.

At the end of the front row of prisoners is a boy who looks only sixteen. His eyes speak utter misery. I walk over to him and he greets me and does not avoid my eyes like the others do. The major allows me to interview him. He tells me: 'I am from Kinshasa but I was studying in Lubumbashi. I was a first-year student at the university studying law. One day the soldiers came into the classroom and took us away. We were sent for military training with the North Koreans for three months. Then I was sent here.'

I ask him if he is in touch with his parents. 'No, my parents think I am still in Lubumbashi.'

So I ask him what he will do now – a stupid question since he will have no say in the matter. 'What will I do now?' he asks in a tone that should be mocking but isn't. 'Please take me with you to Britain.'

No begging, no irony, just a straightforward request like 'Give me a lift, will you?'

I can find nothing to say in reply and I stare at the line of prisoners squeezing out the words of the song. It strikes me that not so long ago I could have bought them all as slaves. I probably could now. Can I buy this young man his freedom and give him his chance? If he stays here he would be forced to fight for Bemba – months, maybe years in the forest with bad food and no medicine if he gets sick. There are tens of thousands of such young men. If by chance he manages to get to the government side he might be executed as a deserter. He goes back to the line and starts singing again. I do nothing. He is twenty-four years old and his name is Serge Franco.

I go for a walk around the village and the impression of the night was right. The village has been badly battered. On the highest point, overlooking the river, a single-storey building has exploded, its roof and walls flung outwards. Another nearby has been crushed inwards, its corrugated iron roof crumpled downwards as if it had been stamped on by a giant boot. The buildings are surrounded by a network of trenches. Posters of Kabila have been torn up and stamped into the mud. Abandoned anti-aircraft guns point their barrels horizontally into the bush. One of them has taken a direct hit and its barrels and sights are twisted and snapped off as if they were plastic. All around are boxes and boxes of ammunition, stacks of machine guns and mortars of all shapes and sizes. Why was this place so heavily defended? Apparently it was a supply base for a government advance that was supposed to go all the way up the river to Gbadolite.

It begins to rain, huge fast-falling drops that soak you in seconds. We dash to a hut by the side of the path and stoop under the thatched eaves to enter. Is it inhabited? It is hard to tell. There are two broken beds in one room and blackened stones on the earth floor of another. Nothing else. Two soldiers join us to escape the rain. They greet us in English and I realize they are Ugandans, army officers. They tell us how they have won a great victory here. We ask them about the MLC and they shrug as if to say, 'Where were they?'

We wander down along the trenches. Suddenly the smell hits us. That smell which goes deeper into the senses than any other. At the bottom of the trench something quivers like a ball of shimmering gold and black jewels. As I approach the gorgeous mask suddenly dissolves in an angry whine. Beneath there is a face: goggle eyes bulging like boiled eggs out of a face-shaped mass of pale slime.

Teeth protrude from a black mouth-hole in a terrible scream. A yellowing black hand is thrown up across the head as if warding off a blow. I stop and the mask of gold and black flies resettles as if to mock the horror with beauty.

Further on the smell comes again. We are told that the massacre took place on the edge of the town. About fifty people had been hiding in the forest and had been found by Kabila's troops, who treated them like spies and slit their throats. It seems just as likely it could have been the MLC but we are not going to find out the truth. We walk to the edge of the village to a house sitting on its own. Outside, a patch of front garden has been recently dug over. The doorway is smeared with red-brown, as if a leaking sack has been dragged across it. I go inside. The smear leads me to a room at the back. It is dark out of the sun. My shoes seems to stick to the floor as if I am walking in treacle and I look down at a black coagulated pool on the floor. Flies seethe. One lands on my lip. I flee.

It took four years of tortuous negotiations to reach a peace agreement in Congo. But it was not a deal of reconciliation. The leaders of the various groups and the invading armies that supported them simply agreed to stop fighting over the spoils and get on with enjoying them. The process was an inclusive African one so the price of peace was that those who started the war were rewarded with positions in government. Joseph Kabila stayed on as President. He inherited the presidency from his father who was murdered by Rwandan agents in 2001. The leaders of the rebel movements became Vice-Presidents. In December 2005 a new constitution was confirmed by a referendum and elections were held in July 2006. The assumption of outsiders was that, forced to govern together, the warlords would check each other's theft and violence. The opposite happened. They kept the country divided, cut deals with each other and filled their pockets.

Many of the bribes on the mining contracts were so blatant that they quickly came to light. Some brave souls were willing to expose and denounce the theft – and not just because they were not getting a cut. Despite the politics of theft, violence and patronage, Congo still inspires great patriotism among its long-suffering citizens. They may have little loyalty to institutions or a ruler, but Congolese believe desperately in the Congolese nation and a few are prepared to fight its looting bosses.

Most payments for mining rights never saw the light of day. An IMF report in 2006 said $70 million was missing from state coffers. That was certainly a huge underestimate. President and Vice-Presidents all grossly 'overspent' their budgets but they did not spend it on the people of Congo.

The election cost more than $500 million and was won by Joseph Kabila. It produced little democracy and no accountability. Shortly afterwards the war broke out again in Kinshasa and Bemba was arrested and sent to the International Criminal Court for trial on charges of war crimes. Had he won the election there is little doubt that it would be Kabila who would have been sent to The Hague. The institutions of the state are no stronger or more accountable than they were under Mobutu.

Meanwhile, in the east of the country, small but horrific civil wars over mines and mining rights continue. Congo has some of the richest veins of minerals on the planet. Artisanal miners and slaves are forced to dig deep shafts to excavate gold, coltan and other valuable minerals which are bought primarily by the Chinese and gangster capitalists. Rwanda's mercenary army, the M23 movement, set up to track down genocidaires, also forced people to dig and collect the mineral wealth of eastern Congo and ship it to Kigali for export. In 2014 the Americans finally realized what Rwanda was up to and there was a glimmer of hope in eastern Congo. M23 was forced to disband. The last major war of the twentieth century seemed to have petered out.

14

Not just another country
South Africa

I still have the photograph: a slim young black man in blue jeans and an open check shirt stands on the bare earth looking at the camera. Behind him are the battered remains of corrugated iron shacks, leaning at crazy angles or flattened. The man's face is a mask of acceptance but his eyes are intense, burning. It is 1979 and we are in Winterveld, a vast, bleak squatter camp for 'excess labour' just north of Pretoria, the capital of white-ruled South Africa. Father Smangaliso Mkhatshwa is the young parish priest of the St Charles Lwanga Catholic church and we have come to inspect the school that he helped construct. It was only a collection of sheds and corrugated iron lean-tos with a few blackboards where children could memorise the basics of literacy. But it has been deemed illegal and the police have destroyed it.

Father Mkhatshwa's reaction is – how shall I put it? – long-term. Although I can see from his eyes that he wants to kill someone right now, he picks through some of the wreckage and shrugs. He says he will get in touch with the authorities and appeal. In the meantime they will rebuild.

Winterveld is one of those illegal but unstoppable encampments that apartheid's mad laws have spawned across South Africa's bleak red plains of thorn scrub and meagre grasses. Nearly a million people are doomed to survive here in mud-brick hovels with corrugated iron roofs and doors. Some have been here since 1951. There is no centre, no organisation, no leadership. It is as if thousands of people with nothing have come to this place of nothingness and must sit and do nothing until the end of time. A few lucky ones have menial jobs in Pretoria but while whites there wanted their labour, they did not want them living anywhere near the city. Father Mkhatshwa and I visit a shack with three rooms that houses a family of fifteen. The latrine is four pieces of battered corrugated iron leaning together three yards from the house.

Jacob Mthemba, the head of the household, the one with a job, is about fifty years old. He earns 120 Rand (£60 at this time) a month and has worked six days a week for twenty years as a cleaner in Pretoria. He pays 8 Rand a month rent, but the biggest problem is water which he has to pay for litre by litre and the price is going up. 'Every month I am left with a debt, an IOU at the store,' he says, watching his exhausted-looking wife bath a baby in a blue plastic bowl filled with reddish brown water. 'There are many diseases here. If a child gets sick it dies. We cannot afford medicine and the hospital is far.' Beds are a pile of mouldering mattresses laid out on the earth floor each night. Pinned to the wall is a tapestry of a gun dog with a dead pheasant in its mouth and a cloth decorated with a scene from Swan Lake; moonlight on the water and ballet dancers in a row. Everything is covered with a film of red dust. Father Mkhatshwa and I visit more homes. He is treated with great respect and tries to provide whatever he can, a few Rand here, a lawyer contact there. Wherever he goes he smiles and exudes a spirit of possibility. But as we drive back his talk is full of anger and despair. It is hard to disagree with him.

Father Mkhatshwa might have stayed a good pastoral priest,

ministering to individuals, helping them survive the worst of apartheid. Instead he chose a more confrontational, prophetic role. A founder of the United Democratic Front which fought apartheid in its last decade, he became a defiant activist, was caught, detained and tortured horribly. But in the 1994 election he stood as an African National Congress candidate and became an MP. President Mandela made him Deputy Minister of Education, then in 2000 he became mayor of Pretoria. When I met him there, he dashed out of a meeting to greet me, burst out laughing and gave me a huge hug. I reminded him of our visit to Winterveld and the school. 'The Winterveld you visited in 1979 looks very different today. Now it has another school,' he says, 'a lot better.' And we shake our heads remembering that day. Could we ever – ever – have dreamed as we stood amid the wreckage of the school in the middle of Winterveld that one day he would be Mayor of Pretoria and see it given an African name, Tshwane?

After my two years in Uganda I did not go back to Africa until 1979. During that time I worked in Northern Ireland and became a journalist. In the last months of the 1970s South Africa was a volcano. The tectonic plates beneath the surface of apartheid were beginning to shift again. Since the sudden explosion of young black anger in the townships in 1976, South Africa had been ominously quiet. Now the relationships between race, class and wealth were realigning, setting the pattern of struggle that would lead into the last violent decade of apartheid. At the time it seemed that white South Africans would fight to the death to keep apartheid – a fight that would last years. South Africa's strategic position would almost certainly draw in the superpowers. Many believed it would be the crucible of a Third World War.

I did not go to South Africa as a journalist. My sponsor was the Christian Fellowship Trust, an innocuous-sounding charity. In

London it was harmless enough, but its other half in South Africa, called the Christian Institute, was deemed so dangerous by the apartheid state that it was banned. Its leader, Dr Beyers Naude, was an Afrikaner aristocrat and *dominee*, minister, and had been moderator of the whites-only Dutch Reformed Church, the theological pillar of apartheid. His father had been a founding member of the Broederbond, the Afrikaners' freemason-like secret society. Naude had defended apartheid as vigorously as any until the massacre at Sharpeville in 1960 transformed him. He abandoned his Afrikaner tribalism, broke out of the white version of the world, left the theological certainties he had grown up with and trekked towards the dream of a non-racial South Africa. He never stopped. Like other great Afrikaner radicals who underwent such a transformation, his change of heart did not settle on the white liberal position which condemned apartheid but continued to enjoy its privileges. He went straight on down the path of radicalism and threw himself into the struggle to overthrow the system.

His former colleagues, the Afrikaner tribalists, declared him a traitor and tried to smother him. They could not tolerate one of their own, a leading light of the Afrikaner Dutch Reformed Church, becoming a 'Communist'. Beyers was confined to his house in Johannesburg, ordered to report regularly to the police and forbidden to meet more than one person at a time – including his wife, Ilse. The Christian Institute was closed down.

Secretly the Christian Fellowship Trust fed funds to surviving members and, if they could get passports, brought them out of South Africa to meet the exiled leaders of the African National Congress and other anti-apartheid activists. It also sent outsiders into South Africa to see for themselves what was going on.

I took a British Airways flight that stopped off at Nairobi to drop tourists bound for Kenya's game parks. I envied them. From the window I watched a group of Kenyan women in blue aprons sweeping – or pretending to sweep – the runway. They horsed around, trying to grab each other's brooms, staggering with laughter at each other's quips. They were the last cheerful Africans I was to see on this trip. The plane was almost empty when we took off and every one of the passengers and crew was white.

Relieved that I got through immigration at Jan Smuts airport with my tourist visa unquestioned, I climbed nervously onto a bus to take me to the centre of Johannesburg. It was mid morning but a crowd of drunken middle-aged Afrikaner men burst onto the bus like a group of overexcited school children. Swigging cans of beer, they knocked off each other's hats and struck boxing poses. Two of them carried a banner reading, 'John Tate RIP 20/10/79'. I had arrived two days before a momentous boxing match between a white South African, Gerrie Coetzee, and an African American, John Tate, who had broken the anti-apartheid sporting boycott to come to South Africa to fight.

This was no ordinary boxing match. This was race war. In other sports, apartheid did not allow teams of different races. Blacks were not permitted to compete with whites. But in boxing, the most brutally physical sport of all, the government allowed a black–white clash. Maybe they were too confident of victory. The drunken whites took great delight in telling the black bus driver what Coetzee would do to Tate. Afrikaans is an extraordinarily expressive language, especially rich in words describing bodily functions and violence. Even I could get the drift of what they were shouting. The driver grinned and laughed at their banter but he did not try to match it. His eyes watched them warily. Just as we were about to leave, one of the Afrikaners decided to go for a pee and leapt off the bus. As he passed the driver he snatched the keys from the ignition. There were roars of laughter. The driver laughed too. When the man returned he threw the keys back at the driver and told him to get going. The driver laughed even more.

At the coach station in the centre of Johannesburg I got off and went to find a lavatory. It was round at the back and stank as if it had not been cleaned for months. As I came out a black man walked in. He looked startled – or was it fear? He said something angrily but I didn't understand. Then I looked back and saw a pale patch on the wall where a notice had been taken down. This was a lavatory for blacks only. It was not the first occasion that I encountered black resentment at a white crossing the apartheid barrier.

At that time the government was taking down the Whites Only signs as part of a new strategy to improve its international image by removing apartheid's more glaring manifestations. Glaring that is, for visitors like me. Signs or no signs, blacks were still kept in their place. The words were ineradicably written on their souls.

Whites and blacks had completely different experiences of what apartheid actually was. In white areas, where only a tiny handful of the black population ever went, apartheid meant the signs saying Whites Only or Non-Whites Only. In black areas like Soweto, however, there were no Non-Whites or Whites Only signs. So while for whites those signs were the most visible manifestation of apartheid, most blacks never even saw them. The removal of the signs – welcomed by white liberals – did not affect blacks at all. Besides, they were replaced in city centres by signs on benches that said Bus Passengers Only or Old People Only. That stopped blacks using them just as effectively.

From a white viewpoint apartheid was only what the word meant: separateness, a way of reserving certain areas for themselves. A common white reaction to questions about apartheid was, 'They have their own areas and if they aren't as nice as ours, it's because the blacks are dirty and lazy.' Whites never went to see Soweto or

Winterveld or New Brighton. They had no conception of what life was like in these officially created slums. These places were what blacks experienced as apartheid. Systematically dispossessed of land, homes and the opportunity to work, to have a family and a future, they were a slave class whose sole purpose was to provide cheap labour for whites. Above all, apartheid stripped them of their rights as citizens and their dignity as human beings.

You did not have to go far outside white areas to see that these minor changes in the public face of apartheid were peripheral, aimed at concealing a stronger grip at the core of the system. That was the government's plan, but it did not work. The act of taking down the signs was not substantial but it was symbolic. It showed that the whole project was already in retreat. Slowly and inexorably black nationalism was stirring again. It could not be stopped. At the heart of separate development and the attempt to make non-white people mere 'hewers of wood and drawers of water' was a contradiction. The creation of wealth in South Africa needed neither wood nor water. It depended on educating skilled labour. Bantu education – as the apartheid system called it – provided few skills beyond literacy, let alone the maths, sciences and technical skills a modern economy needed. But impoverishment forced more and more black people to leave their rural slums and head to urban centres. It was impossible to keep black people out of the modern world, and without them South Africa would itself fail to keep up with modernity.

As early as the late 1960s the apartheid wall had been thoroughly breached by migration. After that the white government could only respond to events. It could not dictate them. The only questions were how apartheid would finally end, whether Western countries would help or hinder its demise and who would take over.

Used to going to big dances at clubs in Uganda, I was determined to see something of South African night life. I heard about the Pelican Club, frequented by a small but growing number of young black professionals in Soweto. In those days whites needed permission to go to Soweto just as blacks needed permits to go to white areas. So I made my way down to the West Rand Administration Board at the bottom end of Johannesburg to obtain a permit. On the second floor in a sparse office I found Mr Phillips reading a newspaper spread out across an empty desk. He produced a form and asked me why I wanted to go, who I would be visiting, which day and hour I would go, which route I would take and the make, colour and registration number of the car I would be going in. The thoroughness of apartheid still astounds. I said I was in the music business looking for new bands. When the huge form was filled, he told me to come back in a week to collect the permit. Then he returned to his newspaper. In contrast to the queues of blacks appearing in the magistrates courts every day charged with being in a white area illegally, I may have been the only white asking to visit Soweto that day, that week, perhaps even that year.

My first attempt to go to Soweto was postponed by an attack on the police station opposite the Pelican Club. The owner, a big cheerful Mozambican named Lucky, called to say it was too dangerous. So we went the following Saturday; two whites and a mixed-race woman who knew the way. At the time she was passing herself off as white so she could live in the northern suburbs but she chose to be black that night. We arrived at the club which lay slightly down a slope from the embattled, floodlit police station. Lucky welcomed us warmly and gave us each a tumbler of neat gin. Then he announced our presence over the DJ system which got us a round of applause. Smartly dressed young men and girls came over and greeted us. It had been three years since the Soweto uprising and they told us no whites had ventured to the club since. Now, these young Sowetans were going out of their way to welcome a posse of whites who dared cross the apartheid boundary – if only for an evening's drinking and dancing in their city.

The music, however, was disappointing; no Miriam Makeba or Hugh Masekela songs, only American soul and Western pop. No-one had heard of Congolese music except Lucky and he said he didn't have any. If whites were cut off from Africa in South Africa, so were blacks. Not for them the gorgeous robes of Senegal, the snazzy Kente cloth of Ghana or the flamboyance of Kitengi from East Africa. South African music had a strong American jazz connection going back to the 1920s, which then merged with traditional Zulu and Xhosa music and church-choir singing. There were few audible links to Congolese music, Ghanaian High Life or other African music.

Two girls and two boys came over and formally introduced themselves, the boys asking my permission to dance with the girls I had come with. I bought some beers and the bottles were passed from mouth to hand round the dance floor. Lucky interrupted the music to announce that someone had lost a watch. 'Whoever finds that watch, Brothers and Sisters, has got to give it back.' A couple of minutes later he announced it had been found and returned. 'Thank you, Brothers and Sisters,' he said, 'and a thank you to those who caused that disturbance last week.' There was a roar of 'Amandla!' – Power – and a show of clenched fists across the dance floor. It was one of the few black political manifestations I saw on that entire visit.

Lucky had an extra reason for hating the police. The Pelican Club did not have an alcohol licence and officers had raided him recently and fined him 500 Rand. That was three nights' takings. Later in the evening he brought us plates of meat and pap which we ate with our fingers. When my friend asked for a napkin to wipe her hands, Lucky told her to find the man with the nicest-looking shirt on the dance floor. 'Go and dance with him and hold him real close.'

In Johannesburg the Christian Institute arranged for me to stay in a convent for a few days. The nuns were a cheerful lot, Irish and white South African. As I sat down to dinner with them on the first evening their old dog waddled in and I was introduced. But no introduction took place when the black cook came in with the soup. She was ignored. Like most whites in South Africa, whether consciously or not, the nuns just didn't get it. Whites just did not see Africa. They lived in it and they owned it. They tried to tame it and control it. But they never listened to Africa's music. They couldn't dance or celebrate. In their own harsh way they loved what they had created here, covering Africa over with an imitation Europe. In this world Africans were either servants or a nuisance to be criticized, even demonized.

Did white South Africans really believe that they would stay in control for ever? Over the past twenty years the European powers – Britain, Belgium, France, Portugal and Spain – had jumped or been pushed off the continent, abandoning the imperial houses they had built. One group of colonists, the Rhodesians, had defied their imperial power and decided to fight on alone. But while I was in South Africa, their leader, Ian Smith, was forced to sit down with the African leaders Robert Mugabe and Joshua Nkomo to negotiate a settlement. South Africa was different. Self-governing from 1902 to 1961, it was a white colony which recognized the sovereignty of imperial Britain. In 1948 the Afrikaner Nationalist Party, many of whose leaders were Nazi sympathizers who had been locked up during the Second World War, came to power and formalized racial separation in law. Imperial Britain saw its role in its colonies as 'balancing' the interests of natives and settlers. In South Africa, now self-governing, that 'balance' was upset by the introduction of apartheid, but Britain lacked the power and will to do anything about it. South Africa was just too valuable. In 1961 the apartheid government broke the last constitutional links with Britain and declared South Africa a republic.

Whites made up 14 per cent of the population and owned almost all of the wealth, including the best land. Some had British passports and had arrived more recently. They were joined by French and Portuguese settlers who had been driven out of Algeria, Angola and Mozambique in the wars for independence. The majority, however, were of Dutch origin: Afrikaners. Their families had been there for 400 years, they spoke a language that was distinct from Dutch and they had no other home in the world. Their culture was rugby, beer and *braaivleis* – barbecues – and jokes about redneck Englishmen – *rooineks*.

For the British South Africans, culture in the 1970s was the shrivelled remains of suburban Britain of the 1950s. They listened desperately to recordings of old BBC comedy shows like the *Goon Show* and *Ray's a Laugh*. They put on awful productions of *Showboat* or *Charlie's Aunt* or attended performances by British artists who could not get bookings in Britain. It was a strange psychosis: nostalgia for memories of a British society which no longer existed and which they had rejected by coming to South Africa.

While working in Northern Ireland in the late 1970s, I had begun to notice the strong parallels with South Africa. The most striking parallel was between the Afrikaners and the Ulster Protestants. Both had arrived as colonists during periods of religious persecution in seventeenth-century Europe. Both embraced orange as their colour, derived from the House of Orange, the Dutch monarchy who had stood out against the Catholic Spanish monarchy. The hero of the Irish Protestants was William III, the Dutch king who finally defeated the Catholic James II and established Protestant British rule in Ireland. The Afrikaners were Dutch Protestants who settled at the Cape to trade and farm. They were joined in South Africa by French Huguenots fleeing Catholic oppression. To the Afrikaners, the *Swart Gevaar* – the Black Threat – and the *Rome Gevaer* – the Threat of Rome – were both seen as real, live threats to their existence. In comparison, the English rooineks who had fought against the Afrikaners in two horrible wars were merely an annoyance.

The Ulster and South African varieties of Protestant fundamentalism had a lot in common. Theirs was a whole world view, an attitude to the meaning of life, self and land. Both believed that they were God's chosen people, rewarded for their faithfulness by the gift of the land they now occupied. The fact they had won the land by conquest reinforced in their minds the idea that God was on their side. They also believed in the puritan values of hard work, thrift and honesty. When I heard an Afrikaner clergyman talk of black Africans as lazy, dirty, unpunctual and untrustworthy, I could have been listening to some of the militant followers of Ian Paisley, the Ulster Protestant political clergyman, talking about Catholics.

Here however, their similarities ended. In Ireland the Orangemen were more British than the British and were, until 1969, backed unquestioningly by Britain's Parliament at Westminster. Since the end of the eighteenth century the British had tried to impose their rule on the Afrikaners, forbidding their practice of slavery and taking their land. At the end of the nineteenth century war broke out between the British and the Afrikaners. The British won the war but the 1902 treaty was generous to the losers and the Afrikaners were allowed to remove rights from non-whites in return for remaining part of the British Empire. Interestingly, in the second South African war some Irish joined the Afrikaners – not their soul brothers, the Ulster Protestants, but the Catholic Irish Republican Brotherhood, forerunner of the IRA. If the Afrikaners were fighting the British they must be the good guys.

A third group of migrating Dutch and English Protestants left their homes at the same time as the Afrikaners first settled in South

Africa. They sailed west rather than south and helped found the most liberal state yet known to humankind, the United States of America. They too were informed by the puritan ethic and the gratifying feeling that God had rewarded them with a land of their own. But although they were liberal towards each other, the new Americans overwhelmed – and virtually exterminated – the native population. If today's white South Africans are colonists, so are the non-indigenous populations of North and South America, Australia and New Zealand. The only difference is in the numbers of surviving native peoples. In the United States, descendants of the original inhabitants represent 0.8 per cent of the population; in Canada it is 4.3 per cent; in Brazil less than 0.4 per cent. Aboriginals make up 2.4 per cent of Australians. The Maori make up 14.6 per cent of New Zealand's population, though only 4.2 per cent use Maori as their first language. In South Africa, the indigenous people are 75 per cent of the population. I once heard an Afrikaner politician quip to an American diplomat trying to foist a non-racial constitution on South Africa, 'At least we left our natives alive.'

The question for the majority black, 'coloured' and Indian population of South Africa was how to wrest power from the white minority. But were the whites, particularly the Afrikaners, to be treated as a dominant and difficult ethnic group or were they alien settlers to be chased out? South Africa's extraordinary history defied conventional analysis. The ANC had been a black organization since its foundation in 1912, formally admitting whites as members only in 1964. Middle class in its leadership and membership, the ANC was not always as close to the people as it liked to claim or as it needed to be. While it stressed that South Africa belonged to *all* its people, a breakaway movement, the Pan Africanist Congress, advocated a more race-based approach: Africa for the Africans. That debate reflected the two strands, Africanist or Marxist, race or class, that ran through the struggle for Africa's liberation from imperial and white rule.

In 1950 the South African Communist Party was banned and ten years later so was the ANC. Better organized, the SACP dictated ANC strategy. But white led, and with close links to Moscow, it could not advocate the expulsion of whites from the country. Its Marxists described South Africa's predicament as 'colonialism of a peculiar type'. Apartheid was, they said, a form of internal colonialism backed by international capitalism. Awkwardly for the Marxists, however, the major capitalists in South Africa were English-speaking, excluded from political power by a party that represented lower-class Afrikaner workers and farmers. During the struggle the SACP and ANC slogans screamed for an uprising of the masses to smash imperialism, capitalism and colonialism. The ANC welcomed and worked with white liberals and Communists and left open the question of what would happen to whites when victory came.

In contrast, the Africanist tradition was more psychological and racial. It demanded Africa for the Africans and wanted to see black states and black leaders who could treat with the rest of the world on an equal footing. Rejecting the imperial oppressor's name 'South Africa', the Africanists called the country Azania, and for a while chanted the slogan 'One Settler, One Bullet'. Since race was the basis of the South African state and society and discrimination was the daily experience of ordinary black people in their everyday lives, this was a far more appealing ideology for many blacks than the broad, revolutionary, anti-capitalist aims of the ANC. The global struggle against capitalism did not motivate as fiercely as the struggle to regain lives and land now.

These two strands often crossed over or became indistinguishable. The Africanists sometimes used even more virulent Marxist language than the Communists. The Communists were happy to play the African race card when Marxist class concepts meant nothing to poor black Africans. And with a discreet presence well established in neighbouring countries, the Communist-supported ANC was ready to receive young black South Africans who had left the country. After 1976 thousands of angry young black South Africans crossed the borders of Lesotho, Botswana and Swaziland to seek military training to fight back. They were met by ANC activists and passed onto Angola and Mozambique, then run by liberation movements allied to the Soviet Union. To compete with the Soviet Union, the Chinese also provided help, but, although also Marxist, they usually backed Africanist groups. They imposed no particular ideology or rhetoric on them.

One of the most important decisions that would affect the future of South Africa was taken shortly before I arrived. I did not see its significance at the time though I had a small part in it. In the 1970s the Africanist cause was reincarnated as Black Consciousness, a philosophy rather than a movement, forged by Steve Biko and other young black intellectuals. Steve Biko, the most charismatic and articulate South African of his generation, was killed in jail by the police in 1977. Many others of his group were imprisoned or fled into exile.

Steve Biko's story was later told by the white journalist Donald Woods. The capture and imprisonment of Nelson Mandela and the leadership of the ANC in the early 1960s decapitated the black leadership for a generation. Only thirty-one when he was battered to death by the police, Biko and his movement reawakened the Africanist strand in the fight against colonialism and white supremacy. Born in 1946, Biko had grown up in the eastern Cape, an industrial area known for the militancy of its black workers. Biko complained that neither the ANC nor the Pan Africanist Congress was doing anything that meant much to ordinary people; their language of class struggle did not touch the lives of ordinary Africans whose main problem was white racism. Their feeling was that the ANC had failed and a new approach was needed.

Pointing out that the most virulent racists were poor whites who should have been closest to black workers according to Marxist theory, Biko forged a different analysis. Being black, he said, was not a matter of skin colour, it was a mental attitude. He wrote: 'Black people are those who can manage to hold their heads high in defiance rather than willingly surrender their souls to the white man.'

He railed against the way in which blacks were willing to accept liberal whites as their leaders because, he argued, liberal whites sought merely to ameliorate a system that was fundamentally evil. On the other hand, he complained that the ANC was neither close to the people nor militant enough. He said it wanted change only through protests and boycotts, hoping that 'the rest could be safely left to the troubled conscience of the fair-minded English folk'.

Drawing on the writings of Franz Fanon and Aimé Césaire, Biko wrote: 'For a long time the black has been listening with patience to the advice he has been receiving on how best to respond to the kick. With painful slowness he is now beginning to show signs that it is his right and duty to respond to the kick *in the way he sees fit.*' (The italics are his.) It was something, he said, every black South African could do, every minute of every day, without having to wait for the revolution.

This realization that blacks were complicit in their own oppression and only blacks could liberate themselves from it, struck a chord with the new generation. Biko's contemporaries were better educated, better off financially and with more access to the outside world than their parents had been. They had not suffered the trauma of the crackdown on the ANC that had smothered opposition to apartheid for more than nearly two decades. The message that Biko delivered with such articulacy was that each black South African must stand up and free himself or herself as an individual from mental apartheid as a starting point and an integral part of liberating their country. When Black Consciousness activists were convicted and sent to Robben Island in 1977, many regarded Nelson Mandela as a sell-out because he and the other ANC prisoners had reached a modus vivendi with the prison warders. The new inmates clashed frequently with the warders because as Anthony Sampson put it in his biography of Mandela, 'they were not prepared to accept the degrading and racist treatment'. They certainly created a dilemma for Mandela who believed in treating all individuals with respect and dignity. He would never call his warders 'baas' as they tried to insist, but neither did he go out of his way to be rude or aggressive towards them. He found the attitude of the new wave of prisoners impetuous and distasteful, but he understood the strategy.

Before I left for South Africa in 1979 I met Barney Pityana, a fugitive of the crackdown on Black Consciousness, in a sparse loft office in north London. A tight, reserved man, it obviously grieved him to ask a white Briton for a favour. He suggested that I find Curtis Nkondo, the leader of Azapo, the Azanian People's Organization, and the only leading figure of the Black Consciousness movement not in jail. Could I, asked Barney, bring news of the survivors inside and ask Nkondo and any others I could find what the remains of the movement inside the country thought the exiles should do.

I met Curtis Nkondo towards the end of my trip. He had been head of the militant teachers' union during the 1976 uprising. Expecting to meet a fierce revolutionary in hiding, I was shocked when he asked me to lunch in an expensive Johannesburg restaurant – so smart that it allowed blacks in. I was even more shocked to meet a young elegantly suited executive. He had a job with an American computer company, Control Data, that was trying to launch an education programme in South Africa, and wanted to give computer training to blacks. Only on condition that blacks ran the programme, came the reply from the black organizations. So Curtis Nkondo was given a well-paid job that afforded him some protection from the South African government.

We sat opposite each other across a small table in a corner and spoke in quiet voices, wary of the other diners. He talked in vague terms about the political scene and had no new ideas or analysis. When the appropriate moment came, I put Barney's question. Without hesitation Nkondo replied, 'Join the ANC.'

He explained that the leaders of the Black Consciousness movement had communicated with each other as best they could and discussed where it should go. The consensus was that it had carried out its task, the struggle was reawakened, young black South Africans were standing up confidently and proudly – and throwing rocks at the police again. Now it was time to reunite and reignite the struggle.

It did. Many of the surviving leaders of the Biko generation were found employment by Desmond Tutu, then secretary general of the South African Council of Churches. That gave them access to resources and a certain degree of protection, but above all it gave them the opportunity to meet people and organize nationwide. As they moved towards rapprochement with the ANC and acceptance of its leadership, they built mass organizations like the United Democratic Front and later the Mass Democratic Movement. They had strength and leadership in depth so that the movement did not collapse when individual leaders were detained. Others immediately took their places. It was this generation of leaders that carried the ANC to victory at the end of the 1980s.

In 1979 a revolution of any sort seemed a very long way off to most observers. On the other side of the apartheid fence, it was beginning to dawn on more reflective members of the white elite that the grand apartheid plan had failed. The homeland policy, to make nominally independent but aid-dependent countries out of the 'native reserves' with their own (carefully vetted) local rulers, was not working. For South Africa's white rulers the big questions increasingly concerned economics and demography, not ideology or ethics. White control over the vast and rapidly growing black urban population was becoming increasingly difficult. The need to keep South Africa modern and competitive demanded more and more skilled people. They were no longer coming from Europe. If whites were going to stay in charge in South Africa they had to bring more blacks on board. Yet in 1979 the primary goal of official government economic strategy was 'to have the Black peoples live and work in their own homelands wherever this is practically possible. Where not, the plan seeks to encourage Blacks to live in their homelands and work in White areas on a daily basis.'

P.W. Botha, the Prime Minister, embarked on a strategy of trying to win allies among other racial groups in South and Southern Africa. His plan was for a white-ruled South Africa to dominate the region, providing the economic dynamism to raise living standards and keep the smaller states safe from revolution and Communism. But if he conceded the principle of democracy, as the rest of the world was urging on South Africa, Botha would need to co-opt other groups and give them a stake in the economic system. If 4.5 million white South Africans could be joined by over 2.5 million Coloureds – people of mixed race – plus a million Asians and the rulers of the 'independent' homelands, the resulting alliance just might be able to defeat the 'Communist-led' urban blacks in an election.

Botha even visited Soweto at the end of 1979, his first trip to any township, and he offered 'collaboration'. Blacks turned out to see him but they were sceptical, unenthusiastic. Under Botha's plan apartheid's laws would have to be relaxed. But to relax apartheid laws undermined the whole security superstructure. In their hearts everyone – black and white – knew that this spelt one thing: an appallingly bloody civil war. No wonder Prime Minister Botha seemed permanently apoplectic with rage. He was not struggling against the forces of godless Communism and black nationalism. He was struggling against reality. The white government's attempts to control that reality turned South Africa into a sandcastle with the tide surging in. From the outside, images of riot police firing tear gas into fleeing crowds gave the impression that the government still had the upper hand. Each surge was turned back. But then another surge would roll forward somewhere else. By the late 1970s the surges were becoming more and more frequent and forceful, the lulls between them shorter and shorter, as the blacks regrouped and consolidated. The sandcastle was slipping and leaking dangerously. The government had already lost control. It was responding defensively, no longer taking the initiative.

Under apartheid South Africans were divided by race. Under Botha's plan South Africans would be kept apart by class and economics. Tough immigration laws would keep the unskilled poor away from urban, wealth-making centres. Like Europe and the United States, wealthy continents protected by policed borders keeping the masses out, white South Africans would also protect their way of life from outsiders and prevent their economy from being destroyed. But if blacks had a skill and a job they could come into the white-controlled economy. Desmond Tutu said it was like saying, 'We have taken the sign saying "prison" off the prison door and are now inviting the inmates to buy their way out of it.'

In 1979 it seemed a distinct possibility that this policy might work. It found favour in Western capitals where all the alternatives seemed to spell bloodshed and destruction. Maybe enough Indian,

Coloured and black South Africans, anxious to keep what economic advantage they had, would buy into this scheme to head off Communist revolution. Under an adapted model of apartheid, whites would retain real power bolstered by other groups with the same economic values. The laager would simply be extended to include those with the same free market economic beliefs. It didn't happen. The Afrikaner Nationalist Party lost the fight.

So did Coetzee. But he lasted ten rounds in the boxing ring and did not go down without hitting back. As did Botha's government. The policy inside South Africa may have been to blur the edges of apartheid but in the region he vigorously attacked neighbours who helped the ANC. The South Africans conducted murderous raids into Zimbabwe, Mozambique, Zambia and Botswana. A whole army was sent to Angola and stayed there until 1989. These countries paid a high price for opposing apartheid.

September 1979 was the turning point. Four events took place that month – and one in October – which were to prove historic. On 10 September talks on the future of Rhodesia/Zimbabwe began at Lancaster House in London. These led to a ceasefire and the restoration of British rule in Rhodesia, then an election that ended white rule and brought independence the following year. That made South Africa and its colony, the occupied territory of Namibia, the last white-ruled countries in Africa.

The second event took place on the 13th when Venda was declared an independent homeland, removing South African citizenship from another half million blacks. Already the people of Ciskei, Transkei, Lebowa, Bophutatswana, Kangwane, Qwaqwa, Gazankulu and Ndebele had been made citizens of fictional states under South African control, often nominally led by a hand-picked brutal dictator. Botha's plan was to create a 'constellation of states' that included these nominally independent homelands as well as small independent countries like Lesotho, Swaziland and Malawi where South African money had built a new capital and a magnificent palace for the dictator, Hastings Banda. The constellation would oppose the 'total onslaught of the Communist menace', as Botha described it. Only KwaZulu, the largest of all, under the leadership of Gatsha Buthelezi, refused independence. Venda was the last homeland to be declared independent. It marked the end of the government's attempt to Balkanize South Africa.

Indeed, a mere two weeks later Botha conceded the right of all black South Africans to join trade unions. Until then blacks from the 'independent homelands' had not been allowed to unionize. This attempt to drive a wedge between blacks with permanent jobs and the right to stay in towns and migrant workers from rural areas had created chaos in the labour market. Now the government allowed the unions to command a national membership, thinking that a well-ordered labour market was preferable to industrial anarchy. But immediately there was a rash of strikes at the Ford Motors plant in Port Elizabeth.

The third and most dramatic event turned out to be the least significant. It was not reported for a month. On 22 September an American reconnaissance plane picked up a bright flash in the Indian Ocean south of South Africa. The conclusion was grim: apartheid had nuclear weapons. Developed with Israeli help and almost certainly the knowledge of London and Washington, the weapon was launched from a naval vessel somewhere in the South Atlantic. Later it emerged at the Truth and Reconciliation Commission that South Africa had chemical and biological weapons too, again developed with the help of Israel. Although its nuclear weapons were never used, this created one of history's most extraordinary and bitter ironies. The Jewish state, born of European racism and forged by Nazi genocide, armed the world's last ideologically Nazi state of the twentieth century with chemical, nuclear and biological weapons, the weapons of genocide.

The final event took place in October. Chief Gatsha – later renamed Mangosuthu – Buthelezi flew to London to meet the exiled leadership of the ANC. Buthelezi was an ambiguous character at the time. A Zulu prince, he had chosen to accept the role of chief minister of the KwaZulu 'homeland', a post created and paid for by the apartheid government. But, unlike other Africans who had accepted an apartheid salary, he refused to accept KwaZulu 'independence' or to implement aspects of the system. He claimed to be fighting apartheid from within by using its structures to build a black power base. He had taken over a Zulu cultural movement known as Inkatha and turned it into a formidable political and frequently violent force. Buthelezi had been a member of the ANC Youth League and claimed when it suited him to be close to the ANC. The meeting in London failed. He didn't persuade the ANC exiles to back his tactics for fighting the system and they didn't convince him to join them on their terms. Buthelezi became a maverick, officially opposing apartheid but secretly accepting arms and training for his Inkatha warrior gangs from the government's undercover paramilitary organizations.

As the war heated up Inkatha's militias increasingly attacked civilians living in pro-ANC areas in KwaZulu Natal. They often collaborated with the police and the secret death squads of the apartheid state. Buthelezi tried to make KwaZulu Natal a no-go area for the ANC and its sister organizations. Thousands of people were killed, most of them fellow Zulus: urban workers and members of the middle classes who tended to support the ANC. Many white commentators inside and outside South Africa dismissed these battles as 'black on black' violence – as if they were inexplicable 'African tribal warfare'. The implication was that this would be the fate of the whole of South Africa if there was democracy.

Buthelezi and Inkatha refused to take part in the lead-up to the 1994 election and would have violently prevented polls taking place in KwaZulu. But at the last minute a deal was done. Buthelezi called off Inkatha's violent campaign against the ANC and was allowed to win the election on its own territory in KwaZulu. Buthelezi became minister for home affairs in Mandela's first government and was for a few days acting President when Mandela was out of the country.

With its two world wars which killed some 90 million people and the violent oppression of Fascism and Communism, the legacy of the twentieth century seemed profoundly nihilistic. But at its dusk shafts of light broke through the depressing gloom. Communism collapsed with a whimper and apartheid, the remnant of Nazism, was brought to an end by negotiation. Nelson Mandela emerged from twenty-seven years in prison, drawing people to him with that huge smile and an eccentric old-fashioned courtesy. Suddenly here was a voice that had earned the right to speak big truths about life and politics. After all the fury and bitterness, all the pain and anger, that voice was gentle, relaxed and full of hope.

I have two stories about him. Just before the 1994 election Mandela held a rally at Umlazi near Durban in the heartland of the Zulu Inkatha Freedom Party. These were dangerous times. Chief Buthelezi, encouraged by many outside South Africa including Mrs Thatcher and her friends, was playing on Zulu nationalism, refusing to take part in the election and demanding Zulu separatism in a post-apartheid South Africa. Many of us thought this was reckless, even suicidal, the moment Mandela would be assassinated and South Africa would explode. Mandela's intention was to woo the Zulus by appealing directly to their king on his territory. It was by far the most dangerous rally of the entire election campaign.

The rally was held in a football field where a wooden platform had been raised. When Mandela arrived I was on the platform talking to the band and did not hear the announcement. As I went to the top of the steps to go down I found Mandela walking slowly up them towards me. I could not push past him. I froze. Here was a man in his opponent's heartland, threatened with assassination, about to make the trickiest speech of his life. As he reached the top of the steps he looked up, grinned and held out his hand to me. 'Hello,' he said, 'I'm Nelson Mandela.'

The speech was clever, especially coming from Mandela, himself a Xhosa prince. He tried to drive a wedge between his audience and Buthelezi's Inkatha party by appealing directly to King Zweletini and offering him a role in an ANC-ruled South Africa. 'I want everybody to stand up and say "*Bayethe*" [the traditional greeting] to the king,' he said. 'We are all his subjects . . . He is my king, but he is also my child. I was his father's adviser.' At the end of the speech the band began to play and a line of Zulu dancing girls swirled and shivered across the stage. A laughing Mandela joined on the end of the line and danced with them. The Mandela magic worked. Zulu audience loved it and three days later Buthelezi caved in and allowed the election to go ahead in KwaZulu.

The second I saw on television. After the election in 1994 England sent its rugby team to South Africa. At that time South Africa had no black players and when the two national sides met there was only one black player on the field: England's Victor Ubogu. President Mandela attended and the two teams lined up to shake his hand. As he came down the line he shook hands with Ubogu exactly as he did with everyone else. It would have been so easy to remark that he was black. Mandela did not even acknowledge the fact. His lack of racism was total.

The future of South Africa has always been a race between economic growth and the expectations of the post-apartheid generation.

Who is winning? Some maintain that the deal that led to the end of apartheid and the 1994 election has merely delayed an inevitable explosion. Will the pessimists be proved right in the long term? It is still too early to say, although by late 2012 there were disturbing signs. The shooting dead by the police of 42 striking miners at the Marikana mine in August 2012 shocked the world. The TV footage of police in blue combat uniforms firing into a crowd was horrifyingly reminiscent of images from the apartheid era. So was the initial reaction of the state. The police were cleared of wrongdoing and instead 270 miners were charged with murder. The protests were so loud and unanimous that the government was forced to drop the charges and investigate the incident.

To deliver fully on those expectations the economy has to grow at around 7–8 per cent and provide employment. After decades of discrimination and apartheid laws that reserved skilled jobs for whites and stopped blacks getting education, that economic growth had to make blacks richer and be seen to do so. Although the governments of Nelson Mandela and Thabo Mbeki retained world-class teams to manage the macroeconomy, South Africa has not grown fast enough or spread the wealth it creates.

First the government launched the Reconstruction and Development Programme which Mandela said would be 'an all-encompassing process of transforming society in its totality to ensure a better life for all'. It took money from the military and spent it on housing, health and education. The RDP also had a special fund for 'presidential projects', such as free medical care for children and pregnant women, a school feeding programme, electrification of poor homes and public works projects for unemployed youths. Fine targets but neither the economy nor the state machinery was able to deliver basic services fast enough.

The wave of enthusiasm produced by the 1994 election did not bring foreign investment in its wake. In 1996 the government produced the Growth, Employment And Redistribution strategy known as GEAR. It aimed for 6 per cent growth and the creation of 400,000 jobs. Considering that the ANC had until recently been committed to nationalization of the mineral wealth, the banks and industry, GEAR was a remarkable document – particularly because it was written by the party's leading Communists. It committed South Africa to developing a 'competitive, fast-growing economy' through tight fiscal and monetary discipline and increased foreign and domestic investment, and by opening the economy to international competition. Public expenditure would be 'reprioritized'. Mrs Thatcher and free marketers would have been proud of it.

Although the economy did begin to pick up, the hoped-for foreign investment did not flow in and the price of gold began to slide. Unemployment grew and people became poorer. For a long time the accepted wisdom was that if people saw others like them doing better they would be patient, living in the expectation that their turn would come. That was not happening. The Finance Ministry declared, 'South Africa remains one of the most unequal countries in the world, with the poorest 40 per cent of households still living below the minimum household subsistence level.' In 2001 a government report found that 65 per cent of South Africans were living below the poverty line. Of these, 46 per cent – 19 million people – were 'trapped in poverty'.

A 2002 report on Social Security for South Africa said that only a few Blacks were benefiting from affirmative action programmes, that unemployment was above 20 per cent – half of those unemployed being Black females – and that poverty had increased from 45 per cent to 55 per cent in less than a decade. In 1998 the economic growth rate had slumped to 0.5 per cent and unemployment levels reached new peaks. Stimulated by consumer spending by those who had cash to spend, the economy picked up, reaching more than 4 per cent after 2004 and expanding for a longer period than at any time in the country's history. But the government's next reaction was an odd one given its Communist background. In 2003 Mbeki introduced Black Economic Empowerment, a code that forced all companies to give a share of ownership to blacks, give a percentage of contracts to black-owned companies and employ a proportion of black workers at specified grades. It is ironic that while the ANC combated apartheid racism by a Marxist non-racialist class-based strategy, it chose to deal with the legacy of apartheid by turning to a race-based Africanist philosophy.

For the black nomenklatura Black Economic Empowerment brought huge benefits – making many of them instant millionaires with highly paid jobs and shares in companies. Other black professionals were given a chance that was denied to generations before them. Released from the shackles of apartheid black entrepreneurs made it to the top on their own. But for many blacks – some would say most – life has not improved since the end of apartheid. In 2012 the South African economist Sampie Terreblanche pointed out that for most of the last century, 20 per cent of the South African population owned 70 per cent of the country's wealth, while 70 per cent of the population owned only 20 per cent of the wealth. This gap has actually widened since the African National Congress came to power. In 1993, the year before Nelson Mandela was elected president, the richest 10 per cent of South Africans owned 53.9 per cent of the country's wealth. In 2008 the richest 10 per cent owned 58.1 per cent. During the same period, the income of the poorest 50 per cent declined from 8.4 to 7.8 per cent. But ten years on poverty levels rose again and by 2015 more than half of South Africans were poor.

The racial element did not seem as important to the majority as it did to Mbeki and the government. An Ipsos Markinor survey carried out in November 2007 showed that a majority of all races in South Africa believed relationships between races were improving. The most optimistic group were blacks: 60 per cent of them thought race relations were getting better, and less than 10 per cent thought they were getting worse. And ironically it is the Afrikaner Chamber of Commerce that is the strongest in the country. As if freed from the burden of running the civil service and the country, Afrikaners are grabbing the opportunity to make money.

For Blacks, however, the issue was and is jobs. If employment equalled 100 in 1980, most middle-income countries were hitting almost 150 by 2000. South Africa had sunk towards 90. In 2007 real unemployment was estimated to be around 43 per cent and there had been a 12 per cent drop in manufacturing jobs since 1994. The 2008 world recession hit South Africa hard, destroying even more jobs. The problems lie deeper than racial redistribution. South Africa's education system is not producing sufficient numbers of skilled people, especially black skilled people. Other Africans – Zimbabweans, Mozambicans, Nigerians – were getting the better-paid, skilled jobs as well as taking low-paid ones. Frustration among the uneducated and unemployed grew. In 2007 four out of five maths teachers in South Africa were Zimbabwean. Of all the black students who take exams when they are fourteen or fifteen years old, only half a per cent achieve sufficient grades in maths by the time they leave school to enable them to study maths – or science-based subjects – at university. And to solve the skills shortage at the highest level the government refuses to bring in skills from outside. Outsiders seeking jobs in South Africa have to wait up to eighteen months for a working visa.

AIDS also takes its toll of the young. In 1997 fewer than 20,000 South Africans died in their thirties. By 2002 that figure had more than doubled. Anti-retroviral drugs are now being distributed but they give a sufferer only about five more years of life. After that the necessary cocktail of drugs is too expensive for most South Africans.

There is also the crime factor. Practically every South African has been a victim or knows someone who has been a victim of crime. Robbers in South Africa often kill after they have stolen. Officers of the poorly paid and ill-trained police force are frequently found to be implicated. Even though the vast majority of victims are black, Mbeki's government has done little to make the police a more effective force.

But the most serious economic factor is failure of the energy supply. In early January 2008 the lights went out. Power cuts have become a regular feature of South African life, sometimes lasting for eight hours. Eskom, the power company, and the government blamed economic growth, arguing that the very success of the new South Africa had created the problem. But then it emerged that the first warnings that this would happen had been made in 1998. A White Paper that year calculated that Eskom would reach full capacity in about 2007. It called on the government to take decisions by the end of the following year. Nothing was done while the government dithered over the privatization of Eskom, hoping that new power companies would come to South Africa. None did because the politics of South Africa demanded that electricity remain cheap – the cheapest in the world. No new power stations were built. The problem is likely to continue until 2013 at the earliest. By 2008, while other middle-income countries in Asia and South America were enjoying the benefits of a mining boom, South Africa, which contains some of the biggest reserves of the most valuable minerals in the world, was stagnating.

In June 2010 South Africa seemed to take a holiday from all its problems to host the World Cup. Despite dire predictions of a crime wave and other disasters, South Africa rekindled the spirit of 1994 and laid on a party to welcome the world. It was a huge success, prompting one commentator to say: 'We have shown we can deliver for the world. Now let's deliver for South Africans.'

Despite the dynamism and hopefulness of South Africans, the country is not a happy place. At worst the whole nation seems consumed by a deep sense of grievance. That miracle in which the new South Africa was born has given way to a feeling of victimhood and injustice. In the 1990s blacks celebrated their freedom while whites were just relieved that the great change had happened without mass violence. Now there is a feeling among blacks that they have not got what they were hoping for while whites feel that something has been taken from them unjustly. They are frightened, sullen, behind bars, their children emigrating, the laager mentality stronger than ever. And blacks and whites do not talk to each other. They live in their separate worlds with their very different thoughts and feelings about South Africa. More and more gated communities are being built – for wealthy blacks as well as whites – but this is now a growing phenomenon throughout Africa. Apartheid now is economic not racial.

When the frustration of South Africa's poor finally boiled over, the anger was not directed at whites but against fellow Africans. Blaming them for crime and for taking 'their' jobs, gangs of xenophobic youths attacked Zimbabweans, Mozambicans and other immigrants. The police could not cope and in two weeks in May 2008 some sixty foreigners were killed, some of them burned to death, while more than 30,000 were driven from their homes. Many fled South Africa for good. The human tragedy was appalling but the implications for South Africa were dire. It showed the ANC government was out of touch with the people it claimed to represent: the poor. It deprived South Africa of much needed skilled – and cheap – labour. Politically it wounded South Africa's pan-

African vision: the rainbow nation and the belief that South Africa was at the heart of Africa and embodied African values that would lead the whole continent towards a united, peaceful and prosperous future.

The attacks occurred as the country was going through a turbulent political storm. In the past the leadership of the African National Congress always made major decisions behind closed doors. Years of suppression, infiltration and exile had disciplined the movement so that ideological differences and personal rivalries were managed in private, after which the leaders' decisions were announced to loyal party members and the world. In 2007 for the first time dissent broke out into the open and for the first time a rival used the ANC's constitution to run for the presidency.

The roots of the crisis go way back. After his release from prison, Nelson Mandela toured South Africa, Africa and the world usually accompanied by Thabo Mbeki, Cyril Ramaphosa and Chris Hani. Mbeki had left South Africa in 1962 to study in Britain and had become the international representative and spokesman for the ANC in exile. He was an intellectual. His father was a Communist who had been imprisoned with Mandela, but they had fought bitterly. Hani was the charismatic head of Umkhonto we Sizwe, the armed though largely ineffective wing of the ANC. Ramaphosa had risen to prominence as the brilliant negotiator for the miners' union in strikes during the 1980s. In the early 90s his skills were deployed as the ANC's chief negotiator at the talks with the apartheid government that led to the total victory of the ANC. Any dreams that the De Klerk government may have had about outwitting or outmanoeuvring the ANC in negotiations were dashed by the sharp mind and tough stance of Ramaphosa.

Following Mandela around capitals in the aftermath of his release, I watched the three men jostling, sometimes literally, for the position of Mandela's bag carrier. Chris Hani was murdered by a right-wing Polish immigrant in 1993. After the election, Mbeki became Deputy President, virtually running the government as Mandela aged. When Mandela did step down, however, it is reported that he preferred Ramaphosa to be his successor but was dissuaded by his old friend Walter Sisulu.

As President, Mbeki demanded complete loyalty and suppressed the tradition of debate within the party. The ANC suddenly became closed and fearful. Many thought that as a former exile, he felt an outsider, threatened by those who had actually organized and fought for freedom on the streets of South Africa. Dissenters were marginalized and discussion kept to a minimum. Mbeki's ideas went unquestioned. His enforcer, the arrogant and thuggish Essop Pahad, dealt with anyone who parted from the Mbeki line.

Mark Gevisser, Mbeki's biographer, has pointed out that Mbeki's favourite play is Shakespeare's *Coriolanus* in which the hero is fatally flawed by his aristocratic arrogance. Although a brave and brilliant warrior for Rome, Coriolanus refuses to beg the people for their votes when he stands for the consulship. He even betrays his country rather than bow to populism. The parallel with Mbeki is striking, but while Coriolanus, defiant, contemptuous of the common people, refuses to engage in politics, Mbeki became increasingly paranoid and power crazy. Every week he wrote a personal 'Letter from the President' on the ANC website in which he deployed venomous sarcasm to attack journalists and others who criticized him. In 2001 his spokesman accused Ramaphosa and two other prominent ANC leaders of plotting to overthrow him.

In December 2007 thousands of ANC delegates met in the northern town of Polokwane to choose the next President of the party. The winner would almost certainly be the ANC candidate for the presidency the following year. Mbeki thought he would win.

Under the constitution he had to stand down as President of the country but there was nothing to stop him continuing as President of the party. That would give him the opportunity of influencing the choice of his successor. Surrounded by sycophants, he had no idea how resentment against his style of government had built up. Meanwhile Jacob Zuma, a former head of intelligence of the ANC and the man he had sacked as Vice-President, had decided to run. In the old days the choice would have been made in secret by consensus among a small clique in the National Executive, but Zuma broke ranks and created a real competition. He won with 60 per cent of the vote. Mbeki and his supporters were jeered at and booed.

The world was stunned. Despite public affirmations of unity, the party was openly split and had to live with two centres of power for several months. Technically there was no difference over policies. The party reaffirmed the ANC's agenda: housing, education, health, crime. But the tone and style of the ANC was utterly changed. The party of Nelson Mandela had chosen as their leader a man whose theme song was 'Bring Me My Machine Gun' and who had faced rape charges in court. Pictures of him dressed in traditional Zulu gear adorned with leopard skins and necklaces of teeth and wielding a spear appeared in all the newspapers. More importantly, he had been charged with corruption connected to the sale of weapons to South Africa. Could such a man lead the country? International confidence in South Africa plummeted.

Polokwane was certainly democracy in action. Resentful of Mbeki's arrogant style and remoteness, the branch organizers of the ANC and trade union leaders planned his overthrow. Mbeki's followers were replaced in the party with candidates more sympathetic to popular demands. But the vote was more anti-Mbeki than pro-Zuma. In essence it represented a deep demand for a more responsive government which would deliver more to ordinary people. Had the election been open with several candidates and a run-off, most people think Ramaphosa would have won by a mile. But because Mbeki insisted on running and the constitution did not allow for a run-off, no-one else stood. Delegates had a stark choice: more Mbeki or Zuma.

Shortly after Polokwane one senior ANC member who had supported Zuma's presidency spoke of 'managing' Zuma, even of the possibility of him being a ceremonial President. It seemed unlikely. He made a bid for power and won. Charming and smart, though with little formal education, Zuma is an immensely self-confident man. He sees himself as a man of the people but tends to say whatever crowds want to hear, continually floating popular and dangerous ideas, such as bringing back the death penalty or taking back the land from whites by force, and then riding the wave of popular support they create without committing himself.

The future of South Africa now lies in the hands of its institutions, mainly the courts and the police. But personal and political rivalries particularly between the national prosecuting service and the police have weakened those institutions. The race between expectation and the economy is still on, but the country is heading into very difficult times. Between 2002 and 2008 the economy soared but then collapsed to minus 1.5 per cent the following year. Were South Africa booming and looking at even higher growth, Zuma could distribute the wealth without damaging its source. But when the economy faced an inevitable downturn he was unable to deliver the jobs and corruption thrived.

In 2018 he was forced from office and replaced by Ramaphosa, the man who organized the successful miners' strike in 1986 and was one of Mandela's bag carriers when he came out of jail. Pushed aside by Thabo Mbeki he went into business with support from the

Oppenheimers. Black South Africans had already waited twenty-four years for real change. Another generation finding promises unfulfilled may be less patient. South Africa is not just another African country. Its extraordinary transition – conducted by face-to-face negotiation without intermediaries – was a miracle. Mandela, constantly building bridges, exuding hope at every turn, became the guiding spirit of the country and the continent. But the economy needs to grow and creating more jobs is difficult. Decades of apartheid left South Africa with a weak education system.

Mandela's death in December 2013 was mourned throughout the world. He was the most respected political leader of the twentieth century and it is hard to find his equal anywhere in history, a man who could relate easily to monarchs and presidents as well as to peasant farmers and workers. A man who suffered for his cause, nearly lost his life for it, went to jail for twenty-seven years, changed his tactics and led his movement and his country into a new world. He took the whole world with him. Only with his family did he fail.

In its transition from being the last Nazi-inspired political system of the twentieth century, South Africa produced the most humanist constitution the world had ever seen, guaranteeing personal freedoms but also protecting minority rights and the weak and vulnerable. It was aspirational as well as protective, aiming to encourage the best in human beings while curbing their darker tendencies. No wonder South Africa carried the hopes of the human race. If it could happen there, politics could bring peace and justice anywhere.

15

Meat and Money Eating in Kenya

News has got round that we are travelling to the Samburu area so when we get up at 4 a.m. we find six or seven young Samburu men waiting at the gate of my friend's house in Nairobi. Koert Lindyer has a long-established friendship with a family near the Resim River. Young men of the family who want to work in Nairobi often stay at his house and he occasionally goes to stay at their *boma* – a group of huts and pens surrounded by a thorn fence.

Dressed in jeans and T-shirts and seeming to carry very little luggage, the lads climb into the back of the Land Rover. We set off before dawn, a journey across one of the most beautiful landscapes of Africa, over the shoulder of Mount Kenya, through the Aberdare Mountains and on up into the dry north. As we drive we talk with the young men about life in Nairobi and their hopes for the future. One is a lawyer, two are students, another works in an office in town and another is a security guard. This is 2000 and these bright young Samburus breathe hope, though they know Kenya is hobbled by bad government. They seem to accept it as if it were like bad weather – beyond their control. It is dark when we arrive and I step out of the Land Rover into a vast dark landscape of silence beneath a billion shimmering stars and the sweet smell of cattle and goats. The family greet us with handshakes – Samburu do not embrace outsiders. While Koert sleeps in the vehicle, I pitch my tent on a pile of soft dried goat shit. The men leave for their family bomas in the neighbourhood.

During the night I am woken by the dull clank of bells every time a goat moves. The bells are tied round their necks. Sometimes the clanking goes on for a long time, as if they are running on the spot. I realize they must be having sex. I am woken again before dawn by soft far-away voices and the dull rumble of cattle hooves as the animals are taken out of the protection of the boma to find grazing. I doze again until I am wakened by the sound of my name being called: 'Riiichad. Riiichad.'

I look out of the tent to find a group of Samburu warriors at the entrance of the boma. They are dressed in long red cloaks, swords at their waists and clubs in their hands, their long hair swept back, dyed with red ochre. They smile and wave. 'But how do they know my name?' I ask myself. Only when I emerge and get close do I recognize them as Lesori and Lelemewa and the others from Nairobi. But they are utterly changed: jeans and T-shirts gone, new hair and clothes and lots of necklaces and bangles.

In much of Africa people dress traditionally only for special rituals or for tourists but the Samburu do so all the time: 'We have to dress properly here,' as one says. But with additions. One wears plastic flowers in his hair and carries a video camera in a skin pouch. Another has a doorkey on his necklace. The lawyer wears new trainers beneath his red cloak. The contrast feels strange. A harsh landscape and a tough life; swords, clubs, spears and blood-red cloaks and flowers in your hair. The Spartans would have understood. The women also dress traditionally with layers of necklaces, and bangles on their wrists and upper arms, their elongated earlobes dangling and swinging with the weight of earrings.

We go with them to water the cattle. This landscape is like

something from another planet: a vast plain of rock, flat-topped thorn trees and crazy mountains that look as if they have been chis-elled by a doodling god. Colour and shape melt in the searing heat haze. The baked ground offers sparse dried grass and spiky ball-head-ed cactus. The only sounds are the bleating of goats, the groaning of camels and an exquisite wren-like song from a little brown bird. Then the distant rumble of a plane passing overhead. In this great emptiness people conduct conversations thirty yards away from each other in normal voices.

Now there is drought so a deep well has been dug in the dried-up river bed. As we approach we can hear chanting. A chain of four young men, perched on ledges on the sides of the well, pass buckets up from the bottom where one scoops up water from a muddy pool. The last one at the top pours it into a trough made from a dug-out tree trunk. As they work they sing – offering phrases and answering each other. The cattle are led in turns to drink at the trough. All the men are naked and when they have finished watering the animals they wash each other down, then sit and comb each other's hair. This well belongs to an old man. It is his because he dug it. No-one here owns space. Only effort and animals. Each herder has his own song and his cattle know his voice so the herdsmen control their own cows as they take turns to drink.

The Samburu can squat, buttocks on heels, for hours but when they stand, they look like tall philosophers, cross-legged, leaning on their spears with a hand cupped around their mouths. These are *Morans*, young men, the third stage in the Samburu rites of passage to manhood. Lesori explains:

> We are Morans, so we look after the cattle. There has been drought
> so most of the herd is far away at present. The first ceremony is
> naming, the name by which you will be known by your age group.

Then there is circumcision which is not the same as becoming a Moran. Then finally you marry. Then you start your own family and build a boma.

Among the Samburu everything is controlled by the old men. They hold the wealth and they make the decisions. A father can even choose a wife for his son. 'If you refuse they can punish you,' says Lesori.

Recently they expelled a man who killed someone. He was expelled because he broke the unity of the people. The usual punishment is a fine of cows. The cows get given to the poorest families. That is justice. Then we have a party and all is forgiven and forgotten.

What is the worst punishment here, I ask.

The worst thing the elders can do to you is to curse you. If they curse you, you die. One young man came from the city to stay here. He slept with a girl he was not supposed to. They called him and he admitted it but he was not sorry so they cursed him. Next day he broke his leg. It happened. I don't know if I believe it or not but it doesn't matter because it happened.

The Samburu do not seem very religious, though they do believe in magic and witchcraft. 'In Samburu religion there is one god. You can pray to the god on the tops of hills or in valleys by water. He is up there somewhere. We have no other gods. Our ancestors are resting, sleeping spirits. We do not forget them.'

We spend the rest of the day walking from boma to boma, meeting and greeting. Each boma is the same, a round fence of thorns enclosing a space for the animals with two or three round domed huts of tree branches and thatch. Inside they are dark and we lie on the floor to keep under the smoke that gathers in the eaves. At least it keeps the flies away.

Everyone here knows that things are changing. There are more people in the area even though there is drought. The old order is breaking down but how it will change is not clear. We spoke to an old woman called Busuke who said her greatest fear was that 'the government will take care of us'. 'Meaning what?' I asked Lesori. 'It means the government will send a helicopter with some police who kill people and then leave,' he replied.

A school has started a few miles away, the first in the area. It's a lonely brick building on a low hill with earth floors and planks on bricks for seating. There is no sign of a book. It has thirty-five pupils and a teacher. Only three people speak English in the area around Resim. Do they need to? Koert asked Busuke if she wanted her grandchildren to go to school. 'They should,' she said, 'but then they will not look after the cattle.' She clearly saw that there was no going back from school. You had to choose between school or a Samburu life with cows.

In the evening Lesori and the others take me down to the dried-up river bed. 'We are going for dinner,' they say, explaining that Morans are not allowed to eat at home. On the way we meet a group of girls looking after goats and a good deal of flirtation begins. The girls giggle into their hands and the boys stick their throwing clubs between their thighs and cross their legs so they look as if they have huge erections. After much teasing and laughter they take a goat from the flock and Lesori slings it across his shoulders and we walk to the river bed. They light a fire and then lay the goat on the ground. Lesori takes the tip of his sword and gently slides it down the neck of the goat, slicing the skin. He pulls back the skin forming a pouch and the goat bleats and wriggles. Then he jabs the sword tip into the goat's throat and blood pumps out into the pouch. He kneels and drinks it – and with a wicked, knowing smile invites me to do the same. So I do, trying not to think or taste the hot blood. The others drink too. Not a drop is spilt.

They skin the animal, lifting the carcass out of the skin which they carefully tuck away. They disembowel the goat, cut up the meat and cook it on a grid of green branches laid across the cinders. The meat is stringy but soft, tasting of earth and milk. Only bones and the innards remain but they say there will be nothing left in the morning. Leopards will find it. There are many around here and a few lions still. There used to be rhinos but they have all gone.

It is a paradox that not far from here is where the earliest humans walked. You might expect the core of civilization to have developed here, but this place remains in its own pre-industrial pastoralist world. Is it that pastoralists have to be more self-reliant than fatalistic farmers, more aware of life around them and prepared to take risks and take control of their lives? Here where life is toughest in Africa – least developed some might say – there is no desire to escape or flee from the past. In this harsh terrain people seem accepting and con- tented and even those who have an education, have been to the big city and have jobs, seem at ease with the life here. They dress tradi- tionally and do not show off their city wealth. They seem happy. The greeting is, 'Everyone is fine.'

I wonder what the rest of the world could give these people – if they asked, which interestingly they do not, despite their material poverty. The only thing I was asked for was a book I was reading. Even if I were rich I could not give them the one thing they need for their survival: regular rain.

A few days later I am sitting on the terrace of the Karen Country Club on the outskirts of Nairobi. A gentle breeze flaps the umbrella and the lace tablecloth covering my table. A waiter in black bow tie

brings me tea and cakes; an English china teapot and cups with a
pretty floral pattern. The beautifully manicured fairway kept green
with sprinklers, stretches away into the distance as smooth as the
tablecloth. In the lounge inside are copies of *Country Life* and the
Tatler. All around me are upper-class English accents: 'How did you
do today, old man?'

'Not bad – only two over. What about yourself?'

'Three, but I birdied the fourth, buggered up the sixth, though.
Is that your new Merc in the car park? First time I've seen the new
model. How does she go?'

'Pure cream. By the way have you heard the one about . . .'

This could be Surrey but I am the only white person at the club
that day.

There is no better example than Kenya of Achebe's colonialist
house – and its golf clubs – being taken over by the 'the smart, and
the lucky and hardly ever the best'. This ruling elite presides with
thoughtless complacency over one of the most unequal societies on
earth. Even teachers and lowly secretaries here have maids and servants who call them sir or madam and cast their eyes down when
speaking to the boss. It reminds me of South Africa under apartheid.

Not half an hour's drive from the club are two of the worst slums
in the world, Kibera and Mathare Valley, shanty towns of indescrib-
able poverty. Rivulets of stinking green-black sewage run between
hovels of mud, plastic, bits of wood and battered old corrugated
iron sheeting. These dwellings are so claustrophobically crammed
together that two people cannot pass between them. Clouds of
wood-fire smoke thickened with the smell of excrement hang permanently over them. Kibera, the larger, is home to nearly a million
people. Legally they do not exist and no-one living in these camps
has any right to his or her shacks. Despite daily murders, rapes and
robberies, the police never go there except as a paramilitary force to

beat down the people and destroy their homes. The government does not provide water, sanitation, roads, schools or clinics. People are forced to shit in plastic bags and throw them into the mud. Yet every day out of this hell step thousands of clean, neatly dressed people, picking their way through the filth and rubbish to walk miles to jobs that pay a dollar or two a day.

Kenya: 'land of contrasts' says Kenyaweb, the tourism website.

To outsiders, until 2008, Kenya was the African success story, the tourist destination with stunning beaches on the Indian Ocean where happy smiling Africans wait on you and teach you to say *Jambo* and *Karibu*. Kenya's gorgeous landscape, game parks heaving with lions, leopards, elephants, giraffes and rhinos, is the setting for *Elsa the Lioness*, *Out of Africa* and *White Mischief*.

So when Kenya exploded in January 2008 after a rigged election, everyone was shocked that such terrible murder and mayhem could happen there. 'But Kenya is such a peaceful, stable country,' said the TV interviewers, as if Kenya had somehow been immune from the political ills that have plagued Africa for the past fifty years.

It is true that Kenya has never had a successful coup, though one nearly succeeded in 1982 when air force personnel tried to depose President Daniel arap Moi. It was stopped at the eleventh hour but some 150 people were killed. Unlike other African countries where political unrest caused the educated middle classes to flee, Kenya has civil servants, lawyers, businessmen and other professionals who can make things work. But, cursed by poisonous and rapacious politicians since independence in 1963, Kenya could hardly be called peaceful. There were the unsolved murders of prominent politicians who upset the President or would not be bought off: J.M. Kariuki, Tom Mboya, Robert Ouko. Moi turned the basement of the 1970s tower block Nyayo House in Nairobi into torture chambers for dissidents, many of whom never re-emerged. And on the streets of cities well-armed gangsterism is rife – often controlled by politicians. Carjackings and house break-ins often end in murder as well. Nairobi is nicknamed Nairobbery.

Murderous local wars fuelled by politicians have often broken out, particularly at election times after multi-party democracy was reintroduced. Kenya's politics are the most ethnicized and monetarized of any on the continent. The primary job of an MP is seen as delivering goodies to his or her own ethnic group. A British parliamentary group visiting Kenya in 2007 were told that one 'scrupulously honest candidate' who campaigned on a bicycle was contesting a 'deeply corrupt' one who drove a shiny new SUV. The people voted for the corrupt one because he was obviously a Big Man who had goodies to bring from government. What could a poor man on a bicycle do for them?

Unsurprisingly Kenyans boil over from time to time. In 1990 I was in Nairobi with a film crew to cover the first rally in favour of multi-party democracy. This was not some Western-inspired call for an end to Kenya's one-party state. Although Britain had called for worldwide multi-party democracy in the wake of the collapse of the Soviet Union, it applied pressure selectively. Of course none was applied to Britain's Middle East oil producers or allies such as Kenya. The British High Commissioner would not even speak to anyone calling for democracy for fear of upsetting Moi. The main external supporter for the call by the two politicians who organized the rally was the ambassador of the United States.

The politicians, who had fallen out of favour with President Moi, called on people to come to Kamakunji, a big open field near the centre of Nairobi, and demonstrate on *Saba Saba*, the seventh of the seventh month, July. Kamakunji was where Jomo Kenyatta, Kenya's founding father, had called for independence. When we arrived in the early afternoon a nervous crowd hung around the edge of the field watching a group of protestors who had gathered in the middle. It was hard to tell if they were supporters or gawpers. We started filming. No Nairobi-based film crew dared to be there for fear of upsetting the government. People came over and thanked us, telling us how important this day was. For the first time people were demonstrating against Moi's government.

Suddenly two police Land Rovers roared onto the field and fired tear gas at the group in the middle. They also appeared to shoot at the crowd around the side which responded with a hail of stones. Within seconds the peaceful but tense demonstration exploded in mayhem. We headed back towards the car and found ourselves surrounded by an angry mob. The friendly welcome we had experienced a few minutes earlier had gone. As I started to drive off, men tried to block the car. I drove into them. I don't know if I hurt anyone but had I stopped I believe we would have been killed.

The rioting lasted three days in Nairobi and spread to other cities. More than twenty people were killed and hundreds injured. This was spontaneous. The militant young turks, mostly lawyers, who had been calling for multi-party democracy, suddenly fell silent at the very moment I would have expected them to call for revolution. Paul Muite, then a human rights lawyer, explained why: 'We are riding a tiger which we cannot control. When the mob attacks like that they are not going to distinguish between Mr Moi's Mercedes and mine.' Muite did indeed drive a Mercedes and later became an MP. Most of that group who led the fight for multi-party democracy in the early nineties later sank in the mire of corruption. One of those who did not was Gibson Kuria, a lawyer then in hiding. I interviewed him in a dark room in the early hours of the morning. He told tales of terrible repression and torture in Britain's closest ally in Africa.

The roots of that violent discontent go a long way back. Kenya was nearly White Man's country, like Algeria, South Africa and

Southern Rhodesia. Ironically it was the great imperialist, Winston Churchill, who argued against it. Demographics made it impossible, he said. But whites did take the best land and drove the Kikuyu and others off their farms. After the Second World War a Kikuyu rebellion began, Mau Mau, aimed at reclaiming the land. White farmers in Kenya had grown rich during the Second World War but at the end of the war they united to force down the wages of farm workers. Mau Mau's tactics were vicious and combined with the violent British reaction Kenya became embroiled in one of the most brutal colonial wars. Only thirty-two white settlers were killed but 3000 African police and soldiers, 12,000 alleged Mau Mau supporters and 1800 African civilians died. It took twelve battalions of the British army and a squadron of Royal Air Force bombers to defeat it. At one stage the heavy aircraft carpet bombed the forests where Mau Mau fighters hid. Those who fled out of them were shot down like rabbits. During the rebellion Britain hanged more than 1000 Kenyans – more than the total number of people executed throughout the rest of the retreating British Empire.

Mau Mau was but one message sent to Britain from the territories it occupied that the days of empire were numbered. Unless the British were prepared to spend much blood and gold in suppressing these revolts, they would have to leave. The British chose to leave Kenya, but the battle against Mau Mau and the independence movement poisoned Kenyan politics for decades. Britain accused Jomo Kenyatta of being the man behind Mau Mau and locked him up. One British governor called him the 'leader unto darkness and death'. Whether Mau Mau was originally an independence movement is fiercely debated but it fed Africa's bid for freedom from European rule.

In fighting the war against Mau Mau, the British recruited other ethnic groups into the police and army. The Kikuyu were the largest ethnic group in Kenya and the one that had lost most land, but they had also gained most from education during colonial rule. Kenyatta's largely Kikuyu Kenyan African National Union (KANU) demanded immediate independence, but as long as he was in jail he was a martyr and he refused to negotiate. As they tried to hang on to Kenya, the British played divide and rule among the ethnic groups and set up a counterweight, the Kenyan Africa Democratic Union (KADU), made up of smaller ethnic groups. Many of these had co-operated with the British during Mau Mau and KADU now co-operated in trying to defeat the independence movement. Its leader was a pliant young schoolteacher, Daniel arap Moi.

But the movement for independence was unstoppable. The Luo, then the second largest ethnic group in Kenya, led by the fiery Communist, Oginga Odinga, joined KANU. The alliance of Kikuyu and Luo spelt the end for British rule and, fearing the firebrand Odinga, the British finally released Kenyatta from jail to lead the country to independence. Having achieved his goal, Kenyatta, then in his mid sixties, sat back and enjoyed wealth and power. He said that Mau Mau should be forgotten, never mentioned again. No truth and reconciliation commission was set up in Kenya. Many British farmers in the 'white highlands' left at independence and other farms were nationalized by the new government, their owners compensated by the British. Incidentally, Britain spent twice as much buying white-owned land in Kenya as it was to offer Zimbabwe to buy out its white farmers two decades later. In Kenya Kenyatta gave the formerly white-owned farms as gifts, largely to his Kikuyu supporters. Unlike in Zimbabwe Britain did not protest.

As Kenyatta grew old and tired two men took over the running of Kenya, Charles Njonjo, the attorney general, and Bruce Mac-kenzie, Britain's placeman in the government, who was appointed Kenyatta's foreign affairs advisor. His main task was to oust Vice-

President Odinga, who was trying to push Kenya towards the Soviet camp and socialism. Tom Mboya, a Luo who was Secretary-General of KANU and a powerful figure, had been murdered in 1969. There was a plan to have Odinga killed as well but Kenyatta overruled it. In 1966 Odinga had been sacked and locked up. Daniel arap Moi became the new Vice-President. Britain had been forced to concede independence but had retained influence and economic power.

Kenya has been a solid pro-Western ally ever since, making its ports available to Western navies and providing training grounds for Western armies. Although it was never to become 'white man's country', several colonists stayed on and gave Kenya a particularly British flavour. That seemed to be confirmed when Mrs Thatcher paid a visit to Kenya, her first trip to Africa as Prime Minister, in 1988. President Daniel arap Moi met her at Nairobi airport and the military band, dressed in white trousers and bright red jackets, played 'Rule Britannia'. She had come to ask for support in her opposition to sanctions against apartheid South Africa and she gave Moi an extra £20 million. Kenya was already Africa's top recipient of British aid. She did not mention Kenya's dreadful human rights record and Moi stayed out of the row between Africa and Britain over sanctions and South Africa.

Today Nairobi hosts the largest United Nations presence in Africa, and many multinational corporates and NGOs base their East African operations there. In recent years it has been a very close ally of the United States in its war on Islamist fundamentalism.

Other African states which relied on a single commodity such as oil, copper or cocoa created a single state-controlled pot in which the ruling elite could collect the country's income. From there they were able to siphon it off into their own pockets and organizations. This was difficult in Kenya where no single commodity provided the bulk of the wealth. To get rich in Kenya you have to work. So how could politicians get rich? Foreign aid was one source, and because Kenya was such a close political ally, no-one investigated how much Western aid went missing. A few politicians set up genuine businesses but the majority had to graft and beg, exchanging government contracts for bribes.

Although Kenya became a one-party state after the 1982 coup attempt, there were elections within the party, and to win an election in Kenya takes money. In the growing culture of chai all voters expected something for their vote. Petty officials and those higher up have always expected something for their services. At the top in business and politics the bribes are huge. It's the corruption pyramid.

Commerce in Kenya was traditionally controlled by Asian Kenyans but in the 1970s and 1980s Kikuyu businessmen and professionals linked to them began to dominate the scene. Behind every wealthy Kenyan business, Asian or African, was a political protector. Money and politics merged in a messy brew.

The *Saba Saba* riots and subsequent pressure on the Moi government for multi-party democracy, which even Britain eventually supported, led the government to abandon one-party rule and hold an election. That needed money. So the senior politicians of the ruling party created an export subsidy scam and passed it into law. Anyone who could show they had exported manufactured gold and diamonds would receive a 35 per cent export subsidy of the estimated value. It sounded fine but there was a problem: apart from some freelance gold panning and diamonds smuggled from Congo, Kenya had no gold or diamonds.

At the heart of what became known as the Goldenberg scam were Moi, his sons and business partners Gideon and Phillip, Kamlesh Pattni, the mastermind behind the schemes and the man who set up the Goldenberg Bank, and his bagman, Ketan Somaia, whose Delphis Bank handled much of the money. Until 2000 Somaia's

Dolphin Holdings Company was chaired by Lord Parkinson, a former chairman of the British Conservative Party. Also involved were the Kenyan finance minister at the time, George Saitoti, who was later education minister, Joshua Kulei, Moi's chief assistant, Nicholas Biwott, Moi's former personal assistant and later minister of industry, and James Kanyotu, Kenya's head of intelligence.

The sheer scale of the looting is still shocking. Four billion dollars left the country fraudulently, but the total loss from 1992 to 2002 may have been three times that – the equivalent of a year's national economic output. It is even more shocking that it was done under the eyes of Western donors, the IMF and the World Bank.

When Central Bank officials queried the scheme Saitoti pushed it through vigorously, breaching bank regulations. Until then gold exports through Kenya were estimated at $1.2 million a year. When the scam was at its height in 1992 Pattni was claiming 'export compensation' of $2.5 million a day. He also claimed compensation for other fantasy goods. Pattni once claimed he was exporting machetes to Britain.

The money went into five banks owned by Moi himself or his accomplices. Then they found another way of multiplying the money they had stolen. Kenya lacked hard currency so exports were encouraged by a pre-export finance scheme funded by the World Bank. Potential exporters were lent 85 per cent of the value of the goods to be exported. Export credit notes were taken to each of five banks collecting that 85 per cent from each. The pre-shipment finance fraud cost Kenyans an estimated $75 million. A further crude alteration of entries on the foreign exchange paperwork added another $23 million.

From the five banks in Nairobi the money shifted all over the world – to London, Dubai, Panama, Geneva, New York and Germany. Pattni and Moi's cronies were not exporting gold or diamonds, they were exporting Kenya's precious foreign reserves and laundering them through the banks of the world. In London the money came to several banks including ANZ Grindlays, Barclays and Standard Chartered Bank. Huge sums went to Union Bancaire Privée in Geneva and Citibank in London and New York. Many of these same banks were used to launder money for the Nigerian military dictator, Sani Abacha. In those days there was no obligation on banks to report suspiciously large movements of money.

Next, the money was sent back to Goldenberg International accounts at the Exchange Bank in Nairobi. The perpetrators then set up scam number three when the government agreed that Pattni and his cronies should receive a special foreign exchange rate. With their new wealth they bought dollars from the Kenya Central Bank at thirty-three Kenya shillings to the dollar. The dollars were sent out of Kenya to banks around the world and shipped from bank to bank to make them virtually untraceable. In late 1992 just in time for the election, the money started to flow back to Kenya and was changed into Kenya shillings at a rate of fifty-seven to the dollar, a profit of nearly 70 per cent.

The shillings were stuffed into boxes and suitcases to pay thugs, bribe officials and buy votes at the December election. Just to make sure of victory, Moi appointed Zaccheus Chesoni, a former Chief Justice who had twice been sacked from the bench for bankruptcy, to run the elections. During the election I discovered that Moi had twice paid off those debts, a fact known to the Commonwealth Observer mission and the British government at the time, but which both decided to keep quiet about. Unsurprisingly Moi won.

Though re-elected, the Moi government was suddenly gripped by panic, perhaps in fear that it might be overthrown or driven into exile. Perhaps it was simply greed or the realization they could get away with anything, but at this late stage the scam turned into a full-scale looting of the treasury. Between March and September

1993 Goldenberg made $407 million from the export subsidy. But by then even the World Bank actually began to complain. The scam suddenly came to a halt on 3 March 1993 with a final request for export compensation for non-existent gold and diamond jewellery worth $48,287,577.

The looting of Kenya by its rulers dragged its economic growth rate down from 4.5 per cent in the late 1980s to 1 per cent in 1991 and less than 1 per cent in subsequent years. The whole country paid the price of their rulers' greed. From 1992 poverty and infant mortality rates increased rapidly and life expectancy and school enrolment fell.

Kenyans might never have discovered the reason for their drastic drop in living standards if there had not been a change of government in 2002. Under the constitution Moi had to step down. Despite misgivings he picked Kenyatta's son, Uhuru, to succeed him. But opposition to Moi was now widespread and for once a broad alliance formed, held together by Mwai Kibaki, a veteran of the independence generation and also a Kikuyu. Furthermore, in the lead-up to the election a new constitution was proposed and the whole country joined in to draw it up. After months of debate and wrangling a draft was agreed at a conference centre near Nairobi called Bomas. It introduced checks and balances, provided for devolution and a powerful Prime Minister and other reforms that diluted the powers of the presidency. A deal was made between Kibaki and Raila Odinga, the son of Oginga Odinga and a powerful politician who had taken a ministerial position in Moi's government and then switched sides. Kibaki would be President and Odinga Prime Minister. They also agreed that if they came to power they would investigate the previous regime for corruption.

A month before the election Kibaki was badly injured in a car crash. Odinga went into overdrive, travelling around the country, addressing rallies and pressing the flesh, pushing Kibaki's bid for the presidency. Kibaki duly won but he and his allies then agreed that the new constitution had been necessary only because of Moi. Now he was gone it was safe to have a strong President again. Kibaki and his allies drew up a new constitution retaining the presidency as it was. Odinga had been double-crossed.

The government set up a huge public inquiry – shown every night on TV – into the Goldenberg fraud. Every day for months Kenyans, rich and poor, dressed in smart suits or shabby shirts, queued outside the Nairobi conference centre to hear lawyers with piles of sworn affidavits cross-examining civil servants, bankers and even Pattni himself. Day by day they sat bug-eyed as the thieves fell out and implicated each other, revealing the astounding tale of the theft of Kenya by its rulers and their business associates. The evidence was overwhelming and appalling. It was wonderful to find that the chief inquisitor was Gibson Kuria, whom I had interviewed back in 1991 as a young lawyer on the run.

The new government also set up inquiries into the murder of Robert Ouko, the foreign minister who had spoken out against corruption. His charred body had been found with a bullet through his head in 1990. The Kenyan government pathologist declared at the inquest that he had committed suicide by setting fire to himself and then shooting himself through the head. John Troon, a British detective, was called in and, declaring the suicide verdict nonsense, cited Biwott and Moi's personal assistant, Hezekiah Oyugi, as witnesses he would like to interview. He fled Kenya shortly afterwards. 'He went far beyond his brief!' spluttered the then British High Commissioner.

The new government sacked or secured the resignation of half the judges including the Chief Justice, confronting them with evidence of their corruption. A well-worn joke in Nairobi was 'Why hire a lawyer when you can buy a judge?' Now at least there was a chance of restoring some respectability to the judiciary. Meanwhile, under Western pressure the government appointed John Githongo, a former accountant and anti-corruption crusader, to be the administration's anti-corruption czar. Githongo commissioned Kroll Associates, a private security company in London, to trace the Goldenberg money. The contract with the Kenya government was that the money would be found, frozen and then returned to the Kenyan treasury. Kroll went to work producing a 45,000-word report and then waited for the order from Nairobi to freeze the accounts and return the stolen money. The order never came. Sent to Nairobi, the report had been studied carefully by Kibaki's associates. Now they spotted a wonderful opportunity. Phone calls were made, deals were done. The money was split between the old thieves and the new thieves. Despite all the evidence no-one was prosecuted for the Goldenberg scam. The money was never returned.

Githongo also discovered that the government he served had started its own Goldenberg to raise funds to win the referendum on the new constitution. It was called Anglo-Leasing, a fictitious company based in Britain into which some £15 million were poured supposedly to provide Kenyans with new passports. In fact the money flowed straight back into party funds and private pockets. When Githongo realized what was happening, he went to see Kibaki personally. After a short interview, he left the President's office and fled for his life.

Kenya's economy grew at around 5 per cent a year during the Kibaki years largely because the government got out of the way and Kenyans worked hard. But in 2005 a poll found that more than half of Kenyans thought the economy was doing badly. Despite the economic turnaround, nearly half the population was living in what the UN defines as poverty – less than a dollar a day. According to the survey by Afrobarometer, the most important issue for most Kenyans was equality, in terms of both opportunity and availability of resources. Was that an indirect way of saying that the Kikuyu, the ethnic group of President Mwai Kibaki and Kenya's largest, was getting everything to the exclusion of everyone else?

Odinga resigned from the government and started to build a new coalition. A brilliant orator and campaigner, he whipped up opposition to the new constitution drafted by Kibaki and heavily defeated it in a referendum. Githongo pointed out that the Kenyan electorate were learning. 'They now know you can go and eat the government's *Nyama Choma* [barbecue] at a rally but then go and vote for what you think is right. They know their vote is secret and can achieve something.'

The voting figures also showed just how ethnically divided the country had become. The Kikuyu voted for the new constitution; most of the rest of Kenya against. Riding the wave – and Kibaki's growing unpopularity – Odinga forged the new Orange coalition, known as the Pentagon, that brought together four other leading politicians and their ethnic communities. Only the Kikuyu were missing. They were certain of victory. Aged sixty-two, Raila Odinga knew that this would be his last chance to fulfil his – and his father's – ambition to be President. On the other side the gang around Kibaki had much to lose if Odinga came to power. They would be out of office, maybe in prison.

The only distinction between Kenya's politicians was between those who were in and those who were out. No policy or ideology divided them. It was all about personal preferment based on ethnic support. So strong had the ethnic element become that a feeling was growing that the Kibaki government, once a broad coalition of all Kenya's ethnicities, had become a Kikuyu clique. Those closest to Kibaki were dubbed the Mount Kenya Mafia. Many saw Kenya becoming Kikuyu land. And some leading Kikuyu even saw this as their right and duty. They are the largest ethnic group with the most education, providing a large proportion of Kenya's professional middle class. Through Mau Mau they led the struggle to free Kenya from colonial rule. Throughout Moi's regime they had been marginalized. Now it was their right to rule again – and eat.

By election time in December 2007 Kenya was facing the perfect political storm. Every election since multi-party politics was reintroduced in 1991 had involved rigging, violence and vote buying. The margin of victory had always been so great that election observers and Western diplomats – keen to maintain 'stability' in Kenya – could claim that the violence and cheating, while regrettable, did not make a difference to the result. 'Voting broadly reflected the will of the people,' was their duplicitous phrase, allowing the ruling elite to play their quinquennial charade.

But in 2007 the margin of victory was too thin. Cheating did make a difference to the result and Raila Odinga, the leader of the main opposition party which won in six out of eight provinces and the largest number of parliamentary seats, refused to concede defeat. Kibera, Nairobi's biggest slum, is in his constituency, providing an instant angry mob whenever he needed to pressurize the government. His own Luo people there and in the Luo town of Kisumu on Lake Victoria immediately started attacking Kikuyus and their businesses. Kalenjin youths did the same in Eldoret and the rest of the Rift Valley. In retaliation organized gangs of Kikuyu youths in the Nairobi slums launched attacks into Luo areas. Gangs with guns, clubs and spears set up roadblocks searching for travellers from the hunted ethnic group. Those they found were dragged out and butchered with machetes or clubs by the roadside. Before long some 1500 Kenyans were dead, scores injured and 600,000 made homeless. Parts of Kenya were war zones, threatening not just Kenyans but 100 million people in the region who depended on

Kenya's ports and roads and its manufacturing and service industries.

Meanwhile the rest of the world was still enjoying Christmas. While the usual remarks were made about irregularities and the fraud and intimidation committed by both sides, the American ambassador congratulated Kibaki on his re-election. The World Bank urged getting back to business as usual as quickly as possible. The Europeans however, were more cautious. For once their election observers had come out with a damning verdict. Gradually the world realized it had a serious problem on its hands.

Despite all the warning signs outsiders had badly misread Kenya. Had anyone bothered to read the report of the Africa Peer Review Mechanism team which was published in 2006 they would have seen this coming and stopped talking about Kenya as a stable, peaceful country. 'There is a need for a healing of the nation. The process of national healing and reconciliation is unlikely to proceed as long as society is still polarized,' the report said. It pointed out the impunity of politicians from past crimes and dwelt on corruption, the nature of presidential power, and the need for devolution and a new constitution. The report called for a 'much-needed political compromise'.

The team had picked up the deep sense of anger and grievance that many Kenyans feel going back to colonial injustices that have never been resolved. They centred on land: Kalenjin and Luo land once seized by whites then handed to Kikuyus. And public, state-owned land enclosed by Kenya's ruling elite, the inhabitants turned into wage labourers picking flowers or beans for foreigners for a few shillings a day.

In the post-election mayhem some positive developments were overlooked. The Kenyan electorate had voted wisely. Kikuyu voters had rejected several leading Kikuyu chauvinists who were ministers.

The Kalenjin electorate voted out Moi's sons and his leading hench-man, Nicholas Biwott. Whatever appalling atrocities the tribal gangs were perpetrating, ordinary Kenyan people seemed to know who, of their own ethnic group, they did not want running the country.

Koert Lindyer, my Dutch colleague in Nairobi married to a Kikuyu, realized the enormity of what had happened when he decided to take a trip up the Rift Valley at the height of the battle. He asked his Kikuyu nephew to come with him and they were actually in the car when he stopped. He could not take a Kikuyu with him to the Rift Valley. Suddenly he realized Kenya was not one country any more. It was a space on the map inhabited by warring ethnic groups. It was the same even among the professionals in the offices of big companies in Nairobi. Several reported that communication around the water dispenser between the Kikuyu and the other Kenyans tailed off as trust in the national social compact began to erode.

When the Europeans and Americans realized what was happening they moved swiftly. First they encouraged the African Union to start negotiations but its envoys were kept waiting then brushed aside by the Kenyans. Kofi Annan, enjoying a quieter life after retiring from the United Nations, was asked to go to sort out the mess. By then African rulers and Western countries had reached consensus. When he arrived in Kenya, Annan spoke for the African Union, the United Nations, the Americans, the Europeans and the rest of the world. Kibaki and Odinga were told in no uncertain terms that they would be international pariahs if they did not reach agreement. Kenya's monetarized politics at least mean that all the players have a bottom line. Although they were prepared to spill a lot of Kenyan blood, once their own interests and wealth were threatened, the politicians caved in. For once international pressure worked in Africa, at least for a while. Kibaki remained President and Raila Odinga became Prime Minister – the deal they had originally made back in 2002.

Part of the deal was that the International Criminal Court should investigate those responsible for ordering, stirring up or paying for the violence. Six people were named and invited to go to The Hague to answer questions. The very announcement cracked the thin veneer of unity. Their political allies insisted that they should be tried in Kenya and their enemies demanded that they be sent to The Hague. Two of those indicted, Uhuru Kenyatta and William Ruto, broadly representing the Kikiuyu and Kalenjin respectively, got together, formed a new alliance called Jubilee and won the 2013 election. The anti-ICC factor played strongly in their favour. Playing the 'anti-colonial' card as if Europe and America held sovereignty over Kenya, they attracted huge support among their peoples, even among the middle class.

Kenya, the most sophisticated country in Africa after South Africa in terms of education and technology, is also the most ethnically divided – again, even at middle-class levels. The devolution of real power and money to its 47 counties under the new constitution may increase that ethnic divide. Broken up into ethnic fiefdoms – most dangerously in urban slums like Kibera and Mathare Valley – Kenya will no longer be one country. More than 600,000 people displaced since January 2008 may never be able to return to their homes again. Kikuyu traders will not be setting up shop in a Luo or Kalenjin area. Thanks to civil war within its ruling class, Kenya has become more dangerously what it has always been: a bomb that politicians can detonate at any time. But despite the dangerous politics, the economic boom has continued, with a growth rate staying at over 5 per cent in the last few years. Kenyans may have been at each other's throats but they were also hard at work and getting richer. Hopefully that will continue to make them pull back from a conflict which may wreck their economy.

Then in September 2013 Kenya was hit again by a merciless Islamist attack on the Westgate shopping centre in Nairobi. In 1998

Islamist bombers had blown up the American embassies in Nairobi and Dar es Salaam but these were attacks by Al-Qaeda on the US, not explicitly on Kenya or Tanzania. The Westgate attack was a direct attack on Kenya's most upmarket shopping mall frequented by wealthy westerners as well as Kenya's middle classes. It was carried out by Al-Qaeda's Somali ally, al-Shabaab, in revenge for Kenya's presence in Somalia and its cooperation with America. The Islamists also attacked holiday hotels on the coast, devastating Kenya's tourist industry. As far as Kenyans are concerned this is nothing to do with their society or politics. It is part of the beginning of a global religious war that already engulfs much of the Middle East and parts of Sahelian Africa.

16

Look out world
Nigeria

Nigeria has had a terrible reputation. Tell someone that you are going to Nigeria and if they haven't been there themselves, they offer sympathy. Tell anyone who has been to Nigeria and they laugh. Then they offer sympathy. Few tourists go there. Only companies rich enough to keep their staff removed from the realities of Nigerian life do business there. And big companies rarely mention Nigeria in their annual reports for fear of what it will do to their share price. Journalists treat it like a war zone. Diplomats regard it as a punishment posting. Everyone has a Nigeria story from beyond the normal bounds of credibility. Some are terrifying. Most are funny. Nigerian politicians try to pretend that its bad image is some Western conspiracy against Nigeria and Africa. The truth is that Nigeria's popular image falls short of the reality. It is not just white visitors who fear it. I told a Ghanaian cab driver in London that I was going to Nigeria. He was quiet for a moment. Then he said: 'I lived in Lagos once. Give me a million – a billion pounds, I would not go back there. Never. It is the most terrible place in the world.'

Lagos is the heart of Nigeria and its gateway to the world. Vast, ugly, sweaty, traffic-jammed, smog-choked, Lagos is a cauldron of superlatives all fighting each other, a frenzy of hustling humanity scrabbling for survival. 'The land of no tomorrow' is how one Nigerian journalist described Nigeria. Lagos is the city of no tomorrow. People here live as if their future depends on what they can grab today. No-one knows how many people live in the city but estimates are that it was 21 million in 2017 and that it will be more than 27 million by 2050. For most of its population water comes from a standpipe that only occasionally works. Cooking is done on wood or charcoal fires. The rich use generators because power is erratic. The national power company NEPA was known as Never Expect Power Always but that has improved slightly. Until recently you could count traffic lights on the fingers of one hand but no-one paid any attention to them. Sleek Mercedes, battered buses and old wrecks, delayed for a second, swerve into oncoming traffic or onto pavements, horns blaring. The city locks daily in traffic jams – or 'go-slows' as they are known here – that can last for hours or even a whole day.

If Lagos was an independent country it would be the fourth largest economy in Africa, sucking in goods and people from all over West Africa. Lagos is like a Hong Kong feeling it's fallen behind, a New York without the good manners. But unlike the prodigious creativity of New York or Hong Kong, the maelstrom of frenetic motion seems like some monstrous machine that has broken its drive shaft, gone into hyperdrive and is whirling itself to pieces. Seems? Impenetrable, incomprehensible to outsiders, Lagos survives. It pulsates. It grows. It works.

So does Nigeria. By any law of political or social science it should have collapsed or disintegrated years ago. Indeed it has been described as a failed state that works. Recalling the image he had used in his novel *A Man of the People*, Chinua Achebe, Nigeria's celebrated novelist, wrote of Nigeria in 1983, 'This house has fallen.' Maybe, but some people are living fabulously wealthy lives amid the ruins. And others survive and get by. How? It's a mystery. The secret lies in the layers of millions upon millions of networks, personal ties, family links, ethnic loyalties, school fraternities, Church connections and scores of other unrecorded, informally organized bonds of trust that make things happen. Forget the government, the formal structures. What makes Nigeria work is a matrix of social, political and economic connections that ensure most people get food and shelter. The hidden wiring also creates Presidents, makes fortunes and prevents wars. But it also ensures that the vast majority of Nigerians are kept outside the ruler-owner circle, never given the chance to fulfil their – or Nigeria's – potential.

A successful Nigeria could transform the continent in the twenty-first century. Its resources grow more valuable as they become globally scarcer. Among the world's biggest oil producers, it is becoming one of America's main suppliers. Nigeria holds the world's seventh-largest gas reserves and production is expected to soar as global demand grows. Its 120 million people – or is it 160 million? – the numbers are disputed like everything else in Nigeria – are a quarter of sub-Saharan Africa's population and among them are astonishing talents. In business, law, science, art, literature, music, sport, Nigeria produces phenomenally talented individuals as if its superheated society throws up brighter, hotter human beings than anywhere else. The leader who manages to harness and direct all that energy – physical and human – will create a formidable country that will change Africa and the world. Were it to implode like its neighbours, Sierra Leone, Liberia and Côte d'Ivoire, the human catastrophe would be unconscionable and it would take much of West Africa with it. Nigeria lives on the edge.

It is ironic that most people's first experience of Nigeria is Murtala Mohammed airport at Lagos, named after the only ruler of Nigeria whom almost all Nigerians revere. Murtala Mohammed came to power in 1975 in a coup committed to order and efficiency.

The airport named after him became a monument to disorder and dishonesty. Visitors vie with each other to recall their most bizarre and alarming experiences there. In 2000 the pilot of a British Airways flight from London taxiing his Boeing 747 for take-off suddenly saw logs in front of him strewn across the runway. He jammed on the brakes and, as the plane juddered to a halt, figures scurried beneath it. They unlocked the hold and unloaded the baggage into trucks before escaping through a hole cut in the perimeter fence. The police arrived a comfortable two minutes later.

Europeans and Americans, coming from lands where spontaneous offers of help are rare, are often enchanted by the warm welcome they receive in Africa. At Murtala Mohammed it can burn you. With smiles wider than their faces men offer to sort out customs and immigration for you, carry your bags or find you a taxi. Unsuspecting visitors who have accepted have been robbed, kidnapped and even murdered. Officials in uniform, often the biggest hyenas of all, tell you, 'You are in big trouble. Come with me,' and lead you to a side room to explain how the 'problem' can be solved. They keep your passport and say, 'Please wait here,' until you pay up. Two hundred dollars is a modest opening bid.

If someone influential does not meet you, you find yourself floundering in a pool of piranhas. It is the same when you leave. Once, after three weeks of exhausting Nigeria, I arrive at the airport carrying a couple of masks I picked up at a tourist shop. While I wait to check in, a huge Nigerian family seeing off their daughter joins the queue behind me. The daughter is going off to study in Britain and carries the biggest suitcase I have ever seen. It exceeds her weight allowance. Having very little baggage, I offer to take some of hers. It is a calculated risk. Arrest for being an inadvertent drug carrier at Heathrow seems preferable to being a friendless foreigner at Murtala Mohammed airport. The family is deeply grateful.

Then I come face to face with a huge, square-faced, scowling woman in the uniform of a customs official. 'Open,' she snaps without even looking at me. She gazes with lazy, heavy-lidded eyes at my belongings. I usually pack my smelliest washing at the top of my bag when expecting customs trouble but she insists I empty it. She spots the masks and her eyes light up.

'Where is your export certificate?' she demands in the voice of one who has asked an unanswerable question. 'Every item leaving Nigeria needs export certificate from the National Museum – like this.' And she whips a green form from under the counter, clearly kept there for dramatic effect. I try to explain that these masks were made recently for tourists and are not old art, but she knows better. 'This is our heritage that you Europeans are stealing. I shall arrest you.' She waddles off telling a subordinate, 'Arrest this man.' The British Airways staff ignore me, even though I am their passenger. But the family with the daughter going to England weigh in to defend me. The mother turns out to be a solicitor and tears into the customs officials. They are polite but they can do nothing, the boss has gone, leaving orders that must be obeyed. A stupendous slanging match ensues. Then the man ordered to arrest me winks at me and helps me repack my bag. I take out my wallet but he shakes his head and points to the departure gate and encourages me to slip away quickly.

I wander casually up the airport concourse still puzzling at Nigeria's ways, while the family and the officials exchange angry insults. After a minute or two the family breaks off the battle and joins me, laughing and celebrating my escape. I am just about to go through immigration when a terrific blow crashes down on my shoulder. I reel round to find myself looking into the eyes of the Amazonian customs chief. 'Where you go now? You under arrest. You have stolen Nigerian heritage property and now you try to escape. You in big, big trouble now. Come!' she shouts, grabbing my arm and dragging me off.

The family grab my other arm and I am pulled in half as I am yanked this way and that across the concourse. A crowd forms. The nice official who had helped me pack intervenes again and has a word in the woman's ear. Then he returns gravely to me. 'She needs an apology,' he announces and tells me to deliver it in her office. I assume she could not be seen to take a bribe in full view of all the passengers but would be happy to accept dash in the privacy of her office.

I follow her, clambering over the check-in desks and making my way through dimly lit corridors to her important-looking office. She squeezes herself behind her desk and fiddles with some papers. Then she launches into a lecture on the evils of European colonialism and neo-colonialism and the looting of Nigeria's cultural heritage. She makes me promise I will never, ever again try to take any object of art out of the country without a certificate – even if it is bought from the airport tourist shop. I grovel and apologize for my wickedness. A smile breaks across her fearsome features and I reach for my wallet. But she puts up her hand and the smile disappears. She looks shocked. I mumble goodbye and totter towards the door completely confused. Can it be that, after all, this woman, head of customs at Murtala Mohammed airport, is letting me go free? Has the customs department, Nigerian officialdom, Nigeria itself, become honest? As I close her office door, the nice official who had managed my rescue springs the trap. 'Fifty dollars for negotiation,' he demands.

I pay.

Colin Powell, the American Secretary of State, once let slip the opinion that all Nigerians are crooks. All? Maybe not, but a lot of Nigerians dedicate their lives to fulfilling the stereotype. And being

Nigerian they are also often world class. An official of the US Drug Enforcement Agency spoke in awe of the Nigerian drug smuggling gangs. 'We thought we knew most of the tricks of the drug trade until we came up against the Nigerians,' he told me. 'Then we realized we were just beginners.'

One area in which Nigeria seems to be deficient is political leadership. With the possible exception of Murtala Mohammed – and he was murdered seven months after coming to power – the country did not have a single decent leader until Olusegun Obasanjo, although many Nigerians would vigorously deny that. When Achebe wrote those lines about the house left behind by the colonialists and taken over by 'the smart and the lucky and hardly ever the best', he was writing about Nigeria. Politics in Nigeria is a business career. Any politician who does not end up a multi-millionaire is regarded as a fool. Not many Nigerians are fools.

In 1996 a commission of inquiry discovered that the $12 billion surplus revenue from oil resulting from the high price during the Gulf War was missing. Much of it was in offshore accounts controlled by President Ibrahim Babangida. None of it was ever recovered. When Babangida's successor, Sani Abacha, died in 1998, his family were forced to pay back $2 billion stolen during his five-year reign. But they were allowed to keep the $100 million that he stole before he seized power. Many Nigerians think that $2 billion is small change compared to what he actually stole.

Corruption is such an important part of the Nigerian political scene that politicians can be quite open about it. Ahmed Sani, the governor of Zamfara state, admits to taking money when he held a senior position at the Central Bank. He says it was given to him by Abacha when he brought cash from the bank to the presidential villa. Theft has spread right down to every level of society. The Catholic Bishop of Sokoto, Matthew Kukah, says he warns Mass attendants to watch their pockets and handbags when they kneel and pray. But theft is not only a Christian vice, he adds: 'No-one goes to the mosque these days in a pair of shoes he cannot afford to lose.'

Yet the rulers who steal Nigeria's future and a poor man who steals a yam at the market are judged very differently. Pinch a yam in the market and you will have a petrol-soaked tyre jammed round your neck and set alight. Trouser a billion dollars of state funds and everyone laughs and fawns on you. No Big Man in Nigeria has ever been punished for theft, though under Olusegun Obasanjo's rule one or two of his political enemies were asked to resign and give back some of what they had stolen.

Corruption exists everywhere, not just Africa. It happens in Europe and America, in India and China. But Nigeria's hilariously brazen corruption puts it in a different league. Elsewhere it is conducted behind closed doors or by nods and euphemisms. In Nigeria it is open and it is everywhere. Internationally the word 'Nigeria' has come to mean corruption and dodgy dealing. The country regularly appears top of the list of the world's most corrupt countries, according to Transparency International. Nigeria is also home to the famous 419 scams named after the law that is supposed to ban them.

The letters are written in a quaintly polite, personal style. 'It is vastly inappropriate for me to contact you in this manner . . . but I received your contact details from the Chamber of Commerce,' says one purporting to be from a son of the late ruler of the Congo, Laurent Kabila. He claims to have found $20 million left over from an arms deal. Help us move this money and you can have 20 per cent, the letter says. Another cheekily claims that half a million $100 bills have been stained in a flood and need to be cleaned. 'If you can kindly help supply us with this service we will give you 15 per cent.'

If you respond you will be invited to meet the agents of the sender, often in a third country. Americans are invited to London,

Britons asked to go to Amsterdam. You will be met by charming, well-dressed, well-spoken Nigerians. Having won your trust, they explain that in order to release the money you need to pay something first, to 'facilitate' the funds. One payment leads to another until the fraudsters recognize signs of suspicion. Then they disappear. Sometimes they obtain details of your bank account – and promptly empty it with a forged cheque.

If you are stupid enough to go to Nigeria, they will take you hostage, but usually there is only the threat of violence and the lure of millions. In one case they created a sophisticated e-bank on the web and gave victims an account and a personal login number so they could be shown the millions that had already apparently been deposited.

These scams grew from a trickle in the late 1980s to a flood. The deluge points to one astounding fact: they worked. The London police received 185,000 419s from the public in 2002, the tip of the iceberg, they say. They used to come by post but with the growth of email and advances in Internet financial activity, the numbers have grown incrementally. The police don't even keep track of the figures any more but they estimate the success rate is about 3 per cent, high enough to keep them flowing. Most victims are too embarrassed to admit they have been conned so the figures are certainly far higher. Still based largely in Nigeria, millions of emails now pour out of servers in West Africa, South Africa and Eastern Europe. And new scams are being invented all the time.

Why do people fall for 419s? Gambling frenzy? Greed? Ironically one factor seems to be Nigeria's very reputation for corruption. People seem to think that they will get away with it because it is Nigeria. The victims are often people who have no record of gambling. Many are middle-aged professionals who already have some savings and blow them in the hope of getting millions more. Some borrow from a bank or friends, some 'borrow' from their employer. Companies have fallen for 419s too, including a leading British advertising company. Some have lost $4 or $5 million. But the largest number of victims are vulnerable people, poor, old or already in debt.

Mention of 419s in Nigeria evokes bursts of ebullient laughter. 'It's called reparations for slavery,' one Nigerian friend told me. I asked him if Nigerians fell for 419s as much as dumb white men appear to do. He looked at me with disdain. 'Richard,' he said, 'Nigerians would never fall for such crude scams. We practise far more sophisticated ones on each other.'

Corruption pervades Nigerian life so broadly and deeply that it is hard to imagine life in Nigeria if it were suddenly to end. Without a little something a policeman will not investigate a crime, a journalist will not write up a politician's speech, a politician will not speak to a constituent, a tax inspector will not sign off your tax return. You may suddenly find your telephone does not work. It has been mysteriously disconnected or 'tossed' as the Nigerians say. Or your electricity is cut off. When you try to find out what has happened you will be presented with a demand for a 'quick quick' reconnection charge.

In Nigeria every contact between an official and an individual seems to involve an extra payment, that personalized VAT. To check your name on the voters' register, to get a passport, to pass through a roadblock, all involve a few notes changing hands. It may be twenty naira for a policeman or it may be $20 million that an international company pays a minister to get an oil concession or a road-building contract. Everybody pays. Even when I went to interview President Obasanjo, the staffer escorting me slipped Obasanjo's bodyguard a few naira. It was not asked for, just slipped discreetly from hand to hand. Why was that necessary? What relationship did that cement?

At the other end of the scale transnational companies operating in Nigeria like to boast that they are so big, so essential to the economy, that they never pay bribes. True. They pay agents for 'facilitation services' instead. Their agents swim into the murky waters like pilot fish and find a way past the sharks so that the big companies remain clean. They settle up with the agents afterwards. In the late 1990s a consortium bidding for a contract to build a liquefied natural gas plant at Bonny in the Niger Delta paid their agent, a British lawyer, $51 million to secure the contract. One member of the consortium was MW Kellogg, a UK-based subsidiary of the American giant Halliburton, which paid over £7 million to the Serious Fraud Office for corrupt dealings by its agents in Nigeria.

So where does the ubiquitous gift-giving or 'tipping' end and real corruption start? Is it tipping or corruption to give an official 500 naira to deal with your application form now rather than putting it in a pile that will not move for a week? What is the difference between that and oil companies paying out millions of dollars in return for contracts or avoiding tax?

Many Nigerians will tell you that it takes two to tango and corruption needs a giver as well as a receiver. They like to blame corruption on foreigners. On the rare occasions when grand corruption has been exposed in Africa there has been an outsider connection: either European or American companies have paid bribes or their banks have received stolen money without question. That is true, but who initiates the bribe? Western companies prefer not to pay bribes and want to operate in well-regulated, transparent environments. They point out that they are never asked for bribes in Norway or America while in most of Africa, particularly Nigeria, they are. Few will admit to paying them since most companies have made it policy not to. Mining companies sign up to the Extractive Industries Transparency Initiative, which supports full verification of company payments and government revenues in the mining, oil and gas industries. But it is hard to believe that these companies which used to pay bribes liberally and still operate in countries like Nigeria, Angola or Congo do not make sure that the local decision makers are not kept happy in some way.

If, on the other hand, corruption comes from within Africa, what traditions within Africa could have evolved into today's ubiquitous systems? In parts of precolonial Africa if you wanted to please a king, you brought him a gift. In return he looked after you, fed you and protected your family. In such an exchange a social bond was created and symbolically cemented by a constant gift-giving and -receiving between ruler and ruled. Gift-giving bound a king to his people, the centre of power to the fringes. Is corruption merely a natural extension of this old glue that binds society together? Is it no more than a bit of old Africa continuing in its own way that has been misnamed corruption by misunderstanding outsiders? No, says President Olusegun Obasanjo, there is nothing traditional about a Swiss bank account.

And the colonial legacy? Both Nigeria and Congo began as territories seized by Europeans for pillage. They were estate states. Congo was created and owned by King Leopold of Belgium. Much of Nigeria was owned and ruled by George Goldie's National Africa Company, chartered by the British government to exploit thousands of square miles and rule hundreds of thousands of Africans. Neither Leopold nor Goldie cared much for ethical business codes, fair trade or transparency. The estate states were created to extract commodities for Europe as cheaply as possible and they made their ruler-owners rich beyond imagining. It is hardly surprising that those who inherited these states imitated their founders.

Whatever the source of corruption in Nigeria and the rest of Africa, much of the ill-gotten gains have been deposited in Western banks with a few polite formalities. Many of them come through secretive trust funds in British offshore islands where few questions are asked unless they are thought to be funding terrorism. From there they feed into the City of London, which explains why the British government is so reluctant to investigate.

Outside my study window in London stood an old hawthorn tree enveloped in a massive growth of ivy. Over the years the tree had become an ivy bush in the shape of a hawthorn tree and I saw it as an image of what corruption does to a country. Mobutu's rule in Zaire seemed like the ivy squeezing the life out of every green shoot, squeezing its wealth and energy, smothering any initiative. When he died I wrote that there was no Zairean state, only corruption in the shape of Zaire, as ivy had taken on the shape of the tree. After seventeen years of military rule Nigeria was close to being like Mobutu's Zaire. All its institutions – the civil service, the law, hospitals, schools, the army, police, business, academics – had become so corrupt that, although Nigeria looks like a functioning state, it is just a shell. It still holds the shape of a nation state from the outside, but within, corruption has become the institution. At around the same time I cut down the hawthorn tree and tore off the ivy. A few months later the hawthorn stump sprouted green shoots and is now thriving again. Ivy does not kill other plants but suppresses and smothers them. Maybe it is not therefore an exact simile for corruption. Corruption does kill in Nigeria.

Nigerians have an ambiguous loyalty to Nigeria. They will tell you it is a great and powerful country but many also rubbish it, cynical about its chances of going anywhere. The World Poverty Clock's Africa-wide survey estimates that 88 million Nigerians live in poverty out of a population of 155 million. Unsurprisingly, Nigerians expressed less belief in their government than any other Africans. Only 12 per cent believed that the country was run by the will of the people and only 7 per cent trusted their government.

Nigerians have a strong sense of being Nigerian, but they do not share with each other the same concept of what this means. For many, loyalty extends little beyond support for the national football side and even that can turn nasty if the Super Eagles lose. Nigerians have never agreed – or been given the chance to agree – what Nigeria is. They feel no loyalty to this house called Nigeria. They are all outsiders, all – except for the few – out in the rain.

One reason that Nigerians disagree about the size of the population is that it is a political issue. If the north has more people than the south it should have more political power. The north is dominated by Hausa-speaking Muslims, the south-east by the Igbos and the south-west by Yorubas. The two latter groups are mostly Christian or follow traditional religions, though there are many Yoruba Muslims too. The British got on well with the aristocratic Muslim rulers of northern Nigeria. They reminded them of the Indian princes and Sultans with whom Britain had ruled India for so long. They tried to recreate that system of 'indirect rule' in Africa too. The Hausas, according to a British government memorandum of 1897, are 'quite the best native material . . . If we could gradually substitute the Hausa for the low-type Coastal Native, there would be a great future for our West African colonies.' To encourage colonization of the south by northerners, the British built a railway linking north and south, and when they left Nigeria in 1960 they bequeathed the country to the northerners, some say by a crudely rigged election.

Religion reinforces some of Nigeria's political divisions but it is not the cause of the division. Nigerians are deeply religious, the vast majority Christian or Muslim. When religion overlays ethnicity and culture, it is easy to claim God or Allah backs your cause. Ahmed Sani – the man who took money when he worked at the Central Bank – used up his cash to get himself elected as governor in 1999 but he needed to get elected again in 2003. In his first term there had been widespread lawlessness and robberies in Zamfara state so he suddenly turned religious, reintroduced full Sharia law to please the largely Muslim electorate and started chopping the hands off thieves. He also demanded that the state be officially Muslim and at one stage he even ordered the destruction of all Christian Churches. This easy political stunt nearly split Nigeria in two. It led to judicial stonings and amputations and caused scores of deaths in Muslim–Christian clashes and riots. It also got Sani re-elected. He nearly ran for President in 2007.

The only non-northerner to rule Nigeria has been Olusegun Obasanjo. As a young general he stepped in when Murtula Mohammed was murdered in 1976 and handed over to an elected civilian government three years later. That stood him in good stead when he ran in the 1999 election. He had also been locked up by General Abacha. He had credibility as a soldier who had opposed military rule, as a general who was respected by other generals, and as a southern Christian who had the trust of the northern Muslims. They largely voted for him in 1999. Soon after the election, however, the northerners accused him of being pro-Yoruba. During his first term his support withered in the north but grew among the Yoruba who gave him a second term in 2003. But when he stepped down in 2007 northern rule resumed with Umaru Yar'Adua. But Yar'Adua was already sick and died in 2010. His successor was his deputy, Goodluck Jonathan, a pleasant charming man who had floated to the top in Nigeria by being in the right place at the right time but had not a clue how to run the country. In 2015 he lost the election to the former military head of state, General Muhammadu Buhari, who had ruled for two years in the 1980s. At that time Buhari was feared and Nigerians recall that they got up earlier and were at work on time and the corruption levels dropped. That made him unpopular among the ruling class and he was pushed aside. In his second coming as president in 2015 he described himself as a converted democrat. But by then so much power had devolved to Nigerian states that the role almost became ceremonial.

Nigerian politics appears to be a zero sum game. The popular assumption is that if the Hausas are in power, they are eating well so the Yoruba and Igbo must be losing out. Northerners will tell you that they should be the rulers because that is what they are good at, and that Yorubas should be the civil servants and Igbos the business-men. This ethnic stereotyping is countered by the southerners' pro-posal that the presidency should rotate between regions. The assumption – spelled out shamelessly at political rallies – is that each group may suffer for a while but every decade it will also 'chop' – meaning gobble up the national resources. In other words, the elite of each region of Nigeria will take it in turns to loot the country. Faced with these alternatives no wonder the military has been allowed to rule for so long in Nigeria. Everyone fears that political breakdown will lead to strife: a bare-fisted, free-for-all fight to the death.

Nigeria is famed for its sudden explosions of violence, usually in cities where a politician has stirred up his own ethnic group or co-religionists to try to wipe out a rival. These brief explosions reg-ularly leave 400 or 500 dead in a couple of days when gangs of thugs take up clubs, machetes and knives. Whole suburbs are burned down – often with people locked in their homes. Then it stops as suddenly as it started. The incidents rarely make more than a paragraph in the Western press. The world sighs and moves on. Violent Africa.

On the contrary, I sometimes feel Africa is not violent enough. If Africans fought back sooner against theft and oppression instead of allowing themselves to be slaves to the rich and powerful, Africa would be a much more peaceful place. Instead African patience allows exploitation and oppression to thrive until everyone loses their temper and explodes.

Nigerians are probably no more tribalist than any other human communities. Nigeria's size in fact makes it more of a melting pot than many smaller African countries and most Nigerians can trace many ethnicities in their family trees. The root of the problem is that the Nigerian state depends not on a constitution but on a commodity: oil.

Nigeria's oil comes from the Niger Delta. In the nineteenth century the Delta produced another desperately needed oil, palm oil. In 1884, the British National Africa Company created a monopoly to purchase and export palm oil from the Niger River. The monopoly wiped out the African middlemen and Africa ended up with little to show for its prized commodity. It was forced at gunpoint to become a primary producer for a British company.

History is repeating itself. Nigeria's first oil was discovered at Olubiri, a village in the Niger Delta. As it reaches the sea the mighty river loses its momentum and splits into hundreds of channels and creeks that meander through dense swamps of mud, mangroves and mosquitoes. Scores of different ethnic groups inhabit thousands of riverside villages as they have done for generations. They once lived on fishing, growing a few crops and taxing passers-by by agreement or force: piracy or kidnapping were always common in the Delta. From the fifteenth century their trade with the outside world consisted of palm oil and slaves whom they seized from their neighbours or bought from other slave traders further up the river and sold on to European traders at the coast.

The Delta inhabitants were a difficult and ferocious people as the Lander brothers discovered when they tried to follow the Niger's course to the sea in 1831. Richard Lander and his brother John wanted to prove that the mighty West African river that flowed past the city of Timbuktu on the edge of the Sahara desert was the same river that flowed into the Bight of Benin. They tracked it towards the sea by canoe and had reached the Delta when they were attacked by huge war canoes with cannons mounted front and back and manned by forty paddlers. These monsters crashed into their little craft and John Lander's was overturned.

The brothers were rescued from the river but taken prisoner by King Obie, the Igbo king. Thinking that he might have a seriously valuable commodity in two white slaves, he decided to take them to the king of Brass on the coast who in turn thought to sell them to an English vessel that happened to be buying palm oil. King Boy, one of the kings of Brass, set off down the river with the Lander brothers lying in the bottom of the boat. Richard records that the king and his wife used his head as a foot-rest.

Have things changed much since the Landers' time? The Delta retains a reputation for banditry and lawlessness. I visited it soon after the death of Ken Saro-Wiwa, the Ogoni activist who tried to force the oil companies and the government to give more oil revenue to the local people. His strategy was direct confrontation, and when his supporters killed four Ogoni chiefs who opposed his movement, he was accused of murder. Convicted by a military tribunal, he was executed in 1995.

Nelson Aziba Olanari, a tough, shrewd 'youth leader', offers to take me on a tour of the Delta. Youth in Nigeria means anyone who is not a grey-haired elder. Nelson must be in his late thirties. We met at a peace conference in Port Harcourt that ended in a brawl. He insists that we go in his car and tells me to be ready early next morning. He picks me up promptly and we drive west out of the sprawling, ugly, oil city. Nelson talks little, using words carefully and firmly, rarely employing the inflammatory language of other self-styled Delta leaders. He reminds me at first of those street-hardened militants who fought apartheid in the townships of South Africa in the 1970s and 1980s.

As we turn off the main road and head southwards we cross into Bayelsa state which covers the southern part of the Delta. Nelson informs me that we are on the only hardtop road in the newly created state even though it produces 95 per cent of Nigeria's wealth, billions of dollars' worth of oil. Straightaway we run into an army roadblock where two men have been forced out of their car and are being made to do press-ups while a bored-looking soldier stands over them casually hitting them with a stick whenever their pace slackens.

Nelson winds down the window and chats to the soldiers and when they finally let us go with quite a small payment, he laughs out loud. He is on their wanted list but they did not recognize him. My presence could work either way. If the soldiers think I am an oil worker they may protect me, but if they find I am a journalist we are in trouble. The roadblock is simply a private tax point for the soldiers to extract a toll on every traveller. Going to town for shopping is expensive for the people of Bayelsa state. Our first stop is the village of Otuasega, a rough collection of plastered cement-block buildings with rusty corrugated iron roofs and a few square, wood-framed, mud houses. Chickens, pigs and goats scratch around in the piles of rubbish. There is a church but no shops. Women sit under umbrellas selling cigarettes and sweets and tiny paper twists of soap powder and salt. The men sit in the shade on old chairs or logs. We wait in a small hut while a delegation assembles, summoned by Nelson. A gaggle of ragged children, some with bellies swollen with hunger, gather in wide-eyed silence around the door to stare at the strange white visitor.

The hut has a mud floor, crude benches and a table. There is an old carpet on the floor and on the wall an out-of-date calendar and a picture of a tragic-looking, long-haired Aryan Jesus looking sky-wards and pointing to his bleeding heart. The chief welcomes us gravely and sends a small boy off to buy Coca-Cola. He comes scurrying back and, before the boy opens them and pours, the chief reaches out and touches each bottle in turn, a gesture to show he is the giver. In the corner is an old-fashioned domed electric hairdryer that you used to see in 1950s hairdressing salons. Beneath its film of oily grime it has clearly never been used. Bought in the expectation that modernity in the form of perms and curls would soon reach Otuasega, it looks like a signpost to a city that was never built, a dream unfulfilled for nearly half a century. Electricity never got here.

A delegation of youth leaders assembles. The oil companies, they tell me, have bought off the traditional chiefs of the villages. Whatever the oil companies give for the local community is kept by the chiefs who buy cars or houses in town. Nothing is ever spent in the village. If people protest the army is sent in. One man tells how his nephew was shot dead by the soldiers a month ago with two others right here in the street. He explains:

> We demanded a dialogue with the elders and gave them ten days'
> grace. Then we launched Operation Climate Change. We all dressed
> in black to show we were mourning the future and danced the Ogle,
> a traditional masked dance, as a form of protest. My nephew was
> pushing a barrow along the road and joined in. When the dance
> reached the soldiers they shot and he died.

In the village we swap Nelson's car for a red pick-up truck. It has a tachometer on the dashboard. It looks like a Shell vehicle to me. Nelson laughs. 'Borrowed,' he says. In the next village two young men spot me in the front seat: a white man in a Shell vehicle. They dash into a hut and re-emerge brandishing machetes. Nelson leaps from the back seat and confronts them. The young men recognize him and there is much laughter as they apologize. But they look disappointed. They must have thought it was Christmas. Hundreds of oil workers have been kidnapped in the Delta recently and the oil companies pay out millions for their release. I think of the Lander brothers.

Now we are down to permanent first gear, grinding along a muddy track in ruts deeper than the wheels. Churned up by the heavy trucks of the oil companies, it has not been repaired for years. On each side a press of rampant vegetation leans across the track and the car has to push through elephant grass and branches. Occasionally patches of open ground have been cleared for oil pipes or pumping stations. Where the pipes are broken the ground is soaked in black oil. Nothing grows. The locals say the oil companies do not repair them, the oil companies say the locals cut the pipes to create a spill then claim compensation. It is more profitable than farming, say the oil companies.

The road suddenly comes into an open area the size of a football pitch. A pipe like a gun barrel sticks out of the earth squirting a massive red-orange flame into the air. The flame becomes a vast balloon of swirling and fluttering fire tailing off into black smoke. The ground and the bushes are scorched and smeared with soot. Look out at night from Port Harcourt and you can see these dragons for miles, thousands of spouts of flame dotted across the Delta, a hellish Mordor. Some say the Niger Delta gas flares are the biggest single contributor to global warming.

We finally pull up on a grassy space. In the middle is an installation of rusting pipes on a small concrete platform with grasses and shrubs sprouting through cracks in the concrete as if the earth is trying to draw the platform back into itself. Hornets' nests like little grey golf balls hang on the pipes. Nelson warns me not to get too close to them. A plaque attached to the pipes reads: 'Olubiri. Well No 1. Drilled June 1956. Depth 12,008 feet.'

This is where it all started, where Nigeria's first oil flowed. It is the story of Midas. Nigeria was suddenly rich. The African country with the most people was blessed with an endless cheap source of energy and wealth. But it turned Nigeria into a nation of junkies. The sweet black juice oozed everywhere, into everything. It suffocated the economy, generated greed, fed regional jealousy, funded terrible regimes, started a war. Oil dreams wrecked Nigeria, and Olubiri was where they all began.

A pipe supported on concrete blocks stretches away along a gash through the trees. Africa's sun burns down on the silent bush. Nothing moves. There is not a building in sight. We get back in the truck but from here the track is so bad that we have to get out and walk ahead to see which set of ruts to take. We have gone about half a mile when thick bush gives way to dark woodland. Suddenly the track stops dead and we are looking down a steep bank into a sluggish brown river. On the far bank under the gloomy forest canopy I can see a village of thatched huts. A hollowed-out log lies on the mud, half out of the water. I close my eyes and open them again. Is there anything here that a visitor 300 years ago would not have seen? Perhaps the ragged clothes of a group of people watching us from the other bank? Yet again I have reached a place in Africa apparently untouched by the outside world. But the outside world has indeed touched this place: fixed it in eternal poverty.

Nelson and I climb into the dugout canoe and we wobble across to the village. The other bank is a fragile dump of slippery palm-nut shells. This place is cursed twice with oil – with the palm oil that enticed the British to take over the Delta in the nineteenth century, and with the petroleum that brought Shell, Exxon Mobil, Texaco, Agip, Elf and all the other companies that came to suck. The bank of palm-nut shells threatens to pitch me back into the river but strong hands haul me up and onto the bank. Those shells represent decades of old-oil toil, crushed by hand for a few cents. Meanwhile Shell sucked out billions of dollars' worth of new oil from under the village. The new oil is pumped away far out of their reach. Even if the village could afford it, it could not obtain it. There is only one petrol station in the whole of the province. No-one here has a car. Canoes and paddles and the odd bicycle are the only methods of transport.

Nelson and I are led to the village meeting place, a thatched building of cement blocks with open sides, and ushered to a low bench in the middle with formal bows. Coca-Cola, the ubiquitous African gift of welcome, is brought. The villagers assemble as if I am an official come to address their problems. Chief Ralph Fabre, a wizened old man dressed in a dirty white robe, arrives and takes his seat at the head of the hall and the formal welcomes and introductions begin.

Chief Fabre tells me that when Shell started looking for oil in the area nearly fifty years ago, he worked as a storeman for the company. 'They knew oil was there but it would not come out,' he said.

So we consulted the oracle. The oracle demanded a white ram and a white cock. So we sacrificed a ram and a cock. Immediately oil was struck. It was the first oil in the whole of Africa.

We were expecting to be living in paradise. We thought we had the only oil on the Niger Delta. But to this day we have never benefited from Shell. They have built no project here. And now the river is polluted with oil spills and there are fewer and fewer fish. We grow food but the black smoke from the oil fires forms on the leaves. There used to be 8000 people in this village, now there are less than 6000. I blame the government and Shell. To us now they are just armed robbers, a den of animals. The only development in this village is a bit of road we have made ourselves by hand, but it takes us two days to get to market. Most of the trade we do now is barter with the next village, fish for yams.

I watch Nelson to see if he is pulling the strings. Activists tend to take you only to people who sing their song. But Chief Fabre seems to speak from the heart. Before I leave he shows me the blackened shell of the school that burned down three or four years before. No-one has rebuilt it – neither the government nor the villagers. Then they take me to a little hut set apart from the village, covered in sacking with little offerings of roots and food in pots around it. This is the oracle that finally permitted oil to be extracted in Nigeria. As a stranger I am not allowed to peep inside but I suggest that the village might now ask the oracle to stop the oil flowing. Everyone laughs. It is hard to tell whether they really believe in it.

As we drive back to Port Harcourt I question Nelson at length. When all his rhetoric about environment and exploitation is spent, Nelson comes to the point: 'The oil companies only employ outsiders. They should give more jobs to local people. I am educated. Why should they not give me a job?'

This may be the heart of Nigerian politics. Everyone is for sale. In a democratic system the ruler derives his power from popular support. In a state totally dependent on oil like Nigeria, the ruler derives his power from outsiders: the companies that extract oil and Western countries that buy it. Power oozes down from the ruler reducing the population to dependency. Until the end of military rule, oil made the President an absolute monarch. At the coronation in England kings and queens are anointed with oil as a symbol of royal power. In Nigeria oil is royal power. Little by little the kings and queens of Britain were forced, over centuries, to negotiate and concede power, drop by drop. Nigeria's military rulers were under no such pressure. The original constitutional arrangement was for half the oil money to be shared among all the states, but successive military rulers drew the oil revenue to themselves and with it, power. Only the constitution stood between the oil-backed ruler and total power, and for twenty-eight of Nigeria's first forty years as an independent state, the constitution was suspended.

King Oil destroyed almost every other economic activity in Nigeria. In 1966 less than 10 per cent of the government's revenue came from oil. By 1990 oil provided 97 per cent. There is no alternative source of wealth to fund a political opposition. In some years the oil revenue doubled. Today it provides more than a third of Nigeria's GDP and three-quarters of government revenue. As the price of oil shot up after 2004, that proportion rose. In the 1970s Nigeria was once so awash with petrodollars that the then President, Yakubu Gowon, said that Nigeria's only problem was how to spend the money. Mostly it was stolen or wasted. In 1997 Pat Utomi, a blunt-speaking economist and head of the Lagos Business School, suggested that all the oil be given to the soldiers. In return, he said, the generals must give Nigeria back to Nigerians. The soldiers called him in and warned him.

King Oil has reinforced the worst aspects of traditional culture and bolstered one of the most hierarchical and unequal societies in the world. An unbridgeable gap divides those who can drink at one of the streams of power and patronage and those who cannot. Those that can are the elite. Is there a single rich Nigerian who made his money honestly and pays tax? The question is greeted with hoots of laughter.

Meanwhile Nigeria's poor get poorer. In 2006 the country contained the largest number of absolutely poor people in the world after China and India – 70 per cent of all Nigerians, some 84 million people.

Abuja, Nigeria's capital since 1991, is ringed and crossed with motorways, its massive green-domed parliament, competing minarets and steeple of mosque and cathedral, the solid black tower of the central bank, luxury hotels and scores of palaces behind high walls topped with razor wire all proclaim a rich, modern city. Barely five miles away lies a traditional African village as poor as any on the continent.

I first went to Durumi in 2003 on the eve of the election and listened to the aged chief, His Excellency Royal Father Shapra Jarumi. He talked about the good old days when they hunted with bows, arrows and spears (he brought them out to show me). Cash was cowrie shells. We met in his house, one of the few buildings to have a corrugated iron roof, and he sat on a chair while everyone else sat on plastic mats on the cement floor. He reckoned that life was better then. Less than half the village had been to Abuja and no-one was working there, but he reckoned Abuja was a good thing. When I asked why he paused and consulted the others then said that if people were sick they could now go there for treatment. The others immediately pointed out that almost no-one could afford medicine. The only thing that linked Durumi to the modern world was a four-roomed school that was being built. The government had promised to pay for two teachers.

I wandered round the mud and thatch village. As in Olubiri there was little from the nineteenth century there, let alone the twenty-first. Water comes from a trickling stream a hundred yards from the edge of the village – a steep climb for the women carrying full pots on their heads. There had recently been an outbreak of diarrhoea caused by pollution further upstream. A few people had oil lamps or candles, the only source of light after dark.

I went back in 2007 to see what, if anything, the government of President Obasanjo, with a windfall budget surplus of some $13 billion, had done for a poor rural village that could not be closer to the capital of the country. If people's lives had not got better here, they were unlikely to have got better anywhere in Nigeria.

I found the village still ate what it grew and grew what it ate. Durumi had not changed much. The kids still scuttled barefoot through the village in rags, young girls pounded guinea corn in the shade of a mango tree and old women tended babies. The mud and thatch grain storage bins perched on stones to keep rats out were as picturesque as ever. Chief Shapra was sick and could not receive me but he sent a message saying things were improving. 'There are more children in the village.' The good news was that the school was functioning and the government had provided four teachers. The chief now wanted a clinic.

By the stream I found the women washing their dishes, bathing their children and filling buckets to take back up to their huts. Jumai, the chief's daughter, told me, 'People are still getting sick from bad water. Most of all we need a borehole for clean water. But we also have fever – malaria. That is the biggest problem.' Eighteen years old, she had just finished six years of secondary school but could go no further because the family could not afford the fees. All she wanted to do was to go to Abuja. Why? 'It has houses, water, light, roads, everything!'

And soon she may be able to go there quite easily. To reach Durumi we had come – mostly in first gear – over a steep hill, down a track of rock and earth, through a ford. We left by a bush path but then, after barely 100 yards, we emerged onto a wide new road in the making. Jumai may soon get to Abuja in minutes, but this road will also bring the squalid shanty town that is spreading fast along the main routes from Abuja. Durumi will be buried and lost within months, part of a sprawling slum growing out of the capital.

Twenty minutes later I was back at the Hilton in Abuja, the mouth for Nigeria's politics of the belly. Streams of Mercedes and smoked-glass four-by-fours sweep up and deposit some of the richest people in the world. Under the shiny copper ceiling in the foyer and in its plush bars, rooms and restaurants, sharp dark suits and gold-threaded robes greet and guffaw, deals are made, plots honed, votes bought, sacks of money handed over, mouths stuffed.

Compare Nigeria with Indonesia, another oil producer which came from a similar economic base. Both suffered dictatorships from the 1960s which both ended in 1998. But when Suharto left power in Indonesia the national output was $221 billion after an average twenty-year growth rate of 7 per cent. Adult literacy in Indonesia was almost 90 per cent and manufacturing represented 40 per cent of exports. When Abacha died Nigeria's output was $33.4 billion after a 2.5 per cent average growth. Adult literacy in Nigeria stood at 60 per cent and non-oil exports were less than 5 per cent. Both were corrupt dictatorships but the difference was that Indonesia's rulers invested in the country and its people. They developed Indonesia and cared about its future, education and health. The Nigerian elite did not believe in Africa. They stole whatever they could and shipped the money out of the country, letting schools, universities and hospitals collapse. In a country awash with oil they did not even keep an oil refinery going and had to import fuel.

Nigeria is now like eighteenth-century Britain, deeply corrupt and with an abyss between classes. The elites, the 'Chosen' as Wole Soyinka, Nigeria's playwright, calls them, are treated as gods by their fawning subjects. Without a hint of irony Nigerians use words like 'elite' and 'breed' to describe their ruling class. The elite – or 'elites' as they are called – own and run Nigeria. You can describe a person as 'an elite', meaning he is a member of this class; he has wealth and power, though not necessarily education.

An elite has a palace in Abuja, another in Lagos and a stupendous mansion on top of the highest hill in his home village. He will have a comfortable detached house in southern England and a flat in New York. These days he may also have a palace in Dubai and a luxury flat in Cape Town. He may keep a different wife in each or at least a mistress and some servants. His money and his children are sent abroad. The money goes to banks in British offshore havens where few questions are asked, the children go to private school in Britain or America. But his most important symbols are his cars and houses, especially the mansion in his village. His first half million dollars will have been spent on a Mercedes Benz and a big house in the village of his ancestors, a demonstration to them and his living relatives that he has become a Big Man. This is also the place where he will be buried. Visit him there and you will sit in a waiting room among relatives and local people who come to beg favours: a loan for school fees, a passport, money for a funeral and, above all, a position. By getting his family into positions in government, he will bolster his power and status. While you are waiting you will be served by maids and servants, relatives from a poor side of the family. They will probably be unpaid and will have been sent to help the Big Man in the hope of hooking onto the money and catching some crumbs from his table.

Dinner with an elite is an unforgettable experience. A car brings me to a house on the edge of Lagos. It is surrounded by a wall higher than the one around Buckingham Palace. Entry is by two immense metal doors, decorated with twisted black ironwork and guarded by armed soldiers. After the security checks the doors swing back and a porter welcomes me into the courtyard containing half a dozen sleek new cars. He indicates a side door of the palace before me. The marbled hallway is the size of a two-storey house, lit by an immense sparkling chandelier. A television the size of a cinema screen dominates a drawing room floored with red and white marble and covered with massive thick-pile white rugs. The windows are draped with heavy gold-tasselled velvet curtains and in the alcoves stand marble plinths with rococo bowls of plastic gold roses. Dinner is about fifteen courses: fish, lamb, shellfish, potatoes, cabbage, beef, more fish, gravy, pumpkin. Served one after the other, each course is piled on top of the last on the same plate, so that just as you are finishing a steak a fish is plonked on top of it.

My host luxuriates in splendour, dressed in a gold-threaded *agbada* and sandals. He is relaxed, informal. A manager of one of his businesses is present but does not speak unless spoken to by the Big Man. When he leaves he bows so low I think he is going to kneel. The Big Man, who distributes oil products, apologizes for being busy that evening. His mobile phone rings every few minutes and he puts it to his ear with a grunt, listens and then says very slowly and calmly, 'Tell them if they go on strike, they will all be sacked. I will shut down the whole business.' A servant comes and tells him that a leader of the strikers has come to negotiate. My host orders the servant to turn the man away, then changes his mind and asks him to wait outside in the courtyard. The man is still waiting when I leave about two hours later.

Individual elites can come unstuck, but only once did a President try to attack them as a class. In the mid 1990s the military dictator, Sani Abacha, took them on head-on. He wanted to show them who was boss and also to make the rest of the world believe he was stamping out corruption. Several Nigerian banks had collapsed because their board members had given themselves loans which they had squandered on new wives, houses, cars, and trips to Europe and America. When they had thoroughly looted the depositors' money, the owners closed the banks. Abacha started arresting the board members.

They were detained at the police station on Victoria Island in Lagos, a pleasant house in its own garden off a tree-lined street. A banker friend invited me to join him when he visited two of the inmates one quiet Sunday afternoon. The contrast with most of Nigeria's jails could not be greater. They are death cells, where hundreds of prisoners are crammed so there is not enough space to sit, let alone lie. They have no toilets or water, and food is thrown into the cells in buckets. They have the highest death rates of any prisons in the world. One of the worst is the Kiri Kiri in Lagos. 'Release, alive, from the Kiri Kiri is rare,' wrote Chris Abani, a poet who was detained there in the 1990s.

This jail has the air of a convalescent home for retired gentlefolk. The thirty-five inmates dress in expensive casual clothes and spend their time sitting under the trees in the walled garden with families and friends. By gentleman's agreement the main gate is left open during the day and the inmates are allowed to pop out to the stall round the corner to buy bottled water, after-shave, shampoo or whatever else they need.

I have come to meet an eminent northern aristocrat, an Alhaji. He is embarrassed by his circumstances but not too discomfited. He has been in 'prison' for three months but bears the suffering stoically. 'I thought I would be here a couple of days but it's dragged on a bit and there's still no sign of going to court.' Police officers come and go at the bidding of the inmates, more like servants than guards. He orders tea for me and we move to some benches under a flowering tree near the gate. 'No-one has yet tried to run away and if anyone is looking itchy and thinks of escape, we have a word with them. We wouldn't want to lose our privileges because someone broke the rules.'

'We are perfectly comfortable here,' says the portly banker complaining that the main problem is boredom. 'We all have radios and there is a colour TV that was once a piece of evidence in a trial that never came to court. Our families provide food. The trouble is that the police realize they are onto a good thing. We have already paid for the septic tank to be repaired and we are doing the water tank on the roof. But now I can see them eyeing the broken generator,' he sighs. 'I'm afraid I will be here until the local police chief puts all his children through school.'

Abacha felt threatened by such rich self-confidence. He was of lowly birth from a minor, widely despised ethnic group and had risen through the army ranks by controlling the intelligence networks. A cold, scowling man, Abacha always wore huge dark glasses. Like many Big Men he was believed to have magical powers. A young university-educated Nigerian told me that Abacha's dark glasses acted like binoculars so he could scrutinize people up close. He thought Abacha might even be able to read your thoughts. With a reputation like that what more did he need to stay in power?

His predecessor, General Ibrahim Babangida, who ruled from 1985 until 1993, used the opposite policy to stay in control. He kept the elites happy. Every politically important Big Man was given a chance to get to the trough and eat. Babangida stayed in power for eight years, promising to return the country to civilian rule. He said he was trying to find a new system of democracy for Nigeria and a new type of Nigerian to run it. He spoke of finding a 'New Breed' of politician, to replace the 'Old Breed', the tribally minded, corrupt and ineffective failures of the past. Of course the Old Breed simply retired to less prominent positions and paid younger men, equally tribally minded, corrupt and ineffective, to pretend they were the New Breed. Politics became a game of complicated ciphers in which you had to know who represented which old network or alliance. In the meantime Babangida kept everyone dancing round him while he pulled the strings, dragging a general or Big Man away from the trough and letting another step forward to eat.

In the end he set up two political parties, one slightly to the right, one slightly to the left, wrote constitutions and manifestos for each, selected their leaders and called it democracy. In 1990 he organized an election, ironically regarded as one of Nigeria's better ones. It was won by Chief Moshood Abiola, but then Babangida panicked. Abiola, a southerner, was not acceptable to the northern lords. At the last moment, after the election but before the result was officially announced, Babangida cancelled it. He tried to set up a civilian administration by decree. But he did not step down as President. A few months later Abacha, his number two, overthrew him and took over.

To the outside world Abacha looked austere and funless. He was not apparently attracted to grotesque accumulation of goods but his bizarre death in 1998 revealed a different side to him. At one time I thought that if I were an African dictator I would salt away a million or so in case I had to take early retirement. I could never understand the scale of theft in places like Nigeria. Then I began to realize that in such places money is power and power is money. That is no different from the rest of the world but it is more naked, more total in Nigeria. Like a lot of dictators Abacha made state funds his own, not to have fun but to buy people. He had to have more money than anyone else to ensure he could outbid anyone for the souls of Nigerians.

Feeding all the elites was expensive. Abacha resorted to awarding bogus contracts to keep them happy. The naira was then at about eighty to the dollar but there was also another rate of twenty-two to the dollar for officially importing essential goods. That required the permission of the President. Once you had been given an import contract with permission to obtain dollars at the lower rate, you hurried off to the Central Bank, obtained your dollars and sold them on the open market. They fetched four times the rate at which you had bought them. With the newly obtained naira, you bribed officials to obtain more dollars and sold them again, quadrupling your money in days. Then when you had done this round trip on the currency a few times, you bought a few second-hand computers or whatever you were supposed to provide, over-invoiced the government and kept the change. You had eaten well.

But Abacha's brutal side made him enemies. He had so many in the end that his death, like *Murder on the Orient Express*, could have been arranged by any number of people. The official version was that he had died of a heart attack. The version put about by Western diplomats was that he died in the arms of an Indian or Lebanese prostitute in a guest house near the presidential palace at Aso Rock in Abuja in the early hours of 8 June 1998. A spiked apple, an overdose of Viagra and various exotic poisons were thrown into the story. There was no autopsy and he was buried the following day in accordance with Islamic custom. People danced in the streets all over Nigeria, even in his home town.

Some of the generals who had served Abacha faithfully through his fifteen years of theft and incompetence decided they could no longer claim to be the guardians of the nation. Under considerable international pressure after Abacha's death, they decided to return the country to civilian rule. It was time for the generals to take a back seat for a while. Many speculated that the soldiers had decided they would allow civilians to rule just long enough to prove yet again that they were incompetent and the soldiers could step back in. Others pointed out that it hardly mattered whether there was an election or not, the elites would still own and run Nigeria.

The coming of democracy in 1999 did not change the Nigerian system: the king is dead, long live whoever-has-got-the-oil-money. Shockingly to outsiders, but not to Nigerians, the new parties that sprang up were stuffed with hangers-on from the military dictatorships. Men who had wished eternal rule on Abacha now proclaimed themselves democrats and stood for election. Policies and principles were non-existent. Politics were about personal alliances. In a desperate gamble to back the right horse, they performed a bewildering dance, merging, splitting, joining, splitting.

Is there no-one outside this dance of the elites? Did anyone oppose military rule? Yes, but you can count them on the fingers of one hand. Here are some of them: General Ishola Williams, a poor retired general who looks like John the Baptist and probably sounds like him to most Nigerians. He worked for Transparency International in Lagos from an office a minicab company would be ashamed of. He is a national joke; a man who had power and position and is poor. Beko Ransome Kuti, a laid-back, chain-smoking human rights lawyer. One brother was the world-famous iconoclastic musician Fela Kuti, another was Babangida's minister of health. Their mother was murdered by soldiers, thrown from a window in a raid on their house. Beko was in and out of jail during the years of military rule, never afraid to take on a case against the soldiers. Another one who stood up to the military junta was Dele Giwa, the editor of *Newswatch* magazine. He was blown to pieces by a parcel bomb delivered to his office by two security men who worked for Babangida.

In most countries these heroes of the resistance would have been swept to power after the collapse of military rule. Not in Nigeria. None of them got anywhere in Nigerian politics. There is no point in voting for a good man. What is the point of that? How can he help you unless he is rich? As Father Kukah said, 'Can you eat democracy?' You vote for a man who can give you a few naira for your vote.

The elites that had joined the People's Democratic Party assembled at Jos in December 1999 to choose a presidential candidate. Jos has been chosen as the venue for the convention because it is Middle Belt, neither north nor south, Muslim nor Christian. It is a pleasant, hilly little town, a former colonial station laid out with avenues of trees and hedges, sensible administration offices, clubby hotels and small villas set in pleasant gardens. Ibrahim Isiaku, who is bankrolling Obasanjo's rival, Alex Ekwueme, has ensconced himself in a chalet at the Plateau Hotel. From here he acts like a gambler who lays bets from a distance but rarely goes to the casino. A flow of runners and messengers keeps him abreast of events while he sits in a plain white robe in a darkened room with CNN blaring but unwatched on the television. His lieutenants supervise the payment of gangs to care for his delegates and protect them from rivals who might try to pay more for their votes.

The town looks like the battleground for a huge game of capturing the flag. We used to play it at school. Two flags, two teams, two bases: the aim is to capture the other team's flag from its base. In the British version you divide your team into attackers and defenders. You run, dodge, hide and try to touch as many of your opponents as possible to capture them. They can be freed only by being touched by one of their own side. The Nigerian version is the same except the flag is the candidacy of the party and you touch people by giving them bags of money. In Jos the delegates are chiefs and village headmen who have been bussed or flown to Jos under close guard. The candidates have paid for their trip and accommodation and some delegates have brought their families with them. The candidates control their supporters by feeding them money and promising them more. But rival candidates try to seek them out and promise even more money to change sides. The challenge is to keep your own supporters corralled and happy, and attack the rival camps.

At the Plateau Hotel, Isiaku's guards are on the gate, keeping out the Obasanjo troops, while their attackers, armed with shopping bags of cash, creep out to the Hill Station Hotel, Obasanjo's camp, trying to probe their defences. Occasionally one is spotted and repulsed by Obasanjo's heavies. The game is afoot.

It swings back and forth for a couple of days: I spot Ekwueme agents near the Obasanjo hotel and vice versa. On the eve of the election Ekwueme's camp is beginning to run out of money. That night a large, well-guarded, heavily laden truck turns up at the Plateau Hotel and backs carefully onto Isiaku's suite. A team of guards hurriedly unload huge cardboard cartons and hump them to Isiaku's rooms. They are stuffed with billions of naira. In Isiaku's rooms the bricks of notes are counted, made up into new bundles, repacked into black plastic bags and handed over to the troops to launch a last raid on the Obasanjo camp.

In the event it isn't enough. Next day the candidates and their entourages take their seats in the stand of the Jos soccer stadium. The delegates are spread out on uncovered benches under a hot sun. Ekwueme and his followers appear to a rousing welcome and he tours the stadium like a conqueror. A sharp-eyed Nigerian journalist points out to me that the serried ranks of northern delegates are only clapping politely. 'He has not given them enough,' he says.

Voting begins eight hours late. Two hours after sundown we are only halfway through. Under arc lights and the roar of generators, voting goes on until 2 a.m. and counting is not complete by dawn. The journalist is right. Isiaku's money has been trumped by Obasanjo's billions. Where did they come from? Obasanjo is not thought to be very rich. Many say from Babangida, adding that he has given money to all the candidates. The northern delegates, a huge bloc who have no candidate from their own area, vote almost unanimously for Obasanjo. Ekwueme is bitterly disappointed but manages to concede defeat with grace. Isiaku is angry. He has lost a truckload.

As the vote begins to go Obasanjo's way, I come across Ekwueme's chief money man surrounded by the members of a band who have played and sung ecstatically for him all night. They are one of those traditional Nigerian bands that play well to start with and then start playing badly, then worse and worse until you have to pay them again to go away. Ekwueme's man is backing away from them holding up his hands but they are in an angry mood. 'More dash or we go play for Obasanjo,' their leader shouts. The bag man picks up his robes and runs for it, hotly pursued by the musicians.

With the legacy of sixteen years of bad military rule, strong international support and a six-fold increase in Nigeria's oil revenues during Obasanjo's eight years as President, it is hard to find exactly how he managed to end his reign as just about the most unpopular man in Nigeria. When he came to power he had all the cards. He could have bought off or charmed opponents, taken easy steps such as providing electricity and clean water. He could have left a legacy of real change, a transformed Nigeria, but Obasanjo left office discredited and disgraced.

One of his reforms reinstated the allocation of oil revenues to the states. Power began to be devolved and aspirant politicians no longer saw their future necessarily at the centre in Abuja. But this does not explain how he lost the trust of Nigerians.

In his first term he deployed a team of old cronies from the 1970s with no idea how to create a modern economy. But in his second term, at the urging of Western countries, Obasanjo appointed a technocratic team to run the economy. Buoyed by the oil price rise, the Nigerian economy began to pick up.

With so much international support and an overflowing pot of largesse to dispense, Obasanjo was well placed to create a new deal for the Delta. He began by trying to suppress revolt there by sending in the army. When soldiers razed the village of Odi killing more than a hundred people, Obasanjo shrugged it off saying that is what soldiers do. Then he tried a more political approach, but the state governors from his own party in the Delta were greedy criminals who stole all the money that might have been used to bring some development. Attacks on oil companies and the kidnapping of foreign oil workers, as well as battles between rival militias for control of oil pipelines that could be tapped, all increased towards the end of the Obasanjo years. It also became clear that while there were elements of real rebellion against years of injustice in the Delta, much of the violence was actually controlled by Big Men and military chiefs. There was growing suspicion that it was they who received the bulk of the kidnap ransom money. The revolution was hijacked by the very people it was originally aimed at.

Internationally Britain and America did not put pressure on Obasanjo. They needed a powerful ally in Africa and Obasanjo provided that, siding with Britain rather than South Africa over Zimbabwe and promoting free market reforms that Western countries urged on the continent.

On corruption and human rights Obasanjo commissioned reports when he came into office. But he never published them. Unwilling to make the thieves accountable to the Nigerian people, he prefered to use the information to blackmail political rivals. 'I keep the reports in the cupboard,' he growled at me in an interview. 'They know what is in them.'

This approach to corruption was confirmed when he appointed the fierce young policeman Nuhu Ribadu to go after stolen money. For a while it seemed that Ribadu could do whatever he wanted. Senior members of the government were summoned for questioning. In time, however, it became clear that although many people were investigated, only those opposed to Obasanjo were brought to account. Meanwhile Obasanjo began to build his family's own fortune. A national development corporation called Transcorp was set up, given billions and awarded concessions and contracts to blandly named Nigerian and offshore companies. Leaked information suggested the ultimate beneficiaries were Obasanjo, his family and a few close cronies. Many suspected it was set up as a war chest to secure him a third term as President.

His falling-out with his deputy Atiku Abubakar and growing unpopularity because of his attempt to run for a third term weakened his ability to choose his successor. His most effective ministers had no political power base and there was no popular support for his free market economic reforms even though, with Nigeria's oil income more than doubling in 2006, economic pressures were off. In his last year in office he suddenly sacked Ngozi Okonjo-Iweala, his finance minister, who had secured a write-off of Nigeria's debt. Was he jealous of her success in winning international approval after he had tried and failed for four years? Or was she just too abrasive in the office?

His greatest political failing was his bad temper and his ability to fall out with friends and demonize enemies. He treated parliament with contempt but under the new constitution it had real teeth. Outraged by his dictatorial tendencies, the people's representatives nearly impeached him. He survived that but as his second term drew to a close, Obasanjo tried to persuade parliament to change the constitution to allow him to run for a third term. Parliament stood firm and blocked him.

Nigeria is one country that Western countries, dependent on oil, cannot afford to bully. They shrug off Nigeria's all-pervasive corruption, happy to talk softly and never waving a big stick. Even when relations were at their lowest during the public outcry following the hanging of Ken Saro-Wiwa, America made it clear they would not impose oil sanctions. To reward Obasanjo for his international support, they lifted the 'burden of debt' from poor Nigeria. In 2006 Britain arranged an $18 billion debt write-off even as Nigeria's oil revenues were beginning to take off.

But what Obasanjo's rule did allow was freedom for a new, younger, entrepreneurial professional class. Mostly the well-connected children of the elites, they are determined to be international business players and that means changing the reputation of Nigeria and Nigerians. Not yet powerful enough to be a political force, they operate increasingly as a like-minded group which might, in time, challenge the ruling political elites. In the meantime they are developing businesses in the non-oil sector that had until recently been a desert created by oil. Maybe all that Nigeria ever needed to be successful was to allow bright people who believed in the country to get on and do business.

Obasanjo's last chance was to leave office gracefully and organize a free and fair election to choose his successor. He picked Umaru Yar'Adua, a Muslim northerner from an old aristocratic family with a relatively clean reputation. There is no evidence that he ever wanted the job. His older brother Shehu Yar'Adua had been a military man and second in command to Obasanjo when he ruled the country in the late 1970s. Umaru rebelled by joining a socialist movement but then left politics and became a university chemistry teacher. When his widely respected brother died in jail in 1997 – almost certainly murdered by the military regime – the quiet-spoken, reclusive Umaru was forced back into politics.

Obasanjo described the vote as a 'do or die election'. The ruling party, the army, local government, the police and secret police collaborated in what must go down as one of the most blatantly stolen elections in the history of democracy. They set about it with brazen vigour, stealing and stuffing ballot boxes, intimidating opposition voters, buying votes and bribing officials. Much of this was in full view of observers and journalists. Only in Lagos and Kano, Nigeria's two biggest cities, did they hold off, fearful of causing a backlash. Both cities voted against the ruling party.

I decide to cover the election for the governorship of Ekiti state north of Lagos, a poor area with high levels of emigration. As the polls open we stop at a polling station where a gang has just stolen one book of ballot papers and filled in another with votes for the ruling party.

Already by 10 a.m. we have heard there has been violence and shooting and we pull up at a village clinic. Two men are being treated for machete wounds. Both members of the opposition Action Party, they had been attacked by officials of Obasanjo's People's Democratic Party. One has a horrible gash in his back. The nurse says he is in trauma.

At our second polling station in front of a line of stalls a few yards off the main road, we find the ballot box has been stolen, and while we are hearing what happened a black BMW comes by. It slows down and as the back window opens, I see a gun barrel sticking out, pointing towards us. When we get up, shaken and scared, and brush the dust off, we find no-one has been hit. The bullets went over our heads. A couple of policemen fire after the car as it accelerates away.

We drive to the small town of Oye where an army truck is blocking the road. Beside it is parked an unmarked silver Toyota but as we approach on foot, it slips away. The soldiers say they have no idea who is in it. But the people in that town are furious, the ballot boxes have been stolen. Our arrival gives them courage and they surround a house and attack it. A few moments later a terrified woman and four men are dragged out and then, with a whoop of triumph, someone comes out carrying the missing ballot boxes. The crowd starts beating the five, kicking them, hitting them with sticks. Some people come running up with head-sized rocks. We are about to witness horrible deaths. At that moment one of the opposition candidates turns up and his bodyguards pull guns from under their agbadas and fire in the air. They wade into the crowd and rescue the five and get them to a car to take them to the police station.

Back at the first polling station we visited, a group of men is now running off with the ballot box. As they see the arrival of foreigners an argument breaks out – presumably between those who don't care and those who think it might not be a good idea to steal ballot boxes in front of foreign observers. The latter group wins and they bring the box back to the polling booth. 'Where were you taking it?' I ask innocently. 'We were taking it for safe-keeping,' comes the defiant reply.

A few calls to other journalists and observers throughout Nigeria establishes that what we have witnessed in Ekiti is widespread if not typical of Nigeria's election day. Obasanjo says nothing – even when urged by his Western friends.

A week later it's the big one, the presidential election. The first signs that this election would be no different from the gubernatorial elections are spotted in Kano on the eve of polling day. Senior officials of the ruling party take over the presidential suite of the Prince Hotel. It happens to be where the journalists are staying and we watch the party agents leaving the hotel carrying bundles of tomorrow's ballot papers.

Next morning at the magnificent arched entrance of the emir of Kano's palace his followers queue in holiday mood, men and women in their finest costumes standing in separate lines in this strict Muslim city. Water and kola nut sellers do a brisk trade in the heat. The emir himself and his family have their own private voting booth inside the palace. Their workers vote openly, proudly holding up their thumb-printed ballots so all can see their allegiance to the opposition All Nigerian People's Party. One election official, Ibrahim Mohammed, says there are no complaints. 'We are going to show that voting can be done in a peaceful and orderly manner here – not like in the south.'

But when we cross into Katsina state, the state governed by Yar'Adua for the past four years, the picture changes. In the beautiful mud-walled village of Yashe we are immediately surrounded by an angry crowd. 'No vote here,' they shout. 'Kwata kwata.' They tell us that as the polling station opened, about forty people drove up led by Abdul Samadu Yussuf, the chairman of the local government area. Among the crowd were policemen and known agents of the ruling People's Democratic Party. They seized the ballot boxes and drove off. The crowd tell us that exactly the same thing had happened in the governorship election last week. We stop at another village further along the road and exactly the same story was repeated. 'Kwata kwata' – not one, not a single person voted.

At the local government offices a few miles down the road Abdul Samadu denies everything. 'I have not left this place. I slept here to make sure distribution went well,' he says. He refuses to come and meet the villagers. 'They should write a written complaint,' he says. When I ask him who might win the election, he replies: 'Yar'Adua. The PDP is the only party here. It is the ruling party.'

We drive on to the local office of the Independent National Electoral Commission where a group of uniformed policemen sit in the shade. Two red Volkswagen Golfs with no number plates are parked outside. Their occupants are three young men in dark glasses and smart jeans who do not greet us. Inside two men in a back room are unloading voting slips from ballot boxes and stuffing them into holdalls. The presiding officer, Yakubu Ahmed, says, 'We are getting good results.' He admits that only 60 per cent of the presidential ballots had arrived. 'But it doesn't matter,' he says, 'because only about half of the people vote.' And the ballots being removed in the back room? 'They are last week's – to make room for today's.'

In the late afternoon, we call colleagues scattered across Nigeria. The picture is consistent: ballot boxes being stolen, people being chased away from polling stations by ruling party thugs, and stolen ballot boxes being stuffed. All with the complicity of the election commission, the army, police and local officials. The reports are so similar that it is hard not to believe that the rigging exercise was centrally controlled with Obasanjo's approval.

We head east into Jigawa state then south back towards Kano. At Dambarta we find the road blocked by a barricade of flaming tyres. Here we are: three white journalists, a northern Nigerian election observer and a southern Nigerian driver. The driver wants to turn back. The observer says we will be OK. 'Just keep moving slowly,' he says. We push into the angry crowd and are surrounded by young men waving machetes and iron bars. They hammer furiously on the roof of the car shouting: 'Kwata kwata – not one person has voted here.' The car stalls with a jerk. We try to smile and wave as the terrified driver restarts the engine and edges forward again. But when I see their eyes I know we are going to be safe. 'We are angry,' is their message, 'but not with you. We want to show you just how angry we are, but we will not harm you.'

I wonder if a couple of black people would be as safe if they drove into an angry white crowd in Europe or America. There is still humanity in Nigeria.

After the election the losers head to the courts. The ruling party admit that they have probably overdone it in the gubernatorial elections and offer to give some seats to the opposition. The courts turn down appeals in the presidential election. I had expected Nigeria to explode but on the day of the announcement there is silence. A week later there is still no sound. When I visit Nigeria eight months later I ask some young Nigerian businessmen what happened.

'What happened about what?' replies one, a former campaigner for good governance, now a businessman.

'About the election.'

'Oh that. Nothing really – the guy who won isn't so bad and we have more important things to worry about now – like making money.'

President Umaru Yar'Adua died of kidney disease in 2010 after a long absence from the country while he was in hospital in Saudi Arabia. His deputy, Chief Goodluck Jonathan, had looked like a token representative from the Niger Delta who would soon be swept aside by the northern power-brokers. But with the death of the President he cautiously slipped onto the throne and then used his newly acquired position and resources to secure his nomination as PDP candidate.

In what has been described as Nigeria's best election – a relative term – Jonathan defeated the former general, Muhammadu Buhari. Suddenly power – political, and therefore economic as well – seemed to be slipping away from the North, which had controlled Nigeria pretty much since independence. The PDP, which had been a national coalition of 'elites', looked like being captured by southerners. And to compound the misery of the North, a new Islamic movement, Boko Haram, emerged and used terror tactics such as car bombings to sow fear and mistrust in the North. The government tried using the full force of the army to suppress it. The army used the only tactics it knows – killing or beating up people, destroying homes and looting property. The Nigerian army has probably been Boko Haram's best recruiting tool, assuming that militant absolutist Islam will grow. Meanwhile, the South, led by Lagos, is surging ahead. Nigeria may not split but it could become two different worlds as divided as it was at independence in 1960.

17

Ethiopia
A Very Different World

In Ethiopia you can find yourself wondering not just where you are but which millennium you are in. Ethiopians do things their way and many of their ways date back to times when we in Europe were tribal, living in mud huts and Ethiopia was already a proud kingdom. Indeed, it has a good claim to being the world's oldest nation state and to having a Christian tradition that predates most of Europe.

Go to a service in one of the Ethiopian Orthodox churches and you will see priests dressed in gorgeous red and gold robes, wearing beautiful crowns and carrying crosses of silver and gold. In a hypnotic wailing chant they read from bulky goatskin-bound Bibles, handwritten in Ge'ez, an ancient language with its own script now used only in church. I went to a three-hour Eucharist in one of the rock-hewn churches at Lalibela. The congregation, young and old, women on the left, men on the right, are wrapped in thick white cotton shawls. They lean on prayer sticks – there are no seats – or sit or lie on the floor. All are barefoot, shoes left at the door. Silver bells are rung as the chant rises and falls and incense pours from the swinging thuribles and floats gently into the dark recesses of the domes. You feel you have just stumbled into a scene from the Old Testament.

You have.

At the city of Aksum next to a huge church built in the 1960s there stands a small simple classical-style building. Here, I am told by my young university student guide, lies the Ark of the Covenant. 'What?' I blink. 'You mean the chest containing the tablets of stone given by God to Moses on Mount Ararat?'

'Yes. It's in there.'

'Can I see it?'

'No. It is kept by a monk who lives there permanently. He is pledged to stay in the building until his death. When he dies another will take his place.'

Along with Babylon, Egypt, the Greek world and the Roman Empire, Aksum, the Ethiopian state that existed in the second and first millennia BC, was one of the great early polities of the world. The Aksumite kingdom, perched up in the mountains but trading through the port of Adulis on the Red Sea, grew rich on the export of ivory to Egypt and beyond to the West and to India in the East, perhaps as far as China. It had an embassy in Constantinople, sent emissaries to other Mediterranean states, and became Christian in about 340 AD.

Possessing literacy from those early times but with no Reformation to modernize its religious beliefs and practice, Ethiopia was ruled until 1974 by a line of emperors who claimed to be descended from King Solomon. The beginnings of Ethiopia's royal story are told in the fourteenth-century history book called the *Kebra Negast*, or *The Glory of the Kings*. As with all Ethiopian history, the story is personal and precise. The Queen of Sheba, Negesta Saaba, travelled from Ethiopia to visit King Solomon in Israel. He asked her to a banquet and invited her to stay the night in his palace but she made him promise that he would not force her to have sex with him. In turn he made her promise that she would take nothing from his house. She agreed. But he put so much salt in her food that in the night she woke with a terrible thirst and reached for a cup of water thereby breaking her promise and absolving him from his. The result is the history of Ethiopia: nine months later she gave birth to a son, Menelik, from whom all Ethiopian kings and emperors are said to be descended. Later the young King Menelik went to Israel to visit his father, Solomon, who gave him the original Tabot, the tablets of stone bearing the Ten Commandments. Solomon told him to take them to Ethiopia for safekeeping. And they have been kept in Aksum ever since.

Wherever you go in Ethiopia you will hear further wonderful tales of divine intervention. Every mountain and village seems to have had a visitation from a well-known archangel or saint or, occasionally, a spectacular devil, whose appearance will be marked by a great annual celebration. The ubiquitous round churches are decorated with vivid and colourful wall paintings depicting biblical and local tales of miracles and divine apparitions. Here is the Archangel Michael striking down a devil on that rock – yes, that one over there – and throwing his body into that ravine down there. Over here is St George rescuing a young queen. And there is a holy snake helping a local saint to climb that sheer cliff face up there. All are painted in the same lively style in bright colours whether they were painted 1500 years ago or last week. These ancient stories and their annual ceremonies are not performed to charm tourists.

My guide told me the story of the Queen of Sheba as if he had seen it happen last week. You do not hear: 'the story goes that...' or 'history has it...' These spectacular stories are set in Ethiopia's vast landscape of high plateaux, deep gorges, lakes like inland seas and gargantuan, fantastically shaped mountains. Ethiopia is like *Raiders of the Lost Ark* meets *Lord of the Rings*. The only word for Ethiopian history is epic.

Ethiopia can also make a good case for being the birthplace of humankind. The museum in Addis Ababa contains the fossil skeleton of Lucy, the early hominid who lived 3.2 million years ago in the Rift Valley. She is the size of a modern eight-year-old, slightly stooping, with a large head and long arms and hands. And around her in the national museum are other fossilized bones of hominids, prototypes of us all. The first workshop is there too. Mankind's oldest tools are found in Ethiopia, made some 200,000 years ago. The level fertile floor of the Rift Valley, with its lakes and open plains between the crazy mountain ranges, feels like an appropriate nursery for our beginnings.

At Yeha in the mountains of Tigray a large building, possibly a palace, is estimated to have been constructed more than 2500 years ago. It is currently being excavated by German archaeologists. It could demonstrate that the Ethiopian state is even older than we thought. Nearby on a hillside above a plain of cornfields is a square tower built with blocks of stone the size of a large fridge. No one knows how these rocks were cut and laid so precisely. They look as if they were cut by machine yesterday and laid in perfect symmetry with the help of a theodolite. Professor David Phillipson, an archaeologist and leading historian of ancient Ethiopia, thinks that beneath an ancient church nearby may lie another even larger building. He bemoans the 'lamentably incomplete' nature of our knowledge of the area but while it was once thought that these buildings were erected by colonizers from southern Arabia, the evidence increasingly suggests that, although the architecture of Yeha may have been influenced by styles prevalent on the other side of the Red Sea, there was no change in the language or culture. The buildings at Yeha are Ethiopian constructions. Certainly the successor state of Aksum was completely indigenous. The language on its coinage is Ge'ez.

Thirty miles away and some 800 years later in the first century AD, the city of Aksum became the capital of a state that ruled the southern coast of the Red Sea for some 700 years and traded with places as far flung as Constantinople and India. The dead kings of the Aksum kingdom were commemorated with massive stone steles like spires set in the ground, many of which still survive, their stonework almost as sharp as the day they were erected. The largest weighs 520 tonnes and would have stood 33 metres high had it not fallen and broken shortly after it was erected. Today you can clamber over it and walk under the vast pieces. Beneath the steles are beautifully carved stairs and corridors leading to the royal tombs, great slabs of neatly cut stone. Nearby are the remains of a substantial palace and further off a small city which has no defensive walls. The people of Aksum did not fear invasion.

Although the story of the Queen of Sheba, recounted above, serves to bind Ethiopia to ancient Israel and give divine legitimacy to the succession of its kings, Ethiopia became Christian in about AD 330. Once again, the story of this conversion is told a personal way: Frumentius, a young man from Tyre, then in the Roman Empire, was captured by the Ethiopian king, Ezana, who made him his secretary and treasurer. Frumentius converted Ezana to his religion, Christianity. The link established however was not to Rome but to the Coptic Church in Egypt. Until recently the head of the Ethiopian Church was always appointed by the Coptic Pope in Alexandria. But there is an even more important link with Egypt: water. Egypt depends on the river Nile, and 80 per cent of the water that reaches Egypt comes from the Blue Nile, which rises in the Ethiopian Highlands. Hence Egypt's deep concern about Ethiopia building dams on the Nile: without the river's annual flood from those highlands, Egypt would be desert.

In the sixth century AD Islam spread across North Africa from Arabia and cut Ethiopia off from the rest of the Christian world. Having spread westwards to Morocco, northwards to Constantinople and Persia, and eastwards to India and beyond, Islam left Ethiopia a mountainous island of Christianity. However the Muslims never tried to conquer Ethiopia. The Prophet Mohammed had praised Christian Ethiopia for giving refuge to his persecuted followers when they fled from Arabia across the Red Sea, and since then the guiding rule in the Islamic world has been not to attack Christian Ethiopia unless it attacks Islam. Ethiopia continued to trade but lost its port on the Red Sea and retreated into the mountains, whose steep escarpments on all sides turned the country into a fortress. The Arab world also blocked European access and influence, so Ethiopia's culture and development remained static for almost a thousand years. Although its existence was vaguely remembered in medieval and renaissance Europe, Ethiopia lost contact with Europe until the fifteenth century. It was largely ignored by the Ottoman Empire too, so for centuries it retained its own culture and religions, embracing in various forms the Judaic, Christian and Islamic traditions. To this day it maintains its own calendar, seven years behind the western one and with thirteen months in the year. Today the country hosts the African Union and other pan-African organizations – a legacy of Haile Selassie's pan-African ambitions. But just how 'African' is Ethiopia? After a trip to Addis Ababa for an African Union meeting a Nigerian friend of mine told me that he was asked three times why there were so many Africans in Addis that week. Ethiopia belongs only to itself. It just happens to be in Africa.

On the steep climb to the Asheton Maryam monastery above Lalibela I pass a barefooted ploughman wrapped in a white shawl and guiding two oxen with a whip. The plough has a wooden share and its parts are tied together with sisal rope. Like all the churches of Lalibela, the monastery church is carved out of the rock. It is not built from blocks of stone, it is excavated, the rock cut away, leaving a church with doors, floors, window frames, arches, niches and walls.

You step out of the dark, smooth rock and into a vast landscape, with ranges of spectacular mountains in all directions. It was here, I am told, that King Lalibela stood when a rainbow formed and he decided to build his new capital where it touched the earth.

When we get to the top a village meeting is taking place in a mud and wattle shed held up by rough-hewn tree trunks. About 70 men and women – no children – sit separately on crudely cut planks kept about three inches off the earth floor by flat stones. They are discussing matters like crop prices and marriages. Most marriages are arranged by parents here. It is the day before Lent starts, so there is millet beer, served in plastic mugs from great plastic barrels. It has a pleasant earthy taste. I look around. The pottery plates are locally made, so are their Sunday outfits. What little furniture there is is also local. I cannot see anything apart from the plastic mugs that would not have existed here in the same form a thousand, two thousand, possibly five thousand years ago. The conversation has probably not changed much either.

In contrast to the rest of Africa, Ethiopian rulers are always referred to as Kings or Rases, nobles rather than chiefs, and ethnic groups are called nations, not tribes. The three big ethnic groups of Ethiopia, the Oromos, the Amharas and the Tigrayans, occupy the mountain heartland of Ethiopia, while the east is inhabited by Somalis and the north by their cousins, the Afars. In the west are Arabic-speaking northern Sudanese, while the south, conquered in the nineteenth century, is largely black African and was traditionally the source of slaves and ivory. Until recently, southerners were commonly referred to as *Abbayid* – slaves.

Ethiopian history is rich in dynastic feuds and family intrigues. Droughts and devastating wars frequently destroyed huge areas of the country, which was ruled by a series of dynastic emperors, the Negus, the King of Kings. But maintaining that position was not easy. The Emperor could only hold the country together by travelling with a substantial army and constantly collecting taxes from the local lords, the Rases, for whom victory and glory in battle was the meaning of life. Rebellions were common but the distances were so vast and travelling so difficult that as soon as one rebellion was suppressed, another would break out. The Rases seem to have fought continually with each other too. Most of the Ethiopian population consisted of either peasants or soldiers.

By the nineteenth century some Rases realized it was safer to control the Negus than to be the Negus, so the title was left to a weak Ras. But whenever there was a real crisis a King of Kings seemed to emerge and prevent complete collapse.

The isolation of Ethiopia has contributed to its self-sufficiency and self-confidence, but outsiders have played a crucial role at key moments. Frumentius brought Christianity to the country and, according to tradition, it was spread by the Seven Saints, a group of non-Ethiopians who performed miracles and converted the entire region to Christianity.

In Europe a story was recounted of a lost Christian kingdom in Africa ruled by 'Prester John' – a priest called John. No one knew whether it was true or merely a medieval romance, but eventually a Portuguese explorer, Pêro da Covilhã, disguised as a Muslim traveller, reached Ethiopia in 1493. The story of a lost Christian kingdom turned out to be true-ish, and da Covilhã stayed on and became a mentor to other delegations that found their way there from Europe. The only other non-Ethiopians were individual Arabs, Portuguese or Indians and the odd Briton or Frenchman who brought skills in metalwork or stonework that emperors valued, such as building or weapon making. Their stylistic additions can be seen in the ancient rock churches at Lalibela and the magnificent medieval castles of Gondar built from the middle of the seventeenth century.

The Ethiopians welcomed these outsiders' knowledge of the wider world but were not interested in other versions of Christianity. After all, if you have possession of the Tabot, you don't expect foreign guests to come and accuse you of heresy. Nor did the Roman Catholics or, later, the Protestants respect the Ethiopian Church, sending missionaries to 'convert' the benighted Ethiopians. The main dispute concerned whether Jesus Christ had a dual or a single nature, the Egyptian school of Alexandria believing that Jesus Christ had only a divine nature and the school of Antioch, from which western Christian belief is derived, believing that Jesus Christ was God and Man, two natures. Welcomed at first, the missionaries ended up being rebuffed when they tried to lure Ethiopians away from their traditions and their understanding of Christianity. Some European missionaries were executed but their successors were not turned away as the Ethiopians still wanted European technology, especially for firearms. They also wanted mutual diplomatic contact. The Europeans would offer them the first of these but not the second.

That refusal to allow diplomatic contact with Europe led to catastrophe in the mid-nineteenth century. The emperor at the time, Tewodros, had been a modernising monarch, introducing reforms and welcoming western education. But as a monarch – indeed, as King of Kings – he naturally wanted a relationship of equality with the British monarch, Queen Victoria. The British could not comprehend an African monarch who felt he could treat the Great White Queen of England as an equal. Tewodros wrote copious elegant letters to Queen Victoria but she did not reply. Somehow he could not get her attention. So he detained several Britons who were working for him building a mighty mortar gun. Relations worsened and, after much diplomatic toing and froing, Britain assembled an army in India and moved it westwards up the Red Sea. The ships carrying the soliders landed at Masawa in early 1868. At every step diplomatic channels were kept open but Tewodros still did not receive the respect he felt he deserved. The British were still demanding the release of the 'hostages', as they called them (Tewodros called them 'guests'), so the 32,000-strong British army began its ascent into the mountains. Many of the Emperor's local rivals joined the invaders. In early April the enhanced army neared the magnificent mountain fortress of Magdala. Tewodros tried to negotiate, challenging the British general, Sir Robert Napier, to a duel to settle the matter. He was turned down. Then, finally, Tewodros released the 'guests'. Too late. Having assembled such a large and expensive army, sailed it all the way from India, and then marched it all the way up the hill, the British had to have a battle. The tax payer back home would not have understood if its army had left without a fight.

The battle of Magdala was a ghastly massacre. The Ethiopians' huge mortar gun failed to work and they were defeated in hours. It was a bloodbath. The fortress was destroyed. The treasures of Magdala, including religious objects of gold and silver and a huge library with several thousand books, were looted or trashed. At the height of the slaughter Tewodros committed suicide. The British army then marched down the mountain and sailed back to India. Britain had no interest in Ethiopia. It was still just too far away and difficult to reach to be brought into the mainstream European or Middle Eastern worlds.

But the following year, 1869, a more world-changing event took place. The Suez Canal opened. Suddenly the route to India was shortened by thousands of miles. Coupled with the development of better, faster steam vessels, this meant that global trade was about to increase enormously. The Red Sea became a major thoroughfare, particularly for the British, for whom India was its key overseas possession. Its old rivalry with France for global domination came to a head again. Britain promptly bought the shares in the canal from the

Egyptian ruler, the Khedive, and took over control of Suez. To rule the Red Sea they had earlier taken the port of Aden on the south coast of Arabia, and towards the end of the nineteenth century the French – Britain's main global rival – took Djibouti on the north coast of Africa.

After Magdala Ethiopia was in chaos. Although the British had left the country, it faced invaders on all its borders. The immediate threat came not from the north but from the west. Here the Ansar, the Islamist Mahdi movement in Sudan, was attacking in the south-west. In the north-east the Egyptians seized Harar, an important trading town, and the Italians had started encroaching from the Red Sea. And there was famine in Tigray.

This might have been the moment when Ethiopia was carved up, but the attacks had the opposite effect and unified the country. A new emperor, Johannes IV, decided to deal with the Mahdist threat from Sudan. He led his army there, but at Metemma on the border with Sudan in March 1889 the Ethiopians were defeated and Johannes was killed. In his place the King of Shoa, Menelik, emerged as the nation's leader, supported by the powerful Ras Alula, an effective military commander.

The Ansar sacked Gondar and destroyed all but one of its churches but then withdrew to Sudan again. That left Menelik free to deal with the Italians who had bought the Red Sea port of Assab and begun to move up the escarpment into Ethiopia. Italy had the support of the British in this, duplicitous as it was, as they were supposed to be allies of Menelik. But they were happy for the Italians, latecomers in the scramble for Africa, to create a base in the Red Sea – at least they weren't the French.

At first the Italians made a treaty with Ethiopia, which gave them a 'protectorate' over Eritrea and the coastline. However its wording also included a phrase which the Ethiopians interpreted as giving them the option of using the Italians as a channel of communication to other European powers. The Italians claimed the phrase obliged Ethiopia to deal exclusively with Italy in its relations with other European countries, which made the whole of Ethiopia a virtual protectorate. When Menelik repudiated the Italians' interpretation, Italy saw a reason for war and claimed overlordship of the whole country.

Despite Emperor Menelik's attempts at diplomacy, the Italians invaded. Menelik therefore realized he would have to fight and assembled an army estimated by the Italians to be 50,000 strong. The Italians for their part had 9000 troops and 11,000 Eritrean and Ethiopian soldiers who opposed Menelik. They met at Adowa on 1 March 1896. Ethiopia's fate lay in the balance that day. Defeat would have meant its colonization. Unlike many other African states, Ethiopia had some of the latest European weaponry. Both sides had repeater rifles and artillery but the Ethiopian tactics were less sophisticated. It was a fearsome close-range, chaotic battle, one of the last to be lost and won in a day. The Ethiopians won comprehensively. Some 7000 Italians were killed and 2000 captured. All their military equipment was lost.

It was Ethiopia's Waterloo, its proudest moment, and it changed what had seemed to be the inevitable course of history. To this day Ethiopians know and feel their history and have a self-confidence that is often lacking in other African countries even after they gained independence. However, Eritrea, a large area of Ethiopia, remained under Italian control and as a result took a different trajectory.

Ethiopia was fortunate too in Haile Selassie, the third emperor after Menelik. A small man of great presence, he was a cautious modernizer though no democrat. He established good relations with America and Britain and became a key ally. However, fascist Italy had ambitions in the Horn of Africa and in 1936 launched a full-scale invasion of Ethiopia. This was revenge for Adowa. Haile Selassie left, but a resistance movement immediately fought back against the Italians, helped by Britain, which sent in troops to assist the Ethiopians when Italy entered the Second World War on Germany's side in 1940. The Italians were defeated and surrendered in Ethiopia in November 1941.

Like their historic forerunners the Romans, the Italians' rule was brutal but their legacy was mixed. They unified the country by building roads and water supplies for Addis Ababa and other towns, but they also left a problem for the Eritreans. Eritrea had been an Italian colony from 1890 to 1947 and, although the highland Eritreans are of the same religion and ethnicity as the Tigrayans, they saw themselves as separate – even superior. Lowland Eritrea is inhabited by Muslims, many of whom settled there from the Middle East. But decades of colonization by the Italians gave Eritreans better education, so that they often became professionals, shopkeepers or traders.

The Italians had invested heavily in Eritrea and by 1942 most of Ethiopia's industry and skilled manpower was concentrated there. Asmara, the capital, was a far more sophisticated city than Addis Ababa, and Eritreans also had a different political outlook.

But at the end of the Second World War, the question was whether Eritrea was to be part of Ethiopia or independent. After all, the boundary was an artificial colonial one and all Ethiopia's trading routes to the rest of the world passed through Eritrea at that time. After much political debate between the British, the Americans and the Ethiopians, it was agreed that Eritrea should be 'an autonomous state federated with Ethiopia'. It did not take long for Ethiopia under Haile Selassie to whittle away its autonomy and forcibly integrate it into Ethiopia. That resulted in the twentieth century's longest war, a 30-year struggle for Eritrean independence.

The British left Ethiopia at the end of the Second World War, and their parting recommendation was that the Ogaden, the lowlands to the east of Ethiopia, should be joined with Somalia and Somaliland since they were largely occupied by Somalis. This recommendation was overruled by the Americans, and to this day the Ogaden has been a problem because most of its people are Somali, so that it is regarded by most Somalis as part of Somalia.

As Haile Selassie grew old he kept his age group in power with him, frustrating the younger, better-educated generation. The new post–World War II generation that had gone through university resented the power of the ruling class and the Rases. In 1973 famine struck in Wollo and other northern areas but it was ignored by Haile Selassie and his government. That led to student protests and demands for a socialist revolution.

The following year a young major, Mengistu Haile Mariam, mounted a coup and deposed the Emperor. He detained him and then had the 84-year-old smothered to death and his body buried secretly. Mengistu's military government was called the Derg, and it consisted of a group of army officers and young communists who believed in state control of the economy. The Soviet Union and Cuba supported him and that ensured he would not be overthrown by a coup as long as he had their support. Although he abolished the feudal power of the aristocracy and nationalized all land, he also destroyed the administration system. So when he tried to turn Ethiopia into a communist state, there simply wasn't the capacity to effect any changes. The army became the instrument of government, tearing down the peasants' scattered homesteads and brutally forcing them into newly created villages with neat rows of huts, away from their fields, now collectivized. They were also paid low prices and taxed heavily. Promises of schools and clinics did not materialize. Production slumped.

Soon after Mengistu came to power radical Tigrayan students at Addis Ababa University founded the Tigrayan People's Liberation

Front (TPLF). Also Marxist Leninist, its supporters wanted a different sort of socialism, not one imposed by ideologues in Moscow or Havana. Their modest aim was to gain more autonomy for Tigray. Meanwhile, in the neighbouring mountains, the Eritrean People's Liberation Front (EPLF) had emerged as the main movement fighting for Eritrean independence. Relations between the movements were not easy, but they needed each other if they were to topple the Derg. It would be a long struggle.

In 1984, two years of drought and the deepening civil war created one of the worst famines in living memory. It was ignored by the government and the rest of the world until on 23 October the BBC Nine O'Clock News led with Michael Buerk's clear, solemn voice: 'Dawn, and as the sun breaks through the piercing chill of night on the plain outside Korem it lights up a biblical famine – now, in the twentieth century.' The pictures of skeletal figures and pot-bellied children at the overwhelmed feeding centre in Korem shocked everyone. As Mohammed Amin's camera showed slow frail fingers picking up grains of wheat one by one, Buerk described how someone, usually a child, was dying every 20 minutes. Nothing had been seen like this since the Biafran war in 1971, but back then the impact was from photographs. Now television pictures, transmitted on the same day, had a far greater impact. Thousands had already died, said Buerk, and the lives of seven million were threatened.

Although Buerk mentioned the war as a complicating factor, the immediate spotlight fell on the aid agencies, Oxfam, Save the Children and others, rather than the politicans or diplomats. Immediately money poured in from the public but the aid agencies admitted helplessness in the face of such a catastrophe. What was needed was for the big UN agencies to move – fast. But the catastrophe looked too far advanced for anyone to do anything meaningful. Suddenly a tall, straggle-haired, highly articulate if occasionally foul-mouthed Irish rock singer called Bob Geldof appeared on the scene. Why, he asked, weren't the United Nations, western governments and others doing something? He expressed the pain and anger that such pictures had elicited around the world. Somehow his rage – including his persistent and unapologetic swearing – felt entirely appropriate. Why indeed wasn't anything been done? Geldof called his friends in the music business and organized a 24-hour rolling rock concert broadcast live all round the world where the performers played for free and the public pledged money.

That put pressure on the politicians, who found more aid and shook up their development agencies. Getting food to starving people was hard enough in itself, but it was also necessary to get the world to understand the deeper causes of the famine. When attempts were made to explain the cause of the war – two Marxist liberation rebel armies fighting a Marxist government – it all became too bizarre and complicated to make sense of. But the concerts were great and the movement inspired a whole generation of people to give money to save starving Ethiopians. Churches, schools, community groups raised funds. It changed a generation. Ask anyone working in the development business today who saw those reports and they will say that it was the Ethiopian famine and Geldof's Band Aid that first inspired them.

The downside of the TV footage of Ethiopia at this time was that it associated Africa with famine and failure. Ethiopia – and Africa as a whole – became the image of a starving, pot-bellied child with stick-thin arms and legs, an image it has taken years to shrug off. Famine caused by war in Ethiopia and elsewhere in Africa began to create layer on layer of images portraying the entire continent as a place of hunger, failure and hopelessness. Aid agencies saw the power that images of starvation had in terms of fundraising and exploited them ruthlessly. Journalists also played their part, bending the rules of objectivity to manipulate images and scenes in the belief that this was in a good cause. Soon after the Ethiopian famine I watched a cameraman in Somalia picking out the most starved-looking children he could find to gather them into a single camera shot. That was in Baidoa. After I left the camp I walked up the main street where people were shopping and meeting friends and going about their business as normal. The cameraman didn't film the shopping street as it would have complicated the simple message of starvation he wanted to convey.

In Ethiopia in 1984 there was little analysis of what had turned one of Ethiopia's usual periodic tough times into a catastrophe: bad politics and war. There had been famines before in the Ethiopian highlands. Over the centuries the country's kings and Rases had periodically created them by putting together large armies to wage war which also consumed vast quantities of food without payment, as well as requisitioning animals and forcibly recruiting young men into their armies. The Ethiopian peasants were used to very hard times, but over millennia they had developed ways of mitigating and surviving them.

In the years leading up to the famine in the mid-1980s, the rebellions in the north had spread, and the army had become increasingly brutal in dealing with the insurgents. Between 1980 and 1985 the Ethiopian army launched three massive attacks into Tigray to try to dislodge the TPLF. The government forcibly resettled thousands of self-sufficient peasants, tearing down their homes and putting them on trucks to take them to resettlement villages in the south or even flying them in aeroplanes and resettling them in the lowlands, where they often died of tropical diseases unknown in the highlands. Western aid agencies such as Oxfam supported these forced removals. I recently met one family near Mekele that had been forcibly removed and taken south to the lowlands around Gambela and given land. They told me that the old women and children were left in the camps while the men and younger women had walked across the border into Sudan. There they had joined the TPLF and gone back into Ethiopia as fighters. Other resettled families made their own way back home, walking hundreds of miles back to the mountains.

My notebooks from Ethiopia at this time are full of endless interviews with aid workers and rows of figures detailing numbers of deaths, bags of food aid distributed and plans to eradicate famine and bring development. In fact the cause of the mid-1980s catastrophe was simple: war had turned food shortages into famine.

I regret never making the month-long journey from Sudan into the mountains to observe the Eritrean and Tigrayan wars in the 1980s first-hand. Those who did came back with astonishing tales of tank battles and massed armies attacking each other from lines of trenches. The Tigrayan People's Liberation Front had entered the war in 1975, helped by the Eritreans who had already been fighting for 14 years. There were reports of the extraordinary ingenuity, creativity and solidarity of the EPLF and TPLF, determined as they were to keep their armies operational, their efforts supported willingly by hard-pressed civilian populations.

The closest I got to the war until I witnessed the arrival of the TPLF in Addis Ababa in 1991 was when I was at the military airport outside Addis Ababa in 1987. The civilian airport was closed because the runway had become badly eroded by the hundreds of food-aid flights landing and taking off from there. Instead, all airlines had to use the military airport at Debre Zeit some 26 miles away. We were ushered off a bus into the passenger departure lounge that was actually the air force pilots' mess. While we waited for our flight to Djibouti I watched the laden MiG fighter aircraft take off and then return one hour later, refuel and rearm with rockets and napalm, as

I was told by a civilian pilot, before taking off again. While they were waiting for their aircraft to be restocked, the air force pilots sat in front of a TV drinking coffee and watching endless episodes of Benny Hill, the buffoonish British comedian. It seemed a bizarre way to relax between trips to drop napalm on helpless villagers.

By the late 1980s the hostilities in Tigray and Eritrea had ceased to be hit-and-run guerrilla warfare and had turned into full-scale conventional wars that were also a regional proxy war on behalf of Sudan and Ethiopia. Sudan helped the Eritrean and Ethiopian rebels, and in retaliation Ethiopia backed the Sudan People's Liberation Army rebellion in south Sudan.

In Ethiopia the Eritrean and Tigrayan rebels had also captured sufficient artillery and tanks as well as anti-aircraft guns to hold their territory, dig deep trenches and take on the army head to head. By the end of 1990 the government's presence in the north was limited to a few garrison towns and the rebels began to push south.

The war was barely reported in Khartoum or Addis Ababa although there were frequent, though unreported, funerals of soldier sons. The rest of the world largely ignored it. Unlike other African liberation movements, the EPLF and TPLF had no western backers and only very small groups of supporters or sympathizers in the West. Meles Zenawi, leader of the TPLF, had said in 1989 that his model was Albania, so he and the TPLF were regarded by most of the western world as so far to the left as to be laughable. What he had actually meant by that was that unlike other Communist regimes, the Albanians were autonomous, not under the control of the Soviet Union or China. But he was so out of touch in the mountains in Tigray that he did not know that in the West the Albanians were regarded as beyond the lunatic fringe of Socialism. This cost the TPLF considerable support from those with influence in Europe and America.

In a sense Ethiopia was to Russia what Vietnam had been to the USA. The Soviet Union and Cuba had backed the Mengistu regime with billions of roubles and when the Soviet Union collapsed, the leader of the Derg lost his global allies. The fact that the rebels were also Marxist Leninist organizations made the war all the more bizarre and ideologically meaningless.

With the end of the Soviet Union, the Derg's main backer, the seemingly endless supply of munitions for Mengistu dried up. He then turned initially to Israel which, at the time, was constantly look-ing for non-Arab African states as allies in its battle for Palestine. Mengistu wanted money and guns, and in return the Israelis wanted the Falashas – Ethiopians who follow the ancient Jewish religious practices. They bought them for millions of dollars and packed them into charter flights to take them to Israel. The Israelis also provided weapons for Mengistu and offered to build dams on the Nile in Ethiopia.

In November 1989, a month after the fall of the Berlin Wall, I was invited to meet a senior representative of the Tigrayan People's Liberation Front in its dingy offices in Stockwell, South London. The breakthrough had been made and the government forces driven out of Tigray. The Eritrean fighters were gearing up to attack Massawa, the country's main port. At the heart of the TPLF was the Marxist Leninist League of Tigray, a group of radical students at Addis Ababa University who had supported the overthrow of the Emperor in 1974 but had then seen the revolution hijacked by Mengistu Haile Mariam. When Mengistu instituted the Red Terror – the annihilation of anyone who questioned him – Meles and his Tigrayan group decided to follow Mao Tse Tung's example and go back to the rural areas to build a peasant army and make the long march back to the capital. They slipped out of Addis and headed north to the mountains of Tigray to begin a guerrilla war. Their allies, the Eritrean rebels, had been fighting for 26 years at that stage. Now – in 1989 – they were about to return to Addis Ababa – in tanks.

Their leader, Meles Zenawi, had come to London to explain their plans and policies. A stocky, neatly bearded, soft-spoken man with an easy manner and chuckle, Meles bore a startling resemblance to Lenin. I found myself having one of the most interesting if perplexing conversations I have ever had. For a revolutionary guerrilla who had just come down from the Tigrayan mountains to visit Stockwell, he was remarkably self-deprecating, more student than Stalin. But the laid-back style masked a razor sharp mind and the ruthless confidence of one who knows history is on his side. Between raids and battles in the mountains he and his companions had held seminars in which they honed their debating skills. There were few clichés. He did not rant. He explained, clearly. We got through a whole packet of Benson and Hedges – his – during the interview.

Meles and his companions had vanished into the mountains and built a movement among the peasants of Tigray which, they hoped, would become strong enough to demand some autonomy for Tigray and space to create a real socialism. The government would control the economy at its highest level, but the peasants would be allowed to make their own decisions and all cooperatives and collectives would be voluntary.

In early 1991 the TPLF and their allies, the Eritrean People's Liberation Front, were only 90 miles from the capital and could cut the road and rail links to the Red Sea ports, Ethiopia's lifeline to the world. But while the Eritreans knew exactly what they wanted – the independence of Eritrea – the TPLF was faced with the prospect of getting far more than it had fought for. It was no longer just a question of autonomy for Tigray. Meles and his comrades had suddenly realized that they were not just going to liberate Tigray, they were about to overthrow the government and take over the whole country.

That realization put the TPLF's leaders in a quandary. They had not expected the Soviet Union to collapse so suddenly. They may have hoped that a long struggle might nibble away at the Mengistu regime and gain greater independence for Tigray, but suddenly they found the entire regime collapsing. It was no longer a question of capturing a slice of Ethiopia. They could have the whole cake.

But how could they claim legitimacy? As the TPLF army approached Addis Ababa, Meles and his colleagues came up with a startling solution. The TPLF would find allies among Ethiopia's other ethnicities and create a national umbrella body, the Ethiopian People's Revolutionary Democratic Front, the EPRDF. A new constitution would allow all of Ethiopia's ethnic groups – four big ones and more than 60 smaller ones – to hold a referendum on the question of leaving Ethiopia. Could Meles persuade the rest of the country to let Eritrea leave Ethiopia? In reality it was an absurd idea, not least because – unlike with Eritrea, a former Italian colony with defined borders – there were no clear boundaries containing specific ethnic groups in the rest of the country. But Meles found like-minded people among Ethiopia's other main ethnic groups, Amharas, Oromos, Somalis and the ethnically mixed southerners, people like the Anuak or the Welayta, and created political parties for them. Like the Eritreans, all these 'nationalities' were given the constitutional right to vote to secede from Ethiopia by referenda. In this way Ethiopia took the opposite direction to other African countries. In the rest of Africa, the fear of breaking countries up along ethnic lines remains the ultimate nightmare, and rulers tried to create nationalism by suppressing ethnicity and even banning ethnic-based political parties. The new Ethiopia based its whole political system on parties and local governments representing the country's constituent ethnic regions. African presidents rarely refer to specific ethnic groups and few politicians would dare to – or be allowed to – form explicitly ethnic or regional parties. Ethiopia, however, made a virtue of doing so, creating the national polity on the basis of different ethnicities and offering it as a constitutional solution. It was an extraordinary gamble.

Yet Meles's proposals and solutions sounded eminently pragmatic and reasonable, and his use of Marxist language made it all sound inevitable and utterly logical. The ideology of the EPRDF was naturally that of the TPLF, and the Tigrayans held all the most powerful positions. All of the EPRDF's policies and programmes bore a remarkable similarity to those of the Marxist Leninist League of Tigray. It might be a crazy fiction, but the alternative – forcing Eritrea to stay part of Ethiopia – would have led to the continuation of a war Ethiopia might not win.

Meles also promised 'real democracy where the people themselves decide and have a right to free speech, peaceful demonstrations and strikes'. That was a promise he was not to keep.

At the end of the interview in London I tried to bait him, suggesting he was a backroom theoretical revolutionary who had never actually fought. He said nothing but took my hand and pressed my forefinger onto his temple. I felt a hard lump. 'Feel that?' he said. 'It is an AK bullet.'

'I think I am talking to the next Emperor of Ethiopia,' I said. Meles's eyes sparkled and he laughed.

On Monday, 21 May 1991, I was in Hargeisa witnessing the independence ceremony of Somaliland, which had decided to split away from the rest of Somalia, when that prediction came true: the BBC announced that President Mengistu had fled Ethiopia. It was the first of three successive and momentous Mondays. I managed to hitch a lift on a plane going to Djibouti and told an official at the Ethiopian embassy there that my wife and children were stuck in Addis Ababa and persuaded him that I needed to join them. I have never told a lie in print but to get to a breaking story, anything goes.

It worked, I got a visa and the next day I caught the last flight from Djibouti to Addis Ababa.

We stopped briefly at Dire Dawa. A crowd tried to force its way onto the plane. I found myself sitting next to a general in civilian dress. He said he was simply heading home to his wife and children. He was afraid of what the future held. Eventually we landed at Addis, the last plane allowed in. The airport was deserted. I did not need that visa after all.

An eerie silence had descended on the city. During the day people stayed at home, only going out to search for food or to go to church. Early each morning thousands flocked to the churches, gathering around the entrances to perform the rituals of prayer, touching the doors or walls with their foreheads and standing in prayer with head bowed and one hand on the church wall. The monks prayed in their wailing chant. There was no sign of police or soldiers on the streets. One day a line of tanks drove rapidly through the city in a show of strength. One fell off a bridge into a ravine and was abandoned. The rest disappeared.

A small group of journalists, including the BBC's Michael Buerk and Mohammed Amin, his cameraman, and John Mathai, the sound man, gathered at the Hilton Hotel. We talked incessantly to each other, swapping information, sifting rumours, trying to piece together what was going on and testing ideas of what might happen next. All we knew was the rebels were close by. The big questions were: when would they come, and would there be a fight for the city?

On the second Monday, shortly after 5 a.m., we got our answer. A massive bang electrocuted me out of sleep. The hotel rocked and the ceiling of my bathroom came crashing down. I pulled on some clothes and ran down the corridor to join other journalists trying to see what was happening less than 400 yards away. I could hear the crackle of machine guns and the stunning bangs of tank fire. Some of the journalists were lying on the balcony trying to record what they were seeing as bullets smacked into the brickwork around them.

Directly outside the hotel sat the cause of the big bangs – a tank that was firing shell after shell into the palace gateway. After a while it stopped shooting and its commander poked his head out of the turret and trained his binoculars on the burning gateway. A group of us crept out and sprinted across the road to crouch behind the tank. 'Are you the TPLF?' I called. 'No,' said the commander. 'We are Eritreans.'

We waited till we saw a single file of fighters walking up the hill towards the palace, in khaki shorts and shirts and wearing open sandals, and with AK-47s or rocket launchers at the ready. We joined them. Not a shot was fired, although we could hear exchanges elsewhere in the city. We got to the burning guardhouse at the smashed gateway, stepped over several dead bodies and walked up through the wooded gardens towards the palace. Suddenly a young soldier stepped out of a small hut and held out his gun to us. He was crying and shaking and had shat himself. We walked back down the hill with him only to discover that we had got ahead of the advancing line of fighters. We handed him over but as we turned to go back up the hill there were bursts of fire ahead of us and then silence. A second palace guard had been in the hut but had decided to go down fighting. We had been only inches away from him but he had waited for us to go back down the hill with his companion before opening fire. He was quickly killed.

Our main aim was to get into the imperial palace that Mengistu had used as his headquarters. Accompanied now by a young Ethiopian civilian determined to seek revenge on a regime that had collapsed, we found an open side door into the palace. I think we were hoping for scenes of a last debauched party or some other indicators of depravity or extravagance. We were disappointed. From the outside the palace was as grand as could be, but inside we found only dull dark rooms, rather sparsely furnished. There were no tell-tale signs of luxurious living – or of panic or despair. The only things of interest were a Soviet-style painting of the army leading the peasants and workers in revolution and a toy model of the battle of Adwa. Mengistu's office was only slightly grander than the other rooms and on his empty desk was a simple pen-holder with a mini wooden shield bearing the Ethiopian flag in red, yellow and black. I stole it. I am not sure why. Maybe I just wanted evidence for myself that I really had been there and witnessed these events. But they were momentous without being extraordinary. Mengistu may have lived in a palace but he had apparently lived very simply.

At that moment we heard gunfire on the north side of the palace and, afraid this might be a counter attack, we quickly left the palace and made our way back down towards the main gate, coming across more bodies of palace guards who had inexplicably decided to fight on.

In the afternoon we decided to visit the British embassy to see if the diplomats knew anything more about what was happening. On the way we stopped at the Russian embassy to see if anyone had claimed political asylum there. They hadn't, but we learned that four generals had fled to the Italian embassy where they have remained ever since. One has now died and the other three will probably die there too. I asked the Russian ambassador if this was the equivalent of the fall of Saigon for Russia. 'Not really,' he said gloomily. 'This embassy has no flat roof for a helicopter to come to rescue me.'

Outside the British embassy we had to step round the body of a dead soldier sprawled in the road and after we had identified ourselves by shouting over the ten-foot high gate, we were let in by two members of the Royal Military Police. We found ourselves in what is probably the most beautiful British embassy in the world, set in luxurious, peaceful gardens. Ten minutes later we were on an immaculately kept lawn playing croquet and drinking Pimm's.

On the third Monday we were woken in the early hours by a series of explosions coming from the south of the city. We gathered in a south-facing room on one of the top floors and watched what looked like a spectacular firework display. From a steady glow on the ground massive explosions were erupting and flares, shells, mines and rockets went shooting into the night sky. We soon realized it was not, as we feared, a counterattack by Mengistu loyalists trying to retake the city but an ammunition dump exploding. A few days before we had seen the remains of an ammunition factory west of the city that had also exploded. It was a gruesome sight. It appeared that people had tried to break into it and had accidentally set off the ammunition. Huge trees near the remains of the building had been snapped off like twigs while in the branches of others we could make out the remains of bodies blown to pieces. All over the surrounding area more bodies lay blackened and bloated. Some said later that both dumps were booby-trapped.

This ammunition store was on the outskirts of the capital near some oil tanks. We knew that people must be dying there but the curfew prevented us leaving the hotel till 6 a.m. So we watched and waited and dozed. By 5.45 the firework display was still continuing with periodic eruptions and explosions. At that point four of us squeezed into a car and I drove as quickly as I could to the source. We passed hundreds of people hurrying away, carrying their goods on their heads or in barrows. We got as close as we dared to the eruptions as rockets and bullets popped and zinged. I decided to drive round the enclosure when something happened that I cannot remember or describe. I only remember getting out of the car and seeing a tower of bright flame and black roiling smoke shooting upwards. Bits of rock, brickwork and earth were falling all round us and my companions were screaming at me to get back in the car. Later a photographer who had remained at the hotel two and a half miles away sent me the picture. The massive mushroom cloud looked like Hiroshima.

Then we learned others had not been so lucky. At least 100 people were killed, probably many more, and thousands hurt. We had been behind some houses that backed onto the dump but Michael Buerk, Mohammed Amin and John Mathai had been in the open and had been hit by the full blast of the explosion. Mike was blown off his feet and very shaken but unhurt. Mo was badly hurt and had lost his arm. John was dead, flung against a concrete wall. I had had dinner with him the night before. He had been sent to Addis at the last moment. He had not wanted to be there. His wife had just had a baby.

In the next few days the Ethiopians showed their feelings about the change of government by looting and trashing every public building they could get near. Every state, UN and aid agency building was looted – not just the food stores and depots, but schools, clinics and community centres. What was not stolen was broken or damaged. Paper was strewn around like confetti. It seemed to me a strange reaction. But after centuries of authoritarian royal rule followed by Communist dictatorship, war and the prospect of another Communist dictatorship, it was perhaps a natural one.

In a small town south of Addis, we found one group of Irish and British NGO workers whose compound had been broken into by the local people, some of whom worked with them. As the looters rampaged through the stores and their houses, the foreigners huddled together in one hut. Everything that was removable was removed and what wasn't taken was smashed. Then a group of men broke in. They paused but then took the aid workers' watches and shoes and anything else they wanted.

The next day the foreigners found their shoes returned, neatly

laid out by the gate. A group from the village later came and apolo-
gized. But elsewhere a pattern of rage and looting was repeated
though not a church or monastery was touched and, as far as I know,
not a single foreigner was hurt.

What a change the new regime brought in. Mengistu had been a
remote, cold figure pushing centrally driven, Soviet-style programmes of development in the name of the masses, where people
were treated as production machines, controlled but never consulted. A few days after the new government came to power, Ethiopia's
civil servants were summoned to the Black Lion Cinema in the centre of town to be addressed by their new political masters. Solemn
male bureaucrats, mainly Amharas, dressed in sober suits and ties,
and notorious for their obfuscating and tangled systems, assembled
gloomily in the cinema foyer. I managed to sneak in as well and
found a seat near the back. Order was called and onto the stage
walked a man in khaki shirt and shorts and wearing plastic sandals,
with his hair in a massive afro. The gasp from the civil servants was
audible. This was Abay Tsehaye, later to be Minister of Federal
Affairs. He strolled across the stage like a hippy at a congress of
bankers. But he greeted the civil servants politely and told them they
must continue to work as usual but would be vetted and reselected.
He lectured them on Ethiopia's new world and what was expected of
them. They left in silence. Shaking with anger, one of them said to
me: 'How did it happen? We had the best army in Africa and we let
ourselves be beaten these *woyane* (bandits).'

It was not just the civil servants. The whole of Ethiopia, fed for
almost 15 years on a diet of lies and propaganda, could not believe
that its huge, glorious army – the biggest in Africa – had been beaten
by bandits. In Addis there were marches and demonstrations, one
outside the American embassy, which many saw as the sponsor of the
rebels. That was partly true. Hank Cohen, the US Assistant Secretary

of State for Africa, had met Meles and been impressed by him. Ethiopia was no longer a Cold War battleground and Meles, though a Marxist, had read the signs of the times better than Mengistu. With the Soviet Union gone, the Americans had inherited the earth. The American ambassador Robert Houdek and his deputy, Robert Frazure – the two Bobs – became the midwives of the new regime and acted as intermediaries between the rebels and the representative of the former government, Tesfai Dinka, the Foreign Minister (later given a post in a Washington think tank). Between them they managed the takeover and the largely peaceful transition. There have not been many other occasions when the United States of America has made an alliance with the Marxist Leninist vanguard party.

I decided to head north-east to the Somali region where it seemed possible that there might be trouble. I took the train to Djibouti, along a rickety, toy-like narrow-gauge railway built by the French in the 1920s. All night it rattled and shook as it wriggled down out of the mountains, stopping at every station where it was besieged by people searching for relatives or wanting news from Addis, or selling bananas, kebabs or peanuts.

I got off at Dire Dawa and found a lift to Harar, where I met up with a TPLF unit. The commander was happy to let me travel with his unit. Some of them had never been out of the mountains before and as we headed into the Ogaden I realized they were in territory they had no knowledge of. On the second day we were approaching a village in the flat, hot drylands at the beginning of the Ogaden, the Somali part of Ethiopia, when suddenly we heard shooting ahead and saw tracers flying in the village. We stopped and the commander, a small, wiry man, told us to wait while he and one other soldier armed only with an AK-47 walked towards the village. After a while the shooting stopped and the officer returned. He squatted down by the side of the road and put his head in his hands. 'I did not know such people existed in my country,' he said quietly. We had just run into a Somali clan dispute, nothing to do with the future of Ethiopia.

Further east in the harsh drylands of the Ogaden we stumbled across another horror, a fifteen-year-old nightmare. The Ogaden was given to Ethiopia at the end of World War II, although the population of the lowland areas is Somali. In 1977 Somalia launched a full-scale war on Ethiopia to grab the Ogaden but after a short campaign, it was defeated. Seeing the Somalis in the Ogaden as a fifth column with the potential to be treacherous, Ethiopia rounded them up and expelled them across the border into Somalia. There they were housed in huge, grim camps run by the UN High Commission for Refugees and western aid agencies.

Many of the men in the camps were recruited by the Somali government, led by Siad Barre, to fight against the Somali National Movement (SNM), an emerging resistance movement in Somaliland in the north-west of Somalia. When the Barre regime in Somalia finally collapsed early in 1991, the SNM took over Somaliland. The first thing it did was to disarm Barre's troops who had been recruited from the Ogaden and drive them back into Ethiopia. Here, being Somali, they were not welcomed by the Ethiopians and found their land and livelihoods gone. Many of them had lived in refugee camps for more than ten years and no longer had the reserves or skills to support themselves in this harsh land. The UN High Commissioner for Refugees (UNHCR) refused to help them because they were returnees, not technically refugees, and at the time the agency's mandate did not extend to them. A few small aid agencies were working in their camps but they were overwhelmed. The death rates were among the worst ever recorded. One I visited on two successive days had more than 20 new graves overnight, mostly small ones.

Back in Addis Ababa one of the first things the new government did was to agree the details of Eritrean independence. Camps were set up in Addis Ababa and in the rest of the country for the Eritreans to return to Eritrea. The new Eritrean government expelled all Ethiopians. For the many mixed families who viewed themselves as both Eritrean and Ethiopian agonising choices had to be made or else were made arbitrarily for them.

Ethiopians were not happy to see Eritrea and their routes to the sea given away. But if the TPLF had reneged on its deal with the EPLF, the war would have continued. In Eritrea the EPLF announced the date for a referendum on independence. If Eritrea became independent, Ethiopia would become landlocked and dependent on it for access to seaports.

Relations between Meles, the new prime minister and leader of the TPLF, and Issiayas Afwerki, the EPLF leader, were efficient but cool. There had been reports of rifts during the war when the Eritreans controlled the routes in and out of Sudan and sometimes blocked supplies destined for the TPLF. Among aid agencies both organizations had good reputations for integrity and straight talking. The EPLF in particular was regarded with awe by aid workers. In an interview with me, Tony Vaux of Oxfam said that 'the Eritrean Relief Association is the most effective relief operation I have ever seen. It has sophisticated, democratic structures at village level and when there is a food shortage the food aid goes very quickly straight to the right people. There is a terrific sense of national morale.'

My own experience of the Eritreans was similar. They were all dedicated and idealistic but practical and although they all made the same political statements, they seemed to do so without looking over their shoulders for some commissar forcing them what to say or think. The liberation struggle had been practical as well as heroic. They had manufactured their own ammunition and uniforms, as well as menstruation pads for the women fighters and the ubiquitous plastic sandals that Issiayas Afwerki continued to wear as president.

The spirit of Eritrea felt too good to be true but as an outsider I could never see any chinks in the wall of Eritrean solidarity. The referendum went ahead in April 1992 and I spent the days beforehand in Asmara searching for an Eritrean who believed the country should stay with Ethiopia or who might vote yes to remaining part of Ethiopia out of fear. I couldn't find one. The result was 99.83 per cent in favour of independence. I believed it.

The separation went ahead and Eritrea created its own central bank and currency. Most people were optimistic. While Ethiopia was a poor hand-to-mouth country with low levels of literacy and little infrastructure, Eritrea had skills, energy, creativity and single-mindedness. Freed from the heavy hand of Ethiopian rule, Eritrea could use the talents that it had developed during the long war for peaceful purposes – it could have become another Singapore, an African Hong Kong.

The separation was not popular with the rest of Ethiopia which had as a result become landlocked and lost its trading ports. It was also bankrupt. Already wary of their new Tigrayan masters, the Amharas and Oromos – Ethiopia's biggest ethnic groups – saw them as puppets of the Eritreans. How could Meles and the Tigrayans – just 6 per cent of the total population of Ethiopia – overcome this suspicion and persuade the rest of the country that they were in control and would make life better for all? In May 1991 they controlled the northern mountains and they had occupied the capital. But how could they run the whole country and – as they had promised – be democratic?

While the war was still going on, they secretly forged links with politicians from other ethnic groups and helped them create their own ethnic-based parties. Unsurprisingly, these matched both the TPLF agenda and its structure. This gave the TPLF the cover it needed for letting Eritrea go.

But an ethnic map of Ethiopia resembles a Jackson Pollock painting with different colours and shapes spattered across a canvas. There are at least 80 ethnic groups among Ethiopia's 93 million people, very few of which had stayed within a defined area, instead wandering off and colonizing other areas while others had mixed and mingled in undefined territories. Would the Amharas and the Oromos, let alone the Anuak or the Welayta, want to walk away and form their own country? The only area that might well want to secede was the Somali-inhabited Ogaden. But that was never going to be allowed to happen – Ethiopia had fought a terrible war in the late 1970s to keep it.

Meanwhile, the peaceful separation of Eritrea had turned sour. In 1998 a small incident occurred on the revived border between Ethiopia and Eritrea in which Eritrean soldiers opened fire on Ethiopian policemen at an insignificant little town called Badme. Was it in Eritrea or Ethiopia? Who cared? 'Two bald men fighting over a comb,' I wrote in the *Economist*.

Knowing that the two presidents knew each other well and could pick up the phone and sort it out, I thought nothing of the incident. There had been disagreements about economic policy and currency values, but they were about the division of the cake, and as such, were negotiable. Destroying the cake did not make sense and so, I thought, would never happen. I was wrong.

The incident at Badme was the spark that rapidly escalated into an all-out war for political, economic and military mastery of the Horn of Africa. It was hard to see which of the two governments had the greater power. The issues involved were trade and transport, their economic interests and currency exchange rates. Eritrea wanted to exploit its position as Ethiopia's gateway to the outside world, and Ethiopia was beginning to feel hemmed in, exploited by Eritrea.

The war led to the deaths of some 100,000 people and cost both countries tens of billions of dollars that could have been used for development. Both sides spent furiously on arms, including the latest fighter aircraft from Russia and the USA. Both sides knew each other too well – particularly the generals. Smart tactics gave way to a slogging match using First World War–style trenches and tactics.

Issiayas Afwerki was the unchallenged leader of Eritrea, but Meles had to manage a much more open, mixed society. Many Ethiopians thought him incapable of standing up to the Eritreans. If he failed or conceded too much, he would be quickly overthrown. He had to give the generals their head. Issiayas in Eritrea had already shown a propensity for military action by attacking Yemeni territory on the Hanish islands in the Red Sea. The Eritreans also saw themselves as the big brother of Ethiopia who had given the TPLF support and space, even controlled it. There had been spats in the past, but now the TPLF, though still quite small as an organization, controlled the whole of Ethiopia with its vast resources. There were other factors too, such as the habit of war on both sides. The Eritreans had experienced 30 years of war on their own territory and the Ethiopians 16 years. Both the new governments had secured power through military victory so it was easy for them to pick up the guns again.

Shortly after the first round of fighting there was a ceasefire and I flew to Asmara and went to the front-line battlefield at Tsorona where Ethiopia had launched an attack in mid-March. Amid the wrecks of about 20 tanks and other armoured vehicles, scores of bodies still lay unburied in the sun, cut down by artillery and machine-gun fire. A severed arm dangled in the branches of one of the few trees still standing and dead bodies stuck out of newly bulldozed ramparts. It seemed that Ethiopia, having a much larger army, had used First World War tactics of mass attacks by armour and infantry against heavily defended Eritrean lines of zigzag trenches and ramparts. Attack helicopters had also been deployed, according to the middle-aged Eritrean officer who showed me round. She said there were about 10,000 Ethiopian dead and 700 prisoners. She would not give me the Eritrean casualty figure.

The next day I interviewed Issiayas. He played the underdog, still fighting to be free from the treacherous Ethiopians, and gave me a long justification for the war and a map that showed the disputed territory that Ethiopia was claiming. I then flew to Addis and saw Meles two days later. I told him I brought greetings from his brother, Issiayas – and the map. Meles looked at it and smiled. 'No,' he said, laughing, 'we are looking for much more than that.'

Under the journalistic code, you must report something if it is true and important unless you are morally sure someone will die as a result. This was the only time in my career that I have had to act on that principle. Issiayas has no sense of humour and something told me that if I quoted what Meles had just said, the war would start again overnight.

In the end the war stalemated with Ethiopia able to call on more fighters, resources and international support than Eritrea. Meles resisted the pressure from some of his generals to march into Eritrean territory, overthrow Issiayas and reincorporate Eritrea into Ethiopia. The USA and Europe had come down on the side of Ethiopia but were urging diplomacy rather than war. Eventually both sides agreed to accept the ruling of a team of experts on where the border lay.

In 2002 those experts from the boundary commission declared that Badme was Eritrean – just. During colonial times it had been administered from Addis Ababa, but technically it was in Eritrea. That must have given personal satisfaction to Issiayas, but by then both sides had had enough. The western world – for its own reasons – backed Ethiopia. Unlike Issiayas, Meles had established good relations with London and Washington and with the African Union which is based in Addis Ababa. Ethiopia had also become a poster boy for development, both human and economic. Eritrea was diplomatically and strategically outgunned. When the Ethiopians delayed implementing the experts' ruling, no pressure was applied to them to comply. When I asked a Foreign Office official why, she said the experts from the boundary commission had come up with the wrong answer.

The war with Eritrea was still on hold in 2014, with the two armies facing each other along the border. But it is unlikely to start again unless Issiayas Afwerki decides to attack. Eritrea turned inwards, away from the western world, and continued the war against Ethiopia through Somali proxies. Instead of being open to the world as an entrepreneurial trading state, Eritrea – like its president – is reclusive, closed and difficult to visit. Issiayas became increasingly dictatorial, imprisoning some of his closest colleagues and driving others into exile.

Meanwhile, Ethiopia became a western ally, open to the world and acting as the region's policeman. Yet internally both governments are desperate to control their people. At times Eritrea is almost North Korean in its repression while in Ethiopia capitalism thrives despite the suppression of any political opposition. Both countries have a dense jungle of bureaucracy and security checks everywhere.

The capital, Addis Ababa, is the heart of the new Ethiopia. At the end of the twentieth century Addis was a city of imperial palaces, stern nineteenth-century government buildings and thousands of single-storey wooden or stucco houses with rust brown corrugated iron roofs set in their own compounds. By the second decade of the twenty-first century new motorways and an urban railway are slicing through the city and heading out into what will soon be new suburban estates. A crop of glass skyscrapers of global design have sprung up in the city centre amid an archipelago of building sites, half-finished concrete and brick blocks six or seven storeys high. Families cashed in on the influx of thousands of young people from rural areas and replaced their rural-style breeze-block or mud-and-corrugated-iron homesteads with small blocks of flats for renting out.

Ethiopia's huge potential and high economic growth rates had persuaded western countries to back it even though it is not run entirely on free market lines. Meles encouraged capitalism to flourish in Ethiopia but it is the free market according to Ethiopian rules, which are frequently imposed arbitrarily and without consultation. The state retains close control over land, the economy and key state-owned companies but some local buccaneer capitalists are given free rein. Ethiopia's ancient and cumbersome bureaucracy still hinders business and development. Meles may have realized the folly of socialism for a country like Ethiopia at this stage in its development, but he did little to reduce the bureaucracy. So he should thus not have been surprised when he opened up Ethiopia for business and only a few investors turned up. When he heard that a German who was a potential investor in flower farms had decided to leave, he is reported to have jumped into his car and chased him all the way to the airport in an effort to persuade him to stay.

Meles also battled with the World Bank complaining of the 'Talmudic' nature of its edicts. In 1993 he said: 'We want broad agreement, we are not opposed to structural adjustment, we are opposed to micro management. Africa is not being given a chance to choose. There is an international one party system operating here… We need trust. There are parts we should do, with or without IMF prodding. These parts just make sense. Others, however we have resisted. How much longer can we resist? They are applying Chinese torture to us. We are reforming because we want to and also because we are forced to. But there are also some parts which don't make sense. And there are fundamental issues on which we differ.'

Nearly ten years later he was still pushing back against western demands for reform. After the global crash of 1998 humbled western donors, the space for alternatives and pushback against western dictates grew in Ethiopia and other African countries. Fortunately the World Bank listened to critics like Meles and by 2000 he was able to say: 'Three years ago I tried to cheat the World Bank man. Now I consult him on a range of economic issues. That is how much I trust him now.'

But Ethiopia set its own development targets and has insisted on building mega dams for hydroelectric power for Ethiopia and the region. Against Western advice, Meles used state funds to build the dams when no one else would help. His view was that if you get the economy, power and infrastructure right, development will follow and the people will benefit. But dam building on the Nile may put the country on a collision course not just with the aid donors but also with Egypt and Sudan with whom Ethiopia has an agreement about the Nile waters, that are of vital strategic interest to Egypt. In 1989 when Israel stepped in to help Mengistu after he had been abandoned by Moscow and offered to build dams on the Blue Nile in exchange for Falashas, I asked an Egyptian general what he thought. He said bluntly: 'If the Israelis build dams on the Nile in Ethiopia, we will bomb them.' Ethiopia also builds many of its own roads. Which other African country except South Africa has that capacity in 2014?

In 2015, the target date for the eight UN Millennium Development Goals, there will be a global reassessment of what the decade of development has achieved. The western formula decreed by the United States and Europe at the end of the Cold War was democracy, respect for human rights and free market economics. But when the league table for successful economic development is published I suspect we shall find that the fastest developers – led by Rwanda and Ethiopia – have adhered to none of these, except – to an extent – the free market.

Ethiopians may be experiencing development but they are unlikely to experience democracy and human rights unless they fight for them. Nor will their human rights be protected if they protest. In elections held in 2005 the EPRDF received a terrible shock when it lost control of the capital even though nationally it probably won. The opposition was jubilant but demonstrations in Addis Ababa were met with gunfire and mass arrests. The government locked up scores of opposition leaders and charged them with serious crimes. Reports of torture and brutal treatment of opposition activists are still common nearly ten years later. Out of the 547 elected members of the country's lower chamber, only one is from an opposition party. I met him. Girma Seifu Maru is a nice man but a lonely one. He rarely gets to speak in Parliament. The tentacles of the security departments stretch everywhere. The Internet is monitored and the press cowed into serving up long detailed reports of development plans rather than political news. Most Ethiopians clam up when asked about politics. The main complaint that I heard from young men and women I spoke to was that they could not choose what topic to study at university. Would-be doctors are sent to study engineering. Wannabe lawyers are sent to be agronomists. Dissent will get you blacklisted.

The Ethiopian government does not deny that it is repressive in the same hypocritical way that other repressive governments do. At the 2012 World Economic Forum meeting in Addis Ababa, only months before he died, Meles Zenawi sat on a panel of presidents and global leaders. He picked the last moment of the closing plenary session to tell the audience bluntly but with his usual understated diffidence: 'there is no connection between democracy and development'.

With those words – his last spoken at a global forum – Meles threw down a challenge to the western consensus that development requires democracy and respect for human rights. For him, development was the priority, and was best delivered by good planning rather than by endless divisive political debates about who should rule. Elections and political rights, he argued, can come later. 'We have set our agenda, now let us get on with it,' Meles was saying. As a result, Ethiopia presented Africa's western donors with a headache. Their formula for Africa is to give aid to countries that are poor and undeveloped, but only if they also respect human rights, hold democratic elections and abide by the rule of law. Knowing that Ethiopia can deliver huge amounts of aid money well, the donors ignore its human rights record because they know that its tight control over society can produce the development results they need to spend their aid budgets.

When Meles appointed Hailemariam Desalegn, a southerner and a Protestant to boot, as Deputy Prime Minister, many saw this as a token gesture to the southerners and a manoeuvre to prevent a rival emerging from one of the powerful highland ethnic groups. But when Meles died in July 2012, Hailemariam became his successor. He sounded more like a technocratic civil servant than a national leader. But by 2014 he was beginning to consolidate his power and appoint his own people in top jobs.

Despite its layers of parliamentary and state structure Ethiopia seems to end up with an authoritarian system bolstered by one or other of the country's 'nations'. Meles's successor could not have been another Tigrayan, and neither could an Amhara have been appointed, because Ethiopia has almost always been ruled by Amharas and should this happen again, the Oromos, a larger group, would be up in arms. Equally, the choice of an Oromo would upset the Amharas. A Somali? Since Ethiopia invaded Somalia in 2006 and again in 2010 and is still interfering there, that would be unthinkable.

In the past a southerner could no more have ruled Ethiopia than an Arab could rule in Israel. But Hailemariam, hard-working, technocratic and controlled by the Tigrayan dominated Central Committee of the EPRDF, was the perfect choice. He was not part of the traditional Ethiopian power struggle and as long as the government continued to deliver an economic boom, he would be given free rein. His appointment also echoes Ethiopian history, when the most powerful Rases did not take the top job but tried to appoint someone weaker whom they could control. As a black African southerner and a Christian protestant from a small ethnic group, Hailemariam was unable to develop his own national constituency. For more than two years after Meles's death, his picture hung in every government office in Ethiopia, not the picture of President Mulatu Teshome, whose name and face few Ethiopians would recognize. Nor that of Prime Minister Hailemariam Desalegn. It was that of Meles Zenawi.

Hailemariam was an energetic manager but by 2018 strikes and protest marches was beginning to make Ethiopia ungovernable. When battles broke out in Tigray, Oromia and the Somali region he resigned and the existing state of emergency was extended. Addis Ababa was brought to a standstill. Step forward Abiy Ahmed, the Oromo leader aged forty-two. His background was in the security sector and he spoke many of the country's languages. He was elected the chairperson of the EPRDF and became prime minister. He immediately freed up the debate and shook up the political system. Within a few weeks the Tigrayans had been pushed aside and the Oromo became the most powerful group. In an even more extraordinary move, Abiy Ahmed reached out to Eritrea and in July 2018 he visited Asmara where he was warmly received. Eritrea opened up its roads and ports to Ethiopian trade and the country. Most importantly, Ahmed conceded that Badme belonged to Eritrea, the tiny town that had been fought over in their border war costing some 70,000 lives.

18

New colonists or old friends?
Asia in Africa

It is late 2006 and I am in a small town in western Uganda sitting in the garden of a new hotel. A group of sunburned Chinese farm-workers dressed in blue overalls arrive in a minibus from a sugar estate outside town. Talking and laughing noisily, they have come to eat in the dining room before they are taken to their hostel on the outskirts of town. The tablecloths at the hotel are made in China, so are the lampshades, plates, cups and cutlery – and the little bunches of plastic flowers on each table. Even the rice they eat comes from China. The cars in the street come from Korea and Japan. In fact almost every manufactured thing I can see has been made in Asia.

A young African man in a suit and tie carrying a briefcase approaches me with a polite greeting. Paul has been well trained and has learned his patter well. He wants to sell me traditional Chinese medicines – or rather he wants me to sign up and pay a certain amount each month by standing order and in return I will receive regular supplies of cures and tonics. To prove its authenticity he gives me a pamphlet about the head of the institute – it does not call itself a company. His name is Mr Li and the pamphlet is full of pictures of Mr Li standing next to the great and good of China. Here is a picture of him shaking hands with President Hu Jintao himself. Paul speaks reverentially of Mr Li and his cures. His sales pitch is delivered with missionary fervour.

At one time Coca-Cola was the only foreign product that reached every corner of the continent. Time and again travelling in Africa over almost fifty years I have found myself in a remote village where I wondered if I was the first foreigner to reach it. Then I would be offered Coca-Cola. Now it is the Chinese and their products who reach everywhere.

China's impact on Africa – and on the rest of the world – is the biggest global geopolitical shift of the early twenty-first century. Globalization that was supposed to establish Western economic mastery of the planet quickly resulted in the economic rise of China and – more slowly – India. India is following in China's path, though its rise is different, less dramatic. In a few years' time maybe every reference to China in this chapter would be followed by 'and India'. While the North Koreans have always found allies among Africa's radical leaders, South Korea is also venturing into Africa. Malaysian and Indonesian companies are stepping up their engagement and Japan has been there for decades and is a major aid donor. Gulf States too, awash with cash, are venturing into Africa. Dubai has become a financial hub for African business. And many of these newcomers are making long-term investments. Asian countries may soon become Africa's predominant outside partners.

China is now the workshop of the world, sucking in oil and minerals from all over the planet and turning them into manufactured goods that undercut traditional suppliers in Europe and America. There has been nothing like it since the rise of America in the late nineteenth and early twentieth centuries. Its state-controlled capitalism and intense, disciplined patriotism have combined to produce year on year growth of nearly 10 per cent over twenty-five years. Its foreign exchange reserves are in trillions of dollars so China could crash the dollar and the American economy with a flick of a finger. That is unlikely, since China's own growth is dependent on the American consumer. China and America now live with the economic equivalent of the Cold War's nuclear MAD – Mutually Assured Destruction.

Chinese state companies have not sat in their offices in Shanghai or Beijing ordering quantities of oil and other minerals on the international exchanges. They have bypassed the London and New York commodity exchanges and gone to the sources of raw materials. Sometimes they pay Western companies to extract and bring the goods to China, sometimes they use their own companies.

In Africa, China's impact is clear from the international airport to the village store. It has diplomatic representation in thirty-nine African capitals, but its presence is felt in every one of Africa's fifty-three countries. This re-engagement – archaeological evidence shows Chinese pottery on the East African coast dating back to the seventh century – began with President Jiang Zemin's tour of Africa in May 1996. He announced the 'second stage' of China's engagement with Africa which, he said, would be 'totally different from before'. It was to be non-ideological with an emphasis on trade – a search for raw materials to feed its factories.

By 2009 Africa was China's biggest trading partner. Since then China's trade with Africa has soared from $5.6 billion in 1996 to $10 billion in 2000, increasing by 19 per cent a year to $40 billion in 2005. The 2006 target of $50 billion was exceeded and by the end of 2009 trade was worth $90 billion and then shot up again to more than $166 billion in 2012 and $200 billion in 2015. But then commodity prices began to fall and in 2017 Africa–China trade was only worth $150 billion.

No-one knows how many Chinese have moved to Africa. There are no official figures. An Angolan minister has spoken of 4 million

Chinese living and working there. That would make them a fifth of the population. In 2017 recession set in and many Chinese were leaving and returning to China. Some may move back and forth to China but many have settled permanently. As I saw in Uganda, they are not all businessmen in suits or technicians. Many are labourers, others are individual entrepreneurs settling in Africa and setting up small businesses.

With economic power, China has gained political power. Beijing points out it has never had imperial ambitions or attacked its neighbours. That is true unless you see China itself as an empire incorporating non-Chinese minorities in its fringe provinces. But it wants African votes in the United Nations. This diplomatic mission began as a stratagem to win support for Beijing's battle with Taiwan. That won – only a handful of odd and insignificant African countries still take aid from Taiwan in exchange for their support to join the UN – China now simply wants to collect as many supporters as possible. It wants African support for its bid for market economy status at the World Trade Organization. If China joins the club and has African support, it will be far harder to prove cases of dumping subsidized Chinese goods in the rest of the world.

In the longer term China may also be seeking diplomatic support for what may come to be that bigger struggle with America for control of resources and sea routes. If it comes to a battle for the world's diminishing resources, the US may choose to fall back on its military might. So wary China is rapidly building a substantial ocean-going navy. Africa's coasts could be the battleground.

This is not the first time the Chinese have come to Africa. In 1414 when Henry V was in his first year on the throne of England, Zheng He, the Grand Eunuch of the Three Treasures, made the first of seven voyages westwards from China to the east coast of Africa. He came with a vast fleet: sixty-two galleons of up to 1500 tons each and some 100 auxiliary vessels. Although they brought nearly 30,000 soldiers, the Chinese came in peace, seeking trade and respect, prestige for the new Ming dynasty. In particular they wanted exotic wild animals, giraffes and zebras, to bring back to the Emperor to demonstrate that he was indeed Emperor of the entire world. The giraffe was thought to be the *qilin*, a magical creature, and its first appearance at the Ming court gave the Emperor's prestige and power a terrific boost. But unlike the Europeans who came later, the Chinese wanted respect, not control. Lesser races must make obeisance to China, but China had no need to rule over them or change them. And unlike the Portuguese who arrived three-quarters of a century later in much smaller vessels – Vasco da Gama's *São Gabriel* was a mere 178 tons – the expedition of Zheng He avoided fighting. From their earliest expeditionary voyages, the Europeans continually clashed with inhabitants, razed towns and took prisoners. The only scrape that the Chinese had on those extraordinary voyages was with the Somalis at Mogadishu. 'Very quarrelsome people,' the voyage log records. Some things in Africa do not change.

The language then was also very similar to today. The Chinese still speak in terms of peace, equality, friendship, trade and mutual benefit. And trade did grow between the continents. China found then what it has found today: Africa is a much richer continent than anyone thought. Chinese pottery from that period discovered on the east coast of Africa suggests that Africans wanted only the best – and were capable of paying for it.

The Chinese made their last diplomatic exploration in 1431 and did not return. Chinese ships continued to trade in the Indian Ocean but politically the country turned in on itself, losing interest in the barbarians beyond its borders, unwilling to fund such large expeditions. And by the nineteenth century Europe dominated the world, making colonies on China's own territory. Finding Africans less satisfactory as workers, the European colonists brought thousands of Chinese to Africa, sometimes as virtual slave labour for their farms and mines. Some 50,000 Chinese contract labourers were brought by British mining companies to South Africa in 1904 and 1905 to break a strike by African workers. Many of them stayed on. In *King Leopold's Ghost*, Adam Hochschild tells the story of the Belgian king bringing Chinese workers to build a railway from the coast to where Kinshasa is today to bring out the rubber more quickly. The king wondered what it would cost to import 2000 Chinese and settle them in villages. Five hundred and forty were brought to Africa in 1892. 'Three hundred of them died on the job or fled into the bush,' writes Hochschild. 'Most of the latter were never seen again, although several were later found more than five hundred miles into the interior. They had walked toward the rising sun, trying to get to Africa's east coast and then home.'

The Chinese did not return to Africa as a political power until the 1960s when Mao Zedong's revolutionary China supported liberation movements and newly independent African countries. They built roads, bridges, stadiums and water systems and established farms and factories. They sent hundreds of doctors and nurses and set up clinics to provide medicines. And they gave military training and weapons to some liberation movements and spread a revolutionary message through posters and calendars and Mao's *Little Red Book*.

The Tanzam Railway is China's biggest legacy of that period. The newly independent states of Southern Africa wanted to shake off their dependency on apartheid South Africa, but all their road and railway links went to South African ports or through the Portuguese territories, Mozambique and Angola. The Africans wanted a new railway running northeast from Zambia's copper-producing area to Dar es Salaam. Western countries, content with the anti-Communist apartheid regime, were unwilling to help in the project. The World

Bank turned it down as uneconomic. The Chinese stepped in and built the railway in five years.

The construction of the railway employed thousands of Chinese male workers, all dressed in identical blue Mao suits and housed in compounds with almost no contact with local people. I travelled the route of the railway in 1971 by hitch-hiking along the US-funded road which was being built at the same time and ran parallel to the line. The Chinese workers were clearly under instructions not to have contact with Westerners. They ignored waves and smiles and even offers of cigarettes.

The railway brought no obvious direct benefit to its builders. The Chinese had little use for anything coming from Zambia at that time. Western countries gave 'aid' projects to Africa that either directly benefited their national companies or bought diplomatic support in the Cold War. The Chinese however, invested in long-term goodwill – international solidarity, they called it. They still do. It is a factor that most Western governments, acting only according to national self-interest and accountable to an electorate, find it hard to match – or comprehend. Although it developed crippling failures after China handed it over at the end of 1975, the Tanzam Railway made the Chinese popular in Africa. It was a huge political success and is still cited by the Chinese as an example of their aid to Africa.

When it came to backing new leaders in the 1960s and 1970s however, the Chinese, driven primarily by rivalry with Russia, picked badly. They supported Robert Mugabe's ZANU in the battle for Zimbabwe. Although he outgunned Joshua Nkomo's Russian-backed ZAPU, when Mugabe came to power he turned to Britain and the West to help him. He turned again to the Chinese only when he had fallen out with Western governments and wrecked Zimbabwe. In Angola the Chinese backed Jonas Savimbi against the Russian-backed MPLA, but when civil war broke out between the two movements,

Savimbi became the protégé of the South Africans and Americans.

The Cold War is always portrayed as a global struggle between Communism and capitalism but in the early 1960s the world's Communist superpowers, China and Russia, also fell out. After a few border skirmishes they decided to continue their struggle in the rest of the world. So the Russia–China Cold War spread to Africa where they competed for allies. After President Richard Nixon's visit to China in 1972, the US and China often found themselves backing the same allies. For example, Angola under the MPLA was a Russian ally, so the Chinese began backing the US ally, Mobutu Sese Seko, across the border in Zaire – as Congo was named then. They even built Mobutu a Chinese palace in his birthplace, Gbadolite: a magical wooden edifice built on stilts on a lake, with a pagoda, a magnificent stone fountain at the entrance and walkways between the halls and living rooms. Every inch was decorated with painted scenes from the Chinese rural idyll. Dragons flew across lintels and lions guarded doors.

After the death of Mao in 1976 and the start of Deng Xiaoping's reforms two years later, China gave up its global ambitions in order to concentrate on internal reform. Chinese missions remained open in Africa and they continued to build roads and bridges, but they had lost their missionary zeal. They turned to Africa again after the 1989 upheavals of the Tiananmen Square protests when they wanted African diplomatic support, and they wanted trade and did not carry ideological baggage. China's economic reforms were working, but China's own soil could not provide all the raw materials its hungry new industries needed. It found them in Africa.

From copper in Congo to cassava in Cameroon, Chinese companies bought up whatever they could to feed China's factories. They bought timber and fishing rights, platinum mines and textile factories. And they did not always pay the market price. Chinese state companies, being state owned, have no bottom line, no shareholders anxious for an annual dividend. Backed by the treasury, they can afford to make long-term investments. Behind every Chinese state-owned firm lies the Chinese government, willing to provide aid and soft loans or write off a previous debt. At the China-Africa Summit in 2003 China wrote off $1.27 billion owed to it by thirty-one African countries; an additional $1.3 billion of debt was due to be written off between 2006 and 2009.

Even where the playing fields are level the Chinese have the edge. They are prepared to go where Western workers no longer dare to tread. Unlike Western professionals who need high salaries, insurance and health cover, air-conditioned houses and staff to run them, business-class tickets home and four-wheeled drives, the Chinese are pretty much content to live at the same level as their workers. Western companies, more vulnerable to public opinion, are signed up to corporate social and environmental principles and programmes. Chinese companies have no such pressure and war zones hold no particular fears for them. When nine Chinese oil workers were killed by rebels in Ethiopia's Ogaden region in April 2007, China did not flinch, though the incident did provoke debate in China and calls for better protection for Chinese workers in Africa. A Western company would probably have withdrawn.

And their work rate is phenomenal: often they complete projects early and under budget. Chinese companies bring their own Chinese workers from managers to labourers. One reason is language, especially on building sites, and unlike Western firms, Chinses companies have no African managers yet. Asked why they don't employ more local Africans – at least as manual workers – one Chinese minister said that the Africans were not prepared to work at night and weekends – and did not work as hard as Chinese. Had a manager of a Western company made such a remark the sky would have fallen.

The Chinese do not just buy. They also sell cheap watches, mobile phones, radios, computers, clothes, and – everywhere – flip-flops. Thanks to affordable Chinese manufacturing, millions of Africans are able to buy their first piece of high-tec electronic equipment. Whatever strategic and diplomatic advantage the Chinese state seeks in Africa, its most visible footprint is trade. Where the West sees Africa as the place to make poverty history, the Chinese see it as the place to make money. And as I found in that remote village in Uganda, not all the Chinese in Africa are working for big state-owned companies. While China's state companies seek strategic raw materials in a few countries, throughout the whole of Africa Chinese families are to be found running corner shops or small hotels – even Chinese medicine pyramid-selling schemes. And Chinese goods have supplanted Africa's traditional European suppliers. From motor cars – now assembled in Ethiopia and Senegal – to medicine, Chinese goods are far cheaper than anything made in Europe and America. 'More appropriately priced for Africa,' is how one US ambassador described it. African traders have moved to China, Guangdong province in particular, to send goods back to Africa and 'traditional African' fabrics are now made in China by Chinese textile companies for export to Africa.

The Centre for Chinese Studies at Stellenbosch University in South Africa monitors Chinese activity in Africa in a weekly newsletter. One week in October 2007 provides a typical sample: $5 billion is lent to Congo for mining and infrastructure projects. Mauritania, China's newest oil supplier, gets a $61 million debt written off. The China National Oil Corporation buys a $2.3 billion stake in an offshore Nigerian oil and gas field. China will build a new dam on the Zambezi River in Mozambique at a cost of $2 billion. China's Minmetal buys a ferrochrome mine in South Africa for $6.5 million and agrees to build a stadium for $70 million in Ndola, Zambia.

In the previous week the centre reported that a Chinese company bought Zimbabwe's largest ferrochrome mine. Another company will construct a gas-fired power plant in Ghana. The following week it announced that Mandarin will be taught in fifty South African schools.

In 2000 the Chinese and African governments founded the Forum on China–Africa Co-operation Conference, known as FOCAC. The Chinese called it 'a grand diplomatic rallying point and a laying down of principles'. Designating 2006 the 'Year of Africa', the symbolic fiftieth anniversary of the establishment of diplomatic ties between African countries and China, the Chinese government celebrated its re-engagement with Africa with a summit of African leaders in Beijing. The city was shut down, polluting factories switched off and traffic kept off the streets as almost fifty African presidents and delegations gathered in the Great Hall of the People in Tiananmen Square. One by one they walked up the red carpet of the main conference centre to be greeted by two small men in suits, President Hu Jintao and Premier Wen Jiabao. It was an extraordinary demonstration of obeisance at the throne of power and no other country in the world could have commanded it. The message was simple. China was acting with 'deepest sincerity and without political conditionalities', said Wen Jiabao.

At that two-day meeting in November 2006 China announced what was in its great sack of goodies for African governments: $5 billion in loans and credits, a $5 billion fund to be managed by the China Development Bank to support investment by Chinese firms in Africa and a promise to double development assistance by 2009, $1.9 billion signed in trade deals. There were promises of skills training in everything from engineering to medicine and Mandarin. The summit was followed up the next February by a ten-day tour of eight African capitals by Hu Jintao. When did a European foreign minister – let alone a head of state – conduct such a tour?

How is all this changing Africa? A spectrum of opinion is marked at one end by the view that China is the new imperial power in Africa and will be as rapacious and careless of Africa as its European predecessors. At the other end is the view that this is Africa's salvation. China will treat Africa as an equal. Its African trade and investment will develop the continent on a scale that far outstrips European aid agencies' dreams of a Marshall Plan for Africa.

Everyone agrees that China is playing a long game for oil and other raw materials in Africa and securing allies who will vote for it in the United Nations. The positive side to the new relationship for Africa is obvious. At the most basic level China's – and India's – demand for Africa's raw materials pushes up their prices. China's greatest need is for oil and its two state oil companies moved in on new producers like Equatorial Guinea, Angola and Sudan. By 2006, 45 per cent of China's imported oil – 30 per cent of its consumption – came from Africa. Angola provided 16 per cent of that, Sudan 7 per cent. Angola sent more of its oil to China than it did to its traditional buyer, the United States. Wherever there were minerals – or rumours of minerals – in Africa, Chinese and Indian companies were sure to be found. The copper price shot up 500 per cent between 1999 and 2007 thanks largely to Chinese demand.

It is also obvious that African rulers, harassed by Western criticism of corruption, human rights and environmental damage, will embrace China's uncritical 'non-interference' policy in its government-to-government relations. China simply accepts that the government is the government and what a government does to its own people is an internal matter and no business of China's. It does not believe in transparency or multi-party democracy and blames many of Africa's ills on 'imposed Western systems'. Given its own political system and its own rejection of outside criticism of its human rights record or any matter concerning its internal affairs, it is hard to see what other policy it would pursue.

African rulers also like the way in which China presents itself as a neutral, non-imperialist, value-free outsider that wants simple relationships of trade and friendship with African governments. In their formal, stylized way the Chinese emphasize the best of Africa, never referring to its failures and explicitly denouncing 'Afropessimism'. They ignore the aid agency images of poverty and war that African rulers so resent. The Beijing summit made no reference to Africa's poverty. Many Africans see this as a mark of respect. Official Chinese websites, for example, stress mutual friendship and co-operation, economic, cultural, social and educational. Compare Britain's Department for International Development websites on Kenya and Ethiopia which begin by describing them as the poorest countries in Africa.

Africans and Westerners who go to China to find out about China's policy in Africa are directed towards Chinese academics at various institutes spread out across Beijing which act as the eyes and ears of the ministries and government departments that fund them. At one level they are also spokesmen for the Chinese government but they listen carefully and will sometimes venture 'a personal view'. Answers to direct questions however, are often formulaic and opaque. Press on and you run into a defensive wall of accusations against Western imperialism and its failure to develop Africa in the past. Any suggestion that China might be following in Europe's footsteps is angrily dismissed. Referring to China in a speech on Africa in 2006, Jack Straw, the British foreign secretary, listed China as a problem for Africa along with war, famine and disease. He ended on a throwaway line: 'Welcome to the new colonists.' Beijing went ballistic and cut off all contact with Britain on issues affecting Africa for fifteen months. Even if you agree about the Europeans' evil colonial effect on Africa, the conversation does not move on because when you ask about the impact that China is having on Africa today, the academics fall back on the mantra that they are not imperialist and have no ambitions to colonize Africa. Oddly for Marxists, they do not seem to recognize the political and social impact on African countries of their trading relationship. Their mantra is develop the economy first and worry about politics and society later.

China also offers Africa an alternative to Europe and America in two ways, as a model and as a partner. China has brought more of its own people out of poverty in the last decade than live in all of sub-Saharan Africa, but without any freedom of expression or democracy. In theory that offers Africa an alternative development model, but it is unlikely that any African country will follow China's Communist route. African states are weak, its societies much less homogeneous and disciplined than the Chinese. It is impossible to imagine China's one-child policy making any headway in Africa where having children is still an almost unqualified good. But African rulers use China's very interest in Africa, and its tempting condition-free loans, as leverage against the demands of the IMF, the World Bank and Western donors. Since the end of the Cold War, African leaders have had almost no foreign partners other than the West and no alternative model except the Western reform agenda based on multi-party democracy, free market and free press. Governments that are resistant to these reforms see China as a lifeline.

China has promised a sackful of loans four times as great as the World Bank is offering. In May 2007, China's Exim Bank pledged to lend some $20 billion to Africa over three years. In the previous year the World Bank approved projects amounting to only $4.8 billion for Africa. However, if another global recession causes raw material prices to fall, Africa's capacity to service or repay these loans will be weakened. For the first time African governments may have some real power. If they use it well, they could obtain much more from the Western donors – and much more on their terms.

Nowhere was this clearer than in 2007 when the European Union tried to rush African countries and other former colonies in Asia and America into signing its Economic Partnership Agreements. These agreements were designed to create virtually free trade between Africa's regions and Europe by removing tariffs over the next two decades. But African governments, nervous of losing tariff revenues and seeing their nascent industries squeezed by European goods, felt they were being strong-armed into disadvantageous deals. In the old days they had no alternative and they would have signed. Now many, including South Africa and Nigeria, refused – thanks to the presence of their new Asia trading partners. The contrast between the Beijing Summit of 2006 and the European Union Lisbon Summit of 2007 was striking, the one celebratory and uncontroversial, the latter ill-tempered and unproductive.

The Chinese are popular with African governments because they build things: energy supplies and infrastructure, especially roads and railways. Western donors have recently not been keen on roads and ports and are positively allergic to dams. They prefer to concentrate on less visible assistance such as education and health or capacity-building. China loves big infrastructure projects such as stadiums, airports, national TV and radio stations and, something puritanical Western donors abhor, presidential palaces. In Angola they have virtually rebuilt the capital, Luanda. African presidents love it: far better to see something concrete – literally – than a page of statistics that shows school attendance is rising.

And the Chinese get on with it. Their aid programme is uncomplicated: a government wants a road or a stadium, it gets a road or a stadium, fast. 'The West makes us wait – but we are a poor country and we don't have time to wait,' said one minister from Sierra Leone. 'We like the Chinese. When they say they will do something, they do it. No consultants, no environmental impact, no delay. You get your road.'

The Chinese have the political space to take a long-term view, planting now to harvest in forty or fifty years' time. In the early part of the new century the director of a British government-owned company, the CDC, received a call from Chinese officials. They wanted to come to talk to him about the CDC and how it worked. It was exactly what China wanted, they said: long-term investments in commodities that would pay off handsomely in the future. The Commonwealth Development Corporation was set up in 1948 to make long-term investments in British colonies which were not paying their way. It embarked on schemes to plant forests and create plantations and other agricultural enterprises that would pay off in half a century or more. In the new capitalist world of the 1980s and 1990s nothing could have been more unfashionable, and when New Labour came to power in 1997 they wanted to privatize it. Unsurprisingly Western capital was not interested, and although some valuable bits of the CDC were stripped out and sold, the rest was left like an orphan no-one wanted. But with careful investment and the rise in commodity prices, it too has done surprisingly well. In 2017 its value had increased to $53 billion with a profit of $5.3 billion.

Given that the Chinese are deeply concerned about their reputation and what others think of them, it is extraordinary that they don't get everything quite right. In that special Year of Africa one slogan plastered on Beijing's billboards for the Forum on China–Africa Co-operation Conference was 'Africa: Land of Myth and Mystery'. The city was hung with pictures of wild animals and one poster the size of a house was of a naked black man in a grass skirt with a spear in his hand and a bone through his nose. The organizers did not seem to know that Papua New Guinea is not part of Africa. A black South African businessman who was there was not amused. 'I don't feel like a myth and I am certainly not a mystery,' he said.

That horrendous mistake as well as offhand remarks by Chinese officials suggest that the Chinese are as likely as Americans and Europeans to make derogatory assumptions about Africans – if not more so. These days a major component of Western business as well as aid projects is the involvement of the local people. While China funds innumerable training projects, when it comes to their own commercial operations they prefer to bring in their own workers rather than employ and train up locals. Western companies and NGOs in Africa are frequently headed by Africans, but I have yet to discover a Chinese project where Africans are in charge of Chinese.

The same issue was raised by President Thabo Mbeki of South Africa, one of the less enthusiastic voices on China's role in Africa. He bluntly warned of the risk that China will replicate Europe's old colonial relationship with Africa: Africa exports cheap raw materials and re-imports them as expensive manufactured goods. It is not hard to see why this might be true. Many of China's biggest transport infrastructure projects replicate the old colonial pattern: a road or railway from a mine to a port. It is hard to find many that link Africa internally. And while African consumers benefit from cheap clothes, radios and watches, African manufacturing is being destroyed.

South Africa is under particular threat and tries to restrict Chinese imports. Its trade unions say that the textile industry has lost 800 firms and 60,000 jobs as a result of cheap clothes from China. Mbeki offered the Chinese better access in return for Chinese help to set up and protect manufacturing in South Africa. But South Africa, a market the size of a medium-sized province of China, has some muscle. Medium and small African countries with populations under 20 million have none. And China makes deals only with the governments of states. It appears to take little account of the regional economic groupings such as the Economic Community of West African States or the Common Market for Eastern and Southern Africa. Even within China the playing field seems not to be level. African traders who go there to buy goods at source say they must pay tax but Chinese exporters working the same trade route do not.

Some clashes between Chinese companies and African communities have already taken place. In July 2006 six workers were shot and wounded at the Chambishi mine in Zambia when they complained about low wages ($2 a day) with no day off, dangerous conditions and lack of union representation. An explosion in an explosives factory in 2005 killed fifty workers. Michael Sata, an opposition candidate for the presidency, threatened to throw out the Beijing Chinese if elected, and recognize Taiwan instead. The Chinese ambassador reacted by publicly criticizing Sata, saying he was not a fit person to run Zambia. If that wasn't interference in Zambia's internal affairs, it is hard to see what might be.

There are also widespread reports of environmental damage and a complete lack of environmental surveys by Chinese mining companies. This is the other side of the 'can do' coin. They just get on with it – sometimes without a feasibility study. In 2007 they caused severe damage to Gabon's Loango National Park while building a pipeline. From Mozambique it was reported in the same year that 531 containers full of illegally mined logs worth $5 million were seized by the authorities at Nacala port. But the rulers let the Chinese get away with it, or even encouraged them. When Ben Mkapa retired as President of Tanzania, the Chinese built him a magnificent new road to his village near the southern border and a bridge across the river into Mozambique. It went straight through a national park.

The attitude of Chinese business in Africa contrasts with a growing social and environmental consciousness in Western countries and their companies. A dramatic turning point occurred in 1995 with the execution by the Nigerian government of Ken Saro-Wiwa, the Nigerian activist who campaigned against Shell's operations in the Niger Delta. Shell said at first his death was nothing to do with them. They were simply doing business there and did not involve themselves in politics. But Shell began to realize it was deeply implicated in Nigeria's politics. It provided the money that kept the government going and never asked who it went to or how it was spent. Ken Saro-Wiwa's death sparked a profound review of all extractive operations by Western companies in other parts of the world. Oil companies which are at the head of the oil well as well as the high street petrol station are vulnerable to public pressure. Their review led to the establishment of the Extractive Industries Transparency Initiative (EITI), a new code of conduct for mining and oil companies.

This was part of a broader reform. Businesses now promise to be transparent in their dealings with poorer countries, anxious to demonstrate that they are committed to development. They offer better health care and housing for workers and publicize their adherence to international safety and environmental standards, anti-corruption and climate change measures. Corporations, caught up in local wars in far-flung places and denounced by activist NGOs, engage with the NGOs and pour money into local community projects. It seems that globalization can be a race to the top in terms of best practice rather than a race to the bottom for the cheapest goods based on exploitation through low wages or poor conditions.

These new principles have been broadly accepted by Western governments, companies and NGOs and seem to be the signpost to a new road that leads to a land called 'sustainable development'. But just as Western companies were about to head cautiously down that road, Chinese and Indian companies sped past them claiming 'non-interference' and 'business only' – the very language Shell and other companies had used more than a decade earlier. Corporates which signed up to these new codes of practice may find it difficult to compete commercially with Chinese companies which did not.

New twenty-first century governance principles are contained in the New Partnership for Africa's Development, an aspirational document drawn up by South Africa and a coalition of other countries that want to improve the governance of the continent. Similar principles are contained in the Charter of the African Union. The charter also commits member states to respect democratic principles, human rights and the rule of law and good governance, and condemns unconstitutional changes of government. While the Chinese, say they are fully committed to all of these in principle, in practice they sidestep them, hiding again behind their maxim that relations with other countries are strictly government to government and based on non-interference in internal affairs.

So China sells arms to bad governments such as those of Sudan or Zimbabwe and gives unconditional billions in loans to countries like Angola where a tiny elite treat the national treasury as their private bank account. China is a Communist state without multiparty democracy or a charter of political freedoms; no-one would expect it to promote multi-party democracy in Africa. But that does not mean Beijing cannot distinguish between governments such as those of Botswana or Ghana, that try to do the best for their people, and ones that commit human rights abuses. When the Sudanese government forcibly removed thousands of people from their land at Merowe so that the Chinese could build a dam on the Nile in exchange for oil concessions, Beijing said it was none of its business. The government also cleared thousands of people out of the oil areas, burning their homes and seizing their livestock to make way for Chinese oil companies. Yet the Chinese government insisted that it had a purely business relationship with Sudan and was not involved in politics though it sells weapons to the Sudan government that it uses to kill its own people. China uses exactly the same argument as that put forward by firms that benefited from apartheid rule in South Africa.

It is no surprise that the African governments that have received most from China are those that are oil rich but the least open and the worst in terms of corruption, war or human rights abuses: Sudan, Angola and Congo. To those countries China came like a man offering a crate of whisky to an alcoholic. Countries where there is more transparency and a more careful audit of the long-term benefit of their natural resources, such as Botswana and, increasingly, Nigeria, are less keen on Chinese largesse.

The first reaction from many Western governments, companies and NGOs, when they finally noticed what China was doing in Africa, was outrage. The US spoke of containing China. Western governments and corporates had not cared much about Africa in the later years of the twentieth century, but they knew that beneath its soil lay a stupendous hoard of minerals. Suddenly the Chinese moved in and made bids that Western companies could not match. They grumbled that Chinese companies were bribing officials and ripping out minerals with complete disregard for the environment or sustainability, but they were too late. The Chinese had landed. Western influence in Africa is permanently reduced. The only sensible option is to work constructively with them, hopefully agreeing standards of environmental and developmental behaviour. For example, when the Chinese build a road, Western aid could manage the environmental and social aspects and bring schools and clinics to the area. As one executive of a Western mining company said, 'The horse has bolted but we can still talk to the rider.'

China may welcome such co-operation. Beijing is beginning to find that a purely government-to-government policy is not sufficient to protect its interests in Africa. An absolute non-interference policy, relying on local governments for law and security, is a recipe for disaster. Like everyone else, China is stubbing its toe on Africa, finding it puzzlingly obstructive. To work with Africa you need to understand it and China is beginning to learn that. In South Africa over the last decade fourteen Chinese companies set up manufacturing industries but by 2008 all had closed. The Chinese work ethic and business model did not work in a country with strong labour laws protecting workers' rights and a forty-hour week. The Zambian election in 2006 and the killing of Chinese oil workers in 2007 have shown that rhetoric about sovereignty and non-interference applies only when China's own interests are safe. If they feel threatened the Chinese protect their interests by all means, like anyone else.

China also responds to threats to its reputation and prestige. The beginnings of a movement in America to boycott the 2008 Olympics in protest against Chinese support for the Sudan government created panic in Beijing. A conference on Darfur was swiftly organized and speakers were invited to Beijing from America and Europe as well as Sudan. Hints were dropped by Chinese officials about pressure being exerted on Khartoum 'under the table'. Sudan then suddenly dropped its refusal to allow the UN into Darfur. The Chinese officials smiled and winked. 'It's a turning point,' they said. Six months later Liu Guijin, China's Special Representative for Darfur, said publicly that 'China had tried its best to engage the government in Sudan to be more flexible to meeting the requests of the international community.' Although he would not criticize the Sudanese government or contemplate stopping selling weapons to it, he admitted that the security and humanitarian situation was very serious.

Many saw Liu's world diplomacy to explain China's position as a sign that Beijing is worried about its international image and needs to express its policies better. China sees itself as resuming its rightful place as one of the most powerful countries in the world. But that means it must act according to international rules and norms. On the other hand China is also very touchy, it hates criticism by outsiders and it was clearly terrified that its showcase Olympics in 2008 would be wrecked by its support for the Sudanese government.

China's commercial engagement with the rest of the world is likely to prove an even more important driver of change in China's international relations. Buying stakes in global corporates such as Standard Bank of South Africa and Rio Tinto will also bring China in line with international standards. But the power of the party and central government in Beijing is no longer absolute. Once it allowed the people to go out and create wealth, the party ceded control. Massive companies that suddenly emerged in the provinces are now going global and can ignore instructions from central government in Beijing. They are often tightly focused on making money and care-less about other implications. In China itself the singlemindedness of these companies creates local problems, environmental and social, but in Africa these problems are also political. One official said, 'We are trying also to educate Chinese businesses who have interests in Africa and involvements there to respect social conventions and observe local laws and regulations.'

In the end the most fundamental decisions do not lie with Beijing. They lie with Africa and its politics. China will either make or break Africa but it is up to Africa to control the relationship. Those who portray Africa as the weak victim of Chinese colonialism do not know their own history in Africa. The greedy elites that have captured African states like Angola and Kenya use China's engage-ment to enrich themselves – just as their forebears, African kings and chiefs, made pacts with Western invaders in the nineteenth century. Gleaning Chinese attitudes to this is difficult. Anecdotes of what lies behind the mask of friendship are hard to come by. But an indicative one comes from a comment by a Chinese official to Robert Calderisi, a former World Bank representative. 'If we had ministers sporting French-made suits and gold watches, and squalid slums right up against garish mansions, we would have another revolution in twenty-four hours,' he said.

Zambia has been the African country most affected by China's renewed engagement with Africa. Direct investment exceeded $1 billion in 2010, with copper mining and agriculture the main focus. Beijing claims that these investments have created over 150,000 jobs. But in that year two Chinese managers shot and injured 13 workers at a coal mine. Immediately Chinese companies raised wages and addressed complaints. Zambia's President, Levy Mwanawasa, was not slow to exploit the position. He accused Western countries of letting Zambia down and called on them to match Chinese investment in his country. 'Those who oppose Chinese investment . . . all they need to do is to equal the help we are getting from China. We only turned to the East when you people in the West let us down,' said Mwanawasa, pointing out that Chinese aid came with no strings attached.

A lesson for Africa lies in other countries that China has been engaged with in recent years. Vietnam, Malaysia and Australia have done well out of Chinese investment because their governments kept control of the relationship. Cambodia on the other hand has weaker governance and no vision of what it wants from the relationship. It was raped by China. It is up to African governments how they manage the relationship. At the moment China has an Africa policy but Africa's fifty-four governments do not have a China policy. There is little sign that they will try, even at a regional level, to agree a pan-African set of principles and standards by which to do business with China – or with Europe or America for that matter. It is one area in which the African Union could have taken a lead but did not. Angola seems to be the only government that appears to be taking control of the relationship. It insists that Chinese projects are checked and audited, and threatens to rescind oil deals unless it gets its way.

Could Angola's policy be made into a set of rules for the continent? What would they look like? They would insist that China's infrastructure plans fitted continent-wide and regional needs as well as China's need to get raw materials out of Africa. It would insist on Chinese investment in manufacturing in Africa and that Africans take control of the Special Economic Processing Zones that China is proposing to set up. And it would have a continent-wide plan to save and invest the windfalls from oil and other minerals. But the fundamental Africa question for China is the same as that posed to the rest of the world: what goods can Africa add value to and exports to create a decent living for its people?

As British aid agencies scurry around Africa trying to save it from poverty, and the Chinese businessmen and workers seek their fortunes there, the Americans are sending in the army. In 2008 Washington formally set up AFRICOM, a new American military command that will co-ordinate the United States' Africa policy. One reason given for the new command is to counter China's increasing influence in Africa and especially its acquisition of African oil and other raw materials. Part of America's 'grand strategy' to compete globally with China, the creation of AFRICOM is a warning to Beijing that Washington will match China's diplomatic and commercial actions in Africa with military might. I asked an American general how he would feel if China had created a similar structure, putting its Africa policy under military command and Chinese boots on the ground there. He paused for a moment. 'Uneasy,' he said.

Africa: where the French see international status and the British see an object of charity, the Chinese see a business opportunity. The Americans, it appears, see Africa as a threat.

19

A new Africa?

Africa: where humans emerged some 4 million years ago. From where, some 100,000 years ago, Homo sapiens spread all over the world. Africa: the mother of us all. It is our past. Could Africa also be our future?

It doesn't feel like that in a dark, stifling room in a Lagos hotel. For a moment there is silence, a pause between yet another power cut that has shut down the lights and air-conditioning and the start-up roar of the generator. It's a daily occurrence in Lagos – sometimes several times a day – and it's a growing phenomenon all over Africa. Some interpret it as a good sign: the growing demand for power in Africa. The economies are on the move. But did nobody realize that an improvement in economic activity would reveal a shortage of power? Didn't anyone believe that Africa's economies would start to grow? Even South Africa, the only truly modern economy south of the Sahara, suddenly introduced power cuts in 2008, forcing mines and businesses to shut down their operations. Power – or lack of it – has become a problem all over the continent. No one planned for a successful Africa. And that is ironic given the amount of oil and gas that Africa exports.

In Lagos power cuts that plunge the city into darkness used to be greeted with exclamations of 'Nepa don kwench!' Roughly translated from Lagos pidgin, it means 'the national power company has put the fire out again!' NEPA, the National Electrical Power Authority, was better known as Never Expect Power Always. So the government renamed it the Power Holding Company of Nigeria – PHCN. Nigerians also renamed it: Problem Has Changed Name. These days, when cuts have become a daily occurrence, people no longer even pause in their conversation. Even if they can no longer see the person they're addressing, they continue talking as if nothing has happened.

The small fifteen-room hotel I'm staying in is a refurbished house behind high walls and massive sheet-metal gates topped with razor wire. Two policemen, hired by the owner directly from the local police chief, guard it. That is how security, the phone system, water and electricity work in Nigeria. The country – together with much of the continent – has been privatized. Instead of paying tax to the government to provide services to all, you pay the manager of the service as if he owns it. This system works for those who have money.

The recent transformation of this house into a hotel reveals one of Africa's greatest needs – for carpenters, plumbers, plasterers, electricians – people with basic technical skills for setting up and repairing modern infrastructure. On the way to my room, I trip on the last step. It is slightly higher than all the others, and there is also a lower one in the middle. The door doesn't close properly without a final tug. The chair wobbles – or is it the uneven floor? And the bathroom tiles, smeared with cement, are askew.

Watching African footballers like Didier Drogba, George Weah and Samuel Eto'o thread millimetre-perfect passes on a windy, rain-soaked football pitch, I know that precision is not an alien concept in Africa. So I have come across another African mystery. Maybe it is another case of Africans not doing the job they were trained for. The plumbers have all become football players.

The next moment, out go the lights and the fridge clicks off. Then there is a series of stuttering, guttural coughs as one generator after another in the area comes to life. Every Nigerian building now houses at least one generator in a newly constructed cabin in the front yard with an exhaust pipe belching out blue diesel smoke directly into streets already jammed with stationary traffic. In the thirty-degree humid heat here, you could make the ultimate horror film about global warming.

I talk to a Nigerian friend about this. He laughs and quotes an oft-repeated phrase that has become the slogan of eternal Nigerian optimism: 'No condition is permanent.' This time I am not going to allow him to escape. 'Right,' I tell him. 'It could get worse.'

The euphoria of independence in many countries gave way to coups, incompetent military rule and, from the mid-1970s, steady economic decline and stagnation. But Africans always remained optimistic, an optimism that comes from enjoying the good times and surviving the bad times, as they have always done in the past. Because of that optimism I have never lost hope that, in its own time and in its own way, Africa would find a better future. But were expectations too high too early? While the rest of what was known as the Third World – the colonized nations of Asia and South America – sorted themselves out and gained skills and wealth and confidence, Africa seemed to be waiting for something to happen, for someone to come and create or pay for its future. I sensed a lack of agency, a lack of belief that development meant a linear progression, each generation improving on the previous one, building a world that replaced tracks with roads and the roads leading to towns where there were houses instead of huts, light bulbs instead of candles. In Africa, I often sensed that the modern world had arrived like a cargo cult brought by aliens, and that it was fun while it lasted but inevitably the wheel of fortune would turn, the road would disintegrate, the light bulb break and everything would be back where it was before.

When I first went to Uganda I saw how Africans reacted to new things brought in by outsiders: ideas, objects, language. They either adapted them to the African world, kept them carefully but unused or allowed them to disintegrate. It was an impression that was repeated again and again as I visited Africa. Useful things were used till they broke, then repaired and repaired again until they finally crumbled away. Maintenance was not a priority. Useless things – often mighty imperial projects – were left to crumble and die. Perhaps that is what will happen to the nation states themselves. They were not created by Africans so what interest did Africans have in them? Or the symbols were preserved but the purpose was lost. Long after democracy was killed in Zimbabwe, its parliament continued to follow the ancient customs of the Westminster Parliament – as happens in many ex-British colonies. Their Chief Justices still wore eighteenth-century wigs and red robes. Only the rituals remained.

In Africa, objects are often used in creative but unintended ways. The road, for example, is certainly good for travelling on, but also good as a meeting place, a market, a hot space for drying grain or fruit or clothes. Useful things become decoration; telephone wire is made into jewellery, flattened tin cans made into a wall. Some useful objects are kept for display: a whole chemistry laboratory transported to a school at great cost but kept locked away. The chemistry teacher proudly showed it to me, pristine.

Whenever Afro-optimists want to persuade people that things are getting better in Africa they quote Pliny the Elder's comment in the first century AD: 'Always something new out of Africa.' Africa does constantly change but not always in the way outsiders expect or want – or when they want. It goes at its own pace. I have wandered around it for the past thirty years, never quite sure when I would reach my destination or when the planned meeting would take place.

'The bus leaves promptly on Thursdays,' says the notice. 'What time?' I ask. 'Just now' is the answer. 'Please wait. Take a seat.' This means it will go when it is ready to go. But eventually we are off, and when I arrive there is always a warm welcome: 'Mister Richard. You are welcome. God has brought you to us. Good to see you. How are you? How is the family?' Africa is a slow place. There is always time, especially time to talk. Africans are the great communicators – linguists, word collectors. You cannot, as you do in Western cities, sit next to someone without talking to them. And time for music, dancing, singing. The hope is in the music.

And in God. Every meeting begins with a prayer, so does every journey, every flight. At every turn, you hear, 'Salam alaikum,' 'Allah akbar,' 'Thanks be to God.' Africans must be the most religious people on earth. They are great joiners and they seem to be networked to God. Sometimes their faith is explicit and noisy as people pack American-funded fundamentalist Christian churches. On Sundays they stay for three or four hours, singing, praising, preaching. But mostly belief is expressed lightly, casually, without fuss or expectation.

These are just some of the African phenomena that have charmed, puzzled, stimulated or frustrated me over the years. But as the continent becomes more and more connected to the rest of the world, they are being morphed into a new modern African culture. Change, when it comes, need not be slow, even in Africa. It may come within one generation. As a boy in the 1960s, I saw children in Ireland without shoes, homes without running water or sanitation. Like Africa in some ways, Ireland was regarded as charming but backward. The Irish were the butt of the universal jokes about stupidity, laziness and drunkenness. Scarcely a generation later, Ireland had a higher per capita GDP than Britain, its former colonizer, and was dubbed the Celtic Tiger. Until the crash in 2008, it had a higher per capita income than Britain and an economic growth rate twice the European average. In 2007 it was second in per capita income only to Luxembourg. Whole worlds can change within a few years. Although much of this wealth evaporated in the economic crash of 2008, no-one tells those Irish jokes any more.

Already, many of the dire predictions made about Africa in the 1990s and 2000s have not come to pass. One was that Africa would be reduced to anarchy by roving gangs of hopeless AIDS-ridden, gun-carrying youths. Another, made by President Festus Mogae of Botswana in 2000, was that his country, the best run in Africa, may not survive the AIDS pandemic. These fears are not being fulfilled thanks, in part, to the delivery of anti-retroviral drugs. The more worrying effect of AIDS has been two very untraditional African reactions – withdrawal and depression.

Today there are two realities in Africa. Much of Africa is actually getting better and has been since the beginning of the century, if not before. But the benefits of a decade of African growth have still not reached the poorest. Most of the world's fastest-growing economies are African. But nine out of ten countries at the bottom of the United Nations Human Development Index are also African.

In June 2010 McKinsey & Company, a management consultancy, produced a report called Lions on the Move, The Progress and Potential of African Economies. It said: '... sometime in the late 1990s, the continent began to stir. GDP growth picked up and then bounded ahead, rising fast through 2008. Today, while Asia's tiger economies continue to expand rapidly, we foresee the potential rise of economic lions in Africa's future.' It took the analysts nearly 20 years to acknowledge this change but there is huge optimism now that this growth is self generating and will continue.

At first I was sceptical. I had seen 'the dawn of a new era in

Africa' several times before, only to see each one dwindle into dusk and sometimes terrible night. But this time there wasn't a sudden collapse with boom turning to bust. The economies went on growing, despite the 2008 global crash. More and more guns fell silent. More and more children survived the critical first five years of life and more and more of them went to school. And although dictators still cling to office, their power is much diminished by the other powerful players in African societies – the private sector, the media and civil society. Even dictatorial rulers have to ride the waves of economic, social and technological change. And it seems that all these are getting faster. The McKinsey report pointed out that this was not just a commodity boom. Services and retail were making up to two-thirds of the growth. New infrastructure was being built, thanks largely to the Chinese, Africa's new partners.

Africa's economies have risen and fallen unpredictably since 2000 dependent as they are on oil and mineral prices. For example in 2008 Equatorial Guinea's economy grew by 17.8 per cent but in 2010 it fell to minus 8.9 per cent. Angola's grew at 22.6 per cent in 2007, two years later it was down to 2.4 per cent. Worst of all Sierra Leone's growth rate dived from 20.7 per cent to minus 20.6 per cent in 2015 because of the Ebola outbreak. Planning economies with such volatility is impossible.

The future all-Africa figures are alarming. The test came at the end of 2012 when the demand for Africa's resources began to flatten and their price began to drop again. But this time the boom has been self-sustaining, not just depending on the outside world's demand for resources, and growth remained at more than 5 per cent. In 2016 it remained steady at 3.89 per cent. But take population growth out of this and more than 40 per cent of Africans will not be able to live above the $1.25 a day poverty line.

On the other hand the growth is being better managed in most countries. More than half of the new growth is in sectors like banking, phones and insurance. This leads many experts to believe that this is not a temporary or cyclical gold rush but a permanent change in Africa's fortunes. But will it also pull up those on less than $1.25 a day?

Already Africa is receiving far more from trade than it received in aid promised by world leaders in 2005. Aid is also far outweighed by remittances sent home by Africans living abroad. It will play only a minor role in the development of Africa. In 2002, according to the African Development Bank, Africa's GDP was $600 billion. Ten years later it was $2.2 trillion.

Much of this growth was among the non-oil producers. Ethiopia's growth rate in 2003 was a mere 2.7 per cent but the following year leapt to 13.6 per cent and has stayed at that level ever since. Even Congo's economy was hitting nearly 8 per cent. In February 2008 when the European and American economies slumped, the IMF cut its growth estimates for every region of the world except Africa, where it increased it. From 2013 the whole continent began to grow at about 5 per cent and some oil and gas producers at more than twice that. The last time this happened, in the commodity boom of the 1970s, African governments borrowed heavily and threw a party, spending on prestige projects rather than investing in their people. When the prices began to fall, the party ended. Most African countries woke up with a hangover which lasted into the 1990s.

So who is driving the new Africa: Africans or outsiders? There are three main motors driving this change: China, mobile phones and the emergence of a new African middle class. None of them was predicted. In 1996 Chinese President Jiang Zemin addressed the Organization of Africa Unity and called for a rejuvenation of ties with Africa. At that time, China Africa relations were mainly political, with a little one-way trade: Chinese goods traded to Africa. That was worth just under $4 billion a year. In the following years the foundations were laid as China's diplomatic presence was transformed into a trading partnership.

The Chinese saw Africa as a place of opportunity to source the raw materials it needed for rapid industrial expansion. Africa did indeed have huge quantities of raw materials but in the West it was marked 'difficult', so investment from the former colonial powers was not forthcoming. The Chinese moved into Africa at the turn of the century when commercial interest in the continent was at an all-time low. They knew that Africa was the last onshore store of untapped minerals but in many places these were unmapped. Physical and political dangers had also kept out the Western mining companies. They were not too worried as they thought the resources would stay in the ground until needed. Like a pudding that was too hot to eat, Africa would wait until later. But suddenly the Chinese slipped in through the back door and started gobbling up that pudding with sweetened deals that Western companies could not match. They behaved like the Europeans had in the nineteenth century, bravely going where others dared not go. Suddenly Western companies which in the past had divided the spoils of Africa in secret deals with governments and each other, found they had real competition.

Chinese engagement has been very good for Africa in many ways. For millions of ordinary Africans China provided their first watch or radio, a second pair of shoes or a shirt. Maybe a suit. African governments found a big rich partner who was prepared to build roads and other infrastructure quickly, projects that Western donors would avoid or give to the World Bank which would study them for years. Chinese demand for raw materials pushed up the prices of African commodities and China was prepared to offer cheap loans to governments as well as what were often little more than cheap loans, which they called aid, to Chinese companies. By 2000 China–Africa trade stood at $10.5 billion. In 2012 it was estimated to have reached more than $166 billion. Their engagement was, they said: 'non-ideological'. Most African rulers, tired of being lectured by Western diplomats and economic experts, liked the Chinese approach. The Chinese did not mention human rights, democracy or the environment but spoke to Africa warmly, as an apparent equal. And African rulers sometimes got a new presidential palace or a road to their home village as a gift.

China also gave African governments an alternative partner. From the end of the Cold War, African governments were faced with a phalanx of Western states flanked by the IMF and the World Bank all saying the same thing: open up your economies to market forces, hold elections and respect human rights. With China's new offer, African governments had the confidence and enough wiggle room to push back against the Western agenda. Even close allies of the West like Rwanda under Paul Kagame and Ethiopia under Meles Zenawi were able to stand up to Western pressure for human rights. Meles was able to tell them in public: 'There is no connection between democracy and development.'

The second driver has been the mobile phone and connectivity. The idea that phone companies would invest in network infrastructure for mobile phones in poverty-stricken Africa seemed far-fetched. The notion that ordinary Africans would buy them and use them seemed even more so. Maybe a few from the Wabenzi tribe who drive Mercedes would have them, along with their Rolex watches and flashy suits. Everyone knew most Africans did not use telephones. When the South African MTN Group investigated Nigeria as a possible market for mobile phones in the late 1990s, their experts estimated that the maximum number of potential subscribers would be 15 million. So they opened in Nigeria in 2001. By 2010 Nigeria was its largest market with over 40 million subscribers using over 100 million phones – Nigerians often have two or more phones.

That wild underestimation of Nigeria's mobile phone market was repeated throughout Africa. It showed two profound misunderstandings of the continent: first, Africa's ability to pay, and second, its desire to communicate. Africa was a lot richer than the economists of the World Bank and the IMF had thought. Africa's mobile market has been the fastest growing in the world. According to the International Telecommunications Union, in 2011 the continent's mobile phone use had increased at an annual rate of 65 per cent in five years, twice the global average. One reason for this was that Africa had few working fixed-line systems. Only 2.8 per cent of Africans have ordinary phone services. Between 1999 and 2012, the number of mobile subscribers in Africa jumped from 7.5 million to 644 million, which represents about 11 per cent of the world's mobile phones. Africans make up about 16 per cent of the world's population so the mobile phone gap is not that wide. Almost 20 per cent of African subscribers have smart phones and in seven African countries penetration is more than 100 per cent. And Internet use is higher in Nigeria than elsewhere in Africa. According to Internet World Statistics, in 2011 there were about 120 million Internet users in Africa, 44 per cent of them in Nigeria.

Connectivity, not yet universal, reaches the remotest places. Suddenly you can call London from a village more than fifty miles from a town in northern Nigeria. It was not, as expected, just the middle-class professionals who wanted a mobile. The mobile phone companies make their money much further down the pyramid. Villages and shanty towns bleep and jingle as much as hi-tech urban offices. Walk through a market in a Nigerian village and you will hear the market women checking the price of potatoes in the nearest town; visit nomads in Somalia and you will find them, herding-stick in one hand, mobile in the other, finding out the best moment to come to market to sell their animals. Fishermen off the Tanzanian coast check which beach or port to bring their catch to. And everywhere in Africa no taxi driver will let you get out before he has given you his mobile number.

Everyone wants a mobile phone, just as much as they once wanted shoes. The pay-as-you-go cards solved the problem of billing. The postal service does not work in much of Africa. Decades of airtime are sold through plastic scratch cards available from private traders in smartly painted booths and shops in every village. And Kenya was the first country in the world to provide money transfers by mobile. The phone companies get their money back instantly and all have made fortunes. This not only proved that Africans were much richer than the World Bank, the donors – and the mobile phone companies – thought, it is also transforming economies from the bottom up. No-one predicted any of this.

The political impact may be even greater. Not only do all the political and business classes talk to each other incessantly, the phones have also played new and vital roles in civil wars. In northern Uganda rebel leaders talked to international diplomats: the LRA leader, Joseph Kony, had his mobile phone bill paid by the British government. In the Niger Delta the kidnapping gangs make their ransom demands by mobile and can be reached by journalists – and peacemakers. The days when terrible massacres would be revealed only months after they had taken place are gone. The news is Tweeted and Facebooked all over Africa, as it is everywhere else in the world. Could it be that the Rwandan genocide of 1994 would have been stopped if mobile phones had been available at that time?

During elections in Ghana in 2000 radio stations deployed reporters at polling stations all over the country or simply asked members of the public to say on air what they were seeing. At the polling booths accounts of irregularities or outbreaks of intimidation were carried live on local FM stations. The 2008 elections in Zimbabwe revealed how quickly news and elections results spread around the world from remote rural areas. The real election results were posted at polling stations and transmitted instantly by mobile phone. In contrast, when the government attempted to suppress the results, their methods looked positively Stone Age. At the next election in 2013, the government closed down the mobile networks to prevent a repetition. But in the rest of Africa election results announced at polling stations are transferred instantly by observers with mobile phones, ensuring that they can be checked against figures announced in the capital. At little cost mobiles have made elections more transparent than all the monitoring by expensive international election observers. Combined with radios, the phones have opened up unimagined political space in Africa. People use their mobiles to call radio stations to spread political news, views and gossip. Suddenly scores of people discover they all feel the same about the government, have the same problems and are able to listen to different solutions. Mobile phones and radio are creating networks of solidarity.

In most countries government ministers and officials can do little to curb their use – they are private commercial operations and government officials also depend on them. But the technology is also available to those with less democratic intentions. In the aftermath of the Kenyan election at the end of 2007 mobiles were swamped with hate messages urging people to rid the country of Kikuyus or telling Kikuyus to pick up arms and fight back against a conspiracy to rob them and kill them. Gangs of killers on both sides used their mobiles to co-ordinate their attacks.

Mobile phones transformed my work as a journalist in Africa. When I lived in Uganda in the early 1970s I used a telephone once. To do so I had to get a taxi to the nearest town and wait in an office for an hour until a very crackly international line was free. As a journalist in the 1980s I found international lines from Africa were little better. After the coup in Uganda in 1985 which overthrew President Obote, I drove across the country to meet rebel guerrillas in the foothills of the Mountains of the Moon. After I had interviewed them I rushed to the hotel in Fort Portal to call my newspaper in London. There was a phone but when I asked for a line, the manager burst out laughing. 'We have had no line here for more than ten years,' he said. So I had to drive seven hours all the way back to Kampala to send the story. Outside South Africa, the continent was barely part of the global telephone system. A scarcity of fixed lines and a lack of maintenance meant that the most common sound on the African telephone network was a polite voice on a loop saying, 'The number you require is unavailable. Please try later.'

For a journalist communications are everything. When I checked into hotels one of the first things I would do was pay a visit to the telephone operators and buy them drinks or perfume. Once, in Sierra Leone, I even went to the telephone exchange to offer presents for getting me a line. They gratefully accepted my gifts, but the problem lay deeper.

For years I sent my dispatches back to my newspaper by telex. Only post offices and a few hotels had them, but the post office was often the first building to go if there was a war. And businesses closed. Telexes were like huge, clunky typewriters that sent a mechanical signal. Telexing meant you had to type word perfect or send a raft of corrections. If there was a gang of busy journalists, competition for the telex was gladiatorial.

The telex was temporarily replaced by the satellite telex, which was like a heavy briefcase. With that, you could communicate from anywhere in the world – in theory. But it took time. You had to charge up the machine, load your article, work out where the satellite was, point it broadly in that direction, and press buttons. It had a habit of breaking off halfway through sending a message, and I have memories of long nights standing over the machine as though it were a sick child, tending, pleading, praying. It also seemed to spell 'spy' in every known language. I remember explaining to an inquisitive Congolese army officer that it was a machine for storing solar power.

Now I can pick up a signal and send stories by mobile phone from almost anywhere in Africa.

Close behind mobile phones comes the Internet, although its penetration has been slower. Between 2000 and 2011 Internet users in Africa increased from 5 million to almost 14 million. But visit any Internet café in Africa and you must fight for a seat, even though they are often more expensive to use than in Europe. Sitting in London I can chat to people via email in villages all over Africa. Social media is as lively and widespread as it is in Europe and America. Only power cuts can stop this phenomenon. Even if state radio stations suppress news, people pick it up from the Net and broadcast it. Africa is no longer cut off from the rest of the world.

The third driver of development in Africa is the burgeoning self-confidence of the middle class. In the 1970s and 1980s the African middle class was very thin. Professionals were rare. Few were in jobs that put into practice what they had studied at university. Engineers were running government ministries, historians were politicians, scientists were diplomats. Most seemed to find a niche in the state system. It was lucrative but not productive. Most of the managers who made things work were outsiders: Europeans, Lebanese, Asians. In the 1980s in Côte d'Ivoire there were twice as many European expatriates working than there had been in colonial times.

Today a third of Africans – some 350 million people – are middle class, according to the African Development Bank, and spend between $2 and $20 a day. At the most senior level the growing numbers of African managers are interchangeable with their counterparts in New York, London or Tokyo. This new professional middle class is local, pan-African and international. It is technically proficient but also able to avoid or negotiate African politics, African ways of doing things and local culture. Internally the same families and schools that produce the bankers and lawyers also produce the civil society activists who try to keep the governments honest by investigating issues, publicizing their findings through the media and campaigning for better governance in all sectors. Externally they are linked to the diaspora who have become serious investors in Africa. The estimated 140 million Africans living outside the continent sent $44 billion back in 2011. In that year 17 per cent of Foreign Direct Investment in Africa came from the diaspora. According to Eric Guichard, founder of Homestrings, a diaspora investment fund, Kenyans sent $891 million home in 2011, and some $222 million of that was invested as capital into the productive sector. That is $42 million more than Kenya received in aid.

Whether in Africa or outside it, this generation is profoundly different to the young generation I taught in Uganda in the early 1970s. Then, the students all saw their future as civil servants or in a profession that would give them a salary, a desk, a suit and a tie. I don't think any of them made it but that was the expectation of everyone who went to school then. They were set on leaving the despised life of the village and becoming like a white man. The current young generation of Africans know they must find their own way. They know there is no job waiting for them so they desperately seek to accumulate skills by attending courses to give themselves several options. So they may end up working in a shop and driving a taxi during the day, studying in the evenings and at weekends, and growing food on a plot near the room they rent on the edge of town. But the bigger difference is that they are far more self-confident than the previous generation. They are comfortable in their African identity as well as being open to ideas from all over the world. The scramble to be 'just like a white man' has ended.

Africans of this generation are confident that they will take control of the continent's development, leaving it neither to outsiders they feel patronised by, nor to their politicians who they despise. They are doing it by themselves, for themselves. They will lead Africa into a new world, releasing the continent's immense energies and potential, creating and spreading wealth. Although they avoid politics, their attitudes affect the broad political and development debate, creating the background against which decisions are made. Thirty years ago each African country had its own state-controlled newspaper, state-controlled radio station and maybe a television station. South Africa only got TV in 1975 and Malawi not until 1999. Unless people could listen to the BBC World Service, most Africans got all their information about their country and the world from state-owned radio and TV. Now there are thousands of newspapers, websites, radio stations and television stations that are both local and globally connected. Although there is considerable censorship and self-censorship, everyone has knows far more about what is going on than they did 20 years ago. And the diaspora can watch and listen to these media as easily as the people in the area. This is the main way in which the voices of the professional middle classes are heard.

What other factors are at play in the new Africa? Most people outside the continent might still think foreign aid is the solution to Africa's development. At the end of 2007 two clear and diametrically opposed images of Africa were dramatically illustrated within one week in the old imperial capital, London. One was an advertisement in the *Evening Standard* calling for investment in Africa. The other, four days later, was an article in the *Guardian* by the editor, describing a village in Uganda as living in the fourteenth century and encouraging readers to volunteer or send their old computers and bicycles to bring the twenty-first century to the area. This was Africa as portrayed by the aid agencies and Live Aid – a pitiable Africa of poverty and helplessness, needing the West to fix it.

In 2005 the leaders of the Group of Eight (G8) – the leading industrial countries – promised to double their aid to Africa. Britain, which hosted their summit that year, talked grandly about a Marshall Plan for Africa as if all Africa needed was the money which would now be provided. The aim was for Africa to meet the Millennium Development Goals (MDGs), a list of targets for good things like reducing infant mortality and getting more children into school by 2015. Good intentions but the goals – like most of Africa's develop-ment plans – were drawn up by outsiders with no serious input from Africans or their governments. Only Rwanda insisted on setting its own targets, and today Rwanda is one of the few countries which is reaching them. Other African countries will miss them badly but, ever anxious for aid, their governments will sing nicely from the West's development hymn sheet and promise to deliver. They are simply not committed to the MDGs. Indeed, aid may actually pre-vent African countries from developing by allowing their ruling elites to avoid real long-term solutions. As they say in Uganda, 'Begged water does not quench thirst.'

Following the 2005 commitments, the donors promised huge new amounts of aid to Africa and wrote off some of its debts, but few of them kept those promises, particularly after the slump in Europe following the 2008 crash when aid budgets were slashed. By 2011, only a handful of donors and aid recipients were fulfilling the deal. The vision was fading. And most African governments did not have the capacity to spend this aid money quickly or efficiently. Small NGOs run locally but helped by outside funding are more useful than Big Aid. The only exceptions to this generalization are the big, essential but simple medical programmes supported by the United

States and big foundations to fund one-off campaigns such as polio vaccination and anti retroviral drugs to combat HIV/AIDS.

Nearly everyone who actually goes to Africa, walks the ground and listens to Africans comes back with more or less the same conclusion: 'Money is not the answer… but it could help if everything else were in place.' When the 'right answers' are found by the Africans themselves, moderate amounts of external funding can help speed up the process of development. If you ask Western governments which African countries they support, the donors reply that they help ones that are doing the right things, like Botswana. But the Botswanas of Africa are already doing the right things, so they don't need much aid. The ones that desperately need development, like Congo, are incapable of managing aid money. So the argument becomes circular.

When outsiders decree the solutions for development and pour in money, most aid is wasted. At worst it can cover up the problem or even prevent a solution. In some places it has destroyed local initiative and held Africa back. Kenya, for example, experienced economic growth because of its diligent and hard-working middle class and despite the continual looting of its resources by its thieving political elite. Ever since independence Kenyans who have gone into politics have stolen huge amounts of money. When Daniel arap Moi retired and the opposition under Mwai Kibaki came to power, the same – if slightly cruder – scams for stealing public money continued. Kenyans were furious but the World Bank continued to prop up the thieves – giving them even more money to steal. World Bank officials do not further their careers by not spending their budgets. So, desperate to 'push money out of the door', as they say at the Bank, they shovelled more and more money down the throats of Kenya's robber barons until, in the memorable words of Edward Clay, the British High Commissioner, they were 'vomiting on their shoes'.

Ironically, it is the capitalist West that still sees Africa as a continent that needs aid, while Communist and former Socialist governments like China and India see it as a business opportunity. And it is significant that none of the most passionate advocates of aid for Africa are African. Aid can speed up development that people have already decided to carry out for themselves and that they have the capacity for but it cannot transform whole societies, whole countries. Emergency aid is obviously vital to help the victims of war or natural disasters, but that is as true in Surrey as it is in Somalia. Small amounts of aid can also work well in local contexts. But real development can only come about by the people themselves producing things or creating services that someone else wants to buy.

Recently it has become clear that most of the African economic figures issued by African governments, the World Bank and the IMF are wrong. The extraordinary success of mobile phones has already shown that there was a lot more wealth further down the social scale than anyone thought. In 2010 Ghana recalculated its national income by rebasing the baseline for its statistics. In 1993, the year established as the baseline for the calculation, there were no mobile phones or many other economic activities that have been the drivers of Ghana's growth. Suddenly Ghana's GDP wasn't $15.7 billion, it was actually $25.6 billion. This sudden 63 per cent leap made it a middle-income country. Other countries – including Nigeria – are making the same recalculation although, in doing so, they will lose the right to certain concessionary loans and other benefits. Africa is, as many of us always thought, a lot richer than it was portrayed by Western media. It is not incapable of development. It had done well in the 1960s and 1970s but then bad governance, wars and a decline in the price of primary goods but a rise in the price of manufactured goods impoverished several countries in the 1980s and 1990s.

What other factors have made life better in Africa? Conflict has diminished and been replaced by non-violent if robust politics. The early 1990s saw twenty-six African countries either at war or suffering violent, state-threatening events. By 2013 most of those had stopped or become sporadic. Even Somalia's 20-year war had come to an end, although there has been a rise in Islamic fundamentalist attacks in Northern Nigeria, Mali and Niger. War can sometimes be creative – horrible but transforming. However Africa's wars have been almost entirely destructive: infrastructure was smashed, skilled professionals died or fled, long-term investment was withdrawn and warlords took over. In countries like Liberia, Sierra Leone, Congo and Somalia, people had to survive among the ruins. Côte d'Ivoire's nine-year devastating war between Muslim north and Christian south ended in 2011.

Only in South Africa and Rwanda did war make life better. Apartheid South Africa's war against its neighbours in the 1980s was entirely destructive, but the battle within South Africa resulted in a negotiated victory that prompted the longest period of economic growth in the country's history. In Rwanda genocide was stopped by the Rwanda Patriotic Front, a Tutsi-led army which then came to power, determined never to let it happen again. This has meant tight political control and no real democracy but a clear vision of a new Rwanda. With careful planning, extraordinary energy, utter determination – and some aid support – Rwanda's new rulers have driven through a positive economic and development agenda. Human rights and political freedom are, however, extremely limited.

Africa's wars ended partly because of more political engagement and peace-making – though not necessarily intervention – by the rest of the world or African governments led by South Africa. Their persistence paid off in countries like Burundi. America patiently helped create Sudan's Comprehensive Peace Agreement which offered peace and independence to the south after some fifty years of war. In

Somalia, however, Washington did the opposite, giving the Ethiopians the green light to invade and destroy the Islamic Courts which had delivered the beginnings of peace after sixteen years of civil war. In West Africa, Liberia and Sierra Leone are now at peace and their wars did not – as many predicted – spread to Guinea.

In 2012 and 2013 there was a sudden outburst of Islamic fundamentalism in the Western Sahel that grew out of the cancellation of the 1991 Algerian election which was won by the Islamic Salvation Front. That handed the incentive to the extreme Islamic groups which, although they were defeated in Algeria, spread south into the Sahara. This development may become very serious. The sudden and rapid implosion of Mali in 2013 was a shock. Mali had been held up as a model of 'good governance', with a coherent development programme and an army trained by the United States. Suddenly the north was taken over by Islamic fundamentalists supported by Algerian exiles with Al-Qaeda training and financial support. There is increasing evidence of such Islamist movements in the region, with easy access to weaponry and money. In Nigeria Boko Haram in the north east linked up with the trans-Saharan smugglers of drugs and arms. The heavy-handed over-reaction of the Nigerian army has strengthened Boko Haram and brought in more recruits.

The end of wars in the rest of Africa may mean national reconciliation and new political alignments in some countries. Elsewhere the killing may have stopped but the fault lines are still there and the volcanoes still smoke. Some might erupt again or continue in a different form and explode again later. It seems unlikely that Côte D'Ivoire will fall into the abyss again, but Congo's more localised wars may continue for some time. The picture is not clear. But politicians exchanging abuse and insults in their parliaments are better than warlords exchanging bullets and planting mines.

Bad politics erupted in Kenya in 2007 after a close-run election was stolen by the ruling party. That triggered an outburst of anger which had been simmering for fifty years. It expressed itself not as a revolt against the ruling thieves, but in tribalism. In six terrible weeks some 1500 people died in a nation-wide outbreak of ethnic cleansing. The violence began and ended as politicians quarrelled or made up. There was strong evidence that almost all were encouraging, even paying, young men to launch attacks on the supporters of their political enemies. A peace deal brokered by Kofi Annan, the former UN Secretary General, created a government of national unity but the deal was only made possible because, for once, the rest of the world, including Africa, put immense pressure on the two Kenyan leaders to reach a deal. They did, and ruled for four years.

The next election was peaceful but was won by an alliance of two tribal leaders who were both charged with crimes against humanity for the 2008 bloodshed. In the meantime a new constitution came into force, devolving power and budgets to 47 newly created counties. Will the localization of Kenya's politics solve the national problem of ethnic competition or worsen it? The violence in Kenya, the stolen Nigerian election, flawed polls in Uganda, Ethiopia, Cameroon and Malawi, the post-election fallout in Congo and Zimbabwe's stolen election in 2008 all raise the question of whether a winner-takes-all, first-past-the-post, multi-party democracy is going to work in parts of Africa where ethnic allegiance is stronger than national identity.

Overall the best contribution that African governments have made has been to create a simple legal framework for development, encourage investment and then get out of the way and concentrate on providing better infrastructure, health and education. The picture has been mixed. In many cases success has been in spite of the rulers rather than because of them.

Foreign investment interest in Africa began to revive in around

2004. A few adventurous Western investors began to sense that something was stirring in the long grass of Africa. At the time there were only two investment funds designed primarily for Africa; by 2007 more than a dozen had sprung up in London, New York, Johannesburg and even Moscow. Investors and bankers who in the past would have looked away in embarrassment if you had mentioned Africa were now selling it as the wonder opportunity. When the world economy faced slowdown in early 2008, giant investor guides like Goldman Sachs, who would have shunned any connection to Africa a few years before, began to explore its potential. The 2008 global recession affected Africa indirectly because, as the demand for Chinese-made goods declined, Chinese demand for African raw materials also declined. But by then Africa had become the new investment destination. The 'last frontier' had been crossed.

Who were the first to spot the opportunity in Africa? Miles Morland spotted openings to make big money in Africa almost twenty years ago. A charming, exuberant former banker, Miles set up Blakeney Management and started investing in African and Middle Eastern stock markets in the early 1990s when the World Bank was forcing African governments to privatise state-owned companies. He explained to me:

> Firstly no-one had a clue what these companies were worth and secondly Africa suffered from a uniquely negative perception. When African countries were going up in smoke, you went as a journalist to describe the smoke. I went along and picked through the rubble. It was a bit like salvage reclamation. No-one else wanted this stuff because of the perception that Africa was an economic black hole and the Middle East a hotbed of dangerous Islamic terrorists. The general wrongness of that perception created a wonderful niche opportunity for anyone who was prepared to trot off to these fledgling markets

*and do the work themselves. In amongst them were some very
profitable companies.*

Miles invested in anything that supported the emerging professional
classes of Africa and avoided the traditional African markets – South
Africa and minerals. Throughout the 1990s his investments in companies on the African stock markets made huge profits, though he
admits that his four attempts to buy majority stakes in African companies and direct them himself were catastrophic. The lesson seemed
to be that Africa, left to itself, was more than capable of managing its
own affairs and could turn out substantial profits. Blakeney
Management stopped accepting new money when it reached $500
million in September 2004. By the end of 2007, having grown at
over 40 per cent a year for the previous five years, the firm managed
around $2 billion. In mid-2007 the *Financial Times* said that Africa
had reached a tipping point. Miles laughs: 'It tipped eight years ago,
but no-one noticed.'

A new generation of Africans was emerging. Many of them had
finished their education outside Africa but instead of staying away,
they decided to return. But unlike their fathers, who mostly went into
politics or government service, this generation has turned to business.

Instant communication is the most important factor that brought
Kofi Bucknor back to Ghana with his family. His office is in a broad,
quiet street close to Accra's international airport. The house is modest and neat, set in a garden behind high walls, though the gates
would not look out of place at Buckingham Palace. The waiting
room is elegantly furnished with Persian carpets, a bark cloth
printed with a map of Africa, African stone carvings and a beautiful
dark wood table. Kofi greets me in a loose white shirt, slacks and
sandals and immediately takes a call from America on his BlackBerry.

His CV looks like that of a high-flying merchant banker: MBA from Columbia, joined the First Boston Corporation, moved to the Chemical Bank where he ran the Abidjan branch, then across to the African Development Bank in 1986 and back to the private sector with a move to London and Lehman Brothers in 1994, then to the Cal Merchant Bank in London. He also serves on numerous policy and advisory committees, holds several directorates and chairs the Ghanaian stock exchange.

But he always wanted his children to experience growing up in Africa and decided to come back. 'Three factors made it possible,' he says. 'One, the Internet; two, mobile phones; and three, satellite TV. Suddenly the world is flat and I can get the same info in Accra as I could in London. I guess I can operate here now at 70 to 80 per cent efficiency. Before, it was about 20 per cent. I could probably have made bigger bucks in the City of London but the quality of life here is much better, especially for my three kids.'

He manages funds for Saudi Prince Alwaleed bin Talal, who has invested nearly $80 million in Africa. But now he also acts as a consultant for companies looking for a pan-African business, mainly in the area of telecoms. 'I'm fifty-two, I have a ten-minute drive to the office. I dress how I like. I have a beach house in a fishing village not far away. It's a good life. My generation are coming back to Ghana and starting to make the country the way it was back in the 1940s and 1950s.'

On my way back into Accra I take a taxi. The driver is Agyekum who is twenty-three and wears a huge smile. He is making $600 a month, he tells me. His wife makes $300 to $400 as a waitress. At the moment he drives his own car but he wants to buy more cars and employ other drivers. 'If you are prepared to work hard in Ghana you can get rich. It is becoming a great place.' He sounds like the happiest man on earth: 'Everything is going well. Life has never been better.'

That weekend I visit an eco-park of dense rainforest with a

guided tour for visitors, about a third of whom are middle-class Ghanaians. When we step out onto the precarious rope bridge slung between massive trees towering above the jungle it is clear they are no more at home in this wild rural environment than the European tourists. Africa will soon be predominantly urban.

Two countries away in Nigeria, Osaze Osifo looks out across the grey Atlantic from the eighth floor of a new sheer glass block on the Lagos seafront. The line of ships at anchor stretches to the horizon, all of them waiting to come into Lagos port. The queue is symbolic of the world's long wait to do business with Nigeria. These ships are idle at anchor for up to three weeks. That's an improvement on the 1970s when the waiting time averaged 240 days.

Osaze, dressed in jeans and a white shirt, wanders around his company's newly furnished open-plan office where everyone is visible and accessible. There is no Big Man here, no hierarchy and nothing flashy or grand. Again the new professionals are not suits. Osaze himself, small, soft-voiced, plain-speaking, calls in other members of his team as we talk and encourages them to join in the discussion. He too has returned to Africa from a lucrative banking career in London, launching a private equity company, Ocean and Oil Holdings. Its $300 million fund is focusing on transport, power and logistics – all essential to revitalising the Nigerian economy.

Unlike Kofi, Osaze admits he will probably make more money in Nigeria than in London. Nigeria is booming at the moment. But he adds that those who are in business just for the money are doing it the Nigerian way. He doesn't want to fawn over the Big Men business-politicians. He needs to operate by international standards of account-ability and transparency because he is bringing in international money.

'The environment is big enough at present,' he says. 'We see opportunities opening up across West Africa from Angola to Senegal, so we can afford not to do things the Nigerian way. The type of people we have on our board shows we don't want to get things with bribes. We are real people with real jobs. Not cronies.'

This space to do business cleanly seems to have opened up during President Olusegun Obasanjo's second term. Heavy international pressure forced him to appoint an economic team who knew what they were doing and where they wanted to take Nigeria. They set up the Economic and Financial Crimes Commission, reduced the number of banks from eighty-nine to twenty-five and cut their non-performing loans to around 10 per cent. They also let the telecoms revolution happen. The Global System for Mobiles licences were sold cleanly. 'It's quite simple,' says Osaze.

> *All the government needs to do is create an environment in which we can do things properly. People are starting to do this instead of being agents for cronies. Bright young Nigerians are coming back. There is a will to have an irreversible change. It's a mindset, a way of doing things in a less corrupt way. There's a lot of people in Nigeria who have never seen things done properly before.*

I ask if this sudden rush of money into Nigeria will create social problems. 'Not at all,' says Osaze. 'In Nigeria wealth produces ambition, not envy. It's a case of "I want one too," not "I want his."'

Outside the street is deserted so I have to walk a couple of blocks to find an ocada – the motorbike pillion taxis that serve the choked Lagos streets. Immediately I am back in the other Africa. Each building has a pipe blasting smoky diesel exhaust into the street. Beside the road is an open drain overflowing with black, treacle-like water. A rat paddles purposefully through offal, shit and floating plastic bags. My lungs almost seize up involuntarily in the unbreathable air. Suddenly, from being in a smart twenty-first-century air-conditioned hi-tech glass-and-steel building, I am back in another Nigeria. Under a thorn tree right beside the drain, women are cooking doughnuts, plantains and corn on charcoal fires. Their kids play barefoot on the twisted, rusting skeletons of a truck and a car that appear to have collided a long time ago and are now locked permanently together in death. A glossy Hummer with darkened windows roars by.

The image of that uncomfortable juxtaposition of the two Africas stuck in my mind. A few years later I revisited Dar es Salaam which I remembered from the 1970s and 1980s as one of the nicest but sleepiest capitals in Africa. No-one walked at more than a stroll. Everyone seemed to have time to talk. Rush hours? They did not exist. Now its biggest problem is traffic jams. One afternoon I met up with an aid worker in his air-conditioned office and we decided to go for a drink in an air-conditioned hotel. We went in his huge air-conditioned 4x4 (which he had on standby 24 seven) and from there we went on to his air-conditioned home. At the end of the day I asked him if he ever breathes the air of Dar es Salaam.

For the rest of my stay in Dar I tried walking everywhere. Suddenly I was in a different city. The centre of Dar is well laid out with some broad tree-lined streets and wide pavements. But the streets are almost permanently locked in traffic jams and the pavements have all become parking lots for the 4x4s. If you walk you have to walk in the street. When the traffic begins to move, it is quite dangerous. Mixing with the worn shirts, patched trousers and second-hand shoes, I realized that this economic growth was happening in an air-conditioned bubble. Outside it are a vast number, the majority, of Tanzanians who dodge the shiny cars on the streets and glimpse the goodies of growth behind the razor wire of walled and gated mansions.

This is the latest style of Achebe's house, a new one that has been built by the elite, not abandoned by the colonialists. It remains the most striking symbol of what is currently happening to Africa; taken over by 'the smart and the lucky but hardly ever the best'. Inside the house the elites and their friends live in luxury and comfort, always ready to welcome political and business associates from the rest of the world. Outside live the majority, who exist from hand to mouth as they always have, untouched by the Africa described in the new Africa reports from international consultancies.

In some cases the house – as Achebe predicted – has been expanded. But everywhere the gulf has grown so wide between those in the house and those outside that some governments are now building new, gated cities where an electronic pass is needed to bring a car in or even to walk the streets. Everywhere the elites have built themselves new houses they are almost always designed exactly like the old ones – European-style baroque mansions behind high walls topped with razor wire and with armed guards on the gate. The more guards they have around them, the more certain you can be that the gap between the few inside and the mass of people outside, is growing ever wider. Everywhere most of the people are still out in the rain. How long will they wait there before they demand to be let into the house and into the dream of a successful, prosperous Africa?

And how long before those inside the house begin to recognize the needs of their fellow citizens outside? One of the slogans that pricked the conscience of Britain in the time of slavery was 'Am I not too a Man?' Could a similar attitude to the poor develop among the middle class in Africa? 'Am I not too a Nigerian, a Kenyan, a South African?' But there is little solidarity in these newly created states. Africans are still working through the fallout from the impact of European powers in the late nineteenth century. African politics are still dominated by ethnic identity, not by nationalism or class.

What does nationalism mean today in Africa beyond football rivalry and economic competition with neighbours? Where do the loyalties of Africans lie today, a century and a quarter after their continent was carved up by foreigners? The 10,000-odd political entities speaking more than 2,000 languages became 54 states after seven European countries divided Africa between them. Only two African states survived that strange, brief but devastating invasion: Ethiopia and Liberia.

How do Nigerians or Mozambicans owe allegiance to states today that their grandfathers had no part in establishing and that they probably opposed? How does your attachment to the national flag and anthem feel when someone who does not speak your language and does not respect your customs becomes president? You may find you have much more in common with people of your ethnic group across the border in the neighbouring country, even though they may speak a different European language. In light of this I am frequently surprised by how much positive patriotic emotion many Africans display. But at the same time, when they talk about the other, the enemy, they are referring to another ethnic group in their own country, not another nation state. To imagine what this might feel like, suppose the United States had not become a melting pot of peoples and that all the immigrant groups had not mixed but had stayed separate from each other, keeping their own languages and customs and flags and memories of past wars.

In 2008–9 data collected by Afrobarometer revealed that traditional ethnic leadership received a startling level of support. Figures from 19 African countries showed that 40 and 50 per cent supported traditional leadership and in some of those countries the figure rose to 70 per cent. Confidence in government, national and local, existed in only a handful of countries.

Some ask whether it is time to redraw the national boundaries. At independence the first presidents all agreed not to tamper with them. Apart from the separation of Eritrea from Ethiopia and the division of Sudan, there has been little attempt to alter them. Independence movements from ethnic groups such as the Igbo in

Nigeria have been ruthlessly crushed with support from the United Nations and there is little support for such movements now. The political struggle today is for control of state resources between politicians heading ethnic coalitions. If a people feel excluded, they feel excluded as a group.

Most African countries have held elections since the African Union insisted on legitimacy based on votes, not coups. Elections are now held almost everywhere and although the sitting president usually wins, they give people an opportunity to think about their lives and express their feelings. In the 1980s thirty-eight presidential elections were held in Africa; in the 1990s seventy-seven were held; and between 2001 and 2011, the total was eighty-seven. Apart from Eritrea's Issias Afwerke and Swaziland's King Mswati, every African head of state has been elected or has promised some form of election. Whether that makes them more truly democratic is debatable. But it is hard to imagine crude dictators like Idi Amin, Sani Abacha or Hastings Banda taking over again. Robert Mugabe was a far more sophisticated tyrant. Ousted in 2018, his scowl still hangs over the continent, divisive to the last. The man who led his country to independence, Africa's most articulate advocate of anti-imperialism, ended up reducing his country to a wasteland, with its people starving, its wealth stashed in foreign banks. Mugabe was prepared to let his country die rather than give up power. He created a fantasy enemy, Britain, which he claimed was plotting to make Zimbabwe into white-ruled Rhodesia again. Every act of violence and breach of law was justified by a titanic battle against this imaginary foe. To shore up national unity, African rulers often play a card that has been obsolete since the 1960s – the notion that they are helpless victims under attack from 'colonialism and imperialism'. Many of them play that card because they are afraid of their own people and would like to return to the time when dictators could control the whole country including the minds of their people. They create a climate of fear in which evil but intangible forces are said to be conspiring against the country's territorial integrity and national sovereignty – a mindset that strongly resembles belief in the powers of witchcraft.

But Zimbabwe has demonstrated that Mugabe was wrong: Britain could not prevent him from seizing power and keeping it. There has been no outsider invasion of Zimbabwe or anywhere else in Africa, except in an effort to prop up a legitimate government under attack. Despite its efforts to double aid for the continent, Britain's influence in Africa is rapidly waning. And not just Britain's influence. The whole weight of Europe and America could not sway either the Zimbabwean junta or a majority of the African Union.

Could the successors of Nelson Mandela and Thabo Mbeki do to their country what Mugabe has done to Zimbabwe? The ugly public split in the ANC culminating in the coup at its 2007 conference at Polokwane that replaced Mbeki with Zuma indicates that South Africa's political stability is far from secure. The rainbow nation has come and gone. Mbeki's vision of an African Renaissance helped make Africans more confident today than their parents' generation were but, despite his Marxist background, Mbeki chose to frame the new South Africa in the same paradigm as that which framed the old South Africa: race. His attempt to create a black middle class in the course of a decade through a system of positive discrimination led to corruption and resentment. Only powerful people in the ANC and their friends got rich, and the scheme created an ethos of entitlement, making many people rich through connections, not merit. His failure to deal with crises in Congo and Zimbabwe and his refusal to engage with the realities of HIV/AIDS left a flawed legacy. Secretive, Mbeki ruled through a small clique. He did not like open debate and accountability let alone criticism, but it was his failure to reach out to people and inspire them that was his downfall. The Polokwane conference was followed by a violent nation-wide uprising against non South African migrants, putting a dagger through the pan-African vision that might have been his legacy.

After the erratic years of Mbeki's rule, just when South Africa needed a manager who could deliver basic needs such as education and health for the poor and energy and support for South African business, the ANC chose Jacob Zuma, the former head of security in the ANC, who had secretly engineered Mbeki's downfall. A smart politician but inexperienced in management, Zuma had stood trial for rape and was facing corruption charges. These were quickly set aside when he became president. Zuma brought thousands of his Zulu people into the ANC and gave many of them senior positions in the party to ensure a second term or at least the power to choose his successor. He built himself a plush mansion in Kwazulu with state funds and took more wives. His language and vision never moved beyond the old slogans of the exiled ANC and under his rule the state's ability to deliver on its promises rapidly shrunk as corruption spread throughout the administration. The ANC became a battleground for ambitious individuals greedily seeking government contracts.

Forged by the horrors of apartheid, the South African constitution is the most liberal humanist constitution in the world, inclusive and protective of minorities, but with strong guarantees for personal freedom. As well as protecting, it promotes the 'achievement of equality and the advancement of human rights and freedoms, non-racialism and non-sexism' and a democratic government to ensure accountability, responsiveness and openness. Because of it and despite changes the new ANC would like to make, South Africa's constitution cannot be rewritten easily. The state is layered with strong institutions staffed with committed people who will not easily give up what they fought for. But for more than twenty years after the release of Mandela, the needs of many South Africans – perhaps the majority – are not being met. Demagogues like Julius Malema, the head of the ANC Youth League, are demanding nationalization and blaming whites or other racial groups for the government's failure to deliver on its promises. The rich are retreating into fortified citadel states, the reverse image of the townships that black South Africans were forced into.

The two biggest African states, Nigeria and Congo, should be the drivers of the new Africa. But both are governed by a mixture of neglect and sudden violence. They are so big however and so dependent on local rather than national conditions, that war at one end of the country may have no effect whatsoever at the other. Parts of both countries are thriving and if that wealth was shared and invested in the longer term, they could become the next Brazils or Indonesias. South-west Nigeria, Lagos in particular, is booming and could have an exceedingly dynamic future. North-east Nigeria is one of the poorest parts of Africa and now suffers from Islamist-inspired violence which could deepen and spread. In the Niger Delta millions live in poverty while the oil beneath them flows out to benefit others. Periodic kidnappings and oil theft could worsen and evolve into a permanent state of gang warfare that might affect the flow of oil. It all depends on the leaders and the politics but, under presidents Yar A'dua and Goodluck Jonathan, the growth of corruption and lack of vision and strategy made that scenario more likely. The return of Muhammadu Buhari to the presidency sent a shockwave through the country but at seventy-six he had lost the energy and grip he once had. Besides so much power has now been devolved to the states that no Nigerian president can rule as the military dictators did.

At a continental level the African Union presents a new vision with a clear shape and identity. The old Organization of African Unity was little more than a rulers' trade union, issuing platitudes and complaints but prevented by mutual agreement from doing anything effective. Based on non-interference in each other's internal affairs, it was indifferent to the horrors of regimes like Idi Amin's in Uganda or Sékou Touré's in Guinea. The African Union reiterates non-interference but has also given itself the right to intervene in countries where war crimes or genocide are being committed. It also rejects the traditional way in which governments changed in Africa – via the coup. Its one tangible achievement has been to deter army officers from seizing power or to persuade those who have tried that they should step aside. The African Union's stated ideals, its commitments to human rights, freedoms and the rule of law, are less well observed. Its failures in Somalia, Darfur, Congo and Zimbabwe have exposed a gap between the dream and the reality. And when sudden intervention is needed, as happened in Mali in 2013, the former colonial power, France, was forced, reluctantly, to step in and save the country from collapse. Despite the energetic but ultra cautious leadership of Nkosasana Dlamini Zuma, it will be some time before the African Union can make a tangible continent-wide impact.

Much of Africa's new dynamism is coming from the local, not the national. Young Africans who have skills and are globally connected are just getting on with it. But can they persuade those in power to create frameworks that encourage investment and allow real development? In the past, African rulers have tended to try to control the economy as much as possible but bend to pressure from donors and allow the reforms to happen. But they do so without changing their statist mindset or offering real vision and leadership. They have often agreed to economic reforms reluctantly, but by making step-by-step changes since the 1990s, they have created far more space for the private sector to drive economic growth.

However the continent is still leaking capital and people. An OECD report in 2014 found that bribery, money laundering and tax evasion had made little progress in preventing the loss of capital from poor countries. Global Financial Integrity, a Washington-based think tank, estimates that, between 1970 and 2008, Africa lost between $854 billion and $1.8 trillion though 'illicit financial outflows'. In 2014 it found these flows to have been between $1.4 trillion and $2.5 trillion. The majority of this was due to mispricing or transfer pricing by transnational companies. Wealthy Africans also exported capital. A World Bank report in 1990 estimated that Africans held up to $360 billion, 40 per cent of their wealth, outside Africa. In contrast, the equivalent figures for East Asia and Latin America were less than 10 per cent. A 2008 study by the Tax Justice Network estimates the African figure to be as much as $607 billion, more than twice Africa's external debt. Transparency International estimates that $140 billion of that was illegally acquired. If Africans move their own wealth out of the continent, how can Africa ask outsiders to invest there? One of the best indicators as to whether Africa and individual African countries are getting better is whether its professional classes are prepared to live in them, bring up their children there and invest their money in them. In this regard, the exodus of people is alarming. Nearly a million leave each year. An estimated 15 million Africans born in the continent are now living outside it. The most common request to a white visitor to Africa these days, particularly from young people, is for help with a visa to Europe or America. Some 70,000 skilled people are reported to be fleeing the continent each year. Tens of thousands trek across the Sahara Desert in buses and lorries in the hope of finding a passage across the Mediterranean, or leave in tiny boats from West African beaches and ports hoping to reach Spain or Portugal. Untold thousands die en route and thousands more are caught and turned back. But, deported, they simply try again.

Tragic in human terms, this exodus is a big problem for Africa. If the migrants represent young, ambitious Africa, the continent is leaking its most precious resource: its people. Yet the exodus is not a complete loss to Africa. Bound by unbreakable ties to family and home, Africa's huge diaspora in Europe and America – and increasingly Asia – send home substantial proportions of their hard-earned wages. No-one knows how much is sent to Africa by Africans outside the continent, but according to the World Bank, the volume increased from $11 billion in 2000 to $60 billion in 2012, though this figure could be far higher because many Africans simply carry the money home rather than send it through banks or money transfer companies. In comparison, in 2010 Africa received about $43 billion in aid.

These remittances keep millions of children in school and enable families to buy medicine or equip siblings to start small businesses. Of course there are also reports that families use the money to build smart new houses to show off that they have a wealthy relative in London, Paris or New York. Africans like Kofi and Osaze can learn new skills outside Africa and return home to set up businesses but they are the minority of those who leave. The evidence is that while those in the diaspora remain connected, send money home and return for visits, they do not come home for good until they retire. The hope that they would return and use their skills to develop their countries is not borne out. Many who left because of poor economic times or war are often resented if they return because they are seen as people who left when the going was tough, returning home only to show off their wealth. On their side many returnees have complained that African institutions and officials are resistant to new ideas from outside. 'I was sucked straight back into the system,' one Ghanaian banker told me. 'I might as well never have been away.' Others are criticized for living it up in the fleshpots of London or New York while those who stayed behind were suffering.

So will the rest of the world invest in the new Africa? Inward investment hit the $50 billion mark just before the 2008 slump in Europe and returned to this level soon after. Much of this was in the extractive sector – oil, gas and minerals – a sector of low employment. Economists will tell you that no country with a substantial population has ever reached middle-income status without manufacturing. That is where Africa needs investment – either in manufacturing or in high-employment agriculture – to create jobs for the increasing number of young Africans. Wages in Chinese manufacturing have risen and this should present Africa with an opportunity, but most of these jobs appear to be going to southeast Asia. Does Africa have the organization, skills and discipline as well as the infrastructure, including reliable power supplies, to manufacture to Chinese standards? It must develop them quickly or its economies based on raw materials will remain at the mercy of fickle prices.

Africa has always been a rich continent for the 'smart and the lucky' as Chinua Achebe put it. Those inside the house he described can become exceedingly rich now, as in the past, by collaborating with foreigners to export Africa's raw materials: people, rubber, ivory, cocoa, coffee, oil and scores of other goods. But how will ordinary Africans in Africa earn their living in the world? Will the continent stay as a heap of raw materials extracted and exported mainly by foreigners, or will it take control and start to process those raw materials to add value?

Africa's other opportunity as the world's population continues to grow is to feed it. The steady increases in the price and demand for food offers such an opportunity. But even if the rich world dropped its subsidies and tariffs tomorrow, could Africa step up its quantity and quality? The continent has vast amounts of unused and underused land but every inch, outside the deserts, is claimed by someone or some group. Africans have more than a commercial relationship with the earth. They do not see land in purely financial terms and claim their rights to it by association and lineage. In colonial times African farmers were brutally cleared off great swathes of land which were turned over to state or commercial farming. That is beginning to be repeated today as foreign investors make deals with governments that are increasingly forcing people off their land which is then rented or sold to big companies for high-tech farms. Employing few people these farms grow genetically modified crops, managed by satellite weather watchers and watered and fertilised by advanced drip-feed irrigation systems. The crops are then shipped out, bringing no development to the area. This, given Africa's heritage of colonization and Africans' almost mystical attachment to land, is a recipe for disaster.

The present system of peasant production is not as productive as it might be. Where the land is already being cultivated, infrastructure is often poor and millions of tons of food are wasted because storage and transport are non-existent or poorly maintained. Currently most small farmers in Africa rely on hand hoes and God's rain. This haphazard system is unlikely to deliver the consistent quality and quantity of food demanded by the global supermarket chains. But much land could be used more productively. Nigeria, incredibly, is a net importer of food. Under present circumstances if the price of food rises globally, countries such as Brazil, India and Indonesia could move more quickly to grow food efficiently.

If Africa is to feed its own increasing and increasingly urban population as well as to make a profitable living in the world, it needs an agricultural revolution, a change in the way land is owned and used. Land ownership lies at the heart of African society, fundamental to the power structures of communities based on the extended family and clan. The temptation to change that system to create an agricultural revolution in Africa is strong. But simply giving land tenure to individuals who could then sell the freehold could destabilise African societies. A more communal system needs to be developed, perhaps one in which traditional African land tenure could be enshrined in law to allow the original owners to lease land long term to outsider investors while retaining a stake in the business and developing their own individual pieces of land in collaboration with the outsiders.

Europe tried to control Africa in the twentieth century. In the twenty-first century maybe Asia – China particularly – will dominate the continent. In the past outsiders imposed the wrong things on Africa in the wrong way at the wrong time. Maybe China's engagement is just another phase which will leave its mark, change Africa in unintended ways, but change nothing deep down. When Asia has taken what it wants from the continent what will be left for Africans? The trick of integrating old ways and new influences seems to be hard to accomplish in Africa but this is its great opportunity. The difficulty is that there is one China to 54 African countries, most of whose economies are minnows compared to the whale that is China. It can thus play divide and rule.

If the rest of the world wants to help Africa, the guiding principles must be: do no harm and remove the barriers that prevent Africa's development. The following are four ways in which governments in the rest of the world could help Africa without paying a penny in aid. At the top of the list comes ending all agricultural export subsidies that undercut African farmers and prevent them from earning their living as equal producers in the world. Second, the West should recognize that there are aspects of globalization that damage countries with weak economies. It is blatantly hypocritical for Western governments to force African countries to remove trade barriers and drop subsidies, while protecting their own markets by imposing similar trade barriers and giving subsidies. The hypocrisy of promoting the free movement of money and goods but preventing the free movement of people is plain. Globalized trade could at least be conducted on a level playing field, but at present it is managed globalization – managed, that is, by the rich countries in their own interests. If there are any exceptions to the rule of open markets, they should surely be poor countries trying to get a foot on the ladder to wealth. That is how today's wealthy nations – Britain, America and the Asian tigers – got rich. They all went through a period of protectionism to get started. Africa should be allowed to do the same.

On the whole, big oil producers are not democratic and care little for human rights. Possessing the life-blood of the world's economy, they get a free ride on human rights and democracy from the Western powers. It is no surprise that Africa's oil producers – Nigeria, Angola, Equatorial Guinea, Gabon, Cameroon – are among the worst-run states in Africa despite their wealth. Or maybe because of it. Having petrodollars pumped directly into the system at the highest level seems to induce the worst forms of megalomania. Ghana, now one of the more democratic African countries, will be the next oil-rich state. Maybe we should weep for Ghana – and insist that occasionally principles and people matter as much as petroleum.

Third, Western countries could manage migration better by balancing their marginal need to recruit the world's brightest and best-educated talent with Africa's desperate need to retain its most talented people. The one-way traffic could easily be balanced by off-setting the brain drain from Africa with an incentive scheme for those in the diaspora to return or move between two homes.

Fourth, Africa's stolen money is often passed through the international banking system without question. Those who stole it are allowed to travel the world unhindered. Corruption kills as surely as terrorism or drug dealing, and the same obligations should be imposed on banks to watch for the funding from all three sources equally. Britain and banks in its offshore territories are the worst offenders and handle billions of illicit capital flowing from poor countries to rich through transfer pricing and mispricing by global companies.

In addition to economic growth, the future of Africa will depend on other very different factors: population growth, climate change and identity. Population is growing faster in Africa than anywhere else in the world. In many African countries it is doubling every generation. The population of Africa reached a billion around 2009 and will reach 2 billion by 2050. Half of the people in sub-Saharan Africa are under eighteen years old. In some countries half are under fifteen. As infant survival rates continue to rise this will represent one of the fastest rates of growth in the history of humanity. AIDS deaths have affected the shape of the population and the sudden thinning out in the middle of the population pyramid but the current rapid increase in population is Africa's biggest challenge for the future. The quality of that future now depends on the ability of governments to deliver economic growth as well as schools, clinics, hospitals, roads and power so that this next generation can support itself, indeed flourish.

Climate change will affect Africa more severely than almost anywhere else on the planet. According to Camilla Toulmin of the International Institute for Environment and Development, the interior of Africa will become hotter. Millions of Africans live on the edge of drylands at the moment and these areas have already been getting drier. Many may become completely arid. Rainfall, often erratic in Africa, will become even more so with long droughts and sudden torrents. Millions of lives will be disrupted. Coastal cities in Africa, vital to the continent's well-being, could be very severely affected by a rise in sea level. Africans are already experiencing strange weather patterns, but little is being done to adapt to changing climate.

How will Africans' identity change? As these populations grow, can African leaders forge common national identities, a common idea of what it means to be Nigerian or Angolan, Ugandan or Malian? Religion may now be a more dangerous fault line in countries that are both Muslim and Christian, but politicians are still capable of exploiting ethnicity. Africans could reinforce the continent's reputation for tribalism, war and hunger. Or they could draw on their profound talent for coexistence and reconciliation and become the world's peacemakers.

In Africa, however, the weight of the past, the traditional way of doing things, is massive. Go anywhere on the continent and you will find people living in traditional ways unaffected by mobile phones, radios, cars or even the nation states they live in. At the other end of society there are still many elites for whom Africa works perfectly as it is now. They have no incentive to change it or even to allow it to develop. In spite of them, Africa is turning the corner slowly but it will not suddenly take off. Socially Africans are conservative and within families and society power still lies with older people. The new Africa is arriving, aspects of it quite dramatically, but deeper change will take generations. Instead of the dramatic Big Push for Africa that Britain tried to secure in 2005, it should have promoted the Long Haul. Make Poverty History should have had a subtitle – 'A Fifty-Year Project'.

In the meantime the two Africas are coexisting. There is the Africa that has found a new self-respect. Confidently African, its coolly dressed young urban professionals take what they want from other cultures. As more and more of them operate as lawyers or engineers in America or Europe and then return home to the village to sit and eat *ugali* with their fingers or slurp pepper soup, there is a growing realization that you do not have to be either African or European or even half and half. You can be both, two cultures integrated and whole. Their very success as global professionals generates the confidence to reassert their Africanness. They are very different from the elites who took over the countries from the colonialists and, incubus-like, grabbed their countries' resources and sat on them, preventing their economies from developing and integrating into the world. This new generation is open to the world and part of the global movement, enabling their countries' economies to expand. Their growing numbers and aspirations also provide a stabilising counterweight to the power-hungry politicians.

Then there is the Africa of Kibera outside Nairobi, one of the worst slums in the world and home to as many as a million people; of Khayelitsha near Cape Town, home to more than a million and growing faster than the government can provide it with services; or of Durimi, that tiny traditional village in Nigeria, once untouched by the megacity capital five miles away, now obliterated by a slum of shacks. People who survive in such places may have one room that you can step across in two paces, a roof of corrugated iron, a single spare shirt or dress hanging on a nail, a cooking pot and a plate and cup. The inhabitants live on a meal day – if they are lucky – and are dependent on earning a few cents a day, maybe carrying or digging. Many of the people who live in these places are dislocated from their cultures and support systems, and all are poor, threatened by disease and violence. They do what Africa does best – survive from day to day. But they dream of a better future.

They live less than ten minutes away from Achebe's house, today surrounded by a high wall topped with razor wire, protected by security cameras and armed guards. It is perfectly possible for them to continue like this indefinitely. Or the gap between them could grow, the guards on the house could be doubled and the two worlds might then explode in a violent collision. Or they could change, converging as more and more on the outside find opportunities to enter the house and make a better life for themselves, until one day Achebe's house is open to all.

Epilogue

Mr Lule died on 16 May 2004 aged about ninety-six. Like most Africans he did not bother much with the date of his birth. I worked it out with some of his sons when we got him to talk about his childhood growing up as the son of a chief near the border with Tanzania. In those days it was German-ruled Tanganyika. He said he remembered his father being given a gun by the British administrators 'in case the Wa-Germani came'. The Germani? That must have been at the outbreak of the First World War in 1914. 'How old were you then?' we asked excitedly. 'I must have been about six years old,' he replied.

The funeral at Nsambya on the outskirts of Kampala was attended by the Cardinal Archbishop of Uganda, three bishops, twenty priests, two ministers and the speaker of the national assembly. His body was buried at Matale, his home village, about ninety miles south. His son Michael wrote:

> Dad always kept time, the service started at 11.00 a.m. and ended at 11.55, the speeches started at 12.00 and ended at 12.55. The body was taken home for an overnight stay. The following morning we left for Matale at 9.00 a.m. The service at Matale started at 1.00 p.m.

*and burial started at 3.00 p.m., we left Matale at 4.00 p.m. and
were back at Nsambya at 6.30 p.m.*

The old man would have appreciated the precise timekeeping – and would know he was being teased.

I thought of his eternal optimism that made a mockery of World Bank figures, doom warnings from Western aid agencies and disaster reporting from journalists like myself. He had seen Africa move from grass huts to glass skyscrapers. The route had not been easy and as he approached old age Uganda had gone into reverse. Bush tracks that had been made into hard-top tarmac roads reverted to bush tracks again. His children's lives that could have been so prosperous were blighted by politics and war. His grandchildren grew up in greater poverty than he had. It was only in his last few years that his great-grandchildren were able to take up the opportunities that had been blocked more than thirty years before.

His solidly made, beautifully kept house of mud bricks and corrugated iron roof, perfect for Uganda's climate, was an African idyll to me. A small shamba around the house provided food for all the family and firewood to cook it. A coffee plantation and scores of hens in open sheds made enough money for the extras in life: sugar, salt, batteries for the radio, clothes and shoes, school fees and the occasional wedding and funeral. It was also ten minutes from the centre of Kampala, the lush green capital of hills and trees. Was I dreaming when I saw a perfect life here: a continent thriving on millions of small family farms that fed the towns and provided school fees for all their children; and when those children grew up, left home and went to the town, they would still come home to the family farm, the core of traditional family life? As the continent moved into the twenty-first century, became commercialized, high-tec and urbanized, could that rural heart of Africa have stayed strong and healthy?

I didn't make Mr Lule's funeral but I did come to the *Olumbe*, the ceremony that marks the end of the mourning period when 'death is chased from the house'. Thirty-two years after I was expelled from Uganda I stepped off the plane at Entebbe, filled in a form and collected a visa almost as easily as buying a newspaper. Waved straight through customs, I took a smart taxi – reconditioned from Japan – to Kampala. I had been back several times, but this time I tried to spot the changes. The road from the new airport skirts around the bullet-spattered remains of the old Entebbe control tower, a monument to the bad old days. Huge white UN aircraft stand on the apron loading crates and vehicles for the Congo peace-keeping operation, a reminder that the bad times have not gone away, just moved.

Entebbe and Kampala – twenty-five miles apart – used to be separated by thick bush, whole stretches of the road between them showing no sign of human habitation. Today you are never out of sight of buildings – schools, clinics, shops, churches and, set back on the hillsides with stupendous views of the lake, grand mansions. Many more are in various stages of completion. Boarding houses are common, advertising safe and cheap accommodation for the thousands of students from far away who struggle to get into schools in the area. Sections of the road are lined with rows of carpentry workshops displaying three-piece suites in the sun in front of them. Elsewhere iron railings and gates, cut and welded in small foundries, sprout along the roadside. Minibus taxis ply the route, bursting with passengers and their bundles and boxes, and even more people walk or cycle. Most cycles are loaded with bulging sacks or sticks of bananas.

The next day I visit Kabuwoko and the school where I taught. Two new blocks have been built for boarders and their gutters feed a huge cistern that has been sunk into the hilltop. It has already served through one dry spell. The older buildings have been reroofed, repainted and given electricity. One room contains fifteen computers. The school had about 150 students in 1971, now it has 600. The carcass of a tank still lies at the bottom of the church steps, a magnificent symbol of the end of military rule. I once thought the school would collapse without me. It has not only survived war – and my departure; it has thrived.

Uganda, the country that produced Idi Amin and political chaos and became famous for AIDS and Ebola, sounds like the stereotype of the typical third world country. A nasty civil war of eighteen years' duration was still smouldering in the north. But my definition of the third world is where everyone sits around staring at what obviously needs to be done. Here everyone is on the move, doing things. And, unlike three decades ago, everyone has shoes. Who says Africa is mired in poverty and going backwards?

In the evening the Olumbe starts with a Mass at dusk in the garden under an awning outside Mr Lule's house in Nsambya. A bishop presides and a group of drummers back a small choir who wail out the Africanized European hymns and rhythms into the evening air. Whiffs of cooking drift round the house from the open kitchens at the back where food is being prepared for 500 people.

At the end of Mass a huge fire is lit in the middle of the garden to keep us warm through the all-night vigil. The clan elders hold a meeting but the tent they have been allocated does not have sides and they are offended. Negotiations follow and money changes hands to placate them. I ask Michael what they need to discuss. 'Nothing,' he says, 'they just eat, drink and gossip.' His sister Professor Josephine Namboze, Mr Lule's eldest child and Uganda's first woman doctor, dons a bark cloth robe over her dress. Now in her seventies and recently retired from the World Health Organization, she begins the ceremony of initiation for members of the clan. The Baganda were organized around the Kabaka, the king, and each of the dozens of clans had a symbol and a role in the royal household. The patriarchal clans are named after animals and plants and no-one can eat the clan symbol or marry within the clan. Michael tells me there is even a shit clan but I suspect he is winding me up.

The ceremony takes place in the house and I am allowed to peep, though this is women's business. The new initiates to the clan – not all of them children – sit with legs straight out before them while Josephine washes their feet and arms with water from a reed basket, sweetened with a cleansing herb. She chants phrases and the women around ululate in reply. In the old days the initiates would have brought their umbilical cords, carefully preserved, and they would have been laid on the water. If they floated they were admitted to the clan – but if they sank? Michael laughs: 'They were probably killed in a terrible way . . . I don't know but it sounds the sort of thing we used to do. They weren't admitted to the clan anyway.'

In the midst of this ancient ceremony Josephine's mobile phone rings and she breaks off from her ancient rituals to take a call from a friend in New York.

Something new is happening here.

Outside, the crowds are gathering, summoned by the drumming that will not stop till dawn. The Olumbe was announced in the newspaper so anyone can turn up for a free meal – and many do even though they may not be known to the family. In the villages where everyone is known this is not a problem, but in the towns such occasions can be overwhelmed by complete strangers. Round the back of the house a dozen wood fires flicker under huge stew pots lighting up the sweating faces of the cooks. One vast metal pan – taller than a man – contains a ton of matooke. Banana leaves have been packed onto it as a lid and the steam rises gently into the night. Two cows and some 250 chickens have been slaughtered and chopped up to feed the crowds. I keep up with the vigil till after 1 a.m. but then go off to bed, setting my alarm to wake me before dawn. I fall asleep to the noise of sawing crickets and the subtle throbbing of the drums.

Dawn in Africa is the most delicious time of all. Stillness and silence, night growing pale and giving way to deep rich colour as if the world is listening for bird calls and preparing itself for the sun. The air is cool and heavy with the scent of vegetation and earth. I make my way up the purple dirt road to the house again. The drums have at last fallen silent but the crowds are still there sitting on the ground or standing in groups, talking softly. Children are curled up asleep in corners of the tent. The family are in the house. A single drummer, his drum wrapped in a special cloth and tucked under his arm, calls out, thumps out a roll, chants again. He comes to the door. Mr Lule's thirteen children emerge from the house with a long piece of bark cloth over their heads and do a sort of conga round the garden and the outhouses. They are chasing death away. The drummer declares that he has called death out of the house. Death has fled. The family can now return to the house and must mourn the dead no more. As the drummer calls, the first shafts of sunlight strike across the garden.

After breakfast comes an hour-long Mass with another bishop presiding. The feeling that something quite profound has changed is growing on me. In the middle of Mass, when there would usually be a sermon, the bishop sits down and a group of drummers emerges from the congregation. One carries a huge spear and another a gourd and other objects. They are led by a young man dressed in bark cloth who leaps forward thrashing his drum. He shouts out something in Luganda and everyone – bishop and all – bursts out laughing. The congregation stands up, whooping and slapping hands. The laughter goes on and on. Just at the most solemn dramatic moment it looks as if the whole ceremony will collapse in levity. The drum is thrashed again and the man leaps forward and chants. More guffaws. Later I learned that he was chanting the anthem of Mr Lule's clan, the yam clan, but most people there had never heard it before. Its old-fashioned political incorrectness induces anarchic, helpless laughter. The yam clan were the Kabaka's hunters and hunters must have dogs. Their chant runs: 'You can get rid of your wife but always keep your dog. The wife may be unfaithful, the dog never. Your wife may not cook for you but a dog will always find you meat.'

Eventually solemnity is restored and Victor, Mr Lule's fourth son, is installed as the family representative in the clan. He is given a spear and a gourd of banana beer and other objects symbolizing his new role as heir. This does not mean he inherits Mr Lule's house and goods. These are shared among the family but Victor is now responsible for the family – a concept that does not exist in our individualized Western world. If a sister is divorced or a niece orphaned, he takes responsibility for her and brings her into his home. He must take care of the whole family and make sure all are cared for and the children educated.

The bishop, I notice, takes part in these ceremonies as everyone else does, answering in chorus and clapping at moments during these old rituals. They are undergoing something of a revival but no-one is sure of the running order. Twice the chanting stops while old men discuss what should come next or correct whoever is singing or speaking. Michael admits he hasn't a clue what some things meant. Yet they are performed and embraced openly by all.

This would not have happened thirty years ago. In the 1970s I had never been invited to witness Kiganda ceremonies like these and knew only vaguely that they were still performed. I knew no other white people, apart from an anthropologist, who had witnessed them either. They were kept very, very separate from the rituals of the

Catholic Church and all the other Christian Churches. The White Man's religion still stood in opposition to African mumbo jumbo, primitive, evil witchcraft that had to be rejected. Africans had been made ashamed of their own rituals, religion and traditions. Yet their symbolism expresses the meaning of fundamentals such as the family, personal responsibility and death, and seemed to deal with the very areas that we in the West cannot deal with.

What I witnessed here was Africa integrating its past and present, reconciling African tradition with Western culture, mixing African spirituality and Christian ritual, suits and spears, magic and mobile phones. Here at last Africans are equally comfortable in both worlds and combining the two within their own new world that is both African and European. The wound that parted Africa from its soul is healing. Its schizophrenia is ending. Africa is finding itself.

Further reading

When I went to Africa for the first time I went armed with Penguin's Africa Handbook and a pile of their African Library series in brown and black covers, covering everything from religion and history to trade unions and social change. Meanwhile Heinemann's wonderful African Writer Series, in orange and white covers, published the classic novels of the independence era by Chinua Achebe, Ngugi Wa Thiong'o and other writers. Almost all of the former and many of the latter are now out of print.

These days James Currey's African Issues series and Zed Books' African Arguments have gone some way to replacing these series. Elsewhere African books compete for space in a global market. A few outstanding books have made it and survive on their merits. Blaine Harden's *Dispatches from a Fragile Continent* (New York, 1990) remains the best attempt by an outsider to dig under the surface of Africa and create a sympathetic understanding of what lies beneath.

Just how Africa came into being and how mankind has survived there is brilliantly described in John Reader's *Africa: A Biography of the Continent* (New York, 1999) which is strikingly illustrated by the author's own pictures. Although the book ends neatly at the moment of the glorious election in South Africa and the ghastly genocide in

Rwanda, it deals little with why modern Africa is the way it is. Thomas Pakenham's *Scramble for Africa* is the best Western account of how Europe took over Africa, and Basil Davidson's books, especially *Black Man's Burden*, *Black Mother* and *The Search for Africa*, give African history a significance and importance that was previously ignored. Then, most writers were sympathetic to Western policy towards Africa but Davidson laid bare the real impact of colonization and imperialism on Africa.

Davidson thought socialism was the answer, Rene Dumont's *False Start in Africa* (London, 1966) picked up the already widening gap between rich and poor and the inappropriate model of development, capitalist or socialist, that was already emerging in Africa.

At the political level, *Africa: A Modern History* by Guy Arnold (Cornwall, 2006) and Martin Meredith's *The State of Africa* (London, 2005) give detailed accounts of Africa's political power struggles, the former from a sympathetic standpoint, the latter less so. Two volumes in the African Issues series made serious attempts to explain the internal reasons for Africa's failure: *The Criminalization of the State in Africa* by Jean-François Bayart, Stephen Ellis and Beátrice Hibou (Oxford, Bloomington and Indianapolis, 1999) and *Africa Works: Disorder as Political Instrument* by Patrick Chabal and Jean-Pascal Daloz (Oxford, 1999). Both were written in the late 1990s when Africa reached its lowest point and reach opposite conclusions from similar insights. That period of Africa's nadir provoked a rash of exhortatory books urging Africa to 'claim the twenty-first century' and some argued it was already succeeding. The only realistic assessment was Matthew Lockwood's *The State They're In* (London, 2005).

The list of books on individual African countries that have informed and influenced me is too long to mention but Karl Maier's *This House Has Fallen* (London, 2002) on Nigeria and Michela

Wrong's *In the Footsteps of Mr Kurtz* (London, 2000) and Adam Hochschild's *King Leopold's Ghost* (London, 1998), both on Congo, are outstanding. The first half of Barbara Kingsolver's *The Poisonwood Bible* (London, 1999) is one of the best descriptions of outsiders misunderstanding Africa.

Exiled Nigerians have dominated fiction writing from Africa and the novels of Chinua Achebe are still as profound and illuminating as they were when written. Since then Ben Okri has given us visions of mystical Africa. Chimamanda Ngozi Adichie is the latest big African story novelist. A lack of publishing houses in Africa has prevented writers getting their works into print there. Creative energy has gone into music and, in Nigeria, films. Maybe that situation is now changing and a revival in Africa's fortunes will be matched by a revival in African writing.

Index

Keep in touch with
Granta Books:

Visit granta.com to discover more.

GRANTA